THE WORKS OF JONATHAN EDWARDS

VOLUME 4

John E. Smith, General Editor

PREVIOUSLY PUBLISHED

PAUL RAMSEY, ed., *Freedom of the Will*
JOHN E. SMITH, ed., *Religious Affections*
CLYDE A. HOLBROOK, ed., *Original Sin*

JONATHAN EDWARDS

The Great Awakening

A FAITHFUL NARRATIVE
THE DISTINGUISHING MARKS
SOME THOUGHTS CONCERNING THE REVIVAL
LETTERS RELATING TO THE REVIVAL
PREFACE TO *TRUE RELIGION* BY JOSEPH BELLAMY

EDITED BY C. C. GOEN

PROFESSOR OF CHURCH HISTORY
WESLEY THEOLOGICAL SEMINARY

New Haven and London

YALE UNIVERSITY PRESS, 1972

Set in Linotype Baskerville type,
and printed in the United States of America by
Vail-Ballou Press, Inc., Binghamton, N.Y.

Distributed in Great Britain, Europe, and Africa by
Yale University Press, Ltd., London; in Canada by
McGill-Queen's University Press, Montreal;
in Latin America by Kaiman & Polon, Inc.,
New York City; in Australasia by Australia and New
Zealand Book Co., Pty., Ltd., Artarmon, New South
Wales; in India by UBS Publishers' Distributors Pvt., Ltd.,
Delhi; in Japan by John Weatherhill, Inc., Tokyo.

CONTENTS

LIST OF ILLUSTRATIONS

ABBREVIATIONS

References to Jonathan Edwards' writings printed in this volume will be to page numbers herein, with titles abbreviated as follows:

FN: *A Faithful Narrative of the Surprising Work of God in the Conversion of Many Hundred Souls* . . .

DM: *The Distinguishing Marks of a Work of the Spirit of God*

ST: *Some Thoughts Concerning the Present Revival of Religion in New England*

In the case of *A Faithful Narrative* the existence of several versions makes it necessary to add an additional symbol for identification (see below, pp. 32–45, for a description of the relation among these versions):

FN: the unpublished letter of May 30, 1735

FN-C: the letter of November 6, 1736, abridged by Benjamin Colman and published as an appendix, separately paged, to William Williams, *The Duty and Interest of a People* (Boston, 1736)

FN-1: the first edition, published in London in 1737

FN-3: the third edition, published in Boston in 1738

THE Great Awakening of the eighteenth century marks the inauguration of the revival tradition in America. While George Whitefield, by virtue of his flamboyant itineracy and its consequent influence on evangelistic method, may be called the "founder" of American revivalism, it was Jonathan Edwards who began the historical documentation and theological defense which have sustained it as an ongoing tradition. The tracts which constitute the present volume show how Edwards initially made his case, and the fact that they are among the most widely reprinted and perennially popular writings of English-speaking Protestantism testifies to their historical importance.

1. *Some Operating Concepts*

For two centuries revivalism has been the chief instrument for spreading evangelical pietism. Though that may be a truism which needs no laboring, it nonetheless invites attention to its key terms. Consider first *pietism.* A competent recent study has defined pietism as the extension to individual Christian experience of principles which the Reformers had applied "chiefly, though by no means exclusively, to the areas of doctrine and polity," resulting in a surging reassertion of Christianity's experiential tradition in post-Reformation Protestantism. Notwithstanding a wide variety of local expressions, all pietists agreed that true Christianity has its main locus in a meaningful relationship of the individual to God. For this reason they stressed personal repentance and faith, warm devotion, and assurance that they were in truth the children of God. Always strongly biblical and intensely missionary, pietism encouraged lively preaching to persuade unbelievers and complacent church members to commit themselves cordially to the obedience of faith. In short, the character of pietism required it to be aggressively conversionist.[1]

1. Mainly following F. Ernest Stoeffler, *The Rise of Evangelical Pietism* (Leiden, 1965), ch. 1. Similar characterizations are offered by James R. Tanis,

1

Its conversionist thrust explains why pietism occurs so often with the adjective *evangelical*. This is an umbrella term of many meanings; but in relation to the revivalistic writings of Jonathan Edwards and the American tradition of which they are so largely the fountainhead, evangelicalism may be defined as the perspective from which the Christian life is viewed as beginning with an experience of personal conversion and issuing in a pursuit of personal piety. Thus understood, evangelicalism is opposed to sacramentalism, which regards the Christian life as beginning with the bestowal of grace at baptism, and to all forms of the *corpus Christianum,* which treats as Christians all who do not deliberately opt out of the church established by the state. It rejects the "mixed multitude" of a territorial church and seeks to gather "true believers" into disciplined companies of committed converts.

This may sound at first like sectarianism, but the case is not so simple. Where evangelicals are a minority under an established church, they must perforce exist in sects seeking whatever toleration they can obtain. But they may also become dominant and revert to a form of establishment *and* strict discipline—as witness (in different ways) Calvin's Geneva, seventeenth-century Scotland, and Puritan New England. In the last case, the authorities permitted only one form of established worship while insisting that church membership be restricted to those who could testify credibly to a conversion experience. This marked an innovation within Puritanism, but with the passing of the first generation of "experienced" church members it broke down, so that on the eve of the Great Awakening most of the parish churches in New England, like the old English churches from which they had fled, harbored a mixed company. That explains why many of the Awakening's converts were church members of one sort or another.[2] Evangelicals seem to flourish best, however, where the civil government is religiously neutral (as in the United States), requiring all churches to maintain themselves on the basis of voluntary commitment and to advance their interests chiefly

---

Dutch Calvinistic Pietism in the Middle Colonies; A Study in the Life and Theology of Theodorus Jacobus Frelinghuysen (The Hague, 1967), pp. 1–7; and Martin Schmidt, "Pietism," *Encyclopedia of the Lutheran Church* (Minneapolis, 1965), *3,* 1898–1906.

2. Edmund S. Morgan, *Visible Saints; The History of a Puritan Idea* (Ithaca, N.Y., 1965), ch. 4.

through persuasion: in such a situation the greatest advantage accrues to evangelicals because of their conversionist dynamic. The upsurge of evangelical pietism in the century of American independence, therefore, is of enormous importance for the direction of religious development in the new nation.

Inasmuch as evangelical Christianity draws a sharp line between world and church, nature and spirit, sinner and saint—a line crossed only as the individual personally experiences conversion and commits his life to obey the Gospel—it is easy to see why *revivalism* became the chief instrument for spreading evangelical pietism. For revivalism is a technique of mass evangelism, and as such is peculiarly adapted to producing the all-important conversion experience (or at least acceptable surrogates therefor) in great numbers. In this way it both fulfills the missionary-evangelistic imperative of pietism and accelerates the growth of Christianity's evangelical contingent.

The fact that pietism, evangelicalism, and revivalism converged within the context of the Reformed tradition is also highly significant. For here, especially in English Puritanism, the regeneration of the individual soul is the central fact of religious experience, and emphatic demands for biblical obedience shape the whole concept of the Christian life.[3] Among the religious leaders of English Puritanism, in fact, one finds evangelical pietism in an almost classical form. And in a way quite beyond what might have been the case in one of the more quietistic expressions of Protestantism, it is augmented by the *activism* of the Reformed tradition. This impulse to activism among children of Reformed Christianity derives chiefly from the high Calvinistic doctrine of divine sovereignty. One who is called to be the obedient servant of a God whose purposes in history cannot be thwarted is prepared to face every foe with indomitable courage: "If God is for us, who can be against us?" (Rom. 8:31). The Calvinist's quest for assurance of his calling, moreover, took him quickly to the question, "How can I know I am of the elect?" Calvin warned that a univocal answer is impossible, since such matters are locked in the inscrutable counsels of God; but he suggested nevertheless some presumptive evidences of election, one of which was an upright life of strict obedience to the

3. Cf. Roger Sharrock, ed., introduction to John Bunyan, *Grace Abounding to the Chief of Sinners* (Oxford, 1962), pp. xxvii–ix; and M. M. Knappen, ed., *Two Elizabethan Puritan Diaries* (Chicago, 1933), pp. 2–8.

divine will.[4] This is why the Reformed tradition bred a race of heroes willing to topple tyrants, carve new kingdoms out of a howling wilderness, and erect holy commonwealths to fulfill the righteousness of God on earth. When applying itself to the crucial business of making converts, this kind of activism naturally found the revival a forceful engine of evangelism. To Reformed Puritan evangelical pietists of eighteenth-century America, revivalism was more than a one-time "surprising work of God"; it was his gracious gift to those who were turning sinners into saints and thus inaugurating his millennial reign (cf. below, pp. 71–72).

2. *The Arminian Threat*

Seasons of spiritual concern in individual parishes, often intense enough to produce several converts for church membership, were not unknown in New England before the "great and general awakening" of the 1740s. Jonathan Edwards recorded in his "Personal Narrative" that his own first "exercises about my soul" occurred "some years before I went to college, at a time of remarkable awakening in my father's congregation" at East Windsor, Connecticut.[5] The elder Edwards' parish stood in young Jonathan's memory as "a place favored with mercies of this nature above any on this western side of New England, excepting Northampton" (FN-1; below, p. 000).[6] Arriving in Northampton, Massachusetts, in 1727 to become assistant to his reverend grandfather, Solomon Stoddard (below, p. 15–17), he learned that "reformations" had been from time

4. Cf. *Institutes of the Christian Religion,* IV, i, 8. Other evidences (for the guidance of "charitable judgment") were profession of the true faith and continued participation in the sacraments. The import of the latter lay in the fact that in the Reformed churches the Lord's Table was the focal point of ecclesiastical discipline; continued participation in the sacraments, therefore, implied subjection to discipline and pursuit of piety—all of which reinforced a strenuous ethical activism.

5. This account, for which the manuscript is now lost, was written about 1740 and printed first by Samuel Hopkins in *The Life and Character of the Late Reverend Mr. Jonathan Edwards* (Boston, 1765). Later editors (Austin, 1808, and Dwight, 1830) sought to "improve" the text but succeeded only in corrupting it, and nearly all modern anthological reprints unhappily follow them. The only exception is David Levin, ed., *Jonathan Edwards: A Profile* (New York, 1969), which contains the complete work by Hopkins; the above quotation appears on p. 26.

6. Quotations from JE's writings printed in this volume will be cited from the page numbers herein. For title abbreviations, see p. xii.

to time "swiftly propagated through the town," and was impressed with Stoddard's "extraordinary success in the conversion of many [souls]" (below, pp. 114, 145). There had been five "harvests" during Stoddard's sixty-year pastorate: in 1679, 1683, 1696, 1712, and 1718. Edwards must have been fascinated by the accounts of these revivals, for he wrote:

> Some of these times were much more remarkable than others, and the ingathering of souls more plentiful. Those that were about 53, and 40, and 24 years ago were much greater than either the first or the last: but in each of them, I have heard my grandfather say, the bigger part of the young people in the town seemed to be mainly concerned for their eternal salvation.[7]

By this count, the revivals of 1734–35 and 1740–43, described in the writings of this volume, would have been Northampton's sixth and seventh harvests.

In publishing defenses of his own manifestly greater awakenings, Edwards was careful not to deny their continuity with Stoddard's (cf. FN-1; below, p. 190). But occasionally he hinted at "some new circumstances" (below, pp. 157–59, 181, 268); and once he revealed, perhaps too ingenuously, that Northampton's people, for all their familiarity with revivals, had imbibed a quite mistaken notion of conversion. "And indeed it appears very plainly in some of [the new converts], that before their own conversion they had very imperfect ideas what conversion was: it is all new and strange, and what there was no clear conception of before." The converts themselves acknowledged, according to Edwards, that the expressions they formerly used so confidently in their talk about conversion had conveyed to them no more idea of the real thing than the names of colors conveyed to men born blind (FN-1; below, p. 174).

The error he discovered and set himself to combat, of course, was "Arminianism"; and during the Great Awakening most evangelicals

7. FN-1; below, p. 146. Curiously, this is not reflected in church membership records. "In 1677 seventy-six persons qualified for communion in Northampton. Despite three 'harvests' and a supposedly easier admissions policy, three decades later the total of communicants had risen to only ninety-six, a figure which represents approximately 43 percent of the adult inhabitants" (Robert G. Pope, *The Half-Way Covenant: Church Membership in Puritan New England* [Princeton, 1969], pp. 256–57; based in part on "Statistics of the First Church in Northampton," an appendix to John Todd, *The Pulpit and Its Influence on Society* [Northampton, 1834], p. 61).

followed his lead in rejecting pre-Awakening ideas of conversion as based in varying degrees on Arminian presuppositions. For massive evidence of this, one need go no farther than the pages of *The Christian History,* a periodical of revival intelligence published in Boston 1743–44 (see below, p. 78). The Rev. Jonathan Parsons, in a well-known report from Lyme, Connecticut, wrote that he had renounced Arminian principles and after changing his preaching had convinced his church members that few of them had ever been "savingly converted." He described persons "who had made themselves easy for some time with the Arminian way of conversion," but who in the present revival "were now convinced that such a scheme of doctrines, embraced, fatally settled persons down short of Christ." [8] Joseph Park, a missionary to the Indians at Westerly, Rhode Island, confessed that while he had never embraced Arminianism entirely, he "had secretly imagined that there was something [good] in men to begin with, and that Gospel grace came to make [it] perfect"; but after being caught up in the revival, he became fully convinced of the doctrines of total depravity and salvation by grace alone.[9] Nathaniel Leonard of Plymouth, Massachusetts, recalled that after Gilbert Tennent (below, pp. 49–50) preached there in March 1741, urging the doctrines of strict Calvinism, "all persons were put upon examining themselves, warned against trusting in their own righteousness and resting in the form of godliness, without the power, etc. [II Tim. 3:5]." The result was a profound alteration in the temper of the whole town.[1] Josiah Crocker of Taunton testified that Arminianism, formality, and moral laxity were so ingrained among his people that they were "filled with wonder" at Tennent's "strange" doctrine; but after hearing him and several other traveling evangelists, some were "plucked off from their false foundations and . . . savingly converted to God." [2] Peter Thatcher of Middleborough reported that converts in his parish had developed a new doctrinal awareness which made them hostile to "Arminian er-

---

8. *The Christian History,* 2, 123, 133–42. Excerpts from Parsons' account are printed in Joseph Tracy, *The Great Awakening; A History of the Revival of Religion in the Time of Edwards and Whitefield* (Boston, 1842), pp. 134–50, 152–55; and in Alan Heimert, *The Great Awakening; Documents Illustrating the Crisis and Its Consequences* (Indianapolis, 1967), pp. 36–40, 188–91, 196–200.
9. *The Christian History,* *1,* 202–03.
1. Ibid., 2, 314–15.
2. Ibid., 2, 323–44.

rors." [3] John Porter of North Bridgewater, who admitted that before he heard Whitefield and Tennent he himself "knew nothing rightly of my sin and danger . . . neither was established in the doctrines of grace," wrote of his new converts: "many of them were, before this day of God's searching our Jerusalem with candles [Zeph. 1:12], as exact and strict in the performance of the externals of religion (as far as could be observed by man) as any among us, and had gained the charity of their neighbors; but now see they built upon the sandy foundation of their own righteousness, and so had perished eternally, notwithstanding their blazing professions and the good opinion of others, had not God in mercy opened their eyes to see the way of salvation by Christ, and enabled them to embrace it." [4] There are many other testimonies of like import.

How far such manifestoes, penned in the flush of revivalistic fervor, reflect without exaggerating the actual theological situation in New England Congregationalism before the Great Awakening is difficult to say. But it is at least obvious that some new battle lines had been drawn. Edwards made it unmistakably plain in a *A Faithful Narrative* that the Northampton conversions of 1734–35, so far as they stemmed from the influence of his preaching, were produced by what he intended as a doctrinal corrective. And William Cooper, in an interim report on religion in Boston, 1741, enumerated the revival's positive results in both society and the lives of individuals, and reiterated the conviction that "these fruits do not grow on Arminian ground" (preface to DM; below, p. 223). The new wave of evangelical harvests clearly grew out of a challenge to something called Arminianism.

But what was the precise identity of this enemy? To formulate an accurate definition, one must explore the historical background very carefully. Anti-Arminianism in New England had been quiescent since the subsiding of shock waves generated by the defection of several Connecticut clergymen to Anglicanism in 1722. Ten years before Edwards wrote *A Faithful Narrative*, Boston's Cotton Mather had been unable to find that, "among all the pastors of two hundred churches, there is one Arminian." [5] Yet at the onset of his first revival at Northampton, Edwards recorded "a great noise that was in this part of the country about Arminianism" and incurred the

3. Ibid., *1*, 172.
4. Ibid., *1*, 406–07.
5. *Ratio Disciplinae Fratrum Nov-Anglorum* (Boston, 1726), p. 5.

wrath of some who faulted him for "meddling with the controversy in the pulpit." [6] Nor was the noise confined to western Massachusetts, for at the time young Jonathan began his meddling the first public accusation against Arminianism among the Congregational clergy was already in Boston bookstalls. John White of Gloucester complained that some of the younger ministers "are under prejudices against, and fall off from, important articles of the faith of these churches and cast a favorable eye upon, embrace, and as far as they dare, argue for, propagate, and preach the Arminian scheme." In a lengthy jeremiad, he denounced Arminianism as "another gospel" and advised his brethren to eschew this "new body of divinity," which "rather deserves the title of *A Bundle of Errors*." Sinners, White admonished, should "labor to know your hearts and state, and don't rest till you have experienced a thorough work of conversion or regeneration." [7]

Francis A. Christie attempted to explain the resurgence of anti-Arminianism as a reaction of the standing order to continued fears of Anglican incursion, and argued that George Whitefield conjured up the "myth of Arminianism" by his "rash and unwarranted aspersions" against the Congregational clergy.[8] But Whitefield did not arrive in New England until September 1740. Perry Miller attributed it mainly to "the steady influx of books from English Nonconformity," but he made his case chiefly on the basis of John Taylor's *The Scripture Doctrine of Original Sin,* which was not published until 1738.[9] Edmund S. Morgan dismissed Arminianism

6. FN-1; below, p. 148. The opposition was personal as well as doctrinal, coming mainly from the powerful Williams family. The Rev. William Williams (1665–1741) of Hatfield, Mass., had married a daughter of Solomon Stoddard, sister to JE's mother, and the rivalry among the cousins was notorious for acrimony. For the bearing of this intrafamily feud on JE's career at Northampton, see Sereno E. Dwight, *The Life of President Edwards* (New York, 1830), pp. 433–34; and Perry Miller, *Jonathan Edwards* (New York, 1959), pp. 101–05. JE's own account is in his letter of Jan. 30, 1753, to Sir William Pepperell, where he began a long and candid recital by writing: "There has for many years appeared a prejudice in the family of the Williams's against me and my family, especially ever since the great awakening at Northampton 18 years ago" (original in Andover MSS).

7. John White, *New England's Lamentations* (Boston, 1734), pp. 16–18, 29, *et passim.*

8. "The Beginnings of Arminianism in New England," *Papers of the American Society of Church History,* 2d ser., *3* (1912), 159.

9. *Jonathan Edwards,* pp. 106–20. On pp. 7–29 Miller suggests other indica-

as "something of a New England bogy man," but his main evidence was the simple fact that pillars of the establishment continued to *call* themselves Calvinists and disowned any label that hinted otherwise—a curious conclusion following his acknowledgment that "New England ministers . . . even while shouting loudest against Arminianism, were themselves gliding unconsciously toward it." [1] Most recently, Gerald J. Goodwin has updated the Christie thesis by arguing "The Myth of 'Arminian-Calvinism' [as opposed to Arminian Anglicanism] in Eighteenth-Century New England." Restricting his definition of Arminianism to the Five Points of the Dutch Remonstrants (1610), and sharply separating formal theological statements from popular piety, he painted a Puritan establishment whose unadulterated Calvinism stood fast against the Arminian Anglicans and promptly unfrocked every Congregational clergyman departing from orthodoxy. The Arminian noise which disturbed western Massachusetts in 1734, according to Goodwin's reading, was due entirely to the controversy over Robert Breck, whose settlement at Springfield was opposed by the Hampshire Ministers Association in 1734–35, in part because of suspicions regarding his orthodoxy.[2]

None of the attempts to deny the Arminian threat or locate it outside the standing order seems very convincing. For one thing, the Congregationalists' dispute with the Anglicans was mainly over ecclesiastical polity rather than doctrine. In an exchange on the doctrinal question aired in the columns of *The Boston Gazette* during the summer of 1735, one polemicist averred without contradiction that "the tenets of neither [Calvinists nor Arminians] are appropriate to either side of the controversy between Episcopalians and anti-Episcopalians" because each side received the Thirty-Nine Arti-

---

tions of Arminianism in New England in the first third of the eighteenth century.

1. *The Gentle Puritan: A Life of Ezra Stiles, 1727–1795* (New Haven, 1961), pp. 15–19.

2. *New England Quarterly, 41* (1968), 213–37. For the Breck case, see below, p. 113. Goodwin might have found himself even more persuaded by the action of the Hampshire Ministers Association, which in April 1734 protested "the increase of missionaries from the Church of England amongst us" and in September addressed a spirited remonstrance to the Bishop of London (MS records at Forbes Library; cf. also Carl Bridenbaugh, *Mitre and Sceptre; Transatlantic Faiths, Ideas, Personalities, and Politics, 1689–1775* [New York, 1967], pp. 78–81). But he is simply wrong on the point; see below, pp. 17–18.

cles and interpreted them in a variety of ways.[3] Goodwin, failing to
recognize this, sought to support his contention regarding the mythi-
cal state of the Arminian bogy by citing the anti-Anglican comments
of such men as Jonathan Parsons and John White; but upon examining the context of his citations one discovers that the Calvinistic protagonists were arguing polity, not doctrine.[4] Neither man
made any explicit connection, in the passages cited, between his
doctrinal and his political concerns.

To verify that Jonathan Edwards' Arminian target was not
simply a straw man, one might start with Conrad Wright's essay
on "Arminianism Before the Great Awakening," which is still the
best summary treatment of the subject.[5] He calls attention to the
fact that for a long while New England had been moving in the
direction of Arminianism because of a "latent ambiguity" in the
traditional patterns of Puritan orthodoxy. This is the point to
pursue, for the significant truth is that for at least half a century the
whole basis of church life in New England had been shifting imper-
ceptibly to human effort and moral striving, so that quite unawares
many orthodox ministers were encouraging a subtle form of salvation by works.[6] Indeed, this is what "Arminianism" meant in mid-
eighteenth-century New England: it had less to do with Jacobus
Arminius (1560–1609), the Dutch theologian from whom it took its
name, than with a mood of rising confidence in man's ability to gain
some purchase on the divine favor by human endeavor. It was, as
Thomas A. Schafer put it, "a native American variety of human self-
sufficiency which expressed itself still within the forms of the
Covenant theology." [7]

3. *The Boston Gazette,* Aug. 18, 1735.
4. Parsons' account is in *The Christian History,* 2, 120–23. John White's
New England's Lamentations is actually three separate tracts bound together:
the second, which I have quoted above, is on "The Danger of Arminian
Principles" among what White called "our young men"; the third, which Goodwin cites, is on "The Declining State of Our Church Order, Government and
Discipline" and warns against presbyterianism (hardly an "Arminian" threat!)
as well as episcopacy.
5. *The Beginnings of Unitarianism in America* (Boston, 1966), ch. 1.
6. Such a shift was already far advanced in England; see Christopher
FitzSimmons Allison, *The Rise of Moralism; The Proclamation of the Gospel
from Hooker to Baxter* (New York, 1966).
7. "Jonathan Edwards and Justification by Faith," *Church History,* 20
(1951), 55. Cf. Clyde A. Holbrook, ed., *Original Sin,* vol. 3 of *The Works of
Jonathan Edwards* (New Haven, 1970), p. 4 n.

Federal Theology (from *foedus,* covenant), though an impressive intellectual structure, was far from impregnable. It contained a built-in equivocacy whereby the Arminian camel could get his nose under the Puritan tent so unobtrusively that few of the insiders noticed when the stakes of orthodoxy began to loosen. Perry Miller argued that Puritan theologians, by emphasizing the doctrine of God's covenant with the elect, softened the harshness of Calvin's "inscrutable deity" and substituted the "reasonable" concept of a God who limited himself to acting in accord with the terms of his gracious promise of redemption. Thus any man who fulfilled the terms of the covenant would be taking God at his word and might in all justice hold God to his promise. According to Miller's understanding of the New England mind,

> God voluntarily undertakes, not only to save those who believe, but to supply the power of belief, to provide the grace that will make possible man's fulfilling the terms of this new and easier covenant. . . . Man has only to pledge that, when it is given to him, he will avail himself of the assistance which makes belief possible. If he can believe, he has fulfilled the compact; God then must redeem him and glorify him.[8]

Theoretically, God still chooses whom he wills, and only the elect can accept the covenant. But practically all of New England's ecclesiastical, political, and social life was interpreted under rubrics derived from the Federal Theology; and the covenant of grace with individual saints was easily transmuted into an external covenant with the nation. As experiential piety waned, it was natural for leaders of the holy commonwealths to stress men's "natural power" to obey the terms of the external covenant, so that if they did what they could in this respect, possibly God would enable them "to exert those acts of religion which are internal"—i.e., to believe unto salvation.[9]

8. Perry Miller, "The Marrow of Puritan Divinity," in *Errand into the Wilderness* (Cambridge, Mass., 1956), p. 62. Miller probably went too far toward reducing the covenant of grace to man's contractual bargain with the Almighty.

9. So preached Cotton Mather (1663–1728); quoted in Perry Miller, "Preparation for Salvation in Seventeenth-Century New England," *Journal of the History of Ideas, 4* (1943), 285.

This suggests another development, a concomitant one turning on the question of what, if anything, a sinner might do to prepare himself for conversion and entrance into the covenant of grace. While some Puritan teachers had seen salvation as entirely due to divine initiative, others encouraged various kinds of pre-conversion responses to the early promptings of grace. Some indeed had gone so far in affirming the efficacy of preparation as to appear almost synergistic; for these, preparation became "an 'ability' on man's part as a wedge into grace." [1] Practitioners of the preparation scheme thus "laid the groundwork for later American Arminianism by obligating God to bestow salvation on those who sufficiently performed their part of the legal bargain by preparing themselves for grace." [2]

But New England's departure from the experiential tradition has been attributed most often to the operation of the Halfway Covenant, adopted 1662, and the effects of the decrees of the Reforming Synod of 1679–80, for the subtle tendency of these decisions was to relax anxiety about personal regeneration and raise tentative hopes for salvation by character.

The Halfway Covenant was a measure designed to hold within the churches those persons who could not qualify for full membership under the terms of the original ecclesiastical constitution, which provided that only the regenerate were to be received as church members. Following a doctrine of the Federal Theology, according to which the offspring of the regenerate are included in the covenant of grace, the first generation of Puritans in New England presented their children for baptism, the sign and seal of the covenant, fully expecting that when such children reached spiritual maturity they would profess conversion as their parents before them had done. When many members of the second generation found that they could not honestly testify to such an experience, their relationship to the visible church was in considerable doubt. When *they* began to have children, whom they naturally wanted baptized, the problem became intolerable. After much discussion, a Massachusetts synod in 1662 finally affirmed:

1. Norman Pettit, *The Heart Prepared: Grace and Conversion in Puritan Spiritual Life* (New Haven, 1966), p. 20; cf. also ch. 6.

2. Conrad Cherry, *The Theology of Jonathan Edwards: A Reappraisal* (Garden City, N.Y., 1966), p. 115. Cf. also Miller, "Preparation for Salvation in Seventeenth-Century New England," *loc. cit.*, pp. 282–86.

Church members who were admitted in minority, understanding the Doctrine of Faith, and publicly professing their assent thereto; not scandalous in life, and solemnly owning the Covenant before the Church, wherein they give up themselves and their Children to the Lord, and subject themselves to the Government of Christ in the Church, their Children are to be baptized.[3]

The synod acknowledged that persons baptized in infancy, though not professing Christians, were connected somehow with the visible church and might therefore pass along to their children the same ecclesiastical status. Providing they were of upright life and would accept the discipline of the church, they might present their children for baptism; but they could not partake of the Lord's Supper or vote in church affairs. They were halfway, rather than full, members.

Some modern historians have argued that this "way of reconciling the Puritans' conflicting commitments to infant baptism and to a church composed exclusively of saints" was "neither a sign of decline in piety nor a betrayal of the standards of the founding fathers, but an honest attempt to rescue the concept of a church of visible saints from the tangle of problems created in time by human reproduction."[4] This is doubtless true with respect to the intentions of the synod, for the halfway arrangement did propose to safeguard the purity of communicant membership. But as with many a good intention, the historical aftermath was something different. By extending baptism and a measure of church membership to the children of unconverted parents, the synod was accepting another generation of unconverted members who would be content generally with no closer relation to the church—or to God—than their parents had enjoyed. As Robert G. Pope put it, "the halfway covenant represented the terminal commitment for most children who took advantage of it. . . . They took hold of the covenant as the easiest way to maintain their relations with the church." In a statistical analysis of selected church records, Pope found "a low percentage of persons who entered communion after owning the covenant," and

3. *Propositions Concerning the Subjects of Baptism* (Cambridge, Mass., 1662), the Fifth Proposition; in Williston Walker, *The Creeds and Platforms of Congregationalism* (Boston, 1960), p. 328.

4. Morgan, *Visible Saints,* pp. 133–38.

concluded that "by the turn of the century purity had been largely sacrificed to community." [5]

Jonathan Edwards, reflecting on this in 1749, observed that " 'tis not unusual, in some churches . . . for persons at the same time that they come into the church, and pretend to own the covenant, freely to declare to their neighbors, they have no imagination that they have any true faith in Christ, or love to him." Owning the covenant, in his view, had "degenerated into a matter of mere form and ceremony . . . it being visibly a prevailing custom for persons to neglect this till they come to be married, and then to do it for their credit's sake, and that their children may be baptized." [6] On the basis of this and similar testimonies, there is no good reason to doubt Williston Walker's description of the way in which the Halfway Covenant actually operated over the years. By about 1719, he wrote,

> many ministers admitted all applicants of good moral character to the covenant and granted them and their children baptism, without question as to whether the recipients were members by birth or not. . . . Indeed, there is reason to believe that in many places admission to the covenant came to be looked upon . . . as a means by which large bodies of young people might be induced to start out in the right path in life. And while some churches admitted to baptism those who had no other claim than a respectable life and a willingness to take the covenant obligations, others granted the rite to the children of those who had themselves been baptized, without requiring any covenant promises from the parents at all. [7]

When the line between halfway and communicant membership began to break down, as it inevitably did in the relaxation of rigor

5. *The Half-Way Covenant*, pp. 235–38, 276. Pope also found that in churches adopting the halfway practice there was an overall increase in communicant membership, converted from the community at large, and this led him to regard the Halfway Covenant as an advance for the churches.

6. *An Humble Inquiry into the Rules of the Word of God, Concerning the Qualifications Requisite to a Complete Standing and Full Communion in the Visible Christian Church* (Boston, 1749), pp. 32, 36.

7. *Creeds and Platforms of Congregationalism*, pp. 278–79. Cf. also Perry Miller, *The New England Mind*, Vol. 2, *From Colony to Province* (Boston, 1961), p. 113; Morgan, *Visible Saints*, p. 150; and Pettit, *The Heart Prepared*, p. 201.

to maintain an ostensibly pure church, the congregational way itself was in danger. The next "attempt to rescue the concept of a church of visible saints" would have either to redefine the concept of sainthood in terms that dispensed entirely with the demand for professions of experiential faith, or else recover the norms of early Congregationalism. Actually both were tried, the former by Solomon Stoddard and other advocates of an inclusive church, the latter by Jonathan Edwards and many New Lights of the Great Awakening.

The struggle to redefine sainthood was led by Solomon Stoddard (1643–1729) in the sense that he fought the public battles which earned him this notoriety, though others had quietly preceded him. He became pastor at Northampton in 1669; and in less than a decade he was discarding the distinction between full and halfway members, baptizing every adult who assented to the articles of faith, and admitting all the baptized to the Lord's Supper. In 1700 he startled traditionalists by publishing his judgment that visible saints are those who "make a serious profession of the true religion, together with those that do descend from them, till rejected of God." [8] By "profession" Stoddard meant an intellectual and verbal acquiescence, what early Puritans had called "a historical faith." In 1709 he announced that visible sainthood had nothing to do with inward grace and conversion.[9] This was his way of interpreting the canons of the Reforming Synod (1679), one of whose crucial formulations he had been able to dictate. When some of the elders at the Synod had pressed for a statement requiring "that persons should make a relation of the work of God's Spirit upon their hearts, in order to coming into full communion," Stoddard moved successfully to substitute the following: "It is requisite that persons be not admitted unto communion in the Lord's Supper without making a personal and public profession of their faith and repentance." [1] As practiced at Northampton and throughout the Connecticut River Valley, where "Pope" Stoddard's influence was strong, such profession had nothing to say about inward religious experience. One of the few churches which resisted the new scheme was Westfield, whose poetically turned pastor, Edward Taylor, suspected a drift

8. *The Doctrine of the Instituted Churches* (Boston, 1700), p. 6.
9. *An Appeal to the Learned* (Boston, 1709), p. 25.
1. *The Necessity of Reformation* (Boston, 1679), p. 10; in Walker, *Creeds and Platforms of Congregationalism*, p. 433. Stoddard related his victory over the traditionalist clergy in *An Appeal to the Learned*, pp. 93–94.

Into ye Realm of Prelates arch, ye place
Where open Sinners vile unmaskt indeed
Are welcome Guests (if they can say ye Creed)
Unto Christ's Table.[2]

At the very least, Stoddardism marked a major break with the experiential tradition, and indeed with the whole congregational way.[3]

It is only fair to say that Stoddard himself was both a Calvinist and a conversionist. Though he discarded the practice of requiring relations of experience from persons entering full communion in the visible church, he still insisted on the necessity of gracious conversion. He regarded conversion as a change which God alone can produce when and as he wills. He rejected the "Arminian" notion that any acts of preparation are efficacious in themselves, and preached the terrors of hell to those who trusted in their own goodness for salvation. And yet, by insisting on what unregenerate men can and must do to prepare themselves for conversion, and by urging them to partake of the Lord's Supper because it is "a converting ordinance," [4] he unwittingly encouraged the idea that God somehow could be bound to reward the more active doers among them. "If men were seeking more earnestly they would have more success," he declared, and quoted Matt.11:12, "The kingdom of heaven suffereth violence, and the violent take it by force." [5] It is hardly remarkable that such exhortations underscored the importance of human striving, nor is it surprising that less theologically sophisticated men easily assumed that their efforts should purchase

2. Quoted in Miller, *The New England Mind*, 2, 240. Taylor died in 1729, the same year as Stoddard, and the Westfield church soon adopted the Stoddardean practice. Cf. Norman Grabo, *Edward Taylor's Treatise Concerning the Lord's Supper* (Lansing, Mich., 1965).

3. See Pope, *The Half-Way Covenant*, pp. 251–58, where some precedents for Stoddard's "presbyterian polity" are cited; also Morgan, *Visible Saints*, p. 149; Pettit, *The Heart Prepared*, p. 203; and Thomas A. Schafer, "Solomon Stoddard and the Theology of the Revival," in *A Miscellany of American Christianity* (Durham, N.C., 1963), p. 332.

4. See his *Doctrine of the Instituted Churches*, p. 22; and *Appeal to the Learned*, p. 25.

5. *Those Taught by God the Father, to Know God the Son; Are Blessed* (Boston, 1712), p. 33; quoted in Schafer, "Solomon Stoddard and the Theology of the Revival," *loc. cit.*, p. 342. Schafer adds: "Stoddard believes that men must achieve a rather high level of personal morality if the work of conversion is to proceed further" (p. 343).

some claim to the favor of God. Stoddard often sought to awaken sleepy sinners and bring them to that "humiliation" which would lead to genuine conversion, and with frequent success at Northampton; but elsewhere most professing Christians, having already gained all the privileges of church membership, simply enjoyed them with less pain and trouble.

Thus on the eve of the Great Awakening New England's churches were a mixed multitude like the ones from which their founders had fled, their outward religious life characterized largely by moral homilies in the pulpit—"Cotton Mather's 'do-good' piety"—and complacent self-confidence in the pew.[6] This is not formal or explicit Arminianism, but it is certainly the prevailing mood which evoked the outcries of 1734 and afterward. Charles Chauncy, to be sure, was to reject the charge that those who opposed the Awakening did so on Arminian grounds.[7] But other antirevivalists were less defensive. "A few years before these commotions began," wrote one in 1743, "some of the clergy began to preach less metaphysical and more practical sermons; on which many people complained of the decay of religion, the absence of that fervor and spirituality that had formerly appeared among ministers and people, and the danger of Arminianism overspreading the land." [8] He was admitting the reality; what one called it was only a matter of semantics.

But what precisely was the occasion of the "great noise" which Jonathan Edwards heard in Hampshire County in 1734? The best clue comes from the Diary of Stephen Williams (1693–1782), minister at Longmeadow, just below Springfield. On November 18, 1734, Williams recorded:

> This day I hear that Mr. Rand of Sunderland has advanced some new notions as to the doctrines of justification. I am fearful

6. Pope, *The Half-Way Covenant*, p. 276. Miller, in a similar context, referred to such deliverances as preaching "as though John Calvin had never lived" ("Preparation for Salvation in Seventeenth-Century New England," *loc cit.*, p. 282); and Walker saw them as emphasizing "morality as a means to a Christian life" rather than the result of "a divinely wrought change in man's nature" (*Creeds and Platforms of Congregationalism*, p. 284). Under such preaching, many evangelists charged, pewsitters rested in "carnal security."

7. *Seasonable Thoughts on the State of Religion in New England* (Boston, 1743), pp. 397–98. On Chauncy, see below, pp. 62–64, 80–83.

8. "A Dissertation of the State of Religion in North America," *American Magazine, 1* (Sept. 1743), 2.

much mischief will be done—people's spirit exasperated and religion deeply wounded.[9]

The "new notions" are not specified in any source yet discovered; but knowing their author, one can easily surmise their character. William Rand (1700–79) had been installed as the second minister at Sunderland in 1723. Classmate of Charles Chauncy (Harvard 1721), he was soon to be known as the most intransigent Old Light in Hampshire County—a stance which would lead to his removal in 1745.[1] For the time being, however, he seems to have contented himself with one outburst of heterodoxy; and in deference to the uneasiness of his brethren, he soon "retracted the errors he was found to be falling into, and professed his principles in terms approved by his church and neighboring ministers."[2] The "exceeding alienation" between Rand and his congregation was healed, at least temporarily, when the revival reached Sunderland in the spring of 1735 (FN; below, p. 103). This little tempest might have brewed and cooled in a private teapot had not Jonathan Edwards, already alerted by the early bubblings of the Breck controversy, chosen to make a public issue of it. The real genie slipping silently out of the bottle, as he perceived it, was Arminianism. When Stoddard's young successor, standing on the threshold of his career called it by name and set his face against it, the Great Awakening in New England was on.[3]

9. MS Diary at Longmeadow, Mass., Public Library. Surprisingly few scholars have exploited this significant source for religious affairs in colonial Hampshire County. A notable exception is Mary Catherine Foster, whose doctoral dissertation, "Hampshire County, Massachusetts, 1729–1754: A Covenant Society in Transition" (Univ. of Michigan, 1967), identifies and documents beyond dispute the crypto-Arminianism of several of the Hampshire ministers, showing how the early factions there "paralleled the [later] lines of division between Calvinism and Arminianism" (p. 315).

1. Rand was called to Kingston, which had just dismissed Thaddeus Maccarty for New Light sympathies.

2. William Williams of Hatfield, letter dated April 28, 1735, to Benjamin Colman; in Colman Papers, Mass. Hist. Soc. A letter from Warham Williams of Watertown, dated March 20, 1734/5, to his brother Stephen Williams also adverts to "the particular state of the difficulties in Hampshire County in the upper [illegible word] parts of it" (Letters of American Clergymen, New York Public Library). The geographical location points not to Springfield, where in any case the Breck controversy was temporarily quiescent, but to Sunderland.

3. Even though the Awakening in the Middle Colonies began several years earlier, there is no evidence of its having any influence on New England. JE

3. *A Surprising Work of God*

"The beginning of the late work of God in this place," Edwards wrote in 1738, "was so circumstanced that I could not but look upon it as a remarkable testimony of God's approbation of the doctrine of justification by faith alone." That statement appears in the preface to the published version of the series of sermons which, so far as human initiatives go, he regarded as having ignited the Valley revival of 1734–35. Published "at the desire and expense of the town," the work was entitled:

> *Discourses on Various Important Subjects, Nearly Concerning the Great Affair of the Soul's Eternal Salvation, Viz.*
>   *I. Justification by Faith Alone*
>   *II. Pressing into the Kingdom of God*
> *III. Ruth's Resolution*
>   *IV. The Justice of God in the Damnation of Sinners*
>   *V. The Excellency of Jesus Christ*
> *Delivered at Northampton, Chiefly at the Time of the Late Wonderful Pouring Out of the Spirit of God There.*[4]

Edwards was convinced that the leading sermon in this series—and its doctrine repeated in all the others—was what really carried the freight.

> By the noise that had a little before been raised in this country concerning that doctrine, people here seemed to have their minds put into an unusual ruffle. . . . The following discourse of Justification that was preached (though not so fully as it is here printed) at two public lectures seemed to be remarkably blessed. . . . So that this was the doctrine on which this work in its beginning was founded, as it evidently was in the whole progress of it.[5]

testified that news of that movement first came to him when he traveled to New Jersey for his health in the summer of 1735 (FN-1; below, pp. 155–56).

4. Boston, 1738. The fifth sermon was not in the original series; it was added, Edwards confided in the preface, "on my own motion" at the request of hearers in another town where it was "occasionally" preached. Perry Miller called this work "the most elaborate intellectual production [Edwards] had yet attempted" (*Jonathan Edwards*, p. 75).

5. *Discourses on Various Important Subjects*, p. ii. In nearby Longmeadow, the Rev. Stephen Williams recorded in his diary on Sunday, Feb. 23, 1734/5: "I have been again upon the article of justification."

Based on Romans 4:5, "To him that worketh not, but believeth on him that justifieth the ungodly, his faith is counted for righteousness," the sermon stated as its doctrine: "We are justified only by faith in Christ, and not by any manner of virtue or goodness of our own." Although Edwards named Arminianism only once, he was contesting throughout "the adverse scheme [which] lays another foundation of man's salvation than God hath laid." [6] Because of the infinite guilt of sin (on this point Edwards followed the medieval theologian, Anselm of Canterbury) no man should hope for God's acceptance on the ground of such imperfect obedience as natural man can concede, for "as we are in ourselves, and out of Christ, we are under the condemnation of that original law, or constitution that God established with mankind; and therefore 'tis no way fit that anything that we do, any virtue or obedience of ours, should be accepted, or we accepted on the account of it." [7] He marshalled Scripture after Scripture to oppose the conceit "that 'tis our own goodness, virtue, or excellency, that instates us in God's acceptance and favor." [8] He underlined the moral ambiguity in every work of man.

> Not only are our best duties defiled, in being attended with the exercises of sin and corruption, that precede them and follow them, and are intermingled with holy acts; but even the holy acts themselves, and the gracious exercises of the godly, though the act most simply considered is good, yet take the acts in their measure and dimensions, and the manner in which they are exerted, and they are corrupt acts; that is, they are defectively corrupt, or sinfully defective; there is that defect in them that may well be called the corruption of them. That defect is properly sin.[9]

He called for repentance, which would bring the sinner to humble himself before God, and faith as an earnest embracing of Christ who alone fulfilled all righteousness, though he warned that "the admitting a soul to an union with Christ is an act of free and sovereign grace." [1] Any other scheme, he concluded, smacked of "the popish doctrine of merit" which led sinners to believe that " 'tis our

6. Ibid., p. 124.
7. Ibid., p. 34.
8. Ibid., p. 74.
9. Ibid., p. 90.
1. Ibid., p. 102.

virtue, as imperfect as it is, that recommends men to God, by which good men come to have a saving interest in Christ and God's favor, rather than others; and [that] these things are bestowed in testimony of God's respect to their goodness." [2] So much for Arminians!

There was "a special fitness in those sermons," mused a nineteenth-century historian, "to produce the effects which followed them." [3] Not even when "thunder fell in Smith's pasture" during the earthquake of 1727 had Northampton been so shaken.[4] In the midst of growing seriousness among the youth, a frivolous young woman professed a dramatic conversion in the fall of 1734, and this touched off several similar experiences. Soon an intense religious concern gripped the whole town. Within six months more than three hundred persons, ranging in age from four to above seventy years, had testified to a lively hope of having been "savingly wrought upon." Edwards was nearly ecstatic: old converts were revived, contentions abated, exercises of public worship enlivened; religion became everybody's chief engagement: "the town seemed to be full of the presence of God: it never was so full of love, nor so full of joy . . . as it was then. There were remarkable tokens of God's presence in almost every house" (FN-1; below, p. 151).

His wonder undiminished, Edwards enumerated thirty-two other communities in the Connecticut River Valley which began to glow with the same sacred fire.[5] In most cases he seems to have thought

2. Ibid., p. 125. There is much more in the printed version of this sermon (130 pages!) than I have indicated here, especially concerning JE's conception of saving faith as not a meritorious "work" on which salvation is conditioned but a gift of God having a "natural fitness" for bringing a sinner to "close with Christ." For an insightful treatment of this doctrine in the context of JE's total thought, see Cherry, *The Theology of Jonathan Edwards*, ch. 6.

3. Tracy, *The Great Awakening*, p. 12.

4. The phrase is from one of JE's undated MS sermons, cited in Ola Elizabeth Winslow, *Jonathan Edwards, 1703–1758* (New York, 1961), p. 137. The authors of the preface to the first American edition of JE's *Faithful Narrative* also advert to the earthquake (below, p. 139), as does Thomas Prince, Jr., in *The Christian History, 1,* 114.

5. JE referred to every organized town in Hampshire County except Somers and Brimfield. He probably could have included Somers (originally the east precinct of Enfield, Mass., now Conn.), where Samuel Allis was pastor 1727–47. The records of this small church show that it received 21 new members in 1735 as compared with a total of 37 who had been admitted to full communion since the church was organized with nine charter members in 1727. See "Church and Town Records of Somers," in Francis O. Allen, *The History of Enfield, Connecticut, 3* (Lancaster, Pa., 1900), 2186–88.

that the igniting spark came from his own congregation, although in a few instances he acknowledged a simultaneous work which began without news of other awakenings. With several situations he had first-hand acquaintance; others he reported on the basis of testimony of varying reliability. In locating these spreading revivals, sometimes he gave the name of a town or parish, sometimes a neighborhood name for part of a town not yet erected as a separate parish. The list below is compiled from the place names given by Edwards, collated from all extant versions of his report on the revival (there are variations in them), with modern names added where they might be useful. He identified the pastors in only a few instances; additional names and dates of service are supplied by the editor. Pastors whose names are preceded by an asterisk generally opposed the "great and general awakening" of the 1740s, and some were cool even toward the revivals which their churches enjoyed in 1735. The absence of an asterisk does not necessarily mean vigorous support of either movement.

NEW ENGLAND COMMUNITIES MENTIONED BY EDWARDS
AS EXPERIENCING REVIVALS IN 1734–5

 1. Northfield, Mass.   *Benjamin Doolittle, 1718–48
 2. "part of Deerfield, called
     Green River"
 3. Deerfield, Mass.   *Jonathan Ashley, 1732–80
 4. Sunderland, Mass.   *William Rand, 1723–45
 5. Hatfield, Mass.   William Williams, 1685–1741
 6. South Hatfield, "a place
     called The Hill"
 7. Hadley, Mass.   Isaac Chauncy, 1695–1745
 8. South Hadley, Mass.   *Grindall Rawson, 1733–41
 9. Westfield, Mass.   Nehemiah Bull, 1726–40
10. West Springfield, Mass.   *Samuel Hopkins, 1720–55
11. Springfield, Mass.   *Robert Breck, 1735–84
12. Longmeadow, Mass.   Stephen Williams, 1714–82
13. West Suffield, Mass.
     (now in Conn.)
14. Suffield, Mass.   Ebenezer Devotion, 1709–41
     (now in Conn.)
15. Enfield, Mass.   Peter Reynolds, 1724–68
     (now in Conn.)

16. Windsor, Conn.   *Jonathan Marsh, 1710–47
17. East Windsor, Conn. (Second   Timothy Edwards, 1694–1758
    Church of South Windsor)
18. Tolland, Conn.   Stephen Steel, 1719–58
19. Bolton, Conn.   *Thomas White, 1725–63
20. [South] Coventry, Conn.   Joseph Meacham, 1714–52
21. Mansfield, Conn.   Eleazar Williams, 1710–42
22. Lebanon Crank (now Col-   Eleazar Wheelock, 1735–70
    umbia), Conn.
23. Hebron, Conn.   Benjamin Pomeroy, 1735–84
24. [North] Preston (now Gris-   Hezekiah Lord, 1720–61
    wold), Conn.
25. Woodbury, Conn.   Anthony Stoddard, 1700–60
26. Durham, Conn.   *Nathaniel Chauncy, 1706–56
27. Ripton (Second Church   Jedediah Mills, 1723–76
    Stratford, now Huntington),
    Conn.
28. Stratford, Conn.   Hezekiah Gold, 1722–52
29. New Haven, Conn.   *Joseph Noyes, 1715–61
30. Guilford, Conn.   *Thomas Ruggles, Jr., 1729–70
31. [Old] Lyme, Conn.   Jonathan Parsons, 1729–45
32. Groton, Conn.   John Owen, 1727–53

Edwards also mentioned revivals in three localities in New Jersey
(below, p. 156).

Confirming the spread of the new awakening, Stephen Williams
recorded on May 9, 1735, that "the election frolics both at Suffield
and Enfield were turned into religious exercises." [6] Eliphalet Adams
of New London, Connecticut, wrote on September 3, 1735, that the
Spirit of God "hath been at work in divers towns, to awaken a concern in many about what they shall do to be saved, that this concern
continues, that it spreads, and that persons are flocking into the
churches as doves to their windows [Isa. 60:8]." [7] And on May 24,
1736, Elisha Williams, rector of Yale College, sent word to Isaac
Watts that "there has been a remarkable revival of religion in
several parts of this country, in ten parishes in the county of Hampshire, in the Massachusetts province, where it first began a little

6. MS Diary at Longmeadow, Mass., Public Library.
7. Preface "To the Reader," in Eleazar Williams, *Sensible Sinners Invited
to Come to Christ* (New London, 1735).

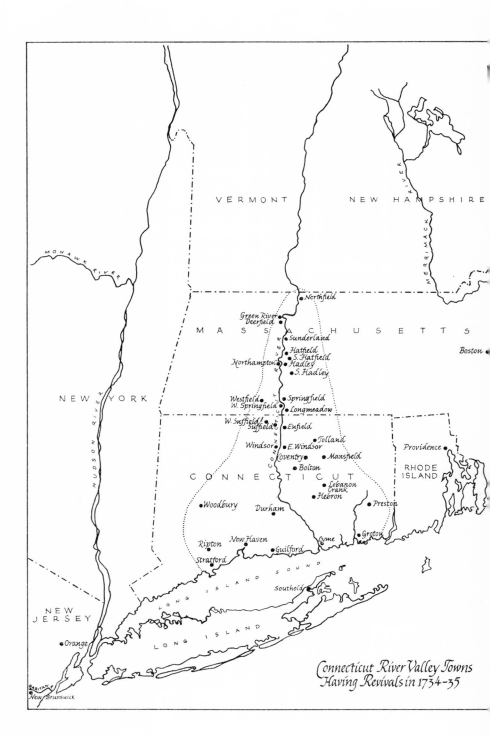

VERMONT

NEW HAMPSHIRE

MONHAWK RIVER

MERRIMACK RIVER

MASSACHUSETTS

Boston

● Northfield

Green River ●
Deerfield ●

● Sunderland

Hatfield ●
S. Hatfield ●
Northampton ● Hadley ●
● S. Hadley

NEW YORK

Westfield ● ● Springfield
W. Springfield ● Longmeadow

HUDSON RIVER

W. Suffield ●
Suffield ● ● Enfield

Windsor ● ● E. Windsor   ● Tolland
● Coventry   ● Mansfield
● Bolton

Providence ●

RHODE
ISLAND

CONNECTICUT

● Lebanon
Crank
● Hebron

● Woodbury   Durham ●

● Preston

Ripton ● New Haven ●
Stratford ● ● Guilford

Lyme ● Groton

LONG ISLAND SOUND

Southold ●

NEW
JERSEY

● Orange

LONG ISLAND

RARITAN R.
New Brunswick

Connecticut River Valley Towns
Having Revivals in 1734-35

more than a year since, and in near twenty parishes of this colony [Connecticut]." [8]

Such was the geographical extent of the "surprising work of God" in 1734–35. Nothing like it had ever occurred before in New England, where previous revivals were largely sporadic and isolated instances which Edwards suspected of resting too often on an implicit Arminianism. An Anglican missionary in Boston, though utterly contemptuous of the new stir in the West, at least concurred in identifying its theological basis. Wrote Timothy Cutler:

> The Calvinistical scheme is in perfection about 100 miles from this place. Conversions are talked of, *ad nauseam usque.* Sixty in a place undergo the work at once . . . and the canting question trumped about is, "Are you gone through?" i.e. conversion. [9]

To Edwards, however, the new awakening was "God glorified in the work of redemption, by the greatness of man's dependence upon him, in the whole of it," [1] not something contrived by man. The element of surprise was real. But what was the nature of the work and of the experiences professed by its subjects?

4. *The Morphology of Conversion*

Jonathan Edwards inherited a tradition which had long occupied itself with analyses of the conversion experience. It is only natural that Puritan teachers should probe here, because as thoroughgoing evangelicals they regarded the Christian life as beginning with an experience of personal conversion (see above, pp. 2–3). They therefore sought to chart the course by which men come to that crucial experience, and "the result of their studies was to establish a morphology of conversion, in which each stage could be distinguished from the next, so that a man could check his eternal condition by a set of temporal and recognizable signs." [2] When the churches of

8. Printed in Thomas Milner, *The Life, Times, and Correspondence of the Rev. Isaac Watts, D.D.* (London, 1834), p. 546. Williams was a son of William Williams of Hatfield; in this letter he described the revival in his father's parish.

9. Letter dated June 5, 1735, to Zachary Grey; in John Nichols, *Illustrations of the Literary History of the Eighteenth Century, 4* (London, 1822), 298.

1. This was the title of JE's lecture when he made his debut before the Boston clergy in 1731. Cf. Miller, *Jonathan Edwards*, pp. 3–34.

2. Morgan, *Visible Saints*, p. 66. William Perkins (1558–1602), whose Cam-

New England introduced the novelty of regenerate church membership and connected this with political privilege in the holy com-
monwealth, it became even more important to have a reliable road-
map to regeneration. Hence Thomas Hooker (1586–1647), Thomas
Shepard (1604–49), and other founding fathers of the New England
Way offered "rich and intricate analyses of the stages on the way
to conversion." [3] Especially did preparationists of varying views seek
to furnish souls under their care with clearly marked guideposts to
grace. By the end of the seventeenth century the steps of the pil-
grim's progress had become so fixed in the New England mind as to
give the religious experiences narrated by applicants for church
membership the appearance of a set form. Professor Morgan has
summarized the traditional pattern:

> First comes a feeble and false awakening to God's commands
> and a pride in keeping them pretty well, but also much back-
> sliding. Disappointments and disasters lead to other fitful heark-
> enings to the word. Sooner or later true legal fear or conviction
> enables the individual to see his hopeless and helpless condition
> and to know that his own righteousness cannot save him, that
> Christ is his only hope. Thereafter comes the infusion of saving
> grace, sometimes but not always so precisely felt that the be-
> liever can state exactly when and where it came to him. A strug-
> gle between faith and doubt ensues, with the candidate careful
> to indicate that his assurance has never been complete and that
> his sanctification has been much hampered by his own sinful
> heart.[4]

The Great Awakening revived this pattern of conversion. Still
more, it established a morphology which would become normative
in the evangelical churches; and as the revivalism then aborning
brought those churches to dominance in American Christianity, this

---

bridge sermons persuaded many hearers, had described no fewer than ten
stages in the reception of saving faith. JE reminded himself at an early stage
of his studies "most nicely and diligently to look into our old divines' opinions
concerning conversion" (Private Diary, entry for May 25, 1723; in Levin,
Jonathan Edwards: A Profile, p. 17).

3. Miller, *Jonathan Edwards*, p. 155.

4. *Visible Saints*, p. 91. Morgan's description rests on narratives of converts
recorded in "The Diary of Michael Wigglesworth," ed. by Edmund S. Morgan,
Publications of the Colonial Society of Massachusetts, 35 (1942–46), 426–44.

pattern of conversion came to be widely accepted as the normal mode of entry into the Christian life. Credit for such a development goes chiefly to Jonathan Edwards, for three reasons: (1) far more than any of his predecessors, he had vast opportunities for clinical observation of sinners in the throes of the conversion experience; (2) he refracted his data through the insights of a new psychology derived from John Locke (1632–1704), thus achieving an interpretation of religious experience that commended the evangelical scheme to many thoughtful persons; [5] and (3) he published a testimonial history of the first wave of revivalism, with the result that the pattern of the Northampton conversions became firmly fixed in the popular mind.[6] During the awakening of 1734–35 Edwards faithfully pursued his pastoral work with reverent wonder, for as already noted, his surprise was genuine. But when he gave his narrative to the world, the simple fact is that no revival could ever be a surprise again. His account showed plainly what kind of preaching would awaken sleepy sinners and what sort of responses could be expected. The day would come too soon when overzealous evangelists would attempt to manipulate audiences so as to elicit the responses described by Edwards, and the revival—if it came—would be not a surprising work of God but a planned contrivance of man.

Edwards' narrative, of course, only testified to what he had learned by experience. As to the preaching that shattered somnolence, he declared: "I think I have found that no discourses have been more remarkably blessed, than those in which the doctrine of God's absolute sovereignty with regard to the salvation of sinners, and his just liberty with regard to answering the prayers, or succeeding the pains of natural men, continuing such, have been insisted on" (FN-1; below, p. 168). His uncompromising sermons on justification by faith alone broke up the "carnal security" of his congregation and brought to him numbers of people anxious for guidance toward the safety of Christ. "The place of resort was now altered; it was no

5. JE's major exposition of the way in which the Spirit of God acts directly on a sinner to give a "new sense of the heart" is *A Treatise Concerning Religious Affections* (Boston, 1746). See Editor John E. Smith's introduction to this work in Vol. 2 of the Yale edition of *The Works of Jonathan Edwards* (New Haven, 1959). Also helpful are Cherry, *The Theology of Jonathan Edwards,* Part One; and Miller, *Jonathan Edwards,* pp. 139–40, 153–58.

6. Thomas Prince, minister at Boston's Old South Church, noted that JE's reports on the Valley revival of 1735 helped to prepare the way for the more pervasive awakening of the 1740s (*The Christian History,* 2, 379).

longer the tavern, but the minister's house, that was thronged far more than ever the tavern had been wont to be" (FN-1; below, p. 161). Far from content with mere repetitions of traditional pieties, the pastor probed and the people wrestled. Anxious that no one think that "for want of judgment, I take every religious pang and enthusiastic conceit for saving conversion" (FN-1; below, p. 159), Edwards compiled for himself a set of "Directions for Judging of Persons' Experiences."

> See to it that the operation be much upon the will or heart, not on the imagination, nor on the speculative understanding or motions of the mind, though they draw great affections after 'em as the consequence. . . . That under their seeming convictions it be sin indeed; that they are convinced of their guilt in offending and affronting so great a God. . . . That it is truly conviction of sin that convinces them of the justice of God in their damnation. . . . That there is to be discerned in their sense of the sufficiency of Christ, a sense of that divine, supreme, and spiritual excellency of Christ, wherein this sufficiency fundamentally consists; and that the sight of this excellency is really the foundation of their satisfaction as to his sufficiency. . . . Whether their experience have a respect to *practice* in these ways. That their behavior at present seems to be agreeable to such experiences. . . . Makes a disposition to ill practices dreadful. Makes 'em long after perfect freedom from sin, and after those things wherein *holiness* consists.[7]

Edwards devoted about one-fourth of *A Faithful Narrative* specifically to describing the morphology of the Northampton conversions (below, pp. 160–76) and another fourth to ringing the changes on each phase (below, pp. 176–91). At times he seemed more impressed by the rich diversity in his people's experiences than by any unifying similarities. But the "endless variety" he professed to see (FN-1; below, p. 185) can be read as little more than an endless way of saying essentially the same things in different words. Edwards' detailed observations are like jottings in the notebook of a clinical psychologist, and from them one can distill a definite pattern of conversion in three basic stages. A typical experience (1) began with "conviction," a troubled sense of sin felt either as fear or misery,

7. Alexander B. Grosart, ed., *Selections from the Unpublished Writings of Jonathan Edwards* (Edinburgh, 1865), pp. 183–85.

(2) descended to some kind of nadir where the subject confessed that he deserved damnation and might even despair of being saved, then (3) mounted to heights of rapture in the joy of sins forgiven.

Careful interpreters of Edwards observe that he was hardly attempting to "fix the work of the Spirit to an inflexible series of stages" or restrict conversion to a uniform pattern.[8] He was always unwilling to reject an experience just because it failed to follow a certain presupposed order, for, as he put it in *Religious Affections,* "no order or method of operations and experiences is any certain sign of their divinity."[9] But in *A Faithful Narrative* he was only reporting what he had actually observed; and notwithstanding the many varieties of religious experience at Northampton, the three-stage pattern which can be extrapolated from his report is a fair summary of what he described. The same sort of eyewitness testimony, joined to a reminder that God is always free to act otherwise, appears in Edwards' account of the revival of 1740–42. He noted that conversions then had been "wrought more sensibly and visibly; the impressions stronger, and more manifest by external effects of them; and the progress of the Spirit of God in conviction, from step to step, more apparent; and the transition from one state to another more sensible and plain; so that it might, in many instances, be as it were seen by bystanders." But then he warned: "The goodness of [a] person's state is not chiefly to be judged of by any exactions of steps, and method of experiences, in what is supposed to be the first conversion" (see below, pp. 549, 556). If Edwards could have foreseen that other evangelists would jettison his warning and erect his clinical reports into a normative pattern, he might have made the warning stronger. The morphology of conversion which emerges from the pages of *A Faithful Narrative* is what revivalists in and after the Great Awakening came to expect of all converts. Indeed, among many of the New Lights anyone who could not (or would not) formulate his Christian testimony in this way was likely to be judged unconverted.[1] Edwards' narrative continues to cast a long shadow, for in various stylized forms its pattern of conversion persists among some evangelicals to this day.

8. Cherry, *The Theology of Jonathan Edwards,* p. 65.

9. Yale ed., p. 159. See Editor John E. Smith's comment on this passage, p. 20.

1. C. C. Goen, *Revivalism and Separatism in New England, 1740–1800,* 2d ed. (Hamden, Conn., 1969), pp. 45–54. Cf. also Daniel B. Shea, Jr., *Spiritual Autobiography in Early America* (Princeton, 1968), p. 209.

Having recorded in rich detail the spiritual travails he observed in more than three hundred parishioners, Edwards climaxed his account with two individual case histories. Abigail Hutchinson, a young single woman slowly starving to death because of some esophageal obstruction, and Phebe Bartlet, a spiritually precocious child of four, were the new converts whose experiences he chose to relate in full (FN-1; below, pp. 191–205). The choices may tell as much about his own pathology as about the work of God, for these were clearly among his most dramatic examples; and the accounts he published were to haunt him and his friends as a few years later they struggled to control the mass hysteria which the revival generated in some places. Ola Winslow remarks:

> When his readers assumed that such behaviors did greater honor to God than less spectacular deliverances their conclusion was fair enough, and when in the next decade extravagance went out of bounds, and revival marvels were induced by a score of bizarre methods, Jonathan Edwards was himself in part to blame. His own very earnest later rebuke to the emphasis on "bodily manifestations" and other sensational forms of hysteria were less effective than the models he had himself set up in this earlier treatise.[2]

For the moment, however, Edwards was innocent of any consideration save to show how God really saves sinners and thus to stop the mouths of all Arminians.

He was able to describe and even in part to guide the experiences of his Northampton converts because he had cast his own religious development in the same idiom. His "Personal Narrative," written about 1740, reveals how during his youth he had been brought to renounce all pride of self, accept the sovereignty of God over his life, and revel in the effulgence of divine love.[3] Perhaps as a settled minister mellowing in the afterglow of a surprising harvest of like-hearted saints he read more back into the impressions of youth than was actually there—at so many points the language of his "Personal Narrative" echoes that of the revival *Narrative*. But in their different times both pastor and people had awakened to the terrible reality of their disobedience to God, and out of their dread of incurring his wrath against their prideful ambition came the "legal terrors"

2. *Jonathan Edwards*, p. 158.
3. In Levin, *Jonathan Edwards: A Profile*, pp. 25–26.

which marked the first step toward conversion. Here may lie one explanation for the rapid spread of the revival, for as Richard L. Bushman has demonstrated, the social history of the Connecticut River Valley is remarkably analogous to Edwards' personal history in that both betray the perennial conflict between inordinate temptations to pride and the known duties of humility. Recent developments in expanding trade, population growth, land speculation, conflicts with authority, and disharmony in personal relationships had given ample opportunity to the Valley's citizens for the expression of prideful ambition. On the other hand, every calamity—earthquake, sudden death, Indian raid, shipwreck—easily aroused fears of the sovereign deity whose judgment stood over all such self-assertion. The "Puritan ethic," as some are pleased to call it, weighed heavily on the Puritan conscience.

> The whole society suffered from a painful confusion of identity. People were taught to work at their earthly callings and to seek wealth; but one's business had to remain subservient to religion and to function within the bounds of seventeenth-century institutions. The opportunities constantly tempted people to overstep both boundaries, thereby evoking the wrath of powerful men who ruled society. Even relations with neighbors deteriorated as expansion multiplied the occasions for hard feelings. At some indeterminate point social values and institutions stopped supporting the man who placed his confidence in worldly success and instead obstructed and condemned his actions. The pleasurable rise which prosperity afforded carried one at last to destruction.[4]

As in the case of an adolescent rebel making peace with his father, religious conversion meant reconciliation with God: as one sub-

---

4. "Jonathan Edwards As a Great Man: Identity, Conversion, and Leadership in the Great Awakening," *Soundings*, 52 (1969), 40–41. Bushman here enlarges a detail of what he painted on a broader canvas in *From Puritan to Yankee; Character and the Social Order in Connecticut, 1690–1765* (Cambridge, Mass., 1967). The whole essay is highly original and suggestive, as is its forerunner, "Jonathan Edwards and the Puritan Consciousness," *Journal for the Scientific Study of Religion*, 5 (1965–66), 383–95. Although Bushman relies heavily on psychoanalytic insights, explaining susceptibility to conversion in terms of guilt produced by drives for wealth and power (and JE's conversion in terms of the resolution of an Oedipal conflict) nowhere does he rule out providence as a "cause" of the awakening.

mitted humbly, love displaced fear and furnished a new ground of confidence; i.e. one acquired a new identity. When this happened on a wide scale, social conflicts were healed and people were united in "affection one to another," as Edwards abundantly testified.[5] From the perspective of two centuries—where admittedly many details are lost from view—it seems possible to suggest that the time was ripe for hundreds throughout the Valley to profess conversion within a few years.

> They followed Edwards, or others like him, because they were ready, not because he personally overpowered them. Something common to all, some prevailing strain on their institutions, some pressure in the culture prepared people for the new life he urged upon them. They listened because the truth of his experience was also the truth of theirs.[6]

The entire epoch of the Great Awakening was thus a critical juncture where old values were failing and a new order was emerging. Jonathan Edwards proved to be the charismatic leader for that moment of *kairos* in American history when a bewildered people groped uncertainly to recapture their faltering sense of destiny. When God surprisingly converted "many hundred souls in Northampton and the neighboring towns," Edwards traced the patterns of his action in the hearts of men and thus began the documentation of what H. Richard Niebuhr has called "our national conversion." [7]

5. *The* Faithful Narrative

On May 30, 1735, Edwards wrote to the Rev. Dr. Benjamin Colman (1673–1747), the urbane and respected pastor of Brattle Street Church in Boston, a letter of eight pages describing the Valley revivals. This is the earliest written account of that event—never published before 1935, when it was included in *Jonathan Edwards: Representative Selections,* edited by Clarence H. Faust and Thomas H. Johnson.[8] Colman included much of Edwards' information in

5. FN; below, p. 103–04. See JE's comments regarding the revival's effect on Northampton's party spirit, below, pp. 557, 563–64.
6. Bushman, "Jonathan Edwards As a Great Man," *loc cit.,* p. 38.
7. *The Kingdom of God in America* (Hamden, Conn., 1956), p. 126.
8. The original (or JE's personal copy) is in the Andover Collection of Edwards' MSS. Almost every Edwards scholar has stated that it was published immediately, but this cannot be verified. No such entry appears in Charles Evans' *American Bibliography* or any other bibliography of colonial America,

his next letter to a friend and correspondent in London, the Rev. Dr. John Guyse (1680–1761), a Dissenting minister at New Broad Street. Guyse greeted the news with appropriate rejoicing and promptly shared it with his fellow minister, Isaac Watts (1674–1748), also a regular correspondent of Colman's, and with his congregation in a sermon. The congregation was so impressed that it asked to have the sermon printed, and Guyse agreed on condition that he could obtain permission to quote parts of Colman's letter. When Colman received Guyse's request, he wrote to William Williams of Hatfield, Edwards' uncle and neighbor, describing the re-

---

including the recent supplements and *The National Index.* So far as I am able to determine, the source of the apparently erroneous claim for publication is Dwight, who asserted that Colman published the letter and then forwarded a copy to friends in London *(Life of President Edwards,* p. 137). Tracy followed Dwight in the mistake *(The Great Awakening,* p. 18), as did Faust and Johnson, who went so far as to identify the letter of May 30, 1735, with a "unique" eighteen-page pamphlet in the Boston Public Library *(Jonathan Edwards: Representative Selections,* p. 420). But what they print in their anthology is a transcription of the manuscript letter. An exhaustive search at the BPL failed to turn up anything of a published version; what is there (and elsewhere) is Colman's abridgment of JE's longer letter of Nov. 6, 1736, appended to William Williams, *The Duty and Interest of a People* (Boston, 1736), which is described more fully below. This abridged version of JE's later letter, more than incidentally, runs to eighteen pages. Thomas H. Johnson repeated the error in *The Printed Writings of Jonathan Edwards,* where on p. 4 he correctly noted the appendix to Williams' sermon but then added: "This is the first draft of *A Faithful Narrative.*" Ola E. Winslow, doubtless misled by all of these, made the same mistake in *Jonathan Edwards: Basic Writings* (New York, 1966), p. 97; so did Perry Miller in his *Jonathan Edwards,* p. 136.

If JE's letter of May 30, 1735, was published at all, it could only have been in one of the newspapers, presumably in Boston. I have checked every extant issue of every Boston paper for the last seven months of 1735, and results were negative. It may be, of course, that the letter did appear in one of the issues which could not be located; these are *The Boston Gazette* for Aug. 25 (No. 817) and *The Boston News Letter* for July 24–Sept. 18. Since in 1735 the *News Letter* was only a single half-sheet printed on both sides, it hardly seems likely that it would carry a letter of this length. This leaves only one real possibility unchecked: the piece could be in the *Gazette* for Aug. 25, but because of the relative lateness of the date I am dubious.

So far as I know, the most accurate account of how Edwards' narrative of the Northampton revival of 1734–35 got into print is Anne Stokely Pratt, *Isaac Watts and His Gift of Books to Yale College* (New Haven, 1938), pp. 32–47. My account must necessarily parallel hers, but every point has been checked and some new details have been added.

ception of revival news in London and suggesting that Edwards write a more detailed account.[9] Edwards' response was immediate. He shared these developments with his own congregation, along with appropriate exhortations to sustain their fervor (FN-1; below, p. 210), and after a brief delay caused by illness in his family, began to write.

This explains why the published version of *A Faithful Narrative* is cast in the form of a letter to Benjamin Colman. Dated November 6, 1737, it reached print primarily through Colman's agency, for Edwards entrusted the whole affair to him (FN-1; below, p. 210). As soon as the lengthy missive arrived, Colman took the liberty of making an "accurate and judicious abridgment," which he attached to a work he had just finished preparing for the press. By a curious coincidence, this latter piece consisted of two sermons preached by William Williams, now past seventy, "at a time of general awakenings"—i.e. during the recent Valley revivals. One sermon is entitled *The Duty and Interest of a People, Among Whom Religion Has Been Planted, to Continue Stedfast and Sincere in the Profession and Practice of It from Generation to Generation*; the other is *Direction for Such as Are Concerned to Obtain a True Repentance and Conversion to God*. The second, probably earlier, sermon is clearly the old man's honest effort to contribute to the spreading revival. In spite of allusions here and there betraying a tacit confidence in human ability, his doctrine of conversion approaches that of Edwards: it is God who grants repentance and awakens faith, the Holy Spirit "enabling the soul to understand the truth of the things that the gospel reveals." But the first sermon, much longer and obviously more characteristic of Williams' preaching, appears to be a post-revival attempt to consolidate gains recently realized; it shows the author lapsing into more traditional terminology. The sermon carries its "Arminianism" in its title, appealing to duty and self-interest; and while it makes the customary threats of wrath and exhortations to faith, it also speaks much of "the reasonableness and amiableness of religion." This work of "honored Uncle Williams" was Colman's vehicle for presenting the first account of Edwards' revival to the American public.

The abridgment itself was offered mainly in Edwards' words rather than Colman's summary. It centered on a description of the awakening at Northampton and its spread throughout the Valley;

9. An extensive search for this letter, dated July 20, 1736, has not been successful.

though it included many details regarding the experiences of the
new converts, it omitted much of Edwards' reiteration and excised
completely the two case histories. Colman thus reduced to eighteen
printed pages what would become later a 132-page book. Isaac Watts
testified that the abridging was "so well performed that had it been
but twice as long as it is we would never have printed Mr. Edwards's
[letter in full]." [1] An unsigned paragraph, evidently by Colman,
introduced the abridged letter and broached the opinion that "the
publishing hereof may be of great use and benefit to souls, and not a
little serve the holy end and design of the preceding excellent
sermons; even to excite under the blessing and power of the Divine
Spirit, a like general concern in towns and churches." At the end
was an advertisement: "If the taste here given of Mr. Edwards his
excellent letter excite in persons of piety a desire to have the whole
of it published; it is hereby notified that subscriptions for that end
will be taken."

Williams' sermons, with the extracts from Edwards' narrative appended, were released by the Boston printers in mid-December
1736. On December 17 Colman sent copies of the appendix to his
London friends, with a covering letter to Watts:

> I send you an extract of a long letter, and another to Dr. Guyse,
> from the Rev. Mr. Edwards of Northampton, relating to that
> work, which will gratify both you and him in the general ac-
> count given; and you may make what use of it you please for the
> good of others. The whole of his letter to me is eight sheets, in
> writing; and whether it will be best to print it all I am in doubt,
> considering the taste of the present day; yet I find Mr. Edwards
> is not altogether pleased with the liberty we have taken of so
> general an extract. If it be not printed here in the whole, as a
> proposal is made by the bookseller, I think to send over to Dr.
> Guyse and you the manuscript, with Mr. Edwards's leave, and I
> think nothing less was his meaning in his labor of writing it; and
> then it will be yours to use as you may judge best for the service
> of souls.[2]

1. Letter dated May 31, 1738, to Benjamin Colman; in *Proceedings of the
Massachusetts Historical Society*, 2d Ser., 9 (1895), 361. (Hereafter cited as
PMHS.) The Mass. Hist. Soc. happily acquired and printed a large number of
Watts' letters in 1895.

2. Printed in Milner, *The Life, Times, and Correspondence of Isaac Watts*,
pp. 553–54. Note that what was to require 132 pages of print was on eight
sheets of JE's handwriting!

Watts replied on February 28, 1737, that Colman's extract had exceeded his expectations and given him such "religious pleasure" that he "longed for a more complete account of it." He added:

> Dr. Guyse has your present to him, and is as much pleased with it as I am. We both agree that your abstract of the letter is very happily drawn; but the hints are brief, and many things are omitted which we long to see, and we are of [the] opinion that so strange and surprising work of God that we have not heard anything like it since the Reformation, nor perhaps since the days of the apostles, should be published, and left upon record with all its attending circumstances, and therefore we join in subscribing five pounds towards the printing of the narrative [in Boston], and let us have as many copies in sheets as may answer the bookseller's encouragement and our desire to spread this narrative in the world. But we entreat also that it may pass under your correction and the approbation of Mr. Edwards; and if some of the neighboring ministers can add anything to make it more complete, it will be more universally acceptable.[3]

Again on April 2 Watts wrote to Colman renewing his offer to help underwrite a printing of the entire narrative in Boston "under your corrections, etc., and with any additions you think proper." The Londoners still longed for it "at large."[4]

The Boston edition proposed by advertisement at the end of Colman's abridgment and urged by Isaac Watts and John Guyse did not appear, for reasons which can only be conjectured. One hint comes from an investigation of the line in Colman's letter of December 17, 1736, quoted above, that Edwards was "not altogether pleased with the liberty we have taken of so general an extract." But Colman was mistaken; it was Uncle Williams who was unhappy. Some time in the spring of 1737 Colman wrote to Edwards a letter (now lost, apparently) apologizing for whatever offense had been caused. Edwards replied on May 19, 1737:

> You mention, Sir, my being displeased at the liberty taken in the extract at the end of my Uncle Williams's sermons: certainly somebody has misrepresented the matter to you. I always looked

3. *PMHS,* 2d ser., *9,* 353.
4. Ibid., p. 356.

upon it an honor too great for me, for you to be at the trouble
to draw an extract of my letter to publish to the world, and that
it should be annexed to my honored Uncle Williams's sermons;
and my main objection against it was that my Uncle Williams
himself never approved of its being put into his book.[5]

What explosions rocked the Hatfield parsonage when Uncle Williams learned that the piece by his upstart nephew had intruded
into his book we do not know, but recalling the long and often
bitter rivalry between Williamses and Edwardses may furnish a
clue. Is it too much to surmise that the powerful Williams clan,
which is known to have had influential friends in Boston, might
have insinuated to the entrepreneurs of printing that they should
ignore Edwards' narrative?

At all events, Colman decided that in view of the local crossfire
and the continuing interest among his friends in London, Edwards'
work might be better handled there. He accordingly packed off the
entire manuscript, probably around the first of May, before Watts'
five-pound subscription arrived. Edwards apparently voiced no objection, for in the same letter that clarified the misunderstanding
over the abridgment he said:

> With regard to the letter itself that I wrote, which you have sent
> to Dr. Watts and Dr. Guyse, I willingly submit it to their cor-
> rection, if they think fit to publish it after they come to see it.
> I am sensible there are some things in it that it would not be
> best to publish in England.

He did not suggest what might be omitted in deference to English
tastes, an oversight he was later to regret.

Upon receiving the manuscript, Watts and Guyse lost no time
getting it to the printer, with the result that the sheets were ready
in October. The London editors had written "a large preface" of
fourteen pages and supplied the title by which (with variations) the
work has been known ever since. Concerning their editorial work
on the narrative, Watts informed Colman in a letter of October 13
that he and Dr. Guyse had "both read it over carefully, and have
omitted many things in it, and by reading it learn more particularly
how judicious your abridgment is, yet upon the whole we thought it

5. The manuscript letter is among the Colman Papers at the Mass. Hist.
Soc.

best to publish the larger account and have made such apologies as we thought needful." [6]

What came from the London press of John Oswald in 1737 is the fullest extant text of *A Faithful Narrative;* and since the original manuscript evidently has perished, Watts' confession that he "omitted many things" could be very disturbing to the modern scholar. But there are two mitigating circumstances. One is a later statement by Watts himself that "we were afraid to leave out very much, lest we should fall under the same censure that Dr. Colman did in his accurate and judicious abridgment." [7] The other is that one of the bound presentation copies of this first edition came to Yale College, where Edwards inspected it and made several corrections in his own hand. Yale still preserves this volume. The author's handwritten note on the flyleaf, to be sure, is not very reassuring:

> It must be noted that the Rev. publishers of the ensuing narrative, by much abridging of it, and altering the phrase and manner of expression, and not strictly observing the words of the original, have through mistake, published some things diverse from fact, which is the reason that some words are crossed out: and besides there are some mistakes in the preface, which are noted in the margin.
>
> J. Edwards

But his annotations on the text of the book are not extensive; the main ones are described below and all are noted in the text of the present edition, along with other variant readings. Further assurance comes from the probability that Edwards exercised some personal oversight of the first American edition,[8] for it incorporates all the corrections he made in Yale's presentation copy and several more besides. So notwithstanding the loss of the manuscript and some unwarranted emendations in the first printed edition, careful

---

6. *PMHS,* 2d ser., *9,* 356–57.

7. Letter dated May 31, 1738, to Colman; ibid., p. 360.

8. Called "The Third Edition." There were three printings of this in 1738: one "Printed and Sold by S. Kneeland and T. Green, and D. Henchman, in Corn Hill"; another "Printed and Sold by S. Kneeland and T. Green, over against the Prison in Queen Street"; and a third "Printed by S. Kneeland and T. Green, for D. Henchman, in Corn Hill." They are identical except that the first lacks the preface by Watts and Guyse.

comparison of these volumes has made possible a reasonably accurate text for most of what Edwards originally wrote.

As for the "apologies" which the London editors felt constrained to make, one hears them mainly in the faintly defensive tone resonating through most of their preface. At one point, for example, they remind readers whose tastes may be offended by some of Edwards' more graphic descriptions that "we must allow every writer his own way; and must allow him to choose what particular instances he would select, from the numerous cases which came before him" (FN-1; below, p. 136). A passage near the end was much too craven to suit Edwards. Watts and Guyse had written:

> Upon the whole, whatever defects any reader may find or imagine in this narrative, we are well satisfied that such an eminent work of God ought not to be concealed from the world: and as it was the reverend author's opinion, so we declare it to be ours also, that 'tis very likely that this account of such an extraordinary and illustrious appearance of divine grace in the conversion of sinners, may, by the blessing of God, have a happy effect upon the minds of men, towards the honor and enlargement of the kingdom of Christ, much more than any supposed imperfection in this representation of it can do injury [FN-1; below, p. 137].

Edwards marked a demurrer in the margin of Yale's copy and rewrote the paragraph almost completely for the American edition of 1738:

> Upon the whole, we declare our opinion that this account of such an extraordinary and illustrious appearance of divine grace in the conversion of sinners, is very like by the blessing of God to have a happy effect, towards the honor and enlargement of the kingdom of Christ.

If they wanted to put words in his mouth, he could play the same game! And as for "defects" in his work, the only ones he could see were those introduced gratuitously by foreign editors.

One can sense the Londoners' defensiveness also by the anxiety they displayed for other witnesses to corroborate Edwards' account. Before Watts ever saw the full narrative, he advised Colman that "if some of the neighboring ministers can add anything to make it more complete, it will be more universally acceptable." [9] After the work was published, Watts' agitation increased. On May 31, 1738, he wrote again:

> Upon the whole I may tell you, Sir, we are called upon from Scotland, and from many of our friends in England, to know if we can give any further attestations of this work by private letters; but I do not know anything that could do it so effectually as if some other minister in New England, who was eye and ear witness to some of these numerous conversions in the other towns thereabout, would draw up a prudent and judicious account in brief of the work of God in some of those other towns at that time, and publish it under the correction of Dr. Colman.[1]

The following month Watts addressed Elisha Williams, who had already written him a description of the awakening of 1735 in his father's parish at Hatfield (above, pp. 23–25). As if in desperation, Watts pleaded:

> I am at every turn desired to inform my friends what further evidence we have of these things from New England. I should be glad to see some short account from one or two more of the ministers in New England who were eye and ear witnesses of this great work in some of the neighboring towns, printed in Boston, and if they were judiciously done I am sure some hundreds of them might be sold in London.[2]

Rector Williams' reply, if he sent one, is unknown.

Much of Watts' concern, of course, arose from the legitimate interest which Edwards' narrative aroused among all evangelicals in Great Britain. The curiosity for revival news was high on both sides of the Atlantic throughout the Great Awakening; and Edwards had already noted that "there is no one thing that I know of that God has made such a means of promoting his work amongst us, as the news of others' conversion" (FN-1; below, p. 176). But in the heart of Isaac Watts there seemed to beat, at least during the late 1730s, a muffled ambivalence in the will to believe Edwards' singular testimony. How far Colman shared this ambivalence is hard to say,

9. Letter dated Feb. 28, 1737; in *PMHS*, 2d ser., *9*, 353.
1. Ibid., p. 361.
2. Letter of June 7, 1738; ibid., p. 335.

but in any case he secured the desired confirmation. On October 11, 1738, six ministers of Hampshire County signed the following attestation: "We take this opportunity to assure you, that the account Mr. Edwards has given in his narrative of our several towns or parishes is true; and that much more of the like nature might have been added with respect to some of them." [3] Watts acknowledged receipt of the testimony in June 1739, but by that time he could make little use of it. To Colman he wrote:

> The letter which you sent subscribed by several country [*sic*; county?] ministers in New England is very agreeable to Dr. Guyse and myself. But our bookseller could not tell how to publish it, because there were so few remaining of the Narrative, and no new edition is demanded. As soon as anything of this nature shall appear we shall publish the ministers' testimony to Mr. Edwards's Narrative.[4]

But no further London edition was to appear until 1791.[5]

Edwards' complaint that his London editors had "published some things diverse from fact" refers in the first instance to their confusion about the geography of New England. On the title page and again in the preface they located "the surprising work of God" in Northampton "and the neighboring towns and villages of New Hampshire," rather than in Hampshire County, Massachusetts. On pages 91 and 125 the Londoners printed "country" where Edwards had written "county." The confusion was persistent, for on September 13, 1736, Watts had written to Colman referring to "the work of God begun in the County of Hampshire (which I also had mistaken for the Province of New Hampshire till your line in Dr. Guyse's letter undeceived me)." [6] The deception returned in 1737, as the title page bears witness, so on May 31, 1738, Watts had to apologize again.

---

3. The testimony, also prefixed to the first American edition of *A Faithful Narrative* (Boston, 1738), was signed by William Williams of Hatfield, Ebenezer Devotion of Suffield, Stephen Williams of Longmeadow, Peter Reynolds of Enfield, Nehemiah Bull of Westfield, and Samuel Hopkins of West Springfield. In June 1743 it was reprinted in *The Christian History, 1,* 128. See below, p. 143.

4. *PMHS*, 2d ser., *9,* 364.

5. John Wesley published a 48-page summary ca. 1744; reprinted 1755. See below, pp. 90–91.

6. *PMHS*, 2d ser., *9,* 349.

The blunder which was made in not distinguishing the
Province of New Hampshire from the County of Hampshire I
take entirely to myself, and I beg your pardon, and the pardon
of everyone concerned for it; but as your letter was not just at
hand, wherein you gave me warning of something of this kind
and I have a map hanging always before me wherein New
Hampshire is printed in large letters, and many of the towns
wherein this work of God was wrought lying under it along the
Connecticut River, without so much as the name of the County
of Hampshire anywhere in the map, this unhappily led me
astray, and we can now do no more than as you direct blot out
the word *New* in the title and in the book.[7]

Since a presentation copy had gone to Yale College, in his next
letter to Rector Elisha Williams, dated June 7, 1738, Watts referred
again to "this great work of God in Hampshire, which by the way
we have unhappily confounded with New Hampshire by a mistake
in a map." [8]

As for the other "things diverse from fact" which provoked
Edwards' complaint on the flyleaf of the Yale copy, one sometimes
wonders whether his notation marks a return to an original sense
distorted by editorial mishandling or represents a shift in his own
thinking. For example, we know that on several occasions Edwards
confessed that for all his caution he had been too hasty in pronounc-
ing many conversions genuine. Such doubts found expression as
early as May 1737, when he declared in a sermon: "I do not know
but I have trusted too much in men, and put too much confidence
in the goodness and piety of the town." [9] Thus when he read in the
Watts edition of his narrative that upon receiving sixty new church
members he had written, "I had very sufficient evidence of the conversion of their souls through divine grace," he crossed out the
whole sentence (FN-1; below, p. 157). No hint of this appears in the
Boston edition of 1738, which may indicate that Edwards simply
took the advantage of retrospect to suppress a premature and ill-

7. Ibid., p. 360. See below, p. 128, where JE himself crossed out "New" on
the title page of Yale's copy.
8. Ibid., p. 335.
9. Sermon on II Sam. 20:19, Andover MSS; excerpt in Perry Miller, "Jonathan Edwards' Sociology of the Great Awakening," *New England Quarterly*, 21
(1948), 61.

considered judgment. Before coming to this conclusion, however, one should note that Benjamin Colman, who read and edited the narrative before Watts ever saw it, does not include the line in his abridgment. Did he omit it at his own discretion, or is it a gratuitous insertion by the London editors? It seems safe to give Edwards the benefit of the doubt, because his settled conviction on the point was that since conversion is a work of God directly on the human soul, no man can know with certainty the spiritual state of another. The church, in his view, can ask only for a testimony of conversion which in the judgment of Christian charity is credible when supported by the visible reality of a genuinely Christian life.[1]

Even more problematical is the quarrel between Edwards and Watts over the course by which a sinner passes from darkness to light, or as some of the eighteenth-century English evangelicals might have put it, whether conversion is gradual or instantaneous. The Watts edition reads:

> If [sinners] are told that they trust too much to their own strength and righteousness, they cannot unlearn this practice all at once, and find not yet the appearance of any good, but all looks as dark as midnight to them [FN-1, orig. ed., p. 41].

Edwards crossed out "all at once." Not content with that, for the Boston edition of 1738 he rewrote the whole sentence:

> If they are told that they trust too much to their own strength and righteousness, they go about to strive to bring themselves off from it, and it may be, think they have done it, when they only do the same thing under a new disguise, and still find no appearance of any good, but all looks as dark as midnight to them [FN-3, p. 26; below, pp. 165–66].

In the Watts edition the same paragraph closes by affirming that the sinner's wandering continues until God reveals to him "the true remedy in a clearer knowledge of Christ and his Gospel." Edwards deleted "a clearer" and substituted "the"; for the Boston edi-

1. JE put the case most directly in *An Humble Inquiry into the Rules of the Word of God, Concerning the Qualifications Requisite to a Complete Standing and Full Communion in the Visible Christian Church* (Boston, 1749). An imaginative modern treatment is James Carse, *Jonathan Edwards and the Visibility of God* (New York, 1967), esp. ch. 8. See also below, pp. 76, 286–87.

tion he struck the ultimate phrase entirely and put a period after "remedy." Apparently he wished to avoid any language from which readers might infer that conversion is a gradual process.[2]

Other changes which Edwards made after he saw his narrative in print seem less consequential. For the most part, they correct minor inaccuracies or reveal differences in emphasis; and since they are all noted in the text of this new edition, the reader may decide for himself what weight each should carry. There is one which is perhaps textually unimportant, but which suggests an interesting nuance for modern urbanites. Of Miss Abigail Hutchinson, the Watts edition says: "She once thought it a pleasant thing to live in the middle of the town, but now, says she, 'I think it much more pleasant to sit and see the wind blowing the trees, and to behold in the country what God has made'" (FN-1; below, p. 195). Edwards crossed out "in the country." Doubtless he did not intend to say so (or did he?), but surely those who spend their days in Megalopolis will be reassured to know that not even Jonathan Edwards thought one needed to withdraw to the country in order to enjoy God and all his works.

In assessing the "errors" of the first edition of *A Faithful Narrative,* one should not judge Watts and Guyse too harshly. Their explanation and defense of gaffes and misconstructions are logical enough—and spirited! Watts wrote:

> As for the other mistakes which Dr. Guyse has informed me of, and which I talked over with him but yesterday, I desire you to take this account of them. Mr. Edwards's Narrative was written in so small a hand and so hard to be read, that if a word or two was mistaken by the printer or by us, I do not wonder at it; for I am sure I was forced to guess at several words in it. As for the alterations we made, we were afraid to leave out very much, lest we should fall under the same censure that Dr. Colman did in his accurate and judicious abridgment; but we both agree that there was not one alteration made which we did not think perfectly agreeable to the sentiments of the writer. It was necessary to make some alterations of the language, lest

2. "Conversion" should be distinguished from "seeking." The latter not only could and often did extend over a long period, but was actually all a sinner could do. JE was suspicious of conversions not preceded by earnest seeking: "Sudden conversions are very often false" (Sermon on Matt. 13:5 [Nov. 1740], in Yale Collection). Cf. below, pp. 106, 160, 346, 549, 556.

we together with the book should have been exposed to much more contempt and ridicule on this account, though I may tell my friend that 'tis not a little of that kind we have both met with. And if Mr. Edwards should be so unwise as to make much talk of any mistakes he supposes we have made, he will do unknown injury to the Narrative itself, whose honor we support in the best manner we can, since we believe it true. We knew and felt it a point of self-denial when we printed it; and therefore we would have been glad that our subscription of £5 toward the printing of it in Boston had reached you before the Narrative came to us; and we took it for granted that the Narrative when it came was desired to be printed, partly from the representations which you made of Mr. Edwards's reasons for sending it to us, and partly from the public advertisement or proposal for the printing of it in Boston at the end of your abridgment. So that we are not conscious we have done anything, nor written or printed one line or word contrary to the meaning of the orders we received. And as it is a most signal account of a wonderful work of God for the conversion of men, we can bear with satisfaction all the reproaches we sustain here, both in conversation and in newspapers, but we hope we shall receive no addition from New England of anything that should make us uneasy.[3]

Anybody who has ever looked at Edwards' handwriting, or followed the acrimonious controversy over revivalism in the eighteenth century, should be able to sympathize with that!

But even the most egregious errors have had an inexcusably long life. The first London edition was soon exhausted, and Watts ordered a new printing before learning of Edwards' reaction. Although the second edition of 1738 was completely reset, with paragraph topics provided by an unknown hand, the text is identical with the first. Even the title page repeats the confusion in geography, naming New Hampshire in place of Hampshire County. Two reprints appeared in Edinburgh in as many years (1737, 1738), repeating most of the errors of the first London edition except that one obvious ungrammaticism was corrected in 1738. Not even the first American edition of the collected works of Jonathan Edwards (ed. Samuel Austin, 8 vols. [Worcester, 1808–09]) reflected the revisions made by the author, and the same is true of the set edited by Sereno Edwards

3. Letter dated May 31, 1738, to Colman; in *PMHS*, 2d ser., 9, 360–61.

Dwight (10 vols. [New York, 1829–30]). Both of these sets in the main follow the English printing of the tract, and except for the grammatical error corrected by the Edinburgh printers, include all its mistakes, even that of sometimes confusing "country" with "county." [4] The title of the Dwight edition, moreover, still locates Northampton in New Hampshire instead of Hampshire County, Massachusetts. Since all subsequent reprints of *A Faithful Narrative* stand at second or further remove from these two standard sets, the present edition is the first to offer an accurate text in modern format of this famous and popular piece.

6. *Premonitions of Controversy*

The Valley revival reached its peak in the spring of 1735, but it was destined to come soon to a stop. The first ominous note sounded on March 25 when Thomas Stebbins, a man of unstable mind, attempted suicide (FN-1; below, pp. 205–06). Then on June 1, two days after Edwards completed his first epistolary account of the revival, his uncle Joseph Hawley, Northampton's leading merchant, cut his throat and died in half an hour. It was Sunday morning, and the community was stunned. "An awful providence!" exclaimed Deacon Ebenezer Hunt.[5] Edwards broke open his letter to Colman to add a postscript, dated June 3, 1735, describing the incident and attributing it to the great rage of Satan against the work of God (FN; below, pp. 109–10). The church, in deep shock, observed a day of fasting. Edwards explained what everybody already knew, that Hawley was "of a family that are exceeding prone to the disease of melancholy," and the coroner had judged him delirious (FN-1; below, p. 206). But this proved to be the turning point in the religious excitement that had possessed the town for months. "The spell was broken, the emotional climate changed at once, . . . the limit of endurable ecstasies had been reached." [6]

Writing his expanded narrative a year later, Edwards told the story candidly and confessed that Hawley's suicide had had an almost hypnotic influence on others, not only in Northampton but elsewhere.

4. The ungrammaticism referred to is on p. 75 of FN-1, the phrase "discoveries with God." It should read, of course, "discoveries *of* God" (below, p. 182).

5. Journal, Judd MSS, *1,* 24; at Forbes Library.

6. Winslow, *Jonathan Edwards,* p. 156.

After this, multitudes in this and other towns seemed to have it strongly suggested to 'em, and pressed upon 'em, to do as this person had done. And many that seemed to be under no melancholy, some pious persons that had no special darkness, or doubts about the goodness of their state, nor were under any special trouble or concern of mind about anything spiritual or temporal, yet had it urged upon 'em, as if somebody had spoke to 'em, "Cut your own throat, now is a good opportunity: *now, NOW!*" So that they were obliged to fight with all their might to resist it, and yet no reason suggested to 'em why they should do it.[7]

The reason, obscure to Edwards in 1736, became clearer in the heightened fervor of the 1740s. One of the most vexing problems in the Great Awakening was the doctrine of personal assurance: how does a convert know he is truly saved, and how does he prove it to others? When some of the more extreme New Lights, much to the dismay of Edwards and other sober evangelicals, began to declare that assurance is the essence of saving faith, various unstable persons began to think within themselves: "I shall know certainly whether I am saved or not only when I die and face God at judgment; according to some of the exhorters I've heard, if I'm saved I'm ready to meet God now; if I'm not I probably never will be, and the longer I live the more I sin and increase my guilt: therefore I must settle the matter now by committing suicide." In such a disordered frame of mind, several tried and some succeeded, though unfortunately whatever they discovered could not be communicated to their puzzled and tempted survivors.[8]

At all events, by the time Edwards wrote his historical narrative in 1736, the revival of 1734–35 was a *late* work of God. During the next few years he struggled unremittingly to retrieve the halcyon days when Northampton was "a city set on a hill." He reminded his congregation how their glory had shone afar, he published the sermons that had shaken the dry bones, he launched a new series

7. FN-1; below, pp. 206–07. Stephen Williams of Longmeadow noted in his diary on Sunday, July 13, 1735: "a most awful providence happened this day in the time of the afternoon exercises—N. Burt 2d cut his own throat" (MS at Longmeadow Public Library). Burt died the next night.

8. Cf. ST; below, pp. 392–94. On the question of assurance as an issue in the Great Awakening, see Goen, *Revivalism and Separatism in New England*, pp. 44–54. On the problem of melancholy, see Gail Thain Parker, "Jonathan Edwards and Melancholy," *New England Quarterly, 41* (1968), 193–212.

on "The History of Redemption" by which he hoped to bring New England once again to the threshold of the millennium, he rebuked resurgent dissension and decried the "very lamentable decay of religious affections." But nothing much happened.[9]

Until 1740. In the fall of that year came George Whitefield (1714–71), "the Grand Itinerant," to set all New England aflame with a revival compared to which the Valley awakening of 1734–35 was but a brush fire. His name already a household word on two continents, Whitefield landed at Newport, Rhode Island, on September 14, preached six times in three days, and took off for Boston. There he received an impressive welcome from ministers and dignitaries, including Governor Jonathan Belcher, and plunged forthwith into a breathtaking round of evangelizing. The response was overwhelming. "A vast congregation in the Rev. Dr. Colman's meetinghouse," reported the newspapers; "at the South Church a crowded audience . . . about 5,000 people on the Common." Sunday afternoon, "having preached to a great number of people at the Old Brick Church, the house not being large enough to hold those that crowded to hear him, when the exercise there was over, he went and preached in the field, to at least 8,000 persons." [10] So it went for eleven days. The next week Whitefield itinerated northward to York, Maine, and back, preaching sixteen times along the way. His final week in Boston occupied him in addressing "very great auditories" daily, and his farewell sermon on October 12 drew more than twenty thousand eager auditors to the Common.

Whitefield next moved overland toward Northampton,[1] preaching en route at Concord, Sudbury, Marlborough, Worcester (Governor Belcher accompanied him this far and wept as they parted), Leicester, Brookfield, Cold Spring, and Hadley. On Friday, October 17, he arrived at Edwards' meetinghouse, preached immediately, and gave another exhortation at the parsonage in the evening. The next

9. See below, p. 544. There had been several occurrences in the daily life of the Valley to turn people away from their preoccupation with religion. JE enumerated some of them in FN-1; below, p. 208.

10. *Boston Weekly News Letter*, Sept. 25, 1740.

1. On Feb. 12, 1739/40, JE had written Whitefield a laudatory letter warmly urging "that in your intended journey through New England next summer, you would be pleased to visit Northampton" (MS letter at the Methodist Archives and Research Center, London).

morning they went to Hatfield (four miles distant) to pay respects
to aged Uncle Williams. Whitefield preached, "but found myself
not much strengthened"; his afternoon sermon to Edwards' congregation was more "affecting." [2] Sunday morning he was again in
the Northampton pulpit.

> Good Mr. Edwards wept during the whole time of exercise. The
> people were equally affected; and, in the afternoon, the power
> increased yet more. . . . Oh, that my soul may be refreshed with
> the joyful news, that Northampton people have recovered their
> first love; that the Lord has revived his work in their souls, and
> caused them to do their first works [Rev. 2:4–5]! [3]

From there Whitefield made his way down the Valley, rekindling
embers now five years cold—"as soon as I mentioned what God
had done for their souls formerly, it was like putting fire to tinder"
—and igniting new flames on every side.[4] From New Haven, after
urging the new birth on ministers and students, governor and popu-
lace, he turned southwestward down the coast. By the time he passed
from Connecticut into New York, his journal showed that he had
spent 45 days, visited 40 towns, and delivered 97 sermons and exhortations. Though he never presumed to count converts, he was
satisfied that New England was about to reap its biggest harvest yet.

Not to take this for granted, however, in New Jersey Whitefield
sought out Gilbert Tennent (1703–64), by now the acknowledged
leader of the Presbyterian revival in the Middle Colonies, and persuaded him to "set out for Boston, in order to blow up the divine

2. *George Whitefield's Journals* (London, 1960), p. 476.

3. Ibid., p. 477. This was exactly what JE was hoping for. A week before
Whitefield arrived, he had written to Eleazar Wheelock bemoaning the "sorrow-
fully dull and dead time" in Northampton's religion and urging Wheelock to
pray that God "would bless Mr. Whitefield's coming here for good to my soul,
and the souls of my people" (letter dated Oct. 9, 1740; in Forbes Library). See
JE's published report of the occasion in his letter to Thomas Prince; below, p.
545.

4. *Whitefield's Journals,* p. 476. The classic document evincing Whitefield's
impact on the common people of New England is "The Spiritual Travels of
Nathan Cole," written by a semiliterate farmer of Kensington, Conn., deposited
at the Connecticut Historical Society. It is examined in some detail by Shea,
Spiritual Autobiography in Early America, pp. 208–21; and Goen, *Revivalism
and Separatism in New England,* pp. 136–43.

fire lately kindled there." [5] By December, in the midst of what a dour Anglican missionary called "the dreadfullest winter that I ever saw," [6] Tennent had launched a three-month mission to New England. Besides the Boston area, still throbbing from the force of the Whitefield whirlwind, Plymouth County, Rhode Island, and eastern Connecticut also felt the hot breath of Tennent's fiery preaching. People responded in droves, notwithstanding the icy weather. To meet the growing popular demand for sermons, other pastors began to itinerate in the manner of Whitefield and Tennent. They preached awakening sermons, appointed special lectures, and spent untold hours counselling the spiritually troubled. William Cooper, Colman's assistant at Brattle Street Church in Boston, testified that "more came to him in one week in deep concern about their souls, than had come in the whole twenty-four years of his preceding ministry." [7] An ecstatic layman reported from East Lyme, Connecticut: "It's a most blessed time, it's a mere heaven upon earth; the people from dull carelessness, now are like the horse-leech at the vein, crying give give!" [8]

Came the spring thaws, popular excitement rose on a steadily ascending curve. In Northampton, Jonathan Edwards observed that new conversions, compared with those in 1734–35, "were frequently wrought more sensibly and visibly; the impressions stronger and

5. Whitefield, letter dated Nov. 9, 1740, to Gov. Jonathan Belcher, written to introduce Tennent to Massachusetts officialdom; in *Works of the Reverend George Whitefield* (London, 1771–72), *1*, 221.

6. Timothy Cutler, letter dated Sept. 24, 1743, to Zachary Grey; in Boston Public Library. Cutler was not exaggerating; all contemporary comments on the winter of 1740–41 agree. Gov. Jonathan Belcher reported in February that Boston's "weather has been so severe for eight or nine weeks past as has hardly been known in the memory of man, and a land of ice for near ten miles from this town into the ocean has in a manner stopped all vessels from coming in or going out, and the excessive snows have rendered the roads unpassable for horses for about a month past" (letter dated Feb. 21, 1740/1; in *Collections of the Mass. Hist. Soc.*, 6th ser., 7, 533). Even so, it still seems appropriate to use incendiary metaphors to describe the warmth of the people's response to the evangelists of the frozen roadways.

7. Thomas Prince, "An Account of the Revival of Religion in New England" (dated Nov. 26, 1744), in *The Christian History*, 2, 391. Prince himself, along with other evangelical pastors, gave similar testimony.

8. J. L., letter in *American Weekly Mercury*, July 16, 1741, p. 1. For a description of the awakening at high tide, see Edwin S. Gaustad, *The Great Awakening in New England* (New York, 1957), ch. 4.

more manifest by external effects of them." By September, he noted, "it was a very frequent thing to see an house full of outcries, faintings, convulsions and such like, both with distress, and also with admiration and joy." [9] After Tennent passed through eastern Connecticut, emotional outbursts in time of worship became common. Preachers sometimes had to stop in mid-sermon, as "weeping, sighs and sobs" mingled with cries of distress: "Alas! I'm undone; I'm undone! O, my sins! How they prey upon my vitals! What will become of me? How shall I escape the damnation of hell, who have spent away a golden opportunity under Gospel light, in vanity?" [1] All-night meetings multiplied—sometimes not by design but simply because people found themselves too wrung out emotionally to travel home. Visions and trances appeared, and some persons began to claim immediate inspiration for occasionally bizarre behavior. This, of course, was "enthusiasm," always an awful threat to orthodox Puritans. Plainly the revival was in danger of getting out of control.

Then came James Davenport (1716–57). Notwithstanding an impeccable pedigree—grandson of the founder of New Haven, graduate of Yale at age 16, tutored in divinity by Elisha Williams, ordained (1738) minister at Southold, Long Island—Davenport suffered from deep feelings of inferiority; and in seeking to compensate, he almost wrecked the revival. Upon hearing of Whitefield's spectacular successes, he gathered his congregation together and harangued them for twenty-four hours straight—and then collapsed. Those whom he regarded as regenerate he called "brother," the rest "neighbor." He waded waist-deep through winter snow to assault a neighboring parish with the Gospel. He visited the Middle Colonies and became personally acquainted with Whitefield and the Presbyterian revivalists, who at the time were much exercised over "the danger of an unconverted ministry." [2] By mid-summer 1741

9. Letter to Prince; below, p. 547. But he added immediately that "after September 1741, there seemed to be some abatement of the extraordinary appearances that had been"—as if to suggest that he had been able to establish some degree of control.

1. Jonathan Parsons, letter dated April 14, 1744; in *The Christian History*, 2, 135. He was describing an experience at East Lyme, Conn., in April 1741. Similar testimony came from layman J. L.; see above, p. 50.

2. This is the title of Gilbert Tennent's famous sermon at Nottingham, Pa., on Mar. 8, 1740, which set off an uproar among Presbyterians. (It is printed in Heimert, *The Great Awakening*, pp. 72–99.) Whitefield's aspersions against

Davenport was ready to lay siege to Connecticut. On July 18 he arrived in New London and preached his first sermon that evening.

> Divers women were terrified and cried out exceedingly. When Mr. Davenport had dismissed the congregation some went out and others stayed; he then went into the broad alley [aisle], which was much crowded, and there he screamed out, "Come to Christ! Come to Christ! Come away!" Then he went into the third pew on the women's side, and kept there, sometimes singing, sometimes praying; he and his companions all taking their turns, and the women fainting and in hysterics. This confusion continued till ten o'clock at night. And then he went off singing through the streets.[3]

From New London Davenport went east to the edge of the colony and started back down the coastline. In parish after parish he imperiously summoned the ministers to recount their spiritual experiences so that he might judge whether they were converted. Those who refused (and most did) he denounced publicly, urging their parishioners to forsake them. At New Haven he branded pastor Joseph Noyes "an unconverted hypocrite and the devil incarnate," and gathered a coterie of admirers, some of whom reported trances and visions under his spell.[4] By that time the summer had ended, and Davenport returned to Southold for the winter. Behind him he left incipient discord and rising hysteria, causing thoughtful men to wonder: Could the revival be controlled? Indeed, if these were its true fruits just now ripening, could it even be defended? Another son of Yale was already preparing an answer.

7. *Testing the Spirits*

A few days after Davenport left town, on September 10, 1741, Jonathan Edwards stood before the faculty and students of Yale College who had gathered, along with an auspicious company of "ministers and other gentlemen," to hear the Commencement address.

New England's "unconverted" clergy and benighted" colleges, published in his *Seventh Journal* (London, 1741), were soon to infuriate a great many of those who had lately welcomed him into that area. The spirituality of the clergy became a subject of major controversy during the Great Awakening.

3. *The Diary of Joshua Hempstead, of New London, Connecticut* (New London, 1901), p. 379. Hempstead was the local Justice of the Peace.

4. Franklin Bowditch Dexter, *Biographical Sketches of Yale College* (New Haven, 1885), *1*, 662.

Keenly conscious of the troubled society's need for sound principles of discrimination in what they all perceived as a gathering storm in the churches, he announced his topic:

> *The Distinguishing Marks of a Work of the Spirit of God, Applied to That Uncommon Operation That Has Lately Appeared on the Minds of Many of the People of This Land: With a Particular Consideration of the Extraordinary Circumstances with Which This Work Is Attended.*[5]

Based on I John 4:1, "Beloved, believe not every spirit, but try the spirits whether they are of God; because many false prophets are gone out into the world," this sermon-address is as simple in structure as anything Edwards ever produced. After a brief examination of his text, he turned his attention first to disarming those who would discredit the revival on the basis of its epiphenomena. Ingenuously admitting nine major flaws in the behavior of the newly awakened, he essayed to show that none is a sign "that we are to judge of a work by, whether it be the work of the Spirit of God or no" (DM; below, p. 228). These "not-signs" are merely extrinsic manifestations from which nothing certain can be concluded either way. Then he enumerated five "sure, distinguishing, Scripture evidences" of a genuine work of God, and treated one "objection" briefly. Finally, in what is almost half the published piece, he developed the "Application" in three parts: his own conclusion that the work "is undoubtedly, in the general, from the Spirit of God," a warning to opposers, and some advice to the friends of the revival. Thus began a critical but sympathetic examination of revivalism which Edwards would continually develop and refine until it issued in the mature statement of 1746, *A Treatise Concerning Religious Affections,* wherein he demonstrated that true religion necessarily involves the whole person, and that it can and must be subjected to discriminating judgment.[6]

The nine flaws, or negative signs, which Edwards dismissed as

5. Published Boston, 1741, "with great enlargements" and a preface by William Cooper; below, pp. 215–25. In 1742 Benjamin Franklin reprinted it in Philadelphia and Isaac Watts arranged for a London edition. Eight subsequent editions appeared, only one of which was in America; of the seven further British editions, four were John Wesley's abridgment. See below, pp. 90–91.

6. See John E. Smith's penetrating comments on "Religion, Revivalism, and Religious Affections" in his introduction to the Yale edition of this work, pp. 43–52.

proving nothing about the revival one way or another, are: (1) that the work is carried on in an unusual or extraordinary way, (2) that it produces strong effects on the bodies of its subjects, (3) that it occasions "a great deal of noise about religion," (4) that it induces lively impressions on people's imaginations, (5) that it is promoted too much by the influence of example, (6) that it results in imprudent and irregular conduct, (7) that errors in judgment and "delusions of Satan" intermingle with it, (8) that some of its professed converts later fall into scandal, and (9) that its preachers insist too much on the terrors of God's wrath. After acknowledging the truth of each charge, Edwards set out to demonstrate that any argument about the validity of the revival based on these premises could lead only to a *non sequitur*. He pointed to precedents in Scripture and history to show that every new movement in the life of the church had elicited many of the same complaints; but so had spurious movements, as well as certain events in secular affairs. How then could such evidence prove that God was, or was not, really at work?

Had Edwards stopped with merely trying to turn aside the rising doubts and criticisms, probably few would have been convinced. But he hastened on to his positive signs, five distinctive marks which would lead unerringly to a valid conclusion. People may recognize the hand of God, he argued, in a work which (1) raises their esteem of Jesus as Son of God and Saviour of the world, (2) leads them to turn from their corruptions and lusts to the righteousness of God, (3) increases their regard for Holy Scripture, (4) establishes their minds in the objective truths of revealed religion, and (5) evokes genuine love for God and man. "These marks," he affirmed confidently, "are sufficient to outweigh a thousand such little objections, as many make from oddities, irregularities, and errors in conduct, and the delusions and scandals of some professors" (DM; below, pp. 258–59).

In the "Application" Edwards put an unequivocal stamp of approval on the work. He insisted that he had judged by "facts and rules"; i.e. he had tested his own experience by the rules of Scripture, and was satisfied that the two corresponded well enough to justify this conclusion. Lest any of his hearers question the extent and authority of his experience as a discerner of revivalistic spirits, he reminded them of Northampton's pre-eminence in the salvation-history of New England (see below, p. 268). He had learned that imprudences, however deplorable, are not decisive, for they are only what one might expect in a new movement of the Spirit following a time of "universal deadness." Since many of the awakened are young people rather than persons of mature years, the exuberance is naturally greater. They need careful pastoral guidance, something they receive all too meagerly because Old Light ministers turn away (and thus share some blame for the excesses they condemn) while New Light ministers are too inexperienced in counseling converts. There are, in short, ample explanations for the irregularities within the human, historical situation; but none of these gives any ground for denying that God is indeed at work in this situation.

In his concluding exhortations, Edwards warned against doing "anything in the least to clog or hinder" the revival. To oppose it is not only to fight against God, thereby invoking on oneself many terrible penalties, but to fall in peril of committing the unpardonable sin against the Holy Spirit. In hurling such a harsh warning against the antirevivalists, he had in mind Matthew 12:22–32, which reports that Jesus performed a miracle and his enemies, recognizing that his work was of God but unwilling to confess it so, attributed it to the Devil. Jesus denounced their sin as unpardonable, not because it was wicked blasphemy against the Father or unknowing rejection of the Son—these were forgivable—but because it was a perverse refusal to confess the spiritual reality they clearly perceived. The "sin against the Holy Spirit," in other words, is a willful sin against light; it cannot be committed unknowingly, and it is unforgivable precisely because it marks a final, deliberate rejection of known truth in an act equivalent to spiritual suicide. Edwards warned that men who contemptuously resist the present work of spiritual renewal may be coming dangerously close to such a judgment. "Those that maliciously oppose and reproach this work, and call it the work of the Devil, want but one thing of the unpardonable sin, and that is doing it against inward conviction." [7]

In order to save these detractors from sealing their doom, and to move honest doubters to positive approval of what he regarded as a latter-day miracle, Edwards urged that they take "thorough

---

7. DM; below, pp. 275–76. JE probably had been thinking about this for some time. According to the records of the Hampshire Ministers Association, which he attended regularly, the doctrinal question discussed at the meeting on April 8, 1741, was "What is the sin that is commonly called the sin against the Holy Ghost?" (MS at Forbes Library).

pains to inform themselves, by going where such things have been to be seen, and narrowly observing them, and diligently inquiring into them; not contenting themselves only with observing two or three instances, nor resting till they were fully informed by their own observation" (DM; below, p. 275). He little dreamed that within a year the arch-opponent of the revival would be doing exactly that, for the purpose of compiling a documented casebook to discredit the entire movement.[8] Friends of the revival, on the other hand, he cautioned to remain humble, resist sudden impulses, seek holiness of life, respect learning, and beware of censorious judging. Those who differ over the source and character of the revival should conduct their disputes at a lower level of sound and heat, seeking patiently for wisdom to discern the true Spirit in his gracious work.

It was doubtless a calculated risk to come to New Haven on the heels of James Davenport and speak so calmly of the turbulence that was threatening to engulf the whole colony. But at the time Edwards was attempting to steer between the hard Scylla of Old Light hostility, soon to turn repressive, and the swirling Charybdis of New Light enthusiasm, soon to exceed all bounds of propriety and sound religion. In September 1741 storm signals were already flying, and the course of moderation would become increasingly hard to find amid the winds of controversy.

8. *Critics' Onslaught*

Edwards' Yale sermon was intended as an irenicon, but instead it marked the beginning of polarization in attitudes toward the revival. Official Yale was unmoved by his address and soon turned rigidly Old Light. Several student hearers, however, were won—or

---

8. The reference, of course, is to Charles Chauncy (below, pp. 62–64). Perry Miller, sometimes too clever at spotting polarities before they have emerged into historical focus, thought that JE's Yale sermon was aimed directly at Chauncy (*Jonathan Edwards,* p. 178). But in 1741 the Old Brick controversialist had barely begun to find his stance. A passage in his sermon of June 4, *The New Creature Described,* is remarkably similar to the famous dangling-spider simile in JE's Enfield sermon of a month later, *Sinners in the Hands of an Angry God;* and only half a page (p. 43) in *The Outpouring of the Holy Ghost,* preached in September, voices reservations about the revival. It is more likely that JE's targets were nearer home. He must have been particularly rankled by those pastors whose parishes were visited by the gracious stirrings of 1735 and who now were resisting the great work; their names are listed (with asterisks) above, pp. 22–23.

at least confirmed—for the evangelical cause. Samuel Hopkins (1721–1803), who received his degree at the 1741 Commencement, switched his hero-worship from Gilbert Tennent to Jonathan Edwards and "concluded to go and live with Mr. Edwards [as a student of divinity] as soon as I should have opportunity." [9] He later achieved fame as a theologian in the Edwardsean tradition. Samuel Buell (1716–98), also graduating in 1741, obtained a preaching license from the New Haven Association and evangelized as an itinerant until settling as pastor of the Presbyterian church at East-hampton, Long Island, in 1746. During January and February 1742 he preached at Northampton while Edwards was away on an evangelistic mission of his own.[1] Sophomore David Brainerd (1718–47), whether inspired by Jonathan Edwards or James Davenport, impetuously aspersed his tutor's piety and was expelled two months after Commencement; he pursued a brief but intense career as missionary to the Indians before succumbing to tuberculosis.[2] Young activists such as these, however, hardly endeared either their mentor or their cause to the Connecticut establishment, which despite Edwards' warning about the unpardonable sin was rapidly gravitating toward the Old Light camp.

There was little correlation between geography and attitudes toward the revival, for every section had both its promoters and its opposers. All over New England "testing the spirits" quickly became a popular pulpit exercise. On October 14, a few weeks before *The Distinguishing Marks* came off the press, the Irish Presbyterian John Caldwell of Blandford (Hampshire County), Massachusetts, preached at Londonderry, New Hampshire, on *An Impartial Trial of the Spirit Operating in This Part of the World.* Taking the same text that Edwards had expounded at New Haven, Caldwell charged that the preponderance of conversions claimed so far smacked of "an epidemical distemper . . . especially [among] the

---

9. "Autobiography," in Edwards A. Park, "Memoir," *The Works of Samuel Hopkins* (Boston, 1852), *1*, 18. He was a nephew of the Samuel Hopkins who was pastor at West Springfield, Mass.; see below, p. 102 n.

1. Ibid., p. 19. Cf. below, pp. 69, 549–50.

2. He died at the Northampton parsonage in the arms of Edwards' daughter Jerusha, his fiancée. Cf. Sereno E. Dwight, ed., *Memoirs of the Rev. David Brainerd* (New Haven, 1822), which contains Brainerd's journals and the account by JE which immortalized the young missionary in the sagas of evangelical Christendom.

younger women and children." [3] The following week David Mc-
Gregore of the Second Presbyterian Church in Londonderry responded with *The Spirits of the Present Day Tried,* which he repeated a fortnight later in a lecture at Brattle Street Church in
Boston. Using the same text and even harsher language, he casti-
gated antirevivalists as "men of Arminian, Pelagian, and Deistical
principles," possessed by a lying, envious, partisan and profane
spirit. [4] At Harvard, meanwhile, some of the students were conducting their own trials, if not inspired by the Northampton oracle, at
least drawing on the vocabulary he had created at Yale. On February 4, 1742, one wrote to his British cousin:

> [It is] a mark of the true Spirit: if it excites immoral and pro-
> fane persons to reformation of their lives and conversations,
> and to an entire change of life; to profess a sweetness and
> pleasure in the ways of God, they could never have found [in]
> the paths of sin; if it excites outward professors to a strict
> examination of their hearts with regard to the power of god-
> liness, and to a discovery of their own self-righteousness, and of
> the all-sufficient righteousness of Christ, and enables them to
> depend on that alone for pardon and life. In fine, if it actuates
> young and old to crowd around the banner of the great Re-
> deemer, and . . . if it makes people careful to evidence their
> faith in the eye of the world by a life of holy obedience, and the
> fruits of righteousness, peace and joy in the Holy Ghost; and
> if this has appeared in multitudes a year or two ago, so as to
> evidence it not to be a sudden motion of the animal spirits, or a
> work barely on the passions, there is a great and glorious work
> of the Spirit of God among us. [5]

3. Boston, 1742; p. 23. On Caldwell, who later was accused of imposture and
scandal, see Barney L. Jones, "John Caldwell, Critic of the Great Awakening,"
in *A Miscellany of American Christianity* (Durham, N.C., 1963), pp. 168–82.

4. Boston, 1742. Excerpts printed in Heimert, *The Great Awakening,* pp.
215–27. McGregore described Caldwell's visit to Londonderry in a letter dated
Jan. 30, 1742, to David Cargill; MS at Mass. Hist. Soc.

5. B. B., possibly Benjamin Brandon (Harvard 1742), letter dated Feb. 4,
1742; printed (from *The Glasgow Weekly History*) in *PMHS,* 53 (1920), 209.
There is abundant evidence of the early impact of the revival at Harvard.
Josiah Willard, Secretary of the Province of New England, sent to George
Whitefield a report fully as glowing as any written by his ministerial friends:
"That which forebodes a more lasting advantage is the new face of things at

But like Yale, Harvard was soon to veer sharply toward the opposition side; and even in Hampshire County Edwardsean evangelicals would find themselves more and more in the minority.[6]

William Cooper (1694–1743), Colman's colleague at Brattle Street, wrote the preface for the published version of Edwards' Yale sermon. After commending the author's learning and wisdom as an interpreter of evangelical experience, Cooper scored opposers as acting from ignorance, jealousy, prejudice, or—*extremitas erroris*—Arminianism. Suspecting that Old Lights would quickly become more vocal, and hoping to retain for evangelicals the initiative which Edwards' publications had captured, Cooper closed with the wish that "those who have been conversant in this work, in one place and another, would transmit accounts of it to such a hand as the reverend author of this discourse, to be compiled into a narrative like that of the conversions at Northampton which was published a few years ago" (below, p. 224). Edwards himself reiterated this suggestion the following year, though he declined to serve as chief intelligencer of revival news on the ground that he was not "conveniently situated" near the press (below, pp. 529, 538). The idea came to fruition in March 1743, when *The Christian History* began weekly publication at Boston under the editorial hand of Thomas Prince, Jr. (cf. below, p. 78).

Benjamin Colman sent copies of *The Distinguishing Marks* to his friends in London, who were delighted. Isaac Watts responded:

> Mr. Edwards's account of the marks of a divine spirit I think are good and just, and the many errors, mistakes, follies, and seeming irregularities which may attend the divine operation in different persons will never prove that a sanctifying work is not divine. I have no fault to find with that book as yet but what you mention (both in the book and in the preface) of their being both exceptionable to many persons in the solemn cautions of sinning against the Holy Spirit by despising this glorious work

---

the College, where the impressions of religion have been, and still are very general and many in a judgment of charity brought home to Christ; and divers gentlemen's sons, that were sent there only for a more polite education, are now so full of zeal for the cause of Christ, and of love to souls, as to devote themselves entirely to the studies of divinity" (letter dated April 25, 1741; ibid., p. 197).

6. Foster, "Hampshire County, Massachusetts, 1729–1754," p. 181.

in New England; and yet I think there should be cautions of that kind.[7]

Watts showed his copy to a neighbor, who "read it with so much delight, that by my encouragement and hers 'tis printed here." [8] The London edition of 1742 included extracts from three of Colman's letters, along with one from Jonathan Parsons of Lyme, Connecticut, which Watts hoped would disarm British critics. "Those short extracts," he explained to Colman, "represent the same work of God in Boston as more calm and rational and discover that 'tis not all a mere flash of imagination and warm passion, but will approve itself to the reason of man and to the work of God, which Mr. Edwards has happily attempted even in those instances where passion and imprudence appear." [9] Two Scotch editions of *The Distinguishing Marks* also appeared in 1742, with a preface by the Rev. John Willison of Dundee praising the sermon as "a most excellent, solid, judicious and scriptural performance." [1]

The euphoria of the prorevival forces, however, was due to come soon to "an unhappy period." In the spring of 1742 James Davenport (above, pp. 51–52) resumed his ill-starred journey across southern Connecticut. During his absence the colony had enacted strong laws against vagrant preaching, and he got no farther than Stratford before being arrested. After a riotous trial in Hartford, where the court leniently judged him "disturbed in the rational faculties of his mind," he was carried forcibly back to Southold. Three weeks later he turned up in Boston—an intrusion which the friends of the revival had reason to fear more than its enemies. When private remonstrances failed to quiet him, the local ministers denied him their pulpits and published a "Declaration" against his acting on impulses, judging ministers, singing in the streets, and encouraging laymen to usurp ministerial prerogatives.[2] Davenport retaliated by

7. Letter dated Feb. 24, 1741/2, to Colman; in *PMHS*, 2d ser., 9, 389.

8. Letter dated April 16, 1742, to Colman; ibid., p. 392. Watts added regretfully that "through the want of foresight in a young bookseller 'tis printed too close and in too small a character. . . . I wish it had been printed in the same form as the New England edition."

9. Letter dated April 22, 1742; ibid., p. 395.

1. Edinburgh and Glasgow. Willison (1680–1750) had been pastor of the South Presbyterian Church in Dundee since 1716.

2. Dated July 1, 1742, and published in *The Boston Weekly Post-Boy*, July 5, 1742.

denouncing some of the clergy as unconverted, "representing the rest as Jehoshaphats in Ahab's army [I Kings 22], and exhorting the people to separate from us; which so diverted the minds of many from being concerned about their own conversion, to think and dispute about the case of others; as not only seemed to put an awful stop to their awakenings, but also on all sides to roil our passions and provoke the Holy Spirit in a gradual and dreadful measure to withdraw his influence."[3] Soon the authorities intervened. Davenport was arrested, tried, and judged *"non compos mentis,* and therefore . . . not guilty." As before, he was deported.

The following spring he reached the zenith of fanaticism when on March 6 he summoned his followers to the wharf at New London, Connecticut, and ordered them to purify themselves from "idolatrous love of worldly things" by burning all their wigs, fine clothes, jewelry, and dangerous books. In a frenzy sufficient to shock all but the wildest enthusiasts, the mob danced dervishlike around the pyre praising God and shouting "Hallelujah!" But for Davenport the dénouement came quickly, inexorably. When the fire died down, he hobbled home, utterly spent, and began to come to himself. The next year he was to publish his *Confession and Retractations,* deploring the "false spirit" that had fastened on his disordered mind and body: "I had the long fever on me and the cankry humor raging at once."[4] But it was too late. He had unleashed the demons of hysteria and fanaticism which no retractation could recall, and furnished the antirevival arsenal with more ammunition than even Jonathan Edwards could repulse.

Inasmuch as some interpreters of the Great Awakening have followed rationalist critics in claiming that the disorders erupting in the wake of Davenport's misadventure differed only in degree from responses encouraged by Whitefield and Tennent, it is worth emphasizing that responsible contemporary observers did not think

3. Thomas Prince, in *The Christian History,* 2, 408.

4. James Davenport, *Confession and Retractations* (Boston, 1744), p. 7; printed in Heimert, *The Great Awakening,* pp. 259–62. Joseph Croswell, a new convert of Groton, Conn., had testified on March 16, 1743, that "Mr. Davenport, in my audience, the last week, before a considerable number, has retracted those strange opinions which he had lately unhappily broached, as enthusiastical and delusive, taking shame to himself, and acknowledging the justice of God in leaving him to himself" (letter printed in *The Boston Evening Post,* March 28, 1743). Davenport later moved to New Jersey and completed his ministerial career with no further aberrations.

so. Thomas Prince, pastor of Old South Church in Boston and chief collector of revival news from all over New England (and elsewhere), testified: "I don't remember any crying out, or falling down, or fainting, either under Mr. Whitefield's or Mr. Tennent's ministry all the while they were here." [5] Benjamin Colman, dean of the Boston clergy, reported as late as June 3, 1742: "The work of God goes on yet calmly at Boston." [6] On June 25 Davenport arrived. In him the festering opposition of the Old Lights found a target against which to vent openly the resentment they had been nursing in secret for some time.

Captain of the antirevival forces was Charles Chauncy (1705–87), copastor of Boston's First Church. "Dull, liberal, Arminian, and a profound scholar, Dr. Chauncy was a ready-made Old Light." [7] While Davenport was still in town, he fired the first overt charge against the revival: *Enthusiasm Described and Cautioned Against; A Sermon Preached at the Old Brick Meeting House in Boston, the Lord's Day after Commencement 1742.* [8] In some ways it was as intemperate as the accusations Davenport was hurling at the local pastors. Chauncy called enthusiasm "a kind of religious frenzy," and lumped it with other such New England horrors as antinomianism,

5. *The Christian History, 2,* 386. Charles Chauncy recognized Prince as a man of extensive learning, possessing "all the intellectual powers in a degree far beyond what is common," though "apt to give too much credit, especially to surprising stories" (letter dated May 6, 1768, to Ezra Stiles; in *Collections of the Mass. Hist. Soc., 10* [1809], 164).

6. Letter to Whitefield; in *PMHS, 53* (1920), 216. Colman added that "the overboiling zeal of some from far, visiting Charlestown, has not served the interest of religion there." These outside agitators were probably from eastern Connecticut, where overboiling zeal was first manifested; they probably came under the leadership of the erratic hotspur, Andrew Croswell (1709–85, Harvard 1728), a native of Charlestown and now pastor of the Second Church in Groton, Conn.

7. Clifford K. Shipton, *Sibley's Harvard Graduates, 6* (Cambridge, Mass., 1942), 444.

8. Boston, 1742; printed in Heimert, *The Great Awakening,* pp. 228–56. "Enthusiasm," from ἔνθεός, ἐνθουσιάζειν, is belief in God's immediate inspiration or possession, leading often to claims of divine authority. Chauncy applied it to Davenport "in a bad sense, as intending an imaginary, not a real inspiration: according to which sense, the Enthusiast is one who has a conceit of himself as a person favored with the extraordinary presence of the Deity. He mistakes the workings of his own passions for divine communications, and fancies himself immediately inspired by the Spirit of God, when all the while he is under no other influence than that of an overheated imagination" (p. 3).

popery, communism, and infidelity. He berated Davenport for daring to "assume a divine prerogative, and act as though you were the constituted judge of your brethren." To his readers he offered a "rule by which you may judge [!] of persons, whether they are enthusiasts, mere pretenders to the immediate influence of the Spirit." The rule was the Bible, interpreted in a reasonable way.[9]

The following month Chauncy stepped up the momentum of his attack on the revival by writing *A Letter from a Gentleman in Boston, to Mr. George Wishart, One of the Ministers of Edinburgh, Concerning the State of Religion in New England,* which was published anonymously in Scotland.[1] Before a foreign audience—the ultimate affront to Americans—he vilified the whole revival as "the effect of enthusiastic heat," and described Gilbert Tennent in terms as lurid as those most people reserved for James Davenport at his worst. To climax this phase of his assault, Chauncy next published an anonymous account of the French Prophets, a group of Huguenots from the mountains of southern France who after the revocation of the Edict of Nantes in 1685 were driven by fierce persecution into bizarre and sometimes fanatical behavior.[2] This shabby *coup de pied* was "devoid of subtlety in its attempt to damn by association, for [in the popular mind] the French Prophets were the epitome of enthusiasm, as Münster was of Anabaptism."[3]

Having set up this appalling scarecrow in the garden of the Lord, Chauncy found that results were not long coming. Old Lights flocked to him and rapidly coalesced as a distinguishable party, with him as confidante and counsellor. When they resorted to the press, as they frequently did now, he served as editor-in-chief. Years later he confided to Ezra Stiles of Newport:

9. Ibid., p. 7.
1. Edinburgh, 1742.
2. *The Wonderful Narrative; Or, A Faithful Account of the French Prophets, Their Agitations, Extasies, and Inspirations. To Which Are Added, Several Other Remarkable Instances of Persons Under the Influence of the Like Spirit, in Various Parts of the World, Particularly in New England* (Boston, 1742). For summary accounts of the French Prophets by responsible historians, see Henry Martyn Baird, *The Huguenots and the Revocation of the Edict of Nantes* (New York, 1895), 2, 183–90; and Ronald Knox, *Enthusiasm: A Chapter in the History of Religion* (New York, 1961), pp. 356–71. JE took brief notice of the French Prophets in ST (below, pp. 313, 330, 341), the only public response he ever made to printed attacks on the revival.
3. Gaustad, *The Great Awakening in New England,* p. 89.

I wrote and printed in that day more than two volumes in octavo. A vast number of pieces were published also as written by others; but there was scarce a piece against the times but was sent to me, and I had the labor sometimes of preparing it for the press, and always of correcting the press.[4]

To an Anglican friend Chauncy boasted that "he could have printed more flagrant accounts, if his intelligencers would have allowed him."[5] But, like their leader, they preferred the cloak of anonymity wherever possible.

By the end of 1742, the year of Davenport's dementia and Chauncy's blitz, the religious situation in New England had become sharply polarized. "We are crumbling into sects," moaned a concerned Old Light, "which time must find a name for."[6] Wrote another: "The glorious work appears to me now as changed into a ruinous war."[7] John Moorhead, a Boston Presbyterian sympathetic to the revival, foresaw the division and labeled the factions with peculiar poignancy:

> O how Satan spews out his flood! God direct us what to do, particularly with *pious zealots* and *cold, diabolical opposers!*[8]

4. Letter dated May 6, 1768; in *Collections of the Mass. Hist. Soc., 10* (1809), 162.

5. Timothy Cutler, letter dated Sept. 24, 1743, to Zachary Grey; in Boston Public Library. The reference was to Chauncy's book, *Seasonable Thoughts on the State of Religion in New England* (below, pp. 80–83).

6. *The Late Religious Commotions in New England Considered. An Answer to the Reverend Mr. Jonathan Edwards's Sermon Entitled,* The Distinguishing Marks of a Work of the Spirit of God . . . *In a Letter to a Friend. Together with a Preface, Containing an Examination of the Rev. Mr. William Cooper's Preface to Mr. Edwards's Sermon. By a Lover of Truth and Peace* (Boston, 1743), p. 18. Published anonymously in March, this tract was long attributed to Chauncy; more recent evidence, however, points to his friend William Rand (above, p. 18). It essays to refute JE's Yale sermon point by point, and concludes that what has been called an extraordinary work of God is nothing more than an extraordinary agitation, an extravagant excess which has had no "tendency to make [people] better, but worse" (p. 34).

7. Ebenezer Gay of Hingham, letter dated Dec. 6, 1742, to his nephew of the same name at Suffield; MS at Historical Society of Pennsylvania.

8. Letter dated July 30, 1742, to John Willison (above, p. 60); printed (from *The Glasgow Weekly History*) in *PMHS, 53* (1920), 212–13. Italics mine; I take these terms to symbolize enthusiasts on the left and supernatural rationalists on the right, with Edwardsean evangelicals somewhere in between.

If that prayer had an answer, it lay with Jonathan Edwards. Having enjoyed titular leadership of the evangelical movement in New England for eight years, he was inexpressibly saddened by the emergence of hostile parties called New Lights and Old Lights. "Such distinguishing names of reproach," he lamented, "do as it were divide us into two armies, separated and drawn up in battle array, ready to fight one with another" (ST; below, p. 499). After another year of warfare he would regard the breach as irreparable, the two parties so far apart that "there is at length raised a wall between them up to heaven; so that one party is very much out of the reach of all influence of the other" (see below, p. 536). But in 1742 he threw himself into the midst of the fray in one last heroic effort to make peace. In the name of all the sober friends of evangelical Christianity he had to search for solid ground between "pious zealots" and "diabolical opposers." The quest led him to expand the principles of discrimination he had enunciated in the Yale sermon and to address his apologetic to an opposition that had become much more articulate and intransigent. At the end of the year he sent to the printer a manuscript of *Some Thoughts Concerning the Present Revival of Religion in New England,* a treatise in five parts.[9]

9. *Thoughts from the Heart*

At the outset of his most ambitious work yet (378 pages), Edwards observed that his efforts to vindicate the revival and confute its critics ought to persuade those whose "error has been in the understanding, and not in the disposition." But this was small ground for hope, as he himself knew: the problem was not so much with the wrong-headed as with the hard-hearted. Rationalistic objections to

9. *Some Thoughts* was advertised as "Just Published" for the first time in *The Boston Gazette* for March 15, 1743. The title pages of all known first editions, however, bear the imprint date 1742. Frequently eighteenth-century publishers set the title page of a work first, so that a book begun near the end of a year might not be actually published until the following year. In any event, a publication date of mid-March 1743 is practically irrefutable. On March 16, Charles Chauncy informed a correspondent that "Mr. Edwards' book of 378 pages upon the good work is at last come forth"; and the next day in *The Boston News Letter,* he advertised a prospectus of his "antidote" for the evangelical virus and invited subscriptions for printing it. His *Seasonable Thoughts* appeared the following September (below, p. 80).

the revival, he asserted, rested on a false philosophy that divorced "the affections of the soul" from the will. This is a point that the Old Lights never understood. They espoused the classical view of man according to which the "passions" are sub-rational appetites to be held in check by the reason, a perspective requiring that religion seek to enlighten the mind rather than raise the affections.[1] Against such a view Edwards set his adaptation of Locke's sensationalist psychology, a position he not only hammered out in the study but expounded in the pulpit. While composing *Some Thoughts* he was also preaching a series of sermons which he would refine and publish in 1746 as *A Treatise Concerning Religious Affections,* and the theme of that later work appears here in crisp summary: man is a unitary being in whom "all acts of the affections . . . are in some sense acts of the will, and all acts of the will are acts of the affections." He therefore concluded that true religion consists in holy affections. "The things of religion take place in men's hearts, no further than they are affected with them. The informing of the understanding is all vain, any farther than it affects the heart; or, which is the same thing, has influence on the affections." [2] Edwards was far from denying the noetic dimension of religious address and response, but he held firmly that the dynamic center of a willing, acting, personal being lies not in the intellect but in the disposition. *Some Thoughts,* in fact, proceeds directly from his own "new sense of the heart."

In Part I of this work Edwards expanded the answer he gave in *The Distinguishing Marks* to judgments of the revival based on external manifestations. The epiphenomena are simply irrelevant, he insisted again; and any argument from this kind of evidence is bound to be barren. Accusing the antirevivalists of judging the whole work by a part, he declared that they rejected the entire movement because of some unworthy things "that are accidental to it." Such undiscriminating critics forget that corruption remains even in the most mature Christians. Thus any work of God among men will be mixed with imperfections, and it is fatuous either to approve or condemn "all in the lump" (ST; below, p. 315). He argued that "an high degree of love to God, is consistent with these

1. According to Chauncy, "an enlightened mind and not raised affections ought always to be the guide of those who call themselves men; and this in the affairs of religion as well as other things" (*Seasonable Thoughts,* p. 327).

2. ST; below, pp. 297–98. Cf. also *Religious Affections,* Part I.

two things, viz. a considerable degree of remaining corruption, and also many errors in judgment . . . [and] may accidentally move a person to that which is very wrong, and contrary to the mind and will of God" (ST; below, p. 316). On this premise he could explain and disavow the *excesses* of the revival while still attributing its *essence* to the gracious working of God.

The philosophical basis of his position at this point is a form of *Occasionalism*. Somewhat to the rationalists' mystification, Edwards wrote:

> They that are studied in logic have learned that the nature of the cause is not to be judged of by the nature of the effect, nor the nature of the effect from the nature of the cause, when the cause is only *causa sine qua non,* or an occasional cause; yea, that in such a case, oftentimes the nature of the effect is quite contrary to the nature of the cause [ST; below, p. 316].

In equating *causa sine qua non* with "occasional cause," he was referring to the finite conditions without which a particular event could not occur, at least in the way it actually does. While such conditions may be necessary to the event, they are never sufficient of themselves to produce it or to determine its essential nature; and that is why one cannot argue the nature of the cause from the nature of the effect, or vice versa. God is the only "true cause," and Edwards did not want His work judged on the basis of the accidents of the historical situation within which God was working. His point was simply that in New England's religious ferment, "occasional causes" might include such things as corruption, errors in judgment, misguided love for God, false zeal, etc.—and these might function as *causae sine qua non* for the accidental disturbances of the revival—but the *essential* effect may be due nonetheless to God's gracious action. In any case, occasions in the finite situation could provide no reliable guide for judging the nature of the true cause; for that a keener principle of discrimination must be invoked, and this is what Edwards proceeded to do in the following pages.[3]

3. Cf. Smith, "Editor's Introduction" to JE's *Religious Affections,* p. 7. Chauncy, not surprisingly, was unimpressed; if observation and experience provide documentary evidence for "bad things" almost universally prevailing in the revival, he retorted, "can it be thought they are nothing more than *accidental effects* of a good cause?" (*Seasonable Thoughts,* p. 308).

Granting (but not condoning) all the imprudences and disorders, passions and heats, transports and ecstasies, errors in judgment and indiscreet zeal, he insisted that there had been an astonishing alteration in personal piety and social morality all over New England. In the face of what to him was luminously *en évidence,* it was exceeding strange—nay, positively shameful—that any should profess not to know whether this was "the work of God or the work of the Devil" (ST; below, p. 330). But if skeptics still wanted to cavil about "enthusiasm," he had one more pearl to cast. Alongside Abigail Hutchinson and Phebe Bartlet he would place a final case history, the supreme example of heartfelt religion experienced as ecstatic transport and lived in sober righteousness. The subject was Sarah, his beloved wife.

Perry Miller (following Joseph Tracy) is unquestionably right in beginning this part of his account with young Jonathan's charming apostrophe to thirteen-year-old Sarah Pierpont, written in 1723. For lovers of the Jonathan Edwards story (and perhaps for other lovers as well) it cannot be repeated too often.

> They say there is a young lady in [New Haven] who is beloved of that great Being who made and rules the world, and that there are certain seasons in which this great Being, in some way or other invisible, comes to her and fills her mind with exceeding sweet delight, and that she hardly cares for anything, except to meditate on him—that she expects after a while to be received up where he is, to be raised up out of the world and caught up into heaven; being assured that he loves her too well to let her remain at a distance from him always. There she is to dwell with him, and to be ravished with his love and delight forever. . . . She has a strange sweetness in her mind, and singular purity in her affections; is most just and conscientious in all her conduct; and you could not persuade her to do anything wrong or sinful, if you would give her all the world, lest she should offend this great Being. She is of a wonderful sweetness, calmness and universal benevolence of mind; especially after this great God has manifested himself to her mind. . . . She loves to be alone, walking in the fields and groves, and seems to have someone invisible always conversing with her.[4]

4. Dwight, *Life of President Edwards,* pp. 114–15. Cf. Miller, *Jonathan Edwards,* pp. 201–06; and Tracy, *The Great Awakening,* pp. 226–30.

Four years later they were married. It was, as Edwards murmured on his deathbed, an "uncommon union . . . of such a nature as I trust is spiritual." [5]

Besides managing his household, bearing his children, and entertaining his numerous guests, Sarah completely shared her husband's religious commitments. From her childhood experiences of communing with God, she came in the Northampton revivals to "a very frequent dwelling, for some considerable time together, in such views of the glory of the divine perfections, and Christ's excellencies, that [her] soul in the meantime has been as it were perfectly overwhelmed, and swallowed up with light and love . . . that was altogether unspeakable; and more than once continuing for five or six hours together." These feelings were strong in 1735, and increased in 1739. Edwards noted dryly, "They arose from no distemper catched from Mr. Whitefield or Mr. Tennent, because they began before either of them came into the country." But in 1742 they reached an overpowering climax. On January 25 Edwards set out on a preaching tour to Leicester that kept him away for two weeks. As he departed, Sarah was uneasy because of a mild rebuke he had administered to her for imprudent remarks to a neighboring minister on the previous day. During Edwards' absence other ministers, notably Samuel Buell, visited Northampton and preached with signal success, causing Sarah to wrestle with feelings of jealousy.[6] But upon resigning herself to God, she soon was able to accept these reversals with sweet serenity. As her sense of God's greatness and goodness increased, she felt herself transported to inexpressible joy, and ultimately to such ecstatic rapture that at times bodily strength failed altogether. For more than a week she drank so deeply of the glories of the heavenly world that her soul was in Paradise, yet all the while she performed her daily duties with humility and efficiency. "Oh how good is it," she exclaimed once, "to work for God in the daytime, and at night to lie down under his smiles!"

When Edwards returned to Northampton he was profoundly moved by the story of Sarah's recent experiences, and asked her to put them in writing. Dutifully she obeyed; and as he composed *Some Thoughts* later that year, her testimony became the final case

5. Hopkins, *Life of Jonathan Edwards*; in Levin, *Jonathan Edwards: A Profile,* p. 80.

6. On Buell, see above, p. 57. JE describes his ministry at Northampton in a letter of 1743; see below, pp. 549–50.

history he would set before the world to authenticate the revival.[7] Changing each personal pronoun to "the person" and carefully suppressing every indication of identity, even of sex, he pictured "one that is [not] in the giddy age of youth, nor a new convert, and unexperienced Christian . . . neither converted nor educated in that enthusiastical town of Northampton." He emphasized that in none of her experiences were any impulses, revelations, superstitions, antinomian delusions, or melancholic seizures. While defending the absolute validity of her transports, he also affirmed the sobriety of her obedient faith. Here was a person "eating for God, and working for God, and sleeping for God, and bearing pain and trouble for God, and doing all as the service of love, and so doing it with a continual, uninterrupted cheerfulness, peace and joy." For sixteen pages he opened her soul's most intimate secrets to the cold stares of hard-hearted rationalists who comprehended such things about as tone-deaf men hear a symphony. Then he allowed his own pent-up heart-cry to escape:

> Now if such things are enthusiasm, and the fruits of a distempered brain, let my brain be evermore possessed of that happy distemper! If this be distraction, I pray God that the world of mankind may be all seized with this benign, meek, beneficent, beatifical, glorious distraction! If agitations of body were found in the French Prophets, and ten thousand prophets more, 'tis little to their purpose, who bring it as an objection against such a work as this, unless their purpose be to disprove the whole of the Christian religion (ST; below, p. 341).

Against "diabolical opposers," when he needed the ultimate experience, Edwards flung the testimony of her who loved to dwell with God and "to be ravished with his love and delight forever." [8]

7. Sarah's original first-person narrative is printed in Dwight, *Life of President Edwards,* pp. 171–86. JE's adaptation of it is in ST; below, pp. 331–41.

8. Chauncy, who can be forgiven only because such things were completely beyond his power to comprehend, remained unmoved. He made only one grumpy comment, a parenthesis within a footnote, that Edwards had taken up sixteen pages "with the character of a single person, who yet was not an instance of conversion in these times" (*Seasonable Thoughts,* p. 332 n). Isaac Watts thought JE had been referring to himself, "because he takes upon him so largely to tell us what passes through his heart" (letter dated Sept. 14, 1743, to Benjamin Colman; in *PMHS,* 2d ser., 9 [1895], 402).

The second part of the treatise underscores the significance of the revival, as Edwards saw it, in the whole of salvation history. The Valley awakening of 1735 had centered his attention on this matter, and he had roughed out his theology of history in a series of sermons on "The History of Redemption" in 1739. Now that the revival had become much more widespread, he was ready to speculate more confidently. *Some Thoughts* carried forward his *heilsgeschichtliches* reading of human events in terms of historical progress toward a goal defined by the providence of God. " 'Tis not unlikely that this work of God's Spirit, that is so extraordinary and wonderful, is the dawning, or at least a prelude, of that glorious work of God, so often foretold in Scripture, which in the progress and issue of it, shall renew the world of mankind" (ST; below, p. 353). The ancient prophecies appeared to him to point toward his own time as presaging an imminent climax in the work of redemption; and he attempted to justify this exciting vision by a series of typological comparisons between the Old World and the New, reinforced by some fanciful allegorizing of biblical prophecies.

What is important here is not the quaint hermeneutic, nor even Edwards' immediate hope of persuading antirevivalists to quit hindering the larger purposes of God in history, but the decisive way in which ideas of this sort reinforce America's persistent self-image as a "redeemer nation." Isaac Watts dismissed the whole notion with the curt remark, "I think his reasonings about America want force," but that was because he read them from the wrong side of the Atlantic.[9] From the time the first settlers mounted their grand errand into the wilderness, Americans have regarded their history as the inauguration of a new—and possibly ultimate—epoch in the work of redemption. A sense of destiny was already becoming manifest when an early historian of America began with the story of creation,[1] when Puritans purposed to complete the Reformation

9. Ibid. Chauncy scoffed at JE's evidence as "absolutely precarious," compared his argument to the delusions of obscure visionaries, and cited testimony of "a worthy gentleman" who had charged JE with claiming that "the millennium began when there was such an awakening at Northampton eight years past.—So that salvation is gone forth from Northampton, and Northampton must have the praise of being first brought into it" (*Seasonable Thoughts*, p. 372 n). JE vigorously denied the charge in a letter; below, p. 560. Miller treats the incident in *Jonathan Edwards*, p. 318.

1. Samuel Purchas, *Purchas His Pilgrimage* (London, 1613).

by planting in America a working model of the true church which all half-reformed churches might see and emulate,[2] and when John Winthrop envisioned leaders of every other society praying, "The Lord make it like that of New England." [3] Edwards' contribution to shaping the idea of a "redeemer nation" was to relate it to biblical prophecies of the millennium, to locate that millennium within history, and to identify its foregleams in a period of spiritual renewal already under way. As America's first postmillennial thinker, he furnished an evangelical basis for the aggressive historical optimism which (in an increasingly secularized form) would support the nation's concept of itself as leader and model for all other peoples.[4] In his urgent call to "all sorts of persons" to acknowledge and promote "the mighty work" because of what it would mean to the country and to the world, Edwards anticipated the messianic impulses of crusading churchmen and politicians for the next two centuries.

The third part is a spirited retort to what Edwards regarded as unjust accusations against the promoters and subjects of the revival. In replying to many criticisms he revealed something of his theory of preaching, though what he said in this section should be read in full awareness of his own style in the pulpit. A fellow minister described him as "a preacher of a low and moderate voice, a natural way of delivery; and without any agitation of body, or anything else in the manner to excite attention; except his habitual and great solemnity, looking and speaking as in the presence of God, and with a weighty sense of the matter delivered." [5] That this was the way in which even his imprecatory sermons were delivered seems to support Edwards' contention that the effects of hearers came not so

2. Cotton Mather, *Magnalia Christi Americana* (London, 1702), Book III, p. 74.

3. "A Model of Christian Charity" (1630), in *The Annals of America,* ed. Mortimer J. Adler (Chicago, 1968), *1,* 115.

4. Cf. C. C. Goen, "Jonathan Edwards: A New Departure in Eschatology," *Church History, 28* (1959), 25–40. The subsequent development of the concept is treated by Ernest Lee Tuveson, *Redeemer Nation; The Idea of America's Millennial Role* (Chicago, 1968). One could argue that a major cause of the widespread frustration in American life today is the thwarting of our primeval messianism in a world of upsurging nationalisms. In this connection, it is instructive to read again Perry Miller's brilliant essay, "Errand into the Wilderness," reprinted in a book of the same title (Cambridge, Mass., 1956), pp. 1–15.

5. Thomas Prince, in *The Christian History, 2,* 390–91.

much from oratorical devices as from the force of the truth declared. "What must have been especially terrifying to Edwards' audience listening to his merciless pictorial representations of the pit was the realization that they were not hearing a sensationalistic ranter striving for an effect, but a prodigious and cool intellect driven by the purest moral earnestness seeking to approach some adequacy of representation for a transcendently awful fact." [6] But Edwards nevertheless sanctioned "an exceeding affectionate way of preaching," provided that "nothing but truth" is declared and the hearers' affections "are not disagreeable to the nature of what they are affected with" (ST; below, pp. 386–87).

A special problem in regard to the preaching of terror was what antirevivalists called "frighting poor innocent children with talk of hell-fire and eternal damnation." Edwards looked upon this as mere sentimentality. Anybody who talks of "innocent" children betrays his deviation from the doctrines of the fathers: children are subjects of God's wrath until they are converted.[7] A true love for them, he argued, would wish them born anew and delivered from the curse of sin as soon as possible, rather than allow them to remain in danger by making them the objects of foolish pity. Therefore he preached to children the same awakening doctrines he urged upon everybody else. When young Billy Sheldon died in February 1741, he called the youth of the town together and on the basis of Job 14:2, "He cometh forth like a flower and is cut down," he labored to "exhort and beseech the young people that are here present to get ready for death." [8] At another private children's meeting the

6. John Gerstner, *Steps to Salvation; The Evangelistic Message of Jonathan Edwards* (Philadelphia, 1960), p. 24.

7. According to Samuel Hopkins, JE diligently instructed his children in the Westminster Shorter Catechism (see Levin, *Jonathan Edwards: A Profile*, p. 43). Q. 19 of the Catechism reads: "What is the misery of that estate whereinto man fell? *Ans.* All mankind by their fall [in Adam] lost communion with God, are under his wrath and curse, and so made liable to all miseries in this life, to death itself, and to the pains of hell forever." On March 9, 1740/1, JE wrote to Benjamin Colman that the past winter had been "a time of the most remarkable and visible blessing of heaven upon my family that ever was. . . . I hope that my four eldest children (the youngest of them between six and seven years of age) have been savingly wrought upon" (MS at Mass. Hist. Soc.).

8. MS Sermon, Yale Collection. He used the same sermon again on Feb. 12, 1748, with "a new application . . . on the occasion of the death of my daughter Jerusha."

same month he used II Kings 2:23–24 to warn that "God is very angry at the sins of children" because they have no love for God, live in neglect of Christ, sin on the Sabbath Day, harbor wicked thoughts and desires, tell many dreadful lies, hate one another, and serve the Devil. Underscoring their "naturally miserable state and condition," he admonished them to seek faith in Christ as "the way to obtain a crown of life." [9] If any doubted the propriety or efficacy of this approach, he could always point to Phebe Bartlet, who was soundly converted at the age of four and was still living a convincing Christian life (see above, p. 30, and below, pp. 199–205).

In all, Edwards endeavored to answer ten of the most common charges against the revival. Had this part of his treatise been left to stand alone, it might have appeared less discriminating than defensive. But he turned next to "what things are to be corrected or avoided." In Part IV, by far the longest section of the book, he undertook the difficult and painful task of rebuking "pious zealots" in full view of "diabolical opposers." The delicacy of the task may be sensed from his careful search for an angle of approach, for the refusal of opposers to do anything more than carp at the whole work had had the most unfortunate result possible: it had convinced the zealots that every word of caution proceeded from the bitterest prejudice and therefore had confirmed them in their belief that "there is no such thing as any prevailing imprudences," and made them "less cautious and suspicious of themselves" than they otherwise might have been (ST; below, p. 410). In short, the revival's critics had made it almost impossible for its friends to correct the disorders of which the critics were complaining!

Painful as it was, however, some plain rebukes had to be administered. Edwards first entreated the careless promoters of the revival to consider three causes of the behavior which had made them an easy target for traducers: spiritual pride, wrong principles, and ignorance of Satan's devices. Spiritual pride is the worst, the "mainspring, or at least the main support of all the rest," and is ever the peculiar trial of the saints. As Edwards saw it, when God seems to bless his saints in a special way, others are provoked to jealousy and criticism, causing the saints to look upon their detractors as cold and dead—and the result is an acerbic polarity in which each side tries to vindicate itself against the other. At the end of an insightful analysis of the tricky way in which pride operates,

9. MS Sermon, Yale Collection. See also MS sermons on Ps. 34:11, dated July 1741; Ps. 71:5, probably in the late 1730s; and Prov. 7:7, dated Nov. 1738.

Edwards urged special precautions toward humility, though he recognized how easy it is even to be proud of one's humility.

Among the "wrong principles," i.e. erroneous beliefs, infecting the revival was the "notion that 'tis God's manner now in these days to guide his saints . . . by inspiration, or immediate revelation; and to make known to 'em what shall come to pass hereafter, or what it is his will that they should do, by impressions that he by his Spirit makes upon their minds" (ST; below, p. 432). This, by definition, is enthusiasm; and Edwards always opposed it as strenuously as anyone. He knew that "this error will defend and support all [other] errors," for as long as one has the notion that he is "guided by immediate direction from heaven," one is oblivious to all counsel and correction. For this reason, he was not very optimistic about the effectiveness of any dissuasive; nevertheless he fired off a barrage of biblical texts and dehortations. A kindred error he traced to those so impatient for reform that they disregarded the need for order. Although he recognized that reformers reject tradition and despise it all the more because they hear reactionary demands for order as thinly veiled calls for suppression, he also knew that the overthrow of fundamental social controls could do nothing but multiply mischief. When certain zealots wanted to ignore ecclesiastical order because "dead forms and ceremonies" had nothing to do with godliness, he had to brand their argument as specious. The immediate issues here were the practice of judging inward spiritual experiences and the itch of some to substitute charismatic in place of institutional qualifications for ministers, but the underlying pressures were much more far-reaching. Edwards failed to carry his point with all— or even most—of the New Lights, and in the next generation the attitudes he could not overcome would help to fuel a movement judging that the traditional forms of English rule were hindering the free exercise of the American spirit.

A third cause of error, he found, was ignorance of the way in which Satan insinuates falsehood into truth, corruption into purity, nature into spirit. In this context Edwards offered another of his keen analyses of the character of religious experience. After observing many hundreds of converts, New Lights of various shades and intensities, he had one word to describe them all: mixed. True piety often coexists with passion, imaginary impressions, self-righteousness, or pride; and true Christians may have serious defects even in their genuinely gracious experiences. New converts especially, as new-born babes, are likely to be undeveloped in Christian character to the extent that in their immaturity they are easily overtaken by corruption. Without questioning the validity of their Christian commitment, Edwards warned them of their need for caution and encouraged them to grow spiritually. He concluded that "the most excellent experiences" are those which have the least mixture with corruption and which are the least deficient. If these qualifications are observed, it matters not how high the experiences are raised— "the higher the better" (ST; below, p. 466).

Following his lengthy examination of the causes of errors, Edwards began to compile a grim catalog of the consequences. Censuring of church members as unconverted he considered "the worst disease that has attended this work," and he devoted a dozen pages to reprimanding it. Censorious judging is beyond the pale of *all* Christian propriety, and should not be allowed even against the revival's worst enemies. God alone has the right and the ability to judge opposers. "We may represent it as exceeding dangerous to oppose this work—for this we have good warrant in the Word of God; but I know of no necessity we are under to determine whether it be possible for those that are guilty of it to be in a state of grace or no" (ST; below, p. 479). Inasmuch as a later controversy over discerning visible sainthood would mark a sharp turn in Edwards' career, it is important to note that neither here nor ever did he advocate the practice of attempting to judge the inward spiritual state of another person. In *Some Thoughts* he recognized that there were churches which received members into full communion only on their testimony of conversion, and that their basis of judgment was properly not some pretense to special spiritual discernment but a testing of converts' professions "in their speech and ordinary behavior." The conviction he was to unveil in 1744, which would finally cost him his pastorate in 1750, was that visible saints (i.e. full communicant members of the visible church) should be *visible* saints, with their verbal profession of sainthood supported by a visible discipleship. It was the visibility of discipleship that should be subject to charitable judgment by the church, he thought, not one's interior spiritual condition. In 1742 he explicitly shunned the controversy over whether to require a personal testimony from applicants for church membership, but what he did affirm was entirely consistent with the position he announced later.[1]

1. Cf. *An Humble Inquiry.* It is sometimes hinted that JE deceived his people by hiding his dissent from Stoddardism for several years. John Searl, a

Part IV closes with a curiously ambivalent mixture of optimism and pessimism: hope that most of the pious zealots would soon correct the errors which were bringing the revival into disrepute, and fear that when they did many of them might begin to doubt the validity of their recent high experiences. "The Devil has driven the pendulum far beyond its proper point of rest; and when he has carried it to the utmost length that he can, and it begins by its own weight to swing back, he probably will set in, and drive it with the utmost fury the other way; and so give us no rest; and if possible prevent our settling in a proper medium." Some readers may dismiss Edwards' desire to blame Satan for driving religion to extremes as simply naive; others may discern a profound insight into the sometimes demonic ambiguity of all religious responses because of the cultural conditioning to which they are inescapably subject. But all should be able to sympathize with the truth that the pendulum of religious experience, heedless of the most devout intentions, never rests at any "proper medium." Not only is every individual located tenuously on some segment of a wide arc, but even the arc itself, as in Foucault's experiment, is always traversing new territory.

In the concluding section Edwards undertook to show what should be done to promote the revival. The first thing needful, he felt, was to remove stumblingblocks, chief among which was what he and other evangelicals regarded as the theological basis of anti-revivalism.

> I would now beseech those that have hitherto been something inclining to Arminian principles, seriously to weigh the matter with respect to this work, and consider whether, if the Scriptures are the Word of God, the work that has been described in the first part of this treatise must not needs be, as to the substance of it, the work of God, and the flourishing of that religion that

younger minister who had "visited at Northampton, at Deacon Pomeroy's" in 1746–47, testified that in his hearing JE "delivered and at sundry times discoursed upon your opinion, that a profession of true godliness was a qualification requisite to full communion in the Christian Church." Searl also recalled several apparently calm discussions with church leaders over a passage in *Religious Affections* (1746) that begins: "I am far from saying that it is not requisite that persons should give any sort of account of their experiences to their brethren" (Yale ed., p. 416). In these years, according to Searl, there was no secret about JE's opinions, nor does he indicate any controversy (letter dated June 4, 1750, to JE; in the Case Memorial Library of the Hartford Seminary Foundation).

is taught by Christ and his apostles; and whether any good medium can be found, where a man can rest with any stability, between owning this work and being a Deist; and also to consider whether or no, if it be indeed so that this be the work of God, it don't entirely overthrow their scheme of religion; and therefore whether it don't infinitely concern 'em, as they would be partakers of eternal salvation, to relinquish their scheme. Now is a good time for Arminians to change their principles [ST; below, p. 503].

With remarkable prescience Edwards foresaw that the Great Awakening was to become a decisive watershed in American religious thought. As history would eventually reveal, many of the rationalistic opposers of the revival were really pre-Unitarians who would develop an ever more self-conscious antithesis to evangelicalism until the result could fairly be called Deism.

Could such stumbling blocks be put out of the way, however, and measures taken to purify the piety and zeal of all Christians, then the revival might prosper not only for the glory of New England but for the entire world. Amid several general exhortations Edwards had three specific proposals: a season of world-wide prayer, a renewing of the people's covenant with God, and the publishing of a comprehensive history of the awakening. The first proposal he enlarged greatly in 1747, when in concert with evangelical friends in Scotland he published *An Humble Attempt to Promote Explicit Agreement and Visible Union of God's People in Extraordinary Prayer for the Revival of Religion and the Advancement of Christ's Kingdom on Earth.*[2] The second he had already implemented at Northampton on March 16, 1742, as an example to be followed by other evangelical churches.[3] And the third, suggested earlier by William Cooper in his preface to *The Distinguishing Marks*, bore prompt fruit in the appearance of *The Christian History, Containing Accounts of the Revival and Propagation of Religion in Great Britain and America,* the first specifically religious magazine in the western hemisphere.[4]

2. Boston, 1747.
3. Below, pp. 85–86; and letter of Dec. 12, 1743; below, pp. 550–54.
4. See Lyon Norman Richardson. *A History of Early American Magazines, 1741–1789* (New York, 1931), pp. 58–73; and above, p. 59. *The Christian History* was edited by Thomas Prince, Jr., whose father was one of the ministers at Boston's Old South Church and a vigorous supporter of the revival. The periodical published two annual volumes before expiring in 1744. A Scottish counterpart,

10. Counterthoughts

Soon after Edwards published *Some Thoughts,* the polarities of New England's religious situation became much sharper. As one indication, in May 1743 the traditional post-Election Day meeting of ministers in Boston devolved into a rump session dominated by Old Lights, who promptly seized the occasion to pass a resolution condemning the revival *in toto* without conceding a shred of integrity to any part of it. Charles Chauncy affixed a presumptuous title to the action and had it printed as *The Testimony of the Pastors of the Churches in the Province of the Massachusetts Bay in New England, at Their Annual Convention in Boston May 25, 1743. Against Several Errors in Doctrine and Disorders in Practice, Which Have of Late Obtained in Various Parts of the Land; As Drawn up by a Committee Chosen by the Said Pastors, Read and Accepted Paragraph by Paragraph, and Voted to Be Signed by the Moderator in Their Name, and Printed.* It was signed by Nathaniel Eells of Scituate alone, thus masking the fact that only seventy of the more than two hundred Massachusetts ministers had been present, with only thirty-eight voting for the resolution. Stung by this brazen attempt to posture the clergy as massively opposed to the revival, evangelicals promptly called a special convocation to meet the day after Commencement and bear a positive witness, which they published as *The Testimony and Advice of an Assembly of Pastors of Churches in New England, at a Meeting in Boston July 7, 1743. Occasioned by the Late Happy Revival of Religion in Many Parts of the Land. To Which Are Added Attestations Contained in Letters from a Number of their Brethren Who Were Providentially Hindered from Giving Their Presence.* This was signed by sixty-eight ministers and supported by letters of approval from forty-three others. Such developments marked the crystallizing of pro- and anti-revival factions into two irreconcilable parties.[5]

The Christian Monthly History, was issued at Edinburgh under the editorship of James Robe, friend and correspondent of JE; appearing irregularly in sixteen numbers between November 1743 and January 1746, it printed many items of American revival intelligence.

5. For a summary account, with convenient references to most of the major sources, see Gaustad, *The Great Awakening in New England,* pp. 63–79. Among the 43 absentees sending letters was JE, who joined six other ministers of Hampshire County in signing a brief testimony dated June 30, 1743; it was printed in *The Christian History, 1,* 178–80. See below, pp. 542–43.

Edwards' thoughts, as it were, had been lobbed into a no-man's land between "two opposing armies." As a consequence, they drew fire from both sides. Besides the expected flak from radical New Lights, there were staunch supporters like William Cooper who felt that he had almost betrayed the revival by exposing its faults before the enemy.

> Some of the friends of the work [Cooper wrote] seem to me to have gone into an extreme this way, I suppose that they might not be accounted partial, and being aware that possibly they might be under a temptation to cover or excuse what was really amiss and blameworthy in the promoters or subjects of this work. I was ready to think Mr. Edwards himself had exceeded this way in his late book.[6]

On the other hand, if Edwards had hoped to dampen the enemy's powder by his frank acknowledgments of the revival's excesses, he was due to be disappointed. One historian (changing the metaphor) opines that "if Old Lights took time to read the fourth part of Edwards' treatise, they found most of the wind taken from their sails." [7] On the contrary, they found here a brisk new wind in which to hoist their sails even higher. Chortled one: "The fourth part of Mr. Edwards's late book . . . contains an account of greater disorders, delusions, errors and extravagances among the subjects of the late work, than the opposers thought of, or could have believed on any lower authority." [8] They lost no time in pressing a new attack.

Chief cannoneer for the Old Lights was Charles Chauncy. In September 1743 he fired from Boston a charge of polemical grapeshot called *Seasonable Thoughts on the State of Religion in New England, a Treatise in Five Parts.* As its title intimates, Chauncy deliberately cast his piece in the same mold as its target. He apparently was already assembling it when Edwards' work appeared, for he wrote the same week to a Connecticut cousin:

> Mr. Edwards' book of 378 pages upon the good work is at last come forth; and I believe will do much hurt; and I am the rather inclined to think so, because there are some good things in it. Error is much more likely to be propagated, when it is mixed

6. Letter dated June 9, 1743, to James Robe; in *The Christian Monthly History, 1* (No. 4, Feb. 1744), 13.

7. Gaustad, *The Great Awakening in New England,* p. 92.

8. *Boston Evening Post,* June 13, 1743.

with truth. This hides its deformity and makes it go down the more easily. I may again trouble myself and the world upon the appearance of this book. I am preparing an antidote, and if the world should see cause to encourage it, it may in time come to light.[9]

Since Edwards had argued extensively from empirical evidence, Chauncy assiduously collected plenty of his own. "I have been a circle of more than three hundred miles," he told his public confidently, "and had, by this means, an opportunity of going through a great number of towns in this, and the neighboring government of Connecticut, and of having personal conversation with most of the ministers, and many other gentlemen, in the country, and of settling a correspondence with several of them, with a particular view to know, as nearly as might be, the truth of things, upon better evidence than that of mere hearsay." [1] Chauncy wanted a direct confrontation, and understandably so, for he conceived of himself, no less than Edwards, as contending for the honor of God and the soul of New England.[2]

On March 24 and again on March 31 the *Boston News Letter* advertised Edwards' *Some Thoughts* as "Just Published," and immediately below was the prospectus for Chauncy's forthcoming *Seasonable Thoughts*. This juxtaposition of the two title pages with their respective tables of contents was, as Edwin S. Gaustad observes, "hardly coincidental." [3] When Chauncy's riposte actually appeared,

9. Letter dated March 16, 1743, to the Rev. Nathaniel Chauncy; in *New England Historical and Genealogical Register, 10* (1956), 332.

1. *Seasonable Thoughts,* p. xxix. Eleazar Wheelock, pastor at Lebanon Crank (now Columbia), Conn., and one of the evangelicals whom Chauncy berated in his book, was suspicious of the Boston traveler's objectivity in collecting evidence. "I was upon that same road to New Haven," Wheelock recalled, "when that Dr. passed through this government . . . to fill his crop with materials for that piece, and I came several times within scent of him (for he left a savour of what he fed upon where he lit) . . . and should have freely given him a full and true account of that whole affair [*in re* enthusiasm at Yale] if he had desired to know the truth. . . . And I suspect he would doubtless have given me the opportunity if the truth had been what he desired" (letter dated Oct. 24, 1759, to Ebenezer Pemberton; in Dartmouth College Library).

2. Alan Heimert, sighting from a longer perspective, might even say, "for the soul of America." Cf. his *Religion and the American Mind from the Great Awakening to the Revolution* (Cambridge, Mass., 1966).

3. *The Great Awakening in New England,* p. 93. Cf. above, p. 65 n.

it fulfilled to the letter its promise. After a predictable preface, "Giving an account of the Antinomians, Familists and Libertines, who infected these churches above an hundred years ago; very needful for these days, the like spirit and errors prevailing now as did then," he set forth the five parts of his treatise:

I. Faithfully pointing out the things of a bad and dangerous tendency, in the late and present religious appearance in the land.

II. Representing the obligations which lie upon the pastors of these churches in particular, and upon all in general, to use their endeavors to suppress prevailing disorders; with the great danger of a neglect in so important a matter.

III. Opening, in many instances, wherein the discouragers of irregularities have been injuriously treated.

IV. Shewing what ought to be corrected, or avoided, in testifying against the evil things of the present day.

V. Directing our thoughts more positively to what may be judged the best expedients, to promote pure and undefiled religion in these times.

Part I, obviously, was what Chauncy regarded as most seasonable: it takes up more than two-thirds of his 424 pages. But though he descanted on every grievance of the Old Lights against the revivalists, he offered little that Edwards had not anticipated.[4] The con-

4. Typical examples of Chauncy's responses to Edwards are given in notes to this edition of Edwards' work and at various places in this Introduction. For those who wish to follow the running quarrel over how to interpret the revival, and particularly its excesses, the table below locates the passages in Edwards' *Some Thoughts* (this volume) which Chauncy quoted or paraphrased and attempted to rebut in *Seasonable Thoughts*.

Topic	Edwards	Chauncy
A priori judgments of the revival	293–96	378–82
Extrabiblical canons for judging	296–313	382–89
Historical examples of religious emotion	307–13	81–92
On distinguishing good from bad effects	314–16	389–90
Causation of aberrant behavior	316–31	307–32
Sarah Edwards' religious experiences	331–41	332 n.
The millennium to begin in America	353–58	371–73
Duties of civil rulers toward the revival	370–73	366–69
Critics of the revival as opposers of God	381–83	392–95
Role of the affections, or "passions"	385–89	301–03
Same: cf. also	296–300	108–13
Propriety of preaching terror	389–94	303–05

troversy was not over whether there were "imprudences and irregularities" in the revival, but whether notwithstanding such excesses the revival was a work of God.

They would never settle this question because of irreconcilable differences between their respective views of man. A veritable chasm separated Edwards and Chauncy with respect to the functions of "reason" and "passion" in religion (cf. above, pp. 65–66). Chauncy's view of human nature required him to insist that "Satan works upon the reason by the passion; the Spirit upon the passion by the reason." [5] That is why he could only reject revivalistic religion as spurious. Edwards, on the other hand, saw man as a sinner who needs to be remade—an event which is possible only as God grants him a "new sense of the heart," a holy affection at the center of his being which radiates its transforming power through the whole man. The revival, therefore, was to him not just a one-time marvel; it was a divinely revealed means of urging latter-day sinners to seek the gracious gift until this fallen world should be renewed in glory. As the revival spread, in God's good time it would eventually usher in the fullness of the kingdom of God. This conflict over the nature of man, expressed during the Great Awakening as an issue of religious address and response, was to stand as a "continental divide" between evangelicals and rationalists. The latter would remain an intellectual élite, flowering in New England and a few other select athenæa, while the former would garner the multitudes into popular churches seeking by means of revivals "to reform the continent and to spread scriptural holiness over these lands." [6]

11. *The Quest for True Religion*

In 1743 Jonathan Edwards and his friends saw the "late work of God" come, as they thought, to "an unhappy period." In wider

Outcries and bodily agitations	399–400	305–07
Accusations of imprudences	409–10	390–92
Character of the revival's critics	410–11	390–92
On judging religious experiences	498–501	395–97
How to promote true religion	496–530	408–12

5. *Seasonable Thoughts*, p. 111.

6. Answer given by American Methodists at their organizing Conference in Baltimore, Christmas 1784, to the question, "What may we reasonably believe to be God's design in raising up the preachers called Methodists?" (*Minutes of Several Conversations . . . Composing a Form of Discipline . . . of the Methodist Episcopal Church in America* [Philadelphia, 1785], p. 3).

perspective, of course, the Great Awakening in New England must be viewed as more than a single surging flood which crested in 1740–41 and ebbed in 1742–43, for the waves generated by the revival maintained their momentum for many more years among the radical New Lights. But while Congregational Separatists and Separate Baptists were bootlegging its main fruits, Old Lights were either quietly taking refuge in the Anglican Church or confirming the crypto-Arminianism that would surface after the Revolution as Unitarianism. Edwards was thus left to contemplate the crumbling ecclesiastical establishment from the confines of Northampton, where he was soon to discover that few even of his most hopeful converts would support him in the controversies looming on the local horizon.

Some of his correspondence during 1743–44 may serve as a footnote to the portion of his career which he devoted to revivalism. One letter, dated May 12, 1743, was addressed to the Rev. James Robe (1688–1753), minister at Kilsyth in Scotland and editor of *The Christian Monthly History,* the Scottish analogue to Boston's pioneer religious periodical, from which it derived much of its material.[7] By this time Edwards' burden was not anger toward critics and opposers but sorrow over the strife which had dissipated the awakening. He candidly attributed all blame to "imprudent management in the friends of the work," and confessed that revivalistic ministers had failed to take sufficient caution for preventing errors and disorders, and had been much too careless in their pastoral counseling of the awakened. While the substantive content of this letter differs little from his previous writings on the revival, its tone is not polemical or hortatory, but confessional.

A similar mood dominated Edwards' letter of the same date to the Rev. William McCulloch (1691–1771) of Cambuslang, Scotland (below, p. 539), except that here he took a longer historical perspective from which to view present reversals as only temporary setbacks. As in *Some Thoughts,* his millennial faith undergirded a robust optimism; and he looked for an imminent reviving of the revival on an even grander scale. McCulloch, replying on August 13, 1743, concurred, except that he feared the enemies of the church might create even "more general and formidable trials" before such hopes were fulfilled.[8] Edwards took this as an invitation to set forth

7. Robe printed the letter in the edition of August 1745, pp. 127–30. See below, pp. 535–38; also above, p. 78 n. 4.

8. The letter is printed in Dwight, *Life of President Edwards,* pp. 198–200.

his view of history more at length. He answered McCulloch on March 5, 1744, and confessed in the most dismal terms yet the "sad delusions" which had permitted "the enemy to come in like a flood," so that "the work is put to a stop everywhere." But he still maintained confidently that the Great Awakening had been but the forerunner of a yet more glorious work of God and that the millennium was imminent. In a decisive departure from traditional millenarianism, he held that the worst trials of the church were already past; whatever "sore conflicts and terrible convulsions" remain to be endured, he still looked upon "the late wonderful revivals of religion" as an earnest of a larger spiritual triumph soon to come.[9]

While the two communications to McCulloch were private, another letter, addressed to Thomas Prince of Boston, was evidently intended for publication. Dated December 12, 1743, and printed in *The Christian History* for January 14, 21, and 28, 1743/4 (Vol. I, pp. 367–81), it stands as Edwards' last public word specifically on the events of the revival at high tide.[1] He still was convinced that the Northampton stirrings had been first and last a work of God; and as always, he was painfully honest about their human defects. He described again the "great and abiding alteration" in the town, beginning in 1734, but admitted that it soon gave way to "a very lamentable decay of religious affections." After Whitefield's visit in October 1740 there had been a general "engagedness of spirit about the things of religion," accompanied by "the most wonderful work among children that ever was in Northampton"; but within a year "a great deal of caution and pains were found necessary to keep the people . . . from running wild." In March 1742 Edwards had led his parishioners to renew their solemn covenant with God—he inserted a full copy—but by summer their religious fervor was declining once again. He closed the letter seemingly resigned to the ebb and flow of piety in the town, though genuinely grateful that "notwithstanding all the corrupt mixtures that have been in the late work here, there are not only many blessed fruits of it, in particular persons that yet remain, but some good effects of it upon the town in general." Perhaps the most significant social result was

9. Letter below, pp. 558–60. Cf. above, pp. 71–72.
1. Letter below, pp. 544–57. Note, "events." He would continue to elaborate the *meaning* of the experience as he developed his doctrine of conversion in *Religious Affections* (1746) and combated Arminianism in *Freedom of the Will* (1754).

that the citizens—*mirabile dictu*—had finally settled "their grand
controversy relating to their common lands." [2]

The new covenant, in spite of its failure to fulfill all of Edwards'
hopes for regulating public morality, perhaps had something to do
with that. Before they reached the recalescence point after Samuel
Buell's visit (above, p. 57), he had been able to persuade the members of his church above fourteen years of age to subscribe a solemn
promise to deal honestly with their neighbors, to make just restitution to whomever they had defrauded, and to resist every temptation
to act out of revenge, enmity, or ill will. Most important for
Christianizing the social order in Northampton was a common
agreement that

> in the management of public affairs, we will not make our own
> worldly gain, or honor, or interest in the affections of others, or
> getting the better of any of a contrary party, that are in any
> respect our competitors, or the bringing or keeping them down,
> our governing aim, to the prejudice of the interest of religion
> and the honor of Christ. . . . We will not wittingly violate jus-
> tice for private interest (below, p. 552).

Even to secure signatures to such a covenant in an acquisitive society
dominated by merchants and land speculators must have been quite
an achievement. To enforce it in a period of expanding trade and
declining religious fervor proved to be impossible. Perry Miller
claims that Edwards "bullied" his people into signing in order to
acquire some leverage for his scheme to overthrow Stoddardism at
Northampton, and that the strategy backfired when the river gods
refused to submit to moral surveillance. Thus "the clash between
Edwards and his people [in 1749–50] . . . was, among other things,
a clash between America's greatest spokesman for absolute Christian
morality and representatives of the American business ethic." [3]

Probably not too much should be made of that, however, for
congregational covenant renewals had long been common in New
England.[4] Besides, Edwards never dominated the social and eco-

2. One of Chauncy's disciples, still imbued with the "thoughts" terminology
of polemic, published a bitter attack on this letter in an unsigned article, "Some
Serious Thoughts on the Late Times," in the *Boston Evening Post,* Jan. 30, 1744.
3. *Jonathan Edwards,* p. 210.
4. See Pope, *The Half-Way Covenant,* pp. 241–46. On May 11, 1742, representatives from seventeen churches in Hampshire County met at Northampton
and considered "what may be proper to promote the interest of religion, and

nomic life of Northampton as his predecessor had done; and in spite of the revivals, his influence over his people waned steadily through the 1740s so that by the end of the decade "he was their leader only in the liturgy . . . [while] the community itself was pursuing a course independent of ministerial influence."[5] He sensed this, and denounced it in uncommonly blunt terms:

> There are some professors, in some of our towns, that are anti-ministerial men; they seem to have a disposition to dislike men of that order; they are apt to be prejudiced against them, and to be suspicious of them, and talk against them; and it seems to be as it were natural to 'em to be unfriendly and unkind towards their own ministers, and to make difficulty for them. But I don't believe there is a true Christian on earth that is of this character; on the contrary . . . everyone that receives Christ, and whose heart is governed by a supreme love to him, has a disposition to receive, love and honor his messengers.[6]

By this test, there would soon be few Christians in Northampton. Plainly enough, the covenant of 1742, like the revival itself, was destined to be compromised by the same human defects, "accidental" or otherwise, which flaw every work of God in history.

The final failure of the covenant, and perhaps of the revival whose fruits it was designed to conserve, came in 1750 when the Northampton church dismissed Jonathan Edwards from its pulpit by a vote of 230 to 23.[7] On July 2 he preached his farewell sermon,

---

good order in the churches"; among other things, they drafted a covenant to be accepted publicly by the people after the fashion of Northampton. Cf. Minutes of the Hampshire Ministers Association for April 13, 1742 (MS at Forbes Library); and *The Christian Monthly History, 1* (No. 1, Nov. 1743), 5–8.

5. T. W. Leavitt, "Northampton after the Halfway Covenant," unpublished ms. (May 1962), p. 37; at the Forbes Library. A case study of transformation in the character of colonial leadership, this is a perceptive work.

6. *The Great Concern of a Watchman for Souls . . . A Sermon Preached at the Ordination of the Rev. Mr. Jonathan Judd, to the Pastoral Office over the Church of Christ in the New Precinct at Northampton, June 8, 1743* (Boston, 1743), pp. 39–40.

7. Cf. above, p. 84. The exact tally is hard to determine because of the ambiguous way in which JE reported it: "About 23 appeared for [my continuance in the pastorate], others stayed away, choosing not to act either way; but the generality of the church, which consists of about 230 male members, voted for my dismission" (letter dated July 5, 1750, to John Erskine, in Andover MSS). Existing church records are silent on the point.

reminding his congregation calmly that "ministers, and the people that have been under their care, must meet one another before Christ's tribunal at the day of judgment." [8] That same month Joseph Bellamy (1719–90), a former pupil and now a beloved colleague in ministry, asked him to write a preface for a new book entitled *True Religion Delineated; Or, Experimental Religion, As Distinguished from Formality on the One Hand, and Enthusiasm on the Other*.[9] In the pain of his defeat, his dearest friend was asking him to stand once again in the no man's land between "pious zealots" and "cold, diabolical opposers," the latter now even more diabolical because of their erstwhile pretenses to piety. Without hesitation he acceded.

Edwards' preface to Bellamy's work, referring as it does to unexpectedly numerous (230?) "counterfeits of grace," betrays a barely veiled bitterness which he had managed to suppress in his farewell sermon. Perhaps some of this arose from self-reproach, for after his repudiation he blamed himself severely for lack of judgment and over-optimism concerning the conversions professed in the revivals. True, his former parishioners had a distressing penchant for controversy, and they had taken his *Faithful Narrative* as a new occasion for spiritual pride; but he was culpable too. One year after his dismissal he confessed to a Scottish friend:

> When I first settled among the [Northampton] people, being young and of but little experience, I was not thoroughly aware of the ill consequences of such a custom [as frivolous testimonies of religious experience]; and so allowed it, or at least did not testify against it as I ought to have done. . . . [My diffidence] was such that I durst not act my own judgment, and had no strength to oppose received notions and established customs, and to testify boldly against some glaring false appearances and counterfeits of religion, till it was too late.[1]

Evidently the same accusing thoughts were on his mind just before he penned his preface for Bellamy, for on July 5, 1750, he wrote to

8. Printed in Dwight, *Life of President Edwards*, pp. 626–53.

9. Boston, 1750. Bellamy graduated from Yale in 1735, studied theology in JE's home, and served as pastor at Bethlehem, Conn., 1740–90. JE described him as "one of the most intimate friends that I have in the world" (letter dated July 5, 1750, to John Erskine; in Andover MSS).

1. Letter to Thomas Gillespie; below, pp. 564–65.

John Erskine: "I am a great enemy to censoriousness, and have opposed it very much in my preaching and writings. But yet I think we should avoid that bastard, mischievous charity, by which Satan keeps men asleep. . . ." [2] All the same, somewhere between sinful censoriousness and complaisant charity, one still must exercise responsible and discerning judgment. Bellamy at least had identified the real problem—and stated it plainly in his title.

Edwards was understandably cautious. Beneath his carefully controlled commendation of his friend's book a sensitive reader can feel the throb of wounds still raw as he speaks of the agonizing difficulty of distinguishing true religion from falsehood on every side. False religion, as he knew by sad experience, "has been the chief thing that has obscured, obstructed and brought to a stand all remarkable revivals of religion, which have been since the beginning of the Reformation; the very chief reason why the most hopeful and promising beginnings have never come to any more than beginnings; being nipped in the bud, and soon followed with a great increase of stupidity, corrupt principles, a profane and atheistical spirit, and the triumph of the open enemies of religion." *That* for Northampton's counterfeit converts! But this heat dissipated quickly, and he closed his preface by noting dispassionately that if the book is read without prejudice it will disclose "the proper essence and distinguishing nature of saving religion" and uncover "falsehood at the very foundation" (below, p. 572).

Perhaps in his humiliation Edwards needed, more than any other reader, Bellamy's gentle reminder that unforeseen trials often follow great victories, as God tests his people in order to winnow false professors from among the truly faithful.[3] A later generation of Christians would say that through all such reversals committed disciples must press on toward a goal whose "truth" is definable only from the perspective of obedient faith. In 1750 neither Edwards nor Bellamy was prepared to confess that so long as men must live within the broken time forms of a historical pilgrimage, an unambiguously *true* religion will always elude them. Revivals may come and go, invariably with mixed results, but the millennium is not yet.

2. Dwight, *Life of President Edwards,* p. 407.
3. *True Religion Delineated,* Author's Preface.

12. *Note on the Texts*

A Faithful Narrative would be a strong competitor for designation as "Edwards' most widely read book." It has been printed at least sixty times—in full, not counting numerous abridgments and extracts—ten times in five countries and three languages during his lifetime.[4] Nor has interest waned, apparently: the present edition is the fifth since the midpoint of the twentieth century.[5] None of the previous editions, however, has attempted to establish an accurate text in even the most elementary sense, as witness the persistence of Isaac Watts' error locating Northampton in New Hampshire—repeated even by a New Hampshire publisher in 1805 and by one in Boston in 1831! Indeed, there seems never to have been any awareness of a problem regarding the text, even though *A Faithful Narrative* is the only one of Edwards' major works to pass through several editors' hands on its haphazard way from his desk to the press. In the absence of the original manuscript, this could represent a serious frustration to any effort at restoring what he actually wrote; but as explained above (pp. 38–39) we have a copy of the first edition annotated in his own hand, and a third edition which he presumably supervised with at least as much care as any of his other Boston publications. By careful comparing of these, together with the abridgment by Benjamin Colman, who was the first to see any part of the work through the press, it is now possible to offer a text which should command reasonable confidence as to its accuracy. Variant readings are given in notes accompanying the text.

The Distinguishing Marks, to judge by the number of printings, has been somewhat less popular. Early distribution, to be sure, was quite wide, as editions appeared within the first year at Boston, Philadelphia, London, Glasgow, and Edinburgh; but with one notable exception there were no more until after the turn of the century. That exception was the 48-page abridgment by John Wesley —a summary rather than excerpts—issued first in 1744 and again

4. See Johnson, *The Printed Writings of Jonathan Edwards,* pp. 4–15.

5. The Banner of Truth Trust in London is reprinting the *textus receptus* of "Select Works of Jonathan Edwards"; the *Faithful Narrative* appeared in 1958 and again in 1965. Kregel Publications (Grand Rapids) issued an abridgment in 1957, and Burt Franklin Publishers (New York) reprinted *The Works of President Edwards* (10 vols., London, 1817–47) in 1968.

in 1755, 1795, 1827, and 1853. Wesley's abridgment of *A Faithful Narrative* also appeared in 1744 and 1755, as well as in his *Christian Library* of 1827; but the Methodists seem to have had a special fondness for *The Distinguishing Marks,* possibly because their revivals, like those of Edwards, were also scorned by rationalists and ecclesiocrats of the establishment. This work passed through at least 46 complete editions (or printings), though some 35 of these were in the various sets of Edwards' collected works.[6] For the text one must rely on the first edition (Boston, 1741), there being no extant manuscript; but there is an errata list printed at the end, and no questionable readings presented themselves. Since previous volumes in the Yale edition of *The Works of Jonathan Edwards* have made a strong case for relying on first editions as authoritative texts of published works for which there is no manuscript original, it does not seem necessary to exhibit again here the ingenuity of nineteenth-century editors who sought to "improve" the work for later readers.

The publication history of *Some Thoughts Concerning the Revival* is similar to that of *The Distinguishing Marks,* except that only one full reprint (Edinburgh, 1743) appeared during Edwards' lifetime. John Wesley's 124-page abridgment was made in 1745, reissued in 1795, and included in his *Christian Library* in 1827. Of special interest is an American edition bearing the imprint, "Lexington, Ky., 1803," recognizable immediately as another time and place in American history when multitudes were greatly exercised by thoughts on revivals. As for the text of the present edition, what is said in the previous paragraph with respect to *The Distinguishing Marks* applies here also.

The same general principles which governed the preparation of earlier volumes in this edition have been observed here.[7] Capitalization is modernized, as is spelling in cases where no rhetorical purpose is served by retaining archaic forms; and italicization is greatly reduced. Quotation marks and abbreviations follow modern usage. Punctuation has been lightly styled, though in the main Edwards'

---

6. Curiously, *The Distinguishing Marks* was missing from the edition of Samuel Austin (8 vols., Worcester, 1808), though it has been included regularly (as one of the "valuable additions") in the numerous four-volume reprints of the Worcester edition.

7. See Paul Ramsey, ed., *Freedom of the Will* (New Haven, 1957), pp. 119–28; Smith, *Religious Affections,* pp. 75–82; and Holbrook, *Original Sin,* pp. 96–97.

custom of punctuating for rhetorical, rather than syntactical, purposes remains intact. The editor has given a more consistent form
to Edwards' irregular numbering of subsections, supplied subhead-
ings where they were clearly indicated, and divided inordinately
long paragraphs to facilitate reading.

The reader of these works will likely notice Edwards' idiosyncratic
use of verbs, especially his penchant for using singular verbs with
plural subjects. If the subject of a sentence consists of two or more
nouns joined by "and," and the last noun is singular, almost invariably the verb is singular: e.g., "those affections and that sense
inclines the mouth to speak" (ST; below, p. 483). On the other
hand, if the noun nearest the verb is plural, the verb usually agrees.
This custom of allowing the nearest noun to govern the verb sometimes led him to match the number of the verb to an interposed
phrase rather than with the actual subject of the sentence, as in:
". . . the creature has fellowship with God himself, with the Father
and the Son, in their beauty and happiness, and *are* made partakers
of the divine nature, and *have* Christ's joy fulfilled in themselves"
(DM; below, p. 280). Occasionally he also shifted the tenses of verbs
in the middle of a paragraph, or even a sentence; witness his paraphrase of a biblical story which proceeds with "they asked . . . he
answers . . . they said . . . he replies, etc." (ST; below, pp. 524).
Although in two instances I have silently changed "begun" to
"began," on the supposition of a typographical error, generally I
have let Edwards' ungrammaticisms stand. To attempt to modernize
him in such usages would rob his writing of its idiomatic color and
cheat students of language and literature out of historical evidence
in which they have a legitimate interest.

Another eighteenth-century device which Edwards frequently
employed was a gerund preceded by the definite article and followed
not with a prepositional phrase but with a direct object, as in "the
giving such rules" (DM; below, p. 226). Occasionally, where this
construction seemed especially awkward, I have supplied "of" in
brackets. Perhaps the most glaring instance left undisturbed is:
"How liberally did the heads of the tribes contribute of their
wealth at the setting up the tabernacle, though it was in a barren
wilderness? These are the days of the erecting the tabernacle of
God amongst us" (ST; below, p. 514). Another idiom one learns to
expect in these writings is Edwards' use of "so" as a modal particle
meaning "in the same manner"; often it includes the sense of

"also" as well. He likewise used "etc.," especially in biblical quotations, to mean "et seq." But editorial insertions and notes purporting to clarify such points have been supplied sparingly, in the conviction that it is usually best to let Edwards speak for himself.

Citations from sources other than Scripture are fewer and less wide-ranging in these revival tracts than in the philosophical and theological treatises. Quotations tend to follow the sources more closely; possibly as a young author Edwards was more meticulous on this point, and less prone to paraphrase. In any case, the variations are few and minor; and as in the other volumes of this edition, quoted material is printed as Edwards wrote it. It has been possible to identify and locate the source of every quotation and allusion save one, the "satisfying exposition" of Cant. 2:7 and parallels, for which he furnished no clue whatsoever (ST; below, pp. 500–01). There, like St. Augustine pondering the problem of the ineffable Trinity, I have been unable to keep silent and so have ventured to suggest some proximate sources that are at least possible. Perhaps this will alert other students of Puritan thought to watch for further hints on this matter.

Seven pieces of correspondence are included because of the further light they shed on how Edwards thought about the revival and described it to his friends. As indicated in the headnotes, three are from contemporary printed sources (no manuscripts found) and four are from original manuscripts. I have taken the texts very much as they stand, and it should be noted that as yet the editing conventions for Edwards' previously unpublished writings have not been fully established. The "Letters" volume of the Yale edition, when it becomes available, will present the definitive form of these texts.

Edwards completed his preface to Joseph Bellamy's *True Religion* on August 4, 1750, and entrusted it to his wife, who delivered it to Samuel Kneeland in Boston three weeks later.[8] It was set in type immediately, and the book appeared the following month. Subsequent editions include Edinburgh, 1788; Morristown, N. J., 1804; London, 1809 and 1852; and Boston, n.d.[9] The present text of Ed-

8. Samuel Kneeland, letter dated Aug. 24, 1750, to Joseph Bellamy; at the Case Memorial Library of the Hartford Seminary Foundation.

9. The Boston edition was a mid-nineteenth-century reprint by the Congregational Board of Publication.

wards' preface, which suffered minor emendations in the nineteenth century, follows that of the first edition.

13. *Acknowledgments*

My enjoyment of this project was considerably enhanced by the expertise of patient librarians and archivists who graciously responded to my calls for bibliographical data, photocopies of rare materials, verifications of minute details, and help in locating fugitive manuscripts. I regret the impossibility of naming all those whose assistance has been so valuable, but I remember with special gratitude Marjorie Wynne and Suzanne Rutter of the Beinecke Rare Book and Manuscript Library at Yale, Roland E. Kircher of the Wesley Theological Seminary Library, Stanley Greenberg of the Forbes Library at Northampton, Walter W. Wright of the Baker Memorial Library at Dartmouth, James E. Mooney of the American Antiquarian Society, Ellis O'Neal of the Andover Newton Theological School Library, Paul R. Wagner of the Princeton University Library, Nafi Donat of the Case Memorial Library at the Hartford Seminary Foundation, and John Alden, Keeper of Rare Books at the Boston Public Library. The staff of the Rare Book Division at the Library of Congress has been unfailingly helpful.

Professors John E. Smith, Edmund S. Morgan, Sydney E. Ahlstrom, and Robert T. Handy read the Introduction and offered many helpful comments. In addition, Professor Smith has fulfilled the task of General Editor with insight and skill. I have profited much from conversations and correspondence with Professor Thomas A. Schafer, editor of Edwards' "Miscellanies," whose extensive acquaintance with the unpublished writings of Edwards is probably unparalleled. Professor George S. Claghorn, who is editing the "Letters" volume, has generously allowed me to consult his transcriptions of the manuscript letters which appear in this volume.

Thanks are due the Wesley Theological Seminary for harboring with true Methodist grace a maverick Baptist whose academic avocation is exploring the influence on their common evangelical tradition of one who had little use for either Methodists or Baptists. The Seminary granted a year of sabbatical leave for the completion of this project, and the American Association of Theological Schools awarded a Faculty Fellowship which permitted me to devote undivided attention to the work.

If one may judge from the paragraphs in which Sarah Edwards is set forth as Northampton's chief paradigm of piety, her spirit breathes through the whole of her husband's writings on the revival. In an analogous way, there is one who by sharing my life as Sarah shared Jonathan's has given her measure of devotion to this book. And I should like to add one further tribute: to Charles Kyle, John Scott, and Robert Curtis, who somehow managed to grow into young manhood while their father was preoccupied with Jonathan Edwards.

C. C. GOEN

Washington, D.C.
May 1970

A FAITHFUL NARRATIVE

Edwards' first report of the revival in the Connecticut River Valley 1734–35 was in a letter to the Rev. Dr. Benjamin Colman, pastor of the Brattle Street Church in Boston (above, pp. 32–34). The original is not extant, but JE's personal copy is in the Andover MSS. It is printed elsewhere only in Clarence H. Faust and Thomas H. Johnson, Jonathan Edwards: Representative Selections *(New York: Hill and Wang, 1935, 1962), pp. 73–84.*

Northampton, May 30, 1735

Dear Sir:

In answer to your desire, I here send you a particular account of the present extraordinary circumstances of this town, and the neighboring towns with respect to religion. I have observed that the town for this several years have gradually been reforming; there has appeared less and less of a party spirit, and a contentious disposition, which before had prevailed for many years between two parties in the town.[1] The young people also have been reforming more and more; they by degrees left off their frolicking, and have been observably more decent in their attendance on the public worship. The winter before last there appeared a strange flexibleness in the young people of the town, and an unusual disposition to hearken to counsel, on this occasion. It had been their manner of a long time, and for aught I know, always, to make Sabbath-day nights and lecture days to be especially times of diversion and company-keeping. I then preached a sermon on the Sabbath before the lecture, to show them the unsuitableness and inconvenience of the practice, and to persuade them to reform it; and urged it on

1. [Northampton had had the usual civil and ecclesiastical controversies afflicting most colonial settlements, and some of these had left lasting scars. What JE specifically refers to here, however, he described more fully in a letter of July 1, 1751, to the Rev. Thomas Gillespie; below, pp. 563–64. The impact of the revival on Northampton's "party spirit" he reported in a letter of Dec. 12, 1743; below, p. 557.]

heads of families that it should be a thing agreed among them to govern their families, and keep them in at those times. And there happened to be at my house the evening after, men that belonged to the several parts of the town, to whom I moved that they should desire the heads of families, in my name, to meet together in their several neighborhoods, that they might know each others' minds, and agree every one to restrain his family; which was done, and my motion complied with throughout the town. But the parents found little or no occasion for the exercise of government in the case; for the young people declared themselves convinced by what they had heard, and willing of themselves to comply with the counsel given them; and I suppose it was almost universally complied with thenceforward.

After this there began to be a remarkable religious concern among some farm houses at a place called Pascommuck,[2] and five or six that I hoped were savingly wrought upon there. And in April [1734] there was a very sudden and awful death of a young man in town, in the very bloom of his youth, who was violently seized with a pleurisy and taken immediately out of his head, and died in two days; which much affected many young people in the town. This was followed with another death of a young married woman, who was in great distress in the beginning of her illness, but was hopefully converted before her death; so that she died full of comfort, and in a most earnest and moving manner, warning and counselling others, which I believe much contributed to the solemnizing of the spirits of the young people in the town; and there began evidently to appear more of a religious concern upon people's minds. In the fall of the year I moved to the young people that they should set up religious meetings, on evenings after lectures, which they complied with; this was followed with the death of an elderly person in the town, which was attended with very unusual circumstances, which much affected many people. About that time began the great noise that there was in this part of the country about Arminianism,[3] which seemed strangely to be overruled for the promoting of religion. People seemed to be put by it upon inquiring, with concern and engagedness of mind, what was the way of salvation, and what were the terms of our acceptance with God; and what was said

2. [A small community three miles from Northampton, where its members worshipped.]

3. [Above, pp. 17–18.]

publicly on that occasion, however found fault with by many elsewhere, and ridiculed by some, was most evidently attended with a very remarkable blessing of heaven, to the souls of the people in this town, to the giving of them an universal satisfaction and engaging their minds with respect to the thing in question, the more earnestly to seek salvation in the way that had been made evident to them.

And then a concern about the great things of religion began, about the latter end of December and the beginning of January [1735], to prevail abundantly in the town, till in a very little time it became universal throughout the town, among old and young, and from the highest to the lowest. All seemed to be seized with a deep concern about their eternal salvation; all the talk in all companies, and upon occasions was upon the things of religion, and no other talk was anywhere relished; and scarcely a single person in the whole town was left unconcerned about the great things of the eternal world. Those that were wont to be the vainest, and loosest persons in town seemed in general to be seized with strong convictions. Those that were most disposed to contemn vital and experimental religion, and those that had the greatest conceit of their own reason, the highest families in the town, and the oldest persons in the town, and many little children were affected remarkably; no one family that I know of, and scarcely a person, has been exempt. And the Spirit of God went on in his saving influences, to the appearance of all human reason and charity, in a truly wonderful and astonishing manner. The news of it filled the neighboring towns with talk, and there were many in them that scoffed and made a ridicule of the religion that appeared in Northampton. But it was observable that it was very frequent and common that those of other towns that came into this town, and observed how it was here, were greatly affected, and went home with wounded spirits, and were never more able to shake off the impression that it made upon them, till at length there began to appear a general concern in several of the towns in the county.

In the month of March the people in New Hadley [4] seemed to be seized with a deep concern about their salvation, all as it were at once, which has continued in a very great degree ever since. About the same time there began to appear the like concern in the west part of Suffield, which has since spread into all parts of the town.

4. [Later South Hadley; below, pp. 119, 152.]

It next began to appear at Sunderland, and soon became universal, and to a very great degree. About the same time it began to appear in part of Deerfield, called Green River, and since has filled the town. It began to appear also at a part of Hatfield, and after that the whole town in the second week in April seemed to be seized at once, and there is a great and general concern there. And there gradually got in a considerable degree of the same concern into Hadley Old Society, and Mr. Hopkins' parish in [West] Springfield,[5] but it is nothing near so great as in many other places. The next place that we heard of was Northfield, where the concern is very great and general. We have heard that there is a considerable degree of it at Longmeadow, and there is something of it in Old Springfield in some parts of the society. About three weeks ago the town of Enfield were struck down as it were at once, the worst persons in the town seemed to be suddenly seized with a great degree of concern about their souls, as I have been informed. And about the same time, Mr. Bull[6] of Westfield [said] that there began to be a great alteration there, and that there had been more done in one week before that time that I spoke with him than had been done in seven years before. The people of Westfield have till now above all other places, made a scoff and derision of this concern at Northampton. There has been a great concern of a like nature at Windsor, on the west side of the [Connecticut] River, which began about the same time that it began to be general here at Northampton; and my father[7] has told me that there is an hopeful beginning on the east side in his society. Mr. Noyes[8] writes me word that there is a considerable revival of religion at New Haven; and I have been credibly informed that there is something of it at Guilford and Lyme, as there also is at Coventry, Bolton, and a society in

5. [Samuel Hopkins (1693–1755, Yale 1718) was pastor at West Springfield, Mass., 1720–55. Married to JE's oldest sister, Esther, he was an uncle of Samuel Hopkins (1721–1803), the celebrated Edwardsean theologian.]

6. [Nehemiah Bull (1701–40, Yale 1723) was pastor at Westfield, Mass., 1726–40.]

7. [Timothy Edwards (1669–1758, Harvard 1691) was pastor at East Windsor, Conn., 1694–1755.]

8. [Joseph Noyes (1688–1761, Yale 1709) was pastor at the First Church in New Haven, Conn., 1715–61. His wife, Abigail Pierpont, was a half-sister to JE's wife. After James Davenport denounced him as unconverted (above, p. 52), he became the target of New Light attacks and lost much support in town and college.]

Lebanon called The Crank. I yesterday saw Mr. White [9] of Bolton, and also last night saw a young man that belongs to [the church at] Coventry, who gave a very remarkable account of that town, of the manner in which the rude debauched young people there were suddenly seized with a concern about their souls.

As to the nature of persons' experiences, and the influences of that spirit that there is amongst us, persons when seized with concern are brought to forsake their vices, and ill practices; the looser sort are brought to forsake and to dread their former extravagances. Persons are soon brought to have done with their old quarrels; contention and intermeddling with other men's matters seems to be dead amongst us. I believe there never was so much done at confessing of faults to each other, and making up differences, as there has lately been. Where this concern comes it immediately puts an end to differences between ministers and people: there was a considerable uneasiness at New Hadley between some of the people and their minister, but when this concern came amongst them it immediately put an end to it, and the people are now universally united to their minister. There was an exceeding alienation at Sunderland, between the minister and many of the people; but when this concern came amongst them it all vanished at once, and the people are universally united in hearty affection to their minister. There were some men at Deerfield, of turbulent spirits, that kept up an uneasiness there with Mr. Ashley; [1] but one of the chief of them has lately been influenced fully and freely to confess his fault to him, and is become his hearty friend.

People are brought off from inordinate engagedness after the world, and have been ready to run into the other extreme of too much neglecting their worldly business and to mind nothing but religion. Those that are under convictions are put upon it earnestly to inquire what they shall do to be saved, and diligently to use appointed means of grace, and apply themselves to all known duty.

9. [Thomas White (1701–63, Yale 1720) was pastor at Bolton, Conn., 1725–63. During the controversies over revivalism in the 1740s his sympathies were with the Old Lights.]

1. [Jonathan Ashley (1712–80, Yale 1730) was pastor at Deerfield, Mass., 1732–80. Married to a daughter of William Williams by Christian Stoddard, sister to JE's mother, he opposed the revival of 1740 and actively aided the anti-Edwards party in the controversy leading to JE's dismissal from Northampton in 1750.]

And those that obtain hope themselves, and the charity of others concerning their good estate, generally seem to be brought to a great sense of their own exceeding misery in a natural condition, and their utter helplessness, and insufficiency for themselves, and their exceeding wickedness and guiltiness in the sight of God; it seldom fails but that each one seems to think himself worse than anybody else, and they are brought to see that they deserve no mercy of God, that all their prayers and pains are exceeding worthless and polluted, and that God, notwithstanding all that they have done, or can do, may justly execute his eternal wrath upon them, and they seem to be brought to a lively sense of the excellency of Jesus Christ and his sufficiency and willingness to save sinners, and to be much weaned in their affections from the world, and to have their hearts filled with love to God and Christ, and a disposition to lie in the dust before him. They seem to have given [to] them a lively conviction of the truth of the Gospel, and the divine authority of the Holy Scriptures; though they can't have the exercise of this at all times alike, nor indeed of any other grace. They seem to be brought to abhor themselves for the sins of their past life, and to long to be holy, and to live holily, and to God's glory; but at the same time complain that they can do nothing, [for] they are poor impotent creatures, utterly insufficient to glorify their Creator and Redeemer. They commonly seem to be much more sensible of their own wickedness after their conversion than before, so that they are often humbled by it; it seems to them that they are really become more wicked, when at the same time they are evidently full of a gracious spirit. Their remaining sin seems to be their very great burden, and many of them seem to long after heaven, that there they may be rid of sin. They generally seem to be united in dear love and affection one to another, and to have a love to all mankind. I never saw the Christian spirit in love to enemies so exemplified in all my life as I have seen it within this half year. They commonly express a great concern for others' salvation; some say that they think they are far more concerned for others' conversion, after they themselves have been converted, than ever they were for their own; several have thought (though perhaps they might be deceived in it) that they could freely die for the salvation of any soul, of the meanest of mankind, of any Indian in the woods.

This town never was so full of love, nor so full of joy, nor so full of distress as it has lately been. Some persons have had those longing desires after Jesus Christ, that have been to that degree as to take away their strength, and very much to weaken them, and make them faint. Many have been even overcome with a sense of the dying love of Christ, so that the home of the body has been ready to fail under it; there was once three pious young persons in this town talking together of the dying love of Christ, till they all fainted away; though 'tis probable the fainting of the two latter was much promoted by the fainting of the first. Many express a sense of the glory of the divine perfections, and of the excellency and fullness of Jesus Christ, and of their own littleness and unworthiness, in a manner truly wonderful and almost unparalleled; and so likewise of the excellency and wonderfulness of the way of salvation by Jesus Christ. Their esteem of the Holy Scriptures is exceedingly increased. Many of them say the Bible seems to be a new book to them, as though they never read it before. There have been some instances of persons that by only an accidental sight of the Bible, have been as much moved, it seemed to me, as a lover by the sight of his sweetheart. The preaching of the Word is greatly prized by them; they say they never heard preaching before: and so are God's Sabbaths, and ordinances, and opportunities of public worship. The Sabbath is longed for before it comes; some by only hearing the bell ring on some occasion in the week time, have been greatly moved, because it has put them in mind of its ringing to call the people together to worship God. But no part of public worship has commonly [had] such an effect on them as singing God's praises. They have a greater respect to ministers than they used to have; there is scarcely a minister preaches here but gets their esteem and affection.

The experiences of some persons lately amongst [us] have been beyond almost all that ever I heard or read of. There is a pious woman in this town that is a very modest bashful person, that was moved by what she heard of the experiences of others earnestly to seek to God to give her more clear manifestations of himself, and evidences of her own good estate, and God answered her request, and gradually gave her more and more of a sense of his glory and love, which she had with intermissions for several days, till one morning the week before last she had it to a more than ordinary degree, and it prevailed more and more till towards the middle of the day, till her nature began to sink under it, as she was alone in the house; but there came somebody into the house, and found her in an unusual, extraordinary frame. She expressed what she saw and felt to him; it came to that at last that they raised the neighbors, [for] they were afraid she would die; I went up to see her and found her perfectly sober and in the exercise of her reason, but having her nature seemingly overborne and sinking, and when she could speak expressing in a manner that can't be described the sense she had of the glory of God, and particularly of such and such perfections, and her own unworthiness, her longing to lie in the dust, sometimes her longing to go to be with Christ, and crying out of the excellency of Christ, and the wonderfulness of his dying love; and so she continued for hours together, though not always in the same degree. At some times she was able to discourse to those about her; but it seemed to me [that] if God had manifested a little more of himself to her she would immediately have sunk and her frame dissolved under it. She has since been at my house, and continues as full as she can hold, but looks on herself not as an eminent saint, but as the worst of all, and unworthy to go to speak with a minister; but yet now beyond any great doubt of her good estate.

There are two persons that belong to other towns that have had such a sense of God's exceeding greatness and majesty, that they were as it were swallowed up; they both of them told me to that purpose that if in the time of it they had had the least fear that they were not at peace with that great God, they should immediately have died. But there is a very vast variety of degrees of spiritual discoveries, that are made to those that we hope are godly, as there is also in the steps, and method of the Spirit's operation in convincing and converting sinners, and the length of time that persons are under conviction before they have comfort.

There is an alteration made in the town in a few months that strangers can scarcely conceive of; our church I believe was the largest in New England before,[2] but persons lately have thronged in, so that there are very few adult persons left out. There have been a great multitude hopefully converted; too many, I find, for me to declare abroad with credit to my judgment. The town seems to be full of the presence of God; our young people when they

2. [Northampton was the shire town of Hampshire County, which at that time embraced nearly half the area of the Bay Colony. Its church numbered 71 members in 1669, when Solomon Stoddard (above, pp. 15–17) became pastor; he admitted 630 persons to membership during his sixty-year ministry. In November 1736 JE claimed 620 communicant adults (below, p. 157).]

get together instead of frolicking as they used to do are altogether on pious subjects; 'tis so at weddings and on all occasions. The children in this and the neighboring towns have been greatly affected and influenced by the Spirit of God, and many of them hopefully changed; the youngest in this town is between nine and ten years of age. Some of them seem to be full of love to Christ and have expressed great longings after him and willingness to die, and leave father and mother and all things in the world to go to him, together with a great sense of their unworthiness and admiration at the free grace of God towards them. And there have been many old people, many above fifty and several near seventy, that seem to be wonderfully changed and hopefully newborn. The good people that have been formerly converted in the town have many of them been wonderfully enlivened and increased.

This work seems to be upon every account an extraordinary dispensation of providence. 'Tis extraordinary upon the account of [the] universality of it in affecting all sorts, high and low, rich and poor, wise and unwise, old and young, vicious and moral; 'tis very extraordinary as to the numbers that are hopefully savingly wrought upon, and particularly the number of aged persons and children and loose livers; and also on the account of the quickness of the work of the Spirit on them, for many seem to have been suddenly taken from a loose way of living, and to be so changed as to become truly holy, spiritual, heavenly persons; 'tis extraordinary as to the degrees of gracious communications, and the abundant measures in which the Spirit of God has been poured out on many persons; 'tis extraordinary as to the extent of it, God's Spirit being so remarkably poured out on so many towns at once, and its making such swift progress from place to place. The extraordinariness of the thing has been, I believe, one principal cause that people abroad have suspected it.

There have been, as I have heard, many odd and strange stories that have been carried about the country of this affair, which it is a wonder some wise men should be so ready to believe. Some indeed under great terrors of conscience have had impressions on their imaginations; and also under the power of spiritual discoveries, they have had livelily impressed ideas of Christ shedding blood for sinners, his blood running from his veins, and of Christ in his glory in heaven and such like things, but they are always taught, and have been several times taught in public not to lay the weight of their hopes on such things and many have nothing of any such imaginations. There have been several persons that have had their natures overborne under strong convictions, have trembled, and han't been able to stand, they have had such a sense of divine wrath; but there are no new doctrines embraced, but people have been abundantly established in those that we account orthodox; there is no new way of worship affected. There is no oddity of behavior prevails; people are no more superstitious about their clothes, or anything else than they used to be. Indeed, there is a great deal of talk when they are together of one another's experiences, and indeed no other is to be expected in a town where the concern of the soul is so universally the concern, and that to so great a degree. And doubtless some persons under the strength of impressions that are made on their minds and under the power of strong affections, are guilty of imprudences; their zeal may need to be regulated by more prudence, and they may need a guide to their assistance; as of old when the church of Corinth had the extraordinary gifts of the Spirit, they needed to be told by the Apostle that the spirit of the prophets were subject to the prophets, and that their gifts were to be exercised with prudence, because God was not the author of confusion but of peace [I Cor. 14:32–33]. There is no unlovely oddity in people's temper prevailing with this work, but on the contrary the face of things is much changed as to the appearance of a meek, humble, amiable behavior. Indeed, the Devil has not been idle, but his hand has evidently appeared in several instances endeavoring to mimic the work of the Spirit of God and to cast a slur upon it, and no wonder. And there has hereby appeared the need of the watchful eye of skillful guides, and of wisdom from above to direct them.

There lately came up hither a couple of ministers from Connecticut, viz. Mr. Lord [3] of [North] Preston, and Mr. Owen [4] of Groton, who had heard of the extraordinary circumstances of this

3. [Hezekiah Lord (1698–1761, Yale 1717) was pastor at North Preston, Conn., 1720–61. He was a cousin of Benjamin Lord (1694–1784) of Norwich, Conn., who also visited Northampton in 1735. Both Lords were active in the revival of the 1740s, though well within the rubrics of the establishment.]

4. [John Owen (1699–1753, Harvard 1723) was pastor at Groton, Conn., 1726–53. He was a vigorous promoter of the revival, itinerating with Benjamin Pomeroy (1704–84) of Hebron, Conn. Returning from Northampton, Lord and Owen stopped in Longmeadow at the home of Stephen Williams, who recorded in his diary that "they give a very wonderful account of things they have seen and heard" (MS at Longmeadow Public Library; entry for May 14, 1735).]

and the neighboring towns, who had heard the affair well represented by some, and also had heard many reports greatly to its disadvantage, who came on purpose to see and satisfy themselves; and
that they might thoroughly acquaint themselves, went about and
spent [the] good part of a day in hearing the accounts of many of
our new converts, and examining of them, which was greatly to
their satisfaction; and they took particular notice, among other
things, of the modesty with which persons gave account of themselves, and said that the one-half was not told them, and could not
be told them; and that if they renounced these persons' experiences they must renounce Christianity itself. And Mr. Owen said
particularly as to their impressions on their imaginations, they were
quite different from what had been represented, and that they were
no more than might naturally be expected in such cases.

Thus, Sir, I have given you a particular account of this affair
which Satan has so much misrepresented in the country. This is a
true account of the matter as far as I have opportunity to know, and
I suppose I am under greater advantages to know than any person
living. Having been thus long in the account, I forbear to make
reflections, or to guess what God is about to do; I leave this to you,
and shall only say, as I desire always to say from my heart, "To God
be all the glory, whose work alone it is." And let him have an interest in your prayers, who so much needs divine help at this day,
and is your affectionate brother and humble servant.

Jonathan Edwards

Northampton, June 3, 1735

Since I wrote the foregoing letter, there has happened a thing of
a very awful nature in the town. My Uncle Hawley,[5] the last Sabbath-day morning [June 1], laid violent hands on himself, and put
an end to his life, by cutting his own throat. He had been for a
considerable time greatly concerned about the condition of his soul;
till, by the ordering of a sovereign providence he was suffered to
fall into deep melancholy, a distemper that the family are very
prone to; he was much overpowered by it; the devil took the advantage and drove him into despairing thoughts. He was kept very
much awake anights, so that he had but very little sleep for two

5. [Joseph Hawley (1682–1735), a leading merchant of Northampton, had
married Rebekah Stoddard, sister to JE's mother. On his suicide, see above, pp.
46–47.]

months, till he seemed not to have his faculties in his own power.
He was in a great measure past a capacity of receiving advice, or
being reasoned with. The coroner's inquest judged him delirious.
Satan seems to be in a great rage, at this extraordinary breaking
forth of the work of God. I hope it is because he knows that he has
but a short time. Doubtless he had a great reach, in this violent
attack of his against the whole affair. We have appointed a day of
fasting in the town this week, by reason of this and other appearances of Satan's rage amongst us against poor souls. I yesterday saw
a woman that belongs to [the church in] Durham [Connecticut],
who says there is a considerable revival of religion there.

I am yours, etc.—

J.E.

THE
DUTY and INTEREST of a *People*,

AMONG WHOM

RELIGION has been planted,

TO

Continue *Stedfast* and *Sincere*

IN THE

Profe*ſſ*ion and *Practice* of it.

FROM

Generation to Generation.

With *Directions* for *ſuch* as are *Concerned* to obtain a true *Repentance* and *Converſion* to GOD.---Preach'd at a Time of

General Awakenings.

By *William Williams*, M.A
Pa*ſt*or of the Church in *Hatfield.*

To which is added,
Part of a large LETTER from the Rev. Mr. *Jonathan Edwards* of *Northampton*.

Giving an *Account* of the late *wonderful Work* of GOD in tho*ſe Parts.*

Pſalm 145. 4. *Iſa.* 38. 19.

Printed and Sold by S KNEELAND and T. GREEN, over again*ſt* the Pri*ſon* in Queen*ſt*reet. M.DCC,XXXVI.

At the request of Benjamin Colman, Edwards expanded his account of the Valley revival in a longer letter dated November 6, 1736. Colman immediately prepared an extract and appended it to William Williams, The Duty and Interest of a People, a small volume of sermons which he was seeing through the press at the end of the year. Since the first edition of A Faithful Narrative was published in London the following year, this abridgment is the first publication in America of any part of Edwards' writings on the Great Awakening (see above, pp. 32-35).

[Colman's Introduction]

A PARTICULAR account of the late wonderful work of God in some of the towns in the County of Hampshire, was earnestly desired and expected by many the last year. It happened that Dr. Colman in some of his letters to the Rev. Dr. Watts and Dr. Guyse of London, made mention of it in such manner that Dr. Watts in his next letter expressed his great joy on that occasion, and Dr. Guyse let him know that he had on a day of solemn prayer communicated to the congregation a part of his letter, which had greatly moved the audience; and they had desired him to publish his sermon, which he was unwilling to do till he had Dr. Colman's leave to print what he had written to him. This explains the occasion of the following letter from the Rev. Mr. Edwards of Northampton to Dr. Colman, a small part of which is here communicated to the public, partly because the foregoing sermons directing how to obtain a true conversion to God, were preached at this time of extraordinary awakenings, but more especially because it is judged that the publishing hereof may be of great use and benefit to souls, and not a little serve the holy end and design of the preceding excellent sermons; even to excite under the blessing and power of the divine Spirit, a like general concern in towns and churches, "What they shall do to be saved" [Acts 16:30].

The Letter Follows

Northampton
Nov. 6, 1736

Rev. and Honored Sir,

Having seen your letter to my honored Uncle Williams [1] of Hatfield, of July 20 [1736], wherein you inform him of the notice taken by the Rev. Dr. Watts and Dr. Guyse of London, of the late wonderful work of God in this and some other towns of this county, and of their desire to be more perfectly informed of it; and at the same time signify your own desires that some of us would send you a full account, and that I would undertake it; I will therefore now do it in as just and faithful a manner as in me lies.

The people of the county in general, I suppose, are as sober, orderly and good sort of people as in any part of New England, and I believe they have been preserved the freest by far of any part in the country from error and variety of sect and opinions. Indeed there has been nothing of it till of late a small number of Baptists at Springfield.[2] Our distance from the seaports, and being so far within the land, in the corner of the country, has doubtless been one reason why we have not been corrupted with vice, as most other parts. But without question the religion and good order of the county, and their purity in doctrine, has under God, been very much owing to the great abilities and eminent piety of my venerable and honored grandfather Stoddard. I suppose we have been the freest of any part of the land from unhappy divisions and quarrels in our ecclesiastical and religious affairs, till the late lamentable Springfield contention.[3]

1. [William Williams (1665–1741, Harvard 1683) was pastor at Hatfield, Mass., 1685–1741. His second wife was Christian Stoddard, sister to JE's mother. See above, pp. 34–37.]

2. [Coming from Boston, where a Baptist church had existed since 1665, these Baptists organized a church at West Springfield in 1740. Note that this reference does not appear in other versions of *A Faithful Narrative*.]

3. [Robert Breck (1713–84, Harvard 1730) was called to the pastorate of the church at Springfield (15 miles from Northampton) in 1735. Alerted by charges from the Rev. Thomas Clap of Windham, Conn., the Hampshire Ministers Association suspected Breck of heterodoxy and misconduct and therefore opposed his ordination. The ensuing controversy became so notorious that Boston authorities intervened, and Breck was finally installed over the protests of Hampshire ministers. JE took little part in these proceedings, but he voted

The town of Northampton is of about eighty-two years' standing, and has now about two hundred families, which mostly dwell more compactly together than any town of such a bigness in these parts of the country; which probably has been some occasion that both our corruption and reformation have been from time to time the more swiftly propagated through the town. In general the people seem as rational and understanding as any I have been acquainted with, and have ever from their beginning been noted for religion, and distinguished by their knowledge in things that relate to heart religion and Christian experience, and their great regard thereto.

I am the third minister that has been settled in the town. The Rev. Mr. Eleazar Mather, who was the first, was ordained in July 1661, and died July 1669.[4] His heart was much in his work, he was abundant in his labors for the good of precious souls, had the high esteem and love of his people, and was blessed with no small success. The Rev. Mr. Stoddard, who succeeded him, came to the town the November after his death, but was not ordained till September 11, 1672, and died February 11, 1728/9, so that he continued in the work of the ministry here near sixty years. And as he was renowned for his gifts and graces, so he was blessed from the beginning with extraordinary success, in the conversion of many. He had five harvests, as he called them; the first was about fifty-seven years ago, the second about fifty-three, the third about forty, the fourth about twenty-four, the fifth and last about eighteen years ago. Some of those times were much more remarkable than others, and the ingathering of souls more plentiful. In each of them, I have heard my grandfather say, that the bigger part of the young people of the town seemed to be mainly concerned for their eternal salvation.

---

with the anti-Breck forces and his name became linked with publications of the Hampshire Association defending the opposition to Breck. A full account is in Foster, "Hampshire County, Massachusetts, 1729–1754," pp. 54–78; summaries are in Shipton, *Sibley's Harvard Graduates, 8,* 661–80, and Ezra H. Byington, "Rev. Robert Breck Controversy," *Papers and Proceedings of the Connecticut Valley Historical Society, 2* (1904), 1–19.]

4. [Eleazar Mather (1637–69, Harvard 1656) began preaching to the early settlers of Northampton in 1658. The church was formally organized June 18, 1661, and Mather was ordained the following week (June 23)—not in July, as JE thought. See *Sibley's Harvard Graduates, 1,* 406; and Joseph Sylvester Clark, *A Historical Sketch of the Congregational Churches in Massachusetts* (Boston, 1858), p. 60.]

After the last of these came a more degenerate time, at least among the young people, by far I suppose than had been ever before. Mr. Stoddard indeed had the comfort before he died of seeing no small moving among some, and a considerable ingathering of souls, even after I was settled with him in the ministry, which was about two years before his death. And I have reason to bless God for the great advantage I had by it. There were near twenty that Mr. Stoddard hoped were then savingly converted, but there was nothing of any general awakening.

After my grandfather's death, it seemed a time of extraordinary dullness in religion. Licentiousness had for many years too much prevailed among the youth of the town. It was the manner of too many of them to get together, in conventions of both sexes for mirth and jollity, which they called frolics; and they would spend the greater part of the night in them, without regard to order in the families they belonged to. And indeed family government did too much fail in the town. But within two or three years after Mr. Stoddard's death, there began to be a sensible amendment of these evils. The young people hearkened to counsel, and by degrees left off their frolicking, and grew observably more decent in their attendance on the public worship and manifested more of a religious concern.

At the latter end of the year 1733, there appeared a very unusual flexibleness and yielding to advice. It had been their manner to make the evening after the Sabbath,[5] and after our public lecture, the times of their mirth and company-keeping. A sermon was therefore preached the Lord's day before the lecture, to shew the evil tendency of the practice, and to persuade them to reform it. And it was urged on heads of families to agree to govern and restrain their households at those times; and withal it was more privately moved to them, to meet the next day in their several neighborhoods to know one another's minds; which was accordingly done, and the motion complied with throughout the town. But parents found little or no occasion for the exercise of government in the case; the young people declared themselves convinced by what they had heard from the pulpit, and there was a thorough reformation of these disorders, which has continued.

Presently after this, there began to appear a remarkable religious

5. It must be noted, that it has never been our manner to observe the evening that follows the Sabbath, but that which precedes it, as part of Holy Time.

concern in a little village [6] about three miles from the main body of the town, where a number of persons seemed to be savingly wrought upon. In the April following, *anno* 1734, there happened a very sudden and awful death of a young man in the bloom of life, which, with what was said publicly on that occasion, much affected many of our young people. This was followed also with another death, of a young married woman, who was in great distress in the beginning of her illness, but died full of comfort, with satisfying evidence of God's saving mercy to her; in a most earnest manner warning and counseling others, which seemed to contribute much to the solemnizing [of] the spirits of many.

In the fall of the year I moved to the young people that they would agree to spend the evenings after the lectures in social religion in various parts of the town, which was accordingly done; and those meetings have been since continued, and the example followed by elder people.

About this time began the noise which was in this part of the country about Arminianism,[7] which seemed to appear with a threatening aspect. The friends of vital piety trembled for fear of the issue, but contrary to their fears it was strangely overruled to the promoting of religion. A sermon concerning "Justification by Faith Alone"[8] (though great fault was found with meddling with the controversy, and it was elsewhere ridiculed, yet) proved a word in season, and it was evidently attended with a remarkable blessing to the souls of the people in this town; giving them universal satisfaction about the main thing in question, which they had been in trembling concern about.

And then it was in the latter part of December that the Spirit of God began extraordinarily to set in, and wonderfully to work among us; so that there were, very suddenly, one after another, five or six persons that were to all appearance savingly converted; and some of them wrought upon in a remarkable manner. Among these, I was surprised with the relation of a young woman that had been one of the greatest company-keepers in the whole town, in whom there appeared evident a glorious work of God's infinite power and sovereign grace; a new and truly broken, sanctified heart. Yet I was filled

6. [Pascommuck; above, p. 100.]

7. [Above, pp. 17–18.]

8. [Preached at two "public lectures" and printed more largely in *Discourses on Various Important Subjects* (Boston, 1738). See above, pp. 19–21.]

with concern about the effect it might have on others, and was
ready to conclude (though too rashly) that some would be hardened
by it in carelessness and looseness of life, and would take occasion to
reproach religion; but the event was the reverse to a wonderful
degree. God made it, I suppose, the greatest occasion of awakening
to others, of anything that ever came to pass in the town. I have had
abundant opportunity to know the effect it had, by my private
conversation with many. The news of it seemed as a flash of lightning upon the hearts, both of young people and others. The persons
farthest from seriousness were greatly affected with it: many went to
talk with her, to their great satisfaction. And presently upon this, a
great and earnest concern about the great things of religion and the
eternal world became universal, in all parts of the town, and among
persons of all degrees and ages. The noise among the dry bones
waxed louder and louder. All other talk but about spiritual and
eternal things was thrown by. All the conversation in all companies,
and upon all occasions, was upon these things only; except so much
as was necessary for people's carrying on their ordinary secular business. Other discourse, than of the things of God, would scarce be
tolerated in any company. The minds of people were wonderfully
taken off from the world: it was treated among us as a thing of very
little consequence. Men seemed to follow their worldly business
more as a part of duty, than from any disposition they had to it.
The temptation now seemed to be on the other hand to neglect
worldly affairs too much, and to spend too much time in the immediate exercises of religion: which thing was, however, misrepresented by reports spread in distant parts of the land, as though the
people here had wholly thrown by all worldly business. Yet true it
was, that religion was with all sorts the main concern, and the
world only a thing by the bye. The only thing was to get the kingdom of heaven, and everyone appeared pressing into it. The engagedness of their hearts herein, could not be hid; it appeared in
their very countenances. It was then a dreadful thing among us to
be out of Christ; and in danger every day of dropping into hell.
People were intent upon this, to escape for their lives, and to flee
from the wrath to come. All eagerly laid hold of opportunities for
their souls, and met often in private houses for religious exercises.
There was scarce a single person in the town, old or young, left
unconcerned. The vainest and loosest formerly, were now greatly
awakened; and the work of conversion went on in an astonishing

manner. Souls came as it were by flocks to Jesus Christ. For many months together from day to day, were evident instances of it.

In the spring and summer following, *anno* 1735, the town seemed to be full of the presence of God, full of love and joy so as never before, and yet full of distress. This was almost in every house, on the account of salvation being brought into them. Parents rejoiced over their children as newborn, and husbands and wives in each other; God's day was a delight, and his tabernacles amiable; our public assemblies indeed beautiful, and the congregation alive in God's service; everyone earnestly intent on the public worship, and eager to drink in the Word from the mouth of the minister; generally in tears while the Word was preached, some weeping with sorrow, others with joy and love, others with pity and concern for the souls of their neighbors. Our public praises were greatly enlivened, and God was served in our psalmody as in the beauties of holiness. There was scarce any part of divine worship wherein God's saints among us had grace so drawn forth, and their hearts so lifted up, as in singing the praises of God. Our congregation had excelled all that ever I knew in the external part of the duty before, generally carrying regularly and well three parts of music, and the women a part by themselves; but now they were evidently wont to sing with unusual elevations of heart and voice, which made the duty pleasant indeed. In all companies on other days, on whatsoever occasions persons were met together, Christ was to be heard of and seen in the midst of them. Our young people, when they met, were wont to spend their time in talking of the excellency of Jesus Christ, the gloriousness of the way of salvation, the wonderful free and sovereign grace of God, and his work in the conversion of a soul, the truth and certainty of God's Word, the sweetness of the views of his perfections, etc. And even at weddings, which were formerly occasions of mirth and jollity, there was now no discourse of anything but religion, and no appearance of any but spiritual mirth. The converted were greatly enlivened, and renewed as with fresh oil, though some much more than others, according to the measure of the gift of Christ; and many who had before labored under difficulties about their own state, had now their doubts removed by more clear discoveries to them of the love of God.

When this work of God first appeared, and was so extraordinarily carried on among us in the winter, others round about us seemed not to know what to make of it, and many scoffed at it; some compared our conversions to certain distempers. But it was very observable of many that occasionally came among us from abroad, with disregardful hearts, that what they saw here cured 'em of this temper of mind. Strangers were generally surprised to find things so much beyond what they had heard, and were wont to tell others that the state of the town could not be conceived by those that had not seen it. The notice taken of it when the Court set here in March was very observable, and so at our lectures, when many were remarkably affected. Many had their consciences smitten and awakened, and went home with wounded hearts, and with impressions that never wore off, but had hopefully a saving issue; and those that before had serious thoughts, had their convictions greatly increased. Others that came only on visits or business appeared to be savingly wrought upon, partook of the shower of blessing rained down on us, and went home rejoicing. Till at length the same work began openly to appear and prevail in several other towns of the county.

In the month of March the people of South Hadley began to be seized with deep concern about the things of religion, which very soon became universal: and it has been there not much if anything short of what it has been here, in proportion to the bigness of the place.

About the same time it began to break forth in the west part of Suffield, and soon spread into all the town, where it has also been very great. It next appeared at Sunderland and soon overspread the town; and for a season was no less remarkable there than here. About the same time it began in a part of Deerfield called Green River, and afterwards filled the town, where there had been a glorious work. It became manifest also in the south part of Hatfield, and in the second week of April the whole town seemed to be seized as it were at once, great numbers resorting to their minister for advice, and many have been added to the church. There has been also a very general awakening at West Springfield and Longmeadow; and at Enfield there was for a time a pretty general concern, observable among some that had been before very loose persons. At the same time, the Rev. Mr. Bull [9] of Westfield informed me of a great alteration there, and that more had been done in one week than in seven years before. Something of this appeared also in the first precinct in Springfield, principally in the north and south extremes of the parish. And at Hadley Old Town there was gradually so much

9. [Above, p. 102 n. 6.]

of a work of God upon souls, as at another time would have been thought worthy of much notice. For a short time there was also a very great and general concern of the like nature at Northfield. And wherever it appeared, it seemed not to be in vain, but in every place God brought saving blessings with him. It might well be said here from place to place, "Who are these that fly as a cloud, and as the doves to their windows?" [Isa. 60:8]. The continual news from town to town kept alive the talk of religion, and as it greatly quickened and rejoiced the hearts of good people, so it much awakened those that looked upon themselves as still left behind, and made them earnest to share in the great blessing that others had obtained.

This remarkable pouring out of the Spirit of God, which extended from one end of the county to the other, was not confined to it. Many places in Connecticut partook of the same mercy: as in the first parish in Windsor, under the pastoral care of the Rev. Mr. Marsh [1] while we had no knowledge of each other's circumstances. Afterwards, also in East Windsor, my honored father's parish, which has been in times past a place favored with like mercy, above any on this western side of New England, excepting Northampton, there having been four or five times of general awakening since my father's settlement among them.[2] Last spring and summer the work of God was wonderful at Coventry, under the ministry of the Rev. Mr. Meacham.[3] At the same time it was great in a part of Lebanon, called The Crank, where Mr. Wheelock,[4] a young gentleman is lately settled. So at Durham, under the ministry of the Rev. Mr. Chauncy,[5] and in Stratford under the ministry of the Rev. Mr.

1. [Jonathan Marsh (1685–1747, Harvard 1705) was pastor at Windsor, Conn., 1710–47. "His parish had an independent revival about the time of that at Northampton, but by 1742 he had definitely turned against the excesses of the Great Awakening" (Shipton, *Sibley's Harvard Graduates*, 5, 280).]

2. [In 1694; above, p. 102 n. 7, and p. 4.]

3. [Joseph Meacham (1686–1752, Harvard 1710) was pastor at South Coventry, Conn., 1714–52. He studied divinity under Solomon Stoddard and was always a hearty supporter of the Awakening.]

4. [Eleazar Wheelock (1711–79, Yale 1733) was pastor at Lebanon Second, or North, Parish ("The Crank"), now Columbia, Conn., 1735–70. After wide-ranging activities during the Great Awakening, he removed to Hanover, N.H., where he became the founder of what is now Dartmouth College.]

5. [Nathaniel Chauncy (1681–1756, Yale 1702) began preaching at the new settlement of Durham, Conn., in 1706 and was ordained there in 1711; he con-

Gold,[6] and in another parish called Ripton under the pastoral care of Mr. Mills.[7] A considerable revival of religion was also at New Haven, Old Town, as I have been informed by the Rev. Mr. Noyes [8] there, and by others; which flourishing of religion there still continues and has lately much increased.

Mention is made of some other places by the Rev. Mr. Edwards, as Mansfield, Tolland, the North Parish in Preston, etc. And then he goes on to observe upon all: [9]

That it seems a very extraordinary dispensation of Providence, beyond God's usual way of working, on the account of the universality of it, affecting all sorts, sober and vicious, high and low, wise and unwise, old and young; so that where anyone seemed to remain senseless, it would be spoken of as a strange thing. So also in the numbers of those on whom we hope it has had a saving effect. We have had about six hundred and twenty communicants, which include almost all our adults: the church was large before, but persons never thronged into it as now. Our sacraments are eight weeks asunder, and I received into our communion about an hundred before one sacrament, and fourscore of them at one time; whose appearance, when they presented themselves to make an open explicit profession of Christianity, was very affecting to the congregation. I took in near sixty before the next sacrament. But it is not the manner here, as in many other churches in the country, to make a relation of experience of a work of conversion. I am far from pretending to determine, but if I might be allowed to say what appears to me probable, more than three hundred souls were savingly brought home to Christ in this town, in the space of half a

---

tinued as pastor until his death. His sympathy with the revival was short-lived, and during the controversies of the 1740s he was identified with the Old Lights.]

6. [Hezekiah Gold (1695–1761, Harvard 1719) was pastor at Stratford, Conn., 1722–52. Staunch supporter of the Awakening and an active revivalist himself, Gold saw many of his members defect to the Episcopalian church under the care of Samuel Johnson, and he was eventually dismissed.]

7. [Jedediah Mills (1697–1776, Yale 1722) was pastor of the Ripton Church (North Parish of Stratford, now Huntington, Conn.) 1724–76. An active revivalist, he enjoyed wide favor among evangelicals. When David Brainerd was expelled from Yale in 1742 (above, p. 57), he repaired to Mills' parsonage to continue his studies.]

8. [Above, p. 102 n. 8.]

9. [Editorial insertions by Benjamin Colman, enclosed within quotation marks in the original, are printed here in italics.]

year, and about the same number of males as females, which was far from what has been usual here. Those of our young people who are here on other accounts most likely and considerable, are mostly, as I hope, truly pious and leading in the ways of religion. Those that were formerly our looser young persons are generally to all appearance become lovers of God and Christ, and spiritual in their dispositions. And I hope that by far the greater part above sixteen years of age have the saving knowledge of Christ; and so by what I have heard, I suppose it is at some other places. I suppose there were [converted] upward of fifty persons in this town above forty years of age, and more than twenty of them above fifty, and ten above sixty and two above seventy. And I suppose near thirty were wrought upon between ten and fourteen, and two between nine and ten, and one about four years old; [1] several Negroes also appeared to have been born again.

The Rev. writer goes on to speak of the hand of God visible in the quickness of the work, and in the degree of saving light, love and joy experienced by many; and is very large in the vast variety of manner wherein persons were wrought on. On this head he says:

As to the manner of persons being wrought upon, there is a vast variety, yet in many things there is a great analogy in all. Persons are first awakened with a sense of their miserable condition by nature, and the danger they are in of perishing eternally. Some are more suddenly seized with convictions, by something they hear in public or in private conference; their consciences are suddenly smitten as if their hearts were pierced through with a dart. Others have their awakenings more gradually; they are thoughtful that it is their wisest way to delay no longer, and set themselves seriously to meditate on those things that have the most awakening tendency, and their awakenings have increased, till a sense of their misery has (by the influence of God's Spirit) taken fast hold of them. Others that before this time had been something religious and concerned, have been made sensible that their slack and dull way of seeking was never like to attain their purpose, and have been roused up to a greater violence for the kingdom of heaven [cf. Matt. 11:12].

These awakenings when they first seized on persons have had two effects. First, they have been brought immediately to quit their

1. Of whom a very large and particular account is given in the manuscript letter. [Note by Colman; see below, pp. 199–205.]

sinful practices, and the looser sort to dread their former vices and extravagances. The other effect was, that it put them upon earnest application of themselves to the means of salvation; reading, prayer, meditation, the ordinances of God's house, and private conference.

There is a very great variety as to the degree of fear and trouble, before they obtain any comfortable evidences of pardon and acceptance with God. Some have had abundantly more encouragement and hope: others have had such a sense of the displeasure of God, and the great danger they were in of damnation, that they could not sleep; the thoughts of sleeping in such a condition have been frightful to them. Sometimes the distemper of melancholy is evidently mixed, of which, when it happens, Satan seems to make great advantage, as a great bar in the way of any good effect. One knows not how to deal with such persons, [for] they turn everything that is said to them the wrong way. But it has been very remarkable, that there has been far less of this now, than there was wont to be in persons under awakenings at other times. Some persons that had before for a long time been entangled with peculiar temptations and hurtful distresses, were soon helped over them; and they have been successfully carried on in the way of life. Yet there have been some instances of persons that have had as great a sense of their danger and misery, as their natures could subsist under; sometimes brought to the borders of despair, and it has looked as black as midnight to them, a little before the day-dawn in their souls.

Some few instances there have been of persons under such a sense of God's wrath for sin, that they have been overborne and made to cry out with amazement. But more commonly persons' distresses have not been to such a degree.

The design of the spirit of God in these legal terrors seems most evidently to be, to make way for, and to bring persons to a conviction of their absolute dependence upon his sovereign power and grace, and universal necessity of a Mediator, by leading them into a sense of their exceeding wickedness and guiltiness in his sight, the pollution and insufficiency of their own righteousness, that they can in no wise help themselves, and that God would be just and righteous in casting them off forever.

In those whose awakenings seem to issue in conversion, commonly the first thing that appears after their legal troubles, is a conviction of the justice of God in their condemnation; from a sense of their exceeding sinfulness and the vileness of all their performances.

Others have the sins of their lives in an extraordinary manner set before them; multitudes of them coming then fresh to their remembrance, with their aggravations. Some have their minds especially fixed upon some particular wicked practice. Some are especially convinced by a sight of the corruption and wickedness of their hearts; or some particular corruption in the time of their awakening, whereby the enmity of their hearts against God has been manifested. Some are convinced by a sense of the greatness of the sin of unbelief, the opposition of their hearts to Christ, and obstinacy in rejecting him, etc.

Commonly persons' minds immediately before this discovery of God's justice are exceeding restless, and in a kind of struggle and tumult; and sometimes in a mere anguish. But generally as soon as they have this conviction, it immediately brings their minds to a calm and composure: and often they then come to a conclusion within themselves, that they will lie at God's foot, in hopes of mercy, and wait his time. And it is observable, that persons when they first have this sense of the justice of God, rarely in the time of it think anything of its being that humiliation which they have often heard insisted on, and whereby they are prepared for mercy.

After this legal humiliation and calm of spirit, in some persons it is some time before any special manifestations are made to their souls of the grace of God as revealed in the Gospel; but very often some comfortable and sweet view of a merciful God and an all-sufficient Saviour, or some of the great and joyful things of the Gospel immediately follow, or in a very little time. And in some, the first sight of their just desert of hell, and of God's sovereignty with respect to their salvation, and a discovery of all-sufficient grace, seem to be as it were together.

The discoveries that are given, whence the first special comforts are derived, are in some respects various; more frequently Christ is distinctly the object of the mind, in his sufficiency and willingness to save sinners; but some have their thoughts more especially fixed on God, in some of his sweet and glorious attributes. In some the truths of the Gospel in general, in some the certainty of some particular promises, etc.

There are many that have lately been converted, who have been accounted very knowing persons, especially in the things of religion, and could talk with more than common understanding of conversion, that declare that all their former wisdom is brought to nought, and that they appear to themselves to have been mere babes. And it has seemed to have been with delight that they have seen themselves thus brought down and become nothing; that free grace and divine power might be exalted in them.

It was very wonderful to see after what manner persons' affections were sometimes moved and wrought upon, when God did suddenly open their eyes and let into their minds a sense of his grace, and the fullness of Christ and his readiness to save; who before were broken with apprehensions of divine wrath, and sunk as into an abyss with a sense of guilt, which they were ready to think was beyond the mercy of God. Their joyful surprise has caused their hearts as it were to leap; tears issuing like a flood, intermingled with their joy; and sometimes they have not been able to forbear expressing with a loud voice their great admiration, and sometimes ready to faint.

The converting influences of God's Spirit very commonly bring an extraordinary conviction of the reality and certainty of the great things of religion. They have that sight and taste of the divinity and divine excellency of the things of the Gospel, that is more to convince them than reading of hundreds of volumes of arguments without it. It seems to me, in many instances amongst us, they have at such times been as far from doubting of the truth of them, as from doubting whether there be a sun, when their eyes behold it in a clear hemisphere.

Some persons have had so great a sense of the glory of God and the excellency of Christ, that nature and life has seemed almost to sink under it. I have seen some (and been in conversation with them) in such frames, who certainly have been perfectly sober, and very remote from anything like enthusiastic wildness, expressing themselves concerning the glory of God's perfections, the wonderfulness of his grace in Christ and their own unworthiness, in a manner that can't be expressed after them. Their sense of their exceeding littleness or vileness, and their disposition to debase themselves before God, has appeared to be great in proportion to their light and joy. Such persons amongst us as have been thus distinguished with most extraordinary discoveries of God, have commonly in no wise appeared with the assuming and self-conceited, and self-sufficient airs of enthusiasts; but exceedingly the contrary: and are eminent for a spirit of meekness, modesty, self-diffidence, and low opinion of themselves.

And those who have been thought to be converted amongst us,

generally express an humbleness of mind desirous to lie in the dust before God: and very often speak of their sense of the excellency of the way of salvation by free and sovereign grace, through the righteousness of Christ alone, and how it is with delight they renounce their own righteousness.

There is a great difference among those that are converted, as to the hope and satisfaction they have of their own state. They generally have an awful apprehension of the dreadfulness of a false hope. And there has been observable in most a great caution lest in giving an account of their experiences they should say too much, or use too strong terms.

This is but a small and broken extract of what the Rev. writer says of the manner wherein souls were wrought on; and he adds a very particular exemplification of it in two instances, too large to be inserted in this appendix. Toward the close of his letter he adds:

After these things,[2] instances of conversion were rare in comparison of what had before been. Yet religion remained the main subject of conversation for several months after. But in general there was a gradual decline of that engaged lively spirit which had been before. Several things happened to give a diversion to people's minds, and turned their conversation to other things.[3]

But as to those that have been thought to be converted among us in this time, the change in them seems abiding. They appear to have a new sense of things, new apprehensions and views of God, and the great things of the Gospel. They have a new sense of the truth of them, and they affect them in a new manner; though it is very far from being always alike with them, nor can they revive a sense of things when they please. Their hearts are often touched, and sometimes filled with new sweetnesses and delights. There seems to be an inward ardor and burning of heart which they express, of which they never experienced the like before. There are yet new kind of breathings and pantings and breakings of soul for the longings it hath.

Some that before were very rough in their temper and manner, seem to be remarkably softened and sweetened. And some have their souls exceedingly filled and overwhelmed with light, love, and comfort, long since the work of God has ceased to be so remarkable.

2. [Joseph Hawley's suicide (above, pp. 109–10) and two instances of "enthusiastic delusions" (below, p. 207).]

3. [Enumerated below, p. 208.]

There is still a great deal of religious conversation maintained in the town, among young and old; and private religious meetings on Sabbath and lecture nights are still maintained; and many children still keep up such meetings among themselves. I know of no one young person in the town that has reverted to former ways of looseness and extravagance in any respect; but we still remain a reformed people, and God has evidently made us a new people. A great part of the country have not received favorable thoughts of this affair, and to this day retain a jealousy about it, and prejudice against it: yet so it has pleased God to work, and we are evidently a people blessed of him; and in this corner of the world God dwells and manifests his glory.

Thus, Rev. Sir, I have given a large and particular account of this remarkable affair, which I leave entirely with you to use as you think best; and if you please to send anything to the Rev. Dr. Guyse, I shall be glad to have it signified to him as my humble desire, that since he and his congregation have been pleased to take so much notice of us, they would still think of us at the throne of grace, and seek there for us that God would not forsake us, but enable us to bring forth fruits answerable to our profession and our mercies.

When I first heard of the notice which the Rev. Dr. Watts and Dr. Guyse took of God's mercies to us, I took occasion to inform our congregation of it in a discourse from those words, "A city set upon an hill cannot be hid" [Matt. 5:14]; and I have since read that part of your letter [4] to my congregation, and labored as much as in me lay to enforce their duty from it; with which they were very sensibly moved and affected. I ask your prayers for this county and town, and a particular interest in them for him who is, with humble respect, Sir, your, etc.,

Jonathan Edwards.

❖❖❖❖❖❖❖❖❖❖❖❖❖❖❖❖❖❖❖❖❖❖❖

ADVERTISEMENT

If the taste here given of Mr. Edwards his excellent letter excite in persons of piety a desire to have the whole of it published; it is hereby notified that subscriptions for that end will be taken in by Messrs. Kneeland and Green, at their printing house in Queen Street, Boston. The whole may be contained in five sheets.

4. [Presumably Colman's letter of July 20, 1736, to William Williams; see above, pp. 33–34, 113.]

A Faithful

NARRATIVE

OF THE

Surprizing Work of GOD

IN THE

CONVERSION

OF

Many Hundred Souls in *Northampton,*
and the Neighbouring Towns and
Villages of ~~New~~-Hamp*shire* in *New-
England.*

In a LETTER to the Rev^d. Dr. BENJAMIN
COLMAN of *Boston.*

Written by the Rev^d. Mr. EDWARDS, Minister of
Northampton, on *Nov.* 6. 1736

And Publish'd,

With a Large PREFACE,

By Dr. WATTS and Dr. GUYSE.

LONDON;
Printed for JOHN OSWALD, at the *Rose and Crown*, in
the *Poultry,* near *Stocks-Market.* M.DCC.XXXVII.

Price stitch'd 1 *s.* Bound in Calf-Leather, 1 *s.* 6 *d.*

A Faithful

NARRATIVE

OF THE

Surprising Work of GOD

IN THE

CONVERSION

OF

Many HUNDRED SOULS in *Northampton*, and
the Neighbouring Towns and Villages of
the County of *Hampſhire*, in the Province
of the *Maſſachuſetts-Bay* in *New-England*.

In a LETTER to the Reverend
Dr. BENJAMIN COLMAN, of *Boſton*.

Written by the Revᵈ Mr. EDWARDS, Miniſter of
Northampton, *Nov. 6. 1736.*

Publiſhed with a Large PREFACE by the Rev.
Dr. WATTS and Dr. GUYSE of *London* :

To which a Shorter is added by Some of the
Reverend Miniſters of *BOSTON*.

ogether with an ATTESTATION from Some of the
Reverend *Miniſters* of *Hampſhire*.

The THIRD EDITION.

OSTON: N.E Printed&Sold byS. KNEELAND
T.GREEN, over againſt thePriſon inQueen-ſtreet. 1738.

PREFACE TO THE FIRST EDITION (LONDON, 1737)

A Faithful Narrative in its complete form appeared first in London under the sponsorship of the Revs. Isaac Watts and John Guyse, who wrote a preface to introduce the work and its author to British readers. For an account of the publication and reception of this edition, see above, pp. 36–45.

THE friendly correspondence which we maintain with our brethren of New England, give us now and then the pleasure of hearing some remarkable instances of divine grace in the conversion of sinners, and some eminent examples of piety in that American part of the world. But never did we hear or read, since the first ages of Christianity, any event of this kind so surprising as the present narrative hath set before us. The reverend and worthy Dr. Colman of Boston had given us some short intimations of it in his letters; and upon our request of a more large and particular account, Mr. Edwards, the happy and successful minister of Northampton, which was one of the chief scenes of these wonders, drew up this history in an epistle to Dr. Colman.

There were some useful sermons of the venerable and aged Mr. William Williams published lately in New England, which were preached in that part of the country during this season of the glorious work of God in the conversion of men; to which Dr. Colman subjoined a most judicious and accurate abridgment of this epistle: [1] and a little after by Mr. Edwards' request,[2] he sent the original to our hands, to be communicated to the world under our care here in London.

1. [William Williams, *The Duty and Interest of a People . . . to Which Is Added Part of a Large Letter from the Rev. Mr. Jonathan Edwards of Northampton* (Boston, 1736). Colman's abridgment of JE's letter is printed above, pp. 113–27.]

2. [JE crossed out the phrase "by Mr. Edwards' request," and wrote in the margin, "a mistake." The words are deleted in the Boston edition of 1738 (FN-3).]

We are abundantly satisfied of the truth of this narrative, not only from the pious character of the writer, but from the concurrent testimony of many other persons in New England; for "this thing was not done in a corner" [Acts 26:26]. There is a spot of ground, as we are here informed, wherein there are twelve or fourteen towns and villages, chiefly situate in New Hampshire [3] near the banks of the River of Connecticut, within the compass of thirty miles, wherein it pleased God two years ago to display his free and sovereign mercy in the conversion of a great multitude of souls in a short space of time, turning them from a formal, cold and careless profession of Christianity to the lively exercise of every Christian grace, and the powerful practice of our holy religion. The great God has seemed to act over again the miracle of Gideon's fleece, which was plentifully watered with the dew of heaven, while the rest of the earth round about it was dry, and had no such remarkable blessing [Judges 6:36–38].

There has been a great and just complaint for many years among the ministers and churches in Old England, and in New (except about the time of the late earthquake there [4]), that the work of conversion goes on very slowly, that the Spirit of God in his saving influences is much withdrawn from the ministrations of his Word, and there are few that receive the report of the Gospel with any eminent success upon their hearts. But as the Gospel is the same divine instrument of grace still, as ever it was in the days of the apostles, so our ascended Saviour now and then takes a special occasion to manifest the divinity of this Gospel by a plentiful effusion of his Spirit where it is preached: then sinners are turned into saints in numbers, and there is a new face of things spread over a town or a [5] country. "The wilderness and the solitary places are glad, the desert rejoices and blossoms as the rose" [Isa. 35:1]; and surely concerning this instance we may add, that "they have seen the glory of the Lord there, and the excellency of our God" [Isa. 35:2]; "they have seen the outgoings of God our King in his sanctuary" [Ps. 68:24].

Certainly it becomes us, who profess the religion of Christ, to take notice of such astonishing exercises of his power and mercy, and give him the glory which is due, when he begins to accomplish any of

3. [FN-3 corrects this to "the County of Hampshire." For the Londoners' confusion over the geography of New England, see above, pp. 41–42.]

4. [In 1727.]

5. [Article omitted in FN-3.]

his promises concerning the latter days: and it gives us further encouragement to pray, and wait, and hope for the like display of his power in the midst of us. "The hand of God is not shortened that it cannot save," but we have reason to fear that our iniquities, our coldness in religion, and the general carnality of our spirits, have raised a wall of separation between God and us [cf. Isa. 59:1]. And we may add, the pride and perverse humor of infidelity, degeneracy and apostasy from the Christian faith, which have of late years broken out amongst us, seem to have provoked the Spirit of Christ to absent himself much from our nation. "Return, O Lord, and visit thy churches, and revive thine own work in the midst of us."[6]

From such blessed instances of the success of the Gospel, as appear in this narrative, we may learn much of the way of the Spirit of God in his dealing with the souls of men, in order to convince sinners and restore them to his favor and his image by Jesus Christ, his Son. We acknowledge that some particular appearances in the work of conversion among men may be occasioned by the ministry which they sit under, whether it be of a more or less evangelical strain, whether it be more severe and affrighting, or more gentle and persuasive. But wheresoever God works with power for salvation upon the minds of men, there will be some discoveries of a sense of sin, of the danger of the wrath of God, of the all-sufficiency of his Son Jesus, to relieve us under all our spiritual wants and distresses, and a hearty consent of soul to receive him in the various offices of grace, wherein he is set forth in the Holy Scriptures. And if our readers had opportunity (as we have had) to peruse several of the sermons which were preached during this glorious season, we should find that it is the common plain Protestant doctrine of the Reformation, without stretching towards the Antinomians on the one side, or the Arminians on the other,[7] that the Spirit of God has been pleased to honor with such illustrious success.

We are taught also by this happy event how easy it will be for our blessed Lord to make a full accomplishment of all his predictions concerning his kingdom, and to spread his dominion from sea to sea, through all the nations of the earth. We see how easy it is for him with one turn of his hand, with one word of his mouth, to awaken whole countries of stupid and sleeping sinners, and kindle divine life in their souls. The heavenly influence shall run from door

6. [A spontaneous prayer in language reminiscent of Ps. 80:14 and Hab. 3:2.]
7. [See above, pp. 4–21.]

to door, filling the hearts and lips of every inhabitant with importunate inquiries, "What shall we do to be saved?" And "How shall we escape the wrath to come?"[8] And the name of Christ the Saviour shall diffuse itself like a rich and vital perfume to multitudes that were ready to sink and perish under the painful sense of their own guilt and danger. Salvation shall spread through all the tribes and ranks of mankind, as the lightning from heaven in a few moments would communicate a living flame through ten thousand lamps or torches placed in a proper situation and neighborhood. Thus "a nation shall be born in a day" [Isa. 66:8] when our Redeemer please,[9] and his faithful and obedient subjects shall become as numerous as the spires of grass in a meadow newly mown, and refreshed with the showers of heaven. But the pleasure of this agreeable hint bears the mind away from our theme.

Let us return to the present narrative. 'Tis worthy of our observation, that this great and surprising work does not seem to have taken its rise from any sudden and distressing calamity or public terror that might universally impress the minds of a people. Here was no storm, no earthquake, no inundation of water, no desolation by fire, no pestilence or any other sweeping distemper, nor any cruel invasion by their Indian neighbors, that might force the inhabitants into a serious thoughtfulness, and a religious temper by the fears of approaching death and judgment. Such scenes as these have sometimes been made happily effectual to awaken sinners in Zion, and the formal professor and the hypocrite have been terrified with the thoughts of divine wrath breaking in upon them, "Who shall dwell with everlasting burnings?" [Isa. 33:14]. But in the present case the immediate hand of God in the work of his Spirit appears much more evident, because there is no such awful and threatening providence attending it.

It is worthy also of our further notice, that when many profane sinners and formal professors of religion have been affrighted out of

8. [Cf. Acts 2:37. In the original passage, conscience-stricken men responded to Peter's preaching with the broader question, "What shall we do?" and were given a fourfold program for Christian living: "Repent . . . be baptized . . . receive the gift of the Holy Spirit . . . [and] save yourselves from this crooked generation." Watts and Guyse reveal their evangelical predilections by characteristically telescoping everything into the all-important question of immediate salvation, which assures one of escape from "the wrath to come" (cf. Rev. 6:17).]

9. [FN-3 has "pleases."]

their present carelessness and stupidity by some astonishing terrors approaching them, those religious appearances have not been so durable, nor the real change of heart so thoroughly effected: many of these sort of sudden converts have dropped their religious concerns in a great measure when their fears of the threatening calamity are vanished. But it is a blessed confirmation of the truth of this present work of grace, that the persons who were divinely wrought upon in this season continue still to profess serious religion, and to practice it without returning to their former follies.

It may not be amiss in this place to take notice, that a very surprising and threatening providence has this last year attended the people of Northampton, among whom this work of divine grace was so remarkable: which providence at first might have been construed by the unthinking world to be a signal token of God's displeasure against that town, or a judgment from heaven upon the people; but soon afterwards, like Paul's shaking the viper off from his hand [Acts 28:1–6], it discovered the astonishing care and goodness of God expressed towards a place where such a multitude of his young converts were assembled: nor can we give a better account of it than in the language of this very gentleman, the Rev. Mr. Edwards, minister of that town, who wrote the following letter, which was published in New England.[1]

Northampton, March 19th, 1737

We in this town, were the last Lord's Day the spectators, and many of us the subjects, of one of the most amazing instances of divine preservation, that perhaps was ever known in the land. Our meetinghouse is old and decayed, so that we have been for some time building a new one, which is yet unfinished. It has been observed of late, that the house that we have hitherto met in has gradually spread at bottom, the cells [2] and walls giving way, especially in the foreside, by reason of the weight of timber at top pressing on the braces that are inserted into the posts and beams of the house. It has so done more than ordinarily this

1. [In *The Boston Gazette*, No. 899 (March 28–April 4, 1737), pp. 2–3. The letter is also printed (with some revisions) in Dwight, *Life of President Edwards,* pp. 139–40.]

2. [JE may have intended "sills." Although "cells" can be used in architectural description to refer to the compartments formed by the framing of a building, "sills" comports more easily with the context here.]

spring; which seems to have been occasioned by the heaving of the ground by the extreme frosts of the winter past, and its now settling again on that side which is next the sun; by the thaws of the spring: by this means the underpinning has been considerably disordered, which people were not sensible of, till the ends of the joists which bore up the front gallery, by the walls giving way, were drawn off from the girts on which they rested; so that in the midst of the public exercise in the forenoon, soon after the beginning of sermon, the whole gallery full of people, with all the seats and timber, suddenly and without any warning sunk, and fell down, with most amazing noise, upon the heads of those that sat under, to the astonishment of the congregation, the house being filled with dolorous shrieking and crying, and nothing else was expected than to find many people dead, and dashed to pieces.

The gallery in falling seemed to break and sink first in the middle, so that those who were upon it were thrown together in heaps before the front door. But the whole was so sudden, that many of them that fell knew nothing in the time of it what it was that had befallen them; and others in the congregation knew not what it was that had happened with so great a noise; many thought it had been an amazing clap of thunder. The falling gallery seemed to be broken all to pieces before it got down; so that some that fell with it, as well as those that went under, were buried in the ruins, and were found pressed under heavy loads of timber, and could do nothing to help themselves.

But so mysteriously and wonderfully did it come to pass, that every life was preserved; and though many were greatly bruised, and their flesh torn, yet there is not, as I can understand, one bone broke, or so much as put out of joint among them all. Some that were thought to be almost dead at first, are greatly recovered; and but one young woman seems yet to remain in dangerous circumstances, by an inward hurt in her breast; but of late there appears more hope of her recovery.

There is none can give any account, or conceive by what means it should come to pass, that people's lives and limbs should be thus preserved, when so great a multitude were thus imminently [3] exposed. It looked as though it was impossible it should be otherwise, than that great numbers should instantly be crushed to

3. [The original newspaper account reads "eminently."]

death or dashed in pieces: it seems unreasonable to ascribe it to anything else, but the care of providence in disposing the motions of every stick of timber, and the precise place of safety where everyone should sit and fall, when none were in any capacity to take care for their own preservation. The preservation seems to be most wonderful with respect to the women and children that were in the middle ally [aisle] under the gallery, where it came down first and with greatest force, and where was nothing to break the force of the falling weight.

Such an event may be a sufficient argument of a divine providence over the lives of men. We thought ourselves called to set apart a day to be spent in the solemn worship of God, to humble ourselves under such a rebuke of God upon us in the time of public service in God's house by so dangerous and surprising an accident; and to praise his name for so wonderful, and as it were miraculous a preservation; and the last Wednesday was kept by us to that end: and a mercy in which the hand of God is so remarkably evident, may be well worthy to affect the hearts of all that hear it.

Thus far the letter.

But it is time to conclude our preface. If there should be anything found in this narrative of the surprising conversion of such numbers of souls, where the sentiments or the style of the relater, or his inferences from matters of fact, do not appear so agreeable to every reader, we hope it will have no unhappy influence to discourage the belief of this glorious event. We must allow every writer his own way; and must allow him to choose what particular instances he would select, from the numerous cases which came before him. And though he might have chosen others perhaps, of more significancy in the eye of the world, than the woman and the child whose experiences he relates at large; [4] yet 'tis evident he chose that of the woman because she was dead, and she is thereby uncapable of knowing any honors or reproaches on this account. And as for the child, those who were present, and saw and heard such a remarkable and lasting change on one so very young, must necessarily receive a stronger impression from it, and a more agreeable surprise than the mere narration of it can communicate to others at a distance. Children's language always loses its striking beauties at second hand.

4. [Abigail Hutchinson and Phebe Bartlet; below, pp. 191–205.]

Upon the whole, whatever defects any reader may find or imagine in this narrative, we are well satisfied that such an eminent work of God ought not to be concealed from the world: and as it was the reverend author's opinion, so we declare it to be ours also, that 'tis very likely that this account of such an extraordinary and illustrious appearance of divine grace in the conversion of sinners, may, by the blessing of God, have a happy effect upon the minds of men, towards the honor and enlargement of the kingdom of Christ, much more than any supposed imperfection in this representation of it can do injury.[5]

May the worthy writer of this epistle, and all those his reverend brethren in the ministry, who have been honored in this excellent and important service, go on to see their labors crowned with daily and persevering success! May the numerous subjects of this surprising work hold fast what they have received, and increase in every Christian grace and blessing! May a plentiful effusion of the blessed Spirit also descend on the British Isles and all their American plantations, to renew the face of religion there! And we entreat our readers in both Englands to join with us in our hearty addresses to the throne of grace, that this wonderful discovery of the hand of God in saving sinners, may encourage our faith and hope of the accomplishment of all his words of grace, which are written in the Old Testament and in the New, concerning the large extent of this salvation in the latter days of the world. "Come, Lord Jesus, come quickly; and spread thy dominion through all the ends of the earth. Amen." [6]

Isaac Watts
John Guyse

London, Oct. 12, 1737

5. [On JE's objection to this paragraph, see above, p. 39.]
6. [A spontaneous prayer in the language of Rev. 22:20 and Dan. 4:22.]

PREFACE TO THE THIRD EDITION (BOSTON, 1738)

Nettled by the liberties which Watts and Guyse had taken with A Faithful Narrative, *introducing errors which were repeated in a second edition (London, 1738), Edwards was pleased with the opportunity to publish a corrected version in New England. Four Boston ministers wrote a preface for this third edition; see above, pp. 39–41.*

WHEN the disciples of our glorious Lord were filled with sorrow upon the heavy tidings of his departure from them, he cheered their drooping spirits with that good word, John 16:7, "Nevertheless, I tell you the truth; it is expedient for you that I go away; for if I go not away, the Comforter will not come unto you; but if I depart, I will send him unto you." And after his ascension, he fulfilled this great and precious promise by the extraordinary effusion of his Spirit, under whose conduct and influence the apostles went forth and preached everywhere, the Lord working with them: so that when we read the Acts of the Apostles, we must say: "Not by might, nor by power, but by the Spirit of the Lord of hosts" [Zech. 4:6]. And though soon after the first days of Christianity, there was a dreadful apostasy, yet God did not wholly take his Spirit from his people; but raised up faithful witnesses to testify against the heresies and corruptions of the times wherein they lived. And since Antichrist "that Wicked One has been revealed," our Lord, according to his Word, has been gradually "consuming him with the spirit of his mouth" [II Thess. 2:8], in the Reformation.

Nor have we in these remote corners of the earth, where Satan had his seat from time immemorial, been left without a witness of the divine power and grace. Very remarkable was the work of God's Spirit stirring up our forefathers to leave a pleasant land, and transport themselves over a vast ocean into this then howling wilderness; that they might enjoy communion with Christ in the purity of his ordinances, and leave their children in the quiet possession of the blessings of his kingdom. And God was eminently present with them by his Word and Spirit.

Yea, we need look no higher than our own times, to find abundant occasion to celebrate the wonderful works of God. Thus when God arose and shook the earth,[1] his loud call to us in that amazing providence was followed, so far as man can judge, with the still voice of his Spirit, in which he was present to awaken many and bring them to say trembling, "What must we do to be saved?" [Acts 16:30]. Yea. as we hope, to turn not a few from sin to God in a thorough conversion. But when the bitterness of death was past, much the greater part of those whom God's terrors affrighted, gave sad occasion to remember those words, Psalm 78:34–36, "When he slew them, then they sought him: and they returned and inquired early after God. And they remembered that God was their rock, and the high God their redeemer. Nevertheless, they did flatter him with their mouths, and they lied unto him with their tongues." And there has since been great reason to complain of our speedy return to our former sins, notwithstanding some hopes given of a more general reformation. Yea, when more lately it pleased God to visit many of our towns with a very mortal distemper,[2] to that time in a manner unknown; whereby great numbers of our hopeful children and youth have been cut off, many very suddenly, and with circumstances exceedingly distressing and awful: yet alas! we have not generally seen, nor duly considered God's hand stretched out against us; but have given him reason to complain, as of his ancient people, "Why should ye be stricken any more? Ye will revolt more and more" [Isa. 1:5]. And accordingly his anger is not turned away; but his hand is stretched out still. A plain proof of this awful truth, that the most awakening dispensations can no farther humble and do us good, than as it pleaseth God to accompany them with his Spirit, and so command his blessing upon them. But when the Almighty will work by such means, or without them, who can hinder him? He acts with sovereign liberty and irresistible power. John 3:8, "The wind bloweth where it listeth, and thou hearest the sound thereof, but canst not tell whence it cometh, and whither it goeth: so is every one that is born of the Spirit." Such was his wonderful work at Northampton, and the neighboring towns in the County of Hampshire, and some

1. The earthquake of October 29, 1727.
2. [Massachusetts had had a devastating epidemic of smallpox in 1721–22, and one of somewhat lesser proportions in 1729–30.]

other places. The Holy Spirit was in a plentiful and extraordinary manner poured out on persons of every age and condition, without such remarkable providences going before to awaken them; as "the dew falls in the night," and yet the effects appeared as "the light which goeth forth" [cf. Hos. 6:4–5]. So that we might well admiring say, "What has God wrought!" [Num. 23:23]. Great was the number of them who published the wonders of the divine power and grace; declaring with humility what God had done for their souls. And others who went among them, acknowledged that the work exceeded the fame of it.

Now the Psalmist observes that "God has made his wonderful works to be remembered" [Ps. 111:4]. We therefore apprehend that our reverend brother has done well to record and publish this surprising work of God; and the fidelity of his account would not have been at all doubted of by us, though there had not been the concurrent testimony of others to it. It is also a pleasure to us to hear what acceptance the following narrative has found in the other England, where it has had two impressions already, and been honored with a recommendatory preface, by two divines of eminent note in London, viz. the Rev. Dr. Watts, and Dr. Guyse: after whom it may seem presumption in us to attempt anything of this kind. But it having been thought proper to reprint this letter here, and disperse it among our people; we thankfully embrace this opportunity to praise the Most High for the exceeding riches of his grace, and earnestly to recommend this epistle to the diligent reading and attentive consideration of all into whose hands these shall come. "He that hath an ear, let him hear what the Spirit saith unto the churches" [Rev. 2:7]. And indeed the particular and distinct account which the author has given of God's dealings with the souls of men, at this remarkable season, in the variety of cases then set before him, and many of his observations thereupon, we apprehend are written with that judgment and skill in divine things, as declare him to be a scribe well instructed unto the kingdom of heaven; and we judge may be very useful to ministers in leading weary souls to Christ for rest, and for the direction and encouragement of all under the like operations of the Holy Spirit.

Yea, as the author observes, "There is no one thing I know of, that God has made such a means of promoting his work among us as the news of others' conversion"; [3] we hope that the further spreading of this narrative may, by the divine blessing, still promote the

3. [Below, p. 176.]

conversion of souls, and quicken God's children to labor after the clearer evidences of their adoption, and to bring forth fruits meet for repentance. And as this wonderful work may be considered as an earnest of what God will do towards the close of the Gospel day, it affords great encouragement to our faith and prayer in pleading those promises which relate to the glorious extent and flourishing of the kingdom of Christ upon earth, and have not yet had their full and final accomplishment. And surely the very threatening degeneracy of our times calls aloud to us all, to be earnest in prayer for this most needed blessing, the plentiful effusion of the Spirit of truth and holiness. Nor ought the sense of our own unworthiness discourage us, when we go to our heavenly Father in the name of his dear Son, who has purchased and received this great gift for his people, and says to us, Luke 11:9–13, "Ask and it shall be given you. . . . If ye then, being evil, know how to give good gifts unto your children; how much more shall your heavenly Father give the Holy Spirit to them that ask him?"

But we must draw to a close. May the worthy author be restored to health, and long continued to be a rich blessing to his people! May he still see the pleasure of the Lord prospering in his hand; and in particular, may the Spirit of grace accompany this pious endeavor to spread the savor of the knowledge of Christ for the everlasting advantage of many! May it please God to revive his work throughout this land; and may all the ends of the earth see his salvation!

Joseph Sewall [4]
Thomas Prince [5]
John Webb [6]
William Cooper [7]

Boston, Nov. 4th, 1738.

P.S. Since the writing this preface, one of us has received a letter from a reverend and very worthy minister in Glasgow, in which is the following passage:

4. [Joseph Sewall (1688–1769, Harvard 1707) was pastor of the Old South Church in Boston 1713–69.]

5. [Thomas Prince (1687–1758, Harvard 1709) was colleague pastor with Joseph Sewall at the Old South Church 1718–58.]

6. [John Webb (1687–1750, Harvard 1708) was pastor of the New North Church in Boston 1714–50.]

7. [William Cooper (1694–1743, Harvard 1712) was colleague pastor with Benjamin Colman at Brattle Street Church in Boston 1716–43.]

The friends of serious religion here were much refreshed with a printed account of the extraordinary success of the Gospel, of late, in some parts of New England. If you can favor me with more particular accounts of those joyful events, when you have opportunity of writing to me, it will much oblige me.[8]

8. [FN-1 was reprinted in Edinburgh in 1737 and again in 1738; see above, p. 45.]

ATTESTATION FROM SIX HAMPSHIRE MINISTERS

In response to requests from British correspondents, Dr. Colman secured from several fellow ministers in Hampshire County testimony corroborating Edwards' account of the revival in their areas. The attestation came too late to be published in London but was prefixed to the third edition of A Faithful Narrative *(Boston, 1738). See above, pp. 40–41.*

To the Reverend Benjamin Colman, D.D.
Pastor of a Church in Boston

Westfield, October 11, 1738

Sir,

In your letter of August 19 you inform us, that the Rev. Dr. Watts and Dr. Guyse desire that some ministers, who were eye and ear witnesses to some of those numerous conversions in the other towns about Northampton, would attest unto what the Rev. Mr. Edwards has written of them.

We take this opportunity to assure you, that the account Mr. Edwards has given in his narrative of our several towns or parishes is true; and that much more of the like nature might have been added with respect to some of them.

We are, Reverend Sir, your brethren and servants.

> William Williams, pastor of Hatfield
> Ebenezer Devotion, of Suffield
> Stephen Williams, of Longmeadow
> Peter Reynolds, of Enfield
> Nehemiah Bull, of Westfield
> Samuel Hopkins, of W. Springfield

TEXT OF *A FAITHFUL NARRATIVE*

The text presented here is that of the first edition (London, 1737), corrected according to notations which Edwards made in the margins of the copy at Yale College (now at Beinecke Rare Book and Manuscript Library of Yale University), and collated with the third edition (Boston, 1738). For an account of the textual problems concerning this work, see above, pp. 38–45.

Reverend and Honored Sir,[1]

Having seen your letter to my honored Uncle Williams[2] of Hatfield of July 20 [1736], wherein you inform him of the notice that has been taken of the late wonderful work of God, in this and some other towns in this county; by the Rev. Dr. Watts and Dr. Guyse of London, and the congregation to which the last of these preached on a monthly day of solemn prayer; as also, of your desire to be more perfectly acquainted with it, by some of us on the spot: and having been since informed by my Uncle Williams that you desire me to undertake it; I would now do it in as just and faithful a manner as in me lies.

The people of the county, in general, I suppose, are as sober, and orderly, and good sort of people, as in any part of New England; and I believe they have been preserved the freest by far, of any part of the country, from error and variety of sects and opinions.[3] Our being so far within the land, at a distance from seaports, and in a corner of the country, has doubtless been one reason why we have not been so much corrupted with vice, as most other parts. But without question, the religion and good order of the county, and their purity in doctrine, has, under God, been very much owing to the great abilities and eminent piety of my venerable and honored grandfather

1. [A letter to Benjamin Colman of Boston; see above, pp. 32–34.]
2. [Above, p. 113 n. 1.]
3. [A sentence apparently deleted by Watts and Guyse referred to a group of Baptists at Springfield; see above, p. 113.]

Stoddard.[4] I suppose we have been the freest of any part of the land from unhappy divisions and quarrels in our ecclesiastical and religious affairs, till the late lamentable Springfield contention.[1]

We being much separated from other parts of the province, and having comparatively but little intercourse with them, have from the beginning till now, always managed our ecclesiastical affairs within ourselves: 'tis the way in which the county, from its infancy, has gone on, by the practical agreement of all, and the way in which our peace and good order has hitherto been maintained.

The town of Northampton is of about 82 years standing, and has now about 200 families; which mostly dwell more compactly together than any town of such a bigness in these parts of the country; which probably has been an occasion that both our corruptions and reformations have been, from time to time, the more swiftly propagated from one to another through the town. Take the town in general, and so far as I can judge, they are as rational and understanding a people as most I have been acquainted with: many of them have been noted for religion, and particularly have been remarkable for their distinct knowledge in things that relate to heart religion and Christian experience, and their great regards thereto.

I am the third minister that has been settled in the town: the Rev. Mr. Eleazar Mather, who was the first, was ordained in [July 1661 and died][2] July 1669. He was one whose heart was much in his work, abundant in labors for the good of precious souls; he had the high esteem and great love of his people, and was blessed with no small success. The Rev. Mr. Stoddard, who succeeded him, came first to the town the November after his death, but was not ordained till September 11, 1672, and died February 11, 1728/9. So that he continued in the work of the ministry here, from his first coming to town, near sixty years. And as he was eminent and renowned for his gifts and grace; so he was blessed, from the beginning, with extraordinary success in his ministry in the conversion of many souls.

4. [See above, pp. 15–17.]

1. The Springfield contention relates to the settlement of a minister there, which occasioned too warm debates between some, both pastors and people, that were for it, and others that were against it, on account of their different apprehensions about his principles, and about some steps that were taken to procure his ordination. [See above, p. 113 n. 3.]

2. [The bracketed phrase appears to have been omitted inadvertently in FN-1 and the error was overlooked in FN-3. The correction has been supplied from FN-C; above, p. 114.]

He had five harvests, as he called them: the first was about 57 years ago; the second about 53 years; the third about 40; the fourth about 24; the fifth and last about 18 years ago. Some of these [3] times were much more remarkable than others, and the ingathering of souls more plentiful. Those that were about 53, and 40, and 24 years ago were much greater than either the first or the last: but in each of them, I have heard my grandfather say, the bigger part of the young people in the town seemed to be mainly concerned for their eternal salvation.

After the last of these came a far more degenerate time (at least among the young people), I suppose, than ever before. Mr. Stoddard, indeed, had the comfort before he died, of seeing a time where there were no small appearances of a divine work amongst some, and a considerable ingathering of souls, even after I was settled with him in the ministry, which was about two years before his death; and I have reason to bless God for the great advantage I had by it. In these two years there were near twenty that Mr. Stoddard hoped to be savingly converted; but there was nothing of any general awakening. The greater part seemed to be at that time very insensible of the things of religion, and engaged in other cares and pursuits. Just after my grandfather's death, it seemed to be a time of extraordinary dullness in religion: licentiousness for some years greatly prevailed among the youth of the town; they were many of them very much addicted to night-walking, and frequenting the tavern, and lewd practices, wherein some, by their example exceedingly corrupted others. It was their manner very frequently to get together in conventions of both sexes, for mirth and jollity, which they called frolics; and they would often spend the greater part of the night in them, without regard to any order in the families they belonged to: and indeed family government did too much fail in the town. It was become very customary with many of our young people, to be indecent in their carriage at meeting, which doubtless would not have prevailed to such a degree, had it not been that my grandfather, through his great age (though he retained his powers surprisingly to the last) was not so able to observe them. There had also long prevailed in the town a spirit of contention between two parties, into which they had for many years been divided, by which was maintained a jealousy one of the other, and they were prepared to oppose one another in all public affairs.[4]

3. [FN-C reads "those."]
4. [Above, p. 99 n.]

But in two or three years after Mr. Stoddard's death, there began to be a sensible amendment of these evils; the young people shewed more of a disposition to hearken to counsel, and by degrees left off their frolicking, and grew observably more decent in their attendance on the public worship, and there were more that manifested a religious concern than there used to be.

[A New Awakening Begins]

At the latter end of the year 1733, there appeared a very unusual flexibleness, and yielding to advice, in our young people. It had been too long their manner to make the evening after the Sabbath,[5] and after our public lecture, to be especially the times of their mirth and company-keeping. But a sermon was now preached on the Sabbath before the lecture, to shew the evil tendency of the practice, and to persuade them to reform it; and it was urged on heads of families, that it should be a thing agreed upon among them, to govern their families and keep their children at home at these [6] times; and withal it was more privately moved that they should meet together the next day, in their several neighborhoods, to know each other's minds; which was accordingly done, and the motion complied with throughout the town. But parents found little or no occasion for the exercise of government in the case: the young people declared themselves convinced by what they had heard from the pulpit, and were willing of themselves to comply with the counsel that had been given: and it was immediately, and I suppose, almost universally complied with; and there was a thorough reformation of these disorders thenceforward, which has continued ever since.

Presently after this, there began to appear a remarkable religious concern at a little village belonging to the congregation, called Pascommuck, where a few families were settled at about three miles distance from the main body of the town. At this place, a number of persons seemed to be savingly wrought upon. In the April following, *anno* 1734, there happened a very sudden and awful death of a young man in the bloom of his youth; who being violently seized with a pleurisy and taken immediately very delirious, died in about two days; which (together with what was preached publicly on that occasion) much affected many young people. This was followed with

5. It must be noted, that it has never been our manner to observe the evening that follows the Sabbath, but that which precedes it, as part of Holy Time.

6. [FN-C reads "those."]

another death of a young married woman, who had been considerably exercised in mind about the salvation of her soul before she was ill, and was in great distress in the beginning of her illness; but seemed to have satisfying evidences of God's saving mercy to her before her death; so that she died very full of comfort, in a most earnest and moving manner warning and counseling others. This seemed much to contribute to the solemnizing of the spirits of many young persons: and there began evidently to appear more of a religious concern on people's minds.

In the fall of that year, I proposed it to the young people, that they should agree among themselves to spend the evenings after lectures in social religion, and to that end divide themselves into several companies to meet in various parts of the town; which was accordingly done, and those meetings have been since continued, and the example imitated by elder people. This was followed with the death of an elderly person, which was attended with many unusual circumstances, by which many were much moved and affected.

About this time, began the great noise that was in this part of the country about Arminianism,[7] which seemed to appear with a very threatening aspect upon the interest of religion here. The friends of vital piety trembled for fear of the issue; but it seemed, contrary to their fear, strongly to be overruled for the promoting of religion. Many who looked on themselves as in a Christless condition, seemed to be awakened by it, with fear that God was about to withdraw from the land, and that we should be given up to heterodoxy and corrupt principles; and that then their opportunity for obtaining salvation would be past; and many who were brought a little to doubt about the truth of the doctrines they had hitherto been taught, seemed to have a kind of a trembling fear with their doubts, lest they should be led into bypaths, to their eternal undoing: and they seemed with much concern and engagedness of mind, to inquire what was indeed the way in which they must come to be accepted with God. There were then some things said publicly on that occasion concerning justification by faith alone.[8]

Although great fault was found with meddling with the controversy in the pulpit, by such a person and at that time, and though it was ridiculed by many elsewhere, yet it proved a word spoken in

7. [See above, pp. 17–18.]
8. [Above, p. 19–21.]

season here; and was most evidently attended with a very remarkable blessing of heaven to the souls of the people in this town. They received thence a general satisfaction with respect to the main thing in question, which they had been in trembling doubts and concern about; and their minds were engaged the more earnestly to seek that they might come to be accepted of God, and saved in the way of the Gospel, which had been made evident to them to be the true and only way. And then it was, in the latter part of December, that the Spirit of God began extraordinarily to set in, and wonderfully to work amongst us; and there were, very suddenly, one after another, five or six persons who were to all appearance savingly converted, and some of them wrought upon in a very remarkable manner.

Particularly, I was surprised with the relation of a young woman, who had been one of the greatest company-keepers in the whole town. When she came to me, I had never heard that she was become in any wise serious, but by the conversation I then had with her, it appeared to me that what she gave an account of was a glorious work of God's infinite power and sovereign grace; and that God had given her a new heart, truly broken and sanctified. I could not then doubt of it, and have seen much in my acquaintance with her since to confirm it.

Though the work was glorious, yet I was filled with concern about the effect it might have upon others: I was ready to conclude (though too rashly) that some would be hardened by it, in carelessness and looseness of life; and would take occasion from it to open their mouths in reproaches of religion. But the event was the reverse, to a wonderful degree; God made it, I suppose, the greatest occasion of awakening to others, of anything that ever came to pass in the town. I have had abundant opportunity to know the effect it had, by my private conversation with many. The news of it seemed to be almost like a flash of lightning, upon the hearts of young people all over the town, and upon many others. Those persons amongst us who used to be farthest from seriousness, and that I most feared would make an ill improvement of it, seemed greatly to be awakened with it; many went to talk with her, concerning what she had met with; and what appeared in her seemed to be the satisfaction of all that did so.

Presently upon this, a great and earnest concern about the great things of religion and the eternal world became universal in all parts of the town, and among persons of all degrees and all ages; the noise amongst the dry bones waxed louder and louder. All other talk about spiritual and eternal things was soon thrown by; all the conversation in all companies and upon all occasions, was upon these things only, unless [9] so much as was necessary for people, carrying on their ordinary secular business. Other discourse than of the things of religion would scarcely be tolerated in any company. The minds of people were wonderfully taken off from the world; it was treated amongst us as a thing of very little consequence. They seemed to follow their worldly business more as a part of their duty than from any disposition they had to it; the temptation now seemed to lie on that hand, to neglect worldly affairs too much, and to spend too much time in the immediate exercise of religion: which thing was exceedingly misrepresented by reports that were spread in distant parts of the land, as though the people here had wholly thrown by all worldly business, and betook themselves entirely to reading and praying, and such like religious exercises.

But although people did not ordinarily neglect their worldly business; yet there then was the reverse of what commonly is: religion was with all sorts the great concern, and the world was a thing only by the bye. The only thing in their view was to get the kingdom of heaven, and everyone appeared pressing into it. The engagedness of their hearts in this great concern could not be hid; it appeared in their very countenances. It then was a dreadful thing amongst us to lie out of Christ, in danger every day of dropping into hell; and what persons' minds were intent upon was to escape for their lives, and to fly from the wrath to come. All would eagerly lay hold of opportunities for their souls; and were wont very often to meet together in private houses for religious purposes: and such meetings when appointed were wont greatly to be thronged.

There was scarcely a single person in the town, either old or young, that was left unconcerned about the great things of the eternal world. Those that were wont to be the vainest and loosest, and those that had been most disposed to think and speak slightly of vital and experimental religion, were now generally subject to great awakenings. And the work of conversion was carried on in a most astonishing manner, and increased more and more; souls did as it were come by flocks to Jesus Christ. From day to day, for many months together, might be seen evident instances of sinners brought out of darkness into marvellous light, and delivered out of an horrible pit, and from the miry clay, and set upon a rock with a new

9. [FN-C reads "except."]

song of praise to God in their mouths [cf. I Pet. 2:9 and Ps. 40:2–3].

This work of God, as it was carried on, and the number of true saints multiplied, soon made a glorious alteration in the town; so that in the spring and summer following, *anno* 1735, the town seemed to be full of the presence of God: it never was so full of love, nor so full of joy; and yet so full of distress, as it was then. There were remarkable tokens of God's presence in almost every house. It was a time of joy in families on the account of salvation's being brought unto them; parents rejoicing over their children as newborn, and husbands over their wives, and wives over their husbands. The goings of God were then seen in his sanctuary [Ps. 68:24], God's day was a delight, and his tabernacles were amiable [Ps. 84:1]. Our public assemblies were then beautiful; the congregation was alive in God's service, everyone earnestly intent on the public worship, every hearer eager to drink in the words of the minister as they came from his mouth; the assembly in general were, from time to time, in tears while the Word was preached; some weeping with sorrow and distress, others with joy and love, others with pity and concern for the souls of their neighbors.

Our public praises were then greatly enlivened; God was then served in our psalmody, in some measure, in the beauty of holiness [Ps. 96:9]. It has been observable that there has been scarce any part of divine worship, wherein good men amongst us have had grace so drawn forth and their hearts so lifted up in the ways of God, as in singing his praises. Our congregation excelled all that ever I knew in the external part of the duty before, generally carrying regularly and well three parts of music, and the women a part by themselves.[10] But now they were evidently wont to sing with unusual elevation of heart and voice, which made the duty pleasant indeed.

In all companies, on other days, on whatever occasions persons met together, Christ was to be heard of, and seen in the midst of them. Our young people, when they met, were wont to spend the time in talking of the excellency and dying love of Jesus Christ, the glorious-

10. [FN-1 inserts "the men" before "generally." In Yale's annotated copy JE changed "men" to "congregation." FN-3 removed the redundancy by striking the word along with its article. On singing at Northampton, see JE's letter to Benjamin Colman, dated May 22, 1744, noting that his congregation began using Watts' hymns in 1742. Before that they presumably sang only psalms in meter, which required considerable talent and effort for any melodic result (*PMHS*, 2d ser., *10* {1896}, 429).]

ness of the way of salvation, the wonderful, free, and sovereign grace of God, his glorious work in the conversion of a soul, the truth and certainty of the great things of God's Word, the sweetness of the views of his perfections, etc. And even at weddings, which formerly were merely occasions of mirth and jollity, there was now no discourse of anything but the things of religion, and no appearance of any but spiritual mirth.

Those amongst us that had been formerly converted, were greatly enlivened and renewed with fresh and extraordinary incomes of the Spirit of God; though some much more than others, according to the measure of the gift of Christ. Many that before had labored under difficulties about their own state, had now their doubts removed by more satisfying experience, and more clear discoveries of God's love.

When this work of God first appeared, and was so extraordinarily carried on amongst us in the winter, others round about us seemed not to know what to make of it; and there were many that scoffed at and ridiculed it; and some compared what we called conversion to certain distempers. But it was very observable of many that occasionally came amongst us from abroad, with disregardful hearts, that what they saw here cured them of such a temper of mind: strangers were generally surprised to find things so much beyond what they had heard, and were wont to tell others that the state of the town could not be conceived of by those that had not seen it. The notice that was taken of it by the people that came to town on occasion of the Court, that sat here in the beginning of March, was very observable. And those that came from the neighborhood to our public lectures, were for the most part remarkably affected. Many that came to town, on one occasion or other, had their consciences smitten and awakened, and went home with wounded hearts and with those impressions that never wore off till they had hopefully a saving issue; and those that before had serious thoughts had their awakenings and convictions greatly increased. And there were many instances of persons that came from abroad on visits or on business, that had not been long here before to all appearance they were savingly wrought upon, and partook of that shower of divine blessing that God rained down here, and went home rejoicing; till at length the same work began evidently to appear and prevail in several other towns in the county.[1]

In the month of March, the people in South Hadley began to be

1. [For other towns having revivals in 1734–35, see map on p. 24.]

seized with deep concern about the things of religion; which very soon became universal: and the work of God has been very wonderful there; not much, if anything, short of what it has been here, in proportion to the bigness of the place. About the same time, it began to break forth in the west part of Suffield (where it has also been very great), and soon spread into all parts of the town. It next appeared at Sunderland, and soon overspread the town; and I believe was, for a season, not less remarkable than it was here. About the same time, it began to appear in a part of Deerfield called Green River, and afterwards filled the town, and there has been a glorious work there. It began also to be manifest in the south part of Hatfield, in a place called The Hill, and after that the whole town, in the second week in April, seemed to be seized as it were at once with concern about the things of religion; and the work of God has been great there.[2] There has been also a very general awakening at West Springfield, and Longmeadow; and in Enfield there was for a time no small [3] concern amongst some that before had been very loose persons. About the same time that this appeared at Enfield, the Rev. Mr. Bull [4] of Westfield informed me that there had been a great alteration there, and that more had been done in one week there than in seven years before. Something of this work likewise appeared in the first precinct in Springfield, principally in the north and south extremes of the parish. And in Hadley Old Town, there gradually appeared so much of a work of God on souls, as at another time would have been thought worthy of much notice. For a short time there was also a very great and general concern of the like nature at Northfield. And wherever this concern appeared, it seemed not to be in vain: but in every place God brought saving blessings with him, and his Word attended with his Spirit (as we have all reason to think) returned not void. It might well be said at that time in all parts of the county, "Who are these that fly as a cloud, and as doves to their windows?" [Isa. 60:8].

As what other towns heard of and found in this was a great means of awakening them, so our hearing of such a swift and extraordinary propagation and extent of this work did doubtless for a time serve to uphold the work amongst us. The continual news kept alive the talk of religion, and did greatly quicken and rejoice the hearts of

2. [Cf. the variant reading of this sentence in FN-C; above, p. 119.]
3. ["No small" follows reading in FN-3. FN-1 reads "a pretty general."]
4. [Above, p. 102 n. 6.]

God's people, and much awakened those that looked on themselves as still left behind, and made them the more earnest that they also might share in the great blessing that others had obtained.

This remarkable pouring out of the Spirit of God, which thus extended from one end to the other of this county, was not confined to it; but many places in Connecticut have partook in the same mercy. As for instance, the first parish in Windsor, under the pastoral care of the Rev. Mr. Marsh,[5] was thus blessed about the same time as we in Northampton, while we had no knowledge of each other's circumstances. There has been a very great ingathering of souls to Christ in that place, and something considerable of the same work began afterwards in East Windsor, my honored father's parish, which has in times past been a place favored with mercies of this nature above any on this western side of New England, excepting Northampton; there having been four or five seasons of the pouring out of the Spirit to the general awakening of the people there, since my father's settlement amongst them.[6]

There was also the last spring and summer a wonderful work of God carried on at Coventry, under the ministry of the Rev. Mr. Meacham.[7] I had opportunity to converse with some of Coventry people, who gave me a very remarkable account of the surprising change that appeared in the most rude and vicious persons there. The like was also very great at the same time in a part of Lebanon called The Crank, where the Rev. Mr. Wheelock,[8] a young gentleman is lately settled. And there has been much of the same at Durham, under the ministry of the Rev. Mr. Chauncy; [9] and to appearance no small ingathering of souls there. And likewise amongst many of the young people in the first precinct in Stratford, under the ministry of the Rev. Mr. Gold; [1] where the work was much promoted by the remarkable conversion of a young woman that had been a great company-keeper, as it was here.

Something of this work appeared in several other towns in those parts, as I was informed when I was there the last fall. And we have since been acquainted with something very remarkable of this na-

5. [Above, p. 120 n. 1.]
6. [In 1694. See above, p. 102 n. 7.]
7. [Above, p. 120 n. 3.]
8. [Above, p. 120 n. 4.]
9. [Above, p. 120 n. 5.]
1. [Above, p. 121 n. 6.]

ture at another parish in Stratford called Ripton, under the pastoral care of the Rev. Mr. Mills.[2] And there was a considerable revival of religion last summer at New Haven Old Town, as I was once and again informed by the Rev. Mr. Noyes,[3] the minister there, and by others; and by a letter which I very lately received from Mr. Noyes, and also by information we have had otherwise. This flourishing of religion still continues, and has lately much increased: Mr. Noyes writes that many this summer have been added to the church, and particularly mentions several young persons that belong to the principal families of that town.

There has been a degree of the same work at a part of Guilford; and very considerable at Mansfield, under the ministry of the Rev. Mr. Eleazar Williams; [4] and an unusual religious concern at Tolland; and something of it at Hebron and Bolton. There was also no small effusion of the Spirit of God in the north parish in Preston, in the eastern part of Connecticut, which I was informed of, and saw something of it, when I was the last autumn at the house and in the congregation of the Rev. Mr. Lord,[5] the minister there; who, with the Rev. Mr. Owen [6] of Groton, came up hither in May, the last year, on purpose to see the work of God here; and having heard various and contradictory accounts of it, were careful when they were here to inform and satisfy themselves, and to that end particularly conversed with many of our people; which they declared to be entirely to their satisfaction; and that the one-half had not been told them, nor could be told them. Mr. Lord told me when he got home, he informed his congregation of what he had seen, and that they were greatly affected with it, and that it proved the beginning of the same work amongst them, which prevailed till there was a general awakening, and many instances of persons who seemed to be remarkably converted. I also have lately heard that there has been something of the same work at Woodbury.

But this shower of divine blessing has been yet more extensive. There was no small degree of it in some parts of the Jerseys; as I was informed when I was at New York (in a long journey I took at that

2. [Above, p. 121 n. 7.]
3. [Above, p. 102 n. 8.]
4. [Eleazar Williams (1688–1742, Harvard 1708) was pastor at Mansfield, Conn., 1710–42.]
5. [Above, p. 108 n. 3.]
6. [Above, p. 108 n. 4.]

time of the year for my health) by some people of the Jerseys, whom I saw: especially the Rev. Mr. William Tennent,[7] a minister who seemed to have such things much at heart, told me of a very great awakening of many in a place called The Mountains, under the ministry of one Mr. Cross; [8] and of a very considerable revival of religion in another place under the ministry of his brother, the Rev. Mr. Gilbert Tennent; [9] and also at another place, under the ministry of a very pious young gentleman, a Dutch minister whose name as I remember was Freelinghousa.[1]

7. [William Tennent, Jr. (1705–77) was a leader of the Presbyterian revival in the Middle Colonies. His father had founded the "Log College" for training evangelical ministers, first among whom were his sons John, Gilbert, and William, Jr. In 1733 the last became pastor at Freehold, N.J., succeeding his brother John, who had died the previous year after a pastorate of only two years.]

8. [John Cross (d. ca. 1750) was "a Scottish worthy" who joined the Synod of Philadelphia and was installed in 1732 as Presbyterian pastor at Basking Ridge, N.J. In 1735 he was censured by the East Jersey Presbytery because "he absented himself from their meetings and removed from one congregation to another without the concurrence of presbytery." It was doubtless during this time that Cross stirred an awakening by itinerating to "The Mountain Society," a second church in Newark constituted in 1719 by sons of Newark colonists who had settled along the slopes of the Orange Mountains west of Newark (later the First Presbyterian Church of Orange). More than 300 conversions were reported during this time, leading Cross to boast that his revival paralleled "the account given by Mr. Edwards of the work of God in Northampton" (*George Whitefield's Journals* {London, 1960}, p. 486). By 1739–40 he was back at Basking Ridge, where he entertained Whitefield, James Davenport, and other revivalists. On June 24, 1741, however, he was accused of "detestable carriage" in relation to a woman and suspended by the New Brunswick Presbytery. After failing in all efforts to be readmitted, he reportedly became involved in other scandals and dropped out of public view around 1748. See "Minutes of the Presbytery of New Brunswick," transcribed by George H. Ingram, in *Journal of the Presbyterian Historical Society*, 7 (1913), 152; John C. Rankin, *The Presbyterian Church at Basking Ridge, N.J.* (n.p., 1872), p. 9; Richard Webster, *History of the Presbyterian Church in America* (Philadelphia, 1857), pp. 413–14; and Stephen Wickes, *History of the Oranges* (Newark, 1892), ch. 6.]

9. [Gilbert Tennent (1703–64) was pastor of the Presbyterian church at New Brunswick, N.J., 1727–43, after which he removed to Philadelphia. By 1740 he had emerged as the titular leader of evangelical Presbyterianism. See Leonard J. Trinterud, *The Forming of an American Tradition* (Philadelphia, 1949), Part I.]

1. [Theodorus Jacobus Frelinghuysen (1691–1748) came from Holland to assume the pastoral care of Dutch Reformed people in the Raritan River Valley of New Jersey in 1720. Within six years his pietistic emphasis on the disciplines

This seems to have been a very extraordinary dispensation of Providence: God has in many respects gone out of, and much beyond his usual and ordinary way. The work in this town and some others about us, has been extraordinary on account of the universality of it, affecting all sorts, sober and vicious, high and low, rich and poor, wise and unwise; it reached the most considerable families and persons, to all appearance, as much as others. In former stirrings of this nature, the bulk of the young people have been greatly affected; but old men and little children have been so now. Many of the last have, of their own accord, formed themselves into religious societies, in different parts of the town. A loose, careless person could scarcely find a companion in the whole neighborhood; and if there was anyone that seemed to remain senseless or unconcerned, it would be spoken of as a strange thing.

This dispensation has also appeared very extraordinary in the numbers of those on whom we have reason to hope it has had a saving effect. We have about six hundred and twenty communicants, which include almost all our adult persons.[2] The church was very large before; but persons never thronged into it as they did in the late extraordinary time. Our sacraments are eight weeks asunder, and I received into our communion about an hundred before one sacrament, and fourscore of them at one time, whose appearance, when they presented themselves together to make an open explicit profession of Christianity, was very affecting to the congregation. I took in near sixty before the next sacrament day;[3] but [it must be noted that][4] it is not the custom here, as it is in many other churches in this country, to make a credible relation of their inward experiences the ground of admission to the Lord's Supper.

I am far from pretending to be able to determine how many have lately been the subjects of such mercy; but if I may be allowed to

---

of experiential Christianity had produced a religious awakening in his five congregations, which in turn decisively influenced Gilbert Tennent at nearby New Brunswick. See James R. Tanis, *Dutch Calvinistic Pietism in the Middle Colonies* (The Hague, 1967); and Charles H. Maxson, *The Great Awakening in the Middle Colonies* (Chicago, 1920), chs. 2 and 3.]

2. [Above, p. 106 n.]

3. [FN-1 inserts here: "And I had very sufficient evidence of the conversion of their souls through divine grace, though . . ."; the clause is omitted for reasons suggested in the "Editor's Introduction," above, pp. 42–43.]

4. [The bracketed words appear in FN-3.]

declare anything that appears to me probable in a thing of this nature, I hope that more than 300 souls were savingly brought home to Christ in this town in the space of half a year (how many more I don't guess) and about the same number of males as females; which, by what I have heard Mr. Stoddard say, was far from what has been usual in years past, for he observed that in his time, many more women were converted than men. Those of our young people that are on other accounts most likely and considerable, are mostly, as I hope, truly pious and leading persons in the ways of religion. Those that were formerly looser young persons are generally, to all appearance, become true lovers of God and Christ, and spiritual in their dispositions. And I hope that by far the greater part of persons in this town, above sixteen years of age, are such as have the saving knowledge of Jesus Christ; and so by what I heard I suppose it is in some other places, particularly at Sunderland and South Hadley.

This has also appeared to be a very extraordinary dispensation, in that the Spirit of God has so much extended not only his awakening, but regenerating influences, both to elderly persons and also those that are very young. It has been a thing heretofore rarely to be heard of, that any were converted past middle age; but now we have the same ground to think that many such have in this time been savingly changed, as that others have been so in more early years. I suppose there were [converted] upwards of fifty persons in this town above forty years of age; and more than twenty of them above fifty, and about ten of them above sixty, and two of them above seventy years of age.

It has heretofore been looked on as a strange thing, when any have seemed to be savingly wrought upon, and remarkably changed in their childhood; but now, I suppose, near thirty were to appearance so wrought upon between ten and fourteen years of age, and two between nine and ten, and one of about four years of age; and because I suppose this last will be most difficultly believed, I will hereafter give a particular account of it.[5] The influences of God's Spirit have also been very remarkable on children in some other places, particularly at Sunderland and South Hadley, and the west part of Suffield. There are several families in this town that are all hopefully pious; yea, there are several numerous families in which, I think, we have reason to hope that all the children are truly godly, and most of them lately become so: and there are very few houses in

5. [Phebe Bartlet; below, pp. 199–205.]

the whole town into which salvation has not lately come, in one or more instances. There are several Negroes, that from what was seen in them then, and what is discernible in them since, appear to have been truly born again in the late remarkable season.

God has also seemed to have gone out of his usual way in the quickness of his work, and the swift progress his Spirit has made in his operations on the hearts of many. 'Tis wonderful that persons should be so suddenly, and yet so greatly, changed: many have been taken from a loose and careless way of living, and seized with strong convictions of their guilt and misery, and in a very little time "old things have passed away, and all things have become new with them" [II Cor. 5:17].

God's work has also appeared very extraordinary in the degrees of the influences of his Spirit, both in the degree of awakening and conviction, and also in the degree of saving light, and love, and joy, that many have experienced. It has also been very extraordinary in the extent of it, and its being so swiftly propagated from town to town. In former times of the pouring out of the Spirit of God on this town, though in some of them it was very remarkable, yet it reached no further than this town; the neighboring towns all around continued unmoved.

The work of God's Spirit seemed to be at its greatest height in this town in the former part of the spring, in March and April; at which time God's work in the conversion of souls was carried on amongst us in so wonderful a manner, that so far as I, by looking back, can judge from the particular acquaintance I have had with souls in this work, it appears to me probable, to have been at the rate at least of four persons in a day, or near thirty in a week, take one with another, for five or six weeks together. When God in so remarkable a manner took the work into his own hands, there was as much done in a day or two as at ordinary times, with all endeavors that men can use, and with such a blessing as we commonly have, is done in a year.

[Responses of the Awakened]

I am very sensible how apt many would be, if they should see the account I have here given, presently to think with themselves that I am very fond of making a great many converts, and of magnifying and aggrandizing the matter; and to think that, for want of judgment, I take every religious pang and enthusiastic conceit for saving conversion; and I don't much wonder if they should be apt to think so: and for this reason I have forborne to publish an account of this great work of God, though I have often been put upon it; but having now as I thought a special call to give an account of it, upon mature consideration I thought it might not be beside my duty to declare this amazing work, as it appeared to me, to be indeed divine, and to conceal no part of the glory of it, leaving it with God to take care of the credit of his own work, and running the venture of any censorious thoughts which might be entertained of me to my disadvantage. But that distant persons may be under as great advantage as may be, to judge for themselves of this matter, I would be a little more large and particular.

I therefore proceed to give an account of the manner of persons being wrought upon: and here there is a vast variety, perhaps as manifold as the subjects of the operation; but yet in many things there is a great analogy in all.

Persons are first awakened with a sense of their miserable condition by nature, the danger they are in of perishing eternally, and that it is of great importance to them that they speedily escape, and get into a better state. Those that before were secure and senseless, are made sensible how much they were in the way to ruin in their former courses. Some are more suddenly seized with convictions; it may be by the news of others' conversion, or something they hear in public, or in private conference, [that] their consciences are suddenly smitten, as if their hearts were pierced through with a dart. Others have awakenings that come upon them more gradually; they begin at first to be something more thoughtful and considerate, so as to come to a conclusion in their minds that 'tis their best and wisest way to delay no longer, but to improve the present opportunity; and have accordingly set themselves seriously to meditate on those things that have the most awakening tendency, on purpose to obtain convictions; and so their awakenings have increased, till a sense of their misery, by God's Spirit setting in therewith, has had fast hold of them. Others that, before this wonderful time, had been something religious and concerned for their salvation, have been awakened in a new manner, and made sensible that their slack and dull way of seeking was never like to attain their purpose, and so have been roused up to a greater violence for the kingdom of heaven.

These awakenings when they have first seized on persons have had two effects: one was, that they have brought them immediately to quit their sinful practices, and the looser sort have been brought to forsake and dread their former vices and extravagancies. When once the Spirit of God began to be so wonderfully poured out in a general way through the town, people had soon done with their old quarrels, backbitings, and intermeddling with other men's matters; the tavern was soon left empty, and persons kept very much at home; none went abroad unless on necessary business, or on some religious account, and every day seemed in many respects like a Sabbath day. And the other effect was, that it put them on earnest application to the means of salvation—reading, prayer, meditation, the ordinances of God's House, and private conference; their cry was "What shall we do to be saved?" [6] The place of resort was now altered; it was no longer the tavern, but the minister's house, that was thronged far more than ever the tavern had been wont to be.

There is a very great variety as to the degree of fear and trouble that persons are exercised with before they obtain any comfortable evidences of pardon and acceptance with God. Some are from the beginning carried on with abundantly more encouragement and hope than others; some have had ten times less trouble of mind than others, in whom yet the issue seems to be the same. Some have had such a sense of the displeasure of God, and the great danger they were in of damnation, that they could not sleep at nights; and many have said that when they have laid down, the thoughts of sleeping in such a condition have been frightful to them, and they have scarcely been free from terror while they have been asleep; and they have awaked with fear, heaviness, and distress still abiding on their spirits. It has been very common that the deep and fixed concern that has been on persons' minds, has had a painful influence on their bodies and given disturbance to animal nature.

The awful apprehensions persons have had of their misery, have for the most part been increasing, the nearer they have approached to deliverance; though they often pass through many changes and alterations in the frame and circumstances of their minds. Sometimes they think themselves wholly senseless, and fear that the Spirit of God has left them, and that they are given up to judicial hardness; [7] yet they appear very deeply exercised about that fear, and are in great earnest to obtain convictions again.

6. [Acts 16:30 (?); cf. above, p. 133 n. 8.]

7. [I.e. that God hardened their hearts as a judgment on their unrepentant state; cf. Exod. 9:12 and parallels, and Rom. 9:18.]

Together with those fears, and that exercise of mind which is rational, and which they have just ground for, they have often suffered many needless distresses of thought, in which Satan probably has a great hand, to entangle them and block up their way; and sometimes the distemper of melancholy has been evidently mixed; of which when it happens the Tempter seems to make great advantage, and puts an unhappy bar in the way of any good effect. One knows not how to deal with such persons, [for] they turn everything that is said to them the wrong way, and most to their own disadvantage: and there is nothing that the Devil seems to make so great a handle of, as a melancholy humor, unless it be the real corruption of the heart.

But it has been very remarkable, that there has been far less of this mixture in this time of extraordinary blessing, than there was wont to be in persons under awakenings at other times; for it is evident that many that before had been exceedingly involved in such difficulties, seemed now strangely to be set at liberty. Some persons that had before, for a long time, been exceedingly entangled with peculiar temptations of one sort or other, and unprofitable and hurtful distresses, were soon helped over former stumbling blocks that hindered any progress towards saving good; and convictions have wrought more kindly, and they have been successfully carried on in the way to life. And thus Satan seemed to be restrained, till towards the latter end of this wonderful time, when God's Spirit was about to withdraw.

Many times persons under great awakenings were concerned, because they thought they were not awakened, but miserable, hardhearted, senseless, sottish creatures still, and sleeping upon the brink of hell. The sense of the need they have to be awakened, and of their comparative hardness, grows upon them with their awakenings; so that they seem to themselves to be very senseless, when indeed most sensible. There have been some instances of persons that have had as great a sense of their danger and misery as their natures could well subsist under, so that a little more would probably have destroyed them; and yet they have expressed themselves much amazed at their own insensibility and sottishness in such an extraordinary time as it then was.

Persons are sometimes brought to the borders of despair, and it looks as black as midnight to them a little before the day dawns in their souls; some few instances there have been of persons who have had such a sense of God's wrath for sin, that they have been over-borne and made to cry out under an astonishing sense of their guilt, wondering that God suffers such guilty wretches to live upon earth, and that he doth not immediately send them to hell; and sometimes their guilt does so glare them in the face, that they are in exceeding terror for fear that God will instantly do it; but more commonly the distresses under legal awakenings have not been to such a degree. In some these terrors don't seem to be so sharp, when near comfort, as before; their convictions have not seemed to work so much that way, but they seem to be led further down into their own hearts, to a further sense of their own universal depravity and deadness in sin.

The corruption of the heart has discovered itself in various exercises, in the time of legal convictions; sometimes it appears in a great struggle, like something roused by an enemy, and Satan the old inhabitant seems to exert himself like a serpent disturbed and enraged. Many in such circumstances have felt a great spirit of envy towards the godly, especially towards those that are thought to have been lately converted, and most of all towards acquaintance[s] and companions, when they are thought to be converted; indeed, some have felt many heart-risings against God, and murmurings at his ways of dealing with mankind, and his dealings with themselves in particular. It has been much insisted on, both in public and private, that persons should have the utmost dread of such envious thoughts, which if allowed tend exceedingly to quench the Spirit of God, if not to provoke him finally to forsake them. And when such a spirit has much prevailed, and persons have not so earnestly strove against it as they ought to have done, it has seemed to be exceedingly to the hindrance of the good of their souls: but in some other instances, where persons have been much terrified at the sight of such wickedness in their hearts, God has brought good to them out of evil; and made it a means of convincing them of their own desperate sinfulness, and bringing them off from all self–confidence.

The drift of the Spirit of God in his legal strivings with persons, has seemed most evidently to be, to make way for, and to bring to, a conviction of their absolute dependence on his sovereign power and grace, and universal necessity of a Mediator, by leading them more and more to a sense of their exceeding wickedness and guiltiness in his sight; the pollution and insufficiency of their own righteousness, that they can in no wise help themselves, and that God would be wholly just and righteous in rejecting them, and all that they do, and in casting them off forever: though there be a vast variety as to the manner and distinctness of persons' convictions of these things.

As they are gradually more and more convinced of the corruption and wickedness of their hearts, they seem to themselves to grow worse and worse, harder and blinder, and more desperately wicked, instead of growing better: they are ready to be discouraged by it, and oftentimes never think themselves so far off from good [8] as when they are nearest. Under the sense which the Spirit of God gives them of their sinfulness, they often think that they differ from all others; their hearts are ready to sink with the thought that they are the worst of all, and that none ever obtained mercy that were so wicked as they.

When awakenings first begin, their consciences are commonly most exercised about their outward vicious course, or other acts of sin; but afterwards, are much more burdened with a sense of heart sins, the dreadful corruption of their nature, their enmity against God, the pride of their hearts, their unbelief, their rejection of Christ, the stubbornness and obstinacy of their wills, and the like. In many, God makes much use of their own experience, in the course of their awakenings and endeavors after saving good, to convince them of their own vile emptiness and universal depravity.

Very often under first awakenings, when they are brought to reflect on the sin of their past lives, and have something of a terrifying sense of God's anger, they set themselves to walk more strictly, and confess their sins, and perform many religious duties, with a secret hope of appeasing God's anger and making up for the sins they have committed. And oftentimes, at first setting out, their affections are moved, and they are full of tears, in their confessions and prayers, which they are ready to make very much of, as though they were some atonement, and had power to move correspondent affections in God too; and hence they are for a while big with expectation of what God will do for them, and conceive that they grow better apace, and shall soon be thoroughly converted. But these affections are but short-lived; they quickly find that they fail, and then they think themselves to be grown worse again; they don't find such a prospect of being soon converted, as they thought: instead of being nearer,

8. Both FN-1 and FN-3 read "good," and JE noted no correction. (FN-C omits the passage.) Some Edwardsean scholars perhaps would prefer "God" as better suited to the context.]

they seem to be farther off; their hearts they think are grown harder, and by this means their fears of perishing greatly increase. But though they are disappointed, they renew their attempts again and again; and still as their attempts are multiplied, so are their disappointments; all fails, they see no token of having inclined God's heart to them, they don't see that he hears their prayers at all, as they expected he would; and sometimes there have been great temptations arising hence to leave off seeking, and to yield up the case. But as they are still more terrified with fears of perishing, and their former hopes of prevailing on God to be merciful to them in a great measure fail; sometimes their religious affections have turned into heart-risings against God, because that he won't pity them, and seems to have little regard to their distress and piteous cries, and to all the pains that they take. They think of the mercy that God has shown to others, how soon, and how easily others have obtained comfort, and those too that were worse than they, and have not labored so much as they have done, and sometimes they have had even dreadful blasphemous thoughts in these circumstances.

But when they reflect on these wicked workings of heart against God, if their convictions are continued, and the Spirit of God is not provoked utterly to forsake them, they have more distressing apprehensions of the anger of God towards those whose hearts work after such a sinful manner about him; and it may be have great fears that they have committed the unpardonable sin,[9] or that God will surely never shew mercy to them that are such vipers; and are often tempted to leave off in despair. But then perhaps by something they read or hear of the infinite mercy of God and all-sufficiency of Christ for the chief of sinners, they have some encouragement and hope renewed; but think that as yet they are not fit to come to Christ; they are so wicked that Christ will never accept of them: and then it may be they set themselves upon a new course of fruitless endeavors in their own strength to make themselves better, and still meet with new disappointments. They are earnest to inquire what they shall do. They don't know but there is something else to be done, in order to their obtaining converting grace, that they have never done yet. It may be they hope that they are something better than they were; but then the pleasing dream all vanishes again. If they are told that they trust too much to their own strength and righteousness, they go about to strive to bring themselves off from it, and it may be,

9. [Cf. above, p. 55.]

think they have done it, when they only do the same thing under a new disguise, and still find no appearance of any good, but all looks as dark as midnight to them. Thus they wander about from mountain to hill, seeking rest and finding none: when they are beat out of one refuge they fly to another, till they are as it were debilitated, broken, and subdued with legal humblings; in which God gives them a conviction of their own utter helplessness and insufficiency, and discovers the true remedy.[1]

When they begin to seek salvation, they are commonly profoundly ignorant of themselves; they are not sensible how blind they are, and how little they can do towards bringing themselves to see spiritual things aright, and towards putting forth gracious exercises in their own souls: they are not sensible how remote they are from love to God, and other holy dispositions, and how dead they are in sin. When they see unexpected pollution in their own hearts, they go about to wash away their own defilements and make themselves clean; and they weary themselves in vain, till God shows them that 'tis in vain, and that their help is not where they have sought it, but elsewhere.

But some persons continue wandering in such a kind of labyrinth ten times as long as others, before their own experience will convince them of their insufficiency; and so it appears not to be their own experience only, but the convincing influence of God's Spirit with their experience, that attains the effect: and God has of late abundantly shown, that he don't need to wait to have men convinced by long and often repeated fruitless trials; for in multitudes of instances he has made a shorter work of it: he has so awakened and convinced persons' consciences, and made them so sensible of their exceeding great vileness, and given 'em such a sense of his wrath against sin as has quickly overcome all their vain self-confidence, and borne them down into the dust before a holy and righteous God.

There have been some who have not had great terrors, but have had a very quick work. Some of those that han't had so deep a conviction of these things before their conversion have, it may be, much more of it afterwards. God has appeared far from limiting himself to any certain method in his proceedings with sinners under legal convictions. In some instances it seems easy for our reasoning powers to discern the methods of divine wisdom, in his dealings with the soul under awakenings; in others his footsteps can't be traced,

1. [This paragraph follows FN-3. For the variata see above, pp. 43–44.]

and his ways are past finding out: and some that are less distinctly wrought upon, in what is preparatory to grace, appear no less eminent in gracious experiences afterwards.

There is in nothing a greater difference, in different persons, than with respect to the time of their being under trouble; some but a few days, and others for months or years. There were many in this town that had been, before this effusion of God's Spirit upon us, for years, and some for many years, concerned about their salvation; though probably they were not thoroughly awakened, yet they were concerned to such a degree as to be very uneasy, so as to live an uncomfortable disquieted life, and so as to continue in a way of taking considerable pains about their salvation, but had never obtained any comfortable evidence of a good estate, who now in this extraordinary time have received light; but many of them were some of the last. They first saw multitudes of others rejoicing, and with songs of deliverance in their mouths, who seemed wholly careless and at ease, and in pursuit of vanity, while they had been bowed down with solicitude about their souls; yea, some had lived licentiously, and so continued till a little before they were converted, and grew up to a holy rejoicing in the infinite blessings God had bestowed upon them.

And whatever minister has a [2] like occasion to deal with souls, in a flock under such circumstances, as this was in the last year, I can't but think he will soon find himself under a necessity greatly to insist upon it with them, that God is under no manner of obligation to shew mercy [3] to any natural man, whose heart is not turned to God: and that a man can challenge nothing, either in absolute justice or by free promise, from anything he does before he has believed on Jesus Christ or has true repentance begun in him. It appears to me, that if I had taught those that came to me under trouble any other doctrine, I should have taken a most direct course utterly to have undone them; I should have directly crossed what was plainly the drift of the Spirit of God in his influences [4] upon them; for if they had believed what I said, it would either have promoted self-flattery and carelessness, and so put an end to their awakenings; or cherished and established their contention and strife with God, concerning his dealings with them and others, and blocked up their way to that humiliation before the sovereign disposer of life and death,

2. [FN-3 reads "the."]
3. [FN-1 reads "any mercy."]
4. [FN-3 reads "influence."]

whereby God is wont to prepare them for his consolations. And yet those that have been under awakenings have oftentimes plainly stood in need of being encouraged, by being told of the infinite and all-sufficient mercy of God in Christ; and that 'tis God's manner to succeed [5] diligence and to bless his own means, that so awakenings and encouragements, fear and hope may be duly mixed and proportioned to preserve their minds in a just medium between the two extremes of self–flattery and despondence, both which tend to slackness and negligence, and in the end to security. I think I have found that no discourses have been more remarkably blessed, than those in which the doctrine of God's absolute sovereignty with regard to the salvation of sinners, and his just liberty with regard to answering [6] the prayers, or succeeding the pains of natural men, continuing such, have been insisted on. I never found so much immediate saving fruit, in any measure, of any discourses I have offered to my congregation, as some from those words, Rom. 3:19, "That every mouth may be stopped"; [7] endeavoring to shew from thence that it would be just with God forever to reject and cast off mere natural men.

In those in whom awakenings seem to have a saving issue, commonly the first thing that appears after their legal troubles is a conviction of the justice of God in their condemnation, in a sense of their own exceeding sinfulness and the vileness of all their performances. In giving account [8] of this, they expressed themselves very variously: some [said] that they saw [9] that God was sovereign, and might receive others and reject them; some, that they were convinced that God might justly bestow mercy on every person in the town, and on every person in the world, and damn themselves to all eternity; some, that they see that God may justly have no regard to all the pains they have taken, and all the prayers they have made; some, that they see that if they should seek and take the utmost pains all their lives, God might justly cast them into hell at last, because all

5. ["Succeed" as a transitive verb in the 18th century meant to make successful, prosper, promote. JE's meaning here is that a sinner's efforts may bring him to salvation only as God pleases to inspire and direct them to that end.]

6. [FN-3 reads "his answering."]

7. [This was JE's text for "The Justice of God in the Damnation of Sinners," one of the awakening sermons preached in the winter of 1734–35. See his *Discourses on Various Important Subjects* (Boston, 1738); also above, pp. 19–21.]

8. [FN-1 reads "an account."]

9. [FN-1 omits "they saw."]

their labors, prayers, and tears cannot make an atonement for the least sin, nor merit any blessing at the hands of God; some have declared themselves to be in the hands of God, that he can and may dispose of them just as he pleases; some, that God may glorify himself in their damnation, and they wonder that God has suffered them to live so long, and has not cast 'em into hell long ago.

Some are brought to this conviction by a great sense of their sinfulness, in general, that they are such vile, wicked creatures in heart and life: others have the sins of their lives in an extraordinary manner set before them, multitudes of them coming just then fresh to their memory; [1] and being set before them with their aggravations; some have their minds especially fixed on some particular wicked practice they have indulged; some are especially convinced by a sight of the corruption and wickedness of their hearts; some, from a view they have of the horridness of some particular exercises of corruption, which they have had in the time of their awakening,[2] whereby the enmity of the heart against God has been manifested; some are convinced especially by a sense of the sin of unbelief, the opposition of their hearts to the way of salvation by Christ, and their obstinacy in rejecting him and his grace.

There is a great deal of difference as to persons' distinctness here; some, that han't so clear a sight of God's justice in their condemnation, yet mention things that plainly imply it. They find a disposition to acknowledge God to be just and righteous in his threatenings, and that they are deserving of nothing: and many times, though they had not so particular a sight of it at the beginning, they have very clear discoveries of it soon afterwards, with great humblings in the dust before God.

Commonly persons' minds immediately before this discovery of God's justice are exceeding restless, and in a kind of struggle and tumult, and sometimes in mere anguish; but generally, as soon as they have this conviction, it immediately brings their minds to a calm, and a before-unexpected quietness and composure; and most frequently, though not always, then the pressing weight upon their spirits is taken away, and a general hope arises that some time or other God will be gracious, even before any distinct and particular discoveries of mercy; and often they then come to a conclusion within

1. [FN-3 reads "memories,' which is grammatically more correct but less characteristic of JE's writing.]

2. [FN-3 reads "awakenings."]

themselves, that they will lie at God's feet and wait his time; and they rest in that, not being sensible that the Spirit of God has now brought them to a frame whereby they are prepared for mercy: for 'tis remarkable that persons, when they first have this sense of the justice of God, rarely in the time of it, think anything of its being that humiliation that they have often heard insisted on, and that others experience.

In many persons, the first conviction of the justice of God in their condemnation which they take particular notice of, and probably the first distinct conviction of it that they have, is of such a nature as seems to be above anything merely legal: though it be after legal humblings, and much of a [3] sense of their own helplessness and of the insufficiency of their own duties; yet it does not appear to be forced by mere legal terrors and convictions; but rather from an high exercise of grace, in saving repentance and evangelical humiliation; for there is in it a sort of complacency of soul, in the attribute of God's justice as displayed in his threatenings of eternal damnation to sinners. Sometimes at the discovery of it, they can scarcely forbear crying out, " 'Tis just! 'Tis just!" Some express themselves, that they see the glory of God would shine bright in their own condemnation; and they are ready to think that if they are damned, they could take part with God against themselves and would glorify his justice therein. And when it is thus, they commonly have some evident sense of free and all-sufficient grace, though they give no distinct account of it, but 'tis manifest, by that great degree of hope and encouragement that they then conceive, though they were never so sensible of their own vileness and ill-deservings as they are at that time.

Some, when in such circumstances, have felt that sense of the excellency of God's justice, appearing in the vindictive exercises of it, against such sinfulness as theirs was, and have had such a submission of mind in their idea of this attribute, and of those exercises of it, together with an exceeding loathing of their own unworthiness, and a kind of indignation against themselves, that they have sometimes almost called it a willingness to be damned; though it must be owned they had not clear and distinct ideas of damnation, nor does any word in the Bible require such self-denial as this. But the truth is, as some have more clearly expressed it, that salvation has appeared

3. [FN-3 reads "the."]

too good for them, that they were worthy of nothing but condemnation, and they could not tell how to think of salvation's being bestowed upon them, fearing it was inconsistent with the glory of God's majesty, that they had so much contemned and affronted.

That calm of spirit that some persons have found after their [4] legal distresses, continues some time before any special and delightful manifestation is made to the soul of the grace of God, as revealed in the Gospel; but very often some comfortable and sweet view of a merciful God, of a sufficient Redeemer, or of some great and joyful things of the Gospel, immediately follows, or in a very little time: and in some, the first sight of their just desert of hell, and God's sovereignty with respect to their salvation, and a discovery of all-sufficient grace, are so near that they seem to go as it were together.

These gracious discoveries that are given, whence the first special comforts are derived, are in many respects very various; more frequently Christ is distinctly made the object of the mind, in his all-sufficiency and willingness to save sinners. But some have their thoughts more especially fixed on God, in some of his sweet and glorious attributes manifested in the Gospel, and shining forth in the face of Christ. Some view the all-sufficiency of the mercy and grace of God; some chiefly the infinite power of God, and his ability to save them, and to do all things for them; and some look most at the truth and faithfulness of God. In some, the truth and certainty of the Gospel in general is the first joyful discovery they have; in others, the certain truth of some particular promises; in some, the grace and sincerity of God in his invitations, very commonly in some particular invitation in the mind, and it now appears real to them that God does indeed invite them. Some are struck with the glory and wonderfulness of the dying love of Christ; and some with the sufficiency and preciousness of his blood, as offered to make an atonement for sin; and others with the value and glory of his obedience and righteousness. In some the excellency and loveliness of Christ chiefly engages their thoughts; in some his divinity, that he is indeed the Son of the living God; and in others, the excellency of the way of salvation by Christ and the suitableness of it to their necessities.

Some have an apprehension of these things so given, that it seems more natural to them to express it by sight or discovery; others think

4. [FN-1 reads "the."]

what they experience better expressed by the realizing conviction, or a lively or feeling sense of heart; meaning, as I suppose, no other difference but what is merely circumstantial or gradual.

There is often in the mind some particular text of Scripture, holding forth some evangelical ground of consolation; sometimes a multitude of texts, gracious invitations and promises flowing in one after another, filling the soul more and more with comfort and satisfaction: and comfort is first given to some while reading some portion of Scripture; but in some it is attended with no particular Scripture at all, either in reading or meditation. In some, many divine things seem to be discovered to the soul as it were at once; others have their minds especially fixing on some one thing at first, and afterwards a sense is given of others; in some with a swifter, and others a slower succession, and sometimes with interruptions of much darkness.

The way that grace seems sometimes first to appear after legal humiliation, is in earnest longings of soul after God and Christ, to know God, to love him, to be humbled before him, to have communion with Christ in his benefits; which longings, as they express them, seem evidently to be of such a nature as can arise from nothing but a sense of the superlative excellency of divine things, with a spiritual taste and relish of 'em, and an esteem of 'em as their highest happiness and best portion. Such longings as I speak of, are commonly attended with firm resolutions to pursue this good forever, together with a hoping, waiting disposition. When persons have begun in such frames, commonly other experiences and discoveries have soon followed, which have yet more clearly manifested a change of heart.

It must needs be confessed that Christ is not always distinctly and explicitly thought of in the first sensible act of grace (though most commonly he is); but sometimes he is the object of the mind only implicitly. Thus sometimes when persons have seemed evidently to be stripped of all their own righteousness, and to have stood self-condemned as guilty of death, they have been comforted with a joyful and satisfying view, that the mercy and grace of God is sufficient for them; that their sins, though never so great, shall be no hindrance to their being accepted; that there is mercy enough in God for the whole world, and the like, when they give no account of any particular or distinct thought of Christ; but yet when the account they give is duly weighed, and they are a little interrogated about it, it appears that the revelation of the mercy of God in the Gospel is the ground of this their encouragement and hope; and that it is indeed the mercy of God through Christ that is discovered to them, and that 'tis depended on in him, and not in any wise moved by anything in them.

So sometimes disconsolate souls amongst us, have been revived and brought to rest in God, by a sweet sense given of his grace and faithfulness, in some special invitation or promise, in which is no particular mention of Christ, nor is it accompanied with any distinct thought of him, in their minds; but yet it is not received as out of Christ, but as one of the invitations or promises made of God to poor sinners through his Son Jesus, as it is indeed: and such persons have afterwards had clear and distinct discoveries of Christ, accompanied with lively and special actings of faith and love towards him.

It has more frequently been so amongst us, that when persons have first had the Gospel ground of relief for lost sinners discovered to them, and have been entertaining their minds with the sweet prospect, they have thought nothing at that time of their being converted. To see that there is such an all-sufficiency in God, and such plentiful provision made in Christ, after they have been borne down and sunk with a sense of their guilt and fears of wrath, exceedingly refreshes them; the view is joyful to them, as 'tis in its own nature glorious, and gives them quite new and more delightful ideas of God and Christ, and greatly encourages them to seek conversion, and begets in them a strong resolution to give up themselves, and devote their whole lives to God and his Son, and patiently to wait till God shall see fit to make all effectual; and very often they entertain a strong persuasion that he will in his own time do it for them.

There is wrought in them a holy repose of soul in God through Christ, and a secret disposition to fear and love him, and to hope for blessings from him in this way. And yet they have no imagination that they are now converted, it don't so much as come into their minds; and very often the reason is that they don't see that they do accept of this sufficiency of salvation that they behold in Christ, having entertained a wrong notion of acceptance; not being sensible that the obedient and joyful entertainment which their hearts give to this discovery of grace is a real acceptance of it. They know not that the sweet complacence they feel in the mercy and complete salvation of God, as it includes pardon and sanctification, and is held forth to them only through Christ, is a true receiving of this mercy or a plain evidence of their receiving it. They expected I know not what kind of act of soul, and perhaps they had no distinct idea of it themselves.

And indeed it appears very plainly in some of them, that before their own conversion they had very imperfect ideas what conversion was: it is all new and strange, and what there was no clear conception of before. 'Tis most evident, as they themselves acknowledge, that the expressions that were used to describe conversion and the graces of God's Spirit, such as a spiritual sight of Christ, faith in Christ, poverty of spirit, trust in God, resignedness to God, etc., were expressions that did not convey those special and distinct ideas to their minds which they were intended to signify; in some respects no more than the names of colors are to convey the ideas to one that is blind from birth.[5]

This town is a place where there has always been a great deal of talk of conversion and spiritual experiences; and therefore people in general had before formed a notion in their own minds what these things were; but when they come to be the subjects of them themselves, they find themselves much confounded in their notions and overthrown in many of their former conceits. And it has been very observable that persons of the greatest understanding, and that had studied most about things of this nature, have been more confounded than others. Some such persons that have lately been converted, declare that all their former wisdom is brought to nought, and that they appear to have been mere babes who knew nothing. It has appeared that none have stood more in need of enlightening and instruction even of their fellow Christians, concerning their own circumstances and difficulties than they; and it has seemed to have been with delight that they have seen themselves thus brought down and become nothing, that free grace and divine power may be exalted in them.

It was very wonderful to see after what manner persons' affections were sometimes moved and wrought upon, when God did as it were suddenly open their eyes and let into their minds a sense of the greatness of his grace, and fullness of Christ, and his readiness to save, who before were broken with apprehensions of divine wrath and sunk into an abyss under a sense of guilt, which they were ready to think was beyond the mercy of God. Their joyful surprise has caused their hearts as it were to leap, so that they have been ready to break forth into laughter, tears often at the same time issuing like

5. [In FN-1 this sentence reads, from the semicolon, "perhaps to some of them it was but little more than the names of colors. . . ."]

a flood and intermingling a loud weeping; and sometimes they han't been able to forbear crying out with a loud voice, expressing their great admiration. In some even the view of the glory of God's sovereignty in the exercises of his grace has surprised the soul with such sweetness, as to produce the same effects. I remember an instance of one, who, reading something concerning God's sovereign way of saving sinners as being self-moved, and having no regard to men's own righteousness as the motive of his grace, but as magnifying himself and abasing man, or to that purpose, felt such a sudden rapture of joy and delight in the consideration of it; and yet then suspected himself to be in a Christless condition, and had been long in great distress for fear that God would not have mercy on him.

Many continue a long time in a course of gracious exercises and experiences, and don't think themselves to be converted, but conclude themselves to be otherwise; and none knows how long they would continue so, were they not helped by particular instruction. There are undoubted instances of some that have lived in this way for many years together; and a continuing in these circumstances of being converted and not believing it, has had various consequences with various persons, and with the same persons at various times; some continue in great encouragement and hope that they shall obtain mercy, in a steadfast resolution to persevere in seeking it, and in an humble waiting for it at God's foot; but very often when the lively sense of the sufficiency of Christ and the riches of divine grace begins to vanish, upon a withdraw of the influences of the Spirit of God, they return to greater distress than ever; for they have now a far greater sense of the misery of a natural condition than before, being in a new manner sensible of the reality of eternal things, and the greatness of God, and his excellency, and how dreadful it is to be separated from him, and to be subject to his wrath; so that they are sometimes swallowed up with darkness and amazement. Satan has a vast advantage in such cases to ply them with various temptations, which he is not wont to neglect. In such a case persons do very much need a guide to lead them to an understanding of what we are taught in the Word of God of the nature of grace, and to help them to apply it to themselves.

I have been much blamed and censured by many, that I should make it my practice, when I have been satisfied concerning persons' good estate, to signify it to them: which thing has been greatly misrepresented abroad, as innumerable other things concerning us, to

prejudice the country against the whole affair. But let it be noted
that what I have undertaken to judge of has rather been qualifications and declared experiences, than persons. Not but that I have
thought it my duty as a pastor to assist and instruct persons in applying Scripture rules and characters to their own case (in doing of
which I think many greatly need a guide); and have, where I thought
the case plain, used freedom in signifying my hope of them to others:
but have been far from doing this concerning all that I have had
some hopes of; and I believe have used much more caution than
many have supposed. Yet I should account it a great calamity to be
deprived of the comfort of rejoicing with those of my flock that have
been in great distress, whose circumstances I have been acquainted
with, when there seems to be good evidence that those that were dead
are alive, and those that were lost are found [cf. Luke 15:24]. I am
sensible the practice would have been safer in the hands of one of a
riper judgment and greater experience; but yet there has seemed to
be an absolute necessity of it on the forementioned accounts; and it
has been found to be that which God has most remarkably owned
and blessed amongst us, both to the persons themselves and others.

Grace in many persons, through this ignorance of their state, and
their looking on themselves still as the objects of God's displeasure,
has been like the trees in winter, or like seed in the spring suppressed
under a hard clod of earth; and many in such cases have labored to
their utmost to divert their minds from the pleasing and joyful views
they have had, and to suppress those consolations and gracious affec-
tations that arose thereupon. And when it has once come into their
minds to inquire whether or no this was not true grace, they have
been much afraid lest they should be deceived with common illumi-
nations and flashes of affection, and eternally undone with a false
hope. But when they have been better instructed, and so brought to
allow of hope, this has awakened the gracious disposition of their
hearts into life and vigor, as the warm beams of the sun in the spring
have quickened the seeds and productions of the earth. Grace being
now at liberty, and cherished with hope, has soon flowed out to their
abundant satisfaction and increase.

There is no one thing that I know of, that God has made such a
means of promoting his work amongst us, as the news of others' conversion; in the awakening [of] sinners and engaging them earnestly
to seek the same blessing, and in the quickening of saints. Though I
have thought that a minister's declaring his judgment about par-

ticular persons' experiences might from these things be justified, yet I am often signifying to my people how unable man is to know another's heart, and how unsafe it is depending merely on the judgment of ministers or others, and have abundantly insisted on it with them that a manifestation of sincerity in fruits brought forth, is better than any manifestation they can make of it in words alone, can be; and that without this, all pretenses to spiritual experiences are vain; as all my congregation can witness. And the people in general, in this late extraordinary time, have manifested an extraordinary dread of being deceived, being exceeding fearful lest they should build wrong, and some of them backward to receive hope, even to a great extreme, which has occasioned me to dwell longer on this part of the narrative.[6]

Conversion is a great and glorious work of God's power, at once changing the heart and infusing life into the dead soul; though that grace that is then implanted does more gradually display itself in some than in others. But as to fixing on the precise time when they put forth the very first act of grace, there is a great deal of difference in different persons; in some it seems to be very discernible when the very time of this was; but others are more at a loss. In this respect there are very many that don't know the time (as has been already observed), that when they have the first exercises of grace, don't know that it is the grace of conversion, and sometimes don't think it to be so till a long time after: and many, even when they come to entertain great hope that they are converted, if they remember what they experienced in the first exercises of grace, they are at a loss whether it was any more than a common illumination; or whether some other, more clear and remarkable experience, that they had afterwards, was not the first that was of a saving nature. And the manner of God's work on the soul is (sometimes especially) very mysterious, and 'tis with the kingdom of God as to its manifestation in the heart of a convert, as is said, Mark 4:26–28, "So is the kingdom of God, as if a man should cast seed into the ground, and should sleep, and rise night and day, and the seed should spring and grow up, he knoweth not how; for the earth bringeth forth [fruit] of herself, first the blade, then the ear, then the full corn in the ear."

In some, converting light is like a glorious brightness suddenly shining in upon a person, and all around him: they are in a re-

6. [FN-3 deletes the last thirteen words of this sentence, placing a period in place of the last comma.]

markable manner brought out of darkness into marvellous light
[I Pet. 2:9]. In many others it has been like the dawning of the day,
when at first but a little light appears, and it may be is presently hid
with a cloud; and then it appears again, and shines a little brighter,
and gradually increases, with intervening darkness, till at length, perhaps, it breaks forth more clearly from behind the clouds. And many
are doubtless ready to date their conversion wrong, throwing by
those lesser degrees of light that appeared at first dawning, and calling some more remarkable experience that [7] they had afterwards,
their conversion; which often in great measure arises from a wrong
understanding of what they have always been taught, that conversion
is a great change, wherein old things are done away, and all things
become new [II Cor. 5:17], or at least from a false arguing from that
doctrine.

Persons commonly at first conversion and afterwards, have had
many texts of Scripture brought to their minds, that are exceeding
suitable to their circumstances, which often come with great power,
and as the Word of God or Christ indeed; and many have a multitude of sweet invitations, promises, and doxologies flowing in one
after another, bringing great light and comfort with them, filling
the soul brimful, enlarging the heart, and opening the mouth in religion. And it seems to me necessary to suppose, that there is an immediate influence of the Spirit of God, oftentimes in bringing texts
of Scripture to the mind: not that I suppose 'tis done in a way of
immediate revelation, without any manner of use of the memory;
but yet there seems plainly to be an immediate and extraordinary
influence, in leading their thoughts to such and such passages of
Scripture, and exciting them in the memory. Indeed in some God
seems to bring texts of Scripture to their minds no otherwise than by
leading them into such frames and mediations, as harmonize with
those Scriptures; but in many persons there seems to be something
more than this.

Those that, while under legal convictions, have had the greatest
terrors, have not always obtained the greatest light and comfort; nor
have they always [had] light most suddenly communicated; but yet, I
think, the time of conversion has generally been most sensible in
such persons. Oftentimes the first sensible change after the extremity
of terrors, is a calmness, and then the light gradually comes in; small
glimpses at first, after their midnight darkness, and a word or two

7. [FN-3 omits "that."]

of comfort, as it were softly spoken to 'em; they have a little taste of the sweetness of divine grace, and the love of a Saviour, when terror and distress of conscience begins to be turned into an humble, meek sense of their own unworthiness before God; and there is felt inwardly, perhaps, some disposition to praise God; and after a little while the light comes in more clearly and powerfully. But yet, I think more frequently, great terrors have been followed with more sudden and great light and comfort; when the sinner seems to be as it were subdued and brought to a calm, from a kind of tumult of mind, then God lets in an extraordinary sense of his great mercy through a Redeemer.

The converting influences of God's Spirit very commonly bring an extraordinary conviction of the reality and certainty of the great things of religion (though in some this is much greater, some time after conversion, than at first); they have that sight and taste of the divinity, or divine excellency, that there is in the things of the Gospel, that is more to convince them than reading many volumes of arguments without it. It seems to me that in many instances amongst us, when the divine excellency and glory of the things of Christianity have been set before persons, and they have at the same time as it were seen, and tasted, and felt the divinity of them, they have been as far from doubting of the truth of them as they are from doubting whether there be a sun, when their eyes are open upon it [8] in the midst of a clear hemisphere, and the strong blaze of his light overcomes all objections against his being. And yet many of them, if we should ask them why they believed those things to be true, would not be able well to express or communicate a sufficient reason to satisfy the inquirer, and perhaps would make no other answer but that they see 'em to be true: but a person might soon be satisfied, by a particular conversation with 'em, that what they mean by such an answer is, that they have intuitively beheld, and immediately felt, most illustrious works and powerful evidence of divinity in them.

Some are thus convinced of the truth of the Gospel in general, and that the Scriptures are the Word of God: others have their minds more especially fixed on some particular great doctrine of the Gospel, some particular truths that they are meditating on; or are in a special manner convinced of the divinity of the things they are reading of, in some portion of Scripture. Some have such convictions in a much more remarkable manner than others: and there are

8. [FN-1 omits "upon it."]

some that never had such a special sense of the certainty of divine
things, impressed upon them with such inward evidence and
strength, have yet very clear exercises of grace; i.e. of love to God, repentance and holiness. And if they be more particularly examined,
they appear plainly to have an inward firm persuasion of the reality
of divine things, such as they don't use to have before their conversion. And those that have the most clear discoveries of divine truth,
in the manner that has been spoken of, can't have this always in
view. When the sense and relish of the divine excellency of these
things fades, on a withdraw of the Spirit of God, they han't the medium of the conviction of their truth at command: in a dull frame
they can't recall the idea, and inward sense they had, perfectly to
mind; things appear very dim to what they did before; and though
there still remains an habitual strong persuasion; yet not so as to exclude temptations to unbelief, and all possibility of doubting, as before: but then at particular times, by God's help, the same sense of
things revives again, like fire that lay hid in ashes.

I suppose the grounds of such a conviction of the truth of divine
things to be just and rational, but yet in some God makes use of
their own reason much more sensibly than in others. Oftentimes
persons have (so far as could be judged) received the first saving conviction from reasoning which they have heard from the pulpit; and
often in the course of reasoning which they are led into in their own
meditations.

The arguments are the same that they have heard hundreds of
times; but the force of the arguments, and their conviction by 'em,
is altogether new; they come with a new and before unexperienced
power: before they heard it was so, and they allowed it to be so; but
now they see it to be so indeed. Things now look exceeding plain to
'em, and they wonder that they did not see 'em before.

They are so greatly taken with their new discovery, and things
appear so plain, and so rational to 'em, that they are often at first
ready to think they can convince others; and are apt to engage in
talk with everyone they meet with, almost to this end; and when they
are disappointed, are ready to wonder that their reasonings seem to
make no more impression.

Many fall under such a mistake as to be ready to doubt of their
good estate, because there was so much use made of their own reason
in the convictions they have received; they are afraid that they have
no illumination above the natural force of their own faculties: and

many make that an objection against the spirituality of their convictions, that 'tis so easy to see things as they now see them. They have often heard that conversion is a work of mighty power, manifesting to the soul what no man nor angel can give such a conviction of; but it seems to them that the things that they see are so plain, and easy, and rational, that anybody can see them: and if they are inquired of, why they never saw so before; they say, it seems to them it was because they never thought of it. But very often these difficulties are soon removed by those of another nature, for when God withdraws, they find themselves as it were blind again; they for the present lose their realizing sense of those things that looked so plain to 'em, and by all that they can do they can't recover it, till God renews the influences of his Spirit.

Persons after their conversion often speak of things of religion as seeming new to them; that preaching is a new thing; that it seems to them they never heard preaching before; that the Bible is a new book: they find there new chapters, new psalms, new histories, because they see them in a new light. Here was a remarkable instance of an aged woman,[9] that had spent most of her days under Mr. Stoddard's powerful ministry; who reading in the New Testament concerning Christ's sufferings for sinners, seemed to be surprised and astonished at what she read, as at a thing that was real and very wonderful, but quite new to her, insomuch that at first, before she had time to turn her thoughts, she wondered within herself that she had never heard of it before; but then immediately recollected herself, and thought that she had often heard of it, and read it, but never till now saw it as a thing real; and then cast in her mind how wonderful this was, that the Son of God should undergo such things for sinners, and how she had spent her time in ungratefully sinning against so good a God, and such a Saviour; though she was a person, as to what was visible, of a very blameless and inoffensive life. And she was so overcome by those considerations, that her nature was ready to fail under them: those that were about her, and knew not what was the matter, were surprised, and thought she was dying.

Many have spoken much of their hearts being drawn out in love to God and Christ; and their minds being wrapped up in delightful contemplation of the glory and wonderful grace of God, and the excellency and dying love of Jesus Christ; and of their souls going forth in longing desires after God and Christ. Several of our young chil-

9. [FN-1 adds "of above 70 years."]

dren have expressed much of this; and have manifested a willingnes
to leave father and mother and all things in the world, to go to be
with Christ. Some persons have had longing desires after Christ
which have risen to that degree as to take away their natura
strength. Some have been so overcome with a sense of the dying love
of Christ to such poor, wretched, and unworthy creatures, as to
weaken the body. Several persons have had so great a sense of the
glory of God, and excellency of Christ, that nature and life has
seemed almost to sink under it; and in all probability, if God had
shewed them a little more of himself, it would have dissolved their
frame. I have seen some, and been in conversation with them in
such frames, who have certainly been perfectly sober, and very re
mote from anything like enthusiastic wildness: and [they] have
talked, when able to speak, of the glory of God's perfections, and the
wonderfulness of his grace in Christ, and their own unworthiness, in
such a manner that can't be perfectly expressed after them. Their
sense of their exceeding littleness and vileness, and their disposition
to abase themselves before God, has appeared to be great in propor
tion to their light and joy.

Such persons amongst us as have been thus distinguished with the
most extraordinary discoveries of God, have commonly in no wise
appeared with the assuming, and self-conceited, and self-sufficient
airs of enthusiasts; but exceedingly the contrary; and are eminent
for a spirit of meekness, modesty, self-diffidence, and low opinion of
themselves: no persons seem to be so sensible of their need of instruc
tion, and so eager to receive it, as some of them; nor so ready to
think others better than themselves. Those that have been thought
to be converted amongst us have generally manifested a longing to
lie low, and in the dust before God; withal complaining of their not
being able to lie low enough.

They very often speak much of their sense of the excellency of the
way of salvation by free and sovereign grace, through the righteousness of Christ alone; and how it is with delight that they renounce
their own righteousness, and rejoice in having no account made of it.
Many have expressed themselves to this purpose, that it would
lessen the satisfaction they hope for in heaven to have it by their own
righteousness, or in any other way than as bestowed by free grace,
and for Christ's sake alone. They speak much of the inexpressible-
ness of what they experience, how their words fail, so that they can in
no wise declare it: and particularly speak with exceeding admiration

of the superlative excellency of that pleasure and delight of soul, which they sometimes enjoy; how a little of it is sufficient to pay 'em for all [1] the pains and trouble they have gone through in seeking salvation; and how far it exceeds all earthly pleasures: and some express much of the sense which these spiritual views give 'em of the vanity of earthly enjoyments, how mean and worthless all these things appear to 'em.[2]

Many, while their minds have been filled with spiritual delights, have as it were forgot their food; their bodily appetite has failed, while their minds have been entertained with meat to eat that others knew not of [John 4:32]. The light and comfort which some of them enjoy, gives a new relish to their common blessings, and causes all things about 'em to appear as it were beautiful, sweet and pleasant to them: all things abroad, the sun, moon and stars, the clouds and sky, the heavens and earth, appear as it were with a cast of divine glory and sweetness upon them. The sweetest joy that these good people amongst us express, is not that which consists in a sense of the safety of their own state, and that now they are out of danger of hell; frequently, in times of their highest spiritual entertainment, this seems to be as it were forgotten.[3] The supreme attention of their minds is to the glorious excellencies of God and Christ, which they have in view; not but that there is very often a ravishing sense of God's love accompanying a sense of his excellency, and they rejoice in a sense of the faithfulness of God's promises, as they respect the future eternal enjoyment of God.

The joy that many of them speak of as that to which none is to be paralleled, is that which they find when they are lowest in the dust, emptied most of themselves, and as it were annihilating themselves before God; when they are nothing and God is all, are seeing their own unworthiness, depending not at all on themselves but alone on Christ, and ascribing all glory to God: then their souls are most in the enjoyment of satisfying rest, excepting that at such times they

1. [FN-3 omits "all."]

2. [In FN-3, the previous three paragraphs are run into one.]

3. [This sentence follows FN-3, for which it was much revised. In FN-1 it reads: "The sweetest joy that these good people amongst us express, though it include in it a delightful sense of the safety of their own state, and that now they are out of danger of hell; yet frequently, in times of their highest spiritual entertainment, this seems not to be the chief object of their fixed thought and meditation."]

apprehend themselves to be not sufficiently self-abased; for then above all times do they long to be lower. Some speak much of the exquisite sweetness, and rest of soul that is to be found in the exercises of a spirit of resignation to God, and humble submission to his will. Many express earnest longings of soul to praise God; but at the same time complain that they can't praise him as they would do, and they want to have others help them in praising him: they want to have everyone praise God, and are ready to call upon everything to praise him. They express a longing desire to live to God's glory, and to do something to his honor; but at the same time cry out of their insufficiency and barrenness, that they are poor impotent creatures, can do nothing of themselves, and are utterly insufficient to glorify their Creator and Redeemer.

While God was so remarkably present amongst us by his Spirit, there was no book so delighted in as the Bible; especially the Book of Psalms, the Prophecy of Isaiah, and the New Testament. Some by reason of their esteem and love to God's Word, have at some times been greatly and wonderfully delighted and affected at the sight of a Bible: and then also, there was no time so prized as the Lord's Day, and no place in this world so desired as God's House. Our converts then remarkably appeared united in dear affection to one another, and many have expressed much of that spirit of love which they felt toward all mankind; and particularly to those that had been least friendly to them. Never, I believe, was so much done in confessing injuries, and making up differences as the last year. Persons after their own conversion have commonly expressed an exceeding desire for the conversion of others: some have thought that they should be willing to die for the conversion of any soul, though of one of the meanest of their fellow creatures, or of their worst enemies; and many have indeed been in great distress with desires and longings for it. This work of God had also a good effect to unite the people's affections much to their minister.

There are some persons that I have been acquainted with, but more especially two, that belong to other towns, that have been swallowed up exceedingly with a sense of the awful greatness and majesty of God; and both of them told me to this purpose, that if they in the time of it, had had the least fear that they were not at peace with this so great a God, they should instantly have died.

It is worthy to be remarked, that some persons by their conversion seem to be greatly helped as to their doctrinal notions of religion; it was particularly remarkable in one, who having been taken captive in his childhood, was trained up in Canada in the popish religion; and some years since returned to this his native place, and was in a measure brought off from popery; but seemed very awkward and dull of receiving any true and clear notion of the Protestant scheme, till he was converted; and then he was remarkably altered in this respect.

There is a vast difference, as has been observed, in the degree, and also in the particular manner of persons' experiences, both at and after conversion; some have grace working more sensibly in one way, others in another. Some speak more fully of a conviction of the justice of God in their condemnation; others more of their consenting to the way of salvation by Christ; some more of the actings of love to God and Christ: some more of acts of affiance, in a sweet and assured conviction of the truth and faithfulness of God in his promises; others more of their choosing and resting in God as their whole and everlasting portion, and of their ardent and longing desires after God, to have communion with him; others more of their abhorrence of themselves for their past sins, and earnest longings to live to God's glory for their time to come: some have their minds [4] fixed more on God; others on Christ, as I have observed before,[5] but it seems evidently to be the same work, the same thing done, the same habitual change wrought in the heart; it all tends the same way, and to the same end; and 'tis plainly the same spirit that breathes and acts in various persons. There is an endless variety in the particular manner and circumstances in which persons are wrought on, and an opportunity of seeing so much of such a work of God will shew that God is further from confining himself to certain steps, and a particular method, in his work on souls, than it may be some do imagine. I believe it has occasioned some good people amongst us, that were before too ready to make their own experiences a rule to others, to be less censorious and more extended in their charity.[6] The work of God has been glorious in its variety, it has the more displayed the manifoldness and unsearchableness of the wisdom of God, and wrought more charity among its people.

There is a great difference among those that are converted as to the degree of hope and satisfaction that they have concerning their own

4. [FN-3 reads "mind."]
5. [FN-1 inserts here: "and am afraid of too much repetition."]
6. [FN-1 adds: "and this is an excellent advantage indeed."]

state. Some have a high degree of satisfaction in this matter almost constantly: and yet it is rare that any do enjoy so full an assurance of their interest in Christ, that self-examination should seem needless to them; unless it be at particular seasons, while in the actual enjoyment of some great discovery, that God gives of his glory and rich grace in Christ, to the drawing forth of extraordinary acts of grace. But the greater part, as they sometimes fall into dead frames of spirit, are frequently exercised with scruples and fears concerning their condition.

They generally have an awful apprehension of the dreadfulness and undoing nature of a false hope; and there has been observable in most a great caution, lest in giving an account of their experiences, they should say too much, and use too strong terms. And many after they have related their experiences, have been greatly afflicted with fears, lest they have played the hypocrite, and used stronger terms than their case would fairly allow of; and yet could not find how they could correct themselves.

I think that the main ground of the doubts and fears that persons, after their conversion, have been exercised with about their own state, has been that they have found so much corruption remaining in their hearts. At first their souls seem to be all alive, their hearts are fixed, and their affections flowing; they seem to live quite above the world, and meet with but little difficulty in religious exercises; and they are ready to think it will always be so. Though they are truly abased [7] under a sense of their vileness by reason of former acts of sin, yet they are not then sufficiently sensible what corruption still remains in their hearts; and therefore are surprised when they find that they begin to be in dull and dead frames, to be troubled with wandering thoughts in the time of public and private worship, and to be utterly unable to keep themselves from 'em; also when they find themselves unaffected at seasons in which, they think, there is the greatest occasion to be affected; and when they feel worldly dispositions working in them, and it may be pride and envy, and stirrings of revenge, or some ill spirit towards some person that has injured them, as well as other workings of indwelling sin: their hearts are almost sunk with the disappointment; and they are ready presently to think that all this they have met with is nothing, and that they are mere hypocrites.

They are ready to argue, that if God had indeed done such great

7. [FN-1 reads "abused." JE corrected this in his own hand.]

things for them, as they hoped, such ingratitude would be inconsistent with it. They cry out of the hardness and wickedness of their hearts; and say there is so much corruption, that it seems to them impossible that there should be any goodness there: and many of them seem to be much more sensible how corrupt their hearts are, than ever they were before they were converted; and some have been too ready to be impressed with fear, that instead of becoming better, they are grown much worse, and make it an argument against the goodness of their state. But in truth, the case seems plainly to be, that now they feel the pain of their own wounds; they have a watchful eye upon their hearts, that they don't use to have: they take more notice what sin is there, and sin is now more burdensome to 'em, they strive more against it, and feel more of the strength of it.

They are somewhat surprised that they should in this respect find themselves so different from the idea that they generally had entertained of godly persons; for though grace be indeed of a far more excellent nature than they imagined; yet those that are godly have much less of it, and much more remaining corruption, than they thought. They never realized it, that persons were wont to meet with such difficulties, after they were once converted. When they are thus exercised with doubts about their state, through the deadness of their frames of spirit, as long as these frames last, they are commonly unable to satisfy themselves of the truth of their grace, by all their self-examination. When they hear of the signs of grace laid down for 'em to try themselves by, they are often so clouded that they don't know how to apply them: they hardly know whether they have such and such things in them or no, and whether they have experienced them or not: that which was sweetest, and best and most distinguishing in their experiences, they can't recover a sense or idea of. But on a return of the influences of the Spirit of God, to revive the lively actings of grace, the light breaks through the cloud, and doubting and darkness soon vanish away.

Persons are often revived out of their dead and dark frames by religious conversation: while they are talking of divine things, or ever they are aware, their souls are carried away into holy exercises with abundant pleasure. And oftentimes, while they are relating their past experiences to their Christian brethren, they have a fresh sense of them revived, and the same experiences in a degree again renewed. Sometimes while persons are exercised in mind with several objections against the goodness of their state, they have Scriptures, one after another, coming to their minds, to answer their scruples and unravel their difficulties, exceeding apposite and proper to their circumstances; by which means their darkness is scattered; and often before the bestowment of any new remarkable comforts, especially after long continued deadness and ill frames, there are renewed humblings, in a great sense of their own exceeding vileness and unworthiness, as before their first comforts were bestowed.

Many in the country have entertained a mean thought of this great work that there has been amongst us, from what they have heard of impressions that have been made on persons' imaginations. But there have been exceeding great misrepresentations and innumerable false reports concerning that matter. 'Tis not, that I know of, the profession or opinion of any one person in the town, that any weight is to be laid on anything seen with the bodily eyes: I know the contrary to be a received and established principle amongst us. I cannot say that there have been no instances of persons that have been ready to give too much heed to vain and useless imaginations; but they have been easily corrected, and I conclude it will not be wondered at, that a congregation should need a guide in such cases, to assist them in distinguishing wheat from chaff. But such impressions on the imagination as have been more usual, seem to me to be plainly no other than what is to be expected in human nature in such circumstances, and what is the natural result of the strong exercise of the mind, and impressions on the heart.

I do not suppose that they themselves imagined that they saw anything with their bodily eyes; but only have had within them ideas strongly impressed, and as it were, lively pictures in their minds: as for instance, some when in great terrors, through fear of hell, have had lively ideas of a dreadful furnace. Some, when their hearts have been strongly impressed, and their affections greatly moved with a sense of the beauty and excellency of Christ, it has wrought on their imaginations so, that together with a sense of his glorious spiritual perfections, there has arisen in the mind an idea of one of glorious majesty, and of a sweet and a gracious aspect. So some, when they have been greatly affected with Christ's death, have at the same time a lively idea of Christ hanging upon the cross, and of his blood running from his wounds; which things won't be wondered at by them that have observed how strong affections about temporal matters will excite lively ideas and pictures of different things in the mind.

But yet the vigorous exercise of the mind does doubtless more strongly impress it with imaginary ideas, in some than others; which probably may arise from the difference of constitution, and seems evidently in some, partly to arise from their peculiar circumstances. When persons have been exercised with extreme terrors, and there is a sudden change to light and joy, the imagination seems more susceptive of strong ideas, and the inferior powers, and even the frame of the body, is much more affected and wrought upon, than when the same persons have as great spiritual light and joy afterwards; of which it might, perhaps, be easy to give a reason. The aforementioned Rev. Messrs. Lord and Owen,[8] who, I believe, are esteemed persons of learning and discretion where they are best known, declared that they found these impressions on persons' imaginations quite different things from what fame had before represented to them, and that they were what none need to wonder at, or be stumbled by, or to that purpose.

There have indeed been some few instances of impressions on persons' imaginations, that have been something mysterious to me, and I have been at a loss about them; for though it has been exceeding evident to me by many things that appeared in them, both then (when they related them) and afterwards, that they indeed had a great sense of the spiritual excellency of divine things accompanying them; yet I have not been able well to satisfy myself, whether their imaginary ideas have been more than could naturally arise from their spiritual sense of things. However, I have used the utmost caution in such cases; great care has been taken both in public and in private to teach persons the difference between what is spiritual and what is merely imaginary. I have often warned persons not to lay the stress of their hope on any ideas of any outward glory, or any external thing whatsoever, and have met with no opposition in such instructions. But 'tis not strange if some weaker persons, in giving an account of their experiences, have not so prudently distinguished between the spiritual and imaginary part; which some that have not been well affected to religion, might take advantage of.

There has been much talk in many parts of the country, as though the people have symbolized with the Quakers, and the Quakers themselves have been moved with such reports; and came here, once and again, hoping to find good waters to fish in; but without the least success, and seemed to be discouraged and have left off coming. There

8. [Above, p. 155.]

have also been reports spread about the country, as though the first occasion of so remarkable a concern on people's minds here, was an apprehension that the world was near to an end, which was altogether a false report. Indeed, after this stirring and concern became so general and extraordinary, as has been related, the minds of some were filled with speculation, what so great a dispensation of divine providence might forebode: and some reports were heard from abroad, as though certain divines and others thought the conflagration was nigh; but such reports were never generally looked upon [as] worthy of notice.

The work that has now been wrought on souls is evidently the same that was wrought in my venerable predecessor's days; as I have had abundant opportunity to know, having been in the ministry here two years with him, and so conversed with a considerable number that my grandfather thought to be savingly converted in that time; and having been particularly acquainted with the experiences of many that were converted under his ministry before. And I know no one of them, that in the least doubts of its being the same spirit and the same work. Persons have now no otherwise been subject to impressions on their imaginations than formerly: the work is of the same nature, and has not been attended with any extraordinary circumstances, excepting such as are analogous to the extraordinary degree of it before described. And God's people that were formerly converted, have now partook of the same shower of divine blessing in the renewing, strengthening, edifying influences of the Spirit of God, that others have, in his converting influences; and the work here has also been plainly the same with that which has been wrought in those of other places that have been mentioned, as partaking of the same blessing. I have particularly conversed with persons about their experiences that belong to all parts of the county,[9] and in various parts of Connecticut, where a religious concern has lately appeared; and have been informed of the experiences of many others by their own pastors.

'Tis easily perceived by the foregoing account that 'tis very [1] much the practice of the people here to converse freely one with another of their spiritual experiences; which is a thing that many have been disgusted at. But however our people may have, in some respects, gone

---

9. [FN-1 reads "country."]
1. [FN-1 reads "very very," probably a typographical error.]

to extremes in it, yet 'tis doubtless a practice that the circumstances of this town, and [of] neighboring towns, has naturally led them into. Whatsoever people are in such circumstances, where all have their minds engaged to such a degree in the same affair, that 'tis ever uppermost in their thoughts; they will naturally make it the subject of conversation one with another when they get together, in which they will grow more and more free: restraints will soon vanish; and they will not conceal from one another what they meet with. And it has been a practice which, in the general, has been attended with many good effects, and what God has greatly blessed amongst us. But it must be confessed, there may have been some ill consequences of it; which yet are rather to be laid to the indiscreet management of it than to the practice itself: and none can wonder, if among such a multitude some fail of exercising so much prudence in choosing the time, manner, and occasion of such discourse, as is desirable.

[*Two Notable Converts*]

But to give a clearer idea of the nature and manner of the operations of God's Spirit, in this wonderful effusion of it, I would give an account of two particular instances. The first is an adult person, a young woman whose name was Abigail Hutchinson. I pitch upon her especially because she is now dead, and so it may be more fit to speak freely of her than of living instances: though I am under far greater disadvantages, on other accounts, to give a full and clear narrative of her experiences, than I might of some others; nor can any account be given but what has been retained in the memories of her near friends, and some others, of what they have heard her express in her lifetime.

She was of a rational understanding family: there could be nothing in her education that tended to enthusiasm, but rather to the contrary extreme. 'Tis in no wise the temper of the family to be ostentatious of experiences, and it was far from being her temper. She was before her conversion, to the observation of her neighbors, of a sober and inoffensive conversation; and was a still, quiet, reserved person. She had long been infirm of body, but her infirmity had never been observed at all to incline her to be notional or fanciful, or to occasion anything of religious melancholy. She was under awakenings scarcely a week, before there seemed to be plain evidence of her being savingly converted.

She was first awakened in the winter season, on Monday, by something she heard her brother say of the necessity of being in good earnest in seeking regenerating grace, together with the news of the conversion of the young woman before mentioned, whose conversion so generally affected most of the young people here.[2] This news wrought much upon her, and stirred up a spirit of envy in her towards this young woman, whom she thought very unworthy of being distinguished from others by such a mercy; but withal it engaged her in a firm resolution to do her utmost to obtain the same blessing; and considering with herself what course she should take, she thought that she had not a sufficient knowledge of the principles of religion to render her capable of conversion; whereupon she resolved thoroughly to search the Scriptures; and accordingly immediately began at the beginning of the Bible, intending to read it through. She continued thus till Thursday: and then there was a sudden alteration, by a great increase of her concern, in an extraordinary sense of her own sinfulness, particularly the sinfulness of her nature and wickedness of her heart, which came upon her (as she expressed it) as a flash of lightning, and struck her into an exceeding terror. Upon which she left off reading the Bible in course as she had begun, and turned to the New Testament, to see if she could not find some relief there for her distressed soul.

Her great terror, she said, was that she had sinned against God. Her distress grew more and more for three days; until (as she said) she saw nothing but blackness of darkness before her, and her very flesh trembled for fear of God's wrath: she wondered and was astonished at herself, that she had been so concerned for her body, and had applied so often to physicians to heal that, and had neglected her soul. Her sinfulness appeared with a very awful aspect to her, especially in three things, viz. her original sin, and her sin in murmuring at God's providence, in the weakness and afflictions she had been under, and in want of duty to parents, though others had looked upon her to excel in dutifulness. On Saturday, she was so earnestly engaged in reading the Bible and other books that she continued in it, searching for something to relieve her, till her eyes were so dim that she could not know the letters. Whilst she was thus engaged in reading, prayer, and other religious exercises, she thought of those words of Christ, wherein he warns us not to be as the heathen, that think they shall be heard for their much speaking [Matt. 6:7]; which, she said, led her to see that she had trusted to her

2. [Above, p. 149.]

own prayers and religious performances, and now she was put to a non-plus, and knew not which way to turn herself, or where to seek relief.

While her mind was in this posture, her heart, she said, seemed to fly to the minister for refuge, hoping that he could give her some relief. She came the same day to her brother, with the countenance of a person in distress, expostulating with him, why he had not told her more of her sinfulness, and earnestly inquiring of him what she should do. She seemed that day to feel in herself an enmity against the Bible, which greatly affrighted her. Her sense of her own exceeding sinfulness continued increasing from Thursday till Monday; and she gave this account of it, that it had been an opinion, which till now she had entertained, that she was not guilty of Adam's sin, nor any way concerned in it, because she was not active in it; but that now she saw she was guilty of that sin, and all over defiled by it; and that the sin which she brought into the world with her, was alone sufficient to condemn her.

On the Sabbath day she was so ill that her friends thought it not best that she should go to public worship, of which she seemed very desirous: but when she went to bed on the Sabbath-day night, she took up a resolution that she would the next morning go to the minister, hoping to find some relief there. As she awaked on Monday morning, a little before day, she wondered within herself at the easiness and calmness she felt in her mind, which was of that kind which she never felt before; as she thought of this, such words as these were in her mind: "The words of the Lord are pure words, health to the soul and marrow to the bones." [3] And then these words came to her mind, "The blood of Christ cleanses [us] from all sin" [I John 1:7]; which were accompanied with a lively sense of the excellency of Christ, and his sufficiency to satisfy for the sins of the whole world. She then thought of that expression, " 'tis a pleasant thing for the eyes to behold the sun" [Eccles. 11:7]; which words then seemed to her to be very applicable to Jesus Christ. By these things her mind was led into such contemplations and views of Christ, as filled her exceeding full of joy. She told her brother in the morning that she had seen (i.e. in realizing views by faith) Christ the last night, and that she had really thought that she had not knowledge enough to be converted; "but," says she, "God can make

3. [The first part of the quotation is from Ps. 12:6; the second part appears to be adapted from Prov. 3:8. Cf. also Prov. 16:24.]

it quite easy!" On Monday she felt all day a constant sweetness in her soul. She had a repetition of the same discoveries of Christ three mornings together, that she had on Monday morning, and much in the same manner at each time, waking a little before day; but brighter and brighter every time.

At the last time on Wednesday morning, while in the enjoyment of a spiritual view of Christ's glory and fulness, her soul was filled with distress for Christless persons, to consider what a miserable condition they were in: and she felt in herself a strong inclination immediately to go forth to warn sinners; and proposed it the next day to her brother to assist her in going from house to house; but her brother restrained her, by telling her of the unsuitableness of such a method. She told one of her sisters that day that she loved all mankind, but especially the people of God. Her sister asked her why she loved all mankind. She replied because God had made them. After this, there happened to come into the shop where she was at work, three persons that were thought to have been lately converted; her seeing them as they stepped in one after another into the door so affected her, and so drew forth her love to them, that it overcame her, and she almost fainted: and when they began to talk of the things of religion, it was more than she could bear; they were obliged to cease on that account. It was a very frequent thing with her to be overcome with a flow of affection to them that she thought godly, in conversation with them, and sometimes only at the sight of them.

She had many extraordinary discoveries of the glory of God and Christ; sometimes, in some particular attributes, and sometimes in many. She gave an account that once, as those four words passed through her mind, "wisdom," "justice," "goodness," and "truth," her soul was filled with a sense of the glory of each of these divine attributes, but especially the last; "truth," said she, "sunk the deepest!" And therefore as these words passed, this was repeated, "Truth, truth!" Her mind was so swallowed up with a sense of the glory of God's truth and other perfections, that she said it seemed as though her life was going, and that she saw it was easy with God to take away her life by discoveries of himself. Soon after this she went to a private religious meeting, and her mind was full of a sense and view of the glory of God all the time; and when the exercise was ended, some asked her concerning what she had experienced: and she began to give them an account; but as she was relating it, it revived such a sense of the same things that her strength failed; and they were obliged to take her and lay her upon the bed. Afterwards she was greatly affected, and rejoiced with these words, "Worthy is the Lamb that was slain" [Rev. 5:12].

She had several days together a sweet sense of the excellency and loveliness of Christ in his meekness, which disposed her continually to be repeating over these words, which were sweet to her, "meek and lowly in heart, meek and lowly in heart." [Matt. 11:29] She once expressed herself to one of her sisters to this purpose, that she had continued whole days and whole nights in a constant ravishing view of the glory of God and Christ, having enjoyed as much as her life could bear. Once as her brother was speaking of the dying love of Christ, she told him that she had such a sense of it that the mere mentioning it was ready to overcome her.

Once, when she came to me, she told how that at such and such a time she thought she saw as much of God, and had as much joy and pleasure as was possible in this life, and that yet afterwards God discovered himself yet far more abundantly, and she saw the same things that she had seen before, yet more clearly, and in another, and far more excellent and delightful manner, and was filled with a more exceeding sweetness; she likewise gave me such an account of the sense she once had, from day to day, of the glory of Christ, and of God in his various attributes, that it seemed to me she dwelt for days together in a kind of beatific vision of God; and seemed to have, as I thought, as immediate an intercourse with him as a child with a father: and at the same time, she appeared most remote from any high thought of herself and of her own sufficiency; but was like a little child, and expressed a great desire to be instructed, telling me that she longed very often to come to me for instruction, and wanted to live at my house that I might tell her her duty.

She often expressed a sense of the glory of God appearing in the trees, and growth of the fields, and other works of God's hands. She told her sister that lived near the heart of the town, that she once thought it a pleasant thing to live in the middle of the town, but now, says she, "I think it much more pleasant to sit and see the wind blowing the trees, and to behold⁴ what God has made." She had sometimes the powerful breathings of the Spirit of God on her soul, while reading the Scripture, and would express a sense that she had of the certain truth and divinity thereof. She sometimes would appear with a pleasant smile on her countenance; and once when

4. [FN-1 inserts here, "in the country." See above, p. 44.]

her sister took notice of it, and asked why she smiled, she replied, "I am brimful of a sweet feeling within!" She often used to express how good and sweet it was to lie low before God, and the lower (said [5] she) the better; and that it was pleasant to think of lying in the dust all the days of her life, mourning for sin. She was wont to manifest a great sense of her own meanness and dependence. She often expressed an exceeding compassion and pitiful love, which she found in her heart towards persons in a Christless condition; which was sometimes so strong that as she was passing by such in the streets, or those that she feared were such, she would be overcome by the sight of them. She once said that she longed to have the whole world saved; she wanted, as it were, to pull them all to her; she could not bear to have one lost.

She had great longings to die, that she might be with Christ; which increased till she thought she did not know how to be patient to wait till God's time should come. But once when she felt those longings, she thought with herself, "If I long to die, why do I go to physicians?" Whence she concluded that her longings for death were not well regulated. After this she often put it to herself, which she should choose, whether to live or to die, to be sick, or to be well; and she found she could not tell, till at last she found herself disposed to say these words: "I am quite willing to live, and quite willing to die; quite willing to be sick, and quite willing to be well; and quite willing for anything that God will bring upon me! And then," said she, "I felt myself perfectly easy, in a full submission to the will of God." She then lamented much that she had been so eager in her longings for death, as it argued want of such a resignation to God as ought to be. She seemed henceforward to continue in this resigned frame till death.

After this her illness increased upon her: and once after she had before spent the greater part of the night in extreme pain, she waked out of a little sleep with these words in her heart and mouth: "I am willing to suffer for Christ's sake, I am willing to spend and be spent for Christ's sake; I am willing to spend my life, even my very life for Christ's sake!" [cf. II Cor. 12:15]. And though she had an extraordinary resignation with respect to life or death, yet the thoughts of dying were exceeding sweet to her. At a time when her brother was reading in Job, concerning worms feeding on the dead body [Job 21:26, 24:20], she appeared with a pleasant smile; and

5. [FN-1 reads "says."]

being inquired of about it, she said it was sweet to her to think of her being in such circumstances. At another time, when her brother mentioned to her the danger there seemed to be that the illness she then labored under might be an occasion of her death, it filled her with joy that almost overcame her. At another time, when she met a company following a corpse to the grave, she said it was sweet to her to think that they would in a little time follow her in like manner.

Her illness in the latter part of it was seated much in her throat; and swelling inward, filled up the pipe so that she could swallow nothing but what was perfectly liquid, and but very little of that, and with great and long strugglings and stranglings, that which she took in flying out at her nostrils till she at last could swallow nothing at all. She had a raging appetite to food, so that she told her sister, when talking with her about her circumstances, that the worst bit that she threw to her swine would be sweet to her: but yet when she saw that she could not swallow it, she seemed to be as perfectly contented without it, as if she had no appetite to it. Others were greatly moved to see what she underwent, and were filled with admiration at her unexampled patience. At a time when she was striving in vain to get down a little food, something liquid, and was very much spent with it, she looked up on her sister with a smile, saying, "O Sister, this is for my good!" At another time, when her sister was speaking of what she underwent, she told her that she lived an heaven upon earth for all that. She used sometimes to say to her sister, under her extreme sufferings, "It is good to be so!" Her sister once asked her why she said so. "Why," says she, "because God would have it so: It is best that things should be as God would have 'em: it looks best to me." After her confinement, as they were leading her from the bed to the door, she seemed overcome by the sight of things abroad, as shewing forth the glory of the Being that had made them. As she lay on her deathbed, she would often say these words, "God is my friend!" And once looking up on her sister with a smile, said, "O Sister! How good it is! How sweet and comfortable it is to consider, and think of heavenly things!" And [she] used this argument to persuade her sister to be much in such meditations.

She expressed on her deathbed an exceeding longing, both for persons in a natural state, that they might be converted, and for the godly that they might see and know more of God. And when those that looked on themselves as in a Christless state came to see her, she would be greatly moved with compassionate affection. One in particular that seemed to be in great distress about the state of her soul, and had come to see her from time to time, she desired her sister to persuade not to come any more, because the sight of her so wrought on her compassions that it overcame her nature. The same week that she died, when she was in distressing circumstances as to her body, some of the neighbors that came to see her asked if she was willing to die. She replied that she was quite willing either to live or die; she was willing to be in pain; she was willing to be so always as she was then, if that was the will of God. She willed what God willed. They asked her whether she was willing to die that night. She answered, "Yes, if it be God's will." And [she] seemed to speak all with that perfect composure of spirit, and with such a cheerful and pleasant countenance that it filled them with admiration.

She was very weak a considerable time before she died, having pined away with famine and thirst, so that her flesh seemed to be dried upon her bones; and therefore could say but little, and manifested her mind very much by signs. She said she had matter enough to fill up all her time with talk, if she had but strength. A few days before her death, some asked her whether she held her integrity still, whether she was not afraid of death. She answered to this purpose, that she had not the least degree of fear of death. They asked her why she would be so confident. She answered, "If I should say otherwise, I should speak contrary to what I know: there is," says she, "indeed a dark entry, that looks something dark, but on the other side there appears such a bright shining light, that I cannot be afraid!" She said not long before she died that she used to be afraid how she should grapple with death; but, says she, "God has shewed me that he can make it easy in great pain." Several days before she died, she could scarcely say anything but just yes, and no, to questions that were asked her, for she seemed to be dying for three days together; but seemed to continue in an admirable sweet composure of soul, without any interruption, to the last, and died as a person that went to sleep, without any struggling, about noon, on Friday, June 27, 1735.

She had long been infirm, and often had been exercised with great pain; but she died chiefly of famine. It was, doubtless, partly owing to her bodily weakness that her nature was so often overcome, and ready to sink with gracious affection; but yet the truth was, that she had more grace, and greater discoveries of God and Christ, than the present frail state did well consist with. She wanted to be where strong grace might have more liberty, and be without the clog of a weak body; there she longed to be, and there she doubtless now is. She was looked upon amongst us, as a very eminent instance of Christian experience; but this is but a very broken and imperfect account I have given of her; her eminency would much more appear, if her experiences were fully related, as she was wont to express and manifest them, while living. I once read this account to some of her pious neighbors, who were acquainted with her, who said, to this purpose, that the picture fell much short of the life; and particularly that it much failed of duly representing her humility, and that admirable lowliness of heart, that at all times appeared in her. But there are (blessed be God!) many living instances of much the like nature, and in some things no less extraordinary.

But I now proceed to the other instance that I would give an account of, which is of the little child forementioned.[6] Her name is Phebe Bartlet, daughter of William Bartlet. I shall give the account as I took it from the mouths of her parents, whose veracity none that know them doubt of.

She was born in March, in the year 1731. About the latter end of April, or beginning of May, 1735, she was greatly affected by the talk of her brother, who had been hopefully converted a little before, at about eleven years of age, and then seriously talked to her about the great things of religion. Her parents did not know of it at that time, and were not wont, in the counsels they gave to their children, particularly to direct themselves to her, by reason of her being so young, and as they supposed not capable of understanding: but after her brother had talked to her, they observed her very earnestly to listen to the advice they gave to the other children; and she was observed very constantly to retire several times in a day, as was concluded, for secret prayer; and grew more and more engaged in religion, and was more frequent in her closet; till at last she was wont to visit it five or six times in a day: and was so engaged in it, that nothing would at any time divert her from her stated closet exercises. Her mother often observed and watched her, when such things occurred, as she thought most likely to divert her, either by

6. [Above, p. 158.]

putting it out of her thoughts, or otherwise engaging her inclinations; but never could observe her to fail. She mentioned some very remarkable instances.

She once of her own accord spake of her unsuccessfulness, in that she could not find God, or to that purpose. But on Thursday, the last day of July, about the middle of the day, the child being in the closet where it used to retire, its mother heard it speaking aloud; which was unusual, and never had been observed before. And her voice seemed to be as of one exceeding importunate and engaged; but her mother could distinctly hear only these words (spoken in her childish manner, but seemed to be spoken with extraordinary earnestness, and out of distress of soul): "Pray, blessed Lord, give me salvation! I pray, beg, pardon all my sins!" When the child had done prayer, she came out of the closet, and came and sat down by her mother, and cried out aloud. Her mother very earnestly asked her several times what the matter was, before she would make any answer; but she continued exceedingly crying, and wreathing her body to and fro, like one in anguish of spirit. Her mother then asked her whether she was afraid that God would not give her salvation. She [7] answered, "Yes, I am afraid I shall go to hell!" Her mother then endeavored to quiet her, and told her she would not have her cry; she must be a good girl, and pray every day, and she hoped God would give her salvation. But this did not quiet her at all; but she continued thus earnestly crying, and taking on for some time, till at length she suddenly ceased crying, and began to smile, and presently said with a smiling countenance, "Mother, the kingdom of heaven is come to me!" Her mother was surprised at the sudden alteration, and at the speech; and knew not what to make of it, but at first said nothing to her. The child presently spake again, and said, "There is another come to me, and there is another; there is three." And being asked what she meant, she answered, "One is, 'Thy will be done'; and there is another, 'Enjoy him forever' "; by which it seems that when the child said, "There is three come to me," she meant three passages of its catechism [8] that came to her mind.

After the child had said this, she retired again into her closet; and her mother went over to her brother's, who was next neighbor; and when she came back, the child, being come out of the closet, meets her mother with this cheerful speech, "I can find God now!" referring

7. [FN-1 inserts "then."]
8. [The Westminster Shorter Catechism. Cf. above, p. 73 n. 7.]

to what she had before complained of that she could not find God. Then the child spoke again, and said, "I love God!" Her mother asked her how well she loved God, whether she loved God better than her father and mother; she said, "Yes." Then she asked her whether she loved God better than her little sister Rachel. She answered, "Yes, better than anything!" Then her elder sister, referring to her saying she could find God now, asked her where she could find God. She answered, "In heaven." "Why," said she, "have you been in heaven?" "No," said the child. By this it seems not to have been any imagination of anything seen with bodily eyes, that she called God, when she said, "I can find God now." Her mother asked whether she was afraid of going to hell, and that made her cry. She answered, "Yes, I was; but now I shan't." Her mother asked her whether she thought that God had given her salvation. She answered, "Yes." Her mother asked her, when. She answered, "Today." She appeared all that afternoon exceeding cheerful and joyful. One of the neighbors asked her how she felt herself. She answered, "I feel better than I did." The neighbor asked her what made her feel better. She answered, "God makes me." That evening as she lay abed, she called one of her little cousins to her that was present in the room, as having something to say to him; and when he came, she told him that heaven was better than earth. The next day being Friday, her mother asking her her catechism, asked her what God made her for. She answered, "To serve him," and added, "everybody should serve God, and get an interest in Christ."

The same day the elder children, when they came home from school, seemed much affected with the extraordinary change that seemed to be made in Phebe: and her sister Abigail standing by, her mother took occasion to counsel her, how to improve her time, to prepare for another world: on which Phebe burst out in tears and cried out, "Poor Nabby!" Her mother told her she would not have her cry, she hoped that God would give Nabby salvation; but that did not quiet her, but she continued earnestly crying for some time; and when she had in a measure ceased, her sister Eunice being by her, she burst out again and cried, "Poor Eunice!" and cried exceedingly; and when she had almost done, she went into another room, and there looked upon her sister Naomi: and burst out again, crying "Poor Amy!" Her mother was greatly affected at such a behavior in the child, and knew not what to say to her. One of the neighbors coming in a little after, asked her what she had cried for. She seemed at first backward to tell the reason: her mother told her she might tell that person, for he had given her an apple: upon which she said she cried because she was afraid they would go to hell.

At night a certain minister, that was occasionally in the town, was at the house, and talked considerably [9] with her of the things of religion; and after he was gone she sat leaning on the table, with tears running out of her eyes: and being asked what made her cry, she said it was thinking about God. The next day being Saturday, she seemed [a] great part of the day to be in a very affectionate frame, had four turns of crying, and seemed to endeavor to curb herself and hide her tears, and was very backward to talk of the occasion of it. On the Sabbath day she was asked whether she believed in God; she answered, "Yes." And being told that Christ was the Son of God, she made ready answer and said, "I know it."

From this time there has appeared a very remarkable abiding change in the child: she has been very strict upon the Sabbath; and seems to long for the Sabbath day before it comes, and will often in the week time be inquiring how long it is to the Sabbath day, and must have the days particularly counted over that are between, before she will be contented. And she seems to love God's house, is very eager to go thither. Her mother once asked her why she had such a mind to go, whether it was not to see fine folks. She said no, it was to hear Mr. Edwards preach. When she is in the place of worship, she is very far from spending her time there as children at her age usually do, but appears with an attention that is very extraordinary for such a child. She also appears very desirous at all opportunities to go to private religious meetings; and is very still and attentive at home in prayer time, and has appeared affected in time of family prayer. She seems to delight much in hearing religious conversation: when I once was there with some others that were strangers, and talked to her something of religion, she seemed more than ordinarily attentive; and when we were gone, she looked out very wistly [*sic*, wistfully?] after us, and said, "I wish they would come again!" Her mother asked her why: says she, "I love to hear 'em talk!"

She seems to have very much of the fear of God before her eyes [Ps. 36:1], and an extraordinary dread of sin against him; of which her mother mentioned the following remarkable instance. Some

9. [FN-3 reads "considerable."]

time in August, the last year, she went with some bigger children to get some plums in a neighbor's lot, knowing nothing of any harm in what she did; but when she brought some of the plums into the house, her mother mildly reproved her and told her that she must not get plums without leave, because it was sin: God had commanded her not to steal. The child seemed greatly surprised, and burst out in tears, and cried out, "I won't have these plums!" and turning to her sister Eunice, very earnestly said to her, "Why did you ask me to go to that plum tree? I should not have gone if you had not asked me." The other children did not seem to be much affected or concerned; but there was no pacifying Phebe. Her mother told her she might go and ask leave, and then it would not be sin for her to eat them; and sent one of the children to that end; and when she returned, her mother told her that the owner had given leave, now she might eat them, and it would not be stealing. This stilled her a little while; but presently she broke out again into an exceeding fit of crying: her mother asked her what made her cry again; why she cried now, since they had asked leave. What it was that troubled her now? And asked her several times very earnestly, before she made any answer; but at last [she] said it was because—*because it was sin!* She continued a considerable time crying; and said she would not go again if Eunice asked her an hundred times; and she retained her aversion to that fruit for a considerable time, under the remembrance of her former sin.

She at some times appears greatly affected, and delighted with texts of Scripture that come to her mind. Particularly, about the beginning of November, the last year, that text came to her mind, Rev. 3:20, "Behold, I stand at the door and knock: if any man hear my voice and open the door, I will come in and sup with him, and he with me." She spoke of it to those of the family with a great appearance of joy, a smiling countenance, and elevation of voice, and afterwards she went into another room, where her mother overheard her talking very earnestly to the children about it, and particularly heard her say to them, three or four times over, with an air of exceeding joy and admiration, "Why, it is to sup with God." At some time about the middle of winter, very late in the night, when all were abed, her mother perceived that she was awake, and heard her as though she was weeping. She called to her, and asked her what was the matter. She answered with a low voice, so that her mother could not hear what she said; but thinking that it might be occasioned by some spiritual affection, said no more to her; but perceived her to lie awake, and to continue in the same frame, for a considerable time. The next morning, she asked her whether she did not cry the last night: the child answered, "Yes, I did cry a little, for I was thinking about God and Christ, and they loved me." Her mother asked her whether to think of God and Christ's loving her made her cry: she answered, "Yes, it does sometimes."

She has often manifested a great concern for the good of others' souls: and has been wont many times affectionately to counsel the other children. Once about the latter end of September, the last year, when she and some others of the children were in a room by themselves, a husking Indian corn, the child after a while came out and sat by the fire. Her mother took notice that she appeared with a more than ordinary serious and pensive countenance, but at last she broke silence and said, "I have been talking to Nabby and Eunice." Her mother asked her what she had said to 'em. "Why," said she, "I told 'em they must pray, and prepare to die, that they had but a little while to live in this world, and they must be always ready." When Nabby came out, her mother asked her whether she had said that to them. "Yes," said she, "she said that, and a great deal more." At other times, the child took her opportunities to talk to the other children about the great concern of their souls, sometimes so as much to affect them and set them into tears. She was once exceeding importunate with her mother to go with her sister Naomi to pray: her mother endeavored to put her off; but she pulled her by the sleeve, and seemed as if she would by no means be denied. At last her mother told her that Amy must go and pray herself; "but," says the child, "she will not go"; and persisted earnestly to beg of her mother to go with her.

She has discovered an uncommon degree of a spirit of charity; particularly on the following occasion. A poor man that lives in the woods had lately lost a cow that the family much depended on, and being at the house, he was relating his misfortune, and telling of the straits and difficulties they were reduced to by it. She took much notice of it, and it wrought exceedingly on her compassions; and after she had attentively heard him a while, she went away to her father, who was in the shop, and entreated him to give that man a cow: and told him that the poor man *had no cow!* that the hunters or something else *had killed his cow!* and entreated him to give him one of theirs. Her father told her that they could not spare one. Then she entreated him to let him and his family come and live at his house: and had much more talk of the same nature, whereby she manifested bowels of compassion to the poor [cf. I John 3:17].

She has manifested great love to her minister: particularly when I returned from my long journey for my health, the last fall, when she heard of it, she appeared very joyful at the news, and told the children of it, with an elevated voice, as the most joyful tidings; repeating it over and over, "Mr. Edwards is come home! Mr. Edwards is come home!" She still continues very constant in secret prayer, so far as can be observed (for she seems to have no desire that others should observe her when she retires, but seems to be a child of a reserved temper), and every night before she goes to bed, will say her catechism, and will by no means miss of it: she never forgot it but once, and then after she was abed, thought of it and cried out in tears, "I han't said my catechism!" and would not be quieted till her mother asked her the catechism as she lay in bed. She sometimes appears to be in doubt about the condition of her soul, and when asked whether she thinks that she is prepared for death, speaks something doubtfully about it. At other times [she] seems to have no doubt, but when asked replies "Yes" without hesitation.

[Concluding Observations]

In the former part of this great work of God amongst us, till it got to its height, we seemed to be wonderfully smiled upon and blessed in all respects. Satan (as has been already observed) seemed to be unusually restrained: persons that before had been involved in melancholy, seemed to be as it were waked up out of it; and those that had been entangled with extraordinary temptations, seemed wonderfully to be set at liberty; and not only so, but it was the most remarkable time of health, that ever I knew since I have been in the town. We ordinarily have several bills put up every Sabbath, for persons that are sick; but now we had not so much as one for many Sabbaths together. But after this it seemed to be otherwise, when this work of God appeared to be at its greatest height, a poor weak man [1] that belongs to the town, being in great spiritual trouble, was

---

1. [Thomas Stebbins, identified in the Journal of Deacon Ebenezer Hunt, Judd MSS, *1, 24*; at Forbes Library.]

hurried with violent temptations to cut his own throat, and made an attempt; but did not do it effectually. He after this continued a considerable time exceeding [2] overwhelmed with melancholy; but has now of a long time been very greatly delivered, by the light of God's countenance lifted up upon him [Num. 6:26], and has expressed a great sense of his sin in so far yielding to temptation; and there are in him all hopeful evidences of his having been made a subject of saving mercy.

In the latter part of May, it began to be very sensible that the Spirit of God was gradually withdrawing from us, and after this time Satan seemed to be more let loose, and raged in a dreadful manner. The first instance wherein it appeared was a person's putting an end to his own life, by cutting his throat.[3] He was a gentleman of more than common understanding, of strict morals, religious in his behavior, and an useful honorable person in the town; but was of a family that are exceeding prone to the disease of melancholy, and his mother was killed with it. He had, from the beginning of this extraordinary time, been exceedingly concerned about the state of his soul, and there were some things in his experience, that appeared very hopefully; but he durst entertain no hope concerning his own good estate. Towards the latter part of his time, he grew much discouraged, and melancholy grew amain upon him, till he was wholly overpowered by it, and was in great measure past a capacity of receiving advice, or being reasoned with to any purpose. The Devil took the advantage, and drove him into despairing thoughts. He was kept awake anights, meditating terror; so that he had scarce any sleep at all, for a long time together. And it was observed at last, that he was scarcely well capable of managing his ordinary business, and was judged delirious by the coroner's inquest The news of this extraordinarily affected the minds of people here, and struck them as it were with astonishment. After this, multitudes in this and other towns seemed to have it strongly suggested to 'em, and pressed upon 'em, to do as this person had done. And many that seemed to be under no melancholy, some pious persons that had no special darkness, or doubts about the goodness of their state, nor were under any special trouble or concern of mind about anything spiritual or temporal, yet had it urged upon 'em, as if somebody had spoke to

2. [FN-1 reads "exceedingly."]
3. [Joseph Hawley, JE's uncle by marriage; above, p. 109.]

'em, "Cut your own throat, now is good opportunity: *now, NOW!*"
So that they were obliged to fight with all their might to resist it, and
yet no reason suggested to 'em why they should do it.[4]

About the same time, there were two remarkable instances of persons led away with strange enthusiastic delusions: one at Suffield,
and another at South Hadley. That which has made the greatest
noise in the country was of the man at South Hadley, whose delusion
was that he thought himself divinely instructed to direct a poor man
in melancholy and despairing circumstances, to say certain words
in prayer to God, as recorded in Psalm 116:4, for his own relief. The
man is esteemed a pious man: I have, since this error of his, had a
particular acquaintance with him; and I believe none would question his piety, that had had such an acquaintance. He gave me a particular account of the manner how he was deluded; which is too long
to be here inserted. But in short he was exceedingly rejoiced and
elevated with this extraordinary work, so carried on in this part of
the country; and was possessed with an opinion that it was the beginning of the glorious times of the church spoken of in Scripture:
and had read it as the opinion of some divines, that there would be
many in these times that should be endued with extraordinary gifts
of the Holy Ghost, and had embraced the notion; though he had at
first no apprehensions that any besides ministers would have such
gifts. But he since exceedingly laments the dishonor he has done to
God, and the wound he has given religion in it, and has lain low before God and man for it.

After these things the instances of conversion were rare here in
comparison of what they had before been (though that remarkable
instance of the little child was after this); and the Spirit of God not
long after this time, appeared very sensibly withdrawing from all
parts of the county [5] (though we have heard of its going on in some
places of Connecticut, and that it continues to be carried on even to
this day). But religion remained here, and I believe in some other
places, the main subject of conversation for several months after
this. And there were some turns, wherein God's work seemed something to revive, and we were ready to hope that all was going to be
renewed again: yet in the main there was a gradual decline of that
general, engaged, lively spirit in religion, which had been before.

4. [See above, p. 47.]
5. [FN-1 reads "country." JE noted the correction in his own hand.]

Several things have happened since, that have diverted people's minds, and turned their conversation more to other affairs,[6] particularly His Excellency the Governor's coming up, and the Committee of General Court, on the treaty with the Indians;[7] and afterwards the Springfield controversy;[8] and since that, our people in this town have been engaged in the building of a new meeting-house:[9] and some other occurrences might be mentioned that have seemed to have this effect. But as to those that have been thought to be converted among us, in this time, they generally seem to be persons that have had an abiding change wrought on them: I have had particular acquaintance with many of them since, and they generally appear to be persons that have a new sense of things, new apprehensions and views of God, of the divine attributes, and Jesus Christ, and the great things of the Gospel: they have a new sense of the truth of them, and they affect them in a new manner; though it is very far from being always alike with them, neither can they revive a sense of things when they please. Their hearts are often touched, and sometimes filled, with new sweetnesses and delights; there seems to be an inward ardor and burning of heart that they express, the like to which they never experienced before; sometimes, perhaps, occasioned only by the mention of Christ's name, or some one of the divine perfections: there are new appetites, and a new kind of breathings and pantings of heart, and groanings that cannot be uttered [Rom. 8:26]. There is a new kind of inward labor and struggle of soul towards heaven and holiness.

Some that before were very rough in their temper and manners, seem to be remarkably softened and sweetened. And some have had

6. [FN-3 reads "others affairs," probably a typographical error. FN-1 inserts "as" after the comma.]

7. [Jonathan Belcher (1682–1757) was governor of Massachusetts 1730–41. During the last week of August 1735 he and his councillors came to Deerfield (16 miles north of Northampton) to treat with the Cagnawaga, Housatonic, Scautacook, and Mohawk Indians. (*New England Weekly Journal,* Sept. 2 and 9, 1735. Cf. also Journal of Ebenezer Hunt, Judd MSS, *1,* 26; and Diary of Stephen Williams for Aug. 26–30, 1735.)]

8. [The Breck case; above, p. 113 n. 3. Although this controversy had been simmering since May 1734, it was at its height October–December 1735. Breck was finally ordained on Jan. 26, 1735/6.]

9. [Dedicated Christmas 1737. Assignment of pews in any new meetinghouse invariably roiled the passions of New Englanders; in Northampton it was quite enough to provide the diversion from spiritual concerns which JE lamented.]

their souls exceedingly filled, and overwhelmed with light, love, and comfort, long since the work of God has ceased to be so remarkably carried on in a general way: and some have had much greater experiences of this nature than they had before. And there is still a great deal of religious conversation continued in the town, amongst young and old; a religious disposition appears to be still maintained amongst our people, by their upholding frequent private religious meetings; and all sorts are generally worshipping God at such meetings, on Sabbath nights and in the evening after our public lecture. Many children in the town do still keep such meetings among themselves. I know of no one young person in the town that has returned to former ways of looseness and extravagancy in any respect; but we still remain a reformed people, and God has evidently made us a new people.

I can't say that there has been no instance of any one person that has carried himself so that others should justly be stumbled concerning his profession; nor am I so vain as to imagine that we han't been mistaken concerning any that we have entertained a good opinion of, or that there are none that [1] pass amongst us for sheep, that are indeed wolves in sheep's clothing; who probably may some time or other discover themselves by their fruits.[2] We are not so pure, but that we have great cause to be humbled and ashamed that we are so impure; nor so religious, but that those that watch for our halting may see things in us whence they may take occasion to reproach us and religion: but in the main, there has been a great and marvellous work of conversion and sanctification among the people here; and they have paid all due respects to those who have been blessed of God to be the instruments of it. Both old and young have shewn a forwardness to hearken not only to my counsels, but even to my reproofs from the pulpit.

A great part of the country have not received the most favorable thoughts of this affair; and to this day many retain a jealousy concerning it, and prejudice against it. I have reason to think that the meanness and weakness of the instrument, that has been made use of in this town, has prejudiced many against it; it don't appear to me strange that it should be so: but yet this [3] circumstance of this great work of God is analogous to other circumstances of it. God has so

1. [FN-3 omits "that," probably a typographical error.]
2. [FN-3 reads "fruit."]
3. [FN-1 reads "the." JE noted the correction in his own hand.]

ordered the manner of the work in many respects, as very signally and remarkably to shew it to be his own peculiar and immediate work, and to secure the glory of it wholly to his almighty power and sovereign grace. And whatever the circumstances and means have been, and though we are so unworthy, yet so hath it pleased God to work! And we are evidently a people blessed of the Lord! And here, in this corner of the world, God dwells and manifests his glory.

Thus, Rev. Sir, I have given a large and particular account of this remarkable affair; and yet, considering how manifold God's works have been amongst us, that are worthy to be written, 'tis but a very brief one. I should have sent it much sooner, had I not been greatly hindered by illness in my family, and also in myself. It is probably much larger than you expected, and it may be than you would have chosen. I thought that the extraordinariness of the thing, and the innumerable misrepresentations which have gone abroad of it, many of which have doubtless reached your ears, made it necessary that I should be particular. But I would leave it entirely with your wisdom to make what use of it you think best, to send a part of it to England, or all, or none, if you think it not worthy; or otherwise to dispose of it as you may think most for God's glory, and the interest of religion. If you are pleased to send anything to the Rev. Dr. Guyse, I should be glad to have it signified to him as my humble desire, that since he, and the congregation to which he preached, have been pleased to take so much notice of us as they have, that they would also think of us at the throne of grace, and seek there for us, that God would not forsake us, but enable us to bring forth fruit answerable to our profession, and our mercies, and that our light may so [4] shine before men, that others seeing our good works, may glorify our Father which is in heaven [Matt. 5:16].

When I first heard of the notice the Rev. Dr. Watts and Dr. Guyse took of God's mercies to us, I took occasion to inform our congregation of it in a discourse from these words, "A city that is set upon a hill cannot be hid" [Matt. 5:14]. And having since seen a particular account of the notice the Rev. Dr. Guyse, and the congregation he preached to, took of it, in a letter you wrote to my honored Uncle Williams,[5] I read that part of your letter to the congregation, and labored as much as in me lay to enforce their duty from it. The congregation were very sensibly moved and affected at both times.

4. [FN-3 omits "so."]
5. [Above, p. 113 n. 1.]

I humbly request of you, Rev. Sir, your prayers for this county, in its present melancholy circumstances into which it is brought by the Springfield quarrel,[6] which doubtless above all things that have happened, has tended to put a stop to the glorious work here, and to prejudice this country against it, and hinder the propagation of it. I also ask your prayers for this town, and would particularly beg an interest in them for him who is, honored Sir, with humble respect,

Your obedient son and servant,

Jonathan Edwards.

Northampton
Nov. 6, 1736

6. [Above, p. 113.]

THE DISTINGUISHING MARKS

First delivered as a commencement address at Yale College on September 10, 1741, The Distinguishing Marks *was published later the same year "with great enlargements" and a preface by the Rev. William Cooper of Boston. The texts which follow are those of the first edition, incorporating errata supplied by the printer. For an analysis of the tract and an account of its place in the Great Awakening, see above,* pp. 52–60.

THE
Diſtinguiſhing Marks
Of a Work of the
SPIRIT of GOD.

Applied to that uncommon Opération that has lately appeared on the Minds of many of the People of this Land :

With a particular Conſideration of the extraordinary Circumſtances with which this Work is attended.

A DISCOURSE

Delivered at *New-Haven, September* 10th 1741. Being the Day after the Commencement ;

And now, Publiſhed at the earneſt Deſire of many Miniſters and other Gentlemen that heard it ; with great Enlargements.

By *Jonathan Edwards*, A. M.

Paſtor of the Church of CHRIST at *Northampton.*

With a Preface by the Rev Mr. COOPER of *Boſton.*

Joh 10. 4, 5 *And the Sheep follow him, for they know his Voice ; and a Stranger will they not follow, but will flee from him, for they know not the Voice of Strangers.*

BOSTON : Printed andSold by S. KNEELAND and T. GREEN, in Queenſtreet, over againſt the Priſon. 1741.

PREFACE BY WILLIAM COOPER

THERE are several dispensations, or days of grace, which the church of God has been under from the beginning of time. There is that under the ancient patriarchs; that under the law of Moses; and there is that of the Gospel of Jesus Christ, under which we now are. This is the brightest day that ever shone, and exceeds the other for peculiar advantages. To us who are so happy as to live under the evangelical dispensation, may those words of our Saviour be directed, which he spake to his disciples when he was first setting up the Messiah's kingdom in the world, and Gospel light and power began to spread abroad: "Blessed are the eyes which see the things that ye see. For I tell you, that many prophets and kings have desired to see those things which ye see, and have not seen them; and to hear those things which ye hear, and have not heard them" (Luke 10:23–24).

The Mosaic dispensation, though darkened with types and figures, yet far exceeded the former: but the Gospel dispensation so much exceeds in glory that it doth eclipse the glory of the legal, as the stars disappear when the sun ariseth and goeth forth in his strength. And the chief thing that renders the Gospel so glorious is, that it is the ministration of the Spirit. Under the preaching of it the Holy Spirit was to be poured out in more plentiful measures; not only in miraculous gifts, as in the first times of the Gospel; but in his internal saving operations, accompanying the outward ministry, to produce numerous conversions to Christ, and give spiritual life to souls that were before dead in trespasses and sins, and so prepare them for life eternal. Thus the Apostle speaks, when he runs a comparison between the Old Testament and the New, the law of Moses and the Gospel of Jesus Christ: "For the letter killeth, but the Spirit giveth life. But if the ministration of death, written and engraven in stones was glorious, so that the children of Israel could not steadfastly behold the face of Moses, for the glory of his countenance, which glory was to be done away; how shall not the ministration of the Spirit be rather glorious?" [II Cor. 3:6a–8].

This blessed time of the Gospel, hath several other denominations, which may raise our esteem and value for it. It is called by the evangelical prophet, "the acceptable year of the Lord" [Isa. 61:2], or as it may be read, "the year of liking," or of "benevolence," or of "the good will of the Lord"; because it would be the special period in which he would display his grace and favor in an extraordinary manner, and deal out spiritual blessings with a full and liberal hand. It is also styled by our Saviour, "the regeneration" [Matt. 19:28]; which may refer not only to that glorious restitution of all things, which is looked for at the close of the Christian dispensation, but to the renewing work of grace in particular souls, carried on from the beginning to the end of it.

But few were renewed and sanctified under the former dispensations, compared with the instances of the grace of God in Gospel times. Such numbers were brought into the Gospel church when it was first set up, as to give occasion for that pleasing admiring question, which was indeed a prophecy of it, "Who are these that fly as a cloud, and as the doves to their windows?" [Isa. 60:8]. Then the power of the divine Spirit so accompanied the ministry of the Word, as that thousands were converted under one sermon [Acts 2]. But notwithstanding this large effusion of the Spirit, when Gospel light first dawned upon the world, and that pleasant spring of religion which then appeared on the face of the earth, there was a gradual withdraw of his saving light and influences, and so the Gospel came to be less successful, and the state of Christianity withered in one place and another.

Indeed, at the time of the Reformation from popery, when Gospel light broke in upon the church, and dispelled the clouds of antichristian darkness that covered it, the power of divine grace so accompanied the preaching of the Word, as that it had admirable success in the conversion and edification of souls, and the blessed fruits thereof appeared in the hearts and lives of its professors. That was one of the days of the Son of Man, on which the exalted Redeemer rode forth in his glory and majesty, on the white horse of the pure Gospel, conquering and to conquer; and the bow in his hand, like that of Jonathan's, returned not empty [Rev. 6:2; II Sam. 1:22].

But what a dead and barren time has it now been, for a great while, with all the churches of the Reformation! The golden showers have been restrained; the influences of the Spirit suspended; and the consequence has been that the Gospel has not had any eminent success: conversions have been rare and dubious; few sons and daughters have been born to God; and the hearts of Christians not so quickened, warmed and refreshed under the ordinances, as they have been.

That this has been the sad state of religion among us in this land for many years (except [in] one or two distinguished places, who have at times been visited with a shower of mercy, while other towns and churches have not been rained upon) will be acknowledged by all who have spiritual senses exercised, as it has been lamented by faithful ministers and serious Christians. Accordingly, it has been a constant petition in our public prayers from Sabbath to Sabbath, that God would "pour out his Spirit upon us, and revive his work in the midst of the years" [Joel 2:28; Hab. 3:2]. And besides our annual fast days appointed by the government, most of our churches have set apart days wherein to seek the Lord by prayer and fasting, that he would come and rain down righteousness upon us.

And now, behold! The Lord whom we have sought has suddenly come to his temple [Mal. 3:1]. The dispensation of grace we are now under is certainly such as neither we nor our fathers have seen; and in some circumstances so wonderful, that I believe there has not been the like since the extraordinary pouring out of the Spirit immediately after our Lord's ascension. The apostolical times seem to have returned upon us: such a display has there been of the power and grace of the divine Spirit in the assemblies of his people, and such testimonies has he given to the word of the Gospel.

I remember a remarkable passage of the late reverend and learned Mr. Howe, which I think it may be worth while to transcribe here. It is in his discourse concerning *The Prosperous State of the Christian Church* [sic, *Interest*] *Before the End of Time, by a Plentiful Effusion of the Holy Spirit*, p. 80.[1]

> In such a time (says he), when the Spirit shall be poured forth plentifully, sure ministers shall have their proportionable share. And when such a time as that shall [once] come, I believe you

1. [John Howe (1630–1705) was an English Puritan nonconformist greatly revered in New England. The work here cited consists of fifteen sermons on Ezek. 39:29, preached in 1678, and edited and published by John Evans in London in 1726. The quoted passage extends to p. 81.]

will hear much other kind of sermons, or they will who shall live to such a time, than you are wont to do nowadays: souls will surely be dealt withal at another kind of rate. It is plain (says he), too sadly plain, there is a great retraction of the Spirit of God even from us: we know not how to speak living sense unto souls, how to get within you: our words die in our mouths, or drop and die between you and us. We even faint when we speak; long experienced unsuccessfulness makes us despond: we speak not as persons that hope to prevail, that expect to make you serious, heavenly, mindful of God, and to walk more like Christians. The methods of alluring and convincing souls, even that some of us have known, are lost from amongst us in a great part. There have been other ways taken, than we can tell now how to fall upon, for the mollifying of the obdurate and the awakening of the secure, and the convincing and persuading of the obstinate, and the winning of the disaffected. Sure there will be a large share, that will come even to the part of ministers, when such an effusion of the Spirit shall be, as is [here] expected [*sic,* signified]: that they shall know how to speak to better purpose, with more compassion, [and some] with more seriousness, with more authority and allurement, than we now find we can.

Thus he.

Agreeable to the just expectation of this great and excellent man, we have found it in this remarkable day. A number of preachers have appeared among us, to whom God has given such a large measure of his Spirit, that we are ready sometimes to apply to them the character given of Barnabas, that "he was a good man, and full of the Holy Ghost, and of faith" (Acts 11:24). They preach the Gospel of the grace of God from place to place with uncommon zeal and assiduity. The doctrines they insist on, are the doctrines of the Reformation, under the influence whereof the power of godliness so flourished in the last century. The points on which their preaching mainly turns, are those important ones of man's guilt, corruption, and impotence; supernatural regeneration by the Spirit of God, and free justification by faith in the righteousness of Christ; and the marks of the new birth. The manner of their preaching is not with the enticing words of man's wisdom: howbeit, they speak wisdom among them that are perfect [I Cor. 2:4, 6]. An ardent love to Christ and souls warms their breasts and animates their labors. God has made these his ministers active spirits, a flame of fire in his service: and his word in their mouths has been as a fire; and as a hammer that breaketh the rock in pieces [Ps. 104:4 and Heb. 1:7; Jer. 23:29]. In most places where they have labored, God has evidently wrought with them, and confirmed the Word by signs following [Mark 16:20]. Such a power and presence of God in religious assemblies, has not been known since God set up his sanctuary amongst us: he has indeed glorified the house of his glory [Ezek. 37:26; Isa. 60:7].

This work is truly extraordinary in respect of the extent of it. It is more or less on the several provinces that measure many hundred miles on this continent. "He sendeth forth his commandment upon earth; his word runneth very swiftly" [Ps. 147:15]. It has entered and spread in some of the most populous towns, the chief places of concourse and business. And—blessed be God!—it has visited the seats of learning, both here and in a neighboring colony [Connecticut]. O may the Holy Spirit constantly reside in them both, seize our devoted youth, and form them as polished shafts successfully to fight the Lord's battles against the powers of darkness, when they shall be called out to service!

It is extraordinary also with respect to the numbers that have been the subjects of this operation. Stupid sinners have been awakened by hundreds; and the inquiry has been general in some places, "What must I do to be saved?" [Acts 16:30]. I verily believe in this our metropolis, there were the last winter some thousands under such religious impressions as they never felt before.

The work has been remarkable also for the various sorts of persons that have been under the influence of it. These have been of all ages. Some elderly persons have been snatched as brands out of the burning, made monuments of divine mercy, and born to God, though out of due time; as the Apostle speaks in his own case (I Cor. 15:8). But here with us it has lain mostly amongst the young. Sprightly youth have been made to bow like willows to the Redeemer's scepter, and willingly to subscribe with their own hands to the Lord. And out of the mouths of babes, some little children, has God ordained to himself praise, to still the enemy and the avenger [Ps. 8:2; Matt. 21:16]. Of all ranks and degrees: some of the great and rich, but more of the low and poor. Of other countries and nations: Ethiopia has stretched out her hand; some poor Negroes have, I trust, been vindicated into the glorious liberty of the children of God. Of all qualities and conditions: the most ignorant, the foolish things of the world, babes in knowledge have been made wise unto salvation, and taught those heavenly truths which have been hid from the wise and prudent. Some of the learned and knowing among men have had those things revealed to them of the Father in heaven, which flesh and blood do not teach: and of these, some who had gone into the modern notions, and had no other than the polite religion of the present times, have had their prejudices conquered, their carnal reasonings overcome, and their understandings made to bow to Gospel mysteries; they now receive the truth as it is in Jesus, and their faith no longer stands in the wisdom of man, but in the power of God. Some of the most rude and disorderly are become regular in their behavior, and sober in all things. The gay and airy are become grave and serious. Some of the greatest sinners have appeared to be turned into real saints. Drunkards have become temperate: fornicators and adulterers of a chaste conversation; [2] swearers and profane persons have learned to fear that glorious and fearful name, the Lord their God; and carnal worldlings have been made to seek first the kingdom of God and his righteousness. Yea, deriders and scoffers at this work and the instruments of it, have come under its conquering power. Some of this stamp, who have gone to hear the preacher, as some did Paul—"What will this babbler say?"—have not been able to resist the power and the spirit with which he spake; have sat trembling under the Word, and gone away from it weeping; and afterward did cleave unto the preacher, as Dionysius the Areopagite did unto Paul [Acts 17:18, 34]. Divers instances of this kind have fallen under my knowledge. The virtuous and civil have been convinced that morality is not to be relied on for life; and so excited to seek after the new birth, and a vital union to Jesus Christ by faith. The formal professor likewise has been awakened out of his dead formalities and brought under the power of godliness; taken off from his false rests, and brought to build his hopes only on the Mediator's righteousness. At the same time many of the children of God have been greatly quickened and refreshed; have been awakened out of the sleepy frames they were fallen into, and excited to give diligence to make their calling and election sure [II Pet. 1:10]; and have had precious reviving and sealing times. Thus extensive and general the divine influence has been, at this glorious season.

One thing more is worthy [of] remark; and this is the uniformity

2. [I.e. manner of life.]

of the work. By the accounts I have received in letters, and conversation with ministers and others who live in different parts of the land where this work is going on, it is the same work that is carried on in one place and another: the method of the Spirit's operation on the minds of people is the same; though with some variety of circumstances as is usual at other times: and the particular appearances with which this work is attended, that have not been so common at other times, are also much the same. These are indeed objected by many against the work: but though conversion is the same work, in the main strokes of it, wherever it is wrought; yet it seems reasonable to suppose that at an extraordinary season wherein God is pleased to carry on a work of his grace in a more observable and glorious manner, in a way which he would have to be taken notice of by the world; at such a time, I say, it seems reasonable to suppose, there may be some particular appearances in the work of conversion, which are not common at other times, when yet there are true conversions wrought; or some circumstances attending the work may be carried to an unusual degree and height. If it were not thus, the work of the Lord would not be so much regarded and spoken of; and so God would not have so much of the glory of it: nor would the work itself be like to spread so fast; for God has evidently made use of example and discourse in the carrying of it on.

And as to the fruits of this work (which we have been bid so often to wait for), blessed be God!—so far as there has been time for observation they appear to be abiding. I don't mean that none have lost their impressions, or that there are no instances of hypocrisy and apostasy. Scripture and experience lead us to expect these at such a season. It is to me matter of surprise and thankfulness that as yet there have been no more. But I mean that a great number of those who have been awakened are still seeking and striving to enter in at the strait gate [Matt. 7:13]. The most of those who have been thought to be converted, continue to give evidences of their being new creatures, and seem to cleave to the Lord with full purpose of heart. To be sure, a new face of things continues in this town; though many circumstances concur to render such a work not so observable here, as in smaller and distant places. Many things not becoming the profession of the Gospel are in a measure reformed. Taverns, dancing schools, and such meetings as have been called assemblies, which have always proved unfriendly to serious godliness, are much less frequented. Many have reduced their dress and apparel, so as to make them look more like the followers of the humble Jesus. And it has been both surprising and pleasant to see how some younger people, and of that sex too which is most fond of such vanities, have put off the bravery of their ornaments, as the effect and indication of their seeking the inward glories of the King's daughter. Religion is now much more the subject of conversation at friends' houses, than ever I knew it. The doctrines of grace are espoused and relished. Private religious meetings are greatly multiplied. The public assemblies (especially lectures) are much better attended, and our auditories were never so attentive and serious. There is indeed an extraordinary appetite after the sincere milk of the Word.

It is more than a twelvemonth since an evening lecture was set up in this town; there are now several; two constantly on Tuesday and Friday evenings; when some of our most capacious houses are well filled with hearers who by their looks and deportment seem to come to hear that their souls might live. An evening in God's courts is now esteemed better than many elsewhere. There is also great resort to ministers in private. Our hands continue full of work: and many times we have more than we can discourse with distinctly and separately.

I have been thus large and particular, that persons at a distance, who are desirous to know the present state of religion here, into whose hands these papers will come, may receive some satisfaction.

And now, can any be at a loss to what spirit to ascribe this work? To attribute it, as some do, to the Devil, is to make the old serpent like the foolish woman who plucketh down her house with her hands (Prov. 14:1). Our Saviour has taught us to argue otherwise in such a case as this: "Every kingdom divided against itself is brought to desolation; and every city or house divided against itself shall not stand. And if Satan cast out Satan, he is divided against himself: how then shall his kingdom stand?" (Matt. 12:25–26).

That some entertain prejudices against this work, and others revile and reproach it, does not make it look less like a work of God: it would else want one mark of its being so; for the spirit of this world, and the Spirit which is of God, are contrary the one to the other. I don't wonder that Satan rages, and shews his rage in some that are under his influence, when his kingdom is so shaken, and his subjects desert him by hundreds, I hope by thousands.

The prejudices of some, I make no doubt, are owing to the want of opportunity to be rightly informed, and their having received misrepresentations from abroad. Others may be offended because they have not experienced anything like such a work in themselves; and if these things be so, they must begin again, and get another foundation laid than that on which they have built: and this is what men are hardly brought to. And others, perhaps, may dislike the present work because it supports and confirms some principles which they have not yet embraced, and against which such prejudices hang about their minds, as they cannot easily shake off. For 'tis certain these fruits do not grow on Arminian ground. I hope none dislike the work because they have not been used as instruments in it: for if we love our Lord Jesus Christ in sincerity, we shall rejoice to see him increase, though we should decrease [John 3:30].

If any are resolutely set to disbelieve this work, to reproach and oppose it, they must be left to the free sovereign power and mercy of God to enlighten and rescue them. These, if they have had opportunity to be rightly informed, I am ready to think, would have been disbelievers, and opposers of the miracles and mission of our Saviour, had they lived in his days. The malignity which some of them have discovered, to me approaches near to the unpardonable sin; and they had need beware lest they indeed sin the sin which is unto death: for as I believe it can be committed in these days as well as in the days of the apostles, so I think persons are now in more danger of committing it than at other times. I hope these words have dropped from my pen not in an untemperate zeal, but with due caution, and some suitable solemnity of spirit. At least let them come under the awe of that word, Psalm 28:5, "Because they regard not the works of the Lord, nor the operation of his hands, he shall destroy them, and not build them up."

But if any are disposed to receive conviction, have a mind open to light, and are really willing to know of the present work whether it be of God, it is with great satisfaction and pleasure I can recommend to them the following sheets; in which they will find the distinguishing marks of such a work, as they are to be found in the Holy Scriptures, applied to the uncommon operation that has been on the minds of many in this land. Here the matter is tried by the infallible touchstone of the Holy Scriptures, and is weighed in the balances of the sanctuary, with great judgment and impartiality.

A performance of this kind is seasonable and necessary; and I desire heartily to bless God who inclined this his servant to undertake it, and has graciously assisted him in it. The reverend author is known to be a scribe instructed unto the kingdom of heaven [Matt. 13:52]; the place where he has been called to exercise his ministry has been famous for experimental religion; and he has had opportunities to observe this work in many places where it has powerfully appeared, and to converse with numbers that have been the subjects of it; these things qualify him for this undertaking above most. His arguments in favor of the work, are strongly drawn from Scripture, reason, and experience: and I believe every candid judicious reader will say, he writes very free from an enthusiastic or a party spirit. The use of human learning is asserted; a methodical way of preaching, the fruit of study as well as prayer, is recommended; and the exercise of charity in judging others pressed and urged: and those things which are esteemed the blemishes, and are like to be the hindrances of the work, are with great faithfulness cautioned and warned against. Many I believe will be thankful for this publication. Those who have already entertained favorable thoughts of this work, will be confirmed by it; and the doubting may be convinced and satisfied. But if there are any who cannot after all see the signatures of a divine hand on the work, 'tis to be hoped they will be prevailed on to spare their censures, and stop their oppositions, lest haply they should be found even to fight against God [Acts 5:39].

I had yet several things to say, which I see I must suppress, or I shall go much beyond the limits of a preface: and I fear I need to ask pardon, both of the reader and the publishers, for the length I have run already. Only I can't help expressing my wish, that those who have been conversant in this work, in one place and another, would transmit accounts of it to such a hand as the reverend author of this discourse, to be compiled into a narrative like that of the conversions at Northampton which was published a few years ago: [3] that so the world may know this surprising dispensation, in the beginning, progress, and various circumstances of it. This, I apprehend, would be for the honor of the Holy Spirit, whose work and office has been treated so reproachfully in the Christian world. It would be an open attestation to the divinity of a despised Gospel: and it might have a happy effect on other places, where the sound of this marvel-

---

3. [The reference, of course, is to *A Faithful Narrative*. Cooper's suggestion was renewed by JE the following year in *Some Thoughts Concerning the Revival* (below, p. 529), and came to fruition in Thomas Prince, ed., *The Christian History*, published serially in Boston beginning in March 1743.]

ous work would by this means be heard. I can't but think it would be one of the most useful pieces of church history the people of God are blessed with. Perhaps it would come the nearest to the Acts of the Apostles of anything extant; and all the histories in the world do not come up to that: there we have something as surprising, as in the Book of Genesis; and a new creation, of another kind, seems to open to our view. But I must forbear.

I will only add my prayer, that the worthy author of this discourse may long be continued a burning and shining light in the golden candlestick where Christ has placed him [Rev. 1:20]; and from thence diffuse his light through these provinces! That the divine Spirit, whose cause is here espoused, would accompany this, and the other valuable publications of his servant, with his powerful influences; that they may promote the Redeemer's interest, serve the ends of vital religion, and so add to the author's present joy and future crown!

W. Cooper

Boston
Nov. 20, 1741

Beloved, believe not every spirit, but try the spirits whether they are of God; because many false prophets are gone out into the world" (I John 4:1).

The apostolical age, or the age in which the apostles lived and preached the Gospel, was an age of the greatest outpouring of the Spirit of God that ever was; and that both as to the extraordinary influences and gifts of the Spirit, in inspiration and miracles, and also as to his ordinary operations, in convincing, converting, enlightening and sanctifying the souls of men. But as the influences of the true Spirit abounded, so counterfeits did also then abound: the Devil was abundant in mimicking both the ordinary and extraordinary influences of the Spirit of God, as is manifest by innumerable passages of the apostles' writings. This made it very necessary that the church of Christ should be furnished with some certain rules, and distinguishing and clear marks by which she might proceed safely in judging of spirits, and distinguish the true from the false, without danger of being imposed upon. The giving such rules is the plain design of this chapter, where we have this matter more expressly and fully treated of than anywhere else in the Bible. The Apostle here, of set purpose, undertakes to supply the church of God with such marks of the true Spirit as may be plain and safe, and surely distinguishing, and well accommodated to use and practice; and that the subject might be clearly and sufficiently handled, he insists upon it throughout the chapter: which makes it wonderful that what is said in this chapter, is no more taken notice of in this extraordinary day, when that which is so remarkable appears; such an uncommon operation on the minds of people, that is so extensive; and there is such a variety of opinions concerning it, and so much talk about the work of the Spirit.

The Apostle is led to discourse on this subject by an occasional mention of the indwelling of the Spirit, as the sure evidence of an interest in Christ, in the last verse of the foregoing chapter: "And he that keepeth his commandments dwelleth in him, and he in him; and hereby we know that he abideth in us, by the Spirit which he hath given us." Whence we may infer, that the design of the Apostle in this chapter is not only to give marks whereby to distinguish the true Spirit from false in his extraordinary gifts of prophecy and miracles, but also in his ordinary influences on the minds of his people, in order to their union to Christ, and being built up in him; which is also manifest from the marks themselves that are given, which we shall hereafter take notice of.

The words of the text are an introduction to this discourse, of the distinguishing signs of the true and false spirit. Before the Apostle proceeds to lay down these signs, he exhorts the Christians he writes to, to care in this matter. And, 1. Here is the duty of trying the spirits urged, with a caution annexed, against an over credulousness, and a forwardness to admit everything as the work of a true spirit that has that shew or pretext; "Beloved, believe not every spirit, but try the spirits, whether they are of God." 2. The necessity of this duty is shewn from this, that there were many counterfeits; "because many false prophets are gone out into the world." The false apostles and false prophets, that were in those days, did not only pretend to have the Spirit of God in his extraordinary gifts of inspiration, but also to be the great friends and favorites of heaven, and to be eminently holy persons, and so to have much of the ordinary, saving, sanctifying influences of the Spirit of God on their hearts; and we are to look upon these words as a direction to examine and try their pretenses to the Spirit of God, in both these respects.

After the Apostle had thus counseled and warned the Christians he wrote to, with respect to the trial of spirits, he immediately proceeds to give them rules, by which they may safely proceed in judging of everything that had the pretext of being either the ordinary or extraordinary work of the Spirit of God.

My design therefore at this time is to shew what are the true, certain, and distinguishing evidences of a work of the Spirit of God, by which we may proceed safely in judging of any operation we find in ourselves, or see in others.

And here I would observe that we are to take the Scriptures as our guide in such cases: this is the great and standing rule which God has given to his church, to guide them in all things relating to the great concerns of their souls; and 'tis an infallible and sufficient rule. There are undoubtedly sufficient marks given to guide the church of God in this great affair of judging of spirits, without which it would lie open to woeful delusion, and would be remedilessly exposed to be imposed on and devoured by its enemies: and what rules soever we may find in the Holy Scriptures to this end, we need not be afraid to trust to. Doubtless that Spirit that indited the Scriptures knew how to give us good rules, by which to distinguish his operations from all that is falsely pretended to be from him.

This, as I observed before, the Spirit of God has done of set purpose, in the chapter wherein is the text; and done it more particularly and fully than anywhere else: so that in my present discourse, I shall go nowhere else for rules or marks for the trial of spirits, but shall confine myself to those that I find here.

[Negative Signs]

But before I proceed particularly to speak to these, I would prepare my way by first observing negatively, in some instances, what are not signs that we are to judge of a work by, whether it be the work of the Spirit of God or no; and especially, what are no evidences that a work that is wrought amongst a people, is not the work of the Spirit of God.

1. Nothing can certainly be concluded from this, that the work that appears is carried on in a way very unusual and extraordinary. 'Tis no sign that a work is not the work of the Spirit of God, that it is carried on in such a way as the same Spirit of God heretofore has not been wont to carry on his work, provided the variety or difference be such, as may still be comprehended within the limits of those rules which the Scriptures have given to distinguish a work of the Spirit of God by. What we have been used to, or what the church of God has been used to, is not a rule by which we are to judge whether a work be the work of God, because there may be new and extraordinary works of God. God has heretofore wrought in an extraordinary manner; he has brought those things to pass that have been new things, strange works; and has wrought in such a manner as to surprise both men and angels: and as God has done thus in times past, so we have no reason to think but that he will do so still. The prophecies of Scripture give us reason to think that God has still new things to accomplish, and things to bring to pass that have never yet been seen. No deviation from what has hitherto been usual, let it be never so great, is an argument that a work is not the

work of the Spirit of God, if it be no deviation from the rule that God has given, to judge of a work of his Spirit by. The Spirit of God is sovereign in his operations; and we know that he uses a great variety; and we can't tell how great a variety he may use, within the compass of the rules he himself has fixed. We ought not to limit God where he has not limited himself. If a work be never so different from the work of God's Spirit that has formerly been, yet if it only agrees in those things that the Word of God has given us as the distinguishing signs of a work of his Spirit, that is sufficient to determine us entirely in its favor.

Therefore 'tis not reasonable to determine that a work is not the work of God's Spirit, because of the extraordinary degree in which the minds of persons are influenced and wrought upon. If they seem to have an extraordinary conviction of the dreadful nature of sin, and a very uncommon sense of the misery of a Christless condition, or seem to have extraordinary views of the certainty and glory of divine things; and consequent on these apprehensions, are proportionably moved with very extraordinary affections of fear and sorrow, desire, love or joy: or if the change that seems to be made in persons, the alteration in their affections and frames, be very sudden, and the work that is wrought on people's minds seems to be carried on with very unusual swiftness, and the persons that are thus strangely affected are very many, and many of them are very young; and also be very unusual in many other circumstances, not infringing upon Scripture marks of a work of the Spirit; these things are no argument that the work is not a work of the Spirit of God.

The extraordinary and unusual degree of influence, and power of operation, if in its nature it be agreeable to the rules and marks given in the Scripture, is rather an argument in its favor; for by how much the higher degree that is in, which is in its nature agreeable to the rule, so much the more is there of conformity to the rule, and so much the more evident and manifest is that conformity. When things are in small degrees, though they be really agreeable to the rule, yet the nature of them is more difficultly discerned, and 'tis not so easily seen whether it agrees with the rule or no.

There is a great aptness in persons to doubt of things that are strange; especially it is difficult for elderly persons, those that have lived a great while in the world, to think that to be right which they have been never used to in their day, and have not heard of in the days of their fathers. But if it be a good argument that a work is not from the Spirit of God, that 'tis very unusual, then it always was so, and was so in the apostles' days. The work of the Spirit of God that was wrought then, was carried on in a manner that, in very many respects, was altogether new: there were such things then that the Jews, then living, nor their fathers, had never seen nor heard; yea, such as never had been since the world stood. The work was then carried on with more visible and remarkable power than ever had been before; never were there seen before such mighty and wonderful effects of the Spirit of God, in such sudden changes, and such great engagedness and zeal in such multitudes; such a great and sudden alteration in town, cities and countries; such a swift progress, and vast extent of the work; and many other extraordinary circumstances might be mentioned. The great unusualness of the work surprised the Jews; they knew not what to make of it, but could not believe it to be the work of God; many looked upon the persons that were the subjects of it as bereft of reason; as you may see in Acts 2:13 and 26:24, and I Cor. 4:10.

And we have reason from Scripture prophecy to suppose, that at the commencement of that last and greatest outpouring of the Spirit of God, that is to be in the latter ages of the world, the manner of the work will be very extraordinary, and such as never has yet been seen; so that there shall be occasion then to say, as in Isa. 66:8, "Who hath heard such a thing? Who hath seen such things? Shall the earth be made to bring forth in one day? Shall a nation be born at once? For as soon as Zion travailed, she brought forth her children." It may be reasonably expected that the extraordinary manner of the work then, will bear some proportion to the very extraordinary events, and that glorious change in the state of the world, God will be about to bring to pass by it.

2. A work is not to be judged of by any effects on the bodies of men; such as tears, trembling, groans, loud outcries, agonies of body, or the failing of bodily strength. The influence the minds of persons are under, is not to be judged of one way or the other, whether it be from the Spirit of God or no, by such effects on the body; and the reason is, because the Scripture nowhere gives us any such rule. We can't conclude that persons are under the influence of the true Spirit, because we see such effects upon their bodies, because this is not given as a mark of the true Spirit: nor on the other hand, have

we any reason to conclude, from any such outward appearances, that persons are not under the influence of the Spirit of God, because there is no rule of Scripture given us to judge of spirits by, that does, either expressly or indirectly, exclude such effects on the body; nor does reason exclude them. 'Tis easily accounted for from the consideration of the nature of divine and eternal things, and the nature of man, and the laws of the union between soul and body, how a right influence, a true and proper sense of things, should have such effects on the body, even those that are of the most extraordinary kind; such as taking away the bodily strength, or throwing the body into great agonies, and extorting loud outcries. There are none of us but what suppose, and would have been ready at any time to say it, that the misery of hell is doubtless so dreadful, and eternity so vast, that if a person should have a clear apprehension of that misery as it is, it would be more than his feeble frame could bear; and especially, if at the same time he saw himself in great danger of it, and to be utterly uncertain whether he should be delivered from it, yea, and to have no security from it one day or hour. If we consider human nature, we need not wonder that when persons have a very great sense of that which is so amazingly dreadful, and also have a great view of their own wickedness and God's anger, that things seem to them to forebode speedy and immediate destruction. We see the nature of man to be such, that when he is in danger of some calamity that is very terrible to him, and that he looks upon himself greatly exposed to, he is ready upon every occasion to think that *now* it is coming: as when persons' hearts are full of fear, in time of war, looking upon themselves eminently exposed; they are ready to tremble at the shaking of a leaf, and to expect the enemy every minute, and to say within themselves, *"now* I shall be slain." If we should suppose that a person saw himself hanging over a great pit, full of fierce and glowing flames, by a thread that he knew to be very weak, and not sufficient long to bear his weight, and knew that multitudes had been in such circumstances before, and that most of them had fallen and perished; and saw nothing within reach, that he could take hold of to save him; what distress would he be in? How ready to think that *now* the thread was breaking; *now, this minute,* he should be swallowed up in these dreadful flames? And would not he be ready to cry out in such circumstances? How much more those that see themselves in this manner hanging over an infinitely more dreadful pit, or held over it in the hand of God, who at the same time they see to be exceedingly provoked? No wonder they are ready to expect every moment when this angry God will let them drop; and no wonder they cry out of their misery; and no wonder that the wrath of God when manifested but a little to the soul, overbears human strength.[1]

So it may be easily accounted for, that a true sense of the glorious excellency of the Lord Jesus Christ, and of his wonderful dying love, and the exercise of a truly spiritual love and joy, should be such as very much to overcome the bodily strength. We are all ready to own that no man can see God and live; and that 'tis but a very small part of that apprehension of the glory and love of Christ, and exercise of love to him and joy in him, which the saints in heaven are the subjects of, that our present frame can bear: therefore 'tis not at all strange that God should sometimes give his saints such foretastes of heaven, as to diminish their bodily strength. If it was not unaccountable that the Queen of Sheba fainted, and had her bodily strength taken away, when she came to see the glory of Solomon, much less is it unaccountable that she who is the antitype of the Queen of Sheba, viz. the church, that is brought as it were from the utmost ends of the earth, from being an alien and stranger, far off, in a state of sin and misery, should faint when she comes to see the glory of Christ, who is the antitype of Solomon; and especially will be so in that prosperous, peaceful, glorious kingdom, which he will set up in the world in its latter age.

Some object against such extraordinary appearances, that we have no instances of 'em recorded in the New Testament, in the time of the extraordinary effusions of the Spirit that were then. If this should be allowed, I can see no force in the objection, if neither reason, nor any rule of Scripture excludes such things, especially considering what was observed under the foregoing particular. I don't know that we have any express mention in the New Testament of any person's weeping, or groaning, or sighing, through fear of hell, or a sense of God's anger; but is there anybody so foolish as from hence to argue, that in whomsoever these things appear, their convictions are not from the Spirit of God? And the reason why we don't argue thus is, because these are easily accounted for, from what we know of the nature of man, and from what the Scriptures do inform us in general concerning the nature of eternal things, and the nature of the con-

1. [This language is reminiscent of JE's famous Enfield sermon, preached two months previously.]

victions of God's Spirit, so that there is no need that anything should
be said in particular concerning these external, circumstantial effects.
Nobody supposes that there is any need of express Scripture for
every external, accidental manifestation of the inward motion of the
mind: and though such circumstances are not particularly recorded
in sacred history, yet there is a great deal of reason to think, from
the general accounts we have, that it could not be otherwise than
that such things must be in those days. And there is also reason to
think that that great outpouring of the Spirit that then was, was not
wholly without those more extraordinary effects on persons' bodies.
The jailor in particular, seems to have been an instance of that
nature, when he, in the utmost distress and amazement, came trembling, and fell down before Paul and Silas: his falling down at that
time, don't seem to be a designed putting himself into a posture of
supplication, or humble address to Paul and Silas, for he seems not
to have said anything to 'em then; but he first brought them out, and
then he says to them, "Sirs, what must I do to be saved?" (Acts
16:29–30). But his falling down, seems to be from the same cause as
his trembling. The Psalmist gives an account of his crying out aloud,
and a great weakening of his body under convictions of conscience,
and a sense of the guilt of sin, Ps. 32:3–4, "When I kept silence my
bones waxed old, through my roaring all the day long; for day and
night thy hand was heavy upon me, my moisture is turned into the
drought of summer." We may at least argue so much from it, that
such an effect of conviction of sin, may well in some cases be supposed: for if we should suppose anything of an auxesis in the expressions made use of, yet the Psalmist would not represent what was by
that which would be absurd, and which no degree of that exercise
of mind he spoke of, would have any tendency to.

We read of the disciples, Matt. 14:26, that when they saw Christ
coming to them in the storm, and took him for some terrible enemy,
threatening their destruction in that storm, they cried out for fear:
why therefore should it be thought strange, that persons should cry
out for fear, when God appears to them as their terrible enemy, and
they see themselves in great danger of being swallowed up in the
bottomless gulf of eternal misery?

The spouse once and again speaks of herself as overpowered with
the love of Christ, so as to weaken her body, and make her ready to
faint. Cant. 2:5, "Stay me with flagons, comfort me with apples, for
I am sick of love." And chap. 5:8, "I charge you, O ye daughters of

Jerusalem, if ye find my beloved, that ye tell him that I am sick of love." [2] From whence we may at least argue, that such an effect may well be supposed to arise from such a cause in the saints in some cases, and that such an effect will sometimes be seen in the church of Christ.

'Tis a weak objection, that the impressions that enthusiasts are under, have been wont to have a great effect on their bodies. That the Quakers used to tremble, is no argument that Saul, afterwards Paul, and the jailor, did not tremble from real convictions of conscience. Indeed, all such objections from effects on the body, let them be greater or less, seem to be exceeding frivolous: they that argue from hence, are going in the dark; they knew not what ground they go upon, nor what rule they go by. The root and cause of things is to be looked at, and the nature of the operations and affections that persons' minds are under, are what are to be inquired into, and examined by the rule of God's Word, and not the motions of the blood and animal spirits.

3. 'Tis no argument that an operation that appears on the minds of a people, is not the work of the Spirit of God, that it occasions a great ado, and a great deal of noise about religion. For though true religion be of a contrary nature to that of the Pharisees, that was ostentatious, and delighted to set itself forth to the view of men, for their applause; yet such is human nature, that 'tis morally impossible that there should be a great concern, and strong affection, and engagedness of mind amongst a people, that should be general, and what most of them agree in, and yet there be but little said or done that should be publicly observable; or that it should not cause a notable, visible, and open commotion and alteration amongst that people.

Surely 'tis no argument that the minds of persons are not under the influence of God's Spirit, that they are very much moved: for indeed spiritual and eternal things are so great, and of such vast and infinite concern, that there is a great absurdity in men's being but moderately moved and affected by them; and 'tis no argument that they are not moved by the Spirit of God, that they are affected with these things properly, and in some measure, as they deserve, or in

2. [JE accepted without question the traditional view of the Song of Solomon as a celebration of the love-mystical relationship between Christ and the church, his bride.]

some proportion to their importance. And when was there ever any such thing, since the world stood, as a people in general being greatly affected, in any affair whatsoever, without noise or stir? The nature of man will not allow it.

Indeed, Christ says, Luke 17:20, "The kingdom of God cometh not with observation." That is, it won't consist in what is outward and visible; it shall not be like the kingdoms of earthly kings, set up with outward pomp, in some particular place, which shall be especially the royal city, and seat of the kingdom; as Christ explains himself in the words next following, "Neither shall they say, lo here, or lo there; for behold, the kingdom of God is within you." Not that the kingdom of God shall be set up in the world, on the ruins of Satan's kingdom, without a very notable, observable, great effect; a mighty change in the state of things; to the observation and astonishment of the whole world: for such an effect as this is even held forth in the prophecies of Scripture, and is so by Christ himself, mentioned words, vs. 24, "For as the lightning, that lighteneth out of one part under heaven, shineth unto the other part under heaven, so shall also the Son of Man be in his day." This is to distinguish Christ's coming to set up his kingdom from the coming of false Christs which Christ tells us will be in a private manner, in the deserts, and in the secret chambers; whereas this event of setting up the kingdom of God, should be open and public in the sight of the whole world, with clear manifestation, like lightning that can't be hid, but glares in everyone's eyes, and shines from one side of heaven to the other.

And we find that when Christ's kingdom came, by that remarkable pouring out of the Spirit in the apostles' days, it occasioned a great stir and ado everywhere. What a mighty opposition was there in Jerusalem, on occasion of that great effusion of the Spirit that was there? And so what a great ado in Samaria, Antioch, Ephesus, and Corinth, and other places? The affair filled the world with noise, and gave occasion to some to say of the apostles, that they had turned the world upside down, Acts 17:6.

4. 'Tis no argument that an operation that appears on the minds of a people, is not the work of the Spirit of God, that many that are the subjects of it, have great impressions on their imaginations. That persons have many impressions on their imaginations, don't prove that they have nothing else. It is easy to be accounted for, that there

should be much of this nature amongst a people, where a great multitude, of all kinds of constitutions, have their minds engaged with intense thought and strong affection about those things that are invisible; yea, it would be strange if there should not. Such is our nature that we can't think of things invisible, without a degree of imagination. I dare appeal to any man, of the greatest powers of mind, whether or no he is able to fix his thoughts on God or Christ, or the things of another world, without imaginary ideas attending his meditations? And the more engaged the mind is, and the more intense the contemplation and affection, still the more lively and strong will the imaginary idea ordinarily be; especially when the contemplation and affection of the mind is attended with anything of surprise; as when the view a person has is very new, and takes strong hold of the passions, either fear or joy; and when the change of the state and views of the mind is sudden, from a contrary extreme, as from that which was extremely dreadful, to that which is extremely ravishing and delightful: and it is no wonder that many persons don't well distinguish between that which is imaginary, and that which is intellectual and spiritual; and that they are apt to lay too much weight on the imaginary part, and are most ready to speak of that in the account they give of their experiences, especially persons of less understanding and capacity of distinction.

As God has given us such a faculty as the imagination, and has so made us that we can't think of things spiritual and invisible, without some exercise of this faculty, so it appears to me that such is our state and nature, that this faculty is really subservient and helpful to the other faculties of the mind, when a proper use is made of it; though oftentimes when the imagination is too strong, and the other faculties weak, it overbears 'em, and much disturbs them in their exercise. It appears to me manifest in many instances I have been acquainted with, that God has really made use of this faculty to truly divine purposes; especially in some that are more ignorant: God seems to condescend to their circumstances, and deal with them as babes; as of old he instructed his church while in a state of ignorance and minority by types and outward representations. I can see nothing unreasonable in such a supposition. Let others that have much occasion to deal with souls in spiritual concerns, judge whether experience don't confirm it.

It is no argument that a work is not the work of the Spirit of God, that some that are the subjects of it, have in some extraordinary frames, been in a kind of ecstasy, wherein they have been carried beyond themselves, and have had their minds transported into a train of strong and pleasing imaginations, and kind of visions, as though they were wrapped up even to heaven, and there saw glorious sights. I have been acquainted with some such instances; and I see no manner of need of bringing in the help of the Devil into the account that we give of these things; nor yet of supposing them to be of the same nature with the visions of the prophets, or St. Paul's rapture into paradise [II Cor. 12:1–4]. Human nature, under these vehement and intense exercises and affections of mind, which some persons are the subjects of, is all that need be brought into the account. If it may well be accounted for, that persons under a true sense of the glorious and wonderful greatness and excellency of divine things, and soul-ravishing views of the beauty and love of Christ, should have the strength of nature overpowered, as I have already shewn that it may; then I think it is not at all strange, that amongst great numbers that are thus affected and overborne, there should be some persons of particular constitutions that should have their imaginations thus affected: when it is thus, the effect is no other than what bears a proportion and analogy to other effects of the strong exercise of their minds. 'Tis no wonder that when the thoughts are so fixed, and the affections so strong, and the whole soul so engaged and ravished and swallowed up, that all other parts of the body are so affected as to be deprived of their strength, and the whole frame ready to dissolve; I say, 'tis no wonder that in such a case, the brain in particular (especially in some constitutions) which is a part of the body which we know is nextly and most especially affected by intense contemplations and exercises of mind, should be overborne and affected, so that its strength and spirits should for a season be diverted, and so taken off from impressions made on the organs of external sense, and wholly employed in a train of pleasing delightful imaginations, such as the frame the mind is then in disposes it to.

Some persons are ready to interpret such things wrong, and to lay too much weight on them, as though they were prophetical visions, and to look upon what they imagine they see or hear in them as divine revelations, and sometimes significations from heaven of what shall come to pass; which the issue, in some instances I have known, has shown to be otherwise: but yet it appears to me that such things are evidently sometimes from the Spirit of God, though indirectly; that is, as that extraordinary frame of mind they are in, and that strong and lively sense of divine things that is the occasion of them, is from his Spirit; and also as the mind continues in its holy frame, and retains a divine sense of the excellency of spiritual things, even in its rapture: which holy frame and sense is from the Spirit of God, though the imaginations that attend it are but accidental, and therefore there is commonly something or other in them that is confused, improper and false.

5. 'Tis no sign that a work that appears, and is wrought on the minds of people, is not from the Spirit of God, that example is made use of as a great means of it. 'Tis surely no argument that an effect is not from God, that means are made use of in producing it; for we know that 'tis God's manner to make use of means in carrying on his work in the world: and 'tis no more an argument against the divinity of an effect, that this means is made use of, than if it was by any other means. 'Tis agreeable to Scripture that persons should be influenced by one another's good example: the Scripture directs us to set good examples to that end, Matt. 5:16; I Pet. 3:1; I Tim. 4:12; Tit. 2:7; and also directs us to be influenced by the good examples that others set, and to follow them, II Cor. 8:1–7; Heb. 6:12; Phil. 3:17; I Cor. 4:16 and chap. 11:1; II Thess. 3:9; I Thess. 1:7. By which it appears that example is one of God's means; and certainly 'tis no argument that a work is not the work of God, that God's own means are made use of to effect it.

And as 'tis a scriptural way of carrying on God's work, to carry it on by example, so 'tis a reasonable way. 'Tis no argument that men are not influenced by reason, that they are influenced by example. This way of persons holding forth truth to one another, has a tendency to enlighten the mind, and to convince reason. None will deny but that for persons to signify things one to another by words, may rationally be supposed to tend to enlighten each other's minds; but the same things may be signified by actions, and signified much more fully and effectually. Words are of no use any otherwise than as they convey our own ideas to others; but actions, in some cases, may do it much more fully. There is a language in actions; and in some cases, much more clear and convincing than in words.

'Tis therefore no argument against the goodness of the effect, that one affects and stirs up another; or that persons are greatly affected by seeing others so; yea, though the impression that is made upon them should be only by seeing the tokens of great and extraordinary affection in others in their behavior, taking for granted what they are affected with, without hearing them say one word. There may be language sufficient in such a case in their behavior only, to convey their minds to others, and to signify to them the sense of things they have, more than can possibly be done by words only. If a person should see another under some extreme bodily torment, he might receive much clearer ideas, and more convincing evidence what he suffered by his actions in his misery, than he could do only by the words of an unaffected indifferent relator. In like manner he might receive a greater idea of anything that is excellent and very delightful, from the behavior of one that is in actual enjoyment, or one that is sensible through sight and taste, than by the dull narration of one that is unexperienced and insensible himself. I desire that this matter may be examined by the strictest reason.

And there is this argument, that effects that are produced in persons' minds by example are rational, that 'tis manifest that not only weak and ignorant people are much influenced by it, but nothing can be more evident to anyone that observes the world of mankind, than that all sorts of persons, wise and unwise, and even those that make the greatest boasts of strength of reason, are more influenced by reason held forth in this way than almost any other way.

Indeed when religious affections are raised by this means, it is as when persons affected in hearing the Word preached, or any other means, the affections of many prove flashy, and soon vanish, as Christ represents of the stony-ground hearers; but the affections of some that are thus moved by example are abiding, and prove to be of saving issue.

There never yet was a time of remarkable pouring out of the Spirit, and great revival of religion, but that example had a main hand; so it was in the time of the Reformation, and so it evidently was in that great outpouring of the Spirit that was in the apostles' days, in Jerusalem, and Samaria, and Ephesus, and other parts of the world, as will be most manifest to anyone that attends to the accounts we have in the Acts of the Apostles: as in those days one person was moved by another, so one city or town was influenced by the example of another, I Thess. 1:7–8, "So that ye were ensamples to all that believe in Macedonia, and Achaia; for from you sounded out the Word of the Lord, not only in Macedonia and Achaia, but also in every place your faith to Godward is spread abroad."

'Tis no valid objection against examples being made so much use of, that the Scripture speaks of the Word of God as the principal means of carrying on God's work; for the Word of God is the principal means nevertheless, as that is the means by which other means operate, and are made effectual: the sacraments have no effect but by the Word. And so it is that example becomes effectual; for all that is visible to the eye is unintelligible and vain, without the Word of God to instruct and guide the mind. 'Tis the Word of God that is indeed held forth and applied by example, as the Word of the Lord sounded forth to other towns in Macedonia and Achaia, by the example of those that believed in Thessalonica.

That example should be a great means of propagating the church of God seems to be several ways signified in Scripture: it is signified by Ruth's following Naomi out of the land of Moab, into the land of Israel, when she resolved that she would not leave her; but would go whither she went, and would lodge where she lodged; and that Naomi's people should be her people, and Naomi's God her God [Ruth 1:16]. Ruth, who was the mother of David and of Christ, was undoubtedly a great type of the church; upon which account her history is inserted in the canon of the Scripture: in her leaving the land of Moab and its gods, to come and put her trust under the shadow of the wings of the God of Israel, we have a type, not only of the conversion of the Gentile church, but the conversion of every sinner, that is naturally an alien and stranger, but in his conversion forgets his own people, and father's house, and is made nigh, and becomes a fellow citizen with the saints, and a true Israelite [cf. Eph. 2:12–19]. The same seems to be signified in the effect the example of the spouse, when she was "sick of love," has on the "daughters of Jerusalem," i.e. visible Christians, who are represented as being first awakened by seeing the spouse in such extraordinary circumstances, and then converted. See Cant. 5:8–9 and 6:1. And this is undoubtedly one way that "the Spirit and the bride says, Come," Rev. 22:17; i.e. the Spirit *in* the bride. 'Tis foretold, that the work of God should be carried on very much by this means, in the last great outpouring of the Spirit, that should introduce the glorious day of the church so often spoken of in Scripture. Zech. 8:21–23, "And the inhabitants of one city shall go to another, saying, Let us go speedily to pray before the Lord, and to seek the Lord of hosts; I will go also. Yea, many people and strong nations shall come to seek the Lord of hosts in Jerusalem, and to pray before the Lord. Thus saith the

Lord of hosts, in those days it shall come to pass, that ten men shall take hold, out of all languages of the nations, even shall take hold of the skirt of him that is a Jew, saying, We will go with you, for we have heard that God is with you."

6. 'Tis no sign that a work that is wrought amongst a people is not from the Spirit of God, that many that seem to be the subjects of it, are guilty of great imprudences and irregularities in their conduct. We are to consider that the end for which God pours out his Spirit, is to make men holy, and not to make them politicians. 'Tis no wonder at all, that in a mixed multitude of all sorts, wise and unwise, young and old, of weak and strong natural abilities, that are under strong impressions of mind, there are many that behave themselves imprudently. There are but few that know how to conduct them[selves] under vehement affections of any kind, whether they be of a temporal or spiritual nature: to do so requires a great deal of discretion, and strength and steadiness of mind. A thousand imprudences won't prove a work not to be the work of the Spirit of God; yea, if there be not only imprudences, but many things prevailing that are irregular, and really contrary to the rules of God's holy Word. That it should be thus may be well accounted for from the exceeding weakness of human nature, together with the remaining darkness and corruption of those that are yet the subjects of the saving influences of God's Spirit, and have a real zeal for God.

We have a remarkable instance in the New Testament, of a people that partook largely of that great effusion of the Spirit there was in the apostles' days, among whom there nevertheless abounded imprudences and great irregularities; and that is the church of the Corinthians. There is scarce any church more celebrated in the New Testament for being blessed with large measures of the Spirit of God, both in his ordinary influences, in convincing and converting sinners, and also in his extraordinary and miraculous gifts; yet what manifold imprudences, and great and sinful irregularities, and strange confusion did they run into, at the Lord's Supper, and in the exercise of church discipline, and their indecent manner of attending other parts of public worship, and in jarring and contention about their teachers, and even in the exercise of their extraordinary gifts of prophecy, speaking with tongues, and the like, wherein they spake and acted by the immediate inspiration of the Spirit of God?

And if we see great imprudences, and even sinful irregularities in some that are improved as great instruments to carry on the work, it won't prove it not to be the work of God. The Apostle Peter himself, that was a great and eminently holy and inspired apostle, and one of the chief instruments of setting up the Christian church in the world, and one of the chief of the apostles, when he was actually engaged in this work, was guilty of a great and sinful error in his conduct; of which the Apostle Paul speaks, Gal. 2:11–13, "But when Peter was come to Antioch, I withstood him to the face, because he was to be blamed; for before that certain came from James, he did eat with the Gentiles, but when they were come, he withdrew, and separated himself, fearing them that were of the circumcision; and the other Jews dissembled likewise with him; insomuch that Barnabas also was carried away with their dissimulation." If the great pillar of the Christian church, and he who was one of the chief of those that are the very foundations on which, next to Christ, the whole church is said to be built, was guilty of such an irregularity; is it any wonder if other lesser instruments, that have not that extraordinary conduct of the divine Spirit that he had, should be guilty of many irregularities?

And here in particular, it is no evidence that a work is not the work of God, if many that are the subjects of it, or are improved as instruments to carry it on, are guilty of too great a forwardness to censure others as unconverted, through mistakes they have embraced concerning the marks by which they are to judge of others' hypocrisy and carnality; either not duly apprehending the latitude the Spirit of God uses in the methods of his operations, or for want of making due allowance for that infirmity and corruption that may be left in the hearts of the saints; as well as through want of a due sense of their own blindness and weakness, and remaining corruption, whereby spiritual pride may have a secret vent this way, under some disguise, and not be discovered.

If we allow that truly pious men may have a great deal of remaining blindness and corruption, and may be liable to mistakes about the marks of hypocrisy, as undoubtedly all will allow; then 'tis not unaccountable that they should sometimes run into such errors as these: 'tis as easy, and upon some accounts, more easy to be accounted for, why the remaining corruption of good men should sometimes have an unobserved vent this way than most other ways (though it be exceeding unhappy), and without doubt many holy men have erred this way.

Lukewarmness in religion is abominable, and zeal an excellent grace; yet above all other Christian virtues, it needs to be strictly watched and searched; for 'tis that with which corruption, and particularly pride and human passion, is exceeding apt to mix unobserved. And 'tis observable that there never was a time of great reformation, to cause a revival of much of a spirit of zeal in the church of God, but that it has been attended in some notable instances, with irregularity, running out some way or other into an undue severity. Thus in the apostles' days, a great deal of zeal was spent about unclean meats, with heat of spirit in Christians one against another, both parties condemning and censuring one another, as not true Christians; when the Apostle had charity for both, as influenced by a spirit of real piety: "he that eats," says he, "to the Lord he eats, and giveth God thanks; and he that eateth not, to the Lord he eateth not, and giveth God thanks" [Rom. 14:6]. So in the church of Corinth, they had got into a way of extolling some ministers, and censuring others, and were puffed up for one against another: but yet these things were no sign that the work that was then so wonderfully carried on, was not the work of God. And after this, when religion was still greatly flourishing in the world, and a spirit of eminent holiness and zeal prevailed in the Christian church, the zeal of Christians ran out into a very improper and undue severity, in the exercise of church discipline towards delinquents; in some cases they would by no means admit them into their charity and communion, though they appeared never so humble and penitent. And in the days of Constantine the Great, the zeal of Christians against heathenism, ran out into a degree of persecution. So in that glorious revival of religion, in the time of the Reformation, zeal in many instances appeared in a very improper severity, and even a degree of persecution; yea, in some of the most eminent Reformers, as in the great Calvin in particular: and many in those days of the flourishing of vital religion, were guilty of severely censuring others that differed from them in opinion in some points of divinity.

7. Nor are many errors in judgment, and some delusions of Satan intermixed with the work, any argument that the work in general is not the work of the Spirit of God. However great a pouring out of the Spirit there may be, 'tis not to be expected that the Spirit of God should be given now in the same manner that it was to the apostles, infallibly to guide them in points of Christian doctrine,

so that what they taught might be relied on as a rule to the Christian church. And if many delusions of Satan appear at the same time that a great religious concern prevails, it is not an argument that the work in general is not the work of God, any more than it was an argument in Egypt that there were no true miracles wrought there, by the hand of God, because Jannes and Jambres wrought false miracles at the same time by the hand of the Devil [cf. II Tim. 3:8; Exod. 7:11]. Yea, the same persons may be the subjects of much of the influences of the Spirit of God, and yet in some things be led away by the delusions of the Devil; and this be no more of a paradox than many other things that are true of real saints, in the present state, where grace dwells with so much corruption, and the new man and the old man subsist together in the same person; and the kingdom of God and the kingdom of the Devil remain for a while together in the same heart. Many godly persons have undoubtedly in this and other ages, exposed themselves to woeful delusions, by an aptness to lay too much weight on impulses and impressions, as if they were immediate revelations from God, to signify something future, or to direct them where to go and what to do.

8. If some such as were thought to be wrought upon, fall away into gross errors or scandalous practices, 'tis no argument that the work in general is not the work of the Spirit of God. That there are some counterfeits, is no argument that nothing is true: such things are always expected in a time of reformation. If we look into church history, we shall find no instance of great revival of religion, but what has been attended with many such things: instances of this nature in the apostles' days were innumerable, both of those that fell away into gross heresies, and also vile practices; that yet seemed to be the subjects of that work of the Spirit of God that was then, and were accepted for a while amongst those that were truly so, as their brethren, and some of their company, and were not suspected not to be of them, till they went out from them [I John 2:19]. And they were not only private Christians, but teachers and officers, and eminent persons in the Christian church; and some that God had endowed with miraculous gifts of the Holy Ghost; as appears by the beginning of the sixth chapter of Hebrews. An instance of these was Judas, who was one of the twelve apostles, and had long been constantly united to, and intimately conversant with a company of truly experienced disciples, without being discovered or suspected, till he discovered himself by his scandalous practice; and

had been treated by Jesus himself, in all external things, as if he had truly been a disciple, even to the investing him with the character of apostle, and sending him forth to preach the Gospel, and enduing him with miraculous gifts of the Spirit: for though Christ knew him, yet he did not then clothe himself with the character of omniscient judge, and searcher of hearts, but acted the part of a minister of the visible church of God (for he was his Father's minister); and therefore rejected him not, till he had discovered himself by his scandalous practice; thereby giving an example to other guides and rulers of the visible church, not to take it upon them to act the part of searcher of hearts, but to be influenced in their administrations by what is visible and open.

There were some instances then of such apostates, not only in some that for a while were thought true Christians, but some that were esteemed eminently full of the grace of God's Spirit. An instance of this nature was Nicolas, one of the seven deacons; who was looked upon by the Christians in Jerusalem, in the time of that extraordinary pouring out of the Spirit, as a man full of the Holy Ghost, and was chosen out of the multitude of Christians to that office, for that reason; as you may see in Acts 6:3–5; yet he afterwards fell away, and became the head of a set of vile heretics, of gross practices, called from his name the sect of the Nicolaitans, Rev. 2:6 and 15.[3]

So in the time of the Reformation from popery, how great was the number of those that for a while seemed to join with the Reformers, that fell away into the grossest and most absurd errors, and abominable practices.

And 'tis particularly observable that in times of great pouring out of the Spirit to revive religion in the world, a number of those that for a while seemed to partake in it, have fallen off into whimsical and extravagant errors, and gross enthusiasm, boasting of high degrees of spirituality and perfection, censuring and condemning others as carnal. Thus it was with the Gnostics in the apostles' times; and thus it was with the several sects of Anabaptists in the time of the Reformation, as Anthony Burgess observes, in his book called *Spiritual Refining,* Part I, Sermon 23, p. 132: [4]

3. [A tradition unsupported in any ancient writing before Irenaeus (ca. A.D. 175); see his *Against Heresies,* I, xxvi, 3.]

4. [Anthony Burgess (ca. 1610–80) was an English Puritan nonconformist. *Spiritual Refining: Or a Treatise of Grace and Assurance* was a book of 120 sermons published in 1652; a second part, *Spiritual Refining: A Treatise of*

The first worthy Reformers, and glorious instruments of God found a bitter conflict herein; so that they were exercised not only with formalists and traditionary papists on the one side, but men that pretended themselves to be more enlightened than the Reformers were, on the other side: hence they called those that did adhere to the Scripture, and would try revelations by it, "Literists and Vowelists," [5] as men acquainted with the words and vowels of the Scripture, having nothing of the Spirit of God. And wheresoever in any town the true doctrine of the Gospel brake forth to the displacing of popery, presently such opinions arose, like tares that came up among the good wheat, whereby great divisions were raised, and the Reformation made abominable and odious to the world; as if that had been the sun to give heat and warmth to those worms and serpents to crawl out of the ground. Hence they inveighed against Luther, and said he had only promulged a carnal gospel.

Some of the leaders of those wild enthusiasts, had been for a while, highly esteemed by the first Reformers, and peculiarly dear to them.

So in England at the time when vital religion did much prevail in the days of King Charles I, the Interregnum, and Oliver Cromwell, such things as these abounded. And so in the beginning of New England, in her purest days, when vital piety flourished, such kind of things as these broke out. Therefore the Devil's sowing such tares is no proof that a true work of the Spirit of God is not gloriously carried on.

9. 'Tis no argument that a work is not from the Spirit of God, that it seems to be promoted by ministers insisting very much on the terrors of God's holy law, and that with a great deal of pathos and earnestness. If there be really a hell of such dreadful, and never-ending torments, as is generally supposed, that multitudes are in great danger of, and that the bigger part of men in Christian countries do actually from generation to generation fall into, for want of a sense of the terribleness of it, and their danger of it, and so for

---

Sin, containing 41 sermons, appeared in 1654. Both parts were reissued as a single volume in 1658, and it is from this later edition that JE quotes.]

5. [Burgess had written *"Vocalistas & Literistas, Letterists & Vowalists."* JE probably intended to copy only the English translations but garbled the first word.]

want of taking due care to avoid it; then why is it not proper for those that have the care of souls, to take great pains to make men sensible of it? Why should not they be told as much of the truth as can be? If I am in danger of going to hell, I should be glad to know as much as possibly I can of the dreadfulness of it: if I am very prone to neglect due care to avoid it, he does me the best kindness, that does most to represent to me the truth of the case, that sets forth my misery and danger in the liveliest manner.

I appeal to every one in this congregation, whether this is not the very course they would take in case of exposedness to any great temporal calamity? If any of you that are heads of families, saw one of your children in an house that was all on fire over its head, and in eminent danger of being soon consumed in the flames, that seemed to be very insensible of its danger, and neglected to escape, after you had often spake to it, and called to it, would you go on to speak to it only in a cold and indifferent manner? Would not you cry aloud, and call earnestly to it, and represent the danger it was in, and its own folly in delaying, in the most lively manner you was capable of? Would not nature itself teach this, and oblige you to it? If you should continue to speak to it only in a cold manner, as you are wont to do in ordinary conversation about indifferent matters, would not those about you begin to think you were bereft of reason yourself? This is not the way of mankind, nor the way of any one person in this congregation, in temporal affairs of great moment, that require earnest heed and great haste, and about which they are greatly concerned, to speak to others of their danger, and warn them but a little; and when they do it at all, do it in a cold indifferent manner: nature teaches men otherwise. If we that have the care of souls, knew what hell was, had seen the state of the damned, or by any other means, become sensible how dreadful their case was; and at the same time knew that the bigger part of men went thither; and saw our hearers in eminent danger, and that they were not sensible of their danger, and so after being often warned neglected to escape, it would be morally impossible for us to avoid abundantly and most earnestly setting before them the dreadfulness of that misery they were in danger of, and their great exposedness to it, and warning them to fly from it, and even to cry aloud to them.

When ministers preach of hell, and warn sinners to avoid it, in a cold manner, though they may say in words that it is infinitely terrible; yet (if we look on language as a communication of our minds to others) they contradict themselves; for actions, as I observed before, have a language to convey our minds, as well as words; and at the same time that such a preacher's words represent the sinner's state as infinitely dreadful, his behavior and manner of speaking contradict it, and shew that the preacher don't think so; so that he defeats his own purpose; for the language of his actions, in such a case, is much more effectual than the bare signification of his words.

Not that I think that the law only should be preached: ministers may preach other things too little. The Gospel is to be preached as well as the law, and the law is to be preached only to make way for the Gospel, and in order to an effectual preaching of that; for the main work of ministers of the Gospel is to preach the Gospel: it is the end of the law; Christ is the end of the law for righteousness [Rom. 10:4]. So that a minister would miss it very much if he should insist so much on the terrors of the law, as to forget his end, and neglect to preach the Gospel; but yet the law is very much to be insisted on, and the preaching of the Gospel is like to be in vain without it.

And certainly such earnestness and affection in speaking is beautiful, as becomes the nature and importance of the subject. Not but that there may be such a thing as an indecent boisterousness in a preacher, that is something besides what naturally arises from the nature of his subject, and in which the matter and manner don't well agree together.

Some talk of it as an unreasonable thing to think to fright persons to heaven; but I think it is a reasonable thing to endeavor to fright persons away from hell, that stand upon the brink of it, and are just ready to fall into it, and are senseless of their danger: 'tis a reasonable thing to fright a person out of an house on fire. The word "fright" is commonly used for sudden causeless fear, or groundless surprise; but surely a just fear, that there is good reason for, though it be very great, is not to be spoken against under any such name.

[Positive Evidences]

Having thus shown, in some instance, what are not evidences that a work that is wrought among a people is not a work of the Spirit of God, I now proceed in the second place, as was proposed, to shew positively, what are the sure, distinguishing, Scripture evidences and marks of a work of the Spirit of God, by which we may proceed in judging of any operation we find in ourselves, or see among a people, without danger of being misled.

And in this, as I said before, I shall confine myself wholly to those marks which are given us by the Apostle in the chapter wherein is my text, where this matter is particularly handled, and more plainly and fully than anywhere else in the Bible. And in speaking to these marks, I shall take them in the order in which I find them in the chapter.

1. When that spirit that is at work amongst a people is observed to operate after such a manner, as to raise their esteem of that Jesus that was born of the Virgin, and was crucified without the gates of Jerusalem; and seems more to confirm and establish their minds in the truth of what the Gospel declares to us of his being the Son of God, and the Saviour of men; 'tis a sure sign that that spirit is the Spirit of God. This sign the Apostle gives us in the 2d and 3d verses, "Hereby know ye the Spirit of God; every spirit that confesseth that Jesus Christ is come in the flesh, is of God; and every spirit that confesseth not that Jesus Christ is come in the flesh, is not of God." This implies a confessing, not only that there was such a person that appeared in Palestine, and did and suffered those things that are recorded of him, but that that person was Christ, i.e. the Son of God, the Anointed of God to be Lord and Saviour, as the name Jesus Christ implies. That thus much is implied in the Apostle's meaning, is confirmed by the 15th verse, where the Apostle is still on the same subject of signs of the true Spirit: "Whosoever shall confess that Jesus is the Son of God, God dwelleth in him, and he in God."

And 'tis to be observed that the word "confess," as it is often used in the New Testament, signifies more than merely allowing; it implies an establishing and confirming a thing by testimony, and declaring it with manifestation of esteem and affection: so Matt. 10:32, "Whosoever therefore shall confess me before men, him will I confess also before my Father which is in heaven." Rom. 15:9, "I will confess to thee among the Gentiles, and sing unto thy name." And Phil. 2:11, "That every tongue shall confess that Jesus Christ is Lord, to the glory of God the Father." And that this is the force of the expression, as the Apostle John uses it in this place, is confirmed by that other place in the same epistle, in the next chapter, at the first verse: "Whosoever believeth that Jesus is the Christ, is born of God; and everyone that loveth him that begat, loveth him

also that is begotten of him." And by that parallel place of the
Apostle Paul, where we have the same rule given to distinguish the
true Spirit from all counterfeits, I Cor. 12:3, "Wherefore I give you
to understand, that no man speaking by the Spirit of God, calleth
Jesus accursed (or will shew an ill or mean esteem of him), and that
no man can say that Jesus is the Lord, but by the Holy Ghost."

So that if the spirit that is at work among a people is plainly observed to work after that manner, as to convince them of Christ, and
lead them to Christ; more to confirm their minds in the belief of
the story of Christ, as he appeared in the flesh, and that he is the Son
of God, and was sent of God to save sinners, and that he is the only
Saviour, and that they stand in great need of him; and seems to
beget in them higher and more honorable thoughts of him than
they used to have, and to incline their affections more to him; it is
a sure sign that it is the true and right Spirit; and that [is so]
whether we can determine whether that conviction and affection
be in that manner, or to that degree, as to be saving or no.

But the words of the Apostle are remarkable; the person that the
Spirit gives testimony to, and to whom he raises their esteem and
respect, must be that Jesus that appeared in the flesh, and not
another Christ in his stead; not any mystical, fantastical Christ; such
as the light within, which the spirit of the Quakers extols, while it
diminishes their esteem of, and dependence upon an outward Christ,
or Jesus as he came in the flesh, and leads them off from him; but
the spirit that gives testimony for that Jesus, and leads to him, can
be no other than the Spirit of God.

The Devil has the most bitter and implacable enmity against
that person, especially in his character of the Saviour of men; he
mortally hates the story and doctrine of his redemption; he never
would go about to beget in men more honorable thoughts of him,
and so to incline them more to fear him, and lay greater weight on
his instructions and commands. The spirit that inclines men's
hearts to the seed of the woman, is not the spirit of the serpent, that
has such an irreconcilable enmity against him [cf. Gen. 3:15]. He
that heightens men's esteem of the glorious Michael, that prince of
the angels, is not the spirit of the dragon that is at war with him
[Rev. 12:7].

2. When the spirit that is at work operates against the interest of
Satan's kingdom, which lies in encouraging and establishing sin,

and cherishing men's worldly lusts; this is a sure sign that 'tis a true, and not a false spirit. This sign we have given us in the 4th and 5th verses: "Ye are of God, little children, and have overcome them; because greater is he that is in you, than he that is in the world. They are of the world, therefore speak they of the world, and the world heareth them." Here is a plain antithesis: 'tis evident that the Apostle is still comparing those that are influenced by the two opposite kinds of spirits, the true and the false, and shewing the difference; the one are of God, and overcome the spirit of the world; the other are of the world, and speak and savor the things of the world. The spirit of the devil is here called, "he that is in the world." Christ says, "My kingdom is not of this world" [John 18:36]. But 'tis otherwise with Satan's kingdom; he is the god of this world.

What the Apostle means by "the world," or "the things that are of the world," we learn by his own words in the 2d chapter of this epistle, 15th and 16th verses: "Love not the world, neither the things that are in the world: if any man love the world, the love of the Father is not in him: for all that is in the world, the lust of the flesh, and the lust of the eyes, and the pride of life, is not of the Father, but is of the world." So that by "the world," the Apostle evidently means everything that appertains to the interest of sin, and comprehends all the corruptions and lusts of men, and all those acts and objects by which they are gratified. In these things lies the interest of his kingdom, who is the spirit that is in the world, and is the god of the world.

So that we may safely determine, from what the Apostle says, that the spirit that is at work amongst a people, that is observed to work after such a manner as to lessen men's esteem of the pleasures, profits and honors of the world, and to take off their hearts from an eager pursuit after these things; and to engage them in a deep concern about a future and eternal happiness in that invisible world, that the Gospel reveals; and puts them upon earnest seeking the kingdom of God and his righteousness; and convinces them of the dreadfulness of sin, the guilt that it brings, and the misery that it exposes to: I say, the spirit that operates after such a manner, must needs be the Spirit of God.

It is not to be supposed that Satan would go about to convince men of sin, and awaken the conscience; it can no way serve his end, to make that candle of the Lord shine the brighter, and to open the mouth of that viceregent of God in the soul: it is for his interest, whatever he does, to lull conscience asleep, and keep that quiet; to have that with its eyes and mouth open in the soul, will tend to clog and hinder all his designs of darkness, and evermore to be disturbing his affairs, and crossing his interest in the soul, and disquieting him, so that he can manage nothing to his mind without molestation. Would the Devil when he is about to establish men in a way and state of sin, take such a course, in the first place to enlighten and awaken the conscience to see the dreadfulness of sin, and make them exceedingly afraid of sin, and sensible of their misery by reason of their past sins, and their great need of deliverance from the guilt of them, and more careful, inquisitive and watchful to discern what is sinful; and to avoid future sins; and so more afraid of the Devil's temptations, and careful to guard against them? What do those men do with their reason, that suppose that the spirit that operates thus, is the spirit of the Devil?

Possibly some may say, that the Devil may even awaken men's consciences to deceive them, and make them think they have been the subjects of a saving work of the Spirit of God, while they are indeed still in the gall of bitterness. But to this it may be replied, that the man that has an awakened conscience is the least likely to be deceived of any man in the world: 'tis the drowsy, insensible, stupid conscience that is most easily blinded. The more sensible conscience is in a diseased soul, the less easily is it quieted without a real healing. The more sensible conscience is made of the dreadfulness of sin, and of the greatness of a man's own guilt of it, the less likely is he to rest in his own righteousness, or to be pacified with nothing but shadows. A man that has been thoroughly terrified with a sense of his danger and misery, is not easily flattered and made to believe himself safe, without any good grounds.

To awaken conscience, and convince of the evil of sin, can't tend to establish sin, but certainly tends to make way for sin and Satan's being cast out. Therefore this is a good argument that the spirit that operates thus, can't be the spirit of the Devil; if Christ knew how to argue, who told the Pharisees, that supposed that the spirit that he wrought by, was the spirit of the Devil, that Satan would not cast out Satan, Matt. 12:25–26.

And therefore if we see persons made sensible of the dreadful nature of sin, and of the displeasure of God against it, and of their own miserable condition as they are in themselves, by reason of sin, and earnestly concerned for their eternal salvation, and sensible of their need of God's pity and help, and engaged to seek it in the use of the means that God has appointed, we may certainly conclude that it is from the Spirit of God, whatever effects this concern has on their bodies; though it causes them to cry out aloud, or to shriek, or to faint, or though it throws them into convulsions, or whatever other way the blood and spirits are moved.

The influence of the Spirit of God is yet more abundantly manifest, if persons have their hearts drawn off from the world, and weaned from the objects of their worldly lusts, and taken off from worldly pursuits, by the sense they have of the excellency of divine things, and the affection they have to those spiritual enjoyments of another world, that are promised in the Gospel.

3. That spirit that operates in such a manner, as to cause in men a greater regard to the Holy Scriptures, and establishes them more in their truth and divinity, is certainly the Spirit of God. This rule the Apostle gives us in the 6th verse: "We are of God; he that knoweth God heareth us: he that is not of God, heareth not us: hereby know we the spirit of truth and the spirit of error." "We are of God"—that is, "we the apostles, are sent forth of God, and appointed of him, to teach the world, and to deliver that doctrine, those instructions that are to be their rule; therefore he that knoweth God heareth us, etc." The Apostle's argument in the verse equally reaches all that in the same sense are of God, that is, all those that God has appointed and inspired to deliver to his church its rule of faith and practice; all the prophets and apostles, whose doctrine God has made the foundation on which he has built his church, as in Eph. 2:20; all the penmen of the Holy Scriptures. The Devil never would go about to beget in persons a regard to that divine Word, which God hath given to be the great and standing rule for the direction of his church in all religious matters and concerns of their souls, in all ages. A spirit of delusion won't incline persons to go to seek direction at the mouth of God. "To the law and to the testimony," is never the cry of those evil spirits that have no light in them; for 'tis God's own direction to discover their delusions. Isa. 8:19–20, "And when they shall say unto you, Seek unto them that have familiar spirits, and unto wizards that peep, and that mutter: should not a people seek unto their God? for the living to the dead? To the law and to the testimony; if they speak not according to this word, it is because there is no light in

them." The Devil don't say the same as Abraham did, "They have Moses and the prophets, let them hear them" [Luke 16:29]; nor the same that the voice from heaven did concerning Christ, "Hear ye him" [Matt. 17:5]. Would the spirit of error, in order to deceive men, beget in them an high opinion of the infallible rule, and incline them to think much of it, and be very conversant with it? Would the prince of darkness, in order to promote his kingdom of darkness, lead men to the sun? The Devil has ever shewn a mortal spite and hatred towards that holy book, the Bible: he has done all that has been in his power to extinguish that light, and to draw men off from it: he knows that 'tis that light by which his kingdom of darkness is to be overthrown. He has had for many ages experience of its power to defeat his purposes and baffle his designs. It is his constant plague; 'tis the main weapon which Michael uses in his war with him [Rev. 12:7, 11]; 'tis "the sword of the Spirit" that pierces him and conquers him [Eph. 6:17]; 'tis that "great, and sore, and strong sword" with which God punishes "Leviathan, that crooked serpent" [Isa. 27:1]; 'tis that sharp sword that we read of, Rev. 19:15, that proceeds out of the mouth of him that sat on the horse, with which he smites his enemies. Every text is a dart to torment the old serpent: he has felt the stinging smart thousands of times; therefore he is enraged against the Bible, and hates every word in it: and therefore we may be sure that he never will go about to raise persons' esteem of it, or affection to it. And accordingly we see it to be common in enthusiasts, that they depreciate this written rule, and set up the light within, or some other rule above it.

4. Another rule to judge of spirits may be drawn from those opposite compellations given to the two opposite spirits, in the last words of the 6th verse, "The spirit of truth" and "the spirit of error." These words do exhibit the two opposite characters of the Spirit of God, and other spirits that counterfeit his operations. And therefore, if by observing the manner of the operation of a spirit that is at work among a people, we see that it operates as a spirit of truth, leading persons to truth, convincing them of those things that are true, we may safely determine that 'tis a right and true spirit. As for instance, if we observe that the spirit that is at work, makes men more sensible than they used to be, that there is a God, and that he is a great God, and a sin-hating God; and

makes them more to realize it, that they must die, and that life is short, and very uncertain; and confirms persons in it that there is another world, that they have immortal souls, and that they must give account of themselves to God; and convinces them that they are exceeding sinful by nature and practice; and that they are helpless in themselves; and confirms them in other things that are agreeable to sound doctrine: the spirit that works thus, operates as a spirit of truth: he represents things as they are indeed: he brings men to the light; for whatever makes truth manifest, is light; as the Apostle Paul observes, Eph. 5:13, "But all things that are reproved (or 'discovered,' as it is in the margin) are made manifest by the light; for whatsoever doth make manifest is light." And therefore we may conclude that 'tis not the spirit of darkness, that doth thus discover, and make manifest the truth. Christ tells us that Satan is a liar, and the father of lies [John 8:44]; and his kingdom is a kingdom of darkness. 'Tis upheld and promoted only by darkness and error: Satan has all his power and dominion by darkness. Hence we read of the power of darkness, Luke 22:53 and Col. 1:13. And devils are called the "rulers of the darkness of this world" [Eph. 6:12]. Whatever spirit removes our darkness and brings us to the light, undeceives us, and convinces us of the truth; does us a kindness. If I am brought to a sight of truth, and am made sensible of things as they be, my duty is immediately to thank God for it, without standing first to inquire by what means I have such a benefit.

5. If the spirit that is at work among a people operates as a spirit of love to God and man, 'tis a sure sign that 'tis the Spirit of God. This sign the Apostle insists upon from the 7th verse to the end of the chapter: "Beloved, let us love one another; for love is of God, and everyone that loveth is born of God, and knoweth God. He that loveth not, knoweth not God, for God is love, etc." Here 'tis evident that the Apostle is still comparing those two sorts of persons that are influenced by the opposite kinds of spirits; and mentions love as a mark by which we may know who has the true spirit. But this is especially evident by the 12th and 13th verses: "If we love one another, God dwelleth in us, and his love is perfected in us. Hereby know we that we dwell in him, and he in us, because he hath given us of his Spirit." In these verses love is spoken of as if it were that wherein the very nature of the Holy

Spirit consisted; or as if divine love dwelling in us, and the Spirit of God dwelling in us, were the same thing; as it is also in the two last verses of the foregoing chapter; as also in the 16th verse of this chapter. Therefore this last mark which the Apostle gives of the true Spirit, he seems to speak of as the most eminent; and so insists much more largely upon it, than upon all the rest; and speaks expressly of both love to God and men; of love to men in the 7th, 11th, and 12th verses; and of love to God in the 17th, 18th, and 19th verses; and of both together in the two last verses; and of love to men as arising from love to God in these two last verses.

Therefore when the spirit that is at work amongst a people tends this way, and brings many of them to high and exalting thoughts of the divine Being, and his glorious perfections; and works in them an admiring, delightful sense of the excellency of Jesus Christ; representing him as "the chief among ten thousands, altogether lovely" [Cant. 5:10, 16], and makes him precious to the soul; winning and drawing the heart with those motives and incitements to love which the Apostle speaks of in that passage of Scripture we are upon, viz. the wonderful, free love of God in giving his only begotten Son to die for us, and the wonderful dying love of Christ to us, who had no love to him, but were his enemies; as vss. 9 and 10, "In this was manifested the love of God towards us, because that God sent his only begotten Son into the world, that we might live through him. Herein is love; not that we loved God, but that he loved us, and sent his Son to be the propitiation for our sins." And vs. 16, "And we have known, and believed the love that God hath to us." And vs. 19, "We love him, because he first loved us." The Spirit excites to love on these motives, and makes the attributes of God as revealed in the Gospel and manifested in Christ, delightful objects of contemplation; and makes the soul to long after God and Christ, after their presence and communion, and acquaintance with them, and conformity to them; and to live so as to please and honor them. And also quells contentions among men, and gives a spirit of peace and goodwill, excites to acts of outward kindness and earnest desires of the salvation of others' souls; and causes a delight in those that appear as the children of God and followers of Christ: I say when a spirit operates after this manner among a people, there is the highest kind of evidence of the influence of a true and divine spirit.

Indeed, there is a counterfeit of love that often appears amongst those that are led by a spirit of delusion. There is commonly in the wildest enthusiasts a kind of union and affection that appears in them one towards another, arising from self-love, occasioned by their agreeing one with another in those things wherein they greatly differ from all others, and for which they are the objects of the ridicule of all the rest of mankind; which naturally will cause them so much the more to prize the esteem they observe in each other, of those peculiarities that make them the objects of others' contempt: so the ancient Gnostics, and the wild fanatics that appeared in the beginning of the Reformation, boasted of their great love one to another: one sect of them in particular, calling themselves the Family of Love.[6] But this is quite another thing than that Christian love that I have just described; 'tis only the working of a natural self-love, and no true benevolence, any more than the union and friendship which may be among a company of pirates that are at war with all the rest of the world. There is sufficient said in this passage of St. John that we are upon, of the nature and motive of a truly Christian love, thoroughly to distinguish it from all such counterfeits. It is love that arises from an apprehension of the wonderful riches of free grace and sovereignty of God's love to us in Christ Jesus; being attended with a sense of our own utter unworthiness, as in ourselves the enemies and haters of God and Christ, and with a renunciation of all our own excellency and righteousness. See vss. 9, 10, 11, and 19. The surest character of true divine supernatural love, distinguishing it from counterfeits that do arise from a natural self-love, is that that Christian virtue shines in it, that does above all others renounce and abase and annihilate self, viz. *humility.* Christian love, or true charity, is an humble love. I Cor. 13:4–5, "Charity vaunteth not itself; is not puffed up, doth not behave itself unseemly, seeketh not her own, is not easily provoked." When therefore we see love in persons attended with a sense of their own littleness, vileness, weakness, and utter insufficiency; and so with self-diffidence, self-emptiness, self-renunciation, and poverty of spirit, there are the manifest tokens

6. [A Dutch religious community founded by Hendrik Niclaes (1502–80) about 1540. Familist influence entered England during the reign of Elizabeth I and became strong enough to attract the hostility of both governmental authorities and Puritan heresiographers for three-quarters of a century. Most horrifying to the orthodox were the Familists' alleged enthusiasm and antinomianism. See Friedrich Nippold, "Henrich Niclaes und das Haus der Liebe," *Zeitschrift für die historische Theologie, 32* (1862), 323–94.]

of the Spirit of God: "He that thus dwells in love, dwells in God, and God in him" [I John 4:16]. The love the Apostle speaks of as a great evidence of the true spirit, is God's love or Christ's love; as vs. 12, "His love is perfected in us." What kind of love that is, we may see best in what appeared in Christ, in the example he set us, when he was here upon earth. The love that appeared in that Lamb of God, was not only a love to friends, but to enemies, and a love attended with a meek and humble spirit. "Learn of me," says he, "for I am meek and lowly in heart" [Matt. 11:29].

Love and humility are two things the most contrary to the spirit of the Devil, of anything in the world; for the character of that evil spirit, above all things, consists in pride and malice.

Thus I have spoken particularly to the several marks the Apostle gives us of a work of the true spirit. There are some of these things the Devil would not do if he could. Thus, he would not awaken the conscience, and make men sensible of their miserable state by nature, by reason of sin, and sensible of their great need of a Saviour: and he would not confirm men in a belief that Jesus is the Son of God, and the Saviour of sinners, or raise men's value and esteem of him: he would not beget in men's minds an opinion of the necessity, usefulness and truth of the Holy Scriptures, or incline them to hearken to them, or make much use of them; nor would he go about to shew men the truth, in things that concern their souls' interest; to undeceive 'em, and lead 'em out of darkness into light, and give 'em a view of things as they are indeed. And there are other things that the Devil neither can nor will do: he will not give men a spirit of divine love, or Christian humility and poverty of spirit; nor could he if he would. He can't give those things which he has not himself; these things are as contrary as possible to his nature. And therefore when there is an extraordinary influence or operation appearing on the minds of a people, if these things are found in it, we are safe in determining that 'tis the work of God, whatever other circumstances it may be attended with, whatever instruments are improved, whatever methods are taken to promote it; whatever means a sovereign God, whose "judgments are a great deep" [Ps. 36:6], makes use of to carry it on; and whatever motions there may be of the animal spirits, whatever effects may be wrought on men's bodies. These marks, that the Apostle has given us, are sufficient to stand alone, and support themselves; and wherever they be, they plainly shew the finger of God, and are sufficient to outweigh a thousand such little objections, as many make from oddities, irregularities, and errors in conduct, and the delusions and scandals of some professors.

Objection. But here some may object against the sufficiency of the marks given, what the Apostle Paul says in II Cor. 11:13–14, "For such are false apostles, deceitful workers, transforming themselves into the apostles of Christ; and no marvel, for Satan himself is transformed into an angel of light."

To which I answer, that this can be no objection against the sufficiency of these marks to distinguish the true Spirit from the false spirit, in those false apostles and false prophets, which the Apostle [John] speaks of, in whom the Devil was transformed into an angel of light, because it is principally with a view to them that the Apostle gives these marks; as appears by the words of the text, "Believe not every spirit, but try the spirits, whether they are of God." And this is the reason he gives, "because many false prophets are gone out into the world"; [i.e.] "there are many gone out into the world that are the ministers of the Devil, that transform themselves into the prophets of God, in whom the spirit of the Devil is transformed into an angel of light; therefore try the spirits by these rules that I shall give you, that you may be able to distinguish the true Spirit from the false spirit, under such a crafty disguise." Those false prophets the Apostle John speaks of, are doubtless the same sort of men with those false apostles, and deceitful workers, that the Apostle Paul speaks of, in the place in the second [epistle] of Corinthians, in whom the Devil was "transformed into an angel of light": and therefore we may be sure that these marks the Apostle gives, are especially adapted to distinguish between the true Spirit, and the Devil transformed into an angel of light, because they are given especially for that end; that is the Apostle's declared purpose and design, to give marks by which the true Spirit may be distinguished from that sort of counterfeits.

And if we look over what is said about these false prophets and false apostles (as there is much said about them in the New Testament) and take notice in what manner the Devil was transformed into an angel of light in them, we shall not find anything that in the least injures the sufficiency of these marks to distinguish the true spirit from such counterfeits. The Devil transformed himself into an angel of light, as there was in them a shew, and great boasts of extraordinary knowledge in divine things; Col. 2:8; I Tim. 1:6–7 and chap. 6:3–5; II Tim. 2:14, 16–18; Tit. 1:10, 16. Hence their followers called themselves Gnostics, from their great pretended knowledge: and the Devil in them mimicked the miraculous gifts of the Holy Spirit, in visions, revelations, prophecies, miracles, and the immediate conduct of the Spirit in what they did. Hence they are called false apostles and false prophets: see Matt. 24:24. Again, there was a false shew of, and lying pretenses to great holiness and devotion in words: Rom. 16:17–18; Eph. 4:14. Hence they are called deceitful workers, and wells, and clouds without water: II Cor. 11:13; II Pet. 2:17; Jude 12. There was also in them a shew of extraordinary piety and righteousness in their superstitious worship: Col. 2:16–18, 21–23. So they had a false, proud, and bitter zeal: Gal. 4:17–18; I Tim. 1:6 and chap. 6:4–5. And likewise a false shew of humility, in affecting an extraordinary outward meanness and dejection, when indeed they were vainly puffed up with their fleshly mind; and made a righteousness of their humility, and were exceedingly lifted up with their eminent piety: Col. 2:18, 23. But how do such things as these, in the least injure those things that have been mentioned as the distinguishing evidences of the true spirit?

Besides such vain shews which may be from the Devil, there are common influences of the Spirit, which are often mistaken for saving grace: but these are out of the question, because though they are not saving, yet are the work of the true Spirit.

Having thus fulfilled what I at first proposed, in considering what are the certain, distinguishing marks, by which we may safely proceed in judging of any work that falls under our observation, whether it be the work of the Spirit of God or no, I now proceed to the application.

[*Application*]

1. From what has been said, I will venture to draw this inference, viz. that that extraordinary influence that has lately appeared on the minds of the people abroad in this land, causing in them an uncommon concern and engagedness of mind about the things of religion, is undoubtedly, in the general, from the Spirit of God. There are but two things that need to be known in order to such a work's being judged of, viz. facts and rules. The rules of the Word of God we have had laid before us; and as to facts, there are but

two ways that we can come at them, so as to be in a capacity to compare them with the rules, either by our own observation, or by information from others that have had opportunity to observe.

As to this work that has lately been carried on in the land, there are many things concerning it that are notorious, and known by everybody (unless it be some that have been very much out of the way of observing and hearing indeed) that unless the Apostle John was out in his rules, are sufficient to determine it to be in general, the work of God. 'Tis notorious that the spirit that is at work, takes off persons' minds from the vanities of the world, and engages them in a deep concern about a future and eternal happiness in another world, and puts them upon earnestly seeking their salvation, and convinces them of the dreadfulness of sin, and of their own guilty and miserable state as they are by nature. It is notorious that it awakens men's consciences, and makes 'em sensible of the dreadfulness of God's anger, and causes in them a great desire, and earnest care and endeavor to obtain his favor. It is notorious that it puts them upon a more diligent improvement of the means of grace which God has appointed. It is also notorious that, in general, it works in persons a greater regard to the Word of God, and desire of hearing and reading of it, and to be more conversant with the Holy Scriptures than they used to be. And it is notoriously manifest that the spirit that is at work, in general, operates as a spirit of truth, making persons more sensible of what is really true, in those things that concern their eternal salvation: as that they must die, and that life is very short and uncertain; that there is a great, sin-hating God that they are accountable to, and will fix them in an eternal state in another world; and that they stand in great need of a Saviour. It is furthermore notorious that the Spirit that is at work makes persons more sensible of the value of that Jesus that was crucified, and their need of him; and that it puts them upon earnestly seeking an interest in him. It can't be but that these things should be apparent to people in general through the land: for these things ben't done in a corner; the work that has been wrought has not been confined to a few towns, in some remoter parts of the land, but has been carried on in many places in all parts of the land, and in most of the principal, and most populous, and public places in it (Christ in this respect has wrought amongst us, in the same manner that he wrought his miracles in Judea), and has now been continued for a considerable time; so that there has been a great deal of opportunity to observe the manner of the work. And all such as have been much in the way of observing the work, and have been very conversant with those that have been the subject of it, do see a great deal more that, by the rules of the Apostle, does clearly and certainly shew it to be the work of God.

And here I would observe, that the nature and tendency of a spirit that is at work may be determined with much greater certainty, and less danger of being imposed upon, when it is observed in a great multitude of people of all sorts, and in various different places, than when it is only seen in a few, in some particular place that have been much conversant one with another. A few particular persons may agree to put a cheat upon others, by a false pretense and professing things that they never were conscious to in their own minds: but when the work is spread over [a] great part of a country, in places distant one from another, among people of all sorts and all ages, and in multitudes of persons of sound mind, good understanding, and known integrity; there would be the greatest absurdity in supposing that, by all the observation that can be made by all that is heard from them and seen in them, for many months together, by those that are most intimate with them in these affairs, and have long been acquainted with them, that yet it can't be determined what kind of influence the operation they are under, has upon people's minds, whether it tends to awaken their consciences, or to stupefy them; whether it tends to incline the more to seek their salvation or neglect it; whether it seems to confirm them in a belief of the Scriptures, or to lead them to Deism; whether it makes them have more regard to the great truths of religion, or less; and so in other things. There is probably no particular person here present, that thinks himself to have a right to be treated as one of a sound mind, and common sense, and veracity, but would think himself abused, if he should declare to others, that he had altered his mind in these and those particulars; he now found himself convinced of the truth of this or that, that formerly he did not believe; and that he found in himself such and such fears, that he don't use to have; or found a greater aversion than he was wont to have, or a greater esteem and affection to such and such things; and those that he made such a profession to would not believe him, though they had long been conversant with him, and though he persisted in this profession for many months together, and nothing appeared in him but what agreed thereto. But much more unreasonable it would be, when such professions are made, not by a particular person only, but a great part of a people in a land, to suppose that they all agree in professing what indeed they do not feel in their souls.

And here it is to be observed, that for persons to profess that they are convinced of these or those divine truths; or that they esteem and love such divine things in a saving manner; and for them to profess that they are more convinced or confirmed in the truth of them, than they used to be, and find that they have a greater regard to them than before they had, are two very different things. Persons of honesty and common sense, have much greater right to demand credit to be given to the latter profession than to the former (though in the former it is vastly less likely that a people in general should be deceived, than some particular persons). But whether persons' convictions, and the alteration in their dispositions and affections, be in a degree and manner that is saving, is beside the present question. If there be such effects on peoples' judgments, dispositions and affections, as have been spoken of, whether they be in a degree and manner that is saving or no, it is nevertheless a sign of the influence of the Spirit of God. Scripture rules serve to distinguish the common influences of the Spirit of God, as well as those that are saving, from the influence of other causes.

And as I am one that, by the providence of God, have for some months past, been much amongst those that have been the subjects of that work that has of late been carried on in the land; and particularly, have been abundantly in the way of seeing and observing those extraordinary things that many persons have been much stumbled at; such as persons crying out aloud, shrieking, being put into great agonies of body, and deprived of their bodily strength, and the like; and that in many different towns; and have been very particularly conversant with great numbers of such, both in the time of their being the subjects of such extraordinary influences and afterwards, from time to time, and have seen the manner and issue of such operations and the fruits of them, for several months together; many of them being persons that I have long known, and have been intimately acquainted with them in soul concerns, before and since: so I look upon myself called on this occasion to give my testimony, that so far as the nature and tendency of such a work is capable of falling under the observation of a bystander, to whom those that have been the subjects of it have endeavored to open their hearts, or can be come at by diligent and particular inquiry, this work has all those marks that have been spoken of; in very many instances, in every article; and particularly in many of those that have been the subjects of such extraordinary operations, all those marks have appeared in a very great degree.

Those in whom have been these uncommon appearances have been of two sorts; either those that have been in great distress, in an apprehension of their sin and misery; or those that have been overcome with a sweet sense of the greatness, wonderfulness and excellency of divine things. Of the multitude of those of the former sort, that I have had opportunity to observe, and have been acquainted with, there have been very few, but that by all that could be observed in them, in the time of it, or afterwards, their distress has arisen from real, proper conviction, and a being in a degree sensible of that which was the truth. And though I don't suppose, when such things were observed to be common, that persons have laid themselves under those violent restraints, to avoid outward manifestations of their distress, that perhaps they otherwise would have done; yet there have been very few in whom there has been any appearance of feigning or affecting such manifestations, and very many for whom it would have been undoubtedly utterly impossible for 'em to avoid them. Generally those that have been in these agonies have appeared to be in the perfect exercise of their reason; and those of them that have been able to speak, have been well able to give an account of the circumstances of their minds, and the cause of their distress, in the time of it, and well able to remember, and give an account afterwards. I have known a very few instances of those, that in their great extremity, have for a short space been deprived, in some measure of the use of reason; but among the many hundreds, and it may be thousands, that have lately been brought to such agonies, I never yet knew one, lastingly deprived of their reason. In some that I have known, melancholy has evidently been mixed; and when it is so, the difference is very apparent; their distresses are of another kind, and operate quite after another manner, than when their distress is from mere conviction: 'tis not truth only that distresses them, but many vain shadows and notions, that won't give place either to Scripture or reason. Some in their great distress, have not been well able to give an account of themselves, or to declare the sense they have of things, or to explain the manner and cause of their trouble to others, that yet

I have had no reason to think were not under proper convictions, and in whom there has been manifested a good issue. But this won't be at all wondered at by those who have had much to do with souls under spiritual difficulties. Some things that they are sensible of are altogether new to them, their ideas and inward sensations are new, and what they therefore knew not how to accommodate language to, or to find words to express. And some who on first inquiry, say they know not what was the matter with them, on being particularly examined and interrogated, have been able to represent their case, though of themselves they could not find expressions and forms of speech to do it.

Some say they think that the terrors that such persons are in, that have such effects on their bodies, is only a fright. But certainly there ought to be a distinction made between a very great fear, and extreme distress, arising from an apprehension of some dreadful truth, that is a cause that is fully proportionable to such an effect, and a needless causeless fright: which is of two kinds; either when persons are terrified with that which is not the truth (of this I have seen very few instances, unless in case of melancholy); or secondly, when persons are under a childish fright, only from some terrible outward appearance and noise, and a general notion thence arising, that there is something or other terrible, they know not what; without having in their minds the apprehension of any particular terrible truth whatsoever; of such a kind of fright I have seen very little appearance, either among old or young.

Those that are in such extremity, commonly express a great sense of their exceeding wickedness, the multitude and aggravations of their actual sins, and the dreadful pollution, enmity and perverseness of their hearts, and a dreadful obstinacy and hardness of heart; a sense of their great guilt in the sight of God; and the dreadfulness of the punishment that sin exposes to. Very often they have a lively idea of the horrible pit of eternal misery; and at the same time it appears to them that a great God that has them in his hands, is exceeding angry with them; his wrath appears amazingly terrible to them: God appearing to them so much provoked, and his great wrath so incensed, they are apprehensive of great danger, that he will not bear with them any longer; but will now, forthwith, cut 'em off, and send them down to the dreadful pit they have in view; at the same time seeing no refuge. They see more and more of the vanity of everything they used to trust to, and flatter themselves in; till they are brought wholly to despair in all, and to see that they are at the disposal of the mere will of the God that is so angry with them. Very many, in the midst of their extremity, have been brought to an extraordinary sense of their fully deserving that wrath and destruction, which is then before their eyes; and at the same time, that they have feared every moment, that it would be executed upon them, they have been greatly convinced that it would be altogether just that it should, and that God is indeed absolutely sovereign: and very often, some text of Scripture expressing God's sovereignty, has been set home upon their minds, whereby their minds have been calmed, and they have been brought as it were to lie at God's foot; and after great agonies, a little before light has arisen, they have been composed and quiet, in a kind of submission to a just and sovereign God; but their bodily strength much spent; and sometimes their lives, to appearance almost gone; and then light has appeared, and a glorious Redeemer, with his wonderful, all-sufficient grace, has been represented to them, often in some sweet invitation of Scripture. Sometimes the light comes in suddenly, sometimes more gradually, filling their souls with love, admiration, joy and self-abasement; drawing forth their hearts in longing after the excellent, lovely Redeemer, and longings to lie in the dust before him; and longings that others might behold him, and embrace him, and be delivered by him; and longings to live to his glory: but sensible that they can do nothing of themselves; appearing vile in their own eyes, and having much of a jealousy over their own hearts. And all the appearances of a real change of heart have followed; and grace has acted, from time to time, after the same manner that it used to act in those that were converted formerly, with the like difficulties, temptations, buffetings, and like comforts; excepting that in many, light and comfort has been in higher degree than ordinary. Many very young children have been thus wrought upon. There have been some instances very much like those demoniacs that we read of, Mark 1:26 and chap. 9:26, of whom we read that when the Devil had cried with a loud voice, and rent them sore, he came out of them. And probably those instances were designed for a type of such things as these. Some have several turns of great agonies, before they are delivered: and some have been in such distresses, and it has passed off, and no deliverance at all has followed.

Some object against it as great confusion, when there is a number together in such circumstances, making a noise; and say, God can't be the author of it, because he is the God of order, not of confusion [I Cor. 14:33]. But let it be considered, what is the proper notion of confusion, but the breaking that order of things whereby they are properly disposed, and duly directed to their end, so that the order and due connection of means being broken, they fail of their end; but conviction and conversion of sinners is the obtaining the end of religious means. Not but that I think that persons that are thus extraordinarily moved should endeavor to refrain from such outward manifestations, what they well can, and should refrain to their utmost, in the time of the solemn worship. But if God is pleased to convince the consciences of persons, so that they can't avoid great outward manifestations, even to the interrupting and breaking off those public means they were attending, I don't think this is confusion, or an unhappy interruption, any more than if a company should meet on the field to pray for rain, and should be broken off from their exercise by a plentiful shower. Would to God that all the public assemblies in the land were broken off from their public exercises with such confusion as this the next Sabbath day! We need not be sorry for the breaking the order of the means, by obtaining the end to which that order is directed: he that is going a journey to fetch a treasure, need not be sorry that he is stopped by meeting the treasure in the midst of his journey.

Besides those that are overcome with conviction and distress, I have seen many of late, that have had their bodily strength taken away with a sense of the glorious excellency of the Redeemer, and the wonders of his dying love; with a very uncommon sense of their own littleness, and exceeding vileness attending it, with all expressions and appearances of the greatest abasement and abhorrence of themselves: and not only new converts, but many that were, as we hope, formerly converted, whose love and joy has been attended with a flood of tears, and a great appearance of contrition and humiliation, especially for their having lived no more to God's glory since their conversion; with a far greater sight of their vileness, and the evil of their hearts than ever they had; with an exceeding earnestness of desire to live better for the time to come, but attended with greater self-diffidence than ever. And many have been even overcome with pity to the souls of others, and longing for their salvation.

And many other things I might mention in this extraordinary

work, answering to every one of those marks that have been insisted on. So that if the Apostle John knew how to give signs of a work of the true spirit, this is such a work.

Providence has cast my lot in a place where the work of God has formerly been carried on. I had the happiness to be settled in that place two years with the venerable Stoddard; and was then acquainted with a number that, during that season, were wrought upon under his ministry, and have been intimately acquainted with the experiences of many others, that were wrought upon before under his ministry, in a manner agreeable to his doctrine, and the doctrine of all orthodox divines; and of late that work has been carried on there, with very much of these uncommon operations: but 'tis apparent to all to be the same work, not only that was wrought there six or seven years ago, but elder Christians there know it to be the same work that was carried on there, in their former pastor's days, though there be some new circumstances. And certainly we must throw by all the talk of conversion and Christian experience; and not only so, but we must throw by our Bibles, and give up revealed religion, if this be not in general the work of God. Not that I suppose that the degree of the influence of the Spirit of God, is to be determined by the degree of effect on men's bodies, or that those are always the best experiences, that have the greatest influence on the body.

And as to the imprudences and irregularities and mixture of delusion that have been; it is not at all to be wondered at that a reformation, after a long continued and almost universal deadness, should at first when the revival is new, be attended with such things. In the first creation God did not make a complete world at once; but there was a great deal of imperfection, darkness, and mixture of chaos and confusion, after God first said, "Let there be light" [Gen. 1:3], before the whole stood forth in perfect form. When God at first began his great work for the deliverance of his people, after their long continued bondage in Egypt, there were false wonders mixed with true, for a while; which hardened the unbelieving Egyptians, and made 'em to doubt of the divinity of the whole work. When the children of Israel first went about bringing up the ark of God, after it had long been neglected, and had been long absent, they sought not the Lord "after the due order," I Chron. 15:13. At the time when the sons of God came to present themselves before the Lord, Satan came also among them [Job 1:6; 2:1]. And Solomon's ships, when they brought gold and silver and pearls, also brought apes and peacocks.[10] When daylight first appears, after a night of darkness, we must expect to have darkness mixed with light, for a while, and not to have perfect day, and the sun risen at once. The fruits of the earth are first green, before they are ripe, and come to their proper perfection gradually; and so, Christ tells us, is the kingdom of God. Mark 4:26–28, "So is the kingdom of God; as if a man should cast seed into the ground, and should sleep, and rise night and day; and the seed should spring and grow up, he knoweth not how: for the earth bringeth forth fruit of herself; first the blade; then the ear; then the full corn in the ear."

The imprudences and errors that have attended this work, are the less to be wondered at, if it be considered that it is chiefly young persons that have been the subjects of it, who have less steadiness and experience, and are in the heat of youth, and much more ready to run to extremes. Satan will keep men secure as long as he can; but when he can do that no longer, he often endeavors to drive them to extremes, and so to dishonor God, and wound religion that way. And doubtless it has been one occasion of much of the misconduct there has been, that in many places, people that are the subjects of this work of God's Spirit, see plainly that their ministers have an ill opinion of the work; and therefore with just reason, durst not apply themselves to 'em as their guides in this work; and so are without guides: and no wonder that when a people are as sheep without a shepherd, they wander out of the way. A people, in such circumstances especially, stand in great and continual need of guides, and their guides stand in continual need of much more wisdom than they have of their own. And if a people have ministers that favor the work, and rejoice in it, yet 'tis not to be expected that, either people or ministers should know so well how to conduct themselves in such an extraordinary state of things, while it is new, and what they never had any experience of before, as they may, after they have had experience, and time to see the tendency, consequences and issue of things. The happy influence of experience is very manifest at this day, in the people among whom God has

10. [I Kings 10:22; II Chron. 9:21. Both verses read "ivory" (i.e. elephant's teeth) where JE wrote "pearls."]

settled my abode. The work of God that has been carried on there this year, has been much purer than that which was wrought there six years before.¹ It has seemed to be more purely spiritual; freer from natural and corrupt mixtures, and anything savoring of enthusiastic wildness and extravagance: it has wrought more by deep humiliation and abasement before God and men; and they have been much freer from imprudences and irregularities. And particularly there has been a remarkable difference in this respect, that whereas many before, in their comforts and rejoicings, did too much forget their distance from God, and were ready in their conversation together of the things of God, and of their own experiences, to talk with too much of an air of lightness, and something of laughter; now they seem to have no disposition to it, but rejoice with a more solemn, reverential, humble joy; as God directs the princes of the earth, Ps. 2:11. 'Tis not because the joy is not as great, and in many of them much greater. There are many among us, that were wrought upon in that former season, that have now had much greater communications from heaven than they had then; but their rejoicing operates in another manner: it only abases and solemnizes them; breaks their hearts, and brings them into the dust: now when they speak of their joys, it is not with laughter, but a flood of tears. Thus those that laughed before, weep now; and yet, by their united testimony, their joy is vastly purer and sweeter than that which before did more raise their animal spirits. They are now more like Jacob, when God appeared to him at Bethel, when he saw the ladder that reached to heaven, and said, "How dreadful is this place" [Gen. 28:17]; and like Moses, when God shewed him his glory on the mount, when he made haste, and bowed himself unto the earth [Exod. 34:8].

2. Let us all be hence warned, by no means to oppose, or do anything in the least to clog or hinder that work that has lately been carried on in the land, but on the contrary, to do our utmost to promote it. Now [that] Christ is come down from heaven into this land, in a remarkable and wonderful work of his Spirit, it becomes all his professed disciples to acknowledge him, and give him honor.

The example of the Jews in Christ's and the apostles' times, is enough to beget in those that don't acknowledge this work, a

1. [In 1743 JE again compared the Northampton awakening of 1735 with that of 1741; see below, pp. 548–49.]

great jealousy of themselves, and to make them exceeding cautious of what they say or do. Christ then "was in the world, and the world knew him not: he came to his own professing people, and his own received him not" [John 10:10–11]. That coming of Christ had been much spoken of in the prophecies of Scripture that they had in their hands, and had been long expected; and yet because Christ came in a manner that they did not expect, and that was not agreeable to their carnal reason, they would not own him, but opposed him, counted him a madman, and the spirit that he wrought by the spirit of the Devil [cf. Matt. 12:24]. They stood and wondered at the great things that were done, and knew not what to make of 'em; but yet they met with so many stumbling blocks, that they finally could not acknowledge him. And when the Spirit of God came to be so wonderfully poured out in the apostles' days, they looked upon it to be confusion and distraction. They were astonished by what they saw and heard, but not convinced. And especially was the work of God then rejected by those that were most conceited of their own understanding and knowledge, agreeable to Isa. 29:14, "Therefore behold, I will proceed to do a marvelous work amongst this people, even a marvelous work and a wonder; for the wisdom of their wise men shall perish, and the understanding of their prudent men shall be hid." And many of them that had been in reputation for religion and piety, had a great spite against the work, because they saw it tended to diminish their honor, and to reproach their formality and lukewarmness. Some upon these accounts, maliciously and openly opposed and reproached the work of the Spirit of God, and called it the work of the Devil, against inward conviction; and so were guilty of the unpardonable sin against the Holy Ghost.[2]

There is another coming of Christ, a spiritual coming, to set up his kingdom in the world, that is as much spoken of in Scripture prophecy as that first coming of Christ was, and that has been long expected by the church of God; that we have reason to think, from what is said of it, will be, in many respects, parallel with the other. And certainly, that low state that the visible church of God has lately been sunk into, is very parallel with the state of the Jewish church, when Christ came: and therefore no wonder at all, that when Christ comes, his work should appear a strange work to most; yea, it would be a wonder if it should be otherwise. Whether

2. [See below, p. 275.]

the work that is now wrought be the beginning of that great coming
of Christ to set up his kingdom, that is so much spoken of, or no;
yet it is evident from what has been said that it is a work of the
same Spirit, and of the same nature. And there is no reason to
doubt but that, for persons to continue long to refuse to acknowledge Christ in the work, especially those that are set to be teachers
in his church, will be in like manner provoking to God, as it was in
the Jews of old to refuse to acknowledge Christ; and that notwithstanding what they may plead of the great stumbling blocks
that are in the way, and the cause they have to doubt of the work.
The teachers of the Jewish church found innumerable stumbling
blocks, that were to them insuperable: there were many things
appeared in Christ, and in the work of the Spirit after his ascension,
that were exceeding strange to 'em; they were assured that they had
just cause for their scruples: Christ and his work were to the Jews
a stumbling block. "But blessed is he," says Christ, "whosoever shall
not be offended (or stumbled) in me" [Matt. 11:6]. As strange and
as unexpected as the manner of Christ's appearance was, yet he had
not been long in Judea, working miracles, before all those that had
opportunity to observe, and yet refused to acknowledge him,
brought fearful guilt upon themselves in the sight of God; and
Christ condemned them, that though they could "discern the face
of the sky, and of the earth," yet they could not discern the signs of
these times: "and why," says he, "even of yourselves, judge ye not
what is right?" Luke 12, at the latter end [56–57].

'Tis not to be supposed that the great Jehovah has bowed the
heavens and come down into his land [II Sam. 22:10 and/or Ps.
18:9], and appeared here now for so long a time, in such a glorious
work of his power and grace, in so extensive a manner, in the
most public places of the land, and almost all parts of it, without
giving such evidences of his presence that great numbers, and even
many teachers in his church, can remain guiltless in his sight,
without ever receiving and acknowledging him, and giving him
honor, and appearing to rejoice in his gracious presence; or without
so much as once giving him thanks for so glorious and blessed a
work of his grace, wherein his goodness does more appear, than if
he had bestowed on us all the temporal blessings that the world
affords. A long continued silence in such a case is undoubtedly
provoking to God; especially in ministers: it is a secret kind of opposition, that really tends to hinder the work: such silent ministers

stand in the way of the work of God; as Christ said of old, "He that is not with us is against us." [3] Those that stand wondering at this strange work of God, not knowing what to make of it, and refusing to receive it; and ready, it may be, sometimes to speak contemptibly of it, as it was with the Jews of old; would do well to consider and tremble at St. Paul's words to them, Acts 13:40–41, "Beware therefore lest that come upon you, which is spoken of in the prophets, Behold ye despisers, and wonder, and perish; for I work a work in your days, which you shall in no wise believe, though a man declare it unto you." And those that can't believe the work to be true, because of the extraordinary degree and manner of it, should consider how it was with the unbelieving lord in Samaria, who said, "Behold, if the Lord would make windows in heaven, might this thing be?" To whom Elisha said, "Behold, thou shalt see it with thine eyes, but shall not eat thereof" [II Kings 7:2]. Let all to whom this work is a cloud and darkness, as the pillar of cloud and fire was to the Egyptians, take heed that it ben't their destruction, as that was theirs, while it gave light to God's Israel [cf. Exod. 14:19–20].

I would pray those that quiet themselves with that, that they proceed on a principle of prudence, and are waiting to see what the issue of things will be, and what fruits those that are the subjects of this work will bring forth in their lives and conversations, would consider whether this will justify a long refraining from acknowledging Christ when he appears so wonderfully and graciously present in the land. 'Tis probable that many of those that are thus waiting, know not what they are waiting for: if they wait to see a work of God without difficulties and stumbling blocks, that will be like the fool's waiting at the riverside to have the water all run by. A work of God without stumbling blocks is never to be expected: "It must needs be that offenses come" [Matt. 18:7]. There never yet was any great manifestation that God made of himself to the world, without many difficulties attending it. It is with the *works* of God as 'tis with the *Word* of God; they are full of those things that seem strange and inconsistent and difficult to the carnal unbelieving hearts of men. Christ and his work always was, and always will be a stone of stumbling, and rock of offense; a gin and a snare to many [Hos. 14:9]. The prophet Hosea, in the last chapter

3. [Matt. 12:30; Luke 11:23. Both verses have the first-person pronoun in the singular; JE shifted to the plural.]

of his prophecy, speaking of a glorious revival of religion in God's church, when God would be as the dew to Israel, and he should grow as the lily, and cast forth his roots as Lebanon, his branches should spread, etc., concludes all thus, in the last verse: "Who is wise, and he shall understand these things? prudent, and he shall know them? For the ways of the Lord are right, and the just shall walk in them, but the transgressors shall fall therein" [Hos. 14:9].

'Tis probable that the stumbling blocks that now attend this work will in some respects be increased, and not diminished. Particularly, we probably shall see more instances of apostasy and gross iniquity among professors. And if one kind of stumbling blocks are removed, 'tis to be expected that others will come. 'Tis with Christ's works as it was with his parables: things that are difficult to men's dark minds are ordered of purpose, for the trial of persons' dispositions and spiritual sense, and that persons of corrupt minds, and of an unbelieving, perverse, caviling spirit, seeing might see and not understand [cf. Matt. 13:13]. Those that are now waiting to see the issue of this work, think they shall be better able to determine by and by; but they are probably, many of them, mistaken. The Jews that saw Christ's miracles, waited to see better evidences of his being the Messiah; they wanted a sign from heaven; but they waited in vain; their stumbling blocks did not diminish, but increase; they found no end to 'em; and so were more and more hardened in their unbelief. Many have been praying for that glorious reformation spoken of in Scripture, that knew not what they have been praying for (as it was with the Jews when they prayed for the coming of Christ); if it should come, they would not acknowledge or receive it.

This pretended prudence of persons, in waiting so long before they acknowledge this work, will probably in the end prove the greatest imprudence, in this respect, that hereby they will fail of any share of so great a blessing, and will miss the most precious opportunity of obtaining divine light, grace and comfort, and heavenly and eternal benefits, that ever God gave in New England. While the glorious fountain is set open in so wonderful a manner, and multitudes flock to it, and receive a rich supply of the wants of their souls, they stand at a distance doubting and wondering, and receive nothing, and are like to continue thus till the precious season is past.

It is to be wondered at, that those that have doubted of the work that has been attended with such uncommon external appearances, should be easy in their doubts, without taking thorough pains to inform themselves, by going where such things have been to be seen, and narrowly observing them, and diligently inquiring into them; not contenting themselves only with observing two or three instances, nor resting till they were fully informed by their own observation. I don't doubt but that if this course had been taken, it would have convinced all whose minds are not shut up against conviction, in a great degree indeed. How greatly have they erred, who only from the uncertain reports of others, have ventured to speak slightily of these things? That caution of an unbelieving Jew [Gamaliel] might teach them more prudence, Acts 5:38–39, "Refrain from these men, and let them alone; for if this counsel, or this work be of men, it will come to nought; but if it be of God, ye cannot overthrow it; lest haply ye be found to fight against God." Whether what has been said in this discourse be enough to convince all that have heard it, that the work that is now carried on in the land, is the work of God, or not, yet I hope that for the future, they will at least hearken to the caution of Gamaliel that has been now mentioned; for the future not to oppose it, or say anything against it, or anything that has so much as an indirect tendency to bring it into discredit, lest they should be found to be opposers of the Holy Ghost. There is no kind of sins so hurtful and dangerous to the souls of men, as those that are committed against the Holy Ghost. We had better speak against God the Father, or the Son, than to speak against the Holy Spirit in his gracious operations on the hearts of men: nothing will so much tend forever to prevent our having any benefit of his operations in our own souls.[4]

If there are any that will still resolutely go on to speak contemptibly of these things, I would beg of them to take heed that they ben't guilty of the unpardonable sin against the Holy Ghost. A time when the Holy Spirit is much poured out, and men's lusts, lukewarmness and hypocrisy reproached by its powerful operations, is the most likely time of any whatsoever, for this sin to be committed. If the work goes on, 'tis well if among the many that shew an enmity against it, and reproach it, some ben't guilty of this sin, if none have been already. Those that maliciously oppose and reproach this work, and call it the work of the Devil, want but one thing of the unpardonable sin, and that is doing it against inward

4. [Cf. Matt. 12:22–32; and above, p. 55.]

conviction. And though some are so prudent, as not openly to oppose and reproach the work, yet 'tis to be feared, at this day when the Lord is going forth so gloriously against his enemies, that many that are silent and unactive, especially ministers, will bring that curse of the angel of the Lord upon themselves, Judg. 5:23; "Curse ye Meroz, said the angel of the Lord: curse ye bitterly the inhabitants thereof, because they came not to the help of the Lord, to the help of the Lord against the mighty."

Since the great God has come down from heaven, and manifested himself in so wonderful a manner in this land, it is in vain for any of us to expect any other, than to be greatly affected by it in our spiritual state and circumstances, respecting the favor of God, one way or the other. Those that don't become more happy by it, will become far more guilty and miserable. It is always so: such a season that proves an acceptable year, and a time of great grace and favor to them that will accept it and improve it, proves a day of vengeance to others, Isa. 61:2. When God sends forth his Word it shall not return to him void [Isa. 55:11]; much less his Spirit. When Christ was upon earth in Judea, many slighted and neglected him; but it proved in the issue to be no matter of indifference to them: God made all that people to feel that Christ had been among them; those that did not feel it to their comfort, felt it to their sorrow with a witness. When God only sent the prophet Ezekiel to the children of Israel, he declared that "whether they would hear, or whether they would forbear, yet they should know that there had been a prophet among them" [Ezek. 2:5]. How much more may we suppose that when God has appeared so wonderfully in this land, that he will make everyone to know that the great Jehovah has been in New England?

3. I come now in the third and last place, to apply myself to those that are the friends of this work, and have been partakers of it, and are zealous to promote it. Let me earnestly exhort such to give diligent heed to themselves to avoid all errors and misconduct, and whatsoever may darken and obscure the work, and give occasion to those that stand ready to reproach it. The Apostle [Paul] was careful to "cut off occasion from those that desired occasion" [II Cor. 11:12]. The same apostle exhorts Titus to maintain that strict care and watch over himself, that both his preaching and behavior might be such as "could not be condemned; that he that was

of the contrary part might be ashamed, having no evil thing to say of them," Tit. 2:7–8. We had need to be "wise as serpents and harmless as doves" [Matt. 10:16]. 'Tis of no small consequence that we should at this day behave ourselves innocently and prudently. We must expect that the great Enemy of this work will especially try his utmost with us; and he will especially triumph if he can prevail against any of us, in anything to blind and mislead us: he knows it will do more to further his purpose and interest, than if he prevailed against an hundred others. We had need to watch and pray, for we are but little children; this roaring lion is too strong for us [I Pet. 5:8], and this old serpent too subtile for us [Gen. 3:1].

Humility and self-diffidence, and an entire dependence on our Lord Jesus Christ, will be our best defense. Let us therefore maintain the strictest watch against spiritual pride, or a being lifted up with extraordinary experiences and comforts, and high favors of heaven that any of us may have received. We had need after such favors, in a special manner to keep a strict and jealous eye upon our own hearts, lest there should arise self-exalting reflections upon what we have received, and high thoughts of ourselves as being now some of the most eminent of saints and peculiar favorites of heaven, and that the secret of the Lord is especially with us, and that we above all are fit to be improved as the great instructors and censors of this evil generation: and in an high conceit of our own wisdom and discerning, should as it were naturally assume to ourselves the airs of prophets or extraordinary ambassadors of heaven. When we have great discoveries of God made to our souls, we should not shine bright in our own eyes. Moses when he had been conversing with God in the mount, though his face shone so as to dazzle the eyes of Aaron and the people, yet he did not shine in his own eyes; "he wist not that his face shone" [Exod. 34:29]. Let none think themselves out of danger of this spiritual pride, even in their best frames. God saw that the Apostle Paul (though probably the most eminent saint that ever lived) was not out of danger of it, no, not when he had just been conversing with God in the third heaven; see II Cor. 12:7. Pride is the worst viper that is in the heart; it is the first sin that ever entered into the universe, and it lies lowest of all in the foundation of the whole building of sin, and is the most secret, deceitful and unsearchable in its ways of working, of any lusts whatsoever: it is ready to mix with everything; and nothing is so hateful to God, and contrary to the spirit of the Gospel, or of so dangerous consequence; and there is no one sin that does so much let in the Devil into the hearts of the saints, and expose them to his delusions. I have seen it in many instances, and that in eminent saints. The Devil has come in at this door presently after some eminent experience and extraordinary communion with God, and has woefully deluded and led 'em astray, till God has mercifully opened their eyes and delivered them; and they themselves have afterwards been made sensible that it was pride that betrayed them.

Some of the true friends of the work of God's Spirit have erred in giving too much heed to impulses and strong impressions on their minds, as though they were immediate significations from heaven to them of something that should come to pass, or something that it was the mind and will of God that they should do, which was not signified or revealed anywhere in the Bible without those impulses. These impressions, if they are truly from the Spirit of God, are of a quite different nature from the gracious influences of the Spirit of God on the hearts of the saints; they are of the nature of the extraordinary gifts of the Spirit, and are properly inspiration, such as the prophets and apostles and others had of old; which the Apostle distinguishes from the grace of the Spirit in the 13th chapter of the first of Corinthians.

One reason why some have been ready to lay weight on such impulses, is an opinion they have had, that the glory of the approaching happy days of the church would partly consist in restoring those extraordinary gifts of the Spirit: which opinion I believe arises partly through want of duly considering and comparing the nature and value of those two kinds of influences of the Spirit, viz. his ordinary gracious influences, and his extraordinary influences in inspiration and miraculous gifts. The former are by far the most excellent and glorious; as the Apostle largely shews in the first of Corinthians, beginning with the 31st verse of the 12th chapter; speaking of the extraordinary gifts of the Spirit, he says, "But covet earnestly the best gifts; and yet I shew you a more excellent way," i.e. a more excellent way of the influence of the Spirit: and then he goes on in the next chapter, to shew what that more excellent way is, even that which is in the grace of the Spirit, which summarily consists in charity or divine love. And throughout that chapter he shews the great preference of that above inspiration. God communicates himself in his own nature more to the soul in saving grace in the heart, than in all miraculous gifts. The blessed image of God consists in that, and not in these: the excellency, happiness and glory of the soul, does immediately consist in that, and not in those: that is a root that bears infinitely more excellent fruit. Salvation and the eternal enjoyment of God is promised to divine grace, but not to inspiration: a man may have those extraordinary gifts, and yet be abominable to God, and go to hell: the spiritual and eternal life of the soul don't consist in the extraordinary gifts of the Spirit, but the grace of the Spirit. This, and not those, is that influence of the Spirit of God which God bestows only on his favorites and dear children: he has sometimes thrown out the other to dogs and swine, as he did to Balaam, Saul, and Judas; and some that in the primitive times of the Christian church committed the unpardonable sin, as Heb. 6. Many wicked men at the day of judgment will plead, "Have we not prophesied in thy name, and in thy name cast out devils, and in thy name done many wonderful works?" [Matt. 7:22]. The greatest privilege of the prophets and apostles was not their being inspired and working miracles, but their eminent holiness. The grace that was in their hearts, was a thousand times more their dignity and honor, than their miraculous gifts. The things that we find David comforting himself in, in the Book of Psalms, are not his being a king, or a prophet, but the holy influences of the Spirit of God in his heart, communicating to him divine light, love and joy. The Apostle Paul abounded in visions and revelations and miraculous gifts above all the apostles; but yet he esteems all things but loss for the excellency of the spiritual knowledge of Christ [cf. Phil. 3:8]. It was not the gifts but the grace of the apostles, that was the proper evidence of their names being written in heaven, which Christ directs them to rejoice in, much more than in the devils being subject to them [Luke 10:20]. To have grace in the heart is an higher privilege than the blessed Virgin herself had, in having the body of the second Person in the Trinity conceived in her womb, by the power of the Highest overshadowing her; Luke 11:27–28, "And it came to pass as he spake these things, a certain woman of the company lift[ed] up her voice and said unto them [*sic,* him], Blessed is the womb that bear [*sic,* bare] thee, and the paps that thou has sucked! But he said, Yea, rather blessed are they that hear the Word of God, and keep it." See also to the same purpose, Matt. 12:47, etc.[5]

5. [JE uses "etc." often to mean "et seq." The passage he intends here is Matt. 12:47–50.]

The influence of the Holy Spirit, or divine charity in the heart, is the very greatest privilege and glory of the highest archangel in heaven; yea, this is the very thing by which the creature has fellowship with God himself, with the Father and the Son, in their beauty and happiness, and are made partakers of the divine nature, and have Christ's joy fulfilled in themselves.

The ordinary sanctifying influences of the Spirit of God are the end of all extraordinary gifts, as the Apostle shews, Eph. 4:11–13. They are good for nothing, any further than as they are subordinate to this end; they will be so far from profiting any without it, that they will only aggravate their misery. This is, as the Apostle observes, the most excellent way of God's communicating his Spirit to his church; 'tis the greatest glory of the church in all ages. This glory is what makes the state of the church on earth most like the state of the church in heaven, where prophecy and tongues, and other miraculous gifts cease, and are vanished away, and God communicates his Spirit only in that more excellent way that the Apostle speaks of, viz. charity, or divine love, which never faileth [I Cor. 13:8]. Therefore the glory of the approaching happy state of the church don't at all require these extraordinary gifts. As that state of the church will be the nearest of any to its perfect state in heaven, so I believe it will be like it in this, that all extraordinary gifts shall have ceased and vanished away; and all those stars and moon, with the reflected light they gave in the night, or a more dark season, shall be swallowed up in the sun of divine love. The Apostle speaks of those gifts of inspiration as childish things, in comparison of the influence of the Spirit in divine love, things given to the church only to support it in its minority, till the church should have a complete standing rule established, and the ordinary means of grace should be settled; but as things that should cease, as the church advanced above its childish state, and should entirely vanish when the church should come to the state of manhood; which will be in the approaching glorious times, above any other state of the church on earth: I Cor. 13:11, "When I was a child, I spake as a child, I understood as a child, I thought as a child: but when I became a man, I put away childish things"; compared with the three preceding verses.

When the Apostle in this chapter speaks of prophecies, tongues and revelations ceasing and vanishing away in the church, when the Christian church should be advanced from a state of minority to a state of manhood, he seems to have respect to its coming to an adult state in this world as well as in heaven; for he speaks of such an adult state, or state of manhood, wherein those three things, faith, hope, and charity, should abide or remain after miracles and revelations had ceased; as you may see in the last verse, "And now abideth (μένει, remaineth) faith, hope, charity; these three." The Apostle's manner of speaking here shews an evident reference to what he had just been saying before; and here is a manifest antithesis between that *remaining* spoken of here, and that *failing, ceasing,* and *vanishing away,* spoken of in the 8th verse. The Apostle had been shewing how that all those gifts of inspiration, that were the leading strings of the Christian church in its infancy, should vanish away, when the church came to a state of manhood; and when he has done, then he returns to observe, what things remain after those had failed and ceased; and he observes that those three things shall remain in the church, faith, hope, and charity: and therefore the adult state of the church he speaks of, is the more perfect state which it shall arrive at in this world, which will be above all in that glorious state it shall be brought to in the latter ages of the world. And this was the more properly observed to the church of the Corinthians, upon two accounts: because the Apostle had before observed to that church that they were in a state of infancy, chap. 3:1–2; and because that church seems above all others to have abounded with miraculous gifts. When the expected glorious state of the church comes, the increase of light shall be so great that it will in some respect answer what is said [in] vs. 12, of "seeing face to face." See Isa. 24:23 and 25:7.

Therefore I don't expect a restoration of these miraculous gifts in the approaching glorious times of the church, nor do I desire it: it appears to me that it would add nothing to the glory of those times, but rather diminish from it. For my part, I had rather enjoy the sweet influences of the Spirit, shewing Christ's spiritual divine beauty, and infinite grace, and dying love, drawing forth the holy exercises of faith, and divine love, and sweet complacence, and humble joy in God, one quarter of an hour, than to have prophetical visions and revelations for a whole year. It appears to me much more probable that God should give immediate revelations to his saints in the dark times of popery, than now in the approach of the most glorious and perfect state of his church on earth. It don't appear to me that there is any need of those extraordinary gifts, to introduce this happy state, and set up the kingdom of God through the world: I have seen so much of the power of God in a more excellent way, as to convince me that God can easily do it without [them].

I would therefore entreat the people of God to be very cautious how they give heed to such things. I have seen 'em fail in very many instances; and know by experience that impressions being made with great power, and upon the minds of true saints, yea, eminent saints; and presently after, yea, in the midst of, extraordinary exercises of grace and sweet communion with God, and attended with texts of Scripture strongly impressed on the mind, are no sure signs of their being revelations from heaven: for I have known such impressions [to] fail, and prove vain by the event, in some instances attended with all these circumstances. I know that they that leave the sure word of prophecy, that God has given us to be a light shining in a dark place, to follow such impressions and impulses, leave the guidance of the pole star to follow a Jack-with-a-lanthorn. And no wonder therefore that sometimes they are led a dreadful dance, and into woeful extravagancies.

And seeing inspiration is not to be expected, let us not despise human learning. They that say human learning is of little or no use in the work of the ministry, don't consider what they say; if they did, they would not say it. By human learning I mean, and suppose others mean, that improvement of that common knowledge which men have by human and outward means. And therefore to say that human learning is of no use, is as much as to say that the education of a child, or that the common knowledge that a grown man has, more than a little child, is of no use; and so that a child of four years old is as fit for a teacher in the church of God, with the same degree of grace, and capable of doing as much to advance the kingdom of Christ, by his instruction, as a very understanding knowing man of thirty years of age. If adult persons have greater ability and advantage to do service because they have more human knowledge than a little child, then doubtless if they have more human knowledge still, with the same degree of grace, they would have still greater ability and advantage to do service. An increase of knowledge, without doubt, increases a man's advantage either to do good or hurt, according as he is disposed. 'Tis too manifest to be denied, that God made great use of human learning in the Apostle Paul, as he also did in Moses and Solomon.

And if knowledge obtained by human means is not to be despised, then it will follow that the means of obtaining it are not to be neglected, viz. study; and that this is of great use in order to a preparation for a public instructing [of] others. And though undoubtedly, an having the heart full of the powerful influences of the Spirit of God may at some times enable persons to speak profitably, yea, very excellently, without study; yet this will not warrant us needlessly to cast ourselves down from the pinnacle of the temple, depending upon it that the angel of the Lord will bear us up, and keep us from dashing our foot against a stone [Matt. 4:5–6], when there is another way to go down, though it ben't so quick. And I would pray that method in public discourses, which tends greatly to help both the understanding and memory, mayn't be wholly neglected.

And another thing I would beg the dear children of God more fully to consider of, is: how far, and upon what grounds, the rules of the Holy Scriptures will truly justify their passing censures upon others that are professing Christians, as hypocrites and ignorant of anything of real religion. We all know that there is a judging and censuring of some sort or other, that the Scripture very often, and very strictly forbids. I desire that those rules of Scripture may be looked into, and thoroughly weighed; and that it may be considered whether or no a taking it upon us to discern the state of the souls of others, and to pass sentence upon them as wicked men, that are professing Christians, and of a good visible conversation, be not really forbidden by Christ in the New Testament: if it be, then doubtless the disciples of Christ ought to avoid it, however sufficient they may think themselves for it; or however needful, or of good tendency, they may think it. 'Tis plain that that sort of judging is forbidden, that God claims as his prerogative, whatever that be. We know that there is a certain judging of the hearts of the children of men, that is often spoken of as the great prerogative of God, and which belongs only to him; as in I Kings 8:39, "Forgive, and do, and give to every man according to his ways, whose heart thou knowest: for thou, even thou only, knowest the hearts of all the children of men." And if we examine, we shall find that that judging of hearts that is spoken of as God's prerogative, is not only the judging of the aims and disposition of men's hearts in particular actions, but chiefly a judging the state of the hearts of the professors of religion, with regard to that profession. This will appear very manifest by looking over the following Scriptures: I Chron. 28:9;

Ps. 7:9–11; Ps. 26 throughout; Prov. 16:2 and 17:3 and 21:2; John 2:23–25; Rev. 2:22–23. That sort of judging which is God's proper business is forbidden, as Rom. 14:4, "Who art thou that judgest another man's servant? To his own master he standeth or falleth." Jas. 4:12, "There is one Lawgiver that is able to save and to destroy; who art thou that judgest another?" I Cor. 4:3–4, "But with me it is a very small thing that I should be judged of you, or of man's judgment; yea, I judge not mine own self [. . .] but he that judgeth me is the Lord."

Again, whatsoever kind of judging is the proper work and business of the day of judgment, is a judging that we are forbidden, as in I Cor. 4:5, "Therefore judge nothing before the time, until the Lord come; who both will bring to light the hidden things of darkness, and will make manifest the counsels of the hearts; and then shall every man have praise of God." But to distinguish hypocrites, that have the form of godliness, and the visible conversation of godly men, from true saints; to separate the sheep from goats, is the proper business of the day of judgment; yea, is represented as the main business and end of that great day. They therefore do greatly err that take it upon them positively to determine who are sincere, and who [are] not, and to draw the dividing line between true saints and hypocrites, and to separate between sheep and goats, setting the one on the right and the other on the left [Matt. 25:31–33], and to distinguish and gather out the tares from amongst the wheat. Many of the servants of the owner of the field are very ready to think themselves sufficient for this, and are forward to offer their service to this end; but their lord says, "Nay, lest while ye gather up the tares, ye root up the wheat also: let both grow together until the harvest; and in the time of the harvest I will take care to see a thorough separation made"; as Matt. 13:28–30.[6] Agreeably to that forementioned prohibition of the Apostle, I Cor. 4:5, "Judge nothing before the time," in this parable by the servants that have the care of the fruit of the field, is doubtless meant the same with the servants that have the care of the fruit of the vineyard, Luke 20 [vss. 9–16], and those that are elsewhere represented as servants of the lord of the harvest, that are appointed as laborers in his harvest, which we know are ministers of the Gospel. Now that parable in the 13th [chapter] of Matthew is fulfilled; while men slept (during that long, sleepy, dead time that has been in the church), the enemy

6. [JE has paraphrased only vss. 29 and 30.]

has sowed tares; and now is the time when the blade is sprung up, and religion is reviving; now some of the servants that have the care of the field say, "Let us go and gather up the tares." I know by experience that there is a great aptness in men, that think they have had some experience of the power of religion, to think themselves sufficient to discern and determine the state of others' souls by a little conversation with them; and experience has taught me that 'tis an error. I once did not imagine that the heart of man had been so unsearchable as I find it is. I am less charitable, and less uncharitable than once I was. I find more things in wicked men that may counterfeit, and make a fair shew of piety, and more ways that the remaining corruption of the godly may make them appear like carnal men, formalists and dead hypocrites, than once I knew of. The longer I live, the less I wonder that God challenges it as his prerogative to try the hearts of the children of men, and has directed that this business should be let alone till the harvest. I find that God is wiser than men. I desire to adore the wisdom of God, and his goodness to me and my fellow creatures, that he has not committed this great business into the hands of such poor, weak, dim-sighted a creature as I am; of so much blindness, pride, partiality, prejudice, and deceitfulness of heart; but has committed it into the hands of One infinitely fitter for it, and has made it his prerogative.

The talk of some persons, and the account they give of their experiences is exceeding satisfying, and such as forbids and banishes the least thought of their being any other than the precious children of God; it obliges and as it were forces full charity: but yet we must allow the Scriptures to stand good, that speak of everything in the saint, that belongs to the spiritual and divine life, as hidden. Their life is said to be "hidden," Col. 3:3–4. Their food is the "hidden manna" [Rev. 2:17]; they have meat to eat that others know not of [John 4:32]; a stranger intermeddles not with their joys [Prov. 14:10]: the heart in which they possess their divine distinguishing ornaments is the hidden man, and in the sight of God only, I Pet. 3:4. Their new name, that Christ has given them, "no man knows but he that receives it," Rev. 2:17. The praise of the true Israelites, whose "circumcision is that of the heart," is not of men but of God, Rom. 2:29; that is, they can be certainly known and discerned to be Israelites, so as to have the honor that belongs to such, only of God; as appears by the use of the like expression by the same apostle, I Cor. 4:5. Speaking there of its being God's prerogative to judge who are upright Christians, and that which he will do at the Day of Judgment, he adds, "and then shall every man have praise of God."

The instance of Judas is remarkable; who though he had been so much amongst the rest of the disciples, who were all persons of true experience, yet never seemed to have entertained a thought of his being any other than a true disciple, till he discovered himself by his scandalous practice.

And the instance of Ahithophel is also very remarkable; whom David did not discern, though he was so wise and holy a man, a person of such great experience, and so great a divine, and had such great acquaintance with the Scriptures, and knew more than all his teachers, and more than the ancients; and was grown old in experience, and was in the greatest ripeness of his judgment, and was a great prophet; and though he was so intimately acquainted with Ahithophel, he being his familiar friend and most intimate companion in religious and spiritual concerns: yet David not only never discovered him to be an hypocrite, but relied upon him as a true saint, though he relished and felt his religious discourse, it was sweet to him, and he counted him an eminent saint; so that he made him above any other man his guide and counselor in soul matters: but yet he was not only no saint, but a notoriously wicked man, a murderous, vile wretch. Ps. 55:11–14, "Wickedness is in the midst thereof; deceit and guile depart not from her streets: for it was not an enemy that reproached me; then I could have borne it; neither was it he that hated me that did magnify himself against me; then I would have hid myself from him: but it was thou, a man mine equal, my guide and mine acquaintance: we took sweet counsel together, and walked unto the house of God in company." [Cf. also II Sam. 15–17.]

To suppose that men have ability and right to determine the state of the souls of visible Christians, and so to make an open separation between saints and hypocrites, that true saints may be of one visible company and hypocrites of another, separated by a partition that men make, carries in it an inconsistency: for it supposes that God has given men power to make another visible church within his visible church; for by visible Christians, or those that are of God's visible church, can be understood nothing else than that company that are Christians or saints, *visibly so;* i.e. that have a right to be received as such in the eye of a public charity. None can have [the] right to exclude any one of this visible church, but in the way of that regular ecclesiastical proceeding, which God has established in his visible church.

I beg of those that have a true zeal for promoting this work of God, that God has begun in the land, well to consider these things. I am persuaded that as many of them as have much to do with souls, if they don't hearken to me now, yet will be of the same mind when they have had more experience.

And another thing that I would entreat the zealous friends of this glorious work of God to avoid, is managing the controversy with opposers with too much heat and appearance of an angry zeal; and particularly insisting very much in public prayer and preaching on the persecution of opposers. If their persecution were ten times so great as it is, methinks it would not be best to say so much about it. It becomes Christians to be like lambs, not to be apt to complain and cry when they are hurt; to be dumb and not open their mouth, after the example of our dear Redeemer; and not to be like swine, that are apt to scream aloud when they are touched. We should not be ready presently to think and speak of fire from heaven, when the Samaritans oppose us, and won't receive us into their villages [Luke 9:51–55]. God's zealous ministers would do well to think of the direction the Apostle Paul gave to a zealous minister, II Tim. 2:24–26, "And the servant of the Lord must not strive, but be gentle unto all men, apt to teach, patient; in meekness instructing those that oppose themselves, if God peradventure will give them repentance to the acknowledging of the truth. And that they may recover themselves out of the snare of the Devil, who are taken captive by him at his will."

And another thing that I would humbly recommend to those that love the Lord Jesus Christ, and would advance his kingdom, is a good attendance to that excellent rule of prudence Christ has left us, Matt. 9:16–17, "No man putteth a piece of new cloth into an old garment; for that which is put in to fill it up, taketh from the garment, and the rent is made worse. Neither do men put new wine into old bottles; else the bottles break, and the wine runneth out, and the bottles perish. But they put new wine into new bottles, and both are preserved." I am afraid that the wine is now running out in some parts of this land, for want of attending to this rule. For though I believe we have confined ourselves too much to a certain stated method and form in the management of our religious affairs; which has had a tendency to cause all our religion to degenerate into mere formality; yet whatsoever has the appearance of a great innovation, that tends much to shock and surprise people's minds, and to set them a talking and disputing, tends greatly to hinder the progress of the power of religion, by raising the opposition of some, and diverting the minds of others, and perplexing the minds of many with doubts and scruples, and causing people to swerve from their great business, and turn aside to vain jangling. Therefore that which is very much beside the common practice, unless it be a thing in its own nature of considerable importance, had better be avoided. Herein we shall follow the example of one who had the greatest success in propagating the power of religion in the world, of any man that ever lived, that he himself gives us an account of; I Cor. 9:20–23, "Unto the Jews I became as a Jew, that I might gain the Jews: to them that are under the law, as under the law, that I might gain them that are under the law: to them that are without law, [as without law] (being not without law to God, but under law to Christ), that I might gain them that are without law: to the weak became I as weak, that I might gain the weak: I am made all things to all men, that I might by all means save some. And this I do for the Gospel's sake, that I might be partaker thereof with you."

SOME THOUGHTS CONCERNING
THE REVIVAL

The year 1742 was one of rapidly rising controversy over revivalism. Dismayed that "the glorious work" was threatened on one side by the indiscretions of overzealous promoters and on the other by the stiffening opposition of its critics, Edwards spoke out once again in its defense. In his most ambitious writing yet, he expanded the arguments of The Distinguishing Marks, *seeking more largely to define evangelical experience, rebuke spurious manifestations of it, refute captious criticisms against it, and urge its cordial support by all classes of Christians.* Some Thoughts Concerning the Revival *was completed toward the end of the year and issued by his Boston publishers in March 1743. For a description of its circumstances and an analysis of its contents, see above, pp. 65–78. The text which follows is that of the first edition, corrected according to published errata.*

Some Thoughts

Concerning the prefent

Revival of Religion

IN

NEW-ENGLAND,

And the Way in which it ought to be
acknowledged and promoted,

Humbly offered to the Publick, in a

TREATISE on that Subject.

In Five PARTS ;

PART I. Shewing that the Work that has of late been going on in this Land, is a glorious Work of GOD.

PART II. Shewing the Obligations that all are under, to acknowlege, rejoice in and promote this Work, and the great Danger of the contrary.

ART III. Shewing in many Inftances, where-in the Subjects, or zealous Promoters, of this Work have been injurioufly blamed.

PART IV. Shewing what Things are to be corrected or avoided, in promoting this Work, or in our Behaviour under it.

PART V. Shewing positively what ought to be done to promote this Work.

By *JONATHAN EDWARDS*, A. M.
iftor of the Church of CHRIST at *Northampton.*

Ifai. 40. 3. *Prepare ye the Way of the Lord, make ftrait
in the Defart a high-Way for our God*

BOSTON : Printed and Sold by *S. Kneeland*
and *T. Green* in *Queen-Street*, 1742.

AUTHOR'S PREFACE

IN the ensuing treatise, I condemn ministers' assuming, or taking too much upon them, and appearing as though they supposed that they were the persons to whom it especially belonged to dictate, direct and determine; but perhaps shall be thought to be very guilty of it myself: and some when they read this treatise, may be ready to say that I condemn this in others, that I may have the monopoly of it. I confess that I have taken a great deal of liberty freely to express my thoughts, concerning almost everything appertaining to the wonderful work of God that has of late been carried on in the land, and to declare what has appeared to me to be the mind of God, concerning the duty and obligations of all sorts of persons, and even those that are my superiors and fathers, ministers of the Gospel, and civil rulers: but yet I hope the liberty I have taken is not greater than can be justified. In a free nation, such liberty of the press is allowed, that every author takes leave without offense, freely to speak his opinion concerning the management of public affairs, and the duty of the legislature, and those that are at the head of the administration, though vastly his superiors. As now at this day, private subjects offer their sentiments to the public from the press, concerning the management of the war with Spain; freely declaring what they think to be the duty of the Parliament, and the principal ministers of state, etc.[1] We in New England are at this day engaged in a more important war: and I'm sure, if we consider the sad jangling and confusion that has attended it, we shall confess that it is highly requisite that somebody should speak his mind concerning the way in which it ought to be managed: and that not only a few of the many particulars, that are the matter of strife in the land, should be debated on the one side and the other, in pamphlets (as has of late been done, with heat

---

1. [The so-called "War of Jenkins' Ear" (1739–43), though its North American engagements were mostly in Georgia and Florida, was the subject of occasional comment in New England newspapers.]

and fierceness enough); which don't tend to bring the contention in general to an end, but rather to inflame it, and increase the uproar: but that something should be published, to bring the affair in general, and the many things that attend it, that are the subjects of debate, under a particular consideration. And certainly it is high time that this was done.

If private persons may speak their minds without arrogance; much more may a minister of the kingdom of Christ speak freely about things of this nature, which do so nearly concern the interest of the kingdom of his Lord and Master, at so important a juncture. If some elder minister had undertaken this, I acknowledge it would have been more proper; but I have heard of no such thing a doing, or like to be done. I hope therefore I shall be excused for undertaking such a piece of work. I think that nothing that I have said can justly be interpreted as though I would impose my thoughts upon any, or did not suppose that others have equal right to think for themselves, with myself. We are not accountable one to another for our thoughts; but we must all give an account to him who searches our hearts, and has doubtless his eye especially upon us at such an extraordinary season as this. If I have well confirmed my opinion concerning this work, and the way in which it should be acknowledged and promoted, with Scripture and reason, I hope others that read it will receive it as a manifestation of the mind and will of God. If others would hold forth further light to me in any of these particulars, I hope I should thankfully receive it. I think I have been made in some measure sensible, and much more of late than formerly, of my need of more wisdom than I have. I make it my rule to lay hold of light and embrace it, wherever I see it, though held forth by a child or an enemy. If I have assumed too much in the following discourse, and have spoken in a manner that savors of a spirit of pride, no wonder that others can better discern it than I myself. If it be so, I ask pardon, and beg the prayers of every Christian reader, that I may have more light, humility and zeal; and that I may be favored with such measures of the Divine Spirit, as a minister of the Gospel stands in need of, at such an extraordinary season.

SHEWING THAT THE EXTRAORDINARY WORK THAT HAS OF LATE BEEN
GOING ON IN THIS LAND, IS A GLORIOUS WORK OF GOD

THE error of those who have ill thoughts of the great religious
operation on the minds of men, that has been carried on of late
in New England (so far as the ground of such an error has been
in the understanding, and not in the disposition), seems fundamentally to lie in three things: *first,* in judging of this work a priori;
secondly, in not taking the Holy Scriptures as an whole rule whereby
to judge of such operations; *thirdly,* in not justly separating and
distinguishing the good from the bad.

[*The Revival Not To Be Judged A Priori*]

They have greatly erred in the way in which they have gone
about to try this work, whether it be a work of the Spirit of God
or no, viz. in judging of it a priori; from the way that it began,
the instruments that have been employed, the means that have
been made use of, and the methods that have been taken and
succeeded in carrying it on. Whereas, if we duly consider the matter,
it will evidently appear that such a work is not to be judged of a
priori, but a posteriori: we are to observe the effect wrought; and if,
upon examination of that, it be found to be agreeable to the Word
of God, we are bound without more ado to rest in it as God's work;
and shall be like to be rebuked for our arrogance, if we refuse
so to do till God shall explain to us how he has brought this effect
to pass, or why he has made use of such and such means in doing
of it. Those texts are enough to cause us with trembling to forbear
such a way of proceeding in judging of a work of God's Spirit,
Isa. 40:13–14, "Who hath directed the Spirit of the Lord, or being
his counselor hath taught him? With whom took he counsel, and
who instructed him; and who taught him in the path of judgment,
and taught him knowledge, and shewed to him the way of under-

standing?" John 3:8, "The wind bloweth where it listeth; and thou hearest the sound thereof; but canst not tell whence it cometh, and whither it goeth." We hear the sound, we perceive the effect, and from thence we judge that the wind does indeed blow; without waiting, before we pass this judgment, first to be satisfied what should be the cause of the wind's blowing from such a part of the heavens, and how it should come to pass that it should blow in such a manner, at such a time. To judge a priori is a wrong way of judging of any of the works of God. We are not to resolve that we will first be satisfied how God brought this or the other effect to pass, and why he hath made it thus, or why it has pleased him to take such a course, and to use such and such means, before we will acknowledge his work, and give him the glory of it. This is too much for the clay to take upon it with respect to the potter [cf. Jer. 18:6; Rom. 9:20–21]. "God gives not account of his matters: his judgments are a great deep: he hath his way in the sea, and his path in the great waters, and his footsteps are not known; and who shall teach God knowledge, or enjoin him his way, or say unto him, What doest thou? We know not what is the way of the Spirit, nor how the bones do grow in the womb of her that is with child; even so we know not the works of God who maketh all." [1] No wonder therefore if those that go this forbidden way to work, in judging of the present wonderful operation, are perplexed and confounded. We ought to take heed that we don't expose ourselves to the calamity of those who pried into the ark of God, when God mercifully returned it to Israel, after it had departed from them [I Sam. 6:19].

Indeed God has not taken that course, nor made use of those means, to begin and carry on this great work, which men in their wisdom would have thought most advisable, if he had asked their counsel; but quite the contrary. But it appears to me that the great God has wrought like himself, in the manner of his carrying on this work; so as very much to show his own glory, and exalt his own sovereignty, power and all-sufficiency, and pour contempt on all that human strength, wisdom, prudence and sufficiency, that men have been wont to trust, and to glory in; and so as greatly to cross, rebuke and chastise the pride and other corruptions of men;

1. [JE wrote this as a single quotation. Actually it is a catena of phrases adapted from Job 33:13; Ps. 36:6 and 77:19; Job 21:22, 36:23, and 9:12; and Eccles. 11:5.]

in a fulfilment of that [verse,] Isa. 2:17, "And the loftiness of man shall be bowed down, and the haughtiness of men shall be made low, and the Lord alone shall be exalted in that day." God doth thus, in intermingling in his providence so many stumbling blocks with this work; in suffering so much of human weakness and infirmity to appear; and in ordering so many things that are mysterious to men's wisdom: in pouring out his Spirit chiefly on the common people, and bestowing his greatest and highest favors upon them, admitting them nearer to himself than the great, the honorable, the rich and the learned, agreeable to that prophecy, Zech. 12:7, "The Lord also shall save the tents of Judah first, that the glory of the house of David, and the glory of the inhabitants of Jerusalem, do not magnify themselves against Judah." Those that dwelt in the tents of Judah were the common people, that dwelt in the country, and were of inferior rank. The inhabitants of Jerusalem were their citizens, their men of wealth and figure: and Jerusalem also was the chief place of the habitation or resort of their priests and Levites, and their officers and judges; there sat the great Sanhedrin.[2] The house of David were the highest rank of all, the royal family, and the great men that were round about the king. 'Tis evident by the context that this prophecy has respect to something further than the saving the people out of the Babylonish Captivity.

God in this work has begun at the lower end, and he has made use of the weak and foolish things of the world to carry on his work. The ministers that have been chiefly improved, some of them have been mere babes in age and standing, and some of them such as have not been so high in reputation among their fellows as many others; and God has suffered their infirmities to appear in the sight of others, so as to displease them; and at the same time it has pleased God to improve them, and greatly to succeed them, while he has not so succeeded others that are generally reputed vastly their superiors. Yea, there is reason to think that it has pleased God to make use of the infirmities and sins of some that he has improved and succeeded, as particularly their imprudent and rash zeal and censorious spirit, to chastise the deadness, negligence, earthlymindedness and vanity, that have been found among ministers, in the late times of general declension and deadness; wherein wise virgins and foolish, ministers and people, have sunk into such a

2. [The supreme council and tribunal of the Jews.]

deep sleep. These things in ministers of the Gospel, that go forth as the ambassadors of Christ, and have the care of immortal souls, are extremely abominable to God; vastly more hateful in his sight than all the imprudence and intemperate heats, wildness and distraction (as some call it) of these zealous preachers. A supine carelessness and a vain, carnal, worldly spirit in a minister of the Gospel, is the worst madness and distraction in the sight of God. God may also make use at this day of the unchristian censoriousness of some preachers, the more to humble and purify some of his own children and true servants, that have been wrongfully censured, to fit them for more eminent service, and future honor that he designs them for.

[Scripture as a Whole the Criterion]

Another foundation error of those that don't acknowledge the divinity of this work, is not taking the Holy Scriptures as an whole, and in itself a sufficient rule to judge of such things by. They that have one certain consistent rule to judge by, are like to come to some clear determination; but they that have half a dozen different rules to make the thing they would judge of agree to, no wonder that instead of justly and clearly determining, they do but perplex and darken themselves and others. They that would learn the true measure of anything, and will have many different measures to try it by, and find in it a conformity to, have a task that they will not accomplish.

Those that I am speaking of, will indeed make some use of Scripture, so far as they think it serves their turn; but don't make use of it alone, as a rule sufficient by itself, but make as much, and a great deal more use of other things, diverse and wide from it, to judge of this work by. As particularly:

1. Some make philosophy instead of the Holy Scriptures their rule of judging of this work; particularly the philosophical notions they entertain of the nature of the soul, its faculties and affections. Some are ready to say, "There is but little sober, solid religion in this work; it is little else but flash and noise. Religion nowadays all runs out into transports and high flights of the passions and affections." In their philosophy, the affections of the soul are something diverse from the will, and not appertaining to the noblest part of the soul, but the meanest principles that it has, that belong to

men as partaking of animal nature, and what he has in common with the brute creation, rather than anything whereby he is conformed to angels and pure spirits. And though they acknowledge that there is a good use may be made of the affections in religion, yet they suppose that the substantial part of religion don't consist in them, but that they are rather to be looked upon as something adventitious and accidental in Christianity.[3]

But I can't but think that these gentlemen labor under great mistakes, both in their philosophy and divinity. 'Tis true, distinction must be made in the affections or passions. There's a great deal of difference in high and raised affections, which must be distinguished by the skill of the observer. Some are much more solid than others. There are many exercises of the affections that are very flashy, and little to be depended on; and oftentimes there is a great deal that appertains to them, or rather that is the effect of them, that has its seat in animal nature, and is very much owing to the constitution and frame of the body; and that which sometimes more especially obtains the name of passion, is nothing solid or substantial. But it is false philosophy to suppose this to be the case with all exercises of affection in the soul, or with all great and high affections; and false divinity to suppose that religious affections don't appertain to the substance and essence of Christianity: on the contrary, it seems to me that the very life and soul of all true religion consists in them.

I humbly conceive that the affections of the soul are not properly distinguished from the will, as though they were two faculties in the soul. All acts of the affections of the soul are in some sense acts of the will, and all acts of the will are acts of the affections. All exercises of the will are in some degree or other, exercises of the soul's appetition or aversion; or which is the same thing, of its love or hatred. The soul wills one thing rather than another, or chooses one thing rather than another, no otherwise than as it loves one thing more than another; but love and hatred are affections of the soul: and therefore all acts of the will are truly acts of the affections; though the exercises of the will don't obtain the name of passions, unless the will, either in its aversion or opposition, be exercised in a high degree, or in a vigorous and lively manner.

All will allow that true virtue or holiness has its seat chiefly in

3. [On the differences between JE's anthropology and that of his critics, see above, p. 83.]

the heart, rather than in the head: it therefore follows from what has been said already, that it consists chiefly in holy affections. The things of religion take place in men's hearts, no further than they are affected with them. The informing of the understanding is all vain, any farther than it affects the heart; or, which is the same thing, has influence on the affections.

Those gentlemen that make light of these raised affections in religion, will doubtless allow that true religion and holiness, as it has its seat in the heart, is capable of very high degrees, and high exercises in the soul. As for instance: they will doubtless allow that the holiness of the heart or will, is capable of being raised to an hundred times as great a degree of strength as it is in the most eminent saint on earth, or to be exerted in an hundred times so strong and vigorous exercises of the heart; and yet be true religion or holiness still, but only in an high degree. Now therefore I would ask them, by what name they will call these high and vigorous exercises of the will or heart? Ben't they high affections? What can they consist in, but in high acts of love; strong and vigorous exercises of benevolence and complacence; high, exalting and admiring thoughts of God and his perfections; strong desires after God, etc.? And now what are we come to but high and raised affections? Yea, those very same high and raised affections that before they objected against, or made light of, as worthy of little regard?

I suppose furthermore that all will allow that there is nothing but solid religion in heaven; but that there, religion and holiness of heart is raised to an exceeding great height, to strong, high, exalted exercises of heart. Now what other kinds of such exceeding strong and high exercises of the heart, or of holiness as it has its seat in their hearts, can we devise for them, but only holy affections, high degrees of actings of love to God, rejoicing in God, admiring of God, etc.? Therefore these things in the saints and angels in heaven, are not to be despised and cashiered by the name of great heats and transports of the passions.

And it will doubtless be yet further allowed, that the more eminent the saints are on earth, and the stronger their grace is, and the higher its exercises are, the more they are like the saints in heaven—i.e. (by what has been just now observed) the more they have of high or raised affections in religion.

Though there are false affections in religion, and affections that in some respects are raised high, that are flashy, yet undoubtedly there are also true, holy and solid affections; and the higher these are raised, the better: and if they are raised to an exceeding great height, they are not to be thought meanly of or suspected, merely because of their great degree, but on the contrary to be esteemed and rejoiced in. Charity, or divine love, is in Scripture represented as the sum of all the religion of the heart; but this is nothing but an holy affection: and therefore in proportion as this is firmly fixed in the soul, and raised to a great height, the more eminent a person is in holiness. Divine love, or charity, is represented as the sum of all the religion of heaven, and that wherein mainly the religion of the church in its more perfect state on earth shall consist, when knowledge, and tongues, and prophesyings shall cease [I Cor. 13:8]; and therefore the higher this holy affection is raised in the church of God, or in a gracious soul, the more excellent and perfect is the state of the church, or a particular soul.

If we take the Scriptures for our rule, then the greater and higher are the exercises of love to God, delight and complacence in God, desires and longings after God, delight in the children of God, love to mankind, brokenness of heart, abhorrence of sin, and self-abhorrence for sin; and the "peace of God which passeth all understanding" [Phil. 4:7], and "joy in the Holy Ghost" [Rom. 14:17], "joy unspeakable and full of glory" [I Pet. 1:8]; admiring thoughts of God, exulting and glorying in God; so much the higher is Christ's religion, or that virtue which he and his apostles taught, raised in the soul.

It is a stumbling to some that religious affections should seem to be so powerful, so that they should be so violent (as they express it) in some persons: they are therefore ready to doubt whether it can be the Spirit of God, or whether this vehemence ben't rather a sign of the operation of an evil spirit. But why should such a doubt arise from no other ground than this? What is represented in Scripture as more powerful in its effects than the Spirit of God, which is therefore called "the power of the highest," Luke 1:35? And its saving effect in the soul [is] called "the power of godliness." [4] So we read of the "demonstration of the Spirit and of power," I Cor. 2:4. And it is said to operate in the minds of men with "the exceeding greatness of divine power," and "according to

4. [There is no such specific phrase in the version of Scripture (AV) used by JE; perhaps he was thinking of II Tim. 3:5.]

the working of God's mighty power," Eph. 1:19. So we read of "the effectual working of his power," Eph. 3:7; and of "the power that worketh in" Christians, vs. 20; and of the "glorious power" of God in the operations of the Spirit, Col. 1:11; and of "the work of faith," its being wrought "with power," II Thess. 1:11; and in II Tim. 1:7 the Spirit of God is called the Spirit of "power, and [of] love, and of a sound mind." So [also] the Spirit is represented by a mighty wind, and by fire [Acts 2:2–3], things most powerful in their operation.

2. Many are guilty of not taking the Holy Scriptures as a sufficient and whole rule, whereby to judge of this work, whether it be the work of God, in that they judge by those things which the Scripture don't give as any signs or marks whereby to judge one way or the other, and therefore do in no wise belong to the Scripture rule of judging, viz. the effects that religious exercises and affections of mind have upon the body. Scripture rules respect the state of the mind, and persons' moral conduct, and voluntary behavior, and not the physical state of the body. The design of the Scripture is to teach us divinity, and not physic and anatomy. Ministers are made the watchmen of men's souls, and not their bodies; and therefore the great rule which God has committed into their hands is to make them divines, and not physicians. Christ knew what instructions and rules his church would stand in need of better than we do; and if he had seen it needful in order to the church's safety, he doubtless would have given ministers rules to judge of bodily effects, and would have told 'em how the pulse should beat under such and such religious exercises of mind; when men should look pale, and when they should shed tears; when they should tremble, and whether or no they should ever be faint or cry out; or whether the body should ever be put into convulsions. He probably would have put some book into their hands that should have tended to make them excellent anatomists and physicians: but he has not done it, because he did not see it to be needful. He judged that if ministers thoroughly did their duty as watchmen and overseers of the state and frame of men's souls, and of their voluntary conduct, according to the rules he had given, his church would be well provided for, as to its safety in these matters. And therefore those ministers of Christ and overseers of souls that busy

themselves, and are full of concern about the involuntary motions of the fluids and solids of men's bodies, and from thence full of doubts and suspicions of the cause, when nothing appears but that the state and frame of their minds, and their voluntary behavior is good, and agreeable to God's Word; I say, such ministers go out of the place that Christ has set them in, and leave their proper business, as much as if they should undertake to tell who are under the influence of the Spirit by their looks or their gait. I can't see which way we are in danger, or how the Devil is like to get any notable advantage against us, if we do but thoroughly do our duty with respect to those two things, viz. the state of persons' minds and their moral conduct, seeing to it that they be maintained in an agreeableness to the rules that Christ has given us. If things are but kept right in these respects, our fears and suspicions arising from extraordinary bodily effects seem wholly groundless.

The most specious thing that is alleged against these extraordinary effects on the body, is that the body is impaired and health wronged; and that it's hard to think that God, in the merciful influences of his Spirit on men, would wound their bodies and impair their health. But if it were so pretty commonly or in multiplied instances (which I don't suppose it is) that persons received a lasting wound to their health by extraordinary religious impressions made upon their minds, yet 'tis too much for us to determine that God shall never bring an outward calamity, in bestowing a vastly greater spiritual and eternal good. Jacob in doing his duty in wrestling with God for the blessing, and while God was striving with him, at the same time that he received the blessing from God, suffered a great outward calamity from his hand; God impaired his body so that he never got over it as long as he lived: he gave him the blessing, but sent him away halting on his thigh, and he went lame all his life after. And yet this is not mentioned as if it were any diminution of the great mercy of God to him, when God blessed him, and he received his name Israel, because as a prince he had power with God, and had prevailed [Gen. 32:24–32].

But, say some, the operations of the Spirit of God are of a benign nature; nothing is of a more kind influence on human nature than the merciful breathings of God's own Spirit. But it has been a thing generally supposed and allowed in the church of God, till now, that there is such a thing as being sick of love to Christ, or having the bodily strength weakened by strong and vigorous exercises of love to him.[5] And however kind to human nature the influences of the Spirit of God are, yet nobody doubts but that divine and eternal things, as they may be discovered, would overpower the nature of man in its present weak state; and that therefore the body in its present weakness, is not fitted for the views and pleasures and employments of heaven: and that if God did discover but a little of that which is seen by the saints and angels in heaven, our frail natures would sink under it. Indeed, I know not what persons may deny now, to defend themselves in a cause they have had their spirits long engaged in; but I know these things don't use to be denied, or doubted of.

Let us rationally consider what we profess to believe of the infinite greatness of the things of God, the divine wrath, the divine glory, and the divine infinite love and grace in Jesus Christ, and the vastness and infinite importance of the things of eternity; and how reasonable is it to suppose that if it pleases God a little to withdraw the veil, and let in light into the soul, and give something of a view of the great things of another world in their transcendent and infinite greatness, that human nature, that is as the grass, a shaking leaf, a weak withering flower, should totter under such a discovery. Such a bubble is too weak to bear the weight of a view of things that are so vast. Alas! What is such dust and ashes, that it should support itself under the view of the awful wrath of infinite glory and love of Jehovah! No wonder therefore that it is said, "No man can see me and live" [Exod. 33:20], and "Flesh and blood cannot inherit the kingdom of God" [I Cor. 15:20]. That external glory and majesty of Christ which Daniel saw, when there "remained no strength in him," and "his comeliness was turned in him into corruption," Dan. 10:6–8, and which the Apostle John saw, when he "fell at his feet as dead" [Rev. 1:17], was but an image or shadow of that spiritual glory and majesty of Christ, which will be manifested in the souls of the saints in another world, and which is sometimes, in some degree, manifested to the soul in this world by the influences of the Spirit of God. And if the beholding the image and external representation of this spiritual majesty and glory, did so overpower human nature, is it unreasonable to suppose that a sight of the spiritual glory itself, which is the substance of which that was but the shadow, should have as powerful an effect? The

5. [Cf. above, pp. 232–34.]

prophet Habakkuk, speaking of the awful manifestations God made of his majesty and wrath at the Red Sea, and in the wilderness, and at Mount Sinai, where he gave the law; and of the merciful influence and strong impression God caused it to have upon him, to the end that he might be saved from that wrath, and rest in the day of trouble; says, Hab. 3:16, "When I heard, my belly trembled, my lips quivered at the voice, rottenness entered into my bones, I trembled in myself, that I might rest in the day of trouble." Which is much such an effect as the discovery of the same majesty and wrath, in the same awful voice from Mount Sinai, has had upon many in these days; and to the same purposes, viz. to give 'em rest in the day of trouble, and save 'em from that wrath. The Psalmist also speaks of very much such an effect as I have often seen on persons under religious affections of late, Ps. 119:131, "I opened my mouth and panted, for I longed for thy commandments."

God is pleased sometimes in dealing forth spiritual blessings to his people, in some respect to exceed the capacity of the vessel, in its present scantiness, so that he don't only fill it full, but he makes their cup to run over, agreeable to Ps. 23:5; and pours out a blessing, sometimes, in such a manner and measure that there is not room enough to receive it, Mal. 3:10; and gives 'em riches more than they can carry away, as he did to Jehoshaphat and his people in a time of great favor, by the word of his prophet Jehaziel in answer to earnest prayer, when the people blessed the Lord in the valley of Berachah, II Chron. 20:25-26. It has been with the disciples of Christ, for a long time, a time of great emptiness upon spiritual accounts; they have gone hungry, and have been toiling in vain, during a dark season, a time of night with the church of God; as it was with the disciples of old, when they had toiled all night for something to eat and caught nothing, Luke 5:5 and John 21:3. But now, the morning being come, Jesus appears to his disciples, and takes a compassionate notice of their wants, and says to 'em, "Children, have ye any meat?" And gives some of them such abundance of food, that they are not able to draw their net; yea, so that their net breaks, and their vessel is overloaded, and begins to sink; as it was with the disciples of old, Luke 5:6-7 and John 21:6.

We can't determine that God never shall give any person so much of a discovery of himself, not only as to weaken their bodies, but to take away their lives. 'Tis supposed by very learned and judicious divines, that Moses' life was taken away after this manner [Deut. 34]; and this has also been supposed to be the case with some other saints. Yea, I don't see any solid sure grounds any have to determine that God shall never make such strong impressions on the mind by his Spirit, that shall be an occasion of so impairing the frame of the body, and particularly that part of the body, the brain, that persons shall be deprived of the use of reason. As I said before, it is too much for us to determine that God will not bring an outward calamity in bestowing spiritual and eternal blessings: so it is too much for us to determine, how great an outward calamity he will bring. If God gives a great increase of discoveries of himself, and of love to him, the benefit is infinitely greater than the calamity, though the life should presently after be taken away; yea, though the soul should not immediately be taken to heaven, but should lie some years in a deep sleep, and then be taken to heaven: or, which is much the same thing, if it be deprived of the use of its faculties, and be unactive and unserviceable, as if it lay in a deep sleep for some years, and then should pass into glory. We cannot determine how great a calamity distraction is, when considered with all its consequences, and all that might have been consequent, if the distraction had not happened; nor indeed whether (thus considered) it be any calamity at all, or whether it be not a mercy, by preventing some great sin, or some more dreadful thing, if it had not been. 'Tis a great fault in us to limit a sovereign all-wise God, whose "judgments are a great deep" [Ps. 36:6], and "his ways past finding out" [Rom. 11:33], where he has not limited himself, and in things concerning which he has not told us what his way shall be.

'Tis remarkable, considering in what multitudes of instances, and to how great a degree, the frame of the body has been overpowered of late, that persons' lives have notwithstanding been preserved, and that the instances of those that have been deprived of reason have been so very few, and those, perhaps all of them, persons under the peculiar disadvantage of a weak, vapory habit of body. A merciful and careful divine hand is very manifest in it, that in so many instances where the ship has begun to sink, yet it has been upheld, and has not totally sunk. The instances of such as have been deprived of reason are so few, that certainly they are not enough to cause us to be in any fright, as though this work that has been carried on in the country, was like to be of baneful influence; unless we are disposed to gather up all that we can to darken it, and set it forth in frightful colors.

There is one particular kind of exercise and concern of mind that many have been overpowered by, that has been especially stumbling to some; and that is the deep concern and distress that they have been in for the souls of others. I am sorry that any put us to the trouble of doing that which seems so needless as defending such a thing as this. It seems like mere trifling in so plain a case, to enter into a formal and particular debate, in order to determine whether there be anything in the greatness and importance of the case that will answer, and bear a proportion to the greatness of the concern that some have manifested. Men may be allowed, from no higher a principle than common ingenuity and humanity, to be very deeply concerned, and greatly exercised in mind, at the seeing others in great danger, of no greater a calamity than drowning, or being burnt up in an house on fire. And if so, then doubtless it will be allowed to be equally reasonable, if they saw them in danger of a calamity ten times greater, to be still much more concerned; and so much more still, if the calamity was still vastly greater. And why then should it be thought unreasonable, and looked upon with a very suspicious eye, as if it must come from some bad cause, when persons are extremely concerned at seeing others in very great danger of suffering the fierceness and wrath of Almighty God, to all eternity? And besides, it will doubtless be allowed that those that have very great degrees of the Spirit of God, that is a spirit of love, may well be supposed to have vastly more of love and compassion to their fellow creatures, than those that are influenced only by common humanity. Why should it be thought strange that those that are full of the Spirit of Christ should be proportionably, in their love to souls, like to Christ, who had so strong a love to them and concern for them, as to be willing to drink the dregs of the cup of God's fury for them? And at the same time that he offered up his blood for souls, [he] offered up also, as their High Priest, "strong crying and tears" [Heb. 5:7], with an extreme agony, wherein the soul of Christ was as it were in travail for the souls of the elect; and therefore in saving them he is said to "see of the travail of his soul" [Isa. 53:11]. As such a spirit of love to, and concern for souls was the spirit of Christ, so it is the spirit of the church; and therefore the church, in desiring and seeking that Christ might be brought forth in the world, and in the souls of men, is represented, Rev. 12:2, as a woman crying, "travailing in birth, and pained to be delivered." The spirit of those that have been in distress for the souls of others, so far as I can discern, seems not to be different

from that of the Apostle, who travailed for souls and was ready to
wish himself "accursed from Christ" for others [Rom. 9:3]. And that
of the Psalmist, Ps. 119:53, "Horror hath taken hold upon me, because of the wicked that forsake thy law." And vs. 136, "Rivers of
waters run down mine eyes because they keep not thy law." And
that of the prophet Jeremiah, Jer. 4:19, "My bowels! My bowels!
I am pained at my very heart! My heart maketh a noise in me! I
cannot hold my peace! Because thou hast heard, O my soul, the
sound of the trumpet, the alarm of war!" And so chap. 9:1, and
13:17, and 14:17; and Isa. 22:4. We read of Mordecai, when he
saw his people in danger of being destroyed with a temporal destruction, Esther 4:1, that he "rent his clothes, and put on sack-
cloth with ashes, and went out into the midst of the city, and cried
with a loud and bitter cry." And why then should persons be
thought to be distracted, when they can't forbear crying out at the
consideration of the misery of those that are going to eternal destruction?

3. Another thing that some make their rule to judge of this
work by, instead of the Holy Scriptures, is history, or former observation. Herein they err two ways: *first,*[6] if there be anything new
and extraordinary in the circumstances of this work that was not
observed in former times, that is a rule with them to reject this
work as not the work of God. Herein they make that their rule
that God has not given them for their rule, and limit God where
he has not limited himself. And this is especially unreasonable in
this case: for whosoever has well weighed the wonderful and mysterious methods of divine wisdom, in carrying on the work of the
new creation, or in the progress of the work of redemption, from
the first promise of the "seed of the woman" [Gen. 3:15] to this
time, may easily observe that it has all along been God's manner
to open new scenes, and to bring forth to view things new and
wonderful, such as "eye had not seen, nor ear heard, nor entered
into the heart of man" or angels [I Cor. 2:9], to the astonishment
of heaven and earth, not only in the revelations he makes of his
mind and will, but also in the works of his hands. As the old creation was carried on through six days, and appeared all complete
settled in a state of rest on the seventh; so the new creation, which

6. [Discussion of the second "error" begins below, p. 313.]

is immensely the greatest and most glorious work, is carried on in a gradual progress, from the fall of man to the consummation of all things, at the end of the world. And as in the progress of the old creation, there were still new things accomplished; new wonders appeared every day in the sight of the angels, the spectators of that work; while those "morning stars sang together" [Job 38:7], new scenes were opened or things that they had not seen before, till the whole was finished; so it is in the progress of the new creation. So that that promise, Isa. 64:4, "For since the beginning of the world, men have not heard, nor perceived by the ear, neither hath the eye seen, O God, besides thee, what he hath prepared for him that waiteth for him"; though it had a glorious fulfilment in the days of Christ and the apostles, as the words are applied [in] I Cor. 2:9, yet it always remains to be fulfilled in things that are yet behind, till the new creation is finished at Christ's delivering up the kingdom to the Father [I Cor. 15:24]. And we live in those latter days, wherein we may be especially warranted to expect that things will be accomplished, concerning which it will be said, "Who hath heard such a thing? Who hath seen such things?" [Isa. 66:8].

And besides, those things in this work that have been chiefly complained of as new, are not so new as has been generally imagined: though they have been much more frequent lately, in proportion to the uncommon degree, extent and swiftness, and other extraordinary circumstances of the work, yet they are not new in their kind; but are things of the same nature as have been found and well approved of in the church of God before, from time to time.

We have a remarkable instance in Mr. Bolton, that noted minister of the Church of England, who being awakened by the preaching of the famous Mr. Perkins, minister of Christ in the University of Cambridge, was subject to such terrors as threw him to the ground, and caused him to roar with anguish; and the pangs of the new birth in him were such that he lay pale and without sense, like one dead; as we have an account in *The Fulfilling of the Scripture*, the 5th edition, pp. 103–04.[7] We have an account in the same page

7. [Robert Bolton (1572–1631) was an Oxford scholar who despised Puritans, especially their popular preacher and influential theologian, William Perkins (1558–1602). After a dramatic experience of conversion, Bolton became (according to JE's source) "a chief minister in the Church of England." A biographical sketch by Edward Bagshaw, appended to *Mr. Bolton's Last and Learned Work*

of another, whose comforts under the sunshine of God's presence were so great that he could not forbear crying out in a transport, and expressing in exclamations the great sense he had of forgiving mercy and his assurance of God's love.[8] And we have a remarkable instance in the *Life of [the Reverend] Mr. George Trosse [. . .], Written by Himself* (who, of a notoriously vicious, profligate liver, became an eminent saint and minister of the Gospel) of terrors occasioned by awakenings of conscience, so overpowering the body as to deprive [him] for some time of the use of reason.[9]

Yea, such extraordinary external effects of inward impressions

---

(London, 1632), appears to be the main source for Robert Fleming (1630–94) *The Fulfilling of the Scripture* (Rotterdam, 1669; 5th ed., London, 1726). The passage to which JE refers in the last-mentioned book reads in part as follows: "Mr. Bolton . . . {was} much accustomed to mock at holiness, and {at} those who most shined therein, and particularly {at} that excellent man of God Mr. Perkins, then preacher in Cambridge, whom he much undervalued for his plainness in preaching the truths of God" (p. 103). Fleming's account nowhere intimates that Bolton's awakening or the emotion which attended it was due to Perkins' preaching (and Bagshaw's sketch, which JE probably had not seen, only hints at an indirect influence), a fact on which Charles Chauncy pounced with a stinging indictment of JE for license in the use of sources. Said Chauncy: "How it came about, I know not; but {Mr. Edwards} has very much misunderstood his author in representing from him Mr. Perkins as the person by whose preaching Mr. Bolton was subjected to terrors that threw him to the ground; for it is not so much as insinuated in *The Fulfilling of the Scripture,* either that Mr. Perkins was the instrument of Mr. Bolton's terrors or that he was ever thrown into them in the time of preaching." Chauncy was right, and he labored the point for four pages; see his *Seasonable Thoughts on the State of Religion in New England* (Boston, 1743), pp. 81–85. Fleming's work, incidentally, was reprinted in Boston in October 1743, giving American readers opportunity to check the sources themselves.]

8. [The reference is to a condemned criminal whom Fleming identified only as "a poor buggerer." Converted in prison, he went to his death "crying out to the people, under the sense of pardon . . . 'O he is a great forgiver, he is a great forgiver.'" There is no mention of any "transport," as JE claimed, but Chauncy passed the point in silence.]

9. [George Trosse (1631–1713), in his autobiography published 1714, testified with lurid frankness to a youth of frivolity and profligacy. After a dramatic conversion, which he described in great detail, he became noted for strenuous piety. Chauncy also read his *Life* and concluded that Trosse's terrors arose not from "awakenings of conscience," as JE would have it, but from "an ill habit of body . . . brought upon him by his own follies"; and that his temporary loss of reason was simply a form of mental illness. Cf. *Seasonable Thoughts,* pp. 85–86.]

ave not only been to be found in here and there a single person,
ut there have also before now been times wherein many have been
hus affected, in some particular parts of the church of God; and
uch effects have appeared in congregations, in many at once. So
: was in the year 1625, in the west of Scotland, in a time of great
utpouring of the Spirit of God. It was then a frequent thing for
nany to be so extraordinarily seized with terror in the hearing of
ne Word, by the Spirit of God convincing them of sin, that they
ell down, and were carried out of the church, who afterwards
·roved most solid and lively Christians; as the author of *The
·ulfilling of the Scripture* informs us, p. 185.[1] The same author in
he preceding page informs of many in France that were so won-
erfully affected with the preaching of the Gospel in the time of
hose famous divines Farel and Viret, that for a time they could not
ollow their secular business.[2] And p. 186, of many in Ireland, in a
ime of great outpouring of the Spirit there in the year 1628, that
vere so filled with divine comforts and a sense of God, that they
nade but little use of either meat, drink or sleep, and professed
hat they did not feel the need thereof.[3]

The same author gives an account of very much such things in
Mrs. Catherine Brettergh of Lancashire in England (pp. 391–92)
s have been cried out of here amongst us, as wild and distracted:
ow that after great distress, which very much affected her body,
he sweat sometimes bursting out upon her, God did so break in
upon her mind with light and discoveries of himself, that she was
orced to burst out crying:

1. [JE was faithful to his source here, though Chauncy complained that his
author was too lacking in relevant detail to support any conclusion regarding
he cause and validity of the bodily effects (*Seasonable Thoughts,* pp. 86–88).]

2. [Guillaume Farel (1489–1565) and Pierre Viret (1511–71) were members of
. Swiss-based band of Reformed evangelists who worked aggressively to spread
·rotestant reforms in western Europe. JE again followed Fleming uncritically,
.nd his naive choice of this illustration increased his vulnerability to criticism.
Chauncy, who had "been at the pains to consult all the writers I could meet
with in some of the best and largest libraries in New England"—*that* for the
imited scholars of Hampshire County!—cited both Reformation contemporaries
.nd historical interpreters to claim that Farel was a preacher more in "need of
he rein than the spur," and often excited his hearers into a frenzy (*Seasonable
Thoughts,* pp. 88–90).]

3. [JE captured the spirit of Fleming's paragraph accurately enough. The
·nly thing Chauncy could find to complain about was that the source mentioned
to "strange bodily effects" and therefore afforded no support for JE's argument.]

O the joys, the joys, the joys, that I feel in my soul! O they wonderful, they be wonderful! The place where I now am sweet and pleasant! How comfortable is the sweetness I fe that delights my soul! The taste is precious; do you not feel Oh, so sweet as it is!

And at other times:

O my sweet Saviour, shall I be one with thee, as thou art o with the Father? And dost thou so love me that am but du to make me partaker of glory with Christ? O how wonderful thy love!

And "Oh that my tongue and heart were able to sound forth t praises as I ought." At another time she burst forth thus:

Yea, Lord, I feel thy mercy, and I am assured of thy love! A so certain am I thereof, as thou art that God of truth; even certainly do I know myself to be thine, O Lord my God; a this my soul knoweth right well!

Which last words she again doubled. To a grave minister, one M Harrison, then with her, she said:

My soul hath been compassed with the terrors of death, the s rows of hell were upon me, and a wilderness of woe was in n but blessed, blessed, blessed be the Lord my God! He ha brought me to a place of rest, even to the sweet running wat of life. The way I now go in is a sweet and easy way, strow with flowers; he hath brought me into a place more sweet th the Garden of Eden. O the joy, the joy, the delights and j that I feel! O how wonderful! [4]

Great outcries under awakenings were more frequently heard in former times in the country than they have been of late, as so aged persons now living do testify. Particularly I think fit here

4. [Mrs. Catherine Bruen Brettergh, or Brettargh (1579–1601), as both ch and young matron—she married at twenty—was regarded as a model of Puri piety and virtue. The accounts which celebrated her exemplary life are two funeral sermons by William Harrison and William Leygh, *Death's* vantage Little Regarded, and The Soul's Solace Against Sorrow,* printed w *A Brief Discourse of the Christian Life and Death of Mistress Katherin Bretter* in 1605/6. These popular pieces appeared in three later editions, thus coming the basis for many abstracts in subsequent works such as the one fr which JE here quoted. Even Chauncy found the passage unexceptiona *(Seasonable Thoughts,* p. 91).]

nsert a testimony of my honored father, of what he remembers
ormerly to have heard.

I well remember that one Mr. Alexander Allyn, a Scots gentleman of good credit, that dwelt formerly in this town, shewed
me a letter that came from Scotland, that gave an account of a
sermon preached in the city of Edinburgh (as I remember) in
the time of the sitting of the General Assembly of divines in
that kingdom, that so affected the people, that there was a great
and loud cry made throughout the Assembly. I have also been
credibly informed, and how often I cannot now say, that it was a
common thing, when the famous Mr. John Rogers of Dedham
in England was preaching, for some of his hearers to cry out;
and by what I have heard, I conclude that it was usual for many
that heard that very awakening and rousing preacher of God's
Word, to make a great cry in the congregation.

Timothy Edwards

[East] Windsor
May 5, 1742

Mr. Flavel gives a remarkable instance of a man that he knew,
hat was wonderfully overcome with divine comforts; which it is
upposed he knew, as the Apostle Paul knew the man that was
aught up to the third heaven. He relates that

as the person was traveling alone, with his thoughts closely fixed
on the great and astonishing things of another world, his
thoughts began to swell higher and higher, like the water in
Ezekiel's vision [47:1–5], till at last they became an overflowing
flood. Such was the intenseness of his mind, such the ravishing
tastes of heavenly joys, and such his full assurance of his interest therein, that he utterly lost all sight and sense of this
world, and the concernments thereof; and for some hours, knew
not where he was, nor what he was about. But having lost a
great quantity of blood at the nose, he found himself so faint
that it brought him a little more to himself. And after he had
washed himself at a spring, and drank of the water for his
refreshment, he continued to the end of his journey, which
was thirty miles; and all this while was scarce sensible: and
says he had several trances of considerable continuance. The
same blessed frame was preserved all that night, and in a lower
degree, great part of the next day. The night passed without one
wink of sleep; and yet he declares he never had a sweeter night's

rest in all his life. Still (adds the story) the joy of the Lor
overflowed him, and he seemed to be an inhabitant of anothe
world. And he used for many years after to call that day one o
the days of heaven; and professed that he understood more o
the life of heaven by it, than by all the books he ever read, o
discourses he ever entertained about it.[5]

There have been instances before now, of persons crying out i
transports of divine joy in New England. We have an instance i
Capt. Clap's *Memoirs,* published by the Rev. Mr. Prince, not of
silly woman or child, but a man of solid understanding, that in
high transport of spiritual joy, was made to cry out aloud on he
bed. His words (p. 9) are: "God's Holy Spirit did witness (I d
believe) together with my spirit, that I was a child of God [Ron
8:16]; and did fill my heart and soul with such full assurance tha
Christ was mine, that it did so transport me as to make me cry ou
upon my bed with a loud voice, He is come, he is come!" [6]

There has before now been both crying out and falling dow
in this town, under awakenings of conscience and in the pangs o
the new birth, and also in some of the neighbor towns. In one o
them, more than seven years ago, was a great number together tha
cried out and fell down under convictions; in most of which, I
good information, was a hopeful and abiding good issue. And th
Rev. Mr. Williams [7] of Deerfield gave me an account of an age
man in that town, many years before that, that being awakene

5. [John Flavel (1630–91) was an English Presbyterian whose writin
had long been a staple of New England devotional literature. The quote
passage (somewhat compressed) is from *Pneumatologia: A Treatise of the So
of Man* (London, 1685), pp. 238–40; it may be found conveniently in *The Wor
of John Flavel* (London: Banner of Truth Trust, 1968), *3,* 57–58. JE surmise
that the account was autobiographical in the same way that II Cor. 12:2–4
often assumed to be, while Chauncy commented with customary testiness th
"good men may differ in their sentiments as to the cause of such effects; an
if any should think they are not to be wholly ascribed to a divine influence,
would not be too peremptory in saying, their judgment was not according
truth" (*Seasonable Thoughts,* p. 92).]

6. [Roger Clap, *Memoirs of Capt. Roger Clap* (Boston, 1731). The wo
contains a preface by Thomas Prince.]

7. [John Williams (1664–1729) was pastor at Deerfield, Mass., 1686–172
Note that JE truly did receive this account "many years" earlier. Of th
paragraph Chauncy remarked that he did not "think that such accounts te
much to the credit of religion" (*Seasonable Thoughts,* p. 92).]

y his preaching, cried out aloud in the congregation. There have
een many instances in this and some neighbor towns, before now,
f persons fainting with joyful discoveries made to their souls:
nce several together in this town. And there also formerly have
een several instances here, of persons' flesh waxing cold and be-
umbed, and their hands clinched, yea, their bodies being set
ito convulsions, being overpowered with a strong sense of the
stonishingly great and excellent things of God and the eternal
/orld.

Secondly,[8] another way that some err in making history and
ormer observation their rule to judge of this work, instead of the
Ioly Scripture, is in comparing some external, accidental circum-
:ances of this work, with what has appeared sometimes in enthu-
iasts; and as they find an agreement in some such things, so they
eject the whole work, or at least the substance of it, concluding
t to be enthusiasm. So great use has been made to this purpose
f many things that are found amongst the Quakers; however totally
nd essentially different in its nature this work is, and the principles
t is built upon, from the whole religion of the Quakers. So, to the
ame purpose, some external appearances that were found amongst
he French Prophets, and some other enthusiasts in former times,
ave been of late trumped up with great assurance and triumph.[9]

4. I would propose it to be considered whether or no some, in-
tead of making the Scriptures their only rule to judge of this work,
lon't make their own experience the rule, and reject such and
uch things as are now professed and experienced because they
ever felt 'em themselves. Are there not many that chiefly on this
;round have entertained and vented suspicions, if not peremptory
ondemnations of those extreme terrors, and [of] those great, sudden
nd extraordinary discoveries of the glorious perfections of God,
nd of the beauty and love of Christ; and [of] such vehement affec-
ions, such high transports of love and joy, such pity and distress
or the souls of others, and exercises of mind that have such great
:ffects on persons' bodies; merely, or chiefly, because they knew
iothing about 'em by experience? Persons are very ready to be
uspicious of what they han't felt themselves. 'Tis to be feared
nany good men have been guilty of this error; which yet don't

8. [This sequence began on p. 306 above.]
9. [See above, p. 63.]

make it the less unreasonable. And perhaps there are that upo
this ground don't only reject these extraordinary things, but a
such conviction of sin, and such discoveries of the glory of Goc
and excellency of Christ, and inward conviction of the truth c
the Gospel, by the immediate influence of the Spirit of God, tha
are now supposed to be necessary to salvation.

These persons that thus make their own experiences their rule c
judgment, instead of bowing to the wisdom of God, and yielding t
his Word as an infallible rule, are guilty of casting a great reflectio
upon the understanding of the Most High.

[*The Need for Discrimination*]

Another foundation error of those that reject this work, is thei
not duly distinguishing the good from the bad, and very unjustl
judging of the whole by a part; and so rejecting the work in genera
or in the main substance of it, for the sake of some things that ar
accidental to it, that are evil. They look for more in men that ar
divinely influenced, because subject to the operations of a goo
spirit, than is justly to be expected from them for that reason, i
this imperfect state and dark world, where so much blindness anc
corruption remains in the best. When any profess to have receivec
light and influence and comforts from heaven, and to have hac
sensible communion with God, many are ready to expect that nov
they appear like angels, and not still like poor, feeble, blind anc
sinful worms of the dust. There being so much corruption left ir
the hearts of God's own children, and its prevailing as it sometime
does, is indeed a mysterious thing, and always was a stumblin
block to the world; but won't be so much wondered at by thosc
that are well versed in, and duly mindful of, two things: viz. *first*
the Word of God, which teaches us the state of true Christians in
this world; and *secondly*, their own hearts, at least if they have any
grace, and have experience of its conflicts with corruption. They
that are true saints are most inexcusable in making a great difficulty
of a great deal of blindness, and many sinful errors in those that
profess godliness. If all our conduct, both open and secret, should
be known, and our hearts laid open to the world, how should we
be even ready to fly from the light of the sun, and hide ourselves
from the view of mankind! And what great allowances would it be
found that we should need, that others should make for us?—
perhaps much greater than we are willing to make for others.

The great weakness of the bigger part of mankind, in any affair that is new and uncommon, appears in not distinguishing, but either approving or condemning all in the lump. They that highly approve of the affair in general, can't bear to have anything at all found fault with; and on the other hand, those that fasten their eyes upon some things in the affair that are amiss, and appear very disagreeable to them, at once reject the whole; both which errors oftentimes arise from want of persons' due acquaintance with themselves. It is rash and unjust when we proceed thus in judging either of a particular person, or a people, or of such an affair as the present wonderful influence on the minds of the people of this land. Many, if they see anything very ill in a particular person, a minister or private professor, will at once brand him as an hypocrite. And if there be two or three of a people or society [1] that behave themselves very irregularly, the whole must bear the blame of it. And if there be a few, though it may be not above one in an hundred, that professed and had a shew of being the happy partakers of what are called the saving benefits of this work, that prove nought, and give the world just grounds to suspect 'em, the whole work must be rejected on their account; and those in general, that make the like profession must be condemned for their sakes.

So careful are some persons lest this work should be defended, that now they will hardly allow that the influences of the Spirit of God on the heart, can so much as indirectly and accidentally be the occasion of the exercise of corruption, and commission of sin. Thus far [it] is true, that the influence of the Spirit of God in his saving operations, won't be an occasion of the increase of the corruption of the heart in general, but on the contrary, of the weakening of it: but yet there is nothing unreasonable in supposing that at the same time that it weakens corruption in general, it may be an occasion of the turning what is left into a new channel, and so of there being more of some certain kinds of the exercise of corruption than there was before; as that which tends to hinder and stop the course of a stream, if it don't do it wholly, may give a new course to so much of the water as gets by the obstacle. The influences of the Spirit, for instance, may be an occasion of new ways of the exercise of pride, as has been acknowledged by orthodox divines in general. That spiritual discoveries and comforts may, through the corruption of the heart, be an occasion of the exercises of spiritual pride, don't

1. [I.e., worshipping congregation, or perhaps parish. See below, p. 493 n.]

use to be doubted of, till now it is found to be needful to maintai
the war against this work.

They that will hardly allow that a work of the Spirit of God ca
be a remote occasion of any sinful behavior or unchristian conduc
I suppose will allow that the truly gracious influences of the Spir
of God, yea, and an high degree of love to God, is consistent wit
these two things, viz. a considerable degree of remaining corruptio
and also many errors in judgment in matters of religion, and i
matters of practice. And this is all that need to be allowed, in orde
to its being most demonstratively evident, that a high degree of lov
to God may accidentally move a person to that which is very wrong
and contrary to the mind and will of God. For a high degree of lov
to God will strongly move a person to do that which he believes t
be agreeable to God's will; and therefore, if he be mistaken, an
be persuaded that that is agreeable to the will of God, which indee
is very contrary to it, then his love will accidentally, but strongly
incline him to that which is indeed very contrary to the will of God

They that are studied in logic have learned that the nature of th
cause is not to be judged of by the nature of the effect, nor th
nature of the effect from the nature of the cause, when the cause i
only *causa sine qua non,* or an occasional cause; yea, that in such
a case, oftentimes the nature of the effect is quite contrary to th
nature of the cause.[2]

True disciples of Christ may have a great deal of false zeal, such
as the disciples had of old, when they would have fire called fo
from heaven to come down on the Samaritans, because they did no
receive them. [Luke 9:51–56] And even so eminently holy and grea
and divine a saint as Moses, who conversed with God from time t
time as a man speaks with his friend, and concerning whom Go
gives his testimony, that he "was very meek, above any man upo
the face of the earth" [Num. 12:3], yet may be rash and sinful i
his zeal, when his spirit is stirred by the hard-heartedness and op
position of others, so as to speak very "unadvisedly with his lips,
and greatly to offend God, and shut himself out from the possessio
of the good things that God is about to accomplish for his church o
earth; as Moses was excluded [from] Canaan, though he had brough
the people out of Egypt, Ps. 106:32–33 [cf. also Num. 20:7–12]. And
men, even in those very things wherein they are influenced by a
truly pious principle, yet, through error and want of due considera

2. [For discussion of JE's philosophical premises here, see above, p. 67.]

tion and caution, may be very rash with their zeal. It was a truly good spirit that animated that excellent generation of Israel that was in Joshua's time, in that affair that we have an account of in the 22d chapter of Joshua; and yet they were rash and heady with their zeal, to go about to gather all Israel together to go up so furiously to war with their brethren of the two tribes and [a] half, about their building the altar *Ed,*[3] without first inquiring into the matter, or so much as sending a messenger to be informed. So [also] the Christians that were of the circumcision, with warmth and contention condemned Peter for receiving Cornelius, as we have account, Acts 11. This their heat and censure was unjust, and Peter was wronged in it; but there is all appearance in the story that they acted from a real zeal and concern for the will and honor of God. So the primitive Christians, from their zeal for and against unclean meats, censured and condemned one another: this was a bad effect, and yet the Apostle bears them witness, or at least expresses his charity towards them, that both sides acted from a good principle, and true respect to the Lord, Rom. 14:6. The zeal of the Corinthians with respect to the incestuous man, though the Apostle highly commends it, yet at the same time saw that they needed a caution lest they should carry it too far, to an undue severity, and so as to fail of Christian meekness and forgiveness, II Cor. 2:6–11 and chap. 7:11 to the end. Luther, the great Reformer, had a great deal of bitterness with his zeal.

It surely cannot be wondered at by considerate persons, that at a time when multitudes all over the land have their affections greatly moved, that great numbers should run into many errors and mistakes with respect to their duty, and consequently into many acts and practices that are imprudent and irregular. I question whether there be a man in New England, of the strongest reason and greatest learning, but what would be put to it to keep master of himself, thoroughly to weigh his words, and consider all the consequences of his behavior, so as to behave himself in all respects prudently, if he were so strongly impressed with a sense of divine and eternal things, and his affections so exceedingly moved, as has been frequent of late among the common people. How little do they consider human nature, who look upon it so insuperable a stumbling block, when such multitudes of all kinds of capacities, natural tempers, educations, customs and manners of life, are so greatly and variously

3. [Hebrew עֵד, "witness"; see Josh. 22:34.]

affected, that imprudences and irregularities of conduct should abound; especially in a state of things so uncommon, and when the degree, extent, swiftness and power of the operation is so very extraordinary, and so new, that there has not been time and experience enough to give birth to rules for people's conduct, and so unusual in times past, that the writings of divines don't afford rules to direct us in such a state of things?

A great deal of noise and tumult, confusion and uproar, and darkness mixed with light, and evil with good, is always to be expected in the beginning of something very extraordinary, and very glorious in the state of things in human society, or the church of God. As after nature has long been shut up in a cold dead state, in time of winter, when the sun returns in the spring, there is, together with the increase of the light and heat of the sun, very dirty and tempestuous weather, before all is settled calm and serene, and all nature rejoices in its bloom and beauty. It is in the new creation as it was in the old: the Spirit of God first moved upon the face of the waters, which was an occasion of great uproar and tumult, and things were gradually brought to a settled state, till at length all stood forth in that beautiful, peaceful order, when the heavens and the earth were finished, and God saw everything that he had made; "and behold, it was very good" [cf. Gen. 1]. When God is about to bring to pass something great and glorious in the world, nature is in a ferment and struggle, and the world as it were in travail. As when God was about to introduce the Messiah into the world, and that new and glorious dispensation that he set up, he shook the heavens and the earth, and shook all nations [Hag. 2:6–7]. There is nothing that the church of God is in Scripture more frequently represented by than vegetables; as a tree, a vine, corn, etc., which gradually bring forth their fruit, and are first green before they are ripe. A great revival of religion is expressly compared to this gradual production of vegetables, Isa. 61:11, "As the earth bringeth forth her bud, and as the garden causeth the things that are sown in it to spring forth; so the Lord God will cause righteousness and praise to spring forth before all the nations." The church is in a special manner compared to a palm tree, Cant. 7:7–8; Exod. 15:27; I Kings 6:29; Ps. 92:12. Of which tree this peculiar thing is observed, that the fruit of it, though it be very sweet and good when it is ripe, yet before it has had time to ripen, has a mixture of poison.

The weakness of human nature has always appeared in times of great revival of religion, by a disposition to run to extremes and get into confusion; and especially in these three things—enthusiasm, superstition, and intemperate zeal. So it appeared in the time of the Reformation, very remarkably; and also in the days of the apostles; many were then exceedingly disposed to lay weight on those things that were very notional and chimerical, giving heed to fables and whimsies, as appears by I Tim. 1:4 and 4:7; II Tim. 2:16 and vs. 23; and Tit. 1:14 and 3:9. Many, as ecclesiastical history informs us, fell off into the most wild enthusiasm, and extravagant notions of spirituality, and extraordinary illumination from heaven beyond others; and many were prone to superstition, will-worship and a voluntary humility [Col. 2:18, 23], giving heed to the commandments of men, being fond of an unprofitable bodily exercise [I Tim. 4:8], as appears by many passages in the apostles' writings. And what a proneness then appeared among professors to swerve from the path of duty and the spirit of the Gospel, in the exercises of a rash, indiscreet zeal, censuring and condemning ministers and people; one saying, "I am of Paul"; another, "I of Apollos"; another, "I of Cephas"; judging one another for differences of opinion about smaller matters, unclean meats, holy days and holy places, and their different opinions and practices respecting civil intercourse and communication with their heathen neighbors?] I Cor. 1:12, 6:1–8, 8:1–13; Rom. 14:1–23]. And how much did vain jangling and disputing and confusion prevail through undue heat of spirit, under the name of a religious zeal? I Tim. 6:4–5; II Tim. 2:16; and Tit. 3:9. And what a task had the apostles to keep them within bounds, and maintain good order in the churches? How often are they mentioning their irregularities? The prevailing of such like disorders seems to have been the special occasion of writing many of their epistles. The church in that great effusion of the Spirit that was then, and the strong impressions that God's people were then under, was under the care of infallible guides, that watched over them day and night; but yet so prone were they, through the weakness and corruption of human nature, to get out of the way, that irregularity and confusion rose in some churches, where there was an extraordinary outpouring of the Spirit, to a very great height, even in the apostles' lifetime, and under their eye. And though some of the apostles lived long to settle the state of things, yet presently after they were dead, the Christian church ran into many superstitions and childish notions and practices, and in some respects into a

great severity in their zeal. And let any wise persons that han't, in
the midst of the disputes of the present day, got beyond the calmness of consideration, impartially consider to what lengths, we may
reasonably suppose, many of the primitive Christians, in their heat
of zeal and under their extraordinary impressions, would soon have
gone if they had had no inspired guides; and whether or no 'tis not
probable that the church of Corinth in particular, by an increase of
their irregularities and contentions, would not in a little time have
broke to pieces, and dissolved in a state of the utmost confusion?
And yet this would have been no evidence that there had not been
a most glorious and remarkable outpouring of the Spirit in that
city. But as for us, we have no infallible apostle to guide and
direct us, to rectify disorders, and reclaim us when we are wandering; but everyone does what is right in his own eyes [Judg. 21:25];
and they that err in judgment, and are got into a wrong path,
continue to wander, till experience of the mischievous issue convinces them of their error.

If we look over this affair, and seriously weigh it in its circumstances, it will appear a matter of no great difficulty to account for
the errors that have been gone into, supposing the work in general
to be from a very great outpouring of the Spirit of God. It may
easily be accounted for, that many have run into great errors, and
into just such errors as they have. It is known that some that have
been improved as great instruments to promote this work, have
been very young; and how natural is it for such as are themselves
newly waked out of sleep, and brought out of that state of darkness,
insensibility and spiritual death, which they had been in ever since
they were born; and have a new and wonderful scene opened to
them; and have in view the reality, the vastness, and infinite importance, and nearness of spiritual and eternal things; and at the
same time are surprised to see the world asleep about them; and
han't the advantage of age and experience, and have had but little
opportunity to study divinity, or to converse with aged experienced
Christians and divines; I say, how natural is it for such to fall into
many errors with respect to the state of mankind, with which they
are so surprised, and with respect to the means and methods of
their relief? Is it any wonder that they han't at once learned how
to make all the allowances that are to be made, and that they don't
at once find out that method of dealing with the world, that is
adapted to the mysterious state and nature of mankind? Is it any

wonder that they can't at once foresee what the consequences of things will be, what evils are to be guarded against and what difficulties are like to arise, that are to be provided for?

We have long been in a strange stupor; the influences of the Spirit of God upon the heart have been but little felt, and the nature of them but little taught; so that they are in many respects new to great numbers of those that have lately fallen under them. And is it any wonder that they that never before had experience of the supernatural influence of the divine Spirit upon their souls, and never were instructed in the nature of these influences, don't so well know how to distinguish one extraordinary new impression from another, and so (to themselves insensibly) run into enthusiasm, taking every strong impulse or impression to be divine? How natural is it to suppose, that among the multitudes of illiterate people (most of which are in their youth) that find themselves so wonderfully changed, and brought into such new, and before (to them) almost unheard of circumstances, that many should pass wrong and very strange judgments of both persons and things that are about them; and that now they behold them in such a new light, they in their surprise should go further from the judgment that they were wont to make of them than they ought, and in their great change of sentiments, should pass from one extreme to another? And why should it be thought strange, that those that scarce ever heard of any such thing as an outpouring of the Spirit of God before; or if they did, had no notion of it; don't know how to behave themselves in such a new and strange state of things? And is it any wonder that they are ready to hearken to those that have instructed them, that have been the means of delivering them from such a state of death and misery as they were in before, or have a name for being the happy instruments of promoting the same work among others? Is it unaccountable that persons in these circumstances are ready to receive everything they say, and to drink down error as well as truth from them? And why should there be all indignation and no compassion towards those that are thus misled?

When these persons are extraordinarily affected with a new sense, and recent discovery they have received of the greatness and excellency of the divine Being, the certainty and infinite importance of eternal things, the preciousness of souls, and the dreadful danger and madness of mankind, together with a great sense of God's distinguishing kindness and love to them; no wonder that now they think they must exert themselves, and do something extraordinary for the honor of God and the good of the souls of their fellow creatures, and know not how to sit still, and forbear speaking and acting with uncommon earnestness and vigor. And in these circumstances, if they ben't persons of more than common steadiness and discretion, or han't some person of wisdom to direct them, 'tis a wonder if they don't proceed without due caution, and do things that are irregular, and that will, in the issue, do much more hurt than good.

Censuring others is the worst disease with which this affair has been attended: but yet such a time as this is indeed a time of great temptation to this sinful error. When there has been such a time of great and long continued deadness, and many are brought out of a state of nature into a state of grace, in so extraordinary a manner, and filled with such uncommon degrees of light, 'tis natural to form their notions of a state of grace wholly from what they experience; many of them know no other way, for they never have been taught much about a state of grace, and the different degrees of grace, and the degrees of darkness and corruption that grace is consistent with, nor concerning the manner of the influences of the Spirit in converting a soul, and the variety of the manner of his operations. They therefore forming their idea of a state of grace only by their own experience, no wonder that it appears an insuperable difficulty to them to reconcile such a state, of which they have this idea, with what they observe in professors that are about them. 'Tis indeed in itself a very great mystery, that grace should be consistent with so much and such kind of corruption as sometimes prevails in the truly godly; and no wonder that it especially appears so to uninstructed new converts, that have been converted in an extraordinary manner.

Though censoriousness be a thing that is very sinful, and is most commonly found in hypocrites and persons of a pharisaical spirit, yet it is not so inconsistent with true godliness as some imagine. We have remarkable instances of it in those holy men that we have an account of in the Book of Job: not only were Job's three friends, that seem to have been eminently holy men, guilty of it, in very unreasonably censuring the best man on earth, very positively determining that he was an unconverted man; but Job himself, that was not only a man of true piety, but excelled all men in piety, and particularly excelled in a humble, meek and patient spirit, was guilty of bitterly censuring his three friends as wicked, vile hypocrites. Job 16:9–11, "He teareth me in his wrath who hateth me, he gnasheth upon me with his teeth; mine enemy sharpeneth his eyes upon me: they have gaped upon me with their mouth. . . . God hath delivered me to the ungodly, and turned me over into the hands of the wicked." So he is very positive in it that they are hypocrites, and shall be miserably destroyed as such; in the next chapter, vss. 2–4, "Are there not mockers with me? And doth not mine eye continue in their provocation? Lay down now, put me in surety with thee; who is he that will strike hands with me? For thou hast hid their heart from understanding: therefore shalt thou not exalt them." And again, vss. 8–10, "Upright men shall be astonished at this, and the innocent shall stir up himself against the hypocrite: the righteous also shall hold on his way, and he that hath clean hands shall be stronger and stronger. But as for you all, do you return and come now: for I cannot find one wise man (i.e. one good man) among you."

Thus I think the errors and irregularities that attend this work, may be accounted for, from the consideration of the infirmity and weakness and common corruption of mankind, together with the circumstances of the work, though we should suppose it to be the work of God. And it would not be a just objection in any to say, if these powerful impressions and great affections are from the Spirit of God, why don't the same Spirit give strength of understanding and capacity in proportion, to those persons that are the subjects of them; so that strong affections may not, through their error, drive them to an irregular and sinful conduct? For I don't know that God has anywhere obliged himself to do it. The end of the influences of God's Spirit is to make men spiritually knowing, wise to salvation, which is the most excellent wisdom; and he has also appointed means for our gaining such degrees of other knowledge as we need, to conduct ourselves regularly, which means should be carefully used: but the end of the influence of the Spirit of God is not to increase men's natural capacities, nor has God obliged himself immediately to increase civil prudence in proportion to the degrees of spiritual light.

If we consider the errors that attend this work, not only as from man and his infirmity, but also as from God, and by his permission and disposal, they are not strange, upon the supposition of its being, as to the substance of it, a work of God. If God intends this great revival of religion to be the dawning, or a forerunner of an happy state of his church on earth, it may be an instance of the divine wisdom, in the beginning of it, to suffer so many irregularities and errors in conduct, to which he knew men, in their present weak state, were most exposed, under great religious affections and when animated with great zeal. For it will be very likely to be of excellent benefit to his church, in the continuance and progress of the work afterwards: their experience in the first setting out of the mischievous consequences of these errors, and smarting for them in the beginning, may be an happy defense to them afterwards, for many generations, from these errors, which otherwise they might continually be exposed to. As when David and all Israel went about to bring back the ark into the midst of the land, after it had been long absent, first in the land of the Philistines, and then in Kirjath-jearim, in the utmost borders of the land; they at first sought not the Lord after the due order, and they smarted for their error; but this put them upon studying the law, and more thoroughly acquainting themselves with the mind and will of God, and seeking and serving him with greater circumspection; and the consequence was glorious, viz. their seeking God in such a manner as was accepted of him; and the ark of God's ascending into the heights of Zion, with those great and extraordinary rejoicings of the king and all the people, without any frown or rebuke from God intermixed; and God's dwelling thenceforward in the midst of the people, to those glorious purposes that are expressed in the 68th Psalm [cf. I Sam. 4–6].

And 'tis very analogous to the manner of God dealing with his people, to permit a great deal of error, and suffer the infirmity of his people much to appear, in the beginning of a glorious work of his grace for their felicity, to teach them what they be, to humble them, and fit them for that glorious prosperity he is about to advance them to, and the more to secure to himself the honor of such a glorious work: for by man's exceeding weakness appearing in the beginning of it, 'tis evident that God don't lay the foundation of it in man's strength or wisdom.

And as we need not wonder at the errors that attend this work, if we look at the hand of men that are guilty of them, and the hand of God in permitting them, so neither shall we see cause to wonder at them, if we consider them with regard to the hand that Satan has in them. For as the work is much greater than any other outpouring of the Spirit that ever has been in New England, so no wonder that the Devil is more alarmed and enraged, and exerts himself more vigorously against it, and does more powerfully endeavor to tempt and mislead those that are the subjects of it, or are its promoters.

Whatever imprudences there have been, and whatever sinful irregularities; whatever vehemence of the passions and heats of the imagination, transports and ecstasies; and whatever error in judgment, and indiscreet zeal; and whatever outcries, and faintings, and agitations of body; yet it is manifest and notorious, that there has been of late a very uncommon influence upon the minds of a very great part of the inhabitants of New England, from one end of the land to the other, that has been attended with the following effects: viz. a great increase of a spirit of seriousness, and sober consideration of the things of the eternal world; a disposition to hearken to anything that is said of things of this nature, with attention and affection; a disposition to treat matters of religion with solemnity, and as matters of great importance; a disposition to make these things the subject of conversation; and a great disposition to hear the Word of God preached, and to take all opportunities in order to it; and to attend on the public worship of God, and all external duties of religion in a more solemn and decent manner; so that there is a remarkable and general alteration in the face of New England in these respects. Multitudes in all parts of the land, of vain, thoughtless, regardless persons are quite changed, and become serious and considerate: there is a vast increase of concern for the salvation of the precious soul, and of that inquiry, "What shall I do to be saved?" [Acts 16:30]. The hearts of multitudes have been greatly taken off from the things of the world, its profits, pleasures and honors; and there has been a great increase of sensibleness and tenderness of conscience. Multitudes in all parts have had their consciences awakened, and have been made sensible of the pernicious nature and consequences of sin, and what a dreadful thing it is to lie under guilt and the displeasure of God, and to live without peace and reconciliation with him: they have also been awakened to a sense of the shortness and uncertainty of life, and the reality of another world and future judgment, and of the necessity of an interest in Christ: they are more afraid of sin, more careful and inquisitive that they may know what is contrary to the mind and will of God, that they may avoid it, and what he requires of them, that they may do it; more careful to guard against temptations, more watchful over their own hearts, earnestly desirous of being informed what are the means that God has directed [them] to, for their salvation, and diligent in the use of the means that God has appointed in his Word, in order to it. Many very stupid, senseless sinners, and persons of a vain mind, have been greatly awakened.

There is a strange alteration almost all over New England amongst young people: by a powerful, invisible influence on their minds, they have been brought to forsake those things in a general way, as it were at once, that they were extremely fond of, and greatly addicted to, and that they seemed to place the happiness of their lives in, and that nothing before could induce them to forsake; as their frolicking, vain company-keeping, nightwalking, their mirth and jollity, their impure language, and lewd songs. In vain did ministers preach against those things before, and in vain were laws made to restrain them, and in vain was all the vigilance of magistrates and civil officers; but now they have almost everywhere dropped them as it were of themselves. And there is a great alteration amongst old and young as to drinking, tavern-haunting, profane speaking, and extravagance in apparel. Many notoriously vicious persons have been reformed, and become externally quite new creatures: some that are wealthy, and of a fashionable, gay education; some great beaus and fine ladies, that seemed to have their minds swallowed up with nothing but the vain shews and pleasures of the world, have been wonderfully altered, and have relinquished these vanities, and are become serious, mortified and humble in their conversation.[4] 'Tis astonishing to see the alteration that is in some towns, where before was but little appearance of religion, or anything but vice and vanity: and so remote was all that was to be seen or heard amongst them from anything that savored of vital piety or serious religion, or that had any relation to it, that one would have thought, if they had judged only by what appeared in them, that they had been some other species from the serious and religious, which had no concern with another world, and whose natures were now made capable of those things that appertain to Christian experience, and pious conversation; especially was it thus among young persons. And now they are trans-

4. [Here, and often elsewhere (though not always), JE uses "conversation" in the archaic sense meaning "manner of life."]

formed into another sort of people; their former vain, worldly and vicious conversation and dispositions seem to be forsaken, and they are as it were, gone over to a new world: their thoughts, and their talk, and their concern, affections and inquiries are now about the favor of God, an interest in Christ, a renewed sanctified heart, and a spiritual blessedness, and acceptance and happiness in a future world. And through the greater part of New England, the Holy Bible is in much greater esteem and use than it used to be; the great things that are contained in it are much more regarded, as things of the greatest consequence, and are much more the subjects of meditation and conversation; and other books of piety that have long been of established reputation, as the most excellent, and most tending to promote true godliness, have been abundantly more in use. The Lord's day is more religiously and strictly observed: and abundance has been lately done at making up differences, and confessing faults one to another, and making restitution; probably more within these two years, than was done in thirty years before: it has been so undoubtedly in many places. And surprising has been the power of that Spirit that has been poured out on the land, in many instances, to destroy old grudges, and make up long continued breaches, and to bring those that seemed to be in a confirmed irreconcilable alienation, to embrace each other in a sincere and entire amity.

Great numbers under this influence have been brought to a deep sense of their own sinfulness and vileness; the sinfulness of their lives, the heinousness of their disregard of the authority of the great God, and the heinousness of their living in contempt of a Saviour: they have lamented their former negligence of their souls and neglecting and losing precious time. Their sins of life have been extraordinarily set before them: and they have also had a great sense of their sins of heart; their hardness of heart, and enmity against that which is good, and proneness to all evil; and also of the worthlessness of their own religious performances, how unworthy their prayers, praises, and all that they did in religion, was to be regarded of God. And it has been a common thing that persons have had such a sense of their own sinfulness, that they have thought themselves to be the worst of all, and that none ever was so vile as they. And many seem to have been greatly convinced that they were utterly unworthy of any mercy at the hands of God, however miserable they were, and though they stood in extreme necessity of mercy; and that they deserved nothing but eternal burnings: and have been sensible that God would be altogether just and righteous in inflicting endless damnation upon them, at the same time that they have had an exceeding affecting sense of the dreadfulness of such endless torments, and have apprehended themselves to be greatly in danger of it. And many have been deeply affected with a sense of their own ignorance and blindness, and exceeding helplessness, and so of their extreme need of the divine pity and help. And so far as we are worthy to be credited one by another, in what we say (and persons of good understanding and sound mind, and known and experienced probity, have a right to be believed by their neighbors, when they speak of things that fall under their observation and experience), multitudes in New England have lately been brought to a new and great conviction of the truth and certainty of the things of the Gospel; to a firm persuasion that Christ Jesus is the Son of God, and the great and only Saviour of the world; and that the great doctrines of the Gospel touching reconciliation by his blood, and acceptance in his righteousness, and eternal life and salvation through him, are matters of undoubted truth; together with a most affecting sense of the excellency and sufficiency of this Saviour, and the glorious wisdom and grace of God shining in this way of salvation; and of the wonders of Christ's dying love, and the sincerity of Christ in the invitations of the Gospel, and a consequent affiance and sweet rest of soul in Christ, as a glorious Saviour, a strong rock and high tower, accompanied with an admiring and exalting apprehension of the glory of the divine perfections, God's majesty, holiness, sovereign grace, etc.; with a sensible, strong and sweet love to God, and delight in him, far surpassing all temporal delights, or earthly pleasures; and a rest of soul in him as a portion and the fountain of all good, attended with an abhorrence of sin, and self-loathing for it, and earnest longings of soul after more holiness and conformity to God, with a sense of the great need of God's help in order to holiness of life; together with a most dear love to all that are supposed to be the children of God, and a love to mankind in general, and a most sensible and tender compassion for the souls of sinners, and earnest desires of the advancement of Christ's kingdom in the world. And these things have appeared to be in many of them abiding now for many months, yea, more than a year and [a] half; with an abiding concern to live an holy life, and great complaints of remaining corruption, longing to be more free from the body of sin and death [cf. Rom. 6:6, 7:24, 8:2].

And not only do these effects appear in new converts, but great numbers of those that were formerly esteemed the most sober and pious people have, under the influence of this work, been greatly quickened, and their hearts renewed with greater degrees of light, renewed repentance and humiliation, and more lively exercises of faith, love and joy in the Lord. Many, as I am well knowing, have of late been remarkably engaged to watch, and strive, and fight against sin, and cast out every idol, and sell all for Christ, and give up themselves entirely to God, and make a sacrifice of every worldly and carnal thing to the welfare and prosperity of their souls. And there has of late appeared in some places an unusual disposition to bind themselves to it in a solemn covenant with God.[5] And now instead of meetings at taverns and drinking houses, and meetings of young people in frolics and vain company, the country is full of meetings of all sorts and ages of persons, young and old, men, women and little children, to read and pray, and sing praises, and to converse of the things of God and another world. In very many places the main [subject] of the conversation in all companies turns on religion, and things of a spiritual nature. Instead of vain mirth amongst young people, there is now either mourning under a sense of the guilt of sin, or holy rejoicing in Christ Jesus; and instead of their lewd songs, are now to be heard from them songs of praise to God, and [to] the Lamb that was slain to redeem them by his blood [cf. Rev. 5:6, 9, and 12]. And there has been this alteration abiding on multitudes all over the land, for a year and [a] half, without any appearance of a disposition to return to former vice and vanity. And under the influences of this work, there have been many of the remains of those wretched people and dregs of mankind, the poor Indians, that seemed to be next to a state of brutality, and with whom, till now, it seemed to be to little more purpose to use endeavors for their instruction and awakening, than with the beasts; whose minds have now been strangely opened to receive instruction, and have been deeply affected with the concerns of their precious souls, and have reformed their lives, and forsaken their former stupid, barbarous and brutish way of living; and particularly that sin to which they have been so exceedingly addicted, their drunkenness; and are become devout and serious per-

5. [Northampton had renewed covenant in March 1742; see above, pp. 85–86.]

sons; and many of them to appearance brought truly and greatly to delight in the things of God, and to have their souls very much engaged and entertained with the great things of the Gospel. And many of the poor Negroes also have been in like manner wrought upon and changed. And the souls of very many little children have been remarkably enlightened, and their hearts wonderfully affected and enlarged, and their mouths opened, expressing themselves in a manner far beyond their years, and to the just astonishment of those that have heard them; and some of them from time to time, for many months, greatly and delightfully affected with the glory of divine things, and the excellency and love of the Redeemer, with their hearts greatly filled with love to and joy in him, and have continued to be serious and pious in their behavior.

The divine power of this work has marvelously appeared in some instances I have been acquainted with, in supporting and fortifying the heart under great trials, such as the death of children, and extreme pain of body; wonderfully maintaining the serenity, calmness and joy of the soul, in an immovable rest in God, and sweet resignation to him. There also have been instances of some that have been the subjects of this work, that under the blessed influences of it have, in such a calm, bright and joyful frame of mind, been carried through the valley of the shadow of death.

And now let us consider— Is it not strange that in a Christian, orthodox country, and such a land of light as this is, there should be many at a loss whose work this is, whether the work of God or the work of the Devil? Is it not a shame to New England that such a work should be much doubted of here? Need we look over the histories of all past times, to see if there ben't some circumstances and external appearances that attend this work, that have been formerly found amongst enthusiasts? Whether the Montanists had not great transports of joy, and whether the French Prophets had not agitations of body? [6] Blessed be God! He don't put us to the toil of such inquiries. We need not say, "Who shall ascend into heaven" [Rom. 10:6], to bring us down something whereby to judge of this work. Nor does God send us beyond the seas, nor into past ages, to obtain a rule that shall determine and satisfy us. But we have a rule near at hand, a sacred book that God himself has

6. [Montanism was a second-century attempt to revive pentecostal fervor, along with prophetism and chiliasm, in the churches of Asia Minor. On the French Prophets, see above, p. 63.]

put into our hands, with clear and infallible marks, sufficient to resolve us in things of this nature; which book I think we must reject, not only in some particular passages, but in the substance of it, if we reject such a work as has now been described, as not being the work of God. The whole tenor of the Gospel proves it; all the notion of religion that the Scripture gives us confirms it.

I suppose there is scarcely a minister in this land, but from Sabbath to Sabbath used to pray that God would pour out his Spirit, and work a reformation and revival of religion in the country, and turn us from our intemperance, profaneness, uncleanness, worldliness and other sins; and we have kept from year to year days of public fasting and prayer to God, to acknowledge our backslidings, and humble ourselves for our sins, and to seek of God forgiveness and reformation: and now when so great and extensive a reformation is so suddenly and wonderfully accomplished, in those very things that we have sought to God for, shall we not acknowledge it? Or when we do, do it with great coldness, caution and reserve, and scarcely take any notice of it in our public prayers and praises, or mention it but slightly and cursorily, and in such a manner as carried an appearance as though we would contrive to say as little of it as ever we could, and were glad to pass from it? And that because (although indeed there be such a work attended with all these glorious effects, yet) the work is attended with a mixture of error, imprudences, darkness and sin; because some persons are carried away with impressions, and are indiscreet, and too censorious with their zeal; and because there are high transports of religious affection; and because of some effects on persons' bodies that we don't understand the reason of?

[*An Example of Evangelical Piety*]

I have been particularly acquainted with many persons [7] that have been the subjects of the high and extraordinary transports of the present day; and in the highest transports of any of the instances that I have been acquainted with, and where the affections of admiration, love and joy, so far as another could judge, have been raised to a higher pitch than in any other instances I have observed or been informed of, the following things have been united: viz. a

---

7. [Here JE begins to describe his wife's religious experiences; see above, pp. 68–70.]

very frequent dwelling, for some considerable time together, in such views of the glory of the divine perfections, and Christ's excellencies, that the soul in the meantime has been as it were perfectly overwhelmed, and swallowed up with light and love and a sweet solace, rest and joy of soul, that was altogether unspeakable; and more than once continuing for five or six hours together, without any interruption, in that clear and lively view or sense of the infinite beauty and amiableness of Christ's person, and the heavenly sweetness of his excellent and transcendent love; so that (to use the person's own expressions) the soul remained in a kind of heavenly Elysium, and did as it were swim in the rays of Christ's love, like a little mote swimming in the beams of the sun, or streams of his light that come in at a window; and the heart was swallowed up in a kind of glow of Christ's love, coming down from Christ's heart in heaven, as a constant stream of sweet light, at the same time the soul all flowing out in love to him; so that there seemed to be a constant flowing and reflowing from heart to heart. The soul dwelt on high, and was lost in God, and seemed almost to leave the body; dwelling in a pure delight that fed and satisfied the soul; enjoying pleasure without the least sting, or any interruption, a sweetness that the soul was lost in; so that (so far as the judgment and word of a person of discretion may be taken, speaking upon the most deliberate consideration) what was enjoyed in each single minute of the whole space, which was many hours, was undoubtedly worth more than all the outward comfort and pleasure of the whole life put together; and this without being in any trance, or being at all deprived of the exercise of the bodily senses: and the like heavenly delight and unspeakable joy of soul, enjoyed from time to time, for years together; though not frequently so long together, to such an height: extraordinary views of divine things, and religious affections, being frequently attended with very great effects on the body, nature often sinking under the weight of divine discoveries, the strength of the body taken away, so as to deprive of all ability to stand or speak; sometimes the hands clinched, and the flesh cold, but senses still remaining; animal nature often in a great emotion and agitation, and the soul very often, of late, so overcome with great admiration, and a kind of omnipotent joy, as to cause the person (wholly unavoidably) to leap with all the might, with joy and mighty exultation of soul; the soul at the same time being so strongly drawn towards God and Christ in heaven, that it seemed to the person as though soul and body would, as it were of themselves, of necessity mount up, leave the earth and ascend thither.

These effects on the body did not begin now in this wonderful season, that they should be owing to the influence of the example of the times, but about seven years ago; and began in a much higher degree, and greater frequency, near three years ago, when there was no such enthusiastical season, as many account this, but it was a very dead time through the land. They arose from no distemper catched from Mr. Whitefield or Mr. Tennent, because they began before either of them came into the country; they began, as I said, near three years ago, in a great increase, upon an extraordinary self-dedication, and renunciation of the world, and resignation of all to God, made in a great view of God's excellency, and high exercise of love to him, and rest and joy in him; since which time they have been very frequent; and began in a yet higher degree, and greater frequency, about a year and [a] half ago, upon another new resignation of all to God, with a yet greater fervency and delight of soul; since which time the body has been very often fainting with the love of Christ; and began in a much higher degree still, the last winter, upon another resignation and acceptance of God, as the only portion and happiness of the soul, wherein the whole world, with the dearest enjoyments in it, were renounced as dirt and dung, and all that is pleasant and glorious, and all that is terrible in this world, seemed perfectly to vanish into nothing, and nothing to be left but God, in whom the soul was perfectly swallowed up, as in an infinite ocean of blessedness: since which time there have often been great agitations of body, and an unavoidable leaping for joy; and the soul as it were dwelling almost without interruption, in a kind of paradise; and very often, in high transports, disposed to speak of those great and glorious things of God and Christ, and the eternal world, that are in view, to others that are present, in a most earnest manner, and with a loud voice, so that it is next to impossible to avoid it: these effects on the body not arising from any bodily distemper or weakness, because the greatest of all have been in a good state of health. This great rejoicing has been a rejoicing with trembling, i.e. attended with a deep and lively sense of the greatness and majesty of God, and the person's own exceeding littleness and vileness: spiritual joys in this person never were attended, either formerly or lately, with the least appearance of any laughter or lightness of countenance, or manner of speaking; but with a peculiar abhorrence of such appearances in spiritual rejoicings, especially since joys have been greatest of all. These high transports when they have been past, have had abiding effects in the increase of the sweetness, rest and humility that they have left upon the soul; and a new engagedness of heart to live to God's honor, and watch and fight against sin. And these things not in one that is in the giddy age of youth, nor in a new convert, and unexperienced Christian, but in one that was converted above twenty-seven years ago; and neither converted nor educated in that enthusiastical town of Northampton (as some may be ready to call it), but in a town and family that none that I know of suspected of enthusiasm; and in a Christian that has been long, in an uncommon manner, growing in grace, and rising, by very sensible degrees, to higher love to God, and weanedness from the world, and mastery over sin and temptation, through great trials and conflicts, and long continued struggling and fighting with sin, and earnest and constant prayer and labor in religion, and engagedness of mind in the use of all means, attended with a great exactness of life: which growth has been attended, not only with a great increase of religious affections, but with a wonderful alteration of outward behavior, in many things, visible to those who are most intimately acquainted, so as lately to have become as it were a new person; and particularly in living so much more above the world, and in a greater degree of steadfastness and strength in the way of duty and self-denial, maintaining the Christian conflict against temptations, and conquering from time to time under great trials; persisting in an unmoved, untouched calm and rest; under the changes and accidents of time.

The person had formerly in lower degrees of grace, been subject to unsteadiness, and many ups and downs, in the frame of mind; the mind being under great disadvantages, through a vapory habit of body, and often subject to melancholy, and at times almost overborne with it, it having been so even from early youth: but strength of grace, and divine light has of a long time, wholly conquered these disadvantages, and carried the mind in a constant manner, quite above all such effects of vapors. Since that resignation spoken of before, made near three years ago, everything of that nature seems to be overcome and crushed by the power of faith and trust in God, and resignation to him; the person has remained in a constant uninterrupted rest, and humble joy in God, and assurance of his favor, without one hour's melancholy or darkness, from that day to this; vapors have had great effects on the body, such as they used to have before, but the soul has been always out of their reach. And this steadfastness and constancy has remained through great outward changes and trials; such as times of the most extreme pain, and apparent hazard of immediate death. What has been felt in late great transports is known to be nothing new in kind, but to be of the same nature with what was felt formerly, when a little child of about five or six years of age; but only in a vastly higher degree. These transporting views and rapturous affections are not attended with any enthusiastic disposition to follow impulses, or any supposed prophetical revelations; nor have they been observed to be attended with any appearance of spiritual pride, but very much of a contrary disposition, an increase of a spirit of humility and meekness, and a disposition in honor to prefer others [cf. Rom. 12:10]. And 'tis worthy to be remarked, that at a time remarkably distinguished from all others, wherein discoveries and holy affections were evidently at the greatest height that ever happened, the greatness and clearness of divine light being overwhelming, and the strength and sweetness of divine love altogether overpowering, which began early in the morning of the Holy Sabbath, and lasted for days together, melting all down in the deepest humility and poverty of spirit, reverence and resignation, and the sweetest meekness, and universal benevolence; I say, 'tis worthy to be observed, that there were these two things in a remarkable manner felt at that time, viz. a peculiar sensible aversion to a judging others that were professing Christians of good standing in the visible church, that they were not converted, or with respect to their degrees of grace; or at all intermeddling with that matter, so much as to determine against and condemn others in the thought of the heart; it appearing hateful, as not agreeing with that lamb-like humility, meekness, gentleness and charity, which the soul then, above other times, saw the beauty of, and felt a disposition to. The disposition that was then felt was, on the contrary, to prefer others to self, and to hope that they saw more of God and loved him better; though before, under smaller discoveries and feebler exercises of divine affection, there had been felt a disposition to censure and condemn others. And another thing that was felt at that time, was a very great sense of the importance of moral social duties, and how great a part of religion lay in them: there was such a new sense and conviction of this, beyond what had been before, that it seemed to be as it were a clear discovery then made to the soul. But in general, there has been a very great increase of a sense of these two things, as divine views and divine love have increased.

The things [8] already mentioned have been attended also with the following things, viz. an extraordinary sense of the awful majesty and greatness of God, so as oftentimes to take away the bodily strength; a sense of the holiness of God, as of a flame infinitely pure and bright, so as sometimes to overwhelm soul and body; a sense of the piercing all-seeing eye of God, so as sometimes to take away the bodily strength; and an extraordinary view of the infinite terribleness of the wrath of God, which has very frequently been strongly impressed on the mind, together with a sense of the ineffable misery of sinners that are exposed to this wrath, that has been overbearing: sometimes the exceeding pollution of the person's own heart, as a sink of all manner of abomination, and a nest of vipers, and the dreadfulness of an eternal hell of God's wrath, opened to view both together; with a clear view of a desert of that misery, without the least degree of divine pity, and that by the pollution of the best duties; yea, only by the pollution and irreverence, and want of humility that attended once speaking of the holy name of God, when done in the best manner that ever it was done; the strength of the body very often taken away with a deep mourning for sin, as committed against so holy and good a God, sometimes with an affecting sense of actual sin, sometimes especially indwelling sin, sometimes the consideration of the sin of the heart as appearing in a particular thing, as for instance, in that there was no greater forwardness and readiness to self-denial for God and Christ, that had so denied himself for us; yea, sometimes the consideration of sin that was in only speaking one word concerning the infinitely great and holy God, has been so affecting as to overcome the strength of nature: very great sense of the certain truth of the great things revealed in the Gospel; an overwhelming sense of the glory of the work of redemption, and the way of salvation by Jesus Christ; the glorious harmony of the divine attributes appearing therein, as that wherein "mercy and truth are met together, and righteousness and peace have kissed each other" [Ps. 85:10]; a sight of the fulness

8. [In the original printing this sentence runs for three pages, the paragraph for nine. In the present edition the paragraph has been broken several times, but the sentence structure is modified only slightly.]

and glorious sufficiency of Christ, that has been so affecting as to overcome the body: a constant immovable trust in God through Christ, with a great sense of his strength and faithfulness, the sureness of his covenant, and the immutability of his promises, so that the everlasting mountains and perpetual hills have appeared as mere shadows to these things: sometimes the sufficiency and faithfulness of God as the covenant God of his people, appearing in these words, "I AM THAT I AM" [Exod. 3:14], in so affecting a manner as to overcome the body: a sense of the glorious, unsearchable, unerring wisdom of God in his works, both of creation and providence, so as to swallow up the soul, and overcome the strength of the body: a sweet rejoicing of soul at the thoughts of God's being infinitely and unchangeably happy, and an exulting gladness of heart that God is self-sufficient, and infinitely above all dependence, and reigns over all, and does his will with absolute and uncontrollable power and sovereignty; a sense of the glory of the Holy Spirit, as the great Comforter, so as to overwhelm both soul and body; only mentioning the word, "the Comforter," has immediately taken away all strength; that word, as the person expressed it, seemed great enough to fill heaven and earth: a most vehement and passionate desire of the honor and glory of God's name; a sensible, clear and constant preference of it not only to the person's own temporal interest, but spiritual comfort in this world; and a willingness to suffer the hidings of God's face, and to live and die in darkness and horror if God's honor should require it, and to have no other reward for it but that God's name should be glorified, although so much of the sweetness of the light of God's countenance had been experienced: a great lamenting of ingratitude, and the lowness of the degree of love to God, so as to deprive of bodily strength; and very often vehement longings and faintings after more love to Christ, and greater conformity to him; especially longing after these two things, viz. to be more perfect in humility and adoration; the flesh and heart seems often to cry out for a lying low before God, and adoring him with greater love and humility: the thoughts of the perfect humility with which the saints in heaven worship God, and fall down before his throne, have often overcome the body, and set it into a great agitation.

A great delight in singing praises to God and Jesus Christ, and longing that this present life may be, as it were, one continued song of praise to God; longing, as the person expressed it, to sit and sing this life away; and an overcoming pleasure in the thoughts of spending an eternity in that exercise: a living by faith to a great degree; a constant and extraordinary distrust of own strength and wisdom; a great dependence on God for his help, in order to the performance of anything to God's acceptance, and being restrained from the most horrid sins, and running upon God, even on his neck, and "on the thick bosses of his bucklers" [Job 15:26]: such a sense of the black ingratitude of true saints' coldness and deadness in religion, and their setting their hearts on the things of this world, as to overcome the bodily frame: a great longing that all the children of God might be lively in religion, fervent in their love, and active in the service of God; and when there have been appearances of it in others, rejoicing so in beholding the pleasing sight, that the joy of soul has been too great for the body: taking pleasure in the thoughts of watching and striving against sin, and fighting through the way to heaven, and filling up this life with hard labor, and bearing the cross for Christ, as an opportunity to give God honor; not desiring to rest from labors till arrived in heaven, but abhorring the thoughts of it, and seeming astonished that God's own children should be backward to strive and deny themselves for God: earnest longings that all God's people might be clothed with humility and meekness, like the Lamb of God, and feel nothing in their hearts but love and compassion to all mankind; and great grief when anything to the contrary seems to appear in any of the children of God, as any bitterness, or fierceness of zeal, or censoriousness, or reflecting uncharitably on others, or disputing with any appearance of heat of spirit; a deep concern for the good of others' souls; a melting compassion to those that looked on themselves as in a state of nature, and to saints under darkness, so as to cause the body to faint: an universal benevolence to mankind, with a longing as it were to embrace the whole world in the arms of pity and love; ideas of suffering from enemies the utmost conceivable rage and cruelty, with a disposition felt to fervent love and pity in such a case, so far as it could be realized in thought; fainting with pity to the world that lies in ignorance and wickedness; sometimes a disposition felt to a life given up to mourning alone in a wilderness over a lost and miserable world; compassion towards them being often to that degree, that would allow of no support or rest, but in going to God, and pouring out the soul in prayer for them; earnest desires that the work of God; that is now in the land, may be carried on, and that with greater purity, and freedom from all bitter zeal, censoriousness, spiritual pride, hot disputes, etc.

A vehement and constant desire for the setting up of Christ's kingdom through the earth, as a kingdom of holiness, purity, love, peace and happiness to mankind: the soul often entertained with unspeakable delight, and bodily strength overborne at the thoughts of heaven as a world of love, where love shall be the saints' eternal food, and they shall dwell in the light of love, and swim in an ocean of love, and where the very air and breath will be nothing but love; love to the people of God, or God's true saints, as such that have the image of Christ, and as those that will in a very little time shine in his perfect image, that has been attended with that endearment and oneness of heart, and that sweetness and ravishment of soul, that has been altogether inexpressible; the strength very often taken away with longings that others might love God more, and serve God better, and have more of his comfortable presence, than the person that was the subject of these longings, desiring to follow the whole world to heaven, or that everyone should go before, and be higher in grace and happiness, not by this person's diminution, but by others' increase: a delight in conversing of things of religion, and in seeing Christians together, talking of the most spiritual and heavenly things in religion, in a lively and feeling manner, and very frequently overcome with the pleasure of such conversation: a great sense often expressed, of the importance of the duty of charity to the poor, and how much the generality of Christians come short in the practice of it: a great sense of the need God's ministers have of much of the Spirit of God, at this day especially; and most earnest longings and wrestlings with God for them, so as to take away the bodily strength: the greatest, fullest, longest continued, and most constant assurance of the favor of God, and of a title to future glory, that ever I saw any appearance of in any person, enjoying, especially of late (to use the person's own expression) the riches of full assurance: formerly longing to die with something of impatience, but lately, since that resignation forementioned about three years ago, an uninterrupted entire resignation to God with respect to life or death, sickness or health, ease or pain, which has remained unchanged and unshaken, when actually under extreme and violent pains, and in times of threatenings of immediate death; but though there be this patience and submission, yet the thoughts of death and the day of judgment are always exceeding sweet to the soul. This resignation is also attended with a constant resignation of the lives of dearest earthly friends; and sometimes when some of their lives have been imminently threatened, often expressing the sweetness of the liberty of having wholly left the world, and renounced all for God, and having nothing but God, in whom is an infinite fulness.

These things have been attended with a constant sweet peace and calm and serenity of soul, without any cloud to interrupt it; a continual rejoicing in all the works of God's hands, the works of nature, and God's daily works of providence, all appearing with a sweet smile upon them; a wonderful access to God by prayer, as it were seeing him, and sensibly immediately conversing with him, as much oftentimes (to use the person's own expressions) as if Christ were here on earth, sitting on a visible throne, to be approached to and conversed with; frequent, plain, sensible and immediate answers of prayer; all tears wiped away; all former troubles and sorrows of life forgotten, and all sorrow and sighing fled away, excepting grief for past sins and for remaining corruption, and that Christ is loved no more, and that God is no more honored in the world, and a compassionate grief towards fellow creatures; a daily sensible doing and suffering everything for God for a long time past, eating for God, and working for God, and sleeping for God, and bearing pain and trouble for God, and doing all as the service of love, and so doing it with a continual, uninterrupted cheerfulness, peace and joy. "Oh how good," said the person once, "is it to work for God in the daytime, and at night to lie down under his smiles!" High experiences and religious affections in this person have not been attended with any disposition at all to neglect the necessary business of a secular calling, to spend the time in reading and prayer, and other exercises of devotion; but worldly business has been attended with great alacrity, as part of the service of God: the person declaring that it being done thus, 'tis found to be as good as prayer. These things have been accompanied with an exceeding concern and zeal for moral duties, and that all professors may with them adorn the doctrine of God their Saviour; and an uncommon care to perform relative and social duties, and a noted eminence in them; a great inoffensiveness of life and conversation in the sight of others; a great meekness, gentleness and benevolence of spirit and behavior; and a great alteration in those things that formerly used to be the person's failings; seeming to be much overcome and swallowed up by the late great increase of grace, to the observation of those that are most conversant and most intimately acquainted: in times of the brightest light and highest flights of love and joy, finding no disposition to any opinion of being now perfectly free from sin (agreeable to the notion of the Wesleys and their followers, and some other high pretenders to spirituality in these days); [9] but exceedingly the contrary: at such times especially, seeing how loathsome and polluted the soul is, soul and body and every act and word appearing like rottenness and corruption in that pure and holy light of God's glory: not slighting instruction or means of grace any more for having had great discoveries; on the contrary, never more sensible of the need of instruction than now. And one thing more may be added, viz. that these things have been attended with a particular dislike of placing religion much in dress, and spending much zeal about those things that in themselves are matters of indifference, or an affecting to shew humility and devotion by a mean habit, or a demure and melancholy countenance, or anything singular and superstitious.

Now if such things are enthusiasm, and the fruits of a distempered brain, let my brain be evermore possessed of that happy distemper! If this be distraction, I pray God that the world of mankind may be all seized with this benign, meek, beneficent, beatifical, glorious distraction! If agitations of body were found in the French Prophets, and ten thousand prophets more, 'tis little to their purpose, who bring it as an objection against such a work as this, unless their purpose be to disprove the whole of the Christian religion. The great affections and high transports that others have lately been under, are in general of the same kind with those in the instance that has been given, though not to so high a degree, and many of them, not so pure and unmixed, and so well regulated. I have had

9. [JE unjustly implies that John Wesley (1703–91) is to be linked with the antinomian perfectionists who were beginning to appear on the fringes of the evangelical revival. Wesley's doctrine of Christian (not sinless) perfection rested on the presumed possibility of purity of intention, or singleness of devotion—quite similar, in fact, to the virtuous condition of JE's extended paradigm here. The difference between them can be seen more sharply in their divergent views of sin: JE followed Calvin in regarding sin as corruption, never entirely purged even from the regenerate, whereas Wesley operated with an atomistic view of sins which enabled him to define "Christian perfection" as freedom from willful transgression of known law. Both emphatically rejected antinomianism and warned of the ever-present danger of self-deception before God.]

opportunity to observe many instances here and elsewhere; and though there are some instances of great affections in which there has been a great mixture of nature with grace, and in some a sad degenerating of religious affections; yet there is that uniformity observable, that 'tis easy to be seen that in general 'tis the same spirit from whence the work in all parts of the land has originated. And what notions have they of religion, that reject what has been described as not true religion? What shall we find to answer those expressions in Scripture, "The peace of God that passes all understanding" [Phil. 4:7]; "rejoicing with joy unspeakable and full of glory," in believing in and loving an unseen Saviour [I Pet. 1:8]; "all joy and peace in believing" [Rom. 15:13]; God's "shining into our hearts, to give the light of the knowledge of the glory of God, in the face of Jesus Christ" [II Cor. 4:6]; "with open face, beholding as in a glass, the glory of the Lord, and being changed into the same image, from glory to glory, even as by the Spirit of the Lord" [II Cor. 3:18]; having the love of God "shed abroad in our hearts, by the Holy Ghost given to us" [Rom. 5:5]; having "the Spirit of God, and of glory rest upon us" [I Pet. 4:14]; a being called "out of darkness into marvelous light" [I Pet. 2:9]; and having "the Day Star arise in our hearts" [II Pet. 1:19].—I say, if those things that have been mentioned don't answer these expressions, what else can we find out that does answer them? Those that don't think such things as these to be the fruits of the true Spirit, would do well to consider what kind of spirit they are waiting and praying for, and what sort of fruits they expect he should produce when he comes. I suppose it will generally be allowed that there is such a thing as a glorious outpouring of the Spirit of God to be expected, to introduce very joyful and glorious times upon religious accounts; times wherein holy love and joy will be raised to a great height in true Christians: but if those things that have been mentioned be rejected, what is left that we can find wherewith to patch up a notion, or form an idea, of the high, blessed, joyful religion of these times? What is [it] that any have a notion of, that is very sweet, excellent and joyful, of a religious nature, that is entirely of a different nature from these things?

Those that are waiting for the fruits in order to determine whether this be the work of God or no, would do well to consider two things: 1. What they are waiting for: whether it ben't this; to have this wonderful religious influence that is on the minds of people over and past, and then to see how they will behave themselves? That is, to have grace subside, and the actings of it in a great measure to cease, and to have persons grow cold and dead, and then to see whether after that, they will behave themselves with that exactness and brightness of conversation that is to be expected of lively Christians, or those that are in the vigorous exercises of grace. There are many that will not be satisfied with any exactness or laboriousness in religion now, while persons have their minds much moved, and their affections are high; for they lay it to their flash of affection and heat of zeal, as they call it; they are waiting to see whether they will carry themselves as well when these affections are over. That is, they are waiting to have persons sicken and lose their strength, that they may see whether they will then behave themselves like healthy strong men. I would desire that they would also consider whether they ben't waiting for more than is reasonably to be expected, supposing this to be really a great work of God, and much more than has been found in former great outpourings of the Spirit of God, that have been universally acknowledged in the Christian church. Don't they expect fewer instances of apostasy, and evidences of hypocrisy in professors, and those that for the present seem to be under the influences of the Spirit, than were after that great outpouring of the Spirit in the apostles' days, or that which was in the time of the Reformation? And don't they stand prepared to make a mighty argument of it against this work, if there should be half so many? And 2. They would do well to consider how long they will wait to see the good fruit of this work, before they will determine in favor of it. Is not their waiting unlimited? The visible fruit that is to be expected of a pouring out of the Spirit of God on a country, is a visible reformation in that country. What reformation has lately been brought to pass in New England by this work, has been before observed: and has it not continued long enough already, to give reasonable satisfaction? If God can't work on the hearts of a people after such a manner, as to shew his hand so plainly, as reasonably to expect it should be acknowledged in a year and [a] half, or two years' time; yet surely it is unreasonable that our expectations and demands should be unlimited, and our waiting without any bounds.

As there is the clearest evidence, from those things that have been observed, that this is the work of God, so it is evident that it is a very great and wonderful, and exceeding glorious work of God.

This is certain that it is a great and wonderful event, a strange revolution, an unexpected, surprising overturning of things, suddenly brought to pass; such as never has been seen in New England, and scarce ever has been heard of in any land. Who that saw the state of things in New England a few years ago, the state that it was settled in, and the way that we had been so long going on in, would have thought that in so little a time there would be such a change? This is undoubtedly either a very great work of God, or a great work of the Devil, as to the main substance of it. For though undoubtedly, God and the Devil may work together at the same time, and in the same land; and when God is at work, especially if he be very remarkably at work, Satan will do his utmost endeavor to intrude, and by intermingling his work, to darken and hinder God's work; yet God and the Devil don't work together in producing the same event, and in effecting the same change in the hearts and lives of men: but 'tis apparent that there are some things wherein the main substance of this work consists, a certain effect that is produced, and alteration that is made in the apprehensions, affections, dispositions and behavior of men, in which there is a likeness and agreement everywhere. Now this I say, is either a wonderful work of God, or a mighty work of the Devil; and so is either a most happy event, greatly to be admired and rejoiced in, or a most awful calamity. Therefore if what has been said before, be sufficient to determine it to be as to the main, the work of God, then it must be acknowledged to be a very wonderful and glorious work of God.

Such a work is in its nature and kind, the most glorious of any work of God whatsoever; and is always so spoken of in Scripture. It is the work of redemption (the great end of all other works of God, and of which the work of creation was but a shadow) in the event, success and end of it: it is the work of new creation, that is infinitely more glorious than the old. I am bold to say, that the work of God in the conversion of one soul, considered together with the source, foundation and purchase of it, and also the benefit, end and eternal issue of it, is a more glorious work of God than the creation of the whole material universe: it is the most glorious of God's works, as it above all others manifests the glory of God. It is spoken of in Scripture as that which shews the exceeding greatness of God's power, and the glory and riches of divine grace, and wherein Christ has the most glorious triumph over his enemies, and wherein God is mightily exalted: and it is a work above all others glorious, as it concerns the happiness of mankind; more happiness, and a greater benefit to man, is the fruit of each single drop of such a shower, than all the temporal good of the most happy revolution in a land or nation amounts to, or all that a people could gain by the conquest of the world.

And as this work is very glorious in its nature, so it is in its degree and circumstances. It will appear very glorious if we consider the unworthiness of the people that are the subjects of it; what obligations God has laid us under by the special privileges we have enjoyed for our souls' good, and the great things God did for us at our first settlement in the land; and how he has followed us with his goodness to this day, and how we have abused his goodness; how long we have been revolting more and more (as all confess), and how very corrupt we were become at last; in how great a degree we had cast off God, and forsaken the fountain of living waters: how obstinate we have been under all manner of means that God has used with us to reclaim us; how often we have mocked God with hypocritical pretenses of humiliation, as in our annual days of public fasting, and other things, while instead of reforming, we only grew worse and worse; how dead a time it was everywhere before this work began. If we consider these things, we shall be most stupidly ungrateful, if we don't acknowledge God's visiting of us as he has done, as an instance of the glorious triumph of free and sovereign grace.

The work is very glorious if we consider the extent of it; being in this respect vastly beyond any former outpouring of the Spirit that ever was known in New England. There has formerly sometimes been a remarkable awakening and success of the means of grace, in some particular congregation; and this used to be much taken notice of, and acknowledged to be glorious, though the towns and congregations round about continued dead: but now God has brought to pass a new thing; he has wrought a great work of this nature, that has extended from one end of the land to the other, besides what has been wrought in other British colonies in America.

The work is very glorious in the great numbers that have to appearance, been turned from sin to God, and so delivered from a wretched captivity to sin and Satan, saved from everlasting burnings, and made heirs of eternal glory. How high an honor, and great reward of their labors, have some eminent persons of note in the church of God, signified that they should esteem it, if they should be made the instruments of the conversion and eternal salvation of but one soul? And no greater event than that is thought worthy of great notice in heaven, among the hosts of glorious angels, who rejoice and sing on such an occasion: and when there are many thousands of souls thus converted and saved, shall it be esteemed worth but little notice, and be mentioned with coldness and indifference here on earth, by those among whom such a work is wrought?

The work has been very glorious and wonderful in many circumstances and events of it, that have been extraordinary, wherein God has in an uncommon manner made his hand visible, and his power conspicuous; as in the extraordinary degrees of awakening, the suddenness of conversions in innumerable instances, in whom though the work was quick, yet the thing wrought is manifestly durable. How common a thing has it been for great part of a congregation to be at once moved, by a mighty invisible power; and for six, eight or ten souls to be converted to God (to all appearance) in an exercise, in whom the visible change still continues? How great an alteration has been made in some towns; yea, some populous towns, the change still abiding? And how many very vicious persons have been wrought upon, so as to become visibly new creatures? God has also made his hand very visible, and his work glorious, in the multitudes of little children that have been wrought upon: I suppose there have been some hundreds of instances of this nature of late, any one of which formerly would have been looked upon so remarkable as to be worthy to be recorded and published through the land. The work is very glorious in its influences and effects on many that have been very ignorant and barbarous, as I before observed of the Indians and Negroes.

The work is also exceeding glorious in the high attainments of Christians, in the extraordinary degrees of light, love and spiritual joy, that God has bestowed upon great multitudes. In this respect also, the land in all parts has abounded with such instances, any one of which, if they happened formerly, would have been thought worthy to be taken notice of by God's people throughout the British dominions. The New Jerusalem in this respect has begun to come down from heaven,[1] and perhaps never were more of the prelibations of heaven's glory given upon earth.

1. [Cf. Rev. 21:2. On JE's view of the awakening as prelude to the millennium, see above, pp. 71–72.]

There being a great many errors and sinful irregularities mixed with this work of God, arising from our weakness, darkness and corruption, don't hinder this work of God's power and grace from being very glorious. Our follies and sins that we mix, do in some respects manifest the glory of it: the glory of divine power and grace is set off with the greater luster by what appears at the same time of the weakness of the earthen vessel. 'Tis God's pleasure that there should be something remarkably to manifest the weakness and unworthiness of the subject, at the same time that he displays the excellency of his power and riches of his grace. And I doubt not but some of those things that make some of us here on earth to be out of humor, and to look on this work with a sour displeased countenance, do heighten the songs of the angels, when they praise God and the Lamb for what they see of the glory of God's all-sufficiency, and the efficacy of Christ's redemption. And how unreasonable is it that we should be backward to acknowledge the glory of what God has done, because withal, the Devil, and we in hearkening to him, have done a great deal of mischief?

PART II

[Examples and Warnings from Scripture]

THERE are many things in the Word of God that shew that when God remarkably appears in any great work for his church and against his enemies, it is a most dangerous thing, and highly provoking to God, to be slow and backward to acknowledge and honor God in the work, and to lie still and not to put to an helping hand. Christ's people are in Scripture represented as his army; he is the Lord of hosts, or armies: he is the Captain of the host of the Lord, as he called himself when he appeared to Joshua with a sword drawn in his hand, Josh. 5:13–15. He is the Captain of his people's salvation [Heb. 2:10]; and therefore it may well be highly resented if they don't resort to him when he orders his banner to be displayed; or if they refuse to follow him when he blows the trumpet, and gloriously appears going forth against his enemies. God expects that every living soul should have his attention roused on such an occasion, and should most cheerfully yield to the call, and heedfully and diligently obey it; Isa. 18:3, "All ye inhabitants of the world, and dwellers on the earth, see ye when he lifteth up an ensign on the mountains; and when he bloweth the trumpet, hear ye." Especially should all Israel be gathered after their Captain, as we read they were after Ehud, when he blew the trumpet in Mount Ephraim, when he had slain Eglon, king of Moab, Judg. 3:27–28. How severe is the martial law in such a case, when any of an army refuses to obey the sound of the trumpet, and follow his general to the battle? God at such a time appears in peculiar manifestations of his glory; and therefore not to be affected and animated, and to lie still, and refuse to follow God, will be resented as an high contempt of him. If a subject should stand by, and be a spectator of the solemnity of his prince's coronation, and should appear silent and sullen, when all the multitude were testifying their loyalty and joy with loud acclamations; how greatly would he expose himself to be treated as a rebel, and quickly to perish by the authority of the prince that he refuses to honor?

At a time when God manifests himself in such a great work for his church, there is no such thing as being neuters; there is a necessity of being either for or against the king that then gloriously appears: as when a king is crowned, and there are public manifestations of joy on that occasion, there is no such thing as standing by as an indifferent spectator; all must appear as loyal subjects, and express their joy on that occasion, or be accounted enemies. So it always is when God, in any great dispensation of his providence, does remarkably set his king on his holy hill of Zion, and Christ in an extraordinary manner comes down from heaven to the earth, and appears in his visible church in a great work of salvation for his people. So it was when Christ came down from heaven in his Incarnation, and appeared on earth in his human presence; there was no such thing as being neuters, neither on his side nor against him: those that sat still and said nothing, and did not declare for him, and come and join with him, after he, by his word and works, had given sufficient evidence who he was, were justly looked upon as his enemies; as Christ says, Matt. 12:30, "He that is not with me is against me; and he that gathereth not with me, scattereth abroad." So it is in a time when Christ is remarkably spiritually present, as well as when he is bodily present; and when he comes to carry on the work of redemption in the application of it, as well as in the revelation and purchase. If a king should come into one of his provinces, that had been oppressed by its foes, where some of his subjects had fallen off to the enemy, and joined with them against their lawful sovereign and his loyal subjects; I say, if the lawful sovereign himself should come into the province, and should ride forth there against his enemies, and should call upon all that were on his side to come and gather themselves to him; there would be no such thing, in such a case, as standing neuter: they that lay still and stayed at a distance would undoubtedly be looked upon and treated as rebels. So in the day of battle, when two armies join, there is no such thing for any present as being of neither party; all must be on one side or the other; and they that ben't found with the conqueror in such a case, must expect to have his weapons turned against them, and to fall with the rest of his enemies.

When God manifests himself with such glorious power in a work of this nature, he appears especially determined to put honor upon his Son, and to fulfill his oath that he has sworn to him, that he would make every knee to bow, and every tongue to confess to him [Phil. 2:10–11]. God hath had it much on his heart, from all eternity to glorify his dear and only begotten Son; and there are some special seasons that he appoints to that end, wherein he comes forth with omnipotent power to fulfill his promise and oath to him. And these times are times of remarkable pouring out of his Spirit, to advance his kingdom; such a day is a day of his power, wherein his people shall be made willing, and he shall rule in the midst of his enemies; these especially are the times wherein God declares his firm decree that his Son shall reign on his holy hill of Zion: and therefore those that at such a time don't kiss the Son, as he then manifests himself, and appears in the glory of his majesty and grace, expose themselves to perish from the way, and to be dashed in pieces with a rod of iron [Ps. 2:6, 9, 12].

As such a time is a time wherein God eminently sets his king on his holy hill of Zion, so it is a time wherein he remarkably fulfills that in Isa. 28:16, "Therefore thus saith the Lord God, behold, I lay in Zion for a foundation, a stone, a tried stone, a precious cornerstone, a sure foundation": which the two apostles Peter and Paul (I Pet. 2:6–8 and Rom. 9:33) join with that prophecy, Isa. 8:14–15, "And he shall be for a sanctuary; but for a stone of stumbling, and for a rock of offense to both the houses of Israel, for a gin and for a snare to the inhabitants of Jerusalem: and many among them shall stumble and fall, and be broken, and be snared, and taken": as signifying that both are fulfilled together. Yea, both are joined together by the prophet Isaiah himself; as you may see in the context of that forementioned, Isa. 28:16. In vs. 13 preceding it is said, "But the word of the Lord was unto them precept upon precept, precept upon precept; line upon line, line upon line; here a little and there a little, that they might go, and fall backward, and be broken, and snared and taken." And accordingly it always is so, that when Christ is in a peculiar and eminent manner manifested and magnified, by a glorious work of God in his church, as a foundation and a sanctuary for some, he is remarkably a stone of stumbling and a rock of offense, a gin and a snare to others. They that continue long to stumble, and be offended and ensnared in their minds, at such a great and glorious work of Christ, in God's account, stumble at Christ, and are offended in him; for the work is that by which he makes Christ manifest, and shows his glory, and by which he makes the stone that the builders refused, to become the head of the corner [cf. Ps. 118:22, quoted in Matt. 21:42 (and parallels) and I Pet. 2:7.]. This shows how dangerous it is to continue always stumbling at such a work, forever doubting of it, and forbearing fully to acknowledge it and give God the glory of it: such persons are in danger to go, and fall backward, and be broken, and snared and taken, and to have Christ a stone of stumbling to them, that shall be an occasion of their ruin; while he is to others a sanctuary, and a sure foundation.

The prophet Isaiah, Isa. 29:14, speaks of God's proceeding to do a marvelous work and a wonder, which should stumble and confound the wisdom of the wise and prudent; which the Apostle in Acts 13:41 applies to the glorious work of salvation wrought in those days by the redemption of Christ, and that glorious outpouring of the Spirit to apply it that followed; the prophet in the context of that place in Isa. 29, speaking of the same thing, and of the prophets and rulers and seers, those wise and prudent whose eyes God had closed, says to them, vs. 9, "Stay yourselves and wonder." In the original it is, "Be ye slow and wonder." [1] I leave it to others to consider whether it ben't natural to interpret it thus: "wonder at this marvelous work; let it be a strange thing, a great mystery that you know not what to make of, and that you are very slow and backward to acknowledge, long delaying to come to a determination concerning it." And what persons are in danger of that wonder, and are thus slow to acknowledge God in such a work, we learn by that of the Apostle in that forementioned Acts 13:41, "Behold, ye despisers, and wonder and perish; for I work a work in your days, a work which you shall in no wise believe, though a man declare it unto you."

The church of Christ is called upon greatly to rejoice, when at any time Christ remarkably appears, coming to his church to carry on the work of salvation, to enlarge his own kingdom, and to deliver poor

1. [The first verb is מָהַהּ "to linger, tarry";· used in this passage in the Hithpalpel (וְהִתְיַהְמָהוּ), it has the force of an intensive reflexive: "slow yourselves down." JE's translation is strikingly accurate, though his application in the sentence following is somewhat strained.]

souls out of the pit wherein there is no water, in Zech. 9:9–11, "Rejoice greatly, O daughter of Zion; shout, O daughter of Jerusalem; behold thy king cometh unto thee; he is just and having salvation. . . . His dominion shall be from sea to sea. . . . As for thee also, by the blood of thy covenant, I have sent forth thy prisoners out of the pit wherein is no water." Christ was pleased to give a notable typical or symbolical representation of such a great event as is spoken of in that prophecy, in his solemn entry into the literal Jerusalem, which was a type of the church, or daughter of Zion, there spoken of; probably intending it as a figure and prelude of that great actual fulfillment of this prophecy, that was to be after his ascension, by the pouring out of the Spirit in the days of the apostles, and that more full accomplishment that should be in the latter ages of the Christian church. We have an account, that when Christ made this his solemn entry into Jerusalem, and the whole multitude of the disciples were rejoicing and praising God with loud voices, for all the mighty works that they had seen, the Pharisees from among the multitude said to Christ, "Master, rebuke thy disciples"; but we are told, Luke 19:39–40, [that] Christ answered and said unto them, "I tell you, that if these should hold their peace, the stones would immediately cry out": signifying that if Christ's professing disciples should be unaffected on such an occasion, and should not appear openly to acknowledge and rejoice in the glory of God therein appearing, it would manifest such fearful hardness of heart, so exceeding that of the stones, that the very stones would condemn them. Should not this make those consider, who have held their peace so long, since Christ has come to our Zion having salvation, and so wonderfully manifested his glory in this mighty work of his Spirit, and so many of his disciples have been rejoicing and praising God with loud voices?

It must be acknowledged that so great and wonderful a work of God's Spirit, is a work wherein God's hand is remarkably lifted up, and wherein he displays his majesty, and shows great favor and mercy to sinners, in the glorious opportunity he gives them; and by which he makes our land to become much more a land of uprightness: therefore that place, Isa. 26:10–11, shows the great danger of not seeing God's hand, and acknowledging his glory and majesty in such a work: "Let favor be shewed to the wicked, yet will he not learn righteousness; in the land of uprightness he will deal unjustly, and will not behold the majesty of the Lord. Lord, when thy hand is lifted up, they will not see; but they shall see, and be ashamed for their envy at the people; yea, the fire of thine enemies shall devour them."

[*The Millennium Probably To Dawn in America*]

'Tis not unlikely that this work of God's Spirit, that is so extraordinary and wonderful, is the dawning, or at least a prelude, of that glorious work of God, so often foretold in Scripture, which in the progress and issue of it, shall renew the world of mankind. If we consider how long since the things foretold, as what should precede this great event, have been accomplished; and how long this event has been expected by the church of God, and thought to be nigh by the most eminent men of God in the church; and withal consider what the state of things now is, and has for a considerable time been, in the church of God and world of mankind, we can't reasonably think otherwise, than that the beginning of this great work of God must be near. And there are many things that make it probable that this work will begin in America. 'Tis signified that it shall begin in some very remote part of the world, that the rest of the world have no communication with but by navigation, in Isa. 60:9, "Surely the isles shall wait for me, and the ships of Tarshish first, to bring my sons from far." It is exceeding manifest that this chapter is a prophecy of the prosperity of the church, in its most glorious state on earth in the latter days; and I can't think that anything else can be here intended but America by "the isles that are far off," from whence the firstborn sons of that glorious day shall be brought. Indeed, by "the isles," in prophecies of Gospel times, is very often meant Europe: it is so in prophecies of that great spreading of the Gospel that should be soon after Christ's time, because it was far separated from that part of the world where the church of God had till then been, by the sea. But this prophecy can't have respect to the conversion of Europe, in the time of that great work of God, in the primitive ages of the Christian church; for it was not fulfilled then. The isles and ships of Tarshish, thus understood, did not wait for God first; that glorious work did not begin in Europe, but in Jerusalem, and had for a considerable time, been very wonderfully carried on in Asia, before it reached Europe. And as it is not that work of God that is chiefly intended in this chapter, but that more glorious work that should be in the latter ages of the Christian church, therefore some other part of the world is here intended by the isles, that should be as Europe then was, far separated from that part of the world where the church had before been, by the sea, and with which it can have no communication but by the ships of Tarshish. And what is chiefly intended is not the British Isles, nor any isles near the other continent; for they are spoken of as at a great distance from that part of the world where the church had till then been. This prophecy therefore seems plainly to point out America, as the first fruits of that glorious day.

God has made as it were two worlds here below, the old and the new (according to the names they are now called by), two great habitable continents, far separated one from the other. The latter is but newly discovered; it was formerly wholly unknown, from age to age, and is as it were now but newly created: it has been till of late wholly the possession of Satan, the church of God having never been in it, as it has been in the other continent, from the beginning of the world. This new world is probably now discovered, that the new and most glorious state of God's church on earth might commence there; that God might in it begin a new world in a spiritual respect, when he creates the new heavens and new earth.

God has already put that honor upon the other continent, that Christ was born there literally, and there made the purchase of redemption: so, as providence observes a kind of equal distribution of things, 'tis not unlikely that the great spiritual birth of Christ, and the most glorious application of redemption is to begin in this: as the elder sister [Leah] brought forth Judah, of whom came Christ, and so she was the mother of Christ; but the younger sister [Rachel], after long barrenness, brought forth Joseph and Benjamin, the beloved children [Gen. 29, 30, 35]. Joseph, that had the most glorious apparel, the coat of many colors, who was separated from his brethren, and was exalted to such glory out of a dark dungeon, and fed and saved the world when [it was] ready to perish with famine, and was as a fruitful bough by a well, whose branches ran over the wall, and was blessed with all manner of blessings and precious things, of heaven and earth, through the good will of him that dwelt in the bush; and was, as by the horns of a unicorn, to push the people together, to the ends of the earth, i.e. conquer the world. See Gen. 49:22, etc. and Deut. 33:13, etc. [*sic*, et seq.]. And Benjamin, whose mess was five times so great as that of any of his brethren [Gen. 43:34], and to whom Joseph, that type of Christ, gave wealth and raiment far beyond all the rest; Gen. 45:22.

The other continent hath slain Christ, and has from age to age shed the blood of the saints and martyrs of Jesus, and has often been as it were deluged with the church's blood: God has therefore probably reserved the honor of building the glorious temple to the daughter, that has not shed so much blood, when those times of the peace and prosperity and glory of the church shall commence, that were typified by the reign of Solomon [I Chron. 22:7–10].

The Gentiles first received the true religion from the Jews; God's church of ancient times had been among them, and Christ was of them: but that there might be a kind of equality in the dispensations of providence, God has so ordered it, that when the Jews come to be admitted to the benefits of the evangelical dispensation, and to receive their highest privileges of all, they should receive the Gospel from the Gentiles. Though Christ was of them, yet they have been guilty of crucifying him; it is therefore the will of God that that people should not have the honor of communicating the blessings of the kingdom of God in its most glorious state to the Gentiles, but on the contrary they shall receive the Gospel in the beginning of that glorious day, from the Gentiles [Rom. 11:11–32]. In some analogy to this, I apprehend God's dealings will be with the two continents. America has received the true religion of the old continent; the church of ancient times has been there, and Christ is from thence: but that there may be an equality, and inasmuch as that continent has crucified Christ, they shall not have the honor of communicating religion in its most glorious state to us, but we to them.

The old continent has been the source and original of mankind, in several respects. The first parents of mankind dwelt there; and there dwelt Noah and his sons; and there the second Adam was born, and was crucified and rose again: and 'tis probable that, in some measure to balance these things, the most glorious renovation of the world shall originate from the new continent, and the church of God in that respect be from hence. And so 'tis probable that that will come to pass in spirituals, that has in temporals, with respect to America; that whereas, till of late, the world was supplied with its silver and gold and earthly treasures from the old continent, now it's supplied chiefly from the new, so the course of things in spiritual respects will be in like manner turned.

And 'tis worthy to be noted that America was discovered about the time of the Reformation, or but little before: which Reformation was the first thing that God did towards the glorious renovation of the world, after it had sunk into the depths of darkness and ruin under the great antichristian apostasy. So that as soon as this new world is (as it were) created, and stands forth in view, God presently goes about doing some great thing to make way for the introduction of the church's latter-day glory, that is to have its first seat in, and is to take its rise from that new world.

It is agreeable to God's manner of working, when he accomplishes any glorious work in the world, to introduce a new and more excellent state of his church, to begin his work where his church had not been till then, and where was no foundation already laid, that the power of God might be the more conspicuous; that the work might appear to be entirely God's, and be more manifestly a creation out of nothing; agreeable to Hos. 1:10, "And it shall come to pass that in the place where it was said unto them, Ye are not my people, there it shall be said unto them, Ye are the sons of the living God." When God is about to turn the earth into a paradise, he don't begin his work where there is some good growth already, but in a wilderness, where nothing grows, and nothing is to be seen but dry sand and barren rocks; that the light may shine out of darkness, and the world be replenished from emptiness, and the earth watered by springs from a droughty desert; agreeable to many prophecies of Scripture, as Isa. 32:15, "Until the Spirit be poured [upon us] from on high, and the wilderness become a fruitful field." And chap. 41:18–19, "I will open rivers in high places, and fountains in the midst of the valleys; I will make the wilderness a pool of water, and the dry land springs of water: I will plant in the wilderness the cedar, the shittah tree, and the myrtle, and the oil tree: I will set in the desert the fir tree, and the pine, and the box tree together"; and chap. 43:20, "I will give waters in the wilderness, and rivers in the desert, to give drink to my people, my chosen." And many other parallel Scriptures might be mentioned.

I observed before, that when God is about to do some great work for his church, his manner is to begin at the lower end; so when he is about to renew the whole habitable earth, 'tis probable that he will begin in this utmost, meanest, youngest and weakest part of it, where the church of God has been planted last of all; and so the first shall be last, and the last first; and that will be fulfilled in an eminent manner in Isa. 24:16, "From the uttermost part of the earth have we heard songs, even glory to the righteous."

There are several things that seem to me to argue that when the

"Sun of righteousness," the Sun of the new heavens and new earth, comes to rise, and comes forth as the Bridegroom of his church, "rejoicing as a strong man to run his race," having his going forth "from the end of heaven, and his circuit to the end of it, that nothing may be hid from the light and heat of it." [2] That the sun shall rise in the West [is] contrary to the course of this world, or the course of things in the old heavens and earth. The course of God's providence shall in that day be so wonderfully altered in many respects, that God will as it were change the course of nature, in answer to the prayers of his church; as God changed the course of nature, and caused the sun to go from the West to the East when Hezekiah was healed, and God promised to do such great things for his church, to deliver it out of the hand of the king of Assyria, by that mighty slaughter by the angel; which is often used by the prophet Isaiah as a type of the glorious deliverance of the church from her enemies in the latter days: the resurrection of Hezekiah, the king and captain of the church (as he is called, II Kings 20:5), as it were from the dead, is given as an earnest of the church's resurrection and salvation, Isa. 38:6, and is a type of the resurrection of Christ. At the same time there is a resurrection of the sun, or coming back and rising again from the West, whither it had gone down; which is also a type of the Sun of righteousness. The sun was brought back ten degrees; which probably brought it to the meridian. The Sun of righteousness has long been going down from East to West; and probably when the time comes of the church's deliverance from her enemies, so often typified by the Assyrians, the light will rise in the West, till it shines through the world, like the sun in its meridian brightness. [3]

The same seems also to be represented by the course of the waters of the sanctuary, Ezek. 47, which was from West to East; which waters undoubtedly represent the Holy Spirit, in the progress of his saving influences, in the latter ages of the world: for 'tis manifest that the

2. 'Tis evident that the Holy Spirit in those expressions in Ps. 19:4–6 verses has respect to something else besides the natural sun; and that an eye is had to the Sun of righteousness [Mal. 4:2], that by his light converts the soul, makes wise the simple, enlightens the eyes, and rejoices the heart; and by his preached Gospel enlightens and warms the world of mankind: by the Psalmist's own application in vs. 7 [and 8], and the Apostle's application of vs. 4 in Rom. 10:18. [Cf. also Rev. 21:23.]

3. [A strained interpretation of II Kings 20:1–11 and Isa. 38:1–8. The "mighty slaughter" of the Assyrians by the angel of the Lord (II Kings 19:35) actually preceded the illness and healing of Hezekiah.]

whole of those last chapters of Ezekiel are concerning the glorious state of the church that shall then be.

And if we may suppose that this glorious work of God shall begin in any part of America, I think, if we consider the circumstances of the settlement of New England, it must needs appear the most likely of all American colonies, to be the place whence this work shall principally take its rise.

And if these things are so, it gives us more abundant reasons to hope that what is now seen in America, and especially in New England, may prove the dawn of that glorious day: and the very uncommon and wonderful circumstances and events of this work, seem to me strongly to argue that God intends it as the beginning or forerunner of something vastly great.

I have thus long insisted on this point, because if these things are so, it greatly manifests how much it behooves us to encourage and promote this work, and how dangerous it will be to forbear so to do.

[*Further Warnings from Scripture*]

It is very dangerous for God's professing people to lie still, and not to come to the help of the Lord, whenever he remarkably pours out his Spirit, to carry on the work of redemption in the application of it; but above all, when he comes forth in that last and greatest outpouring of his Spirit, to introduce that happy day of God's power and salvation, so often spoken of. That is especially the appointed season of the application of the redemption of Christ: 'tis the proper time of the kingdom of heaven upon earth, the appointed time of Christ's reign: the reign of Satan as god of this world lasts till then. This is the proper time of actual redemption, or new creation, as is evident by Isa. 65:17–18 and 66:12, and Rev. 21:1. All the outpourings of the Spirit of God that are before this, are as it were by way of anticipation.

There was indeed a glorious season of the application of redemption, in the first ages of the Christian church, that began at Jerusalem, on the Day of Pentecost; but that was not the proper time of ingathering; it was only as it were the Feast of the First Fruits; the ingathering is at the end of the year, or in the last ages of the Christian church, as is represented, Rev. 14:14–16, and will probably as much exceed what was in the first ages of the Christian church, though that filled the Roman Empire, as that exceeded all that had been before, under the Old Testament, confined only to the land of Judea.

The great danger of not appearing openly to acknowledge, rejoice in, and promote that great work of God, in bringing in that glorious harvest, is represented in Zech. 14:16–19, "And it shall come to pass, that every one that is left, of all the nations which came against Jerusalem, shall even go up from year to year to worship the king, the Lord of hosts, and to keep the Feast of Tabernacles. And it shall be, that whoso will not come up, of all the families of the earth, unto Jerusalem to worship the king, the Lord of hosts, even upon them shall be no rain. And if the family of Egypt go not up, and come not, that have no rain, there shall be the plague wherewith the Lord will smite the heathen, that come not up to keep the Feast of Tabernacles. This shall be the punishment of Egypt, and the punishment of all nations that come not up to keep the Feast of Tabernacles." 'Tis evident by all the context, that the glorious day of the church of God in the latter ages of the world, is the time spoken of: the Feast of Tabernacles here seems to signify that glorious spiritual feast, which God shall then make for his church, the same that is spoken of [in] Isa. 25:6, and the great spiritual rejoicings of God's people at that time. There were three great feasts in Israel, at which all the males were appointed to go up to Jerusalem; the Feast of the Passover; and the Feast of the First Fruits, or the Feast of Pentecost; and the Feast of Ingathering, at the end of the year, or the Feast of Tabernacles. In the first of these, viz. the Feast of the Passover, was represented the purchase of redemption by Jesus Christ, the paschal lamb that was slain at the time of that feast. The other two that followed it were to represent the two great seasons of the application of the purchased redemption: in the former of them, viz. the Feast of the First Fruits, which was called the Feast of Pentecost, was represented that time of the outpouring of the Spirit, that was in the first ages of the Christian church, for the bringing in the first fruits of Christ's redemption, which began at Jerusalem on the Day of Pentecost: the other, which was the Feast of Ingathering, at the end of the year, which the children of Israel were appointed to keep on occasion of their gathering in their corn and their wine, and all the fruit of their land, and was called the Feast of Tabernacles, represented the other more joyful and glorious season of the application of Christ's redemption, which is to be in the latter days; the great day of ingathering of the elect, the proper and appointed time of gathering in God's fruits, when the angel of the covenant shall thrust in his sickle, and gather the harvest of the earth; and the clusters of the vine of the earth shall also be gathered [cf. Rev. 14:14–18]. This was upon many accounts the greatest feast of the three: there were much greater tokens of rejoicing in this feast, than any other: the people then dwelt in booths of green boughs, and were commanded to take boughs of goodly trees, branches of palm trees, and the boughs of thick trees, and willows of the brook, and to rejoice before the Lord their God: which represents the flourishing, beautiful, pleasant state the church shall be in, rejoicing in God's grace and love, triumphing over all her enemies, at the time typified by this feast. The tabernacle of God was first set up among the children of Israel at the time of the Feast of Tabernacles; but in that glorious time of the Christian church, God will above all other times set up his tabernacle amongst men. Rev. 21:3, "And I heard a great voice out of heaven, saying, The tabernacle of God is with men, and he will dwell with them, and they shall be his people, and God himself shall be with them, and be their God." The world is supposed to have been created about the time of year wherein the Feast of Tabernacles was appointed; so in that glorious time, God will create a new heaven and a new earth. The temple of Solomon was dedicated at the time of the Feast of Tabernacles, when God descended in a pillar of cloud and dwelt in the temple [I Kings 8; II Chron. 7]; so at this happy time, the temple of God shall be gloriously built up in the world, and God shall in a wonderful manner come down from heaven to dwell with his church. Christ is supposed to have been born at the Feast of Tabernacles; so at the commencement of that glorious day, Christ shall be born; then above all other times shall the woman clothed with the sun, with the moon under her feet, that is in travail and pained to be delivered, bring forth her son, to rule all nations, Rev. 12, at the beginning. The Feast of Tabernacles was the last feast that Israel had in the whole year, before the face of the earth was destroyed by the winter; presently after the rejoicings of that feast were past, a tempestuous season began, Acts 27:9, "Sailing was now dangerous, because the feast was now already past." So this great feast of the Christian church will be the last feast she shall have on earth: soon after it is past, this lower world will be destroyed. At the Feast of Tabernacles, Israel left their houses to dwell in booths or green tents, which signifies the great weanedness of God's people from the world, as pilgrims and strangers on the earth [Heb. 11:13], and their great joy therein. Israel were prepared for the Feast of Tabernacles by the Feast of Trumpets and the Day of Atonement, both on the same month; so way shall be made for the joy of the church of God, in its glorious state on earth, by the extraordinary preaching of the Gospel, and deep repentance and humiliation for past sins, and the great and long continued deadness and carnality of the visible church. Christ at the great Feast of Tabernacles stood in Jerusalem and cried, saying, "If any man thirst, let him come unto me and drink: he that believeth on me, as the Scripture hath said, out of his belly shall flow rivers of living waters" [John 7:37–38]: signifying the extraordinary freedom and riches of divine grace towards sinners at that day, and the extraordinary measures of the Holy Spirit that shall be then given; agreeable to Rev. 21:6 and 22:17.

It is threatened here in this 14th chapter of Zechariah that those who at that time shall not come to keep this feast; i.e. that shall not acknowledge God's glorious works, and praise his name, and rejoice with his people, but should stand at a distance, as unbelieving and disaffected; upon them shall be no rain; and that this shall be the plague wherewith they shall all be smitten: that is, they shall have no share in that shower of divine blessing that shall then descend on the earth, that spiritual rain spoken of, Isa. 44:3, but God would give them over to hardness of heart and blindness of mind.

The curse is yet in a more awful manner denounced against such as shall appear as opposers at that time, vs. 12, "And this shall be the plague, wherewith the Lord shall smite all the people that have fought against Jerusalem: their flesh shall consume away while they stand upon their feet, and their eyes shall consume away in their holes, and their tongue shall consume away in their mouth." Here also in all probability it is a spiritual judgment, or a plague and curse from God upon the soul, rather than upon the body, that is intended; that such persons, who at that time shall oppose God's people in his work, shall in an extraordinary manner be given over to a state of spiritual death and ruin, that they shall remarkably appear dead while alive, and shall be as walking rotten corpses, while they go about amongst men.

The great danger of not joining with God's people at that glorious day is also represented, Isa. 60:12, "For the nation and kingdom that will not serve thee shall perish; yea, those nations shall be utterly wasted."

Most of the great temporal deliverances that were wrought for Israel of old, as divines and expositors observe, were typical [i.e. types] of the great spiritual works of God for the salvation of men's souls, and the deliverance and prosperity of his church, in the days of the Gospel; and especially did they represent that greatest of all deliverances of God's church, and chief of God's works of actual salvation, that shall be in the latter days; which, as has been observed, is above all others the appointed time and proper season of actual redemption of men's souls. But it may be observed that if any appeared to oppose God's work in those great temporal deliverances; or if there were any of his professing people that on such occasions lay still, and stood at a distance, and did not arise and acknowledge God in his work and appear to promote it; it was what in a remarkable manner incensed God's anger, and brought his curse upon such persons.

So when God wrought that great work of bringing the children of Israel out of Egypt (which was a type of God's delivering his church out of the spiritual Egypt, at the time of the fall of Antichrist, as is evident by Rev. 11:8 and 15:3), how highly did God resent it, when the Amalekites appeared as opposers in that affair, and how dreadfully did he curse them for it? Exod. 17:14–16, "And the Lord said unto Moses, Write this for a memorial in a book, and rehearse it in the ears of Joshua; for I will utterly put out the remembrance of Amalek from under heaven. And Moses built an altar, and called the name of it Jehovah-Nissi; for he said, Because the Lord will have war with Amalek from generation to generation." And accordingly we find that God remembered it a long time after, I Sam. 15:3. And how highly did God resent it in the Moabites and Ammonites, that they did not lend an helping hand and encourage and promote the affair? Deut. 23:3–4, "An Ammonite or Moabite shall not enter into the congregation of the Lord; even to their tenth generation, shall they not enter into the congregation of the Lord forever; because they met you not with bread and with water in the way when ye came forth out of Egypt." And how were the children of Reuben, and the children of Gad, and the half-tribe of Manasseh threatened, if they did not go and help their brethren in their wars against the Canaanites, Num. 32:20–23, "And Moses said unto them, If ye will do this thing, if ye will go armed before the Lord to war, and will go all of you armed over Jordan before the Lord, until he hath driven out his enemies from before him, and the land be subdued before the Lord, then afterward ye shall return and be guiltless before the Lord, and before Israel; and this land shall be your possession before the Lord: but if ye will not do so, behold, ye have sinned against the Lord, and be sure your sin will find you out."

That was a glorious work of God that he wrought for Israel, when he delivered them from the Canaanites, by the hand of Deborah and Barak: almost everything about it shewed a remarkable hand of God. It was a prophetess, one immediately inspired by God, that called the people to the battle and conducted them in the whole affair. The people seem to have been miraculously animated and encouraged in the matter, when they willingly offered themselves and gathered together to the battle; they jeoparded their lives in the high places of the field, without being pressed or hired; when one would have thought they should have but little courage for such an undertaking; for what could a number of poor, weak, defenseless slaves do, without a shield or spear to be seen among forty thousand of 'em, to go against a great prince, with his mighty host and nine hundred chariots of iron? And the success did wonderfully shew the hand of God; which makes Deborah exultingly to say, Judg. 5:21, "O my soul, thou hast trodden down strength!" Christ with his heavenly host was engaged in that battle; and therefore 'tis said, vs. 20, "They fought from heaven, the stars in their courses fought against Sisera." The work of God therefore in this victory and deliverance that Christ and his host wrought for Israel, was a type of that victory and deliverance which he will accomplish for his church in that great battle, that last conflict that the church shall have with her open enemies, that shall introduce the church's latter-day glory; as appears by Rev. 16:16 (speaking of that great battle, "And he gathered them together into a place called in the Hebrew tongue, Armageddon," i.e. the mountain of Megiddo; alluding, as is supposed by expositors, to the place where the battle was fought with the host of Sisera, Judg. 5:19, "The kings came and fought, the kings of Canaan, in Taanach, by the waters of Megiddo." Which can signify nothing else, than that this battle, which Christ and his church shall have with their enemies, is the antitype of the battle that was fought there. But what a dreadful curse from Christ did some of God's professing people Israel bring upon themselves, by lying still at that time, and not putting to an helping hand? Judg. 5:23, "Curse ye Meroz, said the angel of the Lord, curse ye bitterly the inhabitants thereof, because they came not to the help of the Lord, to the help of the Lord against the mighty." The angel of the Lord was the captain of the host; he that had led Israel, and fought for them in that battle, who is very often called the angel of the Lord, in Scripture; the same that appeared to Joshua with a sword drawn in his hand, and told him that he was come as the captain of the host of the Lord; and the same glorious captain that we have an account of, as leading forth his hosts to that battle of which this was the type, Rev. 19:11, etc. It seems the inhabitants of Meroz were unbelieving concerning this great work, nor would they hearken to Deborah's pretenses, nor did it enter into them that such a poor defenseless company should ever prevail against those that were so mighty; they did not acknowledge the hand of God, and therefore stood at a distance and did nothing to promote the work: but what a bitter curse from God did they bring upon themselves by it!

'Tis very probable that one great reason why the inhabitants of Meroz were so unbelieving concerning this work, was that they argued a priori; [4] they did not like the beginning of it, it being a woman that first led the way, and had the chief conduct in the affair; nor could they believe that such despicable instruments, as a company of unarmed slaves, were ever like to effect so great a thing; and pride and unbelief wrought together in not being willing to follow Deborah to the battle.

It was another glorious work of God that he wrought for Israel, in the victory that was obtained by Gideon over the Midianites and Amalekites, and the children of the East, when they came up against Israel like grasshoppers, a multitude that could not be numbered. This also was a remarkable type of the victory of Christ and his church over his enemies, by the pouring out of the Spirit with the preached Gospel, as is evident by the manner of it, which Gideon was immediately directed to of God; which was not by human sword or bow, but only by blowing of trumpets and by lights in earthen vessels. We read that on this occasion, Gideon called the people together to help in this great affair; and that accordingly, great numbers resorted to him, and came to the help of the Lord, Judg. 7:23–24. But there were some also at that time, that were unbelieving, and would not acknowledge the hand of God in that work, though it was so great

4. [Cf. above, p. 293–96.]

and wonderful, nor would they join to promote it; and they were the inhabitants of Succoth and Penuel: Gideon desired their help when he was pursuing after Zebah and Zalmunna; but they despised his pretenses and his confidence of the Lord's being on his side, to deliver those two great princes into the hands of such a despicable company as he and his three hundred men, and would not own the work of God, nor afford Gideon any assistance: God proceeded in this work in a way that was exceeding cross to their pride. And they also refused to own the work, because they argued a priori; they could not believe that God would do such great things by such a despicable instrument; one of such a poor, mean family in Manasseh, and he the least in his father's house; and the company that was with him appeared very wretched, being but three hundred men, and they weak and faint: but we see how they suffered for their folly in not acknowledging and appearing to promote this work of God. Gideon when he returned from the victory, took them, and taught them with the briers and thorns of the wilderness, and beat down the tower of Penuel (he brought down their pride and their false confidence), and slew the men of the city, Judg., chap. 8. This, in all probability Gideon did as moved and directed by the angel of the Lord, that is Christ, that first called him, and sent him forth in this battle, and instructed and directed him, in the whole affair.

The return of the ark of God to dwell in Zion, in the midst of the land of Israel, after it had been long absent, first in the land of the Philistines, and then in Kirjath-jearim, in the utmost borders of the land, did livelily represent the return of God to a professing people, in the spiritual tokens of his presence, after long absence from them; as well as the ark's ascending up into a mountain, typified Christ's ascension into heaven. 'Tis evident by the psalms that were penned on that occasion, especially the 68th Psalm, that the exceeding rejoicings of Israel on that occasion represented the joy of the church of Christ on his returning to it, after it has been in a low and dark state, to revive his work, bringing his people back, as it were from Bashan and "from the depth of the sea," scattering their spiritual enemies, and causing that "though they had lain among the pots," yet they should be "as the wings of a dove covered with silver, and her feathers with yellow gold"; and giving the blessed tokens of his presence in his house, that his people may "see the goings of God their king in his sanctuary"; and that the gifts which David, with such royal bounty, distributed amongst the people on that occasion

(II Sam. 6:18–19 and I Chron. 16:2–3) represent spiritual blessings, that Christ liberally sends down on his church by the outpourings of his Spirit; see Ps. 68:1, 3, 13, 18–24. And we have an account how that all the people, from Sihor of Egypt even unto the entering in of Hemath, gathered together and appeared to join and assist in that great affair; and that "all Israel brought up the ark of the covenant of the Lord, with shouting and with sound of the cornet, and with trumpets, and with cymbals, making a noise with psalteries and harps," I Chron. 13:2–5 and 15:28. And not only the men, but the women of Israel, the daughters of Zion appeared as publicly joining in the praises and rejoicings that were on that occasion, II Sam. 6:19. But we read of one of David's wives, even Michal, Saul's daughter, whose heart was not engaged in the affair, and did not appear with others to rejoice and praise God on this occasion, but kept away and stood at a distance, as disaffected and disliking the managements; she despised and ridiculed the transports and extraordinary manifestations of joy that then were; and the curse that she brought upon herself by it was that of being barren to the day of her death [II Sam. 6:16, 20–23]. Let this be a warning to us: let us take heed, in this day of the bringing up of the ark of God, that while we are in visibility and profession the spouse of the spiritual David, we don't shew ourselves to be indeed the children of false-hearted and rebellious Saul, by our standing aloof, and not joining in the joy and praises of the day, and disliking and despising the joys and affections of God's people, because they are to so high a degree, and so bring the curse of perpetual barrenness upon our souls.

Let us take heed that we ben't like the son of the bondwoman, that was born after the flesh, that persecuted him that was born after the Spirit, and mocked at the feasting and rejoicings that were made for Isaac when he was weaned; lest we should be cast out of the family of Abraham, as he was (Gen. 21:8–9). That affair contained spiritual mysteries, and was typical of things that come to pass in these days of the Gospel; as is evident by the Apostle's testimony, Gal. 4:22 to the end. And particularly it seems to have been typical of two things: 1. The weaning of the church from its milk of carnal ordinances, ceremonies, shadows, and beggarly elements, upon the coming of Christ, and pouring out of the Spirit in the days of the apostles. The church of Christ in the times of the Old Testament, was in its minority, and was a babe; and the Apostle tells us that babes must be fed with milk, and not with strong meat; but when God weaned his church from these carnal ordinances, on the ceasing of the legal dispensation, a glorious Gospel feast was provided for souls, and God fed his people with spiritual dainties, and filled them with the Spirit, and gave 'em joy in the Holy Ghost. Ishmael, in mocking at the time of Isaac's feast, by the Apostle's testimony, represented the carnal Jews, the children of the literal Jerusalem, who when they beheld the rejoicings of Christians in their spiritual and evangelical privileges, were filled with envy, deriding, contradicting and blaspheming (Acts 2:13, and chap. 13:45, and 18:6), and therefore were cast out of the family of Abraham, and out of the land of Canaan, to wander through the earth. 2. This weaning of Isaac's seems also to represent the conversion of sinners, which is several times represented in Scripture by the weaning of a child; as in Ps. 131 and Isa. 28:9. Because in conversion the soul is weaned from the enjoyments of the world, which are as it were the breast of our Mother Earth; and is also weaned from the covenant of our first parents, which we as naturally hang upon, as a child on its mother's breasts: and the great feast that Abraham made on that occasion, represents the spiritual feast, the heavenly privileges, and holy joys and comforts, which God gives souls at their conversion. Now is a time when God is in a remarkable manner bestowing the blessings of such a feast. Let everyone take heed that he don't now shew himself to be the son of the bondwoman, and born after the flesh, by standing and deriding with mocking Ishmael; lest they be cast out as he was, and it be said concerning them, these sons of the bondwoman shall not be heirs with the sons of the freewoman [Gen. 21:10; Gal. 4:30]. Don't let us stumble at the things that have been, because they are so great and extraordinary; for "if we have run with the footmen, and they have wearied us, how shall we contend with horses?" [Jer. 12:5]. There is doubtless a time coming when God will accomplish things vastly greater and more extraordinary than these.

And that we may be warned not to continue doubting and unbelieving concerning this work, because of the extraordinary degree of it, and the suddenness and swiftness of the accomplishment of the great things that pertain to it; let us consider the example of the unbelieving lord in Samaria; who could not believe so extraordinary a work of God to be accomplished so suddenly as was declared to him. The prophet Elisha foretold that the great famine in Samaria should very suddenly, even in one day, be turned into an extraordinary plenty; but the work was too great, and too sudden for him to believe; says he, "If the Lord should make windows in heaven, might this thing be?" And the curse that he brought upon himself by it was that he saw it with his eyes, and did not eat thereof, but miserably perished, and was trodden down as the mire of the streets, when others were feasting and rejoicing (II Kings, chap. 7).

When God redeemed his people from their Babylonish Captivity, and they rebuilt Jerusalem, it was, as is universally owned, a remarkable type of the spiritual redemption of God's church; and particularly, was an eminent type of the great deliverance of the Christian church from spiritual Babylon, and their rebuilding the spiritual Jerusalem in the latter days; and therefore they are often spoken of under one [head] by the prophets: and this probably was the main reason that it was so ordered in providence, and particularly noted in Scripture, that the children of Israel, on that occasion, kept the greatest Feast of Tabernacles that ever had been kept in Israel since the days of Joshua, when the people were first settled in Canaan (Neh. 8:16–17), because at that time happened that restoration of Israel, that had the greatest resemblance of that great restoration of the church of God, of which the Feast of Tabernacles was the type, of any that had been since Joshua first brought the people out of the wilderness, and settled them in the good land. But we read of some that opposed the Jews in that affair, and weakened their hands, and ridiculed God's people, and the instruments that were improved in that work, and despised their hope, and made as though their confidence was little more than a shadow, and would utterly fail 'em. "What do these feeble Jews?" say they. "Will they fortify themselves? Will they sacrifice? Will they make an end in a day? Will they revive the stones out of the heaps of the rubbish which are burnt? [. . .] Even that which they build, if a fox go up, he shall even break down their stone wall" [Neh. 4:2–3]. Let not us be in any measure like them, lest it be said to us, as Nehemiah said to them, Neh. 2:20, "We his servants will arise and build; but you have no portion, nor right, nor memorial in Jerusalem." And lest we bring Nehemiah's imprecation upon us, chap. 4:5, "Cover not their iniquity, and let not their sin be blotted out from before thee; for they have provoked thee to anger before the builders."

As persons will greatly expose themselves to the curse of God by opposing, or standing at a distance, and keeping silence at such a time as this; so for persons to arise, and readily to acknowledge God, and honor him in such a work, and cheerfully and vigorously to exert themselves to promote it, will be to put themselves much in the way of the divine blessing. What a mark of honor does God put upon those in Israel, that willingly offered themselves, and came to the help of the Lord against the mighty, when the angel of the Lord led forth his armies, and they fought from heaven against Sisera? Judg. 5:2, 9, 14–15, 17–18. And what a great blessing is pronounced on Jael, the wife of Heber the Kenite, for her appearing on the Lord's side, and for what she did to promote this work, vs. 24, which was no less than the curse pronounced in the preceding verse, against Meroz, for lying still: "Blessed above women shall Jael, the wife of Heber the Kenite, be; blessed shall she be above women in the tent." And what a blessing is pronounced on those which shall have any hand in the destruction of Babylon, which was the head city of the kingdom of Satan, and of the enemies of the church of God? Ps. 137:9, "Happy shall he be, that taketh and dasheth thy little ones against the stones." What a particular and honorable notice is taken, in the records of God's Word, of those that arose and appeared as David's helpers, to introduce him into the kingdom of Israel, in the 12th chap. of I Chron. The host of those that thus came to the help of the Lord, in that work of his, and glorious revolution in Israel, by which the kingdom of that great type of the Messiah was set up in Israel, is compared to the host of God, vs. 22, "At that time, day by day, there came to David to help him, until it was a great host, like the host of God." And doubtless it was intended to be a type of that host of God that shall appear with the spiritual David, as his helpers, when he shall come to set up his kingdom in the world; the same host that we read of, Rev. 19:14. The Spirit of God then pronounced a special blessing on David's helpers, as those that were co-workers with God [II Chron. 12], vs. 18, "Then the Spirit came upon Amasai, who was chief of the captains, and he said, Thine are we, David, and on thy side, thou son of Jesse; peace, peace be unto thee, and peace be to thine helpers, for thy God helpeth thee." So we may conclude that God will much more give his blessing to such as come to the help of the Lord, when he sets his own dear Son as king on his holy hill of Zion [Ps. 2:6]; and they shall be received by Christ, and he will put peculiar honor upon them, as David did on those his helpers; as we have an account in the following words, vs. 18, "Then David received them, and made them captains of the band." 'Tis particularly noted of those that "came to David to Hebron, ready armed to the war, to turn the kingdom of Saul to him, according to the word of the Lord," that they were men "that had understanding of the times, to know what Israel ought to do," vss. 23 and 32. Herein they differed from the Pharisees and other Jews, that did not come to the help of the Lord, at the time that the great Son of David appeared to set up his kingdom in the world, whom Christ condemns, that they had not understanding of those times, Luke 12:56, "Ye hypocrites, ye can discern the face of the sky, and of the earth; but how is it, that ye do not discern these times?" So it always will be, when Christ remarkably appears on earth, on a design of setting up his kingdom here, there will be many that will not understand the times, nor what Israel ought to do, and so will not come to turn about the kingdom to David.

The favorable notice that God will take of such as appear to promote the work of God at such a time as this, may also be argued from such a very particular notice being taken in the sacred records, of those that helped in rebuilding the wall of Jerusalem, upon the return from the Babylonish Captivity, Neh. chap. 3.

[Duties of Civil Rulers]

At such a time as this, when God is setting his king on his holy hill of Zion, or establishing his dominion, or shewing forth his regal glory from thence, he expects that his visible people, without exception, should openly appear to acknowledge him in such a work, and bow before him, and join with him. But especially does he expect this of civil rulers: God's eye is especially upon them, to see how they behave themselves on such an occasion. If a new king comes to the throne, when he comes from abroad, and enters into his kingdom, and makes his solemn entry into the royal city, it is expected that all sorts should acknowledge him; but above all others is it expected that the great men, and public officers of the nation should then make their appearance, and attend on their sovereign, with suitable congratulations and manifestations of respect and loyalty: if such as these stand at a distance, at such a time, it will be much more taken notice of, and will awaken the prince's jealousy and displeasure much more than such a behavior in the common people. And thus it is, when that eternal Son of God, and heir of the world, by whom kings reign and princes decree justice, whom his Father has appointed to be King of kings, comes as it were from far, and in the spiritual tokens of his presence, enters into the royal city Zion; God has his eye at such a time especially upon those princes, nobles and judges of the earth, spoken of [in] Prov. 8:16, to see how they behave themselves, whether they bow to him that he has made the head of all principality and power [Col. 2:10]. This is evident by the 2d Psalm, vss. 6–7, 10–12, "Yet have I set my king upon my holy hill of Zion. I will declare the decree: the Lord hath said unto me, thou art my Son; this day have I begotten thee. . . . Be wise now therefore, O ye kings, be instructed ye judges of the earth; serve the Lord with fear, and rejoice with trembling; kiss the Son, lest he be angry, and ye perish from the way, when his wrath is kindled but a little." There seems to be in the words an allusion to a new king's coming to the throne, and making his solemn entry into the royal city (as Zion was the royal city in Israel); when it is expected that all, especially men in public office and authority, should manifest their loyalty, by some open and visible token of respect by the way, as he passes along; and those that refuse or neglect it are in danger of being immediately struck down, and perishing from the way, by which the king goes in solemn procession.

The day wherein God does in an eminent manner send forth the rod of Christ's strength out of Zion, that he may rule in the midst of his enemies, the day of his power wherein his people shall be made willing, is also eminently a day of his wrath, especially to such rulers as oppose him, or won't bow to him; a day wherein he "shall strike through kings," and "fill the places with the dead bodies," and "wound the heads over many countries." Ps. 110 [vss. 5–6]. And thus it is, that when the Son of God girds his sword upon his thigh, with his glory and his majesty, and in his majesty rides prosperously because of truth, meekness and righteousness, his right hand teaches him terrible things [cf. Ps. 45:3–4]. It was the *princes* of Succoth especially that suffered punishment, when the inhabitants of that city refused to come to the help of the Lord, when Gideon was pursuing after Zebah and Zalmunna; we read that Gideon "took the elders of the city, and thorns of the wilderness and briers, and with them he taught the men of Succoth" [Judg. 8:16]. 'Tis especially taken notice of that the rulers and chief men of Israel were called upon to assist in the affair of bringing up the ark of God; they were chiefly consulted, and were principal in the management of the affair, I Chron. 13:1, "And David consulted with the captains of thousands and hundreds, and with every leader." And chap. 15:25, "So David and the elders of Israel, and the captains over thousands, went to bring up the ark of the covenant of the Lord, out of the house of Obed-edom, with joy." So II Sam. 6:1. And so it was when the ark was brought into the temple, I Kings 8:1, 3; and II Chron. 5:2, 4.

And as rulers, by neglecting their duty at such a time, will especially expose themselves to God's great displeasure, so by fully acknowledging God in such a work, and by cheerfully and vigorously exerting themselves to promote it, they will especially be in the way of receiving peculiar honors and rewards at God's hands. 'Tis noted of the princes of Israel, that they especially appeared to honor God with their princely offering, on occasion of the setting up the tabernacle of God in the congregation of Israel (which I have observed already was done at the time of the Feast of Tabernacles, and was a type of the tabernacle of God's being with men, and his dwelling with men in the latter days); and with what abundant particularity is it noted of each prince, how much he offered to God on that occasion, for their everlasting honor, in the 7th chap. of Numbers? And so with how much favor and honor does the Spirit of God take notice of those princes in Israel, that came to the help of the Lord in the war against Sisera? Judg. 5:9, "My heart is towards the governors of Israel, that offered themselves willingly among the people." And vs. 14, "Out of Machir came down governors." Vs. 15, "And the princes of Issachar were with Deborah." And in the account that we have of the rebuilding the wall of Jerusalem, in the 3d chap. of Nehemiah, it is particularly noted what an hand one and another of the rulers had in this affair; we have an account that such a part of the wall was repaired by the ruler of the half part of Jerusalem, and such a part by the ruler of the other half part of Jerusalem, and such a part by the ruler of part of Beth-haccerem, and such a part by the ruler of part of Mizpah, and such a part by the ruler of the half part of Beth-zur; and such a part by the ruler of Mizpah, vss. 9, 12, 14–16, 19. And there it is particularly noted of the rulers of one of the cities, that "they put not their necks to the work of the Lord," though the common people did; and they are stigmatized for it, in the sacred records, to their everlasting reproach, vs. 5, "And next unto them the Tekoites repaired; but their nobles put not their necks to the work of the Lord." So the Spirit of God, with special honor, takes notice of princes and rulers of several tribes, that assisted in bringing up the ark, Ps. 68:27.

And I humbly desire that it may be considered, whether we han't reason to fear that God is provoked with this land, that no more notice has been taken of this glorious work of the Lord that has been lately carried on, by the civil authority; that there has no more been done by them, as a public acknowledgement of God in this work, and no more improvement of their authority to promote it, either by appointing a day of public thanksgiving to God for so unspeakable a mercy, or a day of fasting and prayer, to humble ourselves before God for our past deadness and unprofitableness under the means of grace, and to seek the continuance and increase of the tokens of his presence; or so much as to enter upon any public consultation, what should be done to advance the present revival of religion and great reformation that is begun in the land. Is there not danger that such a behavior, at such a time, will be interpreted by God as a denial of Christ? If but a new governor comes into a province, how much is there done, especially by those that are in authority, to put honor upon him, to arise and appear publicly, and go forth to meet him, to address and congratulate him, and with great expense to attend upon him and aid him? If the authority of the province, on such an occasion, should all sit still, and say and do nothing, and take no notice of the arrival of their new governor, would there not be danger of its being interpreted by him, and his prince that sent him, as a denial of his authority, or a refusing to receive him, and honor him as their governor? And shall the Head of the angels, and Lord of the universe, come down from heaven in so wonderful a manner into the land, and shall all stand at a distance and be silent and unactive on such an occasion? I would humbly recommend it to our rulers, to consider whether God don't now say to them, "Be wise now, ye rulers; be instructed, ye judges of New England: kiss the Son, lest he be angry, and ye perish from the way" [cf. Ps. 2:10].

'Tis prophesied [in] Zech. 12:8 that in the glorious day of the Christian church, the house of David, or the rulers in God's Israel, "shall be as God, as the angel of the Lord," before his people. But how can such rulers expect to have any share in this glorious promise, that don't so much as openly acknowledge God in the work of that Spirit by which the glory of that day is to be accomplished? The days are coming, so often spoken of, when the saints shall reign on earth, and all dominion and authority shall be given into their hands: but if our rulers would partake of this honor, they ought at such a day as this to bring their glory and honor into the spiritual Jerusalem, agreeable to Rev. 21:24.

[*Duties of Ministers*]

But above all others, is God's eye upon ministers of the Gospel, as expecting of them that they should arise and acknowledge and honor him in such a work as this, and do their utmost to encourage and promote it. For to promote such a work is the very business which they are called and devoted to; 'tis the office to which they are appointed, as co-workers with Christ, and as his ambassadors and instruments, to awaken and convert sinners, and establish, build up and comfort saints; 'tis the business they have been solemnly charged with before God, angels and men, and that they have given up themselves to by the most sacred vows. These especially are the officers of Christ's kingdom, that above all other men upon earth do represent his person, into whose hands Christ has committed the sacred oracles and holy ordinances, and all his appointed means of grace, to be administered by them; they are the stewards of his household, into whose hands he has committed its provision; the immortal souls of men are committed to them as a flock of sheep are committed to the care of a shepherd, or as a master commits a treasure to the care of a servant, of which he must give an account. 'Tis expected of them, above all others, that they should have understanding of the times, and know what Israel ought to do; for 'tis their business to acquaint themselves with things pertaining to the kingdom of God, and to teach and enlighten others in things of this nature. We that are employed in the sacred work of the Gospel ministry are the watchmen over the city, to whom God has committed the keys of the gates of Zion; and if when the rightful king of Zion comes to deliver his people from the enemy that oppresses them, we refuse to open the gates to him, how greatly shall we expose ourselves to his wrath? We are appointed to be the captains of the host in this war: and if a general will highly resent it in a private soldier, if he refuses to follow him when his banner is displayed and his trumpet blown; how much more will he resent it in the officers of his army? The work of the Gospel ministry, consisting in the administration of God's Word and ordinances, is the principal means that God has appointed for carrying on his work on the souls of men; and 'tis his revealed will that whenever that glorious revival of religion and reformation of the world, so often spoken of in his Word, is accomplished, it should be principally by the labors of his ministers; and therefore how heinous will it be in the sight of God, if when a work of that nature is begun, we appear unbelieving, slow, backward and disaffected? There was no sort of persons among the Jews that was in any measure treated with such manifestations of God's great displeasure and severe indignation, for not acknowledging Christ and the work of his Spirit, in the days of Christ and his apostles, as the ministers of religion: see how Christ deals with them for it, in the 23d chapter of Matthew; with what gentleness did Christ treat publicans and harlots, in comparison of them?

When the tabernacle was erected in the camp of Israel, and God came down from heaven to dwell in it, the priests were above all others concerned and busily employed in the solemn transactions of that occasion, Lev. chaps. 8 and 9. And so it was at the time of the dedication of the temple of Solomon, I Kings chap. 8, and II Chron. chaps. 5 and 6 and 7, which was at the time of the Feast of Tabernacles, at the same time that the tabernacle was erected in the wilderness: and the Levites were primarily and most immediately concerned in bringing up the ark into Mount Zion; the business properly belonged to them, and the ark was carried on their shoulders. I Chron. 15:2, "Then David said, None ought to carry the ark of God but the Levites; for them hath the Lord chosen to carry the ark of God, and to minister unto him forever." And vss. 11–12, "And David called for Zadok and Abiathar the priests, and for the Levites, for Uriel, Asaiah, and Joel, Shemaiah, and Eliel, and Amminadab; and said unto them, Ye are the chief of the fathers of the Levites; sanctify yourselves, both ye and your brethren, that you may bring up the ark of the Lord God of Israel, unto the place that I have prepared for it." So [also] we have an account that the priests led the way in rebuilding the wall of Jerusalem after the Babylonish Captivity, Neh. 3, at the beginning.

If ministers preach never so good doctrine, and are never so painful and laborious in their work, yet if at such a day as this, they shew to their people that they are not well affected to this work, but are very doubtful and suspicious of it, they will be very likely to do their people a great deal more hurt than good. For the very fame of such a great and extraordinary work of God, if their people were suffered to believe it to be his work, and the example of other towns, together with what preaching they might hear occasionally, would be likely to have a much greater influence upon the minds of their people, to awaken them and animate them in religion, than all their labors with them. And besides, their minister's opinion won't only beget in them a suspicion of the work they hear of abroad, whereby the mighty hand of God that appears in it loses its influence upon their minds, but it will also tend to create a suspicion of everything of the like nature, that shall appear among themselves, as being something of the same distemper that is become so epidemical in the land; and that is, in effect, to create a suspicion of all vital religion, and to put the people upon talking against it and discouraging it wherever it appears, and knocking it in the head as fast as it rises. And we that are ministers, by looking on this work from year to year with a displeased countenance, shall effectually keep the sheep from their pasture, instead of doing the part of shepherds to them, by feeding them; and our people had a great deal better be without any settled minister at all, at such a day as this.

We that are in this sacred office, had need to take heed what we do, and how we behave ourselves at this time: a less thing in a minister will hinder the work of God, than in others. If we are very silent, or say but little about the work, in our public prayers and preaching, or seem carefully to avoid speaking of it in our conversation, it will, and justly may, be interpreted by our people that we who are their guides, to whom they are to have their eye for spiritual instruction, are suspicious of it; and this will tend to raise the same suspicions in them; and so the forementioned consequences will follow. And if we really hinder and stand in the way of the work of God, whose business above all others it is to promote it, how can we expect to partake of the glorious benefits of it? And by keeping others from the benefit of it, we shall keep them out of heaven; therefore those awful words of Christ to the Jewish teachers should be considered by us, Matt. 23:13, "Woe unto you [. . .] for you shut up the kingdom of heaven [against men]; for ye neither go in yourselves, neither suffer ye them that are entering to go in." If we keep the sheep from their pasture, how shall we answer it to the great Shepherd, that has bought the flock with his precious blood, and has committed the care of them to us? I would humbly desire of every minister that has thus long remained disaffected to this work, and has contemptible thoughts of it, to consider whether he has not hitherto been like Michal, without any child, or at least in a great measure barren and unsuccessful in his work: I pray God it may not be a perpetual barrenness as hers was [cf. II Sam. 6:16, 20–23; and above, p. 366].

The times of Christ's remarkably appearing in behalf of his

church, and to revive religion and advance his kingdom in the world, are often spoken [of] in the prophecies of Scripture, as times wherein he will remarkably execute judgments on such ministers or shepherds as don't feed the flock but hinder their being fed, and so deliver his flock from them, as Jer. 23 throughout, and Ezek. 34 throughout, and Zech. 10:3, and Isa. 56:7-9, etc. I observed before that Christ's solemn, magnificent entry into Jerusalem, seems to be designed as a representation of his glorious coming into his church, the spiritual Jerusalem; and therefore 'tis worthy to be noted, to our present purpose, that Christ at that time, cast out all them that sold and bought in the temple, and overthrew the tables of the money-changers, and the seats of them that sold doves; signifying that when he should come to set up his kingdom on earth, he would cast out those out of his house, who, instead of being faithful ministers, officiated there only for worldly gain. Not that I determine that all ministers that are suspicious of this work do so; but I mention these things to shew that it is to be expected, that a time of a glorious outpouring of the Spirit of God to revive religion, will be a time of remarkable judgments on those ministers that don't serve the end of their ministry.

The example of the unbelieving lord in Samaria should especially be for the warning of ministers and rulers. At the time when God turned an extreme famine into a great plenty by a wonderful work of his, the king appointed this lord to have the charge of the gate of the city; where he saw the common people in multitudes, entering with great joy and gladness, loaden with provision, to feed and feast their almost famished bodies; but he himself, though he saw it with his eyes, never had one taste of it, but being weak with famine, sunk down in the crowd and was trodden to death, as a punishment of God for his not giving credit to that great and wonderful work of God, when sufficiently manifested to him to require his belief [II Kings 7]. Ministers are those, that the King of the church has appointed to have the charge of the gate at which his people enter into the kingdom of heaven, there to be entertained and satisfied with an eternal feast; ministers have the charge of the house of God, which is the gate of heaven.

Ministers should especially take heed of a spirit of envy towards other ministers, that God is pleased to make more use of to carry on this work, than they; and that they don't, from such a spirit, reproach some preachers that have the true Spirit, as though they were influenced by a false spirit, or were bereft of reason and were mad, and were proud, false pretenders, and deserved to be put in prison or the stocks as disturbers of the peace; lest they expose themselves to the curse of Shemaiah the Nehelamite, who envied the prophet Jeremiah, and in this manner reviled him, in his letter to Zephaniah the priest, Jer. 29:26–27, "The Lord hath made thee priest in the stead of Jehoiada the priest, that ye should be officers in the house of the Lord, for every man that is mad, and maketh himself a prophet, that thou shouldst put him in prison, and in the stocks. Now therefore, why hast thou not reproved Jeremiah of Anathoth, which maketh himself a prophet to you?" His curse is denounced in the 32d vs., "Therefore, thus saith the Lord, Behold, I will punish Shemaiah the Nehelamite, and his seed; he shall not have a man to dwell among this people, neither shall he behold the good that I will do for my people, saith the Lord, because he hath taught rebellion against the Lord." All those that are others' superiors or elders should take heed, that at this day they ben't like the elder brother, who could not bear it that the prodigal should be made so much of, and should be so sumptuously entertained, and would not join in the joy of the feast; [he] was like Michal, Saul's daughter, offended at the music and dancing that he heard; the transports of joy displeased him; it seemed to him to be an unseemly and unseasonable noise and ado that was made; and therefore stood at a distance, sullen and much offended, and full of invectives against the young prodigal [Luke 15:25–30].

'Tis our wisest and best way, fully and without reluctance, to bow to the great God in this work, and to be entirely resigned to him, with respect to the manner in which he carries it on, and the instruments he is pleased to make use of, and not to shew ourselves out of humor and sullenly to refuse to acknowledge the work, in the full glory of it, because we han't had so great a hand in promoting it, or han't shared so largely in the blessings of it, as some others; and not to refuse to give all that honor that belongs to others as instruments, because they are young, or are upon other accounts much inferior to ourselves and many others, and may appear to us very unworthy, that God should put so much honor upon them. When God comes to accomplish any great work for his church, and for the advancement of the kingdom of his Son, he always fulfills that Scripture, Isa. 2:17, "And the loftiness of man shall be bowed down, and the haughtiness of men shall be made low, and the Lord alone shall be exalted in that day." If God has a design of carrying on this work, everyone, whether he be great or small, must either bow to it or be broken before it: it may be expected that God's hand will be upon everything that is high, and stiff, and strong in opposition, as in Isa. 2:12–15, "For the day of the Lord of hosts shall be upon everyone that is proud and lofty, and upon everyone that is lifted up, and he shall be brought low; and upon all the cedars of Lebanon, that are high and lifted up, and upon all the oaks of Bashan, and upon all the high mountains, and upon all the hills that are lifted up, and upon every high tower, and upon every fenced wall."

[Duties of the Laity]

Not only magistrates and ministers, but every living soul, is now obliged to arise, and acknowledge God in this work, and put to his hand to promote it, as they would not expose themselves to God's curse. All sorts of persons, throughout the whole congregation of Israel, great and small, rich and poor, men and women, helped to build the tabernacle in the wilderness; some in one way, others in another; each one according to his capacity: "Every one whose heart stirred him up, and every one whom his spirit made willing"; all sorts contributed, and all sorts were employed in that affair, in labors of their hands, both men and women. Some brought gold and silver, others blue, purple and scarlet, and fine linen; others offered an offering of brass; others, with whom was found shittim wood, brought it [as] an offering to the Lord: the rulers brought onyx stones, and spice, and oil; and some brought goats' hair; and some rams' skins, and others badgers' skins. See Exod. 35:20, etc. And we are told, vs. 29, "The children of Israel brought a willing offering unto the Lord, every man and woman, whose heart made them willing." And thus it ought to be in this day of building the tabernacle of God; with such a willing and cheerful heart ought every man, woman, and child to do something to promote this work: those that have not onyx stones, or are not able to bring gold or silver, yet may bring goats' hair.

As all sorts of persons were employed in building the tabernacle in the wilderness, so the whole congregation of Israel were called together to set up the tabernacle in Shiloh, after they came into Canaan, Josh. 18:1. And so again, the whole congregation of Israel were gathered together to bring up the ark of God from Kirjath-jearim; and again, they were all assembled to bring it up out of the house of Obed-edom into Mount Zion; so again, all Israel met together to assist in the great affair of the dedication of the temple, and bringing the ark into it: so [also] we have an account, how that all sorts assisted in the rebuilding the wall of Jerusalem, not only the proper inhabitants of Jerusalem, but those that dwelt in other parts of the land; not only the priests and rulers, but the Nethinims[5] and merchants, husbandmen and mechanics, and women. Neh. 3:5, 12, 26, 31–32. And we have an account of one and another, that he repaired over against his house, vss. 10 and 23, 28; and of one that repaired over against his chamber, vs. 30. So now, at this time of the rebuilding the walls of Jerusalem, everyone ought to promote the work of God within his own sphere, and by doing what belongs to him, in the place in which God has set him: men in a private capacity may repair over against their houses: and even those that have not the government of families, and have but part of an house belonging to them, should repair, each one over against his chamber. And everyone should be engaged to do the utmost that lies in his power, laboring with the utmost watchfulness, care and diligence; with united hearts, and united strength, and the greatest readiness, to assist one another in this work: as God's people rebuilt the wall of Jerusalem; who were so diligent in the work that they wrought from break of day till the stars appeared, and did not so much as put off their clothes in the night; and wrought with that care and watchfulness, that with one hand they wrought in the work, and with the other hand held a weapon; besides the guard they set to defend them; and were so well united in it that they took care that one should stand ready, with a trumpet in his hand, that if any were assaulted in one part, those in the other parts, at the sound of the trumpet, might resort to 'em, and help 'em; Neh. 4, at the latter end.

Great care should be taken that the press should be improved to no purpose contrary to the interest of this work. We read that when God fought against Sisera for the deliverance of his oppressed church, "they that handle the pen of the writer came to the help of the Lord" in that affair, Judg. 5:14. Whatever sort of men in Israel they were that were intended, yet as the words were indited by a Spirit that had a perfect view of all events to the end of the world, and had a special eye on this song, to that great event of the

5. [Naturalized foreigners used as temple servants and slaves to the Levites.]

deliverance of God's church in the latter days, of which this deliverance of Israel was a type, 'tis not unlikely that they have respect to authors, those that should fight against the kingdom of Satan with their pens. Those therefore that publish pamphlets to the disadvantage of this work, and tending either directly or indirectly to bring it under suspicion and to discourage or hinder it, would do well thoroughly to consider whether this be not indeed the work of God; and whether if it be, 'tis not likely that God will go forth as fire, to consume all that stands in his way, and so burn up those pamphlets; and whether there be not danger that the fire that is kindled in them, will scorch the authors.[6]

When a people oppose Christ in the work of his Holy Spirit, it is because it touches 'em in something that is dear to their carnal minds; and because they see the tendency of it is to cross their pride, and deprive them of the objects of their lusts. We should take heed that at this day we be not like the Gadarenes, who when Christ came into their country in the exercise of his glorious power and grace, triumphing over a legion of devils and delivering a miserable creature, that had long been their captive, were all alarmed because they lost their swine by it, and the whole multitude of the country came, and besought him to depart out of their coasts: they loved their filthy swine better than Jesus Christ; and had rather have a legion of devils in their country, with their herd of swine, than Jesus Christ without them.

This work may be opposed, not only by directly speaking against the whole of it: persons may say that they believe there is a good work carried on [in] the country; and may sometimes bless God in their public prayers, in general terms, for any awakenings or revivals of religion there have lately been in any parts of the land; and may pray that God would carry on his own work, and pour out his Spirit more and more; and yet, as I apprehend, be in the sight of God great opposers of his work. Some will express themselves after this manner, that are so far from acknowledging and rejoicing in the infinite mercy and glorious grace of God, in causing so happy a change in the land, that they look upon the religious state of the country, take it

6. [Boston publishers were not exactly neutral on the revival. Samuel Kneeland and Timothy Green, Jr., both members of Old South Church, were staunch supporters and therefore the favorite publishers of the evangelicals. Most of the antirevival tracts, as well as the militantly Old Light *Boston Evening Post,* issued from the press of Thomas Fleet.]

in the whole of it, [as] much more sorrowful than it was ten years ago; and whose conversation, to those that are well acquainted with 'em, evidently shews that they are more out of humor with the state of things, and enjoy themselves less, than they did before ever this work began. If it be manifestly thus with us, and our talk and behavior with respect to this work be such as has (though but) an indirect tendency to beget ill thoughts and suspicions in others concerning it, we are opposers of the work of God.

Instead of coming to the help of the Lord, we shall actually fight against him, if we are abundant in insisting on and setting forth the blemishes of the work, so as to manifest that we rather choose, and are more forward to take notice of what is amiss, than what is good and glorious in the work. Not but that the errors that are committed, ought to be observed and lamented, and a proper testimony borne against them, and the most probable means should be used to have 'em amended; but an insisting much upon 'em, as though it were a pleasing theme, or speaking of them with more appearance of heat of spirit, or with ridicule, or an air of contempt, than grief for them, has no tendency to correct the errors; but has a tendency to darken the glory of God's power and grace appearing in the substance of the work, and to beget jealousies and ill thoughts in the minds of others concerning the whole of it. Whatever errors many zealous persons have run into, yet if the work in the substance of it be the work of God, then it is a joyful day indeed; 'tis so in heaven, and ought to be so among God's people on earth, especially in that part of the earth where this glorious work is carried on. 'Tis a day of great rejoicing with Christ himself, the good Shepherd, when he finds his sheep that was lost, lays it on his shoulders rejoicing, and calls together his friends and neighbors, saying, "Rejoice with me!" [Luke 15:6]. If we therefore are Christ's friends, now it should be a day of great rejoicing with us. If we viewed things in a just light, so great an event as the conversion of such a multitude of sinners would draw and engage our attention much more than all the imprudences and irregularities that have been; our hearts would be swallowed up with the glory of this event, and we should have no great disposition to attend to anything else. The imprudences and errors of poor feeble worms don't hinder or prevent great rejoicing, in the presence of the angels of God, over so many poor sinners that have repented; and it will be an argument of something very ill in us, if they prevent our rejoicing.

Who loves, in a day of great joy and gladness, to be much insisting on those things that are uncomfortable? Would it not be very improper, on a king's coronation day, to be much in taking notice of the blemishes of the royal family? Or would it be agreeable to the bridegroom, on the day of his espousals, the day of the gladness of his heart, to be much insisting on the blemishes of his bride? We have an account, how that at the time of that joyful dispensation of providence, the restoration of the church of Israel, after the Babylonish Captivity, and at the time of the Feast of Tabernacles, many wept at the faults that were found amongst the people, but were reproved for taking so much notice of the blemishes of that affair as to overlook the cause of rejoicing. Neh. 8:9–12, "And Nehemiah, which is the Tirshatha,[7] and Ezra the priest, the scribe, and the Levites that taught the people, said unto all the people, This day is holy unto the Lord your God; mourn not nor weep: for all the people wept, when they heard the words of the law. Then he said unto them, Go your way, eat the fat, and drink the sweet, and send portions unto them for whom nothing is prepared; for this day is holy unto our Lord; neither be you sorry, for the joy of the Lord is your strength. So the Levites stilled all the people, saying, Hold your peace, for the day is holy; neither be ye grieved. And all the people went their way, to eat and to drink, and to send portions, and to make great mirth, because they had understood the words that were declared unto them."

God doubtless now expects that all sorts of persons in New England, rulers, ministers and people, high and low, rich and poor, old and young, should take great notice of his hand in this mighty work of his grace, and should appear to acknowledge his glory in it, and greatly to rejoice in it, everyone doing his utmost in the place that God has set them in, to promote it. And God, according to his wonderful patience, seems to be still waiting to give us opportunity, thus to acknowledge and honor him. But if we finally refuse, there is not the least reason to expect any other than that his awful curse will pursue us, and that the pourings out of his wrath will be proportionable to the despised outpourings of his Spirit and grace.

7. [An honorific title for the governor.]

PART III

THIS work that has lately been carried on in the land is the work
of God, and not the work of man. Its beginning has not been of
man's power or device, and its being carried on depends not on our
strength or wisdom; but yet God expects of all that they should use
their utmost endeavors to promote it, and that the hearts of all
should be greatly engaged in this affair, and that we should improve
strength in it, however vain human strength is without the power
of God; and so he no less requires that we should improve our utmost care, wisdom and prudence, though human wisdom of itself
be as vain as human strength. Though God is wont to carry on such
a work in such a manner, as many ways, to shew the weakness and
vanity of means and human endeavors in themselves; yet at the same
time, he carries it on in such a manner as to encourage diligence
and vigilance in the use of proper means and endeavors, and to
punish the neglect of them. Therefore in our endeavors to promote
this great work, we ought to use the utmost caution, vigilance and
skill, in the measures we take in order to it. A great affair should be
managed with great prudence: this is the most important affair
that ever New England was called to be concerned in. When a people
are engaged in war with a powerful and crafty nation, it concerns
them to manage an affair of such consequence with the utmost discretion. Of what vast importance then must it be, that we should be
vigilant and prudent in the management of this great war that New
England now has, with so great a host of such subtle and cruel
enemies, wherein we must either conquer or be conquered; and the
consequence of the victory, on one side, will be our eternal destruction in both soul and body in hell; and on the other side, our
obtaining the kingdom of heaven and reigning in it in eternal glory?
We had need always to stand on our watch [Hab. 2:1], and to be well

384

versed in the art of war, and not to be ignorant of the devices of our enemies, and to take heed lest by any means we be beguiled through their subtlety.

Though the Devil be strong, yet in such a war as this, he depends more on his craft than his strength. And the course he has chiefly taken from time to time, to clog, hinder and overthrow revivals of religion in the church of God, has been by his subtle, deceitful management, to beguile and mislead those that have been engaged therein; and in such a course God has been pleased, in his holy and sovereign providence, to suffer him to succeed, oftentimes in a great measure, to overthrow that, which in its beginning appeared most hopeful and glorious. The work that is now begun in New England is, as I have shown, eminently glorious; and if it should go on and prevail, would make New England a kind of heaven upon earth. Is it not therefore a thousand pities that it should be overthrown, through wrong and improper management, that we are led into by our subtle adversary, in our endeavors to promote it?

In treating of the methods that ought to be taken to promote this work, I would, I. Take notice, in some instances, wherein fault has been found with the conduct of those that have appeared to be the subjects of it, or have been zealous to promote it (as I apprehend), beyond just cause. II. I would shew what things ought to be corrected or avoided. III. I would shew positively, what ought to be done to promote this glorious work of God.[1]

[*Ten Criticisms Answered*]

I would take notice of some things at which offense has been taken without, or beyond, just cause.

[1] One thing that has been complained of, is ministers addressing themselves rather to the affections of their hearers than to their understandings, and striving to raise their passions to the utmost height, rather by a very affectionate manner of speaking and a great appearance of earnestness in voice and gesture, than by clear reasoning and informing their judgment: by which means, it is objected, that the affections are moved without a proportionable enlightening of the understanding.

1. [This is the outline, not of Part III, which has just begun, but of the remainder of the treatise. According to this enumeration, I = Part III, II = Part IV (below, pp. 409–95), and III = Part V (below, pp. 496–530).]

To which I would say, I am far from thinking that it is not very profitable, for ministers in their preaching, to endeavor clearly and distinctly to explain the doctrines of religion, and unravel the difficulties that attend them, and to confirm them with strength of reason and argumentation, and also to observe some easy and clear method and order in their discourses, for the help of the understanding and memory; and 'tis very probable that these things have been of late, too much neglected by many ministers; yet, I believe that the objection that is made, of affections raised without enlightening the understanding, is in a great measure built on a mistake, and confused notions that some have about the nature and cause of the affections, and the manner in which they depend on the understanding. All affections are raised either by light in the understanding, or by some error and delusion in the understanding; for all affections do certainly arise from some apprehension in the understanding; and that apprehension must either be agreeable to truth, or else be some mistake or delusion; if it be an apprehension or notion that is agreeable to truth, then it is light in the understanding. Therefore the thing to be inquired into is, whether the apprehensions or notions of divine and eternal things, that are raised in people's minds by these affectionate preachers, whence their affections are excited, be apprehensions that are agreeable to truth, or whether they are mistakes. If the former, then the affections are raised the way they should be, viz. by informing the mind, or conveying light to the understanding. They go away with a wrong notion, that think that those preachers can't affect their hearers by enlightening their understandings, that don't do it by such a distinct, and learned handling of the doctrinal points of religion, as depends on human discipline, or the strength of natural reason, and tends to enlarge their hearers' learning, and speculative knowledge in divinity. The manner of preaching without this, may be such as shall tend very much to set divine and eternal things in a right view, and to give the hearers such ideas and apprehensions of them as are agreeable to truth, and such impressions on their hearts, as are answerable to the real nature of things: and not only the words that are spoken, but the manner of speaking, is one thing that has a great tendency to this.

I think an exceeding affectionate way of preaching about the great things of religion, has in itself no tendency to beget false apprehensions of them; but on the contrary a much greater tendency to beget true apprehensions of them, than a moderate, dull, indifferent way of speaking of 'em. An appearance of affection and earnestness in the manner of delivery, if it be very great indeed, yet if it be agreeable to the nature of the subject, and ben't beyond a proportion to its importance and worthiness of affection, and there be no appearance of its being feigned or forced, has so much the greater tendency to beget true ideas or apprehensions in the minds of the hearers, of the subject spoken of, and so to enlighten the understanding: and that for this reason, that such a way or manner of speaking of these things does in fact more truly represent them, than a more cold and indifferent way of speaking of them. If the subject be in its own nature worthy of very great affection, then a speaking of it with very great affection is most agreeable to the nature of that subject, or is the truest representation of it, and therefore has most of a tendency to beget true ideas of it in the minds of those to whom the representation is made. And I don't think ministers are to be blamed for raising the affections of their hearers too high, if that which they are affected with be only that which is worthy of affection, and their affections are not raised beyond a proportion to their importance, or worthiness of affection. I should think myself in the way of my duty to raise the affections of my hearers as high as possibly I can, provided that they are affected with nothing but truth, and with affections that are not disagreeable to the nature of what they are affected with. I know it has long been fashionable to despise a very earnest and pathetical way of preaching; and they, and they only have been valued as preachers, that have shown the greatest extent of learning, and strength of reason, and correctness of method and language: but I humbly conceive it has been for want of understanding, or duly considering human nature, that such preaching has been thought to have the greatest tendency to answer the ends of preaching; and the experience of the present and past ages abundantly confirms the same.

Though as I said before, clearness of distinction and illustration, and strength of reason, and a good method, in the doctrinal handling of the truths of religion, is many ways needful and profitable, and not to be neglected, yet an increase in speculative knowledge in divinity is not what is so much needed by our people, as something else. Men may abound in this sort of light and have no heat: how much has there been of this sort of knowledge, in the Christian world, in this age? Was there ever an age wherein strength and penetration of reason, extent of learning, exactness of distinction, correctness of style, and clearness of expression, did so abound? And yet was there ever an age wherein there has been so little sense of the evil of sin, so little love to God, heavenly-mindedness, and holiness of life, among the professors of the true religion? Our people don't so much need to have their heads stored, as to have their hearts touched; and they stand in the greatest need of that sort of preaching that has the greatest tendency to do this.

Those texts, Isa. 58:1, "Cry aloud, spare not, lift up thy voice like a trumpet, and shew my people their transgression, and the house of Jacob their sins"; and Ezek. 6:11, "Thus saith the Lord God, smite with thine hand, and stamp with thy foot, and say, alas, for all the evil abomination of the house of Israel!"—I say, these texts (however the use that some have made of them has been laughed at) will fully justify a great degree of pathos, and manifestation of zeal and fervency in preaching the Word of God. They may indeed be abused, to justify that which would be odd and unnatural amongst us, not making due allowance for difference of manners and custom, in different ages and nations; but let us interpret them how we will, they at least imply that a most affectionate and earnest manner of delivery, in many cases, becomes a preacher of God's Word.

Preaching of the Word of God is commonly spoken of in Scripture, in such expressions as seem to import a loud and earnest speaking; as in Isa. 40:2, "Speak ye comfortably to Jerusalem, and cry unto her [. . .] that her iniquity is pardoned." And vs. 3, "The voice of him that crieth in the wilderness, Prepare ye the way of the Lord." Verse 6, "The voice said, Cry. And he said, What shall I cry? All flesh is grass, and all the goodliness thereof, as the flower of the field." Jer. 2:2, "Go and cry in the ears of Jerusalem, saying, Thus saith the Lord, etc." Jonah 1:2, "Arise, go to Nineveh, that great city, and cry against it." Isa. 61:1–2, "The Spirit of the Lord God is upon me, because the Lord hath anointed me to preach good tidings to the meek . . . to proclaim liberty to the captives, and the opening of the prison to them that are bound, to proclaim the acceptable year of the Lord, and the year [*sic,* day] of vengeance of our God." Isa. 62:11, "Behold, the Lord hath proclaimed unto the end of the world, Say ye to the daughter of Zion, Behold thy salvation cometh, etc." Rom. 10:18, "Their sound went into all the earth, and their words to the end of the world." Jer. 11:6, "Proclaim all these words in the cities of Judah, and in the streets of Jerusalem, saying, Hear ye the words of this covenant, and do them." So

chap. 19:2 and 7:2. Prov. 8:1, "Doth not wisdom cry, and understanding put forth her voice?" Vss. 3–4, "She crieth at the gates, at
the entry of the city, at the coming in at the doors: Unto you, O men,
I call, and my voice is to the sons of men!" And chap. 1:20, "Wisdom
crieth without, she uttereth her voice in the streets." Chap. 9:3, "She
hath sent forth her maidens; she crieth upon the high places of the
city." John 7:37, "In the last day, that great day of the feast, Jesus
stood and cried, saying, If any man thirst, let him come unto me and
drink."

It seems to be foretold that the Gospel should be especially
preached in a loud and earnest manner, at the introduction of the
prosperous state of religion, in the latter days. Isa. 40:9, "O Zion,
that bringeth good tidings, get thee up into the high mountain! O
Jerusalem, that bringeth good tidings, lift up thy voice with
strength! Lift up, and be not afraid! Say unto the cities of Judah,
Behold your God!" Isa. 52:7–8, "How beautiful upon the mountains,
are the feet of him that bringeth good tidings! . . . Thy watchmen
shall lift up the voice." Isa. 27:13, "And it shall come to pass, in that
day, that the great trumpet shall be blown, and they shall come
which were ready to perish." And this will be one way that the
church of God will cry at that time, like a travailing woman, when
Christ mystical is going to be brought forth; as Rev. 12, at the
beginning. It will be by ministers, that are her mouth: and it will
be this way, that Christ will then cry like a travailing woman, as in
Isa. 42:14, "I have long time holden my peace: I have been still, and
refrained myself; now will I cry, like a travailing woman." Christ
cries by his ministers, and the church cries by her officers. And 'tis
worthy to be noted that the word commonly used in the New
Testament, that we translate "preach," properly signifies to proclaim
aloud like a crier.[2]

[2] Another thing that some ministers have been greatly blamed
for, and I think unjustly, is speaking terror to them that are already
under great terrors, instead of comforting them. Indeed, if ministers
in such a case go about to terrify persons with that which is not true,
or to affright 'em by representing their case worse than it is, or
in any respect otherwise than it is, they are to be condemned; but if
they terrify 'em only by still holding forth more light to them, and

2. [Most likely JE had in mind κηρύσσω, "to proclaim publicly as a herald";
the word usually implies authority and gravity.]

giving them to understand more of the truth of their case, they are altogether to be justified. When sinners' consciences are greatly awakened by the Spirit of God, it is by light imparted to the conscience, enabling them to see their case to be, in some measure, as it is; and if more light be let in, it will terrify 'em still more: but ministers are not therefore to be blamed that they endeavor to hold forth more light to the conscience, and don't rather alleviate the pain they are under, by intercepting and obstructing that light that shines already. To say anything to those who have never believed in the Lord Jesus Christ, to represent their case any otherwise than exceeding terrible, is not to preach the Word of God to 'em; for the Word of God reveals nothing but truth; but this is to delude them. Why should we be afraid to let persons that are in an infinitely miserable condition, know the truth, or bring 'em into the light, for fear it should terrify them? 'Tis light that must convert them, if ever they are converted. The more we bring sinners into the light, while they are miserable, and the light is terrible to them, the more likely it is that by and by the light will be joyful to them. The ease, peace and comfort, that natural men enjoy, have their foundation in darkness and blindness; therefore as that darkness vanishes, and light comes in, their peace vanishes and they are terrified: but that is no good argument why we should endeavor to hold their darkness, that we may uphold their comfort. The truth is, that as long as men reject Christ, and don't savingly believe in him, however they may be awakened, and however strict, and conscientious, and laborious they may be in religion, they have the wrath of God abiding on them; they are his enemies, and the children of the Devil (as the Scripture calls all that ben't savingly converted, Matt. 13:38; I John 3:10), and 'tis uncertain whether they shall ever obtain mercy: God is under no obligation to shew 'em mercy, nor will he be, if they fast and pray and cry never so much; and they are then especially provoking God, under those terrors, that they stand it out against Christ, and won't accept of an offered Saviour, though they see so much need of him: and seeing this is the truth, they should be told so, that they may be sensible what their case indeed is.

To blame a minister for thus declaring the truth to those who are under awakenings, and not immediately administering comfort to them, is like blaming a surgeon because when he has begun to thrust in his lance, whereby he has already put his patient to great pain, and he shrinks and cries out with anguish, he is so cruel that he won't stay his hand, but goes on to thrust it in further, till he comes to the core of the wound. Such a compassionate physician, who as soon as his patient began to flinch, should withdraw his hand, and go about immediately to apply a plaster, to skin over the wound, and leave the core untouched, would be one that would heal the hurt slightly, crying, "Peace, peace, when there is no peace" [Jer. 6:14; 8:11].

Indeed, something else besides terror is to be preached to them whose consciences are awakened: the Gospel is to be preached to them. They are to be told that there is a Saviour provided, that is excellent and glorious, who has shed his precious blood for sinners, and is every way sufficient to save 'em, that stands ready to receive 'em, if they will heartily embrace him; for this is also the truth, as well as that they now are in an infinitely dreadful condition: this is the Word of God. Sinners at the same time that they are told how miserable their case is, should be earnestly invited to come and accept of a Saviour, and yield their hearts unto him, with all the winning, encouraging arguments for 'em so to do, that the Gospel affords: but this is to induce 'em to escape from the misery of the condition that they are now in: but not to make 'em think their present condition less miserable than it is, or at all to abate their uneasiness and distress, while they are in it; that would be the way to quiet them, and fasten them in it, and not to excite 'em to fly from it. Comfort, in one sense, is to be held forth to sinners under awakenings of conscience; i.e. comfort is to be offered to 'em in Christ, on condition of their flying from their present miserable state to him: but comfort is not to be administered to 'em in their present state, as anything that they have now any title to, while out of Christ. No comfort is to be administered to 'em, from anything in *them,* any of *their* qualifications, prayers or other performances, past, present or future; but ministers should, in such cases, strive to their utmost to take all such comforts from 'em, though it greatly increases their terror. A person that sees himself ready to sink into hell is ready to strive, some way or other, to lay God under some obligation to him; but he is to be beat off from everything of that nature, though it greatly increases his terror to see himself wholly destitute on every side, of any refuge, or anything of his own to lay hold of; as a man that sees himself in danger of drowning is in terror, and endeavors to catch hold on every twig within his reach, and he that pulls away those twigs from him increases his terror; yet if they are insufficient to save him, and by being in his way, prevent his looking to that which will save him, to pull them away is necessary to save his life.

If sinners are in any distress, from any error that they embrace, or mistake they are under, that is to be removed. For instance, if they are in terror from an apprehension that they have committed the unpardonable sin, or that those things have happened to 'em that are certain signs of reprobation, or any other delusion, such terrors have no tendency to do them any good; for these terrors are from temptation and not from conviction. But that terror which arises from conviction, or a sight of truth, is to be increased; for those that are most awakened have great remaining stupidity; they have a sense of but little of that which is; and 'tis from remaining blindness and darkness that they see no more; and that remaining blindness is a disease that we ought to endeavor to remove. I am not afraid to tell sinners that are most sensible of their misery, that their case is indeed as miserable as they think it to be, and a thousand times more so; for this is the truth. Some may be ready to say that though it be the truth, yet the truth is not to be spoken at all times, and seems not to be seasonable then: but it seems to me, such truth is never more seasonable than at such a time, when Christ is beginning to open the eyes of conscience. Ministers ought to act as co-workers with him; to take that opportunity, and to the utmost to improve that advantage, and strike while the iron is hot, and when the light has begun to shine, then to remove all obstacles, and use all proper means, that it may come in more fully, and the work be done thoroughly then. And experience abundantly shews, that to take this course is not of an hurtful tendency, but very much the contrary: I have seen, in very many instances, the happy effects of it, and oftentimes a very speedy happy issue, and never knew any ill consequence in case of real conviction, and when distress has been only from thence.

I know of but one case, wherein the truth ought to be withheld from sinners in distress of conscience, and that is the case of melancholy: and 'tis not to be withheld from them then because the truth tends to do 'em hurt, but because if we speak the truth to them, sometimes they will be deceived, and led into error by it, through that strange disposition there is in them to take things wrong. So that that which as it is spoken, is truth, as it is heard and received, and applied by them, is falsehood; as it will be, unless the truth be spoken with abundance of caution and prudence, and consideration of their disposition and circumstances. But the most awful truths of God's Word ought not to be withheld from public congregations, because it may happen that some such melancholic persons may be in it; any more than the Bible is to be withheld from the Christian world because it is manifest that there are a great many melancholic persons in Christendom, that exceedingly abuse the awful things contained in the Scripture, to their own wounding. Nor do I think that to be of weight, which is made use of by some, as a great and dreadful objection against the terrifying preaching that has of late been in New England, viz. that there have been some instances of melancholic persons that have so abused it, that the issue has been the murder of themselves. The objection from hence is no stronger against awakening preaching, that it is against the Bible itself: there are hundreds, and probably thousands of instances, might be produced, of persons that have murdered themselves under religious melancholy. These murders probably never would have been, if it had not been for the Bible, or if the world had remained in a state of heathenish darkness. The Bible has not only been the occasion of these sad effects, but of thousands, and I suppose millions, of other cruel murders that have been committed, in the persecutions that have been raised, that never would have been, if it had not been for the Bible. Many whole countries have been, as it were deluged with innocent blood, which would not have been, if the Gospel never had been preached in the world. 'Tis not a good objection against any kind of preaching, that some men abuse it greatly to their hurt. It has been acknowledged by all divines, as a thing common in all ages, and all Christian countries, that a very great part of those that sit under the Gospel, do so abuse it that it only proves an occasion of their far more aggravated damnation, and so of men's eternally murdering their souls; which is an effect infinitely more terrible than the murder of their bodies. 'Tis as unjust to lay the blame of these self-murders to those ministers who have declared the awful truths of God's Word, in the most lively and affecting manner they were capable of, as it would be to lay the blame of hardening men's hearts, and blinding their eyes, and their more dreadful eternal damnation, to the prophet Isaiah, or Jesus Christ, because this was the consequence of their preaching with respect to many of their hearers. Isa. 6:10; John 9:39; Matt. 13:14. Though a very few have abused the awakening preaching that has lately been, to so sad an effect as to be the cause of their own temporal death; yet it may be, to one such instance there have been hundreds, yea thousands, that have been saved by this means from eternal death.

[3] What has more especially given offense to many, and raised a loud cry against some preachers, as though their conduct were intolerable, is their frighting poor innocent children with talk of hell fire and eternal damnation. But if those that complain so loudly of this really believe what is the general profession of the country, viz. that all are by nature the children of wrath and heirs of hell; and that every one that has not been born again, whether he be young or old, is exposed every moment to eternal destruction, under the wrath of Almighty God; I say, if they really believe this, then such a complaint and cry as this bewrays a great deal of weakness and inconsideration. As innocent as children seem to be to us, yet if they are out of Christ, they are not so in God's sight, but are young vipers, and are infinitely more hateful than vipers, and are in a most miserable condition, as well as grown persons; and they are naturally very senseless and stupid, being "born as the wild ass's colt" [Job 11:12], and need much to awaken them. Why should we conceal the truth from them? Will those children that have been dealt tenderly with in this respect, and lived and died insensible of their misery till they come to feel it in hell, ever thank parents and others for their tenderness, in not letting them know what they were in danger of? If parents' love towards their children was not blind, it would affect 'em much more to see their children every day exposed to eternal burnings, and yet senseless, than to see 'em suffer the distress of that awakening that is necesary in order to their escape from them, and that tends to their being eternally happy as the children of God. A child that has a dangerous wound may need the painful lance as well as grown persons; and that would be a foolish pity, in such a case, that should hold back the lance, and throw away the life. I have seen the happy effects of dealing plainly and thoroughly with children in the concerns of their souls, without sparing them at all, in many instances; and never knew any ill consequence of it, in any one instance.[3]

[4] Another thing that a great deal has been said against, is having so frequent religious meetings, and spending so much time in

3. [See above, pp. 73–74.]

religion. And indeed, there are none of the externals of religion but what are capable of excess: and I believe it is true, that there has not been a due proportion observed in religion of late. We have placed religion too much in the external duties of the First Table; [4] we have abounded in religious meetings and in praying, reading, hearing, singing, and religious conference; and there has not been a proportionable increase of zeal for deeds of charity and other duties of the Second Table (though it must be acknowledged that they are also much increased). But yet it appears to me that this objection of persons' spending too much time in religion, has been in the general groundless. Though worldly business must be done, and persons ought not to neglect the business of their particular callings, yet 'tis to the honor of God that a people should be so much in outward acts of religion, as to carry in it a visible, public appearance of a great engagedness of mind in it, as the main business of life. And especially is it fit, that at such an extraordinary time, when God appears unusually present with a people, in wonderful works of power and mercy, that they should spend more time than usual in religious exercises, to put honor upon that God that is then extraordinarily present, and to seek his face; as it was with the Christian church in Jerusalem, on occasion of that extraordinary pouring out of the Spirit, soon after Christ's ascension. Acts 2:46, "And they continued daily with one accord in the temple, and breaking bread from house to house." And so it was at Ephesus, at a time of great outpouring of the Spirit there; the Christians there attended public religious exercises every day, for two years together, Acts 19:8–10, "And he [Paul] went into the synagogue, and spake boldly for the space of three months, disputing and persuading the things concerning the kingdom of God: but when divers were hardened and believed not, but spake evil of that way before the multitude, he departed from them, and separated the disciples, disputing daily in the school of one Tyrannus; and this continued by the space of two years; so that all they which dwelt in Asia heard the word of the Lord, both Jews and Greeks." And as to the grand objection of "six days shalt thou labor" [Exod. 20:9], all that can be understood by it, and all that the very objectors themselves understand by it, is that we may follow our

4. [I.e., of the Decalogue. The "First Table" adumbrates the first four (or five) commandments, which have to do with specifically religious duties and observances. The "Second Table" enjoins duties to fellow men. The Fifth Commandment, on honor to parents, is sometimes regarded as transitional.]

secular labors in those six days that are not the Sabbath, and ought to be diligent in them: not but that sometimes, we may turn from them, even within those six days, to keep a day of fasting, or thanksgiving, or to attend a lecture; [5] and that more frequently or rarely, as God's providence and the state of things shall call us, according to the best judgment of our discretion.

Though secular business, as I said before, ought not to be neglected, yet I can't see how it can be maintained that religion ought not to be attended so as in the least to injure our temporal affairs, on any other principles than those of infidelity. None objects against injuring one temporal affair for the sake of another temporal affair of much greater importance; and therefore, if eternal things are as real as temporal things, and are indeed of infinitely greater importance; then why may we not voluntarily suffer, in some measure, in our temporal concerns, while we are seeking eternal riches and immortal glory? 'Tis looked upon no way improper for a whole nation to spend considerable time, and much of their outward substance, on some extraordinary temporal occasions, for the sake only of the ceremonies of a public rejoicing; and it would be thought dishonorable to be very exact about what we spend, or careful lest we injure our estates, on such an occasion: and why should we be exact only with Almighty God, so that it should be a crime to be otherwise than scrupulously careful, lest we injure ourselves in our temporal interest, to put honor upon him, and seek our own eternal happiness? We should take heed that none of us be in any wise like Judas, who greatly complained of needless expense and waste of outward substance, to put honor upon Christ, when Mary broke her box and poured the precious ointment on his head: he had indignation within himself on that account, and cried out, "Why was this waste of the ointment made? For it might have been sold for more than three hundred pence, and have been given to the poor." Mark 14:3–5, etc.; and John 12:4–5, etc.

And besides, if the matter be justly considered and examined, I believe it will be found that the country has lost no time from their temporal affairs by the late revival of religion, but have rather gained time; and that more time has been saved from frolicking and tavern-haunting, idleness, unprofitable visits, vain talk, fruitless pas-

5. [The lecture at various times during the week was a traditional device of Puritan instruction; it was adapted by many New England pastors to the purposes of the revival.]

times, and needless diversions, than has lately been spent in extraordinary religion; and probably five times as much has been saved in persons' estates, at the tavern and in their apparel, as has been spent by religious meetings.

The great complaint that is made against so much time spent in religion, can't be in general from a real concern that God may be honored, and his will done, and the best good of men promoted; as is very manifest from this, that now there is a much more earnest and zealous outcry made in the country against this extraordinary religion, than was before against so much time spent in tavern-haunting, vain company-keeping, nightwalking, and other things, which wasted both our time and substance, and injured our moral virtue.

[5] The frequent preaching that has lately been, has in a particular manner been objected against as unprofitable and prejudicial. 'Tis objected that when sermons are heard so very often, one sermon tends to thrust out another; so that persons lose the benefit of all: they say two or three sermons in a week is as much as they can remember and digest. Such objections against frequent preaching, if they ben't from an enmity against religion, are for want of duly considering the way that sermons usually profit an auditory. The main benefit that is obtained by preaching is by impression made upon the mind in the time of it, and not by an effect that arises afterwards by a remembrance of what was delivered. And though an after remembrance of what was heard in a sermon is oftentimes very profitable; yet, for the most part, that remembrance is from an impression the words made on the heart in the time of it; and the memory profits as it renews and increases that impression; and a frequent inculcating [of] the more important things of religion in preaching has no tendency to raze out such impressions, but to increase them, and fix them deeper and deeper in the mind, as is found by experience. It never used to be objected against, that persons upon the Sabbath, after they have heard two sermons that day, should go home and spend the remaining part of the Sabbath in reading the Scriptures and printed sermons; which, in proportion as it has a tendency to affect the mind at all, has as much of a tendency to drive out what they have heard, as if they heard another sermon preached. It seems to have been the practice of the apostles to preach every day, in places where they went; yea, though sometimes they continued long in one place, Acts 2:42 and 46; Acts 19:8–10. They

did not avoid preaching one day, for fear they should thrust out of
the minds of their hearers what they had delivered the day before;
nor did Christians avoid going every day to hear, for fear of any such
bad effect, as is evident by Acts 2:42, 46.

There are some things in Scripture that seem to signify as much,
as that there should be preaching in an extraordinary frequency, at
the time when God should be about to introduce that flourishing
state of religion that should be in the latter days; as that in Isa.
62, at the beginning: "For Zion's sake will I not hold my peace,
[and] for Jerusalem's sake I will not rest, until the righteousness
thereof go forth as brightness, and the salvation thereof as a lamp
that burneth. And the Gentiles shall see thy righteousness, and all
kings thy glory." And vss. 5–6, "For as a young man marrieth a
virgin, so shall thy sons marry thee; and as the bridegroom rejoiceth
over the bride, so shall thy God rejoice over thee. I have set watchmen upon thy walls, O Jerusalem, which shall never hold their peace
day nor night." The destruction of the city of Jericho is evidently,
in all its circumstances, intended by God as a great type of the overthrow of Satan's kingdom; the priests blowing with trumpets at that
time, represents ministers preaching the Gospel; the people compassed the city seven days, the priests blowing the trumpets; but
when the day was come that the walls of the city were to fall, the
priests were more frequent and abundant in blowing their trumpets;
there was as much done in one day then, as had been done in seven
days before; they compassed the city seven times that day, blowing
their trumpets, till at length it came to one long and perpetual blast,
and then the walls of the city fell down flat [Josh. 6:1–20]. The extraordinary preaching that shall be at the beginning of that glorious
jubilee of the church is represented by the extraordinary sounding
of trumpets, throughout the land of Canaan, at the beginning of the
year of jubilee [Lev. 25:8–10]; and by the reading of the law before
all Israel in the year of release [Deut. 31:10–11], [and?] at the Feast of
Tabernacles [Neh. 8]. And the crowing of the cock at break of day,
which brought Peter to repentance, seems to me to be intended to
signify the awakening of God's church out of their lethargy, wherein
they had denied their Lord, by the extraordinary preaching of the
Gospel, that shall be at the dawning of the day of the church's light
and glory [cf. Matt. 26:74–75 and parallels]. And there seems at this
day to be an uncommon hand of divine providence in animating,
enabling, and upholding some ministers, in such abundant labors.

[6] Another thing wherein I think some ministers have been injured, is in being very much blamed for making so much of outcries, faintings, and other bodily effects; speaking of them as tokens of the presence of God, and arguments of the success of preaching; seeming to strive to their utmost to bring a congregation to that pass, and seeming to rejoice in it, yea, even blessing God for it, when they see these effects.

Concerning this I would observe, in the first place, that there are many things with respect to cryings out, falling down, etc., that are charged on ministers, that they are not guilty of. Some would have it, that they speak of these things as certain evidences of a work of the Spirit of God on the hearts of their hearers, or that they esteem these bodily effects themselves to be the work of God, as though the Spirit of God took hold of, and agitated the bodies of men; and some are charged with making these things essential, and supposing that persons can't be converted without them; whereas I never yet could see the person that held either of these things.

But for speaking of such effects as probable tokens of God's presence, and arguments of the success of preaching, it seems to me they are not to be blamed; because I think they are so indeed: and therefore when I see them excited by preaching the important truths of God's Word, urged and enforced by proper arguments and motives, or are consequent on other means that are good, I don't scruple to speak of them, and to rejoice in them, and bless God for them as such; and that for this (as I think) good reason, viz. that from time to time, upon proper inquiry and examination, and observation of the consequence and fruits, I have found that there are all evidences that the persons in whom these effects appear, are under the influences of God's Spirit, in such cases. Cryings out, in such a manner and with such circumstances, as I have seen them from time to time, is as much an evidence to me, of the general cause it proceeds from, as language: I have learned the meaning of it the same way that persons learn the meaning of language, viz. by use and experience. I confess that when I see a great crying out in a congregation, in the manner that I have seen it, when those things are held forth to 'em that are worthy of their being greatly affected by, I rejoice in it, much more than merely in an appearance of solemn attention, and a shew of affection by weeping; and that because there have been those outcries, I have found from time to time a much greater and more excellent effect. To rejoice that the work of God is carried on calmly, without much ado, is in effect to rejoice that 'tis carried on with less power, or that there is not so much of the influence of God's Spirit: for though the degree of the influence of the Spirit of God on particular persons, is by no means to be judged of by the degree of external appearances, because of the different constitution, tempers, and circumstances of men; yet if there be a very powerful influence of the Spirit of God on a mixed multitude, it will cause, some way or other, a great visible commotion.

And as to ministers aiming at such effects, and striving by all means to bring a congregation to that pass, that there should be such an uproar among them; I suppose none aim at it any otherwise than as they strive to raise the affections of their hearers to such an height, as very often appears in these effects; and if it be so, that those affections are commonly good, and it be found by experience that such a degree of them commonly has a good effect, I think they are to be justified in so doing.

[7] Again, some ministers have been blamed for keeping persons together that have been under great affections, which have appeared in such extraordinary outward manifestations. Many think this promotes confusion, that persons in such circumstances do but discompose each other's minds, and disturb the minds of others; and that therefore 'tis best they should be dispersed, and that when any in a congregation are [so] strongly seized that they can't forbear outward manifestations of it, they should be removed, that others' minds may not be diverted.

But I can't but think that those that thus object go upon quite wrong notions of things: for though persons ought to take heed that they don't make an ado without necessity, for this will be the way, in time, to have such appearances lose all their effect; yet the unavoidable manifestations of strong religious affections tend to an happy influence on the minds of bystanders, and are found by experience to have an excellent and durable effect; and so to contrive and order things, that others may have opportunity and advantage to observe them, has been found to be blessed as a great means to promote the work of God; and to prevent their being in the way of observation, is to prevent the effect of that which God makes use of as a principal means of carrying on his work at such an extraordinary time, viz. example; which is often spoken of in

Scripture as one of the chief means by which God would carry on his work, in the time of the prosperity of religion in the latter days.

I have mentioned some texts already to this purpose, in what I published before, of *The Marks of a Work of the True Spirit*; [6] but would here mention some others. In Zech. 9:15–16, those that in the latter days should be filled in an extraordinary manner with the Holy Spirit, so as to appear in outward manifestations and making a noise, are spoken of as those that God, in these uncommon circumstances, will set up to the view of others as a prize or ensign, by their example and the excellency of their attainments, to animate and draw others, as men gather about an ensign, and run for a prize, a crown and precious jewels, set up in their view. The words are: "And they shall drink, and make a noise as through wine; and they shall be filled like bowls, and as the corners of the altar: and the Lord their God shall save them, in that day, as the flock of his people; for they shall be as the stones of a crown, lifted up as an ensign upon his land." (But I shall have occasion to say something more of this Scripture afterwards.[7]) Those that make the objection I am upon, instead of suffering this prize or ensign to be in public view, are for having it removed and hid in some corner. To the like purpose is that, Isa. 62:3, "Thou shalt be a crown of glory in the hand of the Lord, and a royal diadem in the hand of thy God." Here it is observable, that 'tis not said, "Thou shalt be a crown upon the head," but "in the hand of the Lord"—i.e. "held forth, in thy beauty and excellency, as a prize, to be bestowed upon others that shall behold thee, and be animated by the brightness and luster which God shall endow thee with." The great influence of the example of God's people, in their bright and excellent attainments, to propagate religion in those days, is further signified in Isa. 60:3, "And the Gentiles shall come to thy light, and kings to the brightness of thy rising." With vs. 22, "A little one shall become a thousand, and a small one a strong nation." And Zech. 10:8–9, "And they shall increase, as they have increased; and I will sow them among the people." And Hos. 2:23, "And I will sow her unto me in the earth." So Jer. 31:27.

[8] Another thing that gives great disgust to many is the disposition that persons shew, under great affections, to speak so much,

6. [See above, pp. 238–41.]
7. [Below, p. 403.]

and with such earnestness and vehemence, to be setting forth the greatness and wonderfulness and importance of divine and eternal things; and to be so passionately warning, inviting and entreating others.

Concerning which I would say, that I am far from thinking that such a disposition should be wholly without any limits or regulation (as I shall more particularly shew afterwards); [8] and I believe some have erred in setting no bounds, and indulging and encouraging this disposition without any kind of restraint or direction: but yet, it seems to me that such a disposition in general, is what both reason and Scripture will justify. Those that are offended at such things, as though they were unreasonable, are not just: upon examination it will probably be found that they have one rule of reasoning about temporal things, and another about spiritual things. They won't at all wonder, if a person on some very great and affecting occasion of extraordinary danger or great joy, that eminently and immediately concerns him and others, is disposed to speak much, and with great earnestness, especially to those to whom he is united in the bonds of dear affection and great concern for their good. And therefore, if they were just, why would not they allow it in spiritual things? And much more in them, agreeably to the vastly greater importance and more affecting nature of spiritual things, and the concern which true religion causes in men's minds for the good of others, and the disposition it gives and excites to speak God's praises, to shew forth his infinite glory, and talk of all his glorious perfections and works?

That a very great sense, of the right kind, of the importance of the things of religion and the danger sinners are in, should sometimes cause an almost insuperable disposition to speak and warn others, is agreeable to Jer. 6:10–11, "To whom shall I speak, and give warning, that they may hear? Behold, their ear is uncircumcised, and they cannot hearken: behold, the word of the Lord is unto them a reproach; they have no delight in it. Therefore I am full of the fury of the Lord; I am weary with holding in; I will pour it out upon the children abroad, and upon the assembly of the young men together; for even the husband with the wife shall be taken, the aged with him that is full of days." And that true Christians, when they come to be as it were waked out of sleep, and to be filled with a sweet and joyful sense of the excellent things of religion, by the preaching of the Gospel, or by other means of grace, should be

8. [Below, pp. 483–89.]

disposed to be much in speaking of divine things, though before they were dumb, is agreeable to what Christ says to his church, Cant. 7:9, "And the roof of thy mouth is like the best wine for my beloved, that goeth down sweetly, causing the lips of those that are asleep to speak." The roof of the church's mouth is the officers in the church that preach the Gospel; their word is to Christ's beloved like the best wine, that goes down sweetly; extraordinarily refreshing and enlivening the saints, causing them to speak, though before they were mute and asleep.

'Tis said by some that the people that are the subjects of this work, when they get together, talking loud and earnestly, in their pretended great joys, several in a room talking at the same time, make a noise just like a company of drunken persons. On which I would observe, that it is foretold that God's people should do so, in that forementioned place, Zech. 9:15–17, which I shall now take more particular notice of. The words are as follows: "The Lord of hosts shall defend them; and they shall devour and subdue with sling stones; and they shall drink, and make a noise as through wine, and they shall be filled like bowls, and as the corners of the altar. And the Lord their God shall save them in that day, as the flock of his people; for they shall be as the stones of a crown, lifted up as an ensign upon his land. For how great is his goodness, and how great is his beauty! Corn shall make the young men cheerful, and new wine the maids." The words are very remarkable: here it is foretold, that at the time when Christ shall set up an universal kingdom upon earth (vs. 20), the children of Zion shall drink till they are filled like the vessels of the sanctuary: and if we would know what they shall be thus filled with, the prophecy does, in effect, explain itself: they shall be filled as the vessels of the sanctuary that contained the drink offering, which was wine; and yet the words imply that it shall not literally be wine that they shall drink, and be filled with, because it is said, "They shall drink, and make a noise, *as through wine*," as if they had drank wine: which implies that they had not literally done it; and therefore we must understand the words [as meaning] that they shall drink into that, and be filled with that, which the wine of the drink offering represented, or was a type of, which is the Holy Spirit, as well as the blood of Christ, that new wine that is drank in our heavenly Father's kingdom. They shall be filled with the Spirit, which the Apostle sets in opposition to a being drunk with wine, Eph. 5:18. This is the new wine spoken of, vs. 17 [of Zech. 9]. 'Tis the same with that best wine, spoken of in Canticles [7:9], "that goes down sweetly, causing the lips of those that are asleep to speak." 'Tis here foretold that the children of Zion, in the latter days, should be filled with that which should make 'em cheerful, and cause 'em to make a noise as through wine, and by which these joyful happy persons that are thus filled, shall be "as the stones of a crown, lifted up as an ensign upon God's land," being made joyful in the extraordinary manifestations of the beauty and love of Christ: as it follows, "How great is his goodness! And how great is his beauty!" And 'tis further remarkable that 'tis here foretold, that it should be thus especially amongst young people; "Corn shall make the young men cheerful, and new wine the maids." It would be ridiculous to understand this of literal bread and wine: without doubt, the same spiritual blessings are signified by bread and wine here, which were represented by Melchizedek's bread and wine [Gen. 14:18], and are signified by the bread and wine in the Lord's Supper. One of the marginal readings is, "shall make the young men to speak"; which is agreeable to that in Canticles, of the best wine's causing the lips of those that are asleep to speak.

We ought not to be, in any measure, like the unbelieving Jews in Christ's time, who were disgusted both with crying out with distress and with joy. When the poor blind man cried out before all the multitude, "Jesus, thou Son of David, have mercy on me!" and continued instantly thus doing, the multitude rebuked him, and charged him that he should hold his tongue, Mark 10:46–48 and Luke 18:38–39. They looked upon it to be a very indecent noise that he made; a thing very ill becoming him to cause his voice to be heard, so much and so loud, among the multitude. And when Christ made his solemn and triumphant entry into Jerusalem (which, I have before observed, was a type of the glory and triumph of the latter days), the whole multitude of the disciples, of all sorts, especially young people, began to rejoice and praise God, with a loud voice, for all the mighty works that they had seen, saying, "Blessed be the king that cometh in the name of the Lord! Peace in heaven, and glory in the highest!" The Pharisees said to Christ, "Master, rebuke thy disciples." They did not understand such great transports of joy; it seemed to them a very unsuitable and indecent noise and clamor that they made, a confused uproar, many crying out together, as though they were out of their wits; they wondered that Christ would tolerate it. But what says Christ? "I tell you, that if these should hold their peace, the stones would immediately cry out" [Luke 19:37–40]. The words seem to intimate as much, as that there was cause enough to constrain those whose hearts were not harder than the very stones, to cry out and make a noise; which is something like that other expression, of causing the lips of those that are asleep to speak.

When many under great religious affections are earnestly speaking together of divine wonders, in various parts of a company, to those that are next to 'em; some attending to what one says, and others to another, there is something very beautiful in it, provided they don't speak so many as to drown each other's voices, that none can hear what any say; there is a greater and more affecting appearance of a joint engagedness of heart, in the love and praises of God. And I had rather see it than to see one speaking alone, and all attending to what he says; it has more of the appearance of conversation. When a multitude meets on any occasion of temporal rejoicing, freely and cheerfully to converse together, they ben't wont to observe the ceremony of but one speaking at a time, while all the rest, in a formal manner, set themselves to attend to what he says; that would spoil all conversation, and turn it into the formality of set speeches, and the solemnity of preaching. It is better for lay persons, when they speak one to another of the things of God, when they meet together, to speak after the manner of Christian conversation, than to observe the formality of but one speaking at a time, the whole multitude silently and solemnly attending to what he says; which would carry in it too much of the air, of the authority and solemnity of preaching. What the Apostle says, I Cor. 14:29–31, "Let the prophets speak, two, or three, and let the other judge: if anything be revealed to another that sitteth by, let the first hold his peace: for ye may all prophesy, one by one, that all may learn, and all may be comforted"; I say, this don't reach this case; because what the Apostle is speaking of, is the solemnity of their religious exercises in public worship, and persons speaking in the church by immediate inspiration, and in the use of the gift of prophecy, or some gift of inspiration, in the exercise of which they acted as extraordinary ministers of Christ.

[9] Another thing that some have found fault with, is abounding so much in singing in religious meetings. Objecting against such a thing as this seems to arise from a suspicion already established of this work: they doubt of the pretended extraordinary love and

joys that attend this work, and so find fault with the manifestations of them. If they thought persons were truly the subjects of an extraordinary degree of divine love, and heavenly rejoicing in God, I suppose they would not wonder at their having a disposition to be much in praise. They won't object against the saints and angels in heaven singing praises and hallelujahs to God, without ceasing day or night; and therefore doubtless will allow that the more the saints on earth are like 'em in their dispositions, the more they will be disposed to do like 'em. They will readily own that the generality of Christians have great reason to be ashamed that they have so little thankfulness, and are no more in praising God, whom they have such infinite cause to praise. And why therefore, should Christians be found fault with for shewing a disposition to be much in praising God, and manifesting a delight in that heavenly exercise? To complain of this is to be too much like the Pharisees, who were disgusted when the multitude of the disciples began to rejoice, and with loud voices to praise God, and cry "Hosanna!" when Christ was entering into Jerusalem.

There are many things in Scripture, that seem to intimate that praising God, both in speeches and songs, will be what the church of God will very much abound in, in the approaching glorious day. So on the seventh day of compassing the walls of Jericho, when the priests blew with the trumpets in an extraordinary manner, the people shouted with a great shout, and the wall of the city fell down flat [Josh. 6:20]. So the ark was brought back from its banishment, with extraordinary shouting and singing of the whole congregation of Israel [II Sam. 6:15]. And the places in the prophecies of Scripture, that signify that the church of God, in that glorious jubilee that is foretold, shall greatly abound in singing and shouting forth the praises of God, are too many to be mentioned. And there will be cause enough for it: I believe it will be a time wherein both heaven and earth, will be much more full of joy and praise than ever they were before.

But what is more especially found fault with in the singing that is now practiced, is making use of hymns of human composure.[9] And I am far from thinking that the Book of Psalms should be thrown by in our public worship, but that it should always be used in the

9. [JE's congregation had begun using Isaac Watts' hymns a few months earlier. See his letter, dated May 22, 1744, to Benjamin Colman; in *PMHS*, 2d ser., *10* (1896), 429.]

Christian church, to the end of the world: but I know of no obligation we are under to confine ourselves to it. I can find no command or rule of God's Word, that does any more confine us to the words of the Scripture in our singing, than it does in our praying; we speak to God in both: and I can see no reason why we should limit ourselves to such particular forms of words that we find in the Bible, in speaking to him by way of praise, in meter, and with music, than when we speak to him in prose, by way of prayer and supplication. And 'tis really needful that we should have some other songs besides the Psalms of David: 'tis unreasonable to suppose that the Christian church should forever, and even in times of her greatest light in her praises of God and the Lamb, be confined only to the words of the Old Testament, wherein all the greatest and most glorious things of the Gospel, that are infinitely the greatest subjects of her praise, are spoken of under a veil, and not so much as the name of our glorious Redeemer ever mentioned, but in some dark figure, or as hid under the name of some type. And as to our making use of the words of others, and not those that are conceived by ourselves, 'tis no more than we do in all our public prayers; the whole worshipping assembly, excepting one only, makes use of the words that are conceived by him that speaks for the rest.

[10] Another thing that many have disliked, is the religious meetings of children, to read and pray together, and perform religious exercises by themselves. What is objected is children's want of that knowledge and discretion that is requisite, in order to a decent and profitable management of religious exercises. But it appears to me the objection is not sufficient: children, as they have the nature of men, are inclined to society; and those of them that are capable of society one with another, are capable of the influences of the Spirit of God in its active fruits; and if they are inclined by a religious disposition, that they have from the Spirit of God, to improve their society one with another, in a religious manner and to religious purposes, who should forbid them? If they han't discretion to observe method in their religious performances, or to speak sense in all that they say in prayer, they may nothwithstanding have a good meaning, and God understands 'em, and it don't spoil or interrupt their devotion one with another. We that are grown persons, have defects in our prayers that are a thousand times worse in the sight of God, and are a greater confusion, and more absurd nonsense

in his eyes, than their childish indiscretions. There is not so much difference, before God, between children and grown persons as we are ready to imagine; we are all poor, ignorant foolish babes in his sight: our adult age don't bring us so much nearer to God as we are apt to think. God in this work has shewn a remarkable regard to little children; never was there such a glorious work amongst persons in their childhood, as has been of late in New England. He has been pleased in a wonderful manner to perfect praise out of the mouths of babes and sucklings [Matt. 21:16]; and many of them have more of that knowledge and wisdom, that pleases him and renders their religious worship acceptable, than many of the great and learned men of the world: 'tis they, in the sight of God, are the ignorant and foolish children. These [little ones] are grown men, and an hundred years old, in comparison with them; and 'tis to be hoped that the days are coming, prophesied of [in] Isa. 65:20, when "the child shall die an hundred years old."

I have seen many happy effects of children's religious meetings; and God has seemed often remarkably to own them in their meetings, and really descended from heaven to be amongst them: I have known several probable instances of children's being converted at such meetings. I should therefore think, that if children appear to be really moved to it, by a religious disposition, and not merely from a childish affectation of imitating grown persons, they ought by no means to be discouraged or discountenanced: but yet 'tis fit that care should be taken of them, by their parents and pastors, to instruct and direct them, and to correct imprudent conduct and irregularities, if they are perceived; or anything by which the Devil may pervert and destroy the design of their meetings. All should take heed that they don't find fault with, and despise the religion of children, from an evil principle, lest they should be like the chief priests and scribes, who were sore displeased at the religious worship and praises of little children, and the honor they gave Christ in the temple. We have an account of it, and of what Christ said upon it, in Matt. 21:15–16, "And when the chief priests and scribes saw the wonderful things that he did, and the children crying in the temple, and saying, Hosanna to the Son of David, they were sore displeased, and said unto him, Hearest thou what these say? And Jesus saith unto them, Yea, have ye never read, Out of the mouths of babes and sucklings, thou hast perfected praise?"

PART IV

HAVING thus observed, in some instances, wherein the conduct of those that have appeared to be the subjects of this work, or have been zealous to promote it, has been objected against or complained of, without or beyond just cause, I proceed now in the second place [1] to shew what things ought to be corrected or avoided.

Many that are zealous for this glorious work of God are heartily sick of the great noise there is in the country about imprudences and disorders; they have heard it so often from the mouths of opposers that they are prejudiced against the sound; and they look upon it that that which is called a being prudent and regular, which is so much insisted on, is no other than being asleep, or cold and dead in religion, and that the great imprudence that is so much cried out of, is only a being alive, and engaged in the things of God: and they are therefore rather confirmed in any practice, than brought off from it, by the clamor they hear against it, as imprudent and irregular. And to tell the truth, the cry of irregularity and imprudence has been much more in the mouths of those that have been enemies to the main of the work than others; for they have watched for the halting of the zealous, and eagerly catched at anything that has been wrong, and have greatly insisted on it, made the most of it, and magnified it; especially have they watched for errors in zealous preachers, that are much in reproving and condemning the wickedness of the times. They would therefore do well to consider that Scripture, Isa. 29:20–21, "The scorner is consumed, and all that watch for iniquity are cut off, that make a man an offender for a word, and lay a snare for him that reproveth in the gate, and turn aside the just for a thing of nought." They han't only too much insisted on, and magnified real errors, but have very injuriously charged them

1. [This enumeration began at p. 385, above.]

as guilty, in things wherein they have been innocent, and have done their duty. This has so prejudiced the minds of some, that they have been ready to think that all that has been said about errors and imprudences, was injurious and from an ill spirit; and has confirmed them in it, that there is no such thing as any prevailing imprudences; and it has made 'em less cautious and suspicious of themselves, lest they should err. Herein the Devil has had an advantage put into his hands, and has taken the advantage; and doubtless has been too subtile for some of the true friends of religion. That would be a strange thing indeed, if in so great a commotion and revolution, and such a new state of things, wherein so many have been engaged, none have been guilty of any imprudence; it would be such a revival of religion as never was yet, if among so many men, not guided by infallible inspiration, there had not been prevailing a pretty many notable errors in judgment and conduct; our young preachers and young converts must in general vastly exceed Luther, the head of the Reformation, who was guilty of a great many excesses, in that great affair in which God made him the chief instrument.

If we look back into the history of the church of God in past ages, we may observe that it has been a common device of the Devil to overset a revival of religion, when he finds he can keep men quiet and secure no longer, then to drive 'em to excesses and extravagances. He holds them back as long as he can, but when he can do it no longer, then he'll push 'em on, and if possible, run 'em upon their heads. And it has been by this means chiefly, that he has been successful, in several instances, to overthrow most hopeful and promising beginnings: yea, the principal means by which the Devil was successful, by degrees, to overset that grand religious revival of the world that was in the primitive ages of Christianity, and in a manner to overthrow the Christian church through the earth, and to make way for and bring on the great antichristian apostasy, that masterpiece of all the Devil's works, was to improve the indiscreet zeal of Christians, to drive them into those three extremes of enthusiasm, superstition, and severity towards opposers; which should be enough for an everlasting warning to the Christian church.

Though the Devil will do his diligence to stir up the open enemies of religion, yet he knows what is for his interest so well, that in a time of revival of religion, his main strength shall be tried with the friends of it, and he'll chiefly exert himself in his attempts upon them, to mislead them. One truly zealous person, in the time of such an event, that seems to have a great hand in the affair, and draws the eyes of many upon him, may do more (through Satan's being too subtle for him) to hinder the work, than an hundred great, and strong, and open opposers.

In the time of a great work of Christ, his hands, with which he works, are often wounded in the house of his friends; and his work hindered chiefly by them: so that if anyone inquires, as in Zech. 13:6, "What are those wounds in thine hands?" he may answer, "Those with which I was wounded in the house of my friends."

The errors of the friends of the work of God, and especially of the great promoters of it, give vast advantage to the enemies of such a work. Indeed, there are many things that are no errors, but are only duties faithfully and thoroughly done, that wound the minds of such persons more, and are more cross to 'em, than real errors: but yet one real error gives opposers as much advantage, and hinders and clogs the work, as much as ten that are only supposed ones. Real errors don't fret and gall the enemies of religion, so much as those things that are strictly right; but they encourage 'em more; they give 'em liberty, and open a gap for 'em; so that some that before kept their enmity burning in their own bowels, and durst not show themselves, will on such an occasion take courage, and give themselves vent, and their rage will be like that of an enemy let loose; and those that lay still before, having nothing to say but what they would be ashamed of (agreeable to Tit. 2:8), when they have such a weapon put into their hands, will fight with all violence. And indeed, the enemies of religion would not know what to do for weapons to fight with, were it not for the errors of the friends of it; and so must soon fall before them. And besides, in real errors, things that are truly disagreeable to the rules of God's Word, we can't expect the divine protection, and that God will appear on our side, as if our errors were only supposed ones.

Since therefore the errors of the friends and promoters of such a glorious work of God, are of such dreadful consequence; and seeing the Devil, being sensible of this, is so assiduous, and watchful and subtle in his attempts with them, and has thereby been so successful to overthrow religion heretofore, certainly such persons ought to be exceeding circumspect and vigilant, diffident and jealous of themselves, and humbly dependent on the guidance of the good Shepherd. I Pet. 4:7, "Be sober, and watch unto prayer." And chap. 5:8,

"Be sober, be vigilant; because your adversary the Devil, as a roaring lion, walketh about." For persons to go on resolutely, in a kind of heat and vehemence, despising admonition and correction, being confident that they must be in the right, because they are full of the Spirit, is directly contrary to the import of these words, "Be sober, be vigilant."

'Tis a mistake I have observed in some, by which they have been greatly exposed, to their wounding, that they think they are in no danger of going astray, or being misled by the Devil, because they are near to God; and so have no jealous eye upon themselves, and neglect vigilance and circumspection, as needless in their case. They say, they don't think that God will leave them to dishonor him, and wound religion, as long as they keep near to him: and I believe so too, as long as they keep near to God in that respect, that they maintain an universal and diligent watch, and care to do their duty, and avoid sin and snares, with diffidence in themselves and humble dependence and prayerfulness: but not merely because they are near to God, in that respect that they now are receiving blessed communications from God, in refreshing views of him; if at the same time they let down their watch, and are not jealous over their own hearts, by reason of its remaining blindness and corruption, and a subtile adversary. 'Tis a grand error for persons to think they are out of danger of the Devil, and a corrupt, deceitful heart, even in their highest flights, and most raised frames of spiritual joy. For persons in such a confidence, to cease to be jealous of themselves, and to neglect watchfulness and care, is a presumption by which I have known many woefully ensnared. However highly we may be favored with divine discoveries and comforts, yet as long as we are in the world, we are in the enemy's country; and therefore that direction of Christ to his disciples is never out of date in this world, Luke 21:36, "Watch and pray always, that ye may be accounted worthy to escape all these things [. . .] and to stand before the Son of Man." It was not out of date with the disciples, to whom it was given, after they came to be filled so full of the Holy Ghost, and out of their bellies flowed rivers of living water [John 7:38], by that great effusion of the Spirit upon them, that began on the Day of Pentecost. And though God stands ready to protect his people, especially those that are near to him, yet he expects great care and labor of all; and that we should put on the whole armor of God, that we may stand in the evil day [Eph. 6:13]: and whatever spiritual privileges we are raised to, we have no warrant to expect protection in any other way; for God has appointed this whole life as a state of labor, to be all as a race or a battle; the state of rest, wherein we shall be so out of danger as to have no need of watching and fighting, is reserved for another world. I have known it in abundance of instances, that the Devil has come in very remarkably, even in the midst of the most exalted, and upon some accounts excellent, frames: it may seem a great mystery that it should be so; but 'tis no greater mystery, than that Christ should be taken captive by the Devil, and carried into the wilderness, immediately after the heavens had been opened to him, and the Holy Ghost descended like a dove upon him, and he heard that comfortable, joyful voice from the Father, saying, "This is my beloved Son, in whom I am well pleased." [2] In like manner Christ in the heart of a Christian, is oftentimes as it were taken by the Devil, and carried captive into a wilderness, presently after heaven has been, as it were opened to the soul, and the Holy Ghost has descended upon it like a dove, and God has been sweetly owning the believer, and testifying his favor to him as his beloved child.

'Tis therefore a great error, and sin in some persons, at this day, that they are fixed in their way in some things that others account errors, and won't hearken to admonition and counsel, but are confident that they are in the right of it, in those practices that they find themselves disposed to, because God is much with them and they have great degrees of the Spirit of God. There were some such in the apostles' days: the Apostle Paul, writing to the Corinthians, was sensible that some of them would not be easily convinced that they had been in any error, because they looked upon themselves [as] spiritual, or full of the Spirit of God. I Cor. 14:37–38, "If any man think himself to be a prophet, or spiritual, let him acknowledge that the things that I write unto you, are the commandment of the Lord; but if any man be ignorant, let him be ignorant."

And although those that are spiritual amongst us have no infallible apostle to admonish them, yet let me entreat them, by the love of Christ, calmly and impartially to weigh what may be said to them, by one that is their hearty and fervent friend (though an in-

2. [Matt. 3:13 ff. and parallels. JE is mistaken in asserting that Satan captured Jesus and carried him into the wilderness. All three Synoptic Gospels credit the withdrawal to the leading of God's Spirit, Mark even saying (1:12) that the Spirit "drove" him into the wilderness.]

ferior worm) in giving his humble opinion concerning the errors that have been committed, or that we may be exposed to, in methods or practices that have been, or may be fallen into, by the zealous friends or promoters of this great work of God.

In speaking of the errors that have been, or that we are in danger of, I would in the

First place, take notice of the causes whence the errors that attend a great revival of religion usually arise; and as I go along, take notice of some particular errors that arise from each of those causes.

Secondly, observe some errors, that some have lately gone into, that have been owing to the influence of several of those causes conjunctly.

[*Causes of Errors*]

As to the first of these, the errors that attend a great revival of religion usually arise from these three things: 1. Undiscerned spiritual pride. 2. Wrong principles. 3. Ignorance of Satan's advantages and devices.

[1] The first, and the worst cause of errors that prevail in such a state of things, is spiritual pride. This is the main door, by which the Devil comes into the hearts of those that are zealous for the advancement of religion. 'Tis the chief inlet of smoke from the bottomless pit, to darken the mind, and mislead the judgment: this is the main handle by which the Devil has hold of religious persons, and the chief source of all the mischief that he introduces, to clog and hinder a work of God. This cause of error is the mainspring, or at least the main support of all the rest. Till this disease is cured, medicines are in vain applied to heal other diseases. 'Tis by this that the mind defends itself in other errors, and guards itself against light by which it might be corrected and reclaimed. The spiritually proud man is full of light already; he don't need instruction, and is ready to despise the offer of it. But if this disease be healed, other things are easily rectified. The humble person is like a little child; he easily receives instruction; he is jealous over himself, sensible how liable he is to go astray; and therefore if it be suggested to him that he does so, he is ready most narrowly and impartially to inquire. Nothing sets a person so much out of the Devil's reach as humility, and so prepares the mind for true divine light, without darkness, and so clears the eye to look on things as they

truly are. Ps. 25:9, "The meek will he guide in judgment, and the meek he will teach his way." Therefore we should fight neither with small nor with great, but with the king of Israel [II Chron. 18:30]: our first care should be to rectify the heart, and pull the beam out of our eye, and then we shall see clearly [Matt. 7:5].

I know that a great many things at this day are very injuriously laid to the pride of those that are zealous in the cause of God. When any person appears, in any respect, remarkably distinguished in religion from others, if he professes those spiritual comforts and joys that are greater than ordinary, or if he appears distinguishingly zealous in religion, if he exerts himself more than others do in the cause of religion, or if he seems to be distinguished with success, ten to one but it will immediately awaken the jealousy of those that are about him; and they'll suspect (whether they have cause or no) that he is very proud of his goodness, and that he affects to have it thought that nobody is so good as he; and all his talk is heard, and all his behavior beheld, with this prejudice. Those that are themselves cold and dead, and especially such as never had any experience of the power of godliness on their own hearts, are ready to entertain such thoughts of the best Christians; which arises from a secret enmity against vital and fervent piety.

But then those that are zealous Christians should take heed that this injuriousness of those that are cold in religion, don't prove a snare to them, and the Devil don't take advantage from it, to blind their eyes from beholding what there is indeed of this nature in their hearts, and make 'em think, because they are charged with pride wrongfully, and from an ill spirit, in many things, that therefore it is so in everything. Alas, how much pride have the best of us in our hearts! 'Tis the worst part of the body of sin and death: 'tis the first sin that ever entered into the universe, and the last that is rooted out; 'tis God's most stubborn enemy!

The corruption of nature may all be resolved into two things, pride and worldly-mindedness, the Devil and the beast, or self and the world. These are the two pillars of Dagon's temple, on which the whole house leans.[3] But the former of these is every way the worst part of the corruption of nature; 'tis the first-born son of the Devil, and his image in the heart of man chiefly consists in it; 'tis the last thing in a sinner that is overborne by conviction, in order to

3. [Dagon was the tribal deity of the Philistines, with temples at Gaza and Ashdod. Cf. Judg. 16:21, 23; I Sam. 5:1–7.]

conversion; and here is the saint's hardest conflict: 'tis the last thing that he obtains a good degree of conquest over, and liberty from; 'tis that which most directly militates against God, and is most contrary to the Spirit of the Lamb of God; and 'tis most like the Devil its father, in a serpentine deceitfulness and secrecy; it lies deepest, and is most active, is most ready secretly to mix itself with everything.

And of all kinds of pride, spiritual pride is upon many accounts the most hateful; 'tis most like the Devil; 'tis most like the sin that he committed in an heaven of light and glory, where he was exalted high in divine knowledge, honor, beauty and happiness.[4] Pride is much more difficultly discerned than any other corruption, for that reason that the nature of it does very much consist in a person's having too high a thought of himself: but no wonder that he that has too high a thought of himself don't know it; for he necessarily thinks that the opinion he has of himself is what he has just grounds for, and therefore not too high; if he thought such an opinion of himself was without just grounds, he would therein cease to have it. But of all kinds of pride, spiritual pride is the most hidden and difficultly discovered; and that for this reason, because those that are spiritually proud, their pride consists much in an high conceit of those two things, viz. their light and their humility; both which are a strong prejudice against a discovery of their pride. Being proud of their light, that makes 'em not jealous of themselves; he that thinks a clear light shines around him is not suspicious of an enemy lurking near him, unseen: and then being proud of their humility, that makes 'em least of all jealous of themselves in that particular, viz. as being under the prevalence of pride. There are many sins of the heart that are very secret in their nature, and difficultly discerned. The Psalmist says, Ps. 19:12, "Who can understand his errors? Cleanse thou me from secret faults." But spiritual pride is the most secret of all sins. The heart is so deceitful and unsearchable in nothing in the world, as it is in this matter, and there is no sin in the world, that men are so confident in, and so difficultly convinced of: the very nature of it is to work self-confidence, and drive away self-diffidence, and jealousy of any evil of that kind. There is no sin so much like the Devil as this, for secrecy and subtlety, and appearing in a great many shapes, undiscerned and unsuspected, and appearing as an

4. [An ancient tradition, allusions to which some have seen in such Scriptures as Job 1:6; Rev. 12:9; I Tim. 3:6; Jude 6.]

angel of light: it takes occasion to arise from everything; it perverts and abuses everything, and even the exercises of real grace and real humility, as an occasion to exert itself. It is a sin that has, as it were, many lives; if you kill it, it will live still; if you mortify and suppress it in one shape, it rises in another; if you think it is all gone, yet it is there still. There are a great many kinds of it, that lie in different forms and shapes, one under another, and encompass the heart like the coats of an onion; if you pull off one there is another underneath. We had need therefore to have the greatest watch imaginable, over our hearts, with respect to this matter, and to cry most earnestly to the great Searcher of hearts, for his help. "He that trusts his own heart is a fool" [Prov. 28:26].

God's own people should be the more jealous of themselves, with respect to this particular, at this day, because the temptations that many have to this sin are exceeding great: the great and distinguishing privileges to which God admits many of his saints, and the high honors that he puts on some ministers, are great trials of persons in this respect. 'Tis true that great degrees of the spiritual presence of God tends greatly to mortify pride and all corruption; but yet, though in the experience of such favors there be much to restrain pride one way, there is much to tempt and provoke it another; and we shall be in great danger thereby without great watchfulness and prayerfulness. There was much in the circumstances that the angels that fell, were in, in heaven, in their great honors and high privileges, in beholding the face of God, and view of his infinite glory, to cause in them exercises of humility, and to keep 'em from pride; yet through want of watchfulness in them, their great honor and heavenly privilege proved to be to them an undoing temptation to pride, though they had no principle of pride in their hearts to expose 'em. Let no saint therefore, however eminent, and however near to God, think himself out of danger of this: he that thinks himself most out of danger, is indeed most in danger. The Apostle Paul, who doubtless was as eminent a saint as any are now, was not out of danger, even just after he was admitted to see God in the third heavens, by the information he himself gives us, II Cor. 12th chap. And yet doubtless what he saw in heaven of the ineffable glory of the divine Being, had a direct tendency to make him appear exceeding little and vile in his own eyes.

Spiritual pride in its own nature is so secret, that it is not so well discerned by immediate intuition on the thing itself, as by the effects and fruits of it; some of which I would mention, together with the contrary fruits of pure Christian humility.

Spiritual pride disposes to speak of other persons' sins, their enmity against God and his people, the miserable delusion of hypocrites and their enmity against vital piety, and the deadness of some saints, with bitterness, or with laughter and levity, and an air of contempt; whereas pure Christian humility rather disposes either to be silent about 'em, or to speak of them with grief and pity.

Spiritual pride is very apt to suspect others; whereas an humble saint is most jealous of himself, he is so suspicious of nothing in the world as he is of his own heart. The spiritually proud person is apt to find fault with other saints, that they are low in grace, and to be much in observing how cold and dead they be, and crying out of them for it, and to be quick to discern and take notice of their deficiencies: but the eminently humble Christian has so much to do at home, and sees so much evil in his own heart, and is so concerned about it, that he is not apt to be very busy with others' hearts; he complains most of himself, and cries out of his own coldness and lowness in grace, and is apt to esteem others better than himself, and is ready to hope that there is nobody but what has more love and thankfulness to God than he, and can't bear to think that others should bring forth no more fruit to God's honor than he. Some that have spiritual pride mixed with high discoveries and great transports of joy, that dispose 'em in an earnest manner to talk to others, are apt, in such frames, to be calling upon other Christians that are about them, and sharply reproving them for their being so cold and lifeless. And there are some others that behave themselves very differently from these, who in their raptures are overwhelmed with a sense of their own vileness; and when they have extraordinary discoveries of God's glory, are all taken up about their own sinfulness; and though they also are disposed to speak much and very earnestly, yet it is very much in crying out of themselves, and exhorting fellow Christians, but in a charitable and humble manner. Pure Christian humility disposes a person to take notice of everything that is in any respect good in others, and to make the best of it, and to diminish their failings; but to have his eye chiefly on those things that are bad in himself, and to take much notice of everything that aggravates them.

In a contrariety to this, it has been the manner in some places, or at least the manner of some persons, to speak of almost everything that they see amiss in others in the most harsh, severe and terrible language. 'Tis frequent with them to say of others' opinions or conduct or advice, or of their coldness, their silence, their caution, their moderation, and their prudence, and many other things that appear in them, that they are from the Devil, or from hell; that such a thing is devilish or hellish or cursed, and that such persons are serving the Devil, or the Devil is in them, that they are soul-murderers and the like; so that the words "Devil" and "hell" are almost continually in their mouths. And such kind of language they will commonly use, not only towards wicked men, but towards them that they themselves allow to be the true children of God, and also towards ministers of the Gospel and others that are very much their superiors. And they look upon it a virtue and high attainment thus to behave themselves. "Oh," say they, "we must be plain-hearted and bold for Christ, we must declare war against sin wherever we see it, we must not mince the matter in the cause of God and when speaking for Christ." And to make any distinction in persons, or to speak the more tenderly because that which is amiss is seen in a superior, they look upon as very mean for a follower of Christ when speaking in the cause of his Master.

What a strange device of the Devil is here, to overthrow all Christian meekness and gentleness, and even all shew and appearance of it, and to defile the mouths of the children of God, and to introduce the language of common sailors among the followers of Christ, under a cloak of high sanctity and zeal and boldness for Christ! And it is a remarkable instance of the weakness of the human mind, and how much too cunning the Devil is for us!

The grand defense of this way of talking is, that they say no more than what is true; they only speak the truth without mincing the matter; and that true Christians that have a great sight of the evil of sin, and acquaintance with their own hearts know it to be true, and therefore won't be offended to hear such harsh expressions made use of concerning them and their sins; 'tis only (say they) hypocrites, or cold and dead Christians, that are provoked and feel their enmity rise on such an occasion.

But 'tis a grand mistake to think that we may commonly use concerning one another all such language as represents the worst of each other, according to strict truth. 'Tis really true, that every kind of sin, and every degree of it, is devilish and from hell, and is cursed, hellish, and condemned or damned: and if persons had a full sight of their hearts they would think no terms too bad for them; they would look like beasts, like serpents and like devils to themselves; they would be at a loss for language to express what they see in themselves, the worst terms they could think of would seem as it were faint to represent what they see in themselves. But shall a child therefore, from time to time, use such language concerning an excellent and eminently holy father or mother, as that the Devil is in them, that they have such and such devilish, cursed dispositions, that they commit every day hundreds of hellish, damned acts, and that they are cursed dogs, hellhounds and devils? And shall the meanest of the people be justified in commonly using such language concerning the most excellent magistrates, or their most eminent ministers? I hope nobody has gone to this height: but the same pretenses of boldness, plain-heartedness, and declared war against sin, will as well justify these things as the things they are actually made use of to justify. If we proceed in such a manner, on such principles as these, what a face will be introduced upon the church of Christ, the little beloved flock of that gentle Shepherd, the Lamb of God? What a sound shall we bring into the house of God, into the family of his dear little children? How far off shall we soon banish that lovely appearance of humility, sweetness, gentleness, mutual honor, benevolence, complacence, and an esteem of others above themselves, which ought to clothe the children of God all over? Not but that Christians should watch over one another, and in any wise reprove one another, and be much in it, and do it plainly and faithfully; but it don't thence follow that dear brethren in the family of God, in rebuking one another, should use worse language than Michael the archangel durst use when rebuking the Devil himself [Jude 9].

Christians that are but fellow worms ought at least to treat one another with as much humility and gentleness as Christ that is infinitely above them treats them. But how did Christ treat his disciples when they were so cold towards him and so regardless of him, at the time when his soul was exceeding sorrowful even unto death, and he in a dismal agony was crying and sweating blood for them, and they would not watch with him and allow him the comfort of their company one hour in his great distress, though he once and again desired it of them? One would think that then was a proper time if ever to have reproved 'em for a devilish, hellish cursed and damned slothfulness and deadness. But after what manner does Christ reprove them? Behold his astonishing gentleness! Says he, "What, could ye not watch with me one hour? The spirit indeed is willing, but the flesh is weak" [Matt. 26:36–41]. And how did he treat Peter when he was ashamed of his Master, while he was made a mockingstock and a spittingstock for him? Why, he looked upon him with a look of love, and melted his heart [Luke 22:61].

And though we read that Christ once turned and said unto Peter, on a certain occasion, "Get thee behind me, Satan" [Matt. 16:23], and this may seem like an instance of harshness and severity in reproving Peter; yet I humbly conceive that this is by many taken wrong, and that this is indeed no instance of Christ's severity in his treatment of Peter, but on the contrary, of his wonderful gentleness and grace, distinguishing between Peter and the Devil in him, not laying the blame of what Peter had then said, or imputing it to him, but to the Devil that influenced him. Christ saw the Devil then present, secretly influencing Peter to do the part of a tempter to his Master; and therefore Christ turned him about to Peter, in whom the Devil then was, and spake to the Devil, and rebuked him. Thus the grace of Christ don't behold iniquity in his people [and] imputes not what is amiss in 'em to them, but to sin that dwells in them, and to Satan that influences them.

But to return—

Spiritual pride often disposes persons to singularity in external appearance, to affect a singuar way of speaking, to use a different sort of dialect from others, or to be singular in voice, or air of countenance or behavior: but he that is an eminently humble Christian, though he will be firm to his duty, however singular he is in it; he'll go in the way that leads to heaven alone, all the world forsakes him; yet he delights not in singularity for singularity's sake, he don't affect to set up himself to be viewed and observed as one distinguished, as desiring to be accounted better than others, or despising their company, or an union and conformity to them; but on the contrary is disposed to become "all things to all men" [I Cor. 9:22], and to yield to others, and conform to them and please 'em, in everything but sin. Spiritual pride commonly occasions a certain stiffness and inflexibility in persons, in their own judgment and their own ways; whereas the eminently humble person, though he be inflexible in his duty, and in those things wherein God's honor is concerned; and with regard to temptation to those things he apprehends to be sinful, though in never so small a degree, he is not at all of a yieldable spirit, but is like a brazen wall; yet in other things he is of a pliable disposition, not disposed to set up his own opinion, or his own will; he is ready to pay deference to others' opinions, and loves to comply with their inclinations, and has a heart that is tender and flexible, like a little child.

Spiritual pride disposes persons to affect separation, to stand at a distance from others, as better than they, and loves the shew and appearance of the distinction: but on the contrary the eminently humble Christian is ready to look upon himself as not worthy that others should be united to him, to think himself more brutish than any man, and worthy to be cast out of human society, and especially unworthy of the society of God's children; and though he will not be a companion with one that is visibly Christ's enemy, and delights most in the company of lively Christians, will choose such for his companions, and will be most intimate with them, and don't at all delight to spend away much time in the company of those that seem to relish no conversation but about worldly things; yet he don't love the appearance of an open separation from visible Christians, as being a kind of distinct company from them that are one visible company with him by Christ's appointment, and will as much as possible shun all appearances of a superiority, or distinguishing himself as better than others. His universal benevolence delights in the appearance of union with his fellow creatures, and will maintain it as much as he possibly can without giving open countenance to iniquity, or wounding his own soul; and herein he follows the example of his meek and lowly Redeemer, who did not keep up such a separation and distance as the Pharisees, but [did] freely eat with publicans and sinners, that he might win them.

The eminently humble Christian is as it were clothed with lowliness, mildness, meekness, gentleness of spirit and behavior, and with a soft, sweet, condescending, winning air and deportment; these things are just like garments to him; he is clothed all over with them. I Pet. 5:5, "And be clothed with humility." Col. 3:12, "Put on therefore, as the elect of God, holy and beloved, bowels of mercies, kindness, humbleness of mind, meekness, longsuffering."

Pure Christian humility has no such thing as roughness, or contempt, or fierceness, or bitterness in its nature; it makes a person like a little child, harmless and innocent, and that none need to be afraid of; or like a lamb, destitute of all bitterness, wrath, anger and clamor, agreeable to Eph. 4:31.

With such a spirit as this ought especially zealous ministers of the Gospel to be clothed, and those that God is pleased to improve as instruments in his hands of promoting his work. They ought indeed to be thorough in preaching the Word of God, without mincing the matter at all; in handling the sword of the Spirit [Eph. 6:17], as the ministers of the Lord of hosts, they ought not to be mild and gentle; they are not to be gentle and moderate in searching and awakening the conscience but should be sons of thunder. The Word of God, which is in itself "sharper than any two-edged sword," ought not to be sheathed by its ministers, but so used that its sharp edges may have their full effect, even to the "dividing asunder soul and spirit, joints and marrow" [Heb. 4:12] (provided they do it without judging particular persons, leaving it to conscience and the Spirit of God to make the particular application); but all their conversation should savor of nothing but lowliness and good will, love and pity to all mankind; so that such a spirit should be like a sweet odor diffused around 'em wherever they go, or like a light shining about 'em; their faces should as it were shine with it: they should be like lions to guilty consciences, but like lambs to men's persons. This would have no tendency to prevent the awakening of men's consciences, but on the contrary would have a very great tendency to awaken them; it would make way for the sharp sword to enter; it would remove the obstacles, and make a naked breast for the arrow. Yea, the amiable Christ-like conversation of such ministers in itself would terrify consciences of men, as well as their terrible preaching; both would co-operate one with another, to subdue the hard, and bring down the proud heart. If there had been constantly and universally observable such a behavior as this in itinerant preachers, it would have terrified the consciences of sinners ten times as much as all the invectives, and the censorious talk there has been concerning particular persons for their opposition, hypocrisy, delusion, pharisaism, etc. These things in general have rather stupefied sinners' consciences; they take 'em up, and make use of 'em as a shield, wherewith to defend themselves from the sharp arrows of the Word that are shot by these preachers: the enemies of the present work have been glad of these things with all their hearts. Many of the most bitter of them are probably such as in the beginning of this work had their consciences something galled and terrified with it; but these errors of awakening preachers are the things they chiefly make use of as plasters to heal the sore that was made in their consciences.

Spiritual pride takes great notice of opposition and injuries that are received, and is apt to be often speaking of them, and to be much in taking notice of the aggravations of 'em, either with an air of bitterness or contempt: whereas pure, unmixed Christian humility disposes a person rather to be like his blessed Lord, when reviled, dumb, not opening his mouth, but committing himself in silence to him that judgeth righteously [Isa. 53:7; I Pet. 2:23]. The eminently humble Christian, the more clamorous and furious the world is against him, the more silent and still will he be; unless it be in his closet, and there he will not be still. Our blessed Lord Jesus seems never to have been so silent as when the world compassed him round, reproaching, buffeting and spitting on him, with loud and virulent outcries, and horrid cruelties.

There has been a great deal too much talk of late, among many of the true and zealous friends of religion, about opposition and persecution. It becomes the followers of the Lamb of God, when the world is in an uproar about them, and full of clamor against them, not to raise another noise to answer it, but to be still and quiet. 'Tis not beautiful, at such a time, to have pulpits and conversation ring with the sound, "Persecution, persecution," or with abundant talk about Pharisees, carnal persecutors, and the seed of the serpent [Gen. 3:15].

Meekness and quietness among God's people, when opposed and reviled, would be the surest way to have God remarkably to appear for their defense. 'Tis particularly observed of Moses, on the occasion of Aaron and Miriam their envying him, and rising up in opposition against him, that he "was very meek, above all men upon the face of the earth," Num. 12:3; doubtless because he remarkably shewed his meekness on that occasion, being wholly silent under the abuse. And how remarkable is the account that follows of God's being as it were suddenly roused to appear for his vindication? And what high honor did he put upon Moses? And how severe were his rebukes of his opposers? The story is very remarkable, and worth everyone's observing. Nothing is so effectual to bring God down from heaven in the defense of his people, as their patience and meekness under sufferings. When Christ girds his sword upon his thigh, with his glory and majesty, and in his majesty rides prosperously, his right hand teaching him terrible things, it is because of truth and *meekness* and righteousness, Ps. 45:3–4. God will cause judgment to be heard from heaven; the earth shall fear and be still, and God will arise to judgment, to save all the *meek* of the earth, [paraphrase of] Ps. 76:8–9. He will lift up the meek, and cast the wicked down to the ground, Ps. 147:6. He will "reprove with equity for the meek of the earth, and will smite the earth with the rod of his mouth, and with the breath of his lips will he slay the wicked," Isa. 11:4. The great commendation that Christ gives the church of Philadelphia is that, "Thou hast kept the word of my patience," Rev. 3:10. And we may see what reward he promises her, in the preceding verse, "Behold, I will make them of the synagogue of Satan, which say they are Jews and are not, but do lie; behold, I will make them to come and worship at thy feet, and to know that I have loved thee." And thus it is, that we might expect to have Christ appear for us, if under all reproaches we are loaded with, we behaved ourselves with a lamb-like meekness and gentleness; but if our spirits are raised, and we are vehement and noisy with our complaints under color of Christian zeal, this will be to take upon us our own defense, and God will leave it with us to vindicate our cause as well as we can: yea, if we go on in a way of bitterness and high censuring, it will be the way to have him rebuke us, and put us to shame before our enemies.

Here some may be ready to say, " 'Tis not in our own cause that we are thus vehement, but it is in the cause of God; and the Apostle directed the primitive Christians to contend earnestly for the faith once delivered to the saints" [Jude 3]. But how was it that the primitive Christians contended earnestly for the faith? They defended the truth with arguments and a holy conversation; but yet gave their reasons with meekness and fear: they contended earnestly for the faith by fighting violently against their own unbelief and the corruptions of their hearts; yea, they resisted unto blood striving against sin [Heb. 12:4]; but the blood that was shed in this earnest strife was their own blood, and not the blood of their enemies. It was in the cause of God that Peter was so fierce, and drew his sword, and began to smite with it; but Christ bids him put up his sword again, telling him that they that take the sword shall perish by the sword; and while Peter wounds, Christ heals.[5] They contend the most violently, and are the greatest conquerors in a time of persecution, who bear it with the greatest meekness and patience.

Great humility improves even the reflections and reproaches of

5. [Matt. 26:51–52 and parallels; only John (18:10) identifies the swordsman as Peter.]

enemies, to put upon serious self-examination, whether or no there be not some just cause, whether they han't in some respect given occasion to the enemy to speak reproachfully: whereas spiritual pride improves such reflections to make 'em the more bold and confident, and to go the greater lengths in that for which they are found fault with. I desire it may be considered whether there has been nothing amiss of late, among the true friends of vital piety in this respect; and whether the words of David, when reviled by Michal, han't been misinterpreted and misapplied to justify them in it, when he said, "I will be yet more vile, and will be base in mine own sight" [II Sam. 6:22]. The import of his words is that he would humble himself yet more before God, being sensible that he was far from being sufficiently abased; and he signifies this to Michal, and that he longed to be yet lower, and had designed already to abase himself more in his behavior: not that he would go the greater length, to shew his regardlessness of her revilings; that would be to exalt himself, and not more to abase himself, as more vile in his own sight.

Another effect of spiritual pride is a certain unsuitable and self-confident boldness before God and men. Thus some in their great rejoicings before God, han't paid a sufficient regard to that rule in Ps. 2:11. They han't rejoiced with a reverential trembling, in a proper sense of the awful majesty of God, and the awful distance between God and them. And there has also been an improper boldness before men, that has been encouraged and defended by a misapplication of that Scripture, Prov. 29:25, "The fear of man bringeth a snare." As though it became all persons, high and low, men, women and children, in all religious conversation, wholly to divest themselves of all manner of shamefacedness, modesty or reverence towards man; which is a great error, and quite contrary to Scripture. There is a fear of reverence [6] that is due to some men: Rom. 13:7, "Fear to whom fear, honor to whom honor." And there is a fear of modesty and shamefacedness, in inferiors towards superiors, that is amiable and required by Christian rules: I Pet. 3:2, "While they behold your chaste conversation, coupled with fear." And I Tim. 2:9, "In like manner also, that women adorn themselves in modest apparel, with shamefacedness and sobriety." And the Apostle means that this virtue shall have place, not only in civil

6. [One is tempted to suspect here a misprint for "fear *or* reverence," but JE quite evidently intended a descriptive genitive. See also the following sentence, "fear of modesty."]

communication, but also in spiritual communication, and in our religious concerns and behavior, as is evident by what follows: vss. 11–12, "Let the women learn in silence, with all subjection. But I suffer not a woman to teach, nor to usurp authority over the man, but to be in silence." Not that I would hence infer that women's mouths should be shut up from Christian conversation; but all that I mean from it at this time is that modesty, or shamefacedness, and reverence towards men, ought to have some place, even in our religious communication one with another. The same is also evident by I Pet. 3:15, "Be ready always to give an answer to every man that asketh you a reason of the hope that is in you, with meekness and fear." 'Tis well if that very fear and shamefacedness which the Apostle recommends, han't sometimes been condemned under the name of a cursed fear of man.

'Tis beautiful for persons when they are at prayer as the mouth of others, to make God only their fear and their dread, and to be wholly forgetful of men that are present; who, let 'em be great or small, are nothing in the presence of the great God. And 'tis beautiful for a minister, when he speaks in the name of the Lord of hosts, to be bold, and put off all fear of men. And 'tis beautiful in private Christians, though they are women and children, to be bold in professing the faith of Christ, and in the practice of all religion, and in owning God's hand in the work of his power and grace, without any fear of men, though they should be reproached as fools and madmen, and frowned upon by great men, and cast off by parents and all the world. But for private Christians, women and others, to instruct, rebuke and exhort, with a like sort of boldness as becomes a minister when preaching, is not beautiful.

Some have been bold in some things that have really been errors; and have gloried in their boldness in practicing them, though cried out of as odd and irregular. And those that have gone the greatest lengths in these things, have been by some most highly esteemed, as those that come out and appear bold for the Lord Jesus Christ, and fully on his side; and others that have professed to be godly, that have condemned such things, have been spoken of as enemies of the cross of Christ, or at least very cold and dead; and many that of themselves were not inclined to such practices have by this means been driven on, being ashamed to be behind, and accounted poor soldiers for Christ.

Another effect of spiritual pride is assuming: it oftentimes makes it natural to persons so to act and speak, as though it in a special manner belonged to them to be taken notice of and much regarded. It is very natural to a person that is much under the influence of spiritual pride, to take all that respect that is paid him: if others shew a disposition to submit to him, and yield him the deference of a preceptor, he is open to it, and freely admits it; yea, 'tis natural for him to expect such treatment, and to take much notice of it if he fails of it, and to have an ill opinion of others that don't pay him that which he looks upon as his prerogative. He is apt to think that it belongs to him to speak, and to clothe himself with a judicial and dogmatical air in conversation, and to take it upon him as what belongs to him, to give forth his sentence, and to determine and decide: whereas pure Christian humility vaunteth not itself, doth not behave itself unseemly, and is apt to prefer others in honor.[7] One under the influence of spiritual pride is more apt to instruct others, than to inquire for himself, and naturally puts on the airs of a master: whereas one that is full of pure humility naturally has on the air of a disciple; his voice is, "What shall I do? What shall I do that I may live more to God's honor? What shall I do with this wicked heart?" He is ready to receive instruction from anybody, agreeable to Jas. 1:19, "Wherefore, my beloved brethren, let every man be swift to hear, slow to speak." The eminently humble Christian thinks he wants help from everybody, whereas he that is spiritually proud thinks that everybody wants his help. Christian humility, under a sense of others' misery, entreats and beseeches; spiritual pride affects to command, and warn with authority.

There ought to be the utmost watchfulness against all such appearances of spiritual pride, in all that profess to have been the subjects of this work, and especially in the promoters of it, but above all in itinerant preachers: the most eminent gifts, and highest tokens of God's favor and blessing will not excuse them. Alas! What is man at his best estate! What is the most highly favored Christian, or the most eminent and successful minister, that he should now think he is sufficient for something, and somebody to be regarded, and that he should go forth, and act among his fellow creatures, as if he were wise and strong and good!

Ministers that have been the principal instruments of carrying on this glorious revival of religion, and that God has made use of, as it were to bring up his people out of Egypt, as he did of Moses,

7. [Cf. I Cor. 13:4–5 (where the subject is love, not humility) and Rom. 12:10.]

should take heed that they don't provoke God as Moses did, by assuming too much to themselves, and by their intemperate zeal, to shut them out from seeing the good things that God is going to do for his church in this world. The fruits of Moses' unbelief, which provoked God to shut him out of Canaan, and not to suffer him to partake of those great things God was about to do for Israel on earth, were chiefly these two things: *First,* his mingling bitterness with his zeal. He had a great zeal for God, and he could not bear to see the intolerable stiff-neckedness of the people, that they did not acknowledge the work of God, and were not convinced by all his wonders that they had seen; but human passion was mingled with his zeal. Ps. 106:32–33, "They angered him also at the waters of strife, so that it went ill with Moses for their sakes: because they provoked his spirit, so that he spake unadvisedly with his lips." "Hear now, ye rebels," says he, with bitterness of language. *Secondly,* he behaved himself, and spake with an assuming air. He assumed too much to himself: "Hear now, ye rebels, must *we* fetch water out of this rock?" [Num. 20:10]. Spiritual pride wrought in Moses at that time. His temptations to it were very great, for he had had great discoveries of God, and had been privileged with intimate and sweet communion with him, and God had made him the instrument of great good to his church; and though he was so humble a person, and by God's own testimony meek above all men upon the face of the whole earth, yet his temptations were too strong for him: which surely should make our young ministers, that have of late been highly favored and have had great success, exceeding careful and distrustful of themselves.

Alas! how far are we from having the strength of holy, meek, aged Moses! The temptation at this day is exceeding great to both those errors that Moses was guilty of: there is great temptation to bitterness and corrupt passion with zeal; for there is so much unreasonable opposition made against this glorious work of God, and so much stiff-neckedness manifested in multitudes of this generation, notwithstanding all the great and wonderful works in which God has passed before them, that it greatly tends to provoke the spirits of such as have the interest of this work at heart, so as to move 'em to speak unadvisedly with their lips. And there is also great temptation to an assuming behavior in some persons: when a minister is greatly succeeded, from time to time, and so draws the eyes of the multitude upon him, and he sees himself flocked after, and resorted to as an oracle, and people are ready to adore him, and to offer sacrifice to him, as it was with Paul and Barnabas at Lystra [Acts 14:11–13], it is almost impossible for a man to avoid taking upon him the airs of a master, or some extraordinary person; a man had need to have a great stock of humility, and much divine assistance, to resist the temptation. But the greater our dangers are, the more ought to be our watchfulness and prayerfulness, and diffidence of ourselves, lest we bring ourselves into mischief. Fishermen that have been very successful, and have caught a great many fish, had need to be careful that they don't at length begin to burn incense to their net. And we should take warning by Gideon, who after God had highly favored and exalted him, and made him the instrument of working a wonderful deliverance for his people, at length made a god of the spoils of his enemies, which became a snare to him and to his house, so as to prove the ruin of his family [Judg. 8:24–27].

All young ministers in this day of the bringing up the ark of God, should take warning by the example of a young Levite in Israel, viz. Uzzah, the son of Abinadab. He seemed to have a real concern for the ark of God, and to be zealous and engaged in his mind on that joyful occasion of bringing up the ark, and God made him an instrument to bring the ark out of its long continued obscurity in Kirjath-jearim, and he was succeeded to bring it a considerable way towards Mount Zion; but for his want of humility, reverence and circumspection, and assuming to himself, or taking too much upon him, God broke forth upon him, and smote him for his error, so that he never lived to see and partake of the great joy of his church, on occasion of the carrying up the ark into Mount Zion, and the great blessings of heaven upon Israel, that were consequent upon it [II Sam. 6:2–7]. Ministers that have been improved to carry on this work have been chiefly of the younger sort, who have doubtless (as Uzzah had) a real concern for the ark; and 'tis evident that they are much animated and engaged in their minds (as he was) in this joyful day of bringing up the ark; and they are afraid what will become of the ark under the conduct of its ministers (that are sometimes in Scripture compared to oxen [I Cor. 9:9]); they see the ark shakes, and they are afraid these blundering oxen will throw it; and some of 'em, it is to be feared, have been over officious on this occasion, and have assumed too much to themselves, and have been bold to put forth their hand to take hold of the ark, as though they were the only fit and worthy persons to defend it.

If young ministers had great humility without a mixture, it would dispose 'em especially to treat aged ministers with respect and reverence, as their fathers, notwithstanding that a sovereign God may have given them greater assistance and success than they have had. I Pet. 5:5, "Likewise ye younger, submit yourselves unto the elder; yea, all of you, be subject one to another; and be clothed with humility; for God resisteth the proud, and giveth grace to the humble." Lev. 19:32, "Thou shalt rise up before the hoary head, and honor the face of the old man, and fear thy God; I am the Lord."

As spiritual pride disposes persons to assume much to themselves, so it also disposes 'em to treat others with neglect: on the contrary, pure Christian humility disposes persons to honor all men, agreeable to that rule, I Pet. 2:17.

There has been in some, that I believe are true friends of religion, too much of an appearance of this fruit of spiritual pride, in their treatment of those that they looked upon to be carnal men; and particularly in refusing to enter into any discourse or reasoning with them. Indeed to spend a great deal of time in jangling and warm debates about religion, is not the way to propagate religion, but to hinder it; and some are so dreadfully set against this work that it is a dismal task to dispute with them; all that one can say is utterly in vain. I have found it so by experience; and to go to enter into disputes about religion, at some times is quite unseasonable, as particularly in meetings for religious conference, or exercises of worship. But yet we ought to be very careful that we don't refuse to discourse with men, with any appearance of supercilious neglect, as though we counted 'em not worthy to be regarded; on the contrary, we should condescend to carnal men, as Christ has condescended to us, to bear with our unteachableness and stupidity, and still to follow us with instructions, line upon line, and precept upon precept [Isa. 28:10], saying, "Come, let us reason together" [Isa. 1:18]; setting light before us, and using all manner of arguments with us, and waiting upon such dull scholars, as it were hoping that we should receive light. We should be ready with meekness and calmness, without hot disputing, to give our reasons, why we think this work is the work of God, to carnal men when they ask us, and not turn them by as not worthy to be talked with; as the Apostle directed the primitive Christians to be ready to give a reason of the Christian faith and hope to the enemies of Christianity, I Pet. 3:15, "Be ready always to give an answer to every man that asketh you a reason of the hope that is in you, with meekness and fear." And we ought not to condemn all reasoning about things of religion under the name of carnal reason. For my part, I desire no better than that those that oppose this work, should come fairly to submit to have the cause betwixt us tried by strict reasoning.

One qualification that the Scripture speaks of once and again, as requisite in a minister, is that he should be διδακτικόν, apt to teach, I Tim. 3:2. And the Apostle seems to explain what he means by it, in II Tim. 2:24–25. Or at least there [he] expresses one thing he intends by it, viz. that a minister should be ready, meekly to condescend to, and instruct opposers: "And the servant of the Lord must not strive, but be gentle unto all men, apt to teach, patient, in meekness instructing those that oppose themselves, if God peradventure will give them repentance to the acknowledging of the truth."

[2] *Secondly,* another thing from whence errors in conduct, that attend such a revival of religion, do arise, is wrong principles.

And one erroneous principle, than which scarce any has proved more mischievous to the present glorious work of God, is a notion that 'tis God's manner now in these days to guide his saints, at least some that are more eminent, by inspiration, or immediate revelation; and to make known to 'em what shall come to pass hereafter, or what it is his will that they should do, by impressions that he by his Spirit makes upon their minds, either with or without texts of Scripture; whereby something is made known to them, that is not taught in the Scripture as the words lie in the Bible. By such a notion the Devil has a great door opened for him; and if once this opinion should come to be fully yielded to and established in the church of God, Satan would have opportunity thereby to set up himself as the guide and oracle of God's people, and to have his word regarded as their infallible rule, and so to lead 'em where he would, and to introduce what he pleased, and soon to bring the Bible into neglect and contempt. Late experience in some instances has shown that the tendency of this notion is to cause persons to esteem the Bible as a book that is in a great measure useless.

This error will defend and support all errors. As long as a person has a notion that he is guided by immediate direction from heaven, it makes him incorrigible and impregnable in all his misconduct: for what signifies it for poor blind worms of the dust to go to argue with a man, and endeavor to convince him and correct him, that is guided by the immediate counsels and commands of the great Jehovah?

This great work of God has been exceedingly hindered by this error; and till we have quite taken this handle out of the Devil's hands, the work of God will never go on without great clogs and hindrances. But Satan will always have a vast advantage in his hands against it, and as he has improved it hitherto, so he will do still: and 'tis evident that the Devil knows the vast advantage he has by it, that makes him exceeding loath to let go his hold.[8]

'Tis strange what a disposition there is in many well disposed and religious persons, to fall in with and hold fast this notion. 'Tis enough to astonish one that such multiplied, plain instances of the failing of such supposed revelations in the event don't open everyone's eyes. I have seen so many instances of the failing of such impressions, that would almost furnish an history: I have been acquainted with them when made under all kinds of circumstances, and have seen 'em fail in the event, when made with such circumstances as have been fairest and brightest, and most promising; as when they have been made upon the minds of such as there was all reason to think were true saints, yea, eminent saints, and at the very time when they have had great divine discoveries, and have been in the high exercise of true communion with God, and made with great strength, and with great sweetness accompanying, and I have had reason to think, with an excellent heavenly frame of spirit, yet continued, and made with texts of Scripture that seemed to be exceeding apposite, yea, many texts following one another, extraordinarily and wonderfully brought to the mind, and with great power and majesty, and the impressions repeated over and over, after prayers to be directed; and yet all has most manifestly come to nothing, to the full conviction of the persons themselves. And God has in so many instances of late in his providence covered such things with darkness, that one would think it should be enough quite to blank the expectations of such as have been ready to think

8. [The Rev. Thomas Gillespie of Carnock, Scotland (below, p. 561 n. 1), chid JE for not saying more on this matter, and admonished: "I humbly think the Lord calls you, dear Sir, to consider every part of that point in the most critical manner, and to represent fully the consequences resulting from the several principles in that matter, good people, as well as others, have been so fond of" (letter dated Nov. 24, 1746; printed in *Religious Affections*, Yale ed., p. 471).]

highly of such things; it seems to be a testimony of God, that he has no design of reviving revelations in his church, and a rebuke from him to the groundless expectations of it.

It seems to me that that Scripture, Zech. 13:5, is a prophecy concerning ministers of the Gospel, in the latter and glorious day of the Christian church, which is evidently spoken of in this and the foregoing chapters. The words are, "I am no prophet; I am an husbandman: for man taught me to keep cattle from my youth." The words, I apprehend, are to be interpreted in a spiritual sense: "I am an husbandman"—the work of ministers is very often in the New Testament compared to the business of the husbandmen, that take care of God's husbandry, to whom he lets out his vineyard, and sends 'em forth to labor in his field, where one plants and another waters, one sows and another reaps; so ministers are called laborers in God's harvest [cf. I Cor. 2:5–9]. And as it is added, "Man taught me to keep cattle from my youth," so the work of a minister is very often in Scripture represented by the business of a shepherd or pastor. And whereas it is said, "I am no prophet, but man taught me from my youth," 'tis as much as to say, I don't pretend to have received my skill, whereby I am fitted for the business of a pastor or shepherd in the church of God, by immediate inspiration, but by education, by being trained up to the business by human learning, and instructions I have received from my youth or childhood, by ordinary means.

And why can't we be contented with the divine oracles, that holy, pure Word of God, that we have in such abundance and such clearness, now since the canon of Scripture is completed? Why should we desire to have anything added to them by impulses from above? Why should not we rest in that standing rule that God has given to his church, which the Apostle teaches us is surer than a voice from heaven? And why should we desire to make the Scripture speak more to us than it does? Or why should any desire any higher kind of intercourse with heaven, than that which is by having the Holy Spirit given in his sanctifying influences, infusing and exciting grace and holiness, love and joy, which is the highest kind of intercourse that the saints and angels in heaven have with God, and the chief excellency of the glorified man Christ Jesus?

Some that follow impulses and impressions go away with a notion that they do no other than follow the guidance of God's Word, and make the Scripture their rule, because the impression is made with a text of Scripture that comes to their mind, though they take that text as it is impressed on their minds, and improve it as a new revelation, to all intents and purposes, or as the revelation of a particular thing that is now newly made, while the text in itself, as it is in the Bible, implies no such thing, and they themselves do not suppose that any such revelation was contained in it before. As for instance, suppose that text should come into a person's mind with strong impression, Acts 9:6, "Arise, and go into the city; and it shall be told thee what thou must do." And he should interpret it as an immediate signification of the will of God, that he should now, forthwith go to such a neighbor town, and as a revelation of that future event, viz. that there he should meet with a further discovery of his duty. If such things as these are revealed by the impression of these words, 'tis to all intents a new revelation, not the less because certain words of Scripture are made use of in the case: here are propositions or truths entirely new, that are supposed now to be revealed, that those words do not contain in themselves, and that till now there was no revelation of anywhere to be found in heaven or earth. These propositions, that 'tis God's mind and will that such a person by name should arise at such a time, and go from such a place to such a place, and that there he should meet with discoveries, are entirely new propositions, wholly different from the propositions contained in that text of Scripture, no more contained or consequentially implied in the words themselves, without a new revelation, than it is implied that he should arise and go to any other place, or that any other person should arise and go to that place. The propositions supposed to be now revealed are as really different from those contained in that Scripture, as they are from the propositions contained in that text, Gen. 5:6, "And Seth lived an hundred and five years, and begat Enos."

This is quite a different thing from the Spirit's enlightening the mind to understand the precepts or propositions of the Word of God, and [to] know what is contained and revealed in them, and what consequences may justly be drawn from them, and to see how they are applicable to our case and circumstances; which is done without any new revelation, only by enabling the mind to understand and apply a revelation already made.

Those texts of Scripture that speak of the children of God as led by the Spirit, have been by some brought to defend a being guided by such impulses; as particularly those [in] Rom. 8:14, "For as many

as are led by the Spirit of God, they are the sons of God"; and Gal.
5:18, "But if ye are led by the Spirit, ye are not under the law."
But these texts themselves confute them that bring them; for 'tis
evident that the leading of the Spirit that the Apostle speaks of is a
gracious leading, or what is peculiar to the children of God, and that
natural men cannot have; for he speaks of it as a sure evidence of
their being the sons of God, and not under the law: but a leading
or directing a person by immediately revealing to him where he
should go, or what shall hereafter come to pass, or what shall be the
future consequence of his doing thus or thus, if there be any such
thing in these days, is not of the nature of the gracious leading of the
Spirit of God that is peculiar to God's children; 'tis no more than a
common gift; there is nothing in it but what natural men are capable
of, and many of them have had in the days of inspiration. A man may
have ten thousand such revelations and directions from the Spirit
of God, and yet not have a jot of grace in his heart: 'tis no more than
the gift of prophecy, which immediately reveals what will be, or
should be hereafter; but this is but a common gift, as the Apostle
expressly shews, I Cor. 13:2, 8. If a person has anything revealed to
him from God, or is directed to anything by a voice from heaven,
or a whisper, or words immediately suggested and put into his mind,
there is nothing of the nature of grace merely in this; 'tis of the nature of a common influence of the Spirit, and is but dross and dung
in comparison of the excellency of that gracious leading of the
Spirit that the saints have. Such a way of being directed where one
shall go, and what he shall do, is no more than what Balaam had from
God, who from time to time revealed to him what he should do,
and when he had done one thing, then directed him what he should
do next; so that he was in this sense led by the Spirit for a considerable time [Num. 22].

There is a more excellent way that the Spirit of God leads the
sons of God, that natural men cannot have, and that is by inclining
them to do the will of God, and go in the shining path of truth
and Christian holiness, from an holy heavenly disposition, which
the Spirit of God gives them, and enlivens in them which inclines
'em and leads 'em to those things that are excellent and agreeable
to God's mind, whereby they are "transformed by the renewing of
their minds, and prove what is that good, and acceptable, and perfect will of God," as in Rom. 12:2. And so the Spirit of God does in
a gracious manner teach the saints their duty; and teaches 'em in

an higher manner than ever Balaam, or Saul, or Judas, were taught, or any natural man is capable of while such. The Spirit of God enlightens 'em with respect to their duty by making their eye single and pure, whereby the "whole body is full of light" [Matt. 6:22]. The sanctifying influence of the Spirit of God rectifies the taste of the soul, whereby it savors those things that are of God, and naturally relishes and delights in those things that are holy and agreeable to God's mind, and like one of a distinguishing taste, chooses those things that are good and wholesome, and rejects those things that are evil; for the sanctified ear tries words, and the sanctified heart tries actions, as the mouth tastes meat. And thus the Spirit of God leads and guides the meek in his way, agreeable to his promises; he enables them to understand the commands and counsels of his Word, and rightly to apply them. Christ blames the Pharisees that they had not this holy distinguishing taste, to discern and distinguish what was right and wrong. Luke 12:57, "Yea, and why, even of your own selves, judge ye not what is right?"

The leading of the Spirit which God gives his children, which is peculiar to them, is that teaching them his statutes, and causing them to understand the way of his precepts, which the Psalmist so very often prays for, especially in the 119th Psalm; and not in giving of them new statutes, and new precepts. He graciously gives them eyes to see, and ears to hear, and hearts to understand; he causes them to understand the fear of the Lord, and so brings the blind by a way they knew not, and leads them in paths that they had not known, and makes darkness light before them, and crooked things straight [Prov. 2:5; Isa. 42:16].

So the assistance of the Spirit in praying and preaching seems by some to have been greatly misunderstood, and they have sought after a miraculous assistance of inspiration, by immediate suggesting of words to them, by such gifts and influences of the Spirit, in praying and teaching, as the Apostle speaks of, I Cor. 14:14, 26 (which many natural men had in those days), instead of a gracious holy assistance of the Spirit of God, which is the far more excellent way (as I Cor. 12:31 and 13:1). The gracious, and most excellent, kind assistance of the Spirit of God in praying and preaching, is not my immediate suggesting of words to the apprehension, which may be with a cold dead heart, but by warming the heart and filling it with a great sense of those things that are to be spoken of, and with holy affections, that that sense and those affections may suggest words. Thus indeed the Spirit of God may be said, indirectly and mediately to suggest words to us, to indite our petitions for us, and to teach the preacher what to say; he fills the heart, and that fills the mouth; as we know that when men are greatly affected in any matter, and their hearts are very full, it fills them with matter for speech, and makes 'em eloquent upon that subject; and much more have spiritual affections this tendency, for many reasons that might be given. When a person is in an holy and lively frame in secret prayer, it will wonderfully supply him with matter and with expressions, as every true Christian knows; and so it will fill his mouth in Christian conversation, and it has the like tendency to enable a person in public prayer and preaching. And if he has these holy influences of the Spirit on his heart in an high degree, nothing in the world will have so great a tendency to make both the matter and manner of his public performances excellent and profitable. But since there is no immediate suggesting of words from the Spirit of God to be expected or desired, they who neglect and despise study and premeditation, in order to a preparation for the pulpit, in such an expectation are guilty of presumption; though doubtless it may be lawful for some persons in some cases (and they may be called to it) to preach with very little study; and the Spirit of God, by the heavenly frame of heart that he gives them, may enable them to do it to excellent purpose.

Besides this most excellent way of the Spirit of God his assisting ministers in public performances, which (considered as the preacher's privilege) far excels inspiration, there is a common assistance which natural men may have in these days, and which the godly may have intermingled with a gracious assistance, which is also very different from inspiration, and that is his assisting natural principles; as his assisting the natural apprehension, reason, memory, conscience and natural affection.

But to return to the head of impressions and immediate revelations; many lay themselves open to a delusion by expecting direction from heaven in this way, and waiting for it: in such a case it is easy for persons to imagine that they have it. They are perhaps at a loss concerning something, undetermined what they shall do, or what course they should take in some affair, and they pray to God to direct them, and make known to 'em his mind and will; and then, instead of expecting to be directed, by being assisted in consideration of the rules of God's Word, and their circumstances, and God's providence, and enabled to look on things in a true light, and justly to weigh them, they are waiting for some secret immediate influence on their minds, unaccountably swaying their minds and turning their thought or inclinations that way that God would have them go, and are observing their own minds to see what arises there, whether some texts of Scripture don't come into the mind, or whether some ideas or inward motions and dispositions don't arise in something of an unaccountable manner that they may call a divine direction. Hereby they are exposed to two things. *First,* they lay themselves open to the Devil, and give him a fair opportunity to lead them where he pleases; for they stand ready to follow the first extraordinary impulse that they shall have, groundlessly concluding it is from God. And *secondly,* they are greatly exposed to be deceived by their own imaginations; for such an expectation awakens and quickens the imagination; and that oftentimes is called an uncommon impression, that is no such thing; and they ascribe that to the agency of some invisible being, that is owing only to themselves.

Again, another way that many have been deceived, is by drawing false conclusions from true premises. Many true and eminent saints have been led into mistakes and snares by arguing too much from that, that they have prayed in faith; and that oftentimes when the premises are true, they have indeed been greatly assisted in prayer for such a particular mercy, and have had the true spirit of prayer in exercise in their asking it of God; but they have concluded more from these premises than is a just consequence from them: that they have thus prayed is a sure sign that their prayer is accepted and heard, and that God will give a gracious answer, according to his own wisdom, and that the particular thing that was asked shall be given, or that which is equivalent; this is a just consequence from it; but it is not inferred by any new revelation now made, but by the revelation that is made in God's Word, the promises made to the prayer of faith in the Holy Scriptures: but that God will answer them in that individual thing that they ask, if it ben't a thing promised in God's Word, or they don't certainly know that it is that which will be most for the good of God's church and the advancement of Christ's kingdom and glory, nor whether it will be best for them, is more than can be justly concluded from it.

If God remarkably meets with one of his children while he is praying for a particular mercy of great importance, for himself, or some other person, or any society of men, and does by the influences of his Spirit greatly humble him and empty him of himself in his prayer, and manifests himself remarkably in his excellency, sovereignty and his all-sufficient power and grace in Jesus Christ, and does in a remarkable manner enable the person to come to him for that mercy, poor in spirit and with humble resignation to God, and with a great degree of faith in the divine sufficiency, and the sufficiency of Christ's mediation, that person has indeed a great deal the more reason to hope that God will grant that mercy than otherwise he would have; the greater probability is justly inferred from that, agreeable to the promises of the Holy Scripture, that the prayer is accepted and heard; and it is much more probable that a prayer that is heard will be returned with the particular mercy that is asked, than one that is not heard. And there is no reason at all to doubt but that God does sometimes especially enable to the exercises of faith, when the minds of his saints are engaged in thoughts of, and prayer for, some particular blessing they greatly desire; i.e. God is pleased especially to give 'em a believing frame, a sense of his fulness, and a spirit of humble dependence on him, at such times as when they are thinking of and praying for that mercy more than for other mercies; he gives 'em a particular sense of his ability to do that thing, and of the sufficiency of his power to overcome such and such obstacles, and the sufficiency of his mercy and of the blood of Christ for the removal of the guilt that is in the way of the bestowment of such a mercy in particular. When this is the case, it makes the probability still much greater that God intends to bestow the particular mercy sought, in his own time and his own way. But here is nothing of the nature of a revelation in the case, but only a drawing rational conclusions from the particular manner and circumstances of the ordinary gracious influences of God's Spirit. And as God is pleased sometimes to give his saints particular exercises of faith in his sufficiency, with regard to particular mercies they seek, so he is sometimes pleased to make use of his Word in order to it, and helps the actings of faith with respect to such a mercy by texts of Scripture that do especially exhibit the sufficiency of God's power or mercy in such a like case, or speak of such a manner of the exercise of God's strength and grace. The strengthening of their faith in God's sufficiency in this case, is therefore a just improvement of such Scriptures; it is no more than what those Scriptures, as they stand in the Bible, do hold forth just cause for. But to take them as new whispers or revelations from heaven is not making a just improvement of them. If persons have thus a spirit of prayer remarkably given them concerning a particular mercy from time to time, so as evidently to be assisted to act faith in God, in that particular, in a very distinguishing manner, the argument in some cases may be very strong that God does design [*sic,* deign?] to grant that mercy, not from any revelation now made of it, but from such a kind and manner of the ordinary influence of his Spirit, with respect to that thing.

But here a great deal of caution and circumspection must be used in drawing inferences of this nature: there are many ways persons may be misled and deluded. The ground on which some expect that they shall receive the thing they have asked for, is rather a strong imagination, than any true humble faith in the divine sufficiency. They have a strong persuasion that the thing asked shall be granted (which they can give no reason for) without any remarkable discovery of that glory and fulness of God and Christ that is the ground of faith. And sometimes the confidence that persons have that their prayers shall be answered, is only a self-righteous confidence, and no true faith: they have a high conceit of themselves as eminent saints and special favorites of God, and have also a high conceit of the prayers they have made, because they were much enlarged and affected in them; and hence they are positive in it that the thing will come to pass. And sometimes when once they have conceived such a notion, they grow stronger and stronger in it; and this they think is from an immediate divine hand upon their minds to strengthen their confidence; whereas it is only by their dwelling in their minds on their own excellency, and high experiences, and great assistances, whereby they look brighter and brighter in their own eyes. Hence 'tis found by observation and experience, that nothing in the world exposes so much to enthusiasm as spiritual pride and self-righteousness.

In order to drawing a just inference from the supposed assistance we have had in prayer for a particular mercy, and judging of the probability of the bestowment of that individual mercy, many things must be considered. We must consider the importance of the mercy sought, and the principle whence we so earnestly desire it; how far it is good and agreeable to the mind and will of God; the degree of love to God that we exercised in our prayer; the degree of discovery that is made of the divine sufficiency, and the degree in which our assistance is manifestly distinguishing with respect to that mercy. And there is nothing of greater importance in the argument than the degree of humility, poverty of spirit, self-emptiness and resignation to the holy will of God, which God gives us the exercise of in our seeking that mercy: praying for a particular mercy with much of these things, I have often seen blessed with a remarkable bestowment of the particular thing asked for.

From what has been said, we may see which way God may, only by the ordinary gracious influences of his Spirit, sometimes give his saints special reason to hope for the bestowment of a particular mercy they desire and have prayed for, and which we may suppose he oftentimes gives eminent saints, that have great degrees of humility and much communion with God. And here, I humbly conceive, some eminent servants of Jesus Christ that have appeared in the church of God, that we read of in ecclesiastical story [history?], have been led into a mistake; and through want of distinguishing such things as these from immediate revelations, have thought that God has favored 'em, in some instances, with the same kind of divine influences that the apostles and prophets had of old.

Another erroneous principle that some have embraced, that has been a source of many errors in their conduct, is that persons ought always to do whatsoever the Spirit of God (though but indirectly) inclines them to. Indeed the Spirit of God in itself is infinitely perfect, and all his immediate actings, simply considered, are perfect, and there can be nothing wrong in them; and therefore all that the Spirit of God inclines us to directly and immediately without the intervention of any other cause that shall pervert and misimprove what is from the Spirit of God, ought to be done; but there may be many things that we may be disposed to do, which disposition may indirectly be from the Spirit of God, that we ought not to do. The disposition in general may be good, and be from the Spirit of God, but the particular determination of that disposition, as to particular actions, objects and circumstances, may be ill, and not from the Spirit of God, but may be from the intervention or interposition of some infirmity, blindness, inadvertence, deceit or corruption of ours; so that although the disposition in general ought to be allowed and promoted, and all those actings of it that are simply from God's Spirit, yet the particular ill direction or determination of that disposition, which is from some other cause, ought not to be followed.

As for instance, the Spirit of God may cause a person to have a dear love to another, and so a great desire of, and delight in his comfort, ease and pleasure: this disposition in general is good, and ought to be followed; but yet through the intervention of indiscretion, or some other bad cause, it may be ill directed, and have a bad determination, as to particular acts; and the person indirectly, through that real love that he has to his neighbor, may kill him with kindness; he may do that out of sincere good will to him that may tend to ruin him. A good disposition may through some inadvertence or delusion, strongly incline a person to that, which if he saw all things as they are, would be most contrary to that disposition. The true loyalty of a general, and his zeal for the honor of his prince, may exceedingly animate him in war; but yet this that is a good disposition, through indiscretion and mistake, may push him forward to those things that give the enemy great advantage, and may expose him and his army to ruin, and may tend to the ruin of his master's interest.

The Apostle does evidently suppose that the Spirit of God in his extraordinary, immediate and miraculous influences on men's minds, may in some respect excite inclinations in men, that if gratified, would tend to confusion, and therefore must sometimes be restrained, and in their exercise, must be under the government of discretion. I Cor. 14:31–33, "For ye may all prophesy one by one, that all may learn, and all may be comforted. And the spirits of the prophets are subject to the prophets; for God is not the author of confusion, but of peace, as in all the churches of the saints." Here by "the spirits of the prophets," according to the known phraseology of the Apostle, is meant the Spirit of God acting in the prophets, according to those special gifts with which each one was endowed. And here it is plainly implied that the Spirit of God, thus operating in them, may be an occasion of their having sometimes an inclination to do that, in the exercise of those gifts, which it was not proper, decent or profitable that they should; and that therefore the inclination, though indirectly from the Spirit of God, should be restrained, and that it ought to be subject to the discretion of the prophets, as to the particular time and circumstances of its exercise.

I can make no doubt but that it is possible for a minister to have given him by the Spirit of God such a sense of the importance of eternal things, and of the misery of mankind, that are so many of them exposed to eternal destruction, together with such a love to souls, that he might find in himself a disposition to spend all his time, day and night, in warning, exhorting and calling upon men,

and so that he must be obliged as it were to do violence to himself
ever to refrain, so as to give himself any opportunity to eat, drink
or sleep. And so I believe there may be a disposition in like manner,
indirectly excited in lay persons, through the intervention of their
infirmity, to do what only belongs to ministers; yea, to do those
things that would not become either ministers or people: through the
influence of the Spirit of God, together with want of discretion and
some remaining corruption, women and children might feel themselves inclined to break forth and scream aloud to great congregations, warning and exhorting the whole multitude, and to go forth
and halloo and scream in the streets, or to leave the families they
belong to, and go from house to house, earnestly exhorting others;
but yet it would by no means follow that it was their duty to do
these things, or that they would not have a tendency to do ten times
as much hurt as good.

Another wrong principle from whence have arisen errors in conduct is, that whatsoever is found to be of present and immediate
benefit, may and ought to be practiced without looking forward
to future consequences. Some persons seem to think that it sufficiently justifies anything that they say or do that it is found to be
for their present edification, and the edification of those that are with
them; it assists and promotes their present affection, and therefore
they think they should not concern themselves about future consequences, but leave them with God. Indeed, in things that are in themselves our duty, being required by moral rules, or absolute positive
commands of God, they must be done, and future consequences must
be left with God; our election and discretion takes no place here:
but in other things we are to be governed by discretion, and must
not only look at the present good, but our view must be extensive,
and we must look at the consequence of things. 'Tis the duty of
ministers especially to exercise this discretion: in things wherein they
are not determined by an absolute rule, and that are not enjoined
them by a wisdom superior to their own, Christ has left them to
their own discretion, with that general rule that they should exercise
the utmost wisdom they can obtain in pursuing that, which upon
the best view of the consequences of things they can get, will tend
most to the advancement of his kingdom. This is implied in those
words of Christ to his disciples, when he sent 'em forth to preach
the Gospel, Matt. 10:16, "Be ye wise as serpents." The Scripture
always represents the work of a Gospel minister by those employ-

ments that do especially require a wise foresight of, and provision for, future events and consequences. So it is compared to the business of a steward, that is a business that in an eminent manner requires forecast, and a wise laying in of provision for the supply of the needs of the family, according to its future necessities; and a good minister is called a wise steward.[9] So 'tis compared to the business of an husbandman, that almost wholly consists in those things that are done with a view to the future fruits and consequences of his labor: the husbandman's discretion and forecast is eloquently set forth in Isa. 28:24–26, "Doth the plowman plow all day to sow? Doth he open and break the clods of his ground? When he hath made plain the face thereof, doth he not cast abroad the fitches, and scatter the cummin, and cast in the principal wheat, and the appointed barley, and the rye, in their place? For his God doth instruct him to discretion, and doth teach him." So the work of the ministry is compared to that of a wise builder or architect, who has a long reach and comprehensive view; and for whom it is necessary, that when he begins a building, he should have at once a view of the whole frame, and all the future parts of the structure, even to the pinnacle, that all may fitly be framed together [I Cor. 3:10; Eph. 2:21]. So also it is compared to the business of a trader or merchant, who is to gain by trading with the money that he begins with: this also is a business that exceedingly requires forecast, and without it, is never like to be followed with any success for any long time [Matt. 25:14–30]. So 'tis represented by the business of a fisherman, which depends on craft and subtlety [Matt. 4:19]. 'Tis also compared to the business of a soldier that goes to war, which is a business that perhaps, above any other secular business, requires great foresight and a wise provision for future events and consequences [II Tim. 2:3].

And particularly ministers ought not to be careless how much they discompose and ruffle the minds of those that they esteem natural men, or how great an uproar they raise in the carnal world, and so lay blocks in the way of the propagation of religion. This certainly is not to follow the example of that zealous Apostle Paul, who though he would not depart from his enjoined duty to please carnal men, yet wherein he might with a good conscience, did exceedingly lay out himself to please them, and if possible to avoid raising in the multitude prejudices, oppositions and tumults against the Gospel;

9. [Cf. Luke 12:42, though the reference of this verse to ministers is questionable.]

and looked upon it that it was of great consequence that it should be, if possible, avoided. I Cor. 10:32–33, "Give none offense, neither to the Jews, nor to the Gentiles, nor to the church of God: even as I please all men in all things, not seeking mine own profit, but the profit of many, that they may be saved." Yea, he declares that he laid himself out so much for this, that he made himself a kind of a servant to all sorts of men, conforming to their customs and various humors, in everything wherein he might, even in things that were very burdensome to him, that he might not fright men away from Christianity and cause them to stand as it were braced and armed against it, but on the contrary, if possible, might with condescension and friendship win and draw them to it; as you may see, I Cor. 9:19–23. And agreeable hereto, are the directions he gives to others, both ministers and people. So he directs the Christian Romans not to please themselves, but everyone [to] please his neighbor for his good, to edification, Rom. 15:1–2, and to follow after the things that make for peace, chap. 14:19. And he presses it in terms exceeding strong, Rom. 12:18, "If it be possible, as much as lieth in you, live peaceably with all men." And he directs ministers to endeavor if possible, to gain opposers by a meek condescending treatment, avoiding all appearance of strife or fierceness, II Tim. 2:24–26. To the like purpose, the same Apostle directs Christians to walk in wisdom towards them that are without, Col. 4:5, and to avoid giving offense to others if we can, that our good mayn't be evil spoken of, Rom. 14:16. So that 'tis evident that the great and most zealous and most successful propagator of vital religion that ever was, looked upon it to be of great consequence to endeavor, as much as possible, by all the methods of lawful meekness and gentleness, to avoid raising the prejudice and opposition of the world against religion. When we have done our utmost there will be opposition enough against vital religion, against which the carnal mind of man has such an enmity (we should not therefore needlessly increase and raise that enmity); as in the Apostle's days, though he took so much pains to please men, yet because he was faithful and thorough in his work, persecution almost everywhere was raised against him.

A fisherman is careful not needlessly to ruffle and disturb the water, lest he should drive the fish away from his net; but he'll rather endeavor if possible to draw them into it. Such a fisherman was the Apostle. II Cor. 12:15–16, "And I will very gladly spend and be spent for you; though the more abundantly I love you, the less I be loved. But be it so, I did not burden you; nevertheless, being crafty, I caught you with guile."

The necessity of suffering persecution in order to being a true Christian, has undoubtedly by some been carried to an extreme, and the doctrine has been abused. It has been looked upon necessary to uphold a man's credit amongst others as a Christian, that he should be persecuted. I have heard it made an objection against the sincerity of particular persons that they were no more hated and reproached. And the manner of glorying in persecution, or the cross of Christ, has in some been very wrong, so as has had too much of an appearance of lifting up themselves in it, that they were very much hated and reviled, more than most, as an evidence of their excelling others in being good soldiers of Jesus Christ. Such an improvement of the doctrine of the enmity between the seed of the woman and the seed of the serpent [Gen. 3:15], and of the necessity of persecution, becoming credible and customary, has a direct tendency to cause those that would be accounted true Christians to behave themselves so towards those that are not well affected to religion as to provoke their hatred, or at least to be but little careful to avoid it, and not very studiously and earnestly to strive (after the Apostle's example and precepts) to please them to their edification, and by meekness and gentleness to win them, and by all possible means to live peaceably with them.

I believe that saying of our Saviour, "I came not to send peace on earth, but division" [Luke 12:51; cf. also Matt. 10:34], has been abused; as though when we see great strife and division arise about religion, and violent heats of spirit against the truly pious, and a loud clamor and uproar against the work of God, it was to be rejoiced in, because it is that which Christ came to send. It has almost been laid down as a maxim by some, that the more division and strife, the better sign; which naturally leads persons to seek it and provoke it, or leads 'em to, and encourages 'em in such a manner of behavior, such a roughness and sharpness, or such an affected neglect, as has a natural tendency to raise prejudice and opposition; instead of striving, as the Apostle did to his utmost, by all meekness, gentleness and benevolence of behavior, to prevent or assuage it. Christ came to send a sword on earth, and to cause division, no otherwise than he came to send damnation; for Christ that is set for the glorious restoration of some is set for the fall of others [Luke 2:34], and to be a stone of stumbling and rock of offense to them

[Isa. 8:14; I Pet. 2:8], and an occasion of their vastly more aggravated and terrible damnation [Matt. 12:41–42]; and this is always the consequence of a great outpouring of the Spirit and revival of vital religion: it is the means of the salvation of some, and the more aggravated damnation of others. But certainly this is no just argument that men's exposedness to damnation is not to be lamented, or that we should not exert ourselves to our utmost, in all the methods that we can devise, that others might be saved, and to avoid all such behavior towards 'em as tends to lead 'em down to hell.

I know there is naturally a great enmity in the heart of man against vital religion; and I believe there would have been a great deal of opposition against this glorious work of God in New England if the subjects and promoters of it had behaved themselves never so agreeably to Christian rules; and I believe if this work goes on and spreads much in the world, so as to begin to shake kingdoms and nations, it will dreadfully stir up the rage of earth and hell, and will put the world into the greatest uproar that ever it was in since it stood; I believe Satan's dying struggles will be the most violent. But yet I believe a great deal might be done to restrain this opposition, by a good conformity to that of the Apostle James, Jas. 3:13, "Who is a wise man, and endued with knowledge [among you]? Let him shew out of a good conversation, his works, with meekness of wisdom." And I also believe that if the rules of Christian charity, meekness, gentleness and prudence had been duly observed by the generality of the zealous promoters of this work, it would have made three times the progress that it has; i.e. if it had pleased God in such a case, to give a blessing to means in proportion as he has done.

Under this head of carelessness of the future consequences of things, it may be proper to say something of introducing things new and strange, and that have a tendency by their novelty to shock and surprise people. Nothing can be more evident from the New Testament, than that such things ought to be done with great caution and moderation, to avoid the offense that may be thereby given, and the prejudices that might be raised, to clog and hinder the progress of religion: yea, that it ought to be thus in things that are in themselves good and excellent, and of great weight, provided they are not things that are of the nature of absolute duty, which though they may appear to be innovations, yet can't be neglected without immorality or disobedience to the commands of God. What great caution and moderation did the apostles use in introducing things that were new, and abolishing things that were old in their day? How gradually were the ceremonial performances of the law of Moses removed and abolished among the Christian Jews? And how long did even the Apostle Paul himself conform to those ceremonies which he calls "weak and beggarly elements" [Gal. 4:9]? Yea, even to the rite of circumcision (Acts 16:3) that he speaks so much in his epistles of the worthlessness of, that he might not prejudice the Jews against Christianity? So it seems to have been very gradually that the Jewish Sabbath was abolished, and the Christian Sabbath introduced, for the same reason. And the apostles avoided teaching the Christians in those early days, at least for a great while, some high and excellent divine truths, because they could not bear 'em yet, I Cor. 3:1–2; Heb. 5:11 to the end. Thus strictly did the apostles observe the rule that their blessed Master gave them, of not putting new wine into old bottles, lest they should burst the bottles and lose the wine [Matt. 9:17 and parallels]. And how did Christ himself, while on earth, forbear so plainly to teach his disciples the great doctrines of Christianity, concerning his satisfaction, and the nature and manner of a sinner's justification and reconciliation with God, and the particular benefits of his death, resurrection and ascension, because in that infant state the disciples were then in, their minds were not prepared for such instructions; and therefore the more clear and full revelation of these things was reserved for the time when their minds should be further enlightened and strengthened by the out-pouring of the Spirit after his ascension? John 16:12–13, "I have yet many things to say unto you, but ye cannot bear them now: howbeit, when he, the Spirit of truth is come, he will guide you into all truth." And Mark 4:33, "And with many such parables spake he the word unto them, as they were able to bear [*sic,* hear] it." These things might be enough to convince anyone, that don't think himself wiser than Christ and his apostles, that great prudence and caution should be used in introducing things into the church of God that are very uncommon, though in themselves they may be very excellent, lest by our rashness and imprudent haste we hinder religion much more than we help it.

Persons that are influenced by an indiscreet zeal are always in too much haste; they are impatient of delays, and therefore are for jumping to the uppermost step first, before they have taken the preceding steps; whereby they expose themselves to fall and break their bones. It is a thing very taking with them to see the building rise very high, and all their endeavor and strength is employed in advancing the building in height, without taking care withal proportionably to enlarge the bottom; whereby the whole is in danger of coming to the ground; or they are for putting on the cupola and pinnacle before they are come to it, or before the lower parts of the building are done; which tends at once to put a stop to the building, and hinder its ever being a complete structure. Many that are thus imprudent and hasty with their zeal have a real eager appetite for that which is good; but are like children that are impatient to wait for the fruit till the proper season of it, and therefore snatch it before it is ripe: oftentimes in their haste they overshoot their mark, and frustrate their own end; they put that which they would obtain further out of reach than it was before, and establish and confirm that which they would remove. Things must have time to ripen: the prudent husbandman waits till he has received the former and the latter rain, and till the harvest is ripe, before he reaps. We are now just as it were beginning to recover out of a dreadful disease that we have been long under; and to feed a man recovering from a fever with strong meat at once, is the ready way to kill him. The reformation from popery was much hindered by this hasty zeal: many were for immediately rectifying all disorders by force, which were condemned by Luther, and were a great trouble to him. See Sleiden's *History of the Reformation,* page 52, etc., and Book V throughout.[1] It is a vain prejudice that some have lately imbibed against such rules of prudence and moderation: they will be forced to come to 'em at last; they'll find themselves that they are not able to maintain their cause without 'em; and if they won't hearken before, experience will convince 'em at last, when it will be too late for them to rectify their mistake.

Another error that is of the nature of an erroneous principle, that some have gone upon, is a wrong notion that they have of an attestation of divine providence to persons or things. We go too far when we look upon the success that God gives to some persons, in making

1. [Johannes Philippi Sleidanus (1506–56) wrote *Commentariorum de statu religionis et reipublicae, Carolo Quinto Caesare, libri XXVI* in 1555. English translations were John Daus, *A Famous Chronicle of Our Time* (1560), and Edmund Bohun, *The General History of the Reformation of the Church from the Errors and Corruptions of the Church of Rome* (1689). JE used the latter. Sleiden's account of Protestant excesses, to which JE shrewdly refers, had angered many Protestants during the Reformation era.]

them the instruments of doing much good, as a testimony of God's approbation of those persons and all the courses they take. It is a main argument that has been made use of to defend the conduct of some of those ministers, that have been blamed as imprudent and irregular, that God has smiled upon them and blessed them, and given them great success, and that however men charge them as guilty of many wrong things, yet 'tis evident that God is with them, and then who can be against them [Rom. 8:31]? And probably some of those ministers themselves, by this very means, have had their ears stopped against all that has been said to convince 'em of their misconduct. But there are innumerable ways that persons may be misled, in forming a judgment of the mind and will of God, from the events of providence. If a person's success be a reward of something that God sees in him, that he approves of, yet 'tis no argument that he approves of everything in him. Who can tell how far the divine grace may go in greatly rewarding some small good that he sees in a person, a good meaning, something good in his disposition, while he at the same time, in sovereign mercy, hides his eyes from a great deal that is bad, that 'tis his pleasure to forgive, and not to mark against the person, though in itself it be very ill? God has not told us after what manner he will proceed in this matter, and we go upon most uncertain grounds when we undertake to determine. It is an exceeding difficult thing to know how far love or hatred are exercised towards persons or actions, by all that is before us. God was pleased in his sovereignty to give such success to Jacob in that, which from beginning to end was a deceitful, lying contrivance and proceeding of his, that in that way, he obtained that blessing that was worth infinitely more than the fatness of the earth and the dew of heaven, that was given to Esau, in his blessing; yea, worth more than all that the world can afford [Gen. 27–33]. God was for a while with Judas, so that he by God's power accompanying him, wrought miracles and cast out devils; but this could not justly be interpreted as God's approbation of his person, or his thievery that he lived in at the same time [Matt. 10:1–4; John 12:6].

The dispensations and events of providence, with their reasons, are too little understood by us to be improved by us as our rule, instead of God's Word; God has his "way in the sea, and his path in the mighty waters, and his footsteps are not known" [Ps. 77:19; Isa. 43:16]; and he gives us "no account of any of his matters" [Job 33:13]; and therefore we can't safely take the events of his providence as a revelation of his mind concerning a person's conduct and behavior; we have no warrant so to do, God has never appointed those things, but something else to be our rule; we have but one rule to go by, and that is his Holy Word, and when we join anything else with it as having the force of a rule, we are guilty of that which is strictly forbidden, Deut. 4:2, Prov. 30:6, and Rev. 22:18. They who make what they imagine is pointed forth to 'em in providence their rule of behavior, do err, as well as those that follow impulses and impressions: we should put nothing in the room of the Word of God. It is to be feared that some have been greatly confirmed and emboldened by the great success that God has given them, in some things that have really been contrary to the rules of God's Holy Word. If it has been so, they have been guilty of presumption, and abusing God's kindness to them, and the great honor he has put upon them: they have seen that God was with them, and made them victorious in their preaching; and this it is to be feared has been abused by some to a degree of self-confidence; it has much taken off all jealousy of themselves; they have been bold therefore to go great lengths, in a presumption that God was with them, and would defend them, and finally baffle all that found fault with them.

Indeed, there is a voice of God in his providence, that may be interpreted and well understood by the rule of his Word; and providence may, to our dark minds and weak faith, confirm the Word of God as it fulfills it: but to improve divine providence thus, is quite a different thing from making a rule of providence. There is a good use may be made of the events of providence, of our own observation and experience, and human histories, and the opinion of the Fathers and other eminent men; but finally all must be brought to one rule, viz. the Word of God, and that must be regarded as our only rule.

Nor do I think that they go upon sure ground that conclude that they have not been in an error in their conduct, because that at the time of their doing a thing, for which they have been blamed and reproached by others, they were favored with special comforts of God's Spirit. God's bestowing special spiritual mercies on a person at such a time, is no sign that he approves of everything that he sees in him at that time. David had very much of the presence of God while he lived in polygamy: and Solomon had some very high favors and peculiar smiles of heaven, and particularly at the dedication of the temple, while he greatly multiplied wives to himself, and horses, and silver and gold; all contrary to the most express command of God to the king, in the law of Moses, Deut. 17:16–17. We can't tell how far God may hide his eyes from beholding iniquity in Jacob, and seeing perverseness in Israel [Num. 23:21]. We can't tell what are the reasons of God's actions any further than he interprets for himself. God sometimes gave some of the primitive Christians the extraordinary influence of his Spirit, when they were out of the way of their duty; and continued it while they were abusing it; as is plainly implied, I Cor. 14:31–33.

Yea, if a person has done a thing for which he is reproached, and that reproach be an occasion of his feeling sweet exercises of grace in his soul, and that from time to time, I don't think that is a certain evidence that God approves of the thing he is blamed for. For undoubtedly a mistake may be the occasion of stirring up the exercise of grace, in a man that has grace. If a person, through mistake, thinks he has received some particular great mercy, that mistake may be the occasion of stirring up the sweet exercises of love to God, and true thankfulness and joy in God. As for instance, if one that is full of love to God should hear credible tidings concerning a remarkable deliverance of a child or other dear friend, or of some glorious thing done for the City of God, no wonder if, on such an occasion, the sweet actings of love to God and delight in God should be excited, though indeed afterwards it should prove a false report that he heard. So if one that loves God is much maligned and reproached for doing that which he thinks God required and approves, no wonder that it is sweet to such an one to think that God is his friend, though men are his enemies; no wonder at all, that this is an occasion of his, as it were, leaving the world, and sweetly betaking himself to God as his sure friend, and finding sweet complacence in God; though he be indeed in a mistake concerning that which he thought was agreeable to God's will. As I have before shewn that the exercise of a truly good affection may be the occasion of error, and may indirectly incline a person to that which is wrong; [2] so on the other hand, error, or a doing that which is wrong, may be an occasion of the exercise of a truly good affection. The reason of it is this, that however all exercises of grace be from the Spirit of God, yet the Spirit of God dwells and acts in the hearts of the saints, in some measure after

2. [Above, pp. 316–25.]

the manner of a vital, natural principle, a principle of new nature in them; whose exercises are excited by means, in some measure as other natural principles are. Though grace ben't in the saints as a mere natural principle, but as a sovereign agent, and so its exercises are not tied to means by an immutable law of nature, as in mere natural principles; yet God has so constituted that grace should dwell so in the hearts of the saints, that its exercises should have some degree of connection with means, after the manner of a principle of nature.

Another erroneous principle that there has been something of, and that has been an occasion of some mischief and confusion, is that external order in matters of religion and use of the means of grace is but little to be regarded: 'tis spoken lightly of, under the names of ceremonies and dead forms, etc. And [it] is probably the more despised by some because their opposers insist so much upon it, and because they are so continually hearing from them the cry of disorder and confusion. 'Tis objected against the importance of external order that God don't look at the outward form, he looks at the heart: but that is a weak argument against its importance, that true godliness don't consist in it; for it may be equally made use of against all the outward means of grace whatsoever. True godliness don't consist in ink and paper, but yet that would be a foolish objection against the importance of ink and paper in religion, when without it we could not have the Word of God. If any external means at all are needful, any outward actions of a public nature, or wherein God's people are jointly concerned in public society, without doubt external order is needful: the management of an external affair that is public, or wherein a multitude is concerned without order, is in everything found impossible. Without order there can be no general direction of a multitude to any particular designed end; their purposes will cross one another, and they won't help but hinder one another. A multitude can't act in union one with another without order; confusion separates and divides them, so that there can be no concert or agreement. If a multitude would help one another in any affair, they must unite themselves one to another in a regular subordination of members, in some measure as it is in the natural body; by this means they will be in some capacity to act with united strength: and thus Christ has appointed that it should be in the visible church, as I Cor. 12:14 to the end, and Rom. 12:4–8.

Zeal without order will do but little, or at least it will be effectual but a little while. Let a company that are very zealous against the enemy go forth to war without any manner of order, everyone rushing forward as his zeal shall drive him, all in confusion, if they gain something at first onset, by surprising the enemy, yet how soon do they come to nothing, and fall an easy helpless prey to their adversaries? Order is one of the most necessary of all external means of the spiritual good of God's church; and therefore it is requisite even in heaven itself, where there is the least need of any external means of grace; order is maintained amongst the glorious angels there. And the necessity of it in order to the carrying on any design wherein a multitude are concerned, is so great that even the devils in hell are driven to something of it, that they may carry on the designs of their kingdom. And 'tis very observable that those kinds of irrational creatures, for whom it is needful that they should act in union and join a multitude together to carry on any work for their preservation, they do by a wonderful instinct that God has put into them observe and maintain a most regular and exact order among themselves; such as bees and some others. And order in the visible church is not only necessary to the carrying on the designs of Christ's glory and the church's prosperity, but it is absolutely necessary to its defense; without it, it's like a city without walls, and can be in no capacity to defend itself from any kind of mischief: and so however it be an external thing, yet is not to be despised on that account; for though it ben't the food of souls, yet it is in some respect their defense. The people of Holland would be very foolish to despise the dikes that keep out the sea from overwhelming them, under the names of dead stones and vile earth, because the matter of which they are built is not good to eat.

It seems to be partly on the foundation of this notion of the worthlessness of external order, that some have seemed to act on that principle that the power of judging and openly censuring others should not be reserved in the hands of particular persons, or consistories appointed thereto, but ought to be left at large for anybody that pleases to take it upon them, or that think themselves fit for it; but more of this afterwards—[3]

On this foundation also, an orderly attending on the stated worship of God in families has been made too light of; and it has

3. [Below, pp. 474–83.]

been in some places too much of a common and customary thing to be absent from family worship, and to be abroad late in the night at religious meetings, or to attend religious conversation. Not but that this may be, on certain extraordinary occasions; I have seen the case to be such in many instances, that I have thought did afford sufficient warrant for persons to be absent from family prayer, and to be from home till very late in the night: but we should take heed that this don't become a custom or common practice; if it should be so, we shall soon find the consequences to be very ill.

It seems to be on the same foundation of the supposed unprofitableness of external order, that it has been thought by some that there is no need that such and such religious services and performances should be limited to any certain office in the church (of which more afterwards); [4] and also that those offices themselves, as particularly that of the Gospel ministry, need not be limited as it used to be, to persons of a liberal education; but some of late have been for having others, that they have supposed to be persons of eminent experience, publicly licensed to preach, yea, and ordained to the work of the ministry; and some ministers have seemed to favor such a thing: but how little do they seem to look forward, and consider the unavoidable consequences of opening such a door? If once it should become a custom, or a thing generally approved and allowed of, to admit persons to the work of the ministry that have had no education for it, because of their remarkable experiences, and being persons of good understanding, how many lay persons would soon appear as candidates for the work of the ministry? I doubt not but that I have been acquainted with scores that would have desired it. And how shall we know where to stop? If one is admitted because his experiences are remarkable, another will think his experiences also remarkable; and we perhaps shall not be able to deny but that they are near as great: if one is admitted because besides experiences, he has good natural abilities, another, by himself and many of his neighbors, may be thought equal to him. It will be found of absolute necessity that there should be some certain, visible limits fixed, to avoid bringing odium upon ourselves, and breeding uneasiness and strife amongst others; and I know of none better, and indeed no other that can well be fixed, than those that the prophet

4. [Below, pp. 483–88.]

Zechariah fixes, viz. that those only should be appointed to be pastors or shepherds in God's church that have been taught to keep cattle from their youth, or that have had an education for that purpose.[5] Those ministers that have a disposition to break over these limits, if they should do so, and make a practice of it, would break down that fence which they themselves after a while, after they have been wearied with the ill consequences, would be glad to have somebody else build up for them. Not but that there may probably be some persons in the land, that have had no education at college, that are in themselves better qualified for the work of the ministry than some others that have taken their degrees, and are now ordained. But yet I believe the breaking over those bounds that have hitherto been set, in ordaining such persons, would in its consequences be a greater calamity, than the missing such persons in the work of the ministry. The opening a door for the admission of unlearned men to the work of the ministry, though they should be persons of extraordinary experience, would on some accounts be especially prejudicial at such a day as this; because such persons, for want of an extensive knowledge, are oftentimes forward to lead others into those things which a people are in danger of at such a time, above all other times, viz. impulses, vain imaginations, superstition, indiscreet zeal, and such like extremes; instead of defending them from them, for which a people especially need a shepherd at such an extraordinary season.

Another erroneous principle that it seems to me some have been, at least, in danger of, is that ministers, because they speak as Christ's ambassadors, may assume the same style and speak as with the same authority that the prophets of old did, yea, that Jesus Christ himself did in the 23d [chapter] of Matthew, "Ye serpents, ye generation of vipers, etc." and other places; and that not only when they are speaking to the people, but also to their brethren in the ministry. Which principle is absurd, because it makes no difference in the different degrees and orders of messengers that God has sent into the world, though God has made a very great difference: for though they all come in some respect in the name of God, and with something of his authority, yet certainly there is a vast difference in the degree of authority with which God has invested them. Jesus Christ was one that was sent into the world as God's messenger, and so was one of his apostles,

5. [Zech. 13:5; see above, p. 434.]

and so also is an ordinary pastor of a church; but yet it don't follow that because Jesus Christ and an ordinary minister are both messengers of God, that therefore an ordinary minister in his office is vested with an equal degree of authority that Christ was in his. As there is a great difference in their authority, and as Christ came as God's messenger in a vastly higher manner, so another style became him, more authoritative than is proper for us worms of the dust, though we also are messengers of inferior degree. It would be strange if God, when he has made so great a difference in the degree in which he has invested different messengers with his authority, should make no difference as to the outward appearance and shew of authority, in style and behavior, which is proper and fit to be seen in them. Though God has put great honor upon ministers, and they may speak as his ambassadors, yet he never intended that they should have the same outward appearance of authority and majesty, either in their behavior or speech, that his Son shall have when he comes to judgment at the last day, though both come, in different respects and degrees, in the name of the Lord. Alas! Can anything ever make it enter into the hearts of worms of the dust that it is fit and suitable that it should be so?

[3] Thus I have considered the two first of those three causes of error in conduct that were mentioned. I come now to the third and last cause of the errors of those that have appeared to be the subjects of zealous promoters of this work, viz. a being ignorant or unobservant of some particular things, by which the Devil has special advantage.

And here I would particularly take notice (1) of some things with respect to the inward experiences of Christians themselves; and (2) something with regard to the external effects of experiences.

(1) There are three things I would take notice of with regard to the experiences of Christians, by which the Devil has many advantages against us.

A. The first thing is the mixture there oftentimes is in the experiences of true Christians; whereby when they have truly gracious experiences, and divine and spiritual discoveries and exercises, they have something else mixed with them besides what is spiritual: there is a mixture of that which is natural, and that which is corrupt, with that which is divine. This is what Christians are liable to in the present exceeding imperfect state: the great imperfection of grace, and feebleness and infancy of the new nature, and the great remains of corruption, together with the circumstances we are in in this world, where we are encompassed all round with what tends to pollute us, exposes to this. And indeed, it is not to be supposed that Christians ever have any experiences in this world that are wholly pure, entirely spiritual, without any mixture of what is natural and carnal. The beam of light, as it comes from the fountain of light upon our hearts, is pure, but as it is reflected thence, it is mixed: the seed as sent from heaven and planted in the heart, is pure, but as it springs up out of the heart, is impure; yea, there is commonly a much greater mixture, than persons for the most part seem to have any imagination of; I have often thought that the experiences of true Christians are very frequently as it is with some sorts of fruits, that are enveloped in several coverings of thick shells or pods, that are thrown away by him that gathers the fruit, and but a very small part of the whole bulk is the pure kernel that is good to eat.

The things, of all which there is frequently some mixture with gracious experiences, yea, with very great and high experiences, are these three: human, or natural affection and passion; impressions on the imagination; and a degree of self-righteousness or spiritual pride. There is very often with that which is spiritual a great mixture of that affection or passion which arises from natural principles: so that nature has a very great hand in those vehement motions and flights of the passions that appear. Hence the same degrees of divine communications from heaven shall have vastly different effects, in what outwardly appears, in persons of different natural tempers. The great mixture of that which is natural with that which is spiritual, is very manifest in the peculiar effects that divine influences have in some certain families, or persons of such a blood, in a distinguishing manner of the operating of the passions and affections, and the manner of the outward expressions of 'em. I know some remarkable instances of this. The same is also evident by the different effects of divine communications on the same person at different times, and in different circumstances: the novelty of things, or the sudden transition from an opposite extreme, and many other things that might be mentioned, greatly contribute to the raising of the passions. And sometimes there is not only a mixture of that which is common and natural with gracious experience, but even that which is animal, that which is in a great measure from the body, and is properly the result of the animal frame. In what true Christians feel of affections towards God, all is not always purely holy and divine; everything that is felt in the affections don't arise from spiritual principles, but common and natural principles have a very great hand; an improper self-love may have a great share in the effect: God is not loved for his own sake, or for the excellency and beauty of his own perfections as he ought to be; nor have these things in any wise that proportion in the effect that they ought to have. So in that love that true Christians have one to another, very often there is a great mixture of what arises from common and natural principles, with grace; and self-love has a great hand: the children of God ben't loved purely for Christ's sake, but there may be a great mixture of that natural love that many sects of heretics have boasted of, who have been greatly united one to another because they were of their company, on their side, against the rest of the world; yea, there may be a mixture of natural love to the opposite sex, with Christian and divine love. So there may be a great mixture in that sorrow for sin that the godly have; and also in their joys; natural principles may greatly contribute to what is felt, a great many ways, as might easily be shown, would it not make my discourse too lengthy. There is nothing that belongs to Christian experience that is more liable to a corrupt mixture than zeal; though it be an excellent virtue, a heavenly flame, when it is pure: but as it is exercised in those who are so little sanctified, and so little humbled, as we are in the present state, 'tis very apt to be mixed with human passion, yea, with corrupt hateful affections, pride and uncharitable bitterness, and other things that are not from heaven but from hell.

Another thing that is often mixed with what is spiritual in the experiences of Christians are impressions on the imagination; whereby godly persons, together with a spiritual understanding of divine things and conviction of their reality and certainty, and a strong and deep sense of their excellency or great importance upon their hearts, have strongly impressed on their minds external ideas or images of things. A degree of imagination in such a case, as I have observed elsewhere,[6] is unavoidable, and neces-

6. [In *Distinguishing Marks;* above, pp. 235–38.]

sarily arises from human nature as constituted in the present state; and a degree of imagination is really useful, and often is of great benefit; but when it is in too great a degree it becomes an impure mixture that is prejudicial. This mixture very often arises from the constitution of the body. It commonly greatly contributes to the other kind of mixture mentioned before, viz. of natural affections and passions; it helps to raise them to a great height.

Another thing that is often mixed with the experiences of true Christians, which is the worst mixture of all, is a degree of self-righteousness or spiritual pride. This is often mixed with the joys of Christians: the joy that they have is not purely the joy of faith, or a rejoicing in Christ Jesus, but is partly a rejoicing in themselves. There is oftentimes in their elevations a looking upon themselves, and a viewing their own high attainments; they rejoice partly because they are taken with their own experiences and great discoveries, which makes 'em in their own apprehensions so to excel; and this heightens all their passions, and especially those effects that are more external.

There is a much greater mixture of these things in the experiences of some Christians than others; in some the mixture is so great as very much to obscure and hide the beauty of grace in them, like a thick smoke that hinders all the shining of the fire.

These things we ought to be well aware of, that we mayn't take all for gold that glisters, and that we may know what to countenance and encourage, and what to discourage; otherwise Satan will have a vast advantage against us, for he works in the corrupt mixture. Sometimes for want of persons distinguishing the ore from the pure metal, those experiences are most admired by the persons themselves that are the subjects of them, and by others, that are not the most excellent. The great external effects and vehemence of the passions, and violent agitations of the animal spirits, is sometimes much owing to the corrupt mixture (as is very apparent in some instances); though it be not always so. I have observed a great difference among those that are under high affections, and seem disposed to be earnestly talking to those that are about them; some insist much more, in their talk, on what they behold in God and Christ, the glory of the divine perfections, Christ's beauty and excellency, and wonderful condescension and grace, and their own unworthiness, and the great and infinite obligations that they themselves and others are under to love and serve God; some [others] insist almost wholly on their own high privileges, their assurance of God's love and favor, and the weakness and wickedness of opposers, and how much they are above their reach. The latter may have much of the presence of God, but their experiences don't appear to be so solid and unmixed as the former. And there is a great deal of difference in persons' earnestness in their talk and behavior; in some it seems to come indeed from the fullness of their hearts, and from the great sense they have of truth, a deep sense of the certainty and infinite greatness, excellency and importance of divine and eternal things, attended with all appearances of great humility; in others their earnestness seems to arise from a great mixture of human passion, and an undue and intemperate agitation of the spirits, which appears by their earnestness and vehemence not being proportioned to the nature of the subject they insist on, but they are violent in everything they say, as much when they are talking of things of smaller importance, as when speaking of things of greater weight. I have seen it thus in an instance or two, in which this vehemence at length issued in distraction. And there have been some few instances of a more extraordinary nature still, even of persons finding themselves disposed earnestly to talk and cry out, from an unaccountable kind of bodily pressure, without any extraordinary view of anything in their minds, or sense of anything upon their hearts; wherein probably there was the immediate hand of the Devil.

B. Another thing by which the Devil has great advantage, is the unheeded defects there sometimes are in the experiences of true Christians, and those high affections wherein there is much that is truly good.

What I now have respect to is something diverse from that defect, or imperfection of degree, which is in every holy disposition and exercise in this life, in the best of the saints. What I aim at is experiences being especially defective in some particular thing that ought to be in them; which though it ben't an essential defect, or such a defect as is in the experiences of hypocrites, which renders them utterly vain, monstrous, and altogether abominable to God, yet is such a defect as maims and deforms the experience; the essence of truly Christian experiences is not wanting, but yet that is wanting that is very needful in order to the proper beauty of the image of Christ in such a person's experiences; but things are very much out of a due proportion: there is indeed much of some things, but at the same time there is so little of some other things that should bear a proportion, that the defect very much deforms the Christian, and is truly odious in the sight of God.

What I observed before was something that deformed the Christian, as it was too much, something mixed, that is not belonging to the Christian as such; what I speak of now is something that deforms the Christian the other way, viz. by there not being enough, something wanting, that does belong to the Christian as such: the one deforms the Christian as a monstrous excrescence, the other as thereby the new creature is maimed, and some member in a great measure wanting, or so small and withering as to be very much out of due proportion. This is another spiritual calamity that the saints are liable to through the great imperfection of grace in this life; like the chicken in the egg, in the beginning of its formation, in which, though there are indeed the rudiments or lineaments of all the parts, yet some few parts are plain to be seen when others are hid, so that without a microscope it appears very monstrous.

When this deficiency and disproportion is great, as sometimes it is in real saints, it is not only a great deformity in itself, but has many ill consequences; it gives the Devil great advantage, and leaves a door open for corruption, and exposes to very deformed and unlovely actions, and issues oftentimes in the great wounding of the soul.

For the better understanding of this matter, we may observe that God in the revelation that he has made of himself to the world by Jesus Christ, has taken care to give a proportionable manifestation of two kinds of excellencies or perfections of his nature, viz. those that especially tend to possess us with awe and reverence, and to search and humble us, and those that tend to win and draw and encourage us. By the one he appears as an infinitely great, pure, holy and heart-searching Judge; by the other, as a gentle and gracious Father and a loving Friend: by the one he is a pure, searching and burning flame; by the other a sweet, refreshing light. These two kinds of attributes are as it were admirably tempered together in the revelation of the Gospel: there is a proportionable manifestation of justice and mercy, holiness and grace, majesty and gentleness, authority and condescension. God hath thus ordered that his diverse excellencies, as he reveals himself in the face of Jesus Christ [II Cor. 4:6], should have a proportionable

manifestation, herein providing for our necessities; he knew it to
be of great consequence that our apprehensions of these diverse
perfections of his nature should be duly proportioned one to
another; a defect on the one hand, viz. having much of a discovery
of his love and grace, without a proportionable discovery of his
awful majesty and his holy and searching purity, would tend to
spiritual pride, carnal confidence and presumption; and a defect
on the other hand, viz. having much of a discovery of his holy
majesty, without a proportionable discovery of his grace, tends to
unbelief, a sinful fearfulness and spirit of bondage: and therefore
herein chiefly consists that deficiency of experiences that I am now
speaking of. The revelation God has made of himself in his Word,
and the provision made for our spiritual welfare in the Gospel,
is perfect; but yet the actual light and communications we have
are not perfect, but many ways exceeding imperfect and maimed.
And experience plainly shews that Christians may have high experiences in some respects, and yet their circumstances may be
unhappy in this regard, that their experiences and discoveries are
no more general. There is a great difference among Christians in
this respect; some have much more general discoveries than others,
who are upon many accounts the most amiable Christians. Christians may have experiences that are very high, and yet there may
be very much of this deficiency and disproportion: their high experiences are truly from the Spirit of God, but sin comes in by
the defect (as indeed all sin is originally from a defective, priva-
tive cause); and in such a case high discoveries, at the same time
that they are enjoyed, may be, and sometimes are the occasion, or
causa sine qua non [7] of sin; sin may come in at that back door, the
gap that is left open, as spiritual pride often does. And many times
the Spirit of God is quenched by this means, and God punishes
the pride and presumption that rises, by bringing such darkness,
and suffering [8] such awful consequences and horrid temptations,
as are enough to make one's hair stand on end to hear them.
Christians therefore should diligently observe their own hearts as
to this matter, and should pray to God that he would give 'em experiences in which one thing may bear a proportion to another,
that God may be honored and their souls edified thereby; and

7. [See above, pp. 67, 316.]
8. [I.e. permitting.]

ministers should have an eye to this, in their private dealings with
the souls of their people.

'Tis chiefly from such a defect of experiences that some things
have arisen that have been pretty common among true Christians
of late, that have been supposed by many to have risen from a good
cause; as particularly talking of divine and heavenly things, and
expressing divine joys with a laughter or a light behavior. I believe in many instances such things have arisen from a good cause,
as their *causa sine qua non;* that high discoveries and gracious joyful affections have been the occasion of them: but the *proper* cause
has been sin, even that odious defect in their experience, whereby
there has been wanting a sense of the awful and holy majesty of God
as present with them, and their nothingness and vileness before
him, proportionable to the sense they have had of God's grace and
the love of Christ. And the same is true in many cases of persons'
unsuitable boldness, their disposition to speak with authority, intemperate zeal, and many other things that sometimes appear in
true Christians under great religious affections.

And sometimes the vehemence of the motion of the animal
spirits, under great affections, is owing in considerable measure to
experiences being thus partial. I have known it in several instances, that persons have been greatly affected with the dying love
of Christ, and the consideration of the happiness of the enjoyment of him in heaven, and other things of that nature, and their
animal spirits at the same time have been in a great emotion, but
in the midst of it have had given 'em a deep sense of the awful,
holy majesty of God; and it has at once composed them, and
quieted animal nature, without diminishing their comfort, but
only has made it of a better, and more solid nature: when they
have had a sense both of the majesty and grace of God, one thing
has as it were balanced another, and caused a more happy sedate-
ness and composure of body and mind.

From these things we may learn how to judge of experiences,
and to estimate their goodness. Those are not always the best experiences that are attended with the most violent affections and
most vehement motions of the animal spirits, or that have the
greatest effects on the body; nor are they always the best that do
most dispose persons to abound in talk to others, and to speak in
the most vehement manner (though these things often arise from

the greatness of spiritual experiences); but those are the most excellent experiences that are qualified as follows: 1. That have the least mixture, or are the most purely spiritual. 2. That are the least deficient and partial, in which the diverse things that appertain to Christian experience are proportionable one to another. And 3. That are raised to the highest degree: 'tis no matter how high they are raised if they are qualified as before mentioned, the higher the better. Experiences thus qualified will be attended with the most amiable behavior, and will bring forth the most solid and sweet fruits, and will be the most durable, and will have the greatest effect on the abiding temper of the soul.

If God is pleased to carry on this work and it should prove to be the dawning of a general revival of the Christian church, it may be expected that the time will come before long, when the experiences of Christians shall be much more generally thus qualified. We must expect green fruits before we have ripe ones. 'Tis probable that hereafter the discoveries which the saints shall have of divine things will be in a much higher degree than yet have been; but yet shall be so ordered of an infinitely wise and all-sufficient God, that they shall not have so great an effect in proportion on the body, and will be less oppressive to nature; and that the outward manifestations will rather be like those that were in Stephen, when he was full of the Holy Ghost, when "all that sat in the Council, looking steadfastly on him, saw his face as it had been the face of an angel" [Acts 6:15]. Their inward fullness of the Spirit of God, in his divine, amiable and sweet influences, shall as it were shine forth in an heavenly aspect, and manner of speech and behavior.

C. But there is another thing concerning experiences of Christians, of which it is of yet greater importance that we should be aware, than either of the preceding, and that is the degenerating of experiences. What I mean is something diverse from the mere decay of experiences, or their gradually vanishing, by persons losing their sense of things; 'tis persons' experiences growing by degrees worse and worse in their kind, more and more partial and deficient, in which things are more out of due proportion, and also have more and more of a corrupt mixture; the spiritual part decreases, and the other useless and hurtful parts greatly increase. There is such a thing, and it is very frequent, as experience abundantly evidences: I have seen it in very many instances; and great are the mischiefs that have risen through want of being more aware of it.

There is commonly, as I observed before, in high experiences, besides that which is spiritual, a mixture of three things, viz. natural or common affections, and workings of the imagination, and a degree of self-righteousness or spiritual pride. Now it often comes to pass, that through persons not distinguishing the wheat from the chaff, and for want of watchfulness and humble jealousy of themselves, and laying great weight on the natural and imaginary part, and yielding to it and indulging of it, that part grows and increases, and the spiritual part decreases; the Devil sets in and works in the corrupt part, and cherishes it to his utmost; till at length the experiences of some persons who began well, come to but little else but violent motions of carnal affections, with great heats of the imagination, and a great degree of enthusiasm, and swelling of spiritual pride; very much like some fruits which bud, blossom and kernel well, but afterwards are blasted with an excess of moisture; so that though the bulk is monstrously great, yet there is little else in it but what is useless and unwholesome. It appears to me very probable that many of the heresies that have arisen, and sects that have appeared in the Christian world in one age and another, with wild enthusiastical notions and practices, began at first by this means, that it was such a degenerating of experiences that first gave rise to 'em, or at least led the way to 'em.

There is nothing in the world that does so much expose to this degenerating of experiences, as an unheeded spiritual pride and self-confidence, and persons being conceited of their own stock, without an humble, daily and continual dependence on God. And this very thing seems to be typified of old, by the corrupting of the manna. Some of the children of Israel, because they had gathered a store of manna, trusted in it, there being, as they apprehended, sufficient in the store they had gathered and laid up, without humbly looking to heaven and stooping to the earth for daily supplies; and the consequence was that their manna "bred worms and stank," Exod. 16:20. Pride above all things promotes this degeneracy of experiences, because it grieves and quenches the Spirit of the Lamb of God, and so kills the spiritual part: and it cherishes the natural part; it inflames the carnal affections, and heats the imagination.

The unhappy person that is the subject of such a degeneracy of experiences, for the most part, is not sensible of his own calamity; but because he finds himself still violently moved, and [in] greater heats of zeal and more vehement motions of his animal spirits, thinks himself fuller of the Spirit of God than ever. But indeed it is with him, as the Apostle says of the Galatians, Gal. 3:3, having "begun in the Spirit," they are "made perfect by the flesh."

By the mixture there is of common affection with love to God, the love of true Christians is liable to degenerate, and to be more and more built on the foundation of a supposition of being his high and peculiar favorites, and less and less on an apprehension of the excellency of God's nature as he is in himself. So the joy of Christians, by reason of the mixture there is with spiritual joy, is liable to degenerate and to come to that at last as to be but little else but joy in self, joy in a person's own supposed eminency, and distinction from others in the favor of God. So zeal, that at first might be in great part spiritual, yet through the mixture there is, in a long continuance of opposition and controversy, may degenerate more and more into human and proud passion, and may come to bitterness and even a degree of hatred. And so love to the brethren may by degrees come to little else but fondness and zeal for a party; yea, through a mixture of a natural love to the opposite sex, may degenerate more and more, till it issues in that which is criminal and gross. And I leave it with those who are better acquainted with ecclesiastical history, to inquire whether such a degeneracy of affections as this might not be the first thing that led the way and gave occasion to the rise of the abominable notions of some sects that have arisen concerning the community of women.[9] However that is, yet certainly the mutual embraces and kisses of persons of different sexes, under the notion of Christian love and holy kisses, are utterly to be disallowed and abominated, as having the most direct tendency quickly to turn Christian love into unclean and brutish lust, which won't be the better, but ten times the worse, for being christened by the name of Christian love. I should also think it advisable that meetings of young people of both sexes, in the evening, by themselves, without a minister

9. [I.e. communitarian experiments practicing (or accused of) polygamy, or more usually, plural marriage. Examples known to JE would have included the Münster "kingdom" of Reformation Germany, the English Familists (above, p. 257), and the French Prophets (above, p. 63).]

or any elder people amongst them, for religious exercises, should be avoided: for though for the present, while their minds are greatly solemnized with lively impressions, and a deep sense of divine things, there may appear no ill consequence; yet we must look to the further end of things, and guard against future dangers and advantages that Satan might gain against us. As a lively, solemn sense of divine things on the minds of young persons may gradually decay, so there will be danger that an ill improvement of these meetings may gradually prevail; if not in any unsuitable behavior while together in the meeting, yet when they break up to go home, they may naturally consort together in couples for other than religious purposes; and it may at last come to that, that young persons may go to such meetings chiefly for the sake of such an opportunity for company-keeping.

The defect there sometimes is in the experiences of Christians exposes 'em to degenerate, as well as the mixture that they have. Deficient maimed experiences do sometimes become more and more so: the mind being wholly intent upon those things that are in view, and those that are most wanting being neglected, there is less and less of them, and so the gap for corruption to come in grows wider and wider. And commonly both these causes of the degenerating of experiences operate together.

We had need to be jealous over ourselves with a godly jealousy, as the Apostle was over the Christian Corinthians, lest by any means, as the serpent beguiled Eve through his subtlety, so our minds should be corrupted from the simplicity that is in Christ. God indeed will never suffer his true saints totally and finally to fall away, but yet may punish their pride and self-confidence, by suffering them to be long led into a dreadful wilderness by the subtle serpent, to the great wounding of their own souls, and the interest of religion.

And before I dismiss this head of the degenerating of experiences, I would mention one thing more that tends to it; and that is persons' aiming in their experience to go beyond the rule of God's Word, i.e. aiming at that which is indeed, in some respect, beyond the rule. Thus some persons have endeavored utterly to root out and abolish all natural affection, or any special affection or respect to their near relations, under a notion that no other love ought to be allowed but spiritual love, and that all other love is to be abolished as carnal, and that it becomes Christians to love none upon the account of anything else but the image of God; and that therefore love should go out to one and another only in that proportion in which the image of God is seen in them. They might as well argue that a man ought utterly to disallow of, and endeavor to abolish all love or appetite to their daily food, under a notion that it is a carnal appetite, and that no other appetite should be tolerated but spiritual appetites. Why should the saints strive after that, as an high attainment in holiness, which the Apostle in Rom. 1:31 mentions as one instance wherein the heathen had got to the most horrid pass in wickedness, viz. a being without natural affection?

Some have doubted whether they might pray for the conversion and salvation of the souls of their children, any more than for the souls of others; because the salvation of the souls of others would be as much to God's glory as the salvation of their children; and they have supposed that to pray most for their own would shew a selfish disposition. So they have been afraid to tolerate a compassionate grief and concern for their nearest friends, for fear it would be an argument of want of resignation to God.

And 'tis true, there is great danger of persons setting their hearts too much upon their earthly friends; our love to earthly friends ought to be under the government of the love of God, and should be attended with a spirit of submission and resignation to his will, and everything should be subordinated to his glory: but that is no argument that these affections should be entirely abolished, which the Creator of the world has put within mankind, for the good of mankind, and because he saw they would be needful for them, as they must be united in society, in the present state, and are of great use when kept in their proper place; and to endeavor totally to root them out would be to reproach and oppose the wisdom of the Creator. Nor is the being of these natural inclinations, if well regulated, inconsistent with any part of our duty to God, or any argument of a sinful selfishness, any more than the natural abhorrence that there is in the human nature of pain, and natural inclination to ease that was in the man Christ Jesus himself.

'Tis the duty of parents to be more concerned, and to pray more for the salvation of their children, than for the children of their neighbors, as much as it is the duty of a minister to be more concerned for the salvation of the souls of his flock, and to pray more for them, than those of other congregations, because they are committed to his care; so our near friends are more committed to our care than others, and our near neighbors, than those that live at a great distance; and the people of our land and nation are more in some sense, committed to our care than the people of China, and we ought to pray more for them, and to be more concerned that the kingdom of Christ should flourish among them, than in another country, where it would be as much and no more for the glory of God. Compassion ought to be especially exercised towards friends, Job 6:14. Christ did not frown upon a special affection and compassion for near friends, but countenanced and encouraged it, from time to time, in those that in the exercise of such an affection and compassion applied to him for relief for their friends; as in the instance of the woman of Canaan, Jairus, Mary and Martha, the centurion, the widow of Nain, and many others.[10] The Apostle Paul, though a man as much resigned and devoted to God, and under the power of his love, perhaps as any mere man that ever lived, yet had a peculiar concern for his countrymen the Jews, the rather on that account that they were his brethren and kinsmen according to the flesh; he had a very high degree of compassionate grief for them, insomuch that he tells us he had great heaviness and continual sorrow of heart for them, and could wish himself accursed from Christ for them [Rom. 9:1–3].

There are many things that are proper for the saints in heaven that are not suitable to the state God has set us in, in this world: and for Christians, in these and other instances, to affect to go beyond the present state of mankind, and what God has appointed as fit for it, is an instance of that which the wise man calls a being righteous overmuch [Eccles. 7:16], and has a tendency to open a door for Satan, and to cause religious affections to degenerate into something very unbecoming of Christians.

(2) Thus I have, as I proposed, taken notice of some things with regard to the inward experiences of Christians, by which Satan has an advantage. I now proceed in the second place, to take notice of something with regard to the external effects of experiences, which also gives Satan an advantage. What I have respect to is the secret and unaccountable influence that custom has

10. [Cf. Matt. 15:22–28; Mark 5:22–24, 35–42; John 11:1–45; Matt. 8:5–13; and Luke 7:11–15. The last case is not parallel with the others and does not illustrate JE's point, inasmuch as the widow of Nain (so far as the record goes) made no request for assistance.]

upon persons, with respect to the external effects and manifestations of the inward affections of the mind. By custom I mean both a person's being accustomed to a thing in himself, in his own common, allowed and indulged practice, and also the countenance and approbation of others amongst whom he dwells, by their general voice and practice. It is well known, and appears sufficiently by what I have said already in this treatise and elsewhere, that I am far from ascribing all the late uncommon effects and outward manifestations of inward experiences to custom and fashion, as some do; I know it to be otherwise, if it be possible for me to know anything of this nature by the most critical observation, under all manner of opportunities of observing. But yet, this also is exceeding evident by experience, that custom has a strange influence in these things: I know it by the different manners and degrees of external effects and manifestations of great affections and high discoveries, in different towns, according to what persons are gradually led into, and insensibly habituated to, by example and custom; and also in the same place, at different times, according to the conduct that they have. If some person is among them to conduct them, that much countenances and encourages such kind of outward manifestations of great affections, they naturally and insensibly prevail, and grow by degrees unavoidable; but when afterwards they come under another kind of conduct, the manner of external appearances will strangely alter: and yet it seems to be without any proper design or contrivance of those in whom there is this alteration; 'tis not properly affected by them, but the influence of example and custom is secret and insensible to the persons themselves. These things have a vast influence in the manner of persons manifesting their joys, whether with smiles and an air of lightness, or whether with more solemnity and reverence; and so they have a great influence as to the disposition persons have under high affections to abound in talk; and also as to the manner of their speaking, the loudness and vehemence of their speech (though it would be exceeding unjust, and against all the evidence of fact and experience, and the reason of things, to lay all dispositions persons have to be much in speaking to others, and to speak in a very earnest manner, to custom). 'Tis manifest that example and custom has some way or other a secret and unsearchable influence on those actions that are involuntary, by the difference that there is in different places, and in the same places at different times, according to the diverse examples and conduct that they have.

Therefore, though it would be very unreasonable and prejudicial to the interest of religion to frown upon all these extraordinary external effects and manifestations of great religious affections (for a measure of them in natural, necessary and beautiful, and the effect is no wise disproportioned to the spiritual cause, and is of great benefit to promote religion); yet I think they greatly err who think that these things should be wholly unlimited, and that all should be encouraged in going in these things to the utmost length that they feel themselves inclined to: the consequence of this will be very bad. There ought to be a gentle restraint held upon these things, and there should be a prudent care taken of persons in such extraordinary circumstances, and they should be moderately advised at proper seasons, not to make more ado than there is need of, but rather to hold a restraint upon their inclinations; otherwise extraordinary outward effects will grow upon them, they will be more and more natural and unavoidable, and the extraordinary outward show will increase, without any increase of the internal cause; persons will find themselves under a kind of necessity of making a great ado, with less and less affection of soul, till at length almost any slight emotion will set them going, and they will be more and more violent and boisterous, and will grow louder and louder, till their actions and behavior becomes indeed very absurd. These things experience proves.[1]

[*Particular Errors*]

Thus I have taken notice of the more general causes whence the errors that have attended this great revival of religion have risen, and under each head have observed some particular errors

1. [Critics of the revival had observed the same thing. Cf. the anonymous (Charles Chauncy?) *Letter from a Gentleman in Boston to Mr. George Wishart, One of the Ministers of Edinburgh, Concerning the State of Religion in New England* (Edinburgh, 1742), p. 9: "The speaker delivers himself with the greatest vehemence both of voice and gesture, and in the most frightful language his genius will allow of. If this has its intended effect upon one or two weak women, the shrieks catch from one to another, till a great part of the congregation is affected; and some are in the thought that it may be too common for those zealous in the new way to cry out themselves, on purpose to move others, and bring forward a general scream."]

that have flowed from these fountains. I now proceed, as I proposed in the second place, to take notice of some particular errors that have risen from several of these causes; in some perhaps they have been chiefly owing to one, and in others to another, and in others to the influence of several, or all conjunctly.

[1] And here the first thing I would take notice of is censuring others that are professing Christians, in good standing in the visible church, as unconverted. I need not repeat what I have elsewhere [2] said to shew this to be against the plain and frequent and strict prohibitions of the Word of God: it is the worst disease that has attended this work, most contrary to the spirit and rules of Christianity, and of worst consequences. There is a most unhappy tincture that the minds of many, both ministers and people, have received that way. The manner of many has been, when they first enter into conversation with any person that seems to have any shew or make any pretenses to religion, to discern him, or to fix a judgment of him, from his manner of talking of things of religion, whether he be converted, or experimentally acquainted with vital piety or not, and then to treat him accordingly, and freely to express their thoughts of him to others, especially those that they have a good opinion of as true Christians, and accepted as brethren and companions in Christ; or if they don't declare their minds expressly, yet by their manner of speaking of them, at least to their friends, they'll show plainly what their thoughts are. So when they have heard any minister pray or preach, their first work has been to observe him on a design of discerning him, whether he be a converted man or no; whether he prays like one that feels the saving power of God's Spirit in his heart, and whether he preaches like one that knows what he says. It has been so much the way in some places, that many new converts don't know but it is their duty to do so; they know no other way. And when once persons yield to such a notion, and give in to such a humor, they'll quickly grow very discerning in their own apprehension; they think they can easily tell a hypocrite: and when once they have passed their censure, everything seems to confirm it; they see more and more in the person that they have censured, that seems to them to shew plainly that he is an un-

2. [In *Distinguishing Marks;* above, pp. 283–87.]

converted man. And then, if the person censured be a minister, everything in his public performances seems dead and sapless, and to do them no good at all, but on the contrary to be of deadening influence, and poisonous to the soul; yea, it seems worse and worse to them, his preaching grows more and more intolerable: which is owing to a secret, strong prejudice that steals in more and more upon the mind, as experience plainly and certainly shows.

When the Spirit of God was wonderfully poured out in this place more than seven years ago, and near thirty souls in a week, take one with another, for five or six weeks together, were to appearance brought home to Christ, and all the town seemed to be alive and full of God, there was no such notion or humor prevailing here; when ministers preached here, as very many did at that time, young and old, our people did not go about to discern whether they were men of experience or not: they did not know that they must: Mr. Stoddard never brought 'em up in that way; it did not seem natural to 'em to go about anything of that nature, nor did any such thing enter into their hearts; but when any minister preached, the business of everyone was to listen and attend to what he said, and apply it to his own heart, and make the utmost improvement of it. And 'tis remarkable, that never did there appear such a disposition in the people to relish, approve of, and admire ministers preaching as at that time: such expressions as these were frequent in the mouths of one and another, on occasion of the preaching of strangers here, viz. that they rejoiced that there were so many such eminent ministers in the country; and they wondered they never heard the fame of 'em before: they were thankful that other towns had so good means; and the like. And scarcely ever did any minister preach here but his preaching did some remarkable service; as I had good opportunity to know, because at that time I had particular acquaintance with most of the persons in the town, in their soul concerns. That it has been so much otherwise of late in many places in the land, is another instance of the secret and powerful influence of custom and example.

There has been an unhappy disposition in some ministers toward their brethren in the ministry in this respect, which has encouraged and greatly promoted such a spirit among some of their people. A wrong improvement has been made of Christ's scourging the buyers and sellers out of the temple [Matt. 21:12 and parallels]; it has been expected by some, that Christ was now about thus to purge his house of unconverted ministers, and this has made it more natural to them to think that they should do Christ service, and act as co-workers with him, to put to their hand, and endeavor by all means to cashier those ministers that they thought to be unconverted. Indeed it appears to me probable that the time is coming, when awful judgments will be executed on unfaithful ministers, and that no sort of men in the world will be so much exposed to divine judgments; but then we should leave that work to Christ, who is the Searcher of hearts, and to whom vengeance belongs; and not, without warrant, take the scourge out of his hand into our own. There has been too much of a disposition in some, as it were to give ministers over as reprobates, that have been looked upon as wolves in sheep's clothing; which has tended to promote and encourage a spirit of bitterness towards them, and to make it natural to treat them too much as if they knew God hated them. If God's children knew that others were reprobates, it would not be required of them to love them; we may hate those that we know God hates; as 'tis lawful to hate the Devil, and as the saints at the Day of Judgment will hate the wicked.

Some have been too apt to look for fire from heaven upon particular ministers; and this has naturally excited that disposition to call for it, that Christ rebuked in his disciples at Samaria [Luke 9:51–56]. For my part, though I believe no sort of men on earth are so exposed to spiritual judgments as wicked ministers, yet I feel no disposition to treat any minister as if I supposed that he was finally rejected of God; for I can't but hope that there is coming a day of such great grace, a time so appointed for the magnifying the riches and sovereignty of divine mercy beyond what ever was, that a great number of unconverted ministers will obtain mercy. There was no sort of persons in Christ's time that were so guilty, and so hardened, and towards whom Christ manifested such great indignation, as the priests and scribes, and there were no such persecutors of Christ and his disciples as they; and yet in that great outpouring of the Spirit that began on the Day of Pentecost, though it began with the common people, yet in the progress of the work, after a while, a great company of priests in Jerusalem were obedient to the faith, Acts 6:7. And Saul, one of the most violent of all the persecuting Pharisees, became afterwards the greatest promoter of the work of God that ever was. I hope we shall yet see in many instances a fulfillment of that in Isa. 29:24, "They also that erred in spirit shall come to understanding, and they that murmured shall learn doctrine."

Nothing has been gained by this practice. The end that some have aimed at in it has not been obtained, nor is ever like to be. Possibly some have openly censured ministers and encouraged their people's uneasiness under them, in hopes that it would soon come to that, that the uneasiness would be so general, and so great, that unconverted ministers in general would be cast off, and that then things would go on happily: but there is no likelihood of it. The Devil indeed has obtained his end; this practice has bred a great deal of unhappiness among ministers and people, has spoiled Christians' enjoyment of Sabbaths, and made 'em their most uneasy, uncomfortable and unprofitable days, and has stirred up great contention, and set all in a flame; and in one place and another where there was a glorious work of God's Spirit begun, it has in a great measure knocked all in the head, and their ministers hold their places. Some have aimed at a better end in censuring ministers; they have supposed it to be a likely means to awaken them: whereas indeed, there is no one thing has had so great a tendency to prevent the awakening of disaffected ministers in general: and no one thing has actually had such influence to lock up the minds of ministers against any good effect of this great work of God in the land, upon their minds, in this respect. I have known instances of some that seemed to be much moved by the first appearance of this work, but since have seemed to be greatly deadened by what has appeared of this nature. And if there be one or two instances of ministers that have been awakened by it, there are ten to one on whom it has had a contrary influence. The worst enemies of this work have been inwardly eased by this practice; they have made a shield of it to defend their consciences, and have been glad that it has been carried to so great a length; at the same time that they have looked upon it, and improved it, as a door opened for 'em to be more bold in opposing the work in general.

There is no such dreadful danger of natural men's being undone by our forbearing thus to censure them, and carrying it towards them as visible Christians; it will be no bloody, hell-peopling charity, as some seem to suppose, when it is known that we don't treat 'em as Christians, because we have taken it upon us to pass a judgment on their state, on any trial or exercise of our skill in examining and discerning them, but only as allowing them to be worthy of a public charity, on their profession and good external behavior; any more than Judas was in danger of being deceived by Christ's treating him a long time as a disciple, and sending him forth as an apostle (because he did not then take it upon him to act as the Judge and Searcher of hearts, but only as the Head of the visible church). Indeed, such a charity as this may be abused by some, as everything is, and will be, that is in its own nature proper, and of never so good tendency. I say nothing against dealing thoroughly with conscience, by the most convincing and searching dispensation of the Word of God: I don't desire that that sword should be sheathed, or gently handled by ministers; but let it be used as a two-edged sword, to pierce, "even to the dividing asunder soul and spirit, joints and marrow" [Heb. 4:12]; let conscience be dealt with, without any complements;[3] let ministers handle it in flaming fire, without having any more mercy on it than the furnace has on those metals that are tried in it. But let us let men's persons alone: let the Word of God judge them, but don't let us take it upon us till we have warrant for it.

Some have been ready to censure ministers because they seem, in comparison of some other ministers, to be very cold and lifeless in their ministerial performances. But then it should be considered that for aught we know, God may hereafter raise up ministers of so much more excellent and heavenly qualifications, and so much more spiritual and divine in their performances, that there may appear as great a difference between them and those that now seem the most lively, as there is now between them and others that are called dead and sapless; and those that are now called lively ministers may appear to their hearers, when they compare them with others that shall excel them, as wretchedly mean, and their performances poor, dead, dry things; and many may be ready to be prejudiced against them as accounting them good for nothing, and it may be, calling them soul-murderers. What a poor figure, may we suppose, the most lively of us, and those that are most admired

3. [In the Worcester and Dwight editions of JE's works, this word is changed to "compliment," meaning doubtless ceremonious approbation approaching flattery. That would suit the context well enough, perhaps; but the first edition has "complement," which in the eighteenth century sometimes signified something added as an ornament, a nonessential accessory.]

by the people, do make in the eyes of one of the saints of heaven, any otherwise than as their deadness, deformity and rottenness is hid by the veil of Christ's righteousness?

Another thing that has been supposed to be sufficient warrant for openly censuring ministers as unconverted, is their opposing this work of God that has lately been carried on in the land. And there can be no doubt with me but that opposition against this work may be such as to render either ministers or people truly scandalous, and expose 'em to public ecclesiastical censure; and that ministers hereby may utterly defeat the design of their ministry (as I observed before), and so give their people just cause of uneasiness: I should not think that any person had power to oblige me, constantly to attend the ministry of one who did from time to time plainly pray and preach against this work, or speak reproachfully of it frequently in his public performances, after all Christian methods had been used for a remedy, and to no purpose.

But as to determining how far opposing this work is consistent with a state of grace, or how far, and for how long time, some persons of good experience in their own souls, through prejudices they have received from the errors that have been mixed with this work, or through some peculiar disadvantages they are under to behold things in a right view of them, by reason of the persons they converse with, or their own cold and dead frames, [this] is, as experience shows, a very difficult thing; I have seen that which abundantly convinces me that the business is too high for me; I am glad that God has not committed such a difficult affair to me; I can joyfully leave it wholly in his hands, who is infinitely fit for it, without meddling at all with it myself. We may represent it as exceeding dangerous to oppose this work—for this we have good warrant in the Word of God; but I know of no necessity we are under to determine whether it be possible for those that are guilty of it to be in a state of grace or no.

God seems so strictly to have forbidden this practice of our judging our brethren in the visible church, not only because he knew that we were too much of babes, infinitely too weak, fallible and blind, to be well capacitated for it, but also because he knew that it was not a work suited to our proud hearts; that it would be setting us vastly too high, and making us too much of lords over our fellow creatures. Judging our brethren and passing a condemnatory sentence upon them seems to carry in it an act of

authority, especially in so great a case, to sentence them with respect to that state of their hearts, on which depends their liable-
ness to eternal damnation; as is evident by such interrogations as
those (to hear which from God's mouth is enough to make us
shrink into nothing with shame and confusion, and sense of our
own blindness and worthlessness). Rom. 14:4, "Who art thou that
judgest another man's servant? To his own master he standeth or
falleth." And Jas. 4:12, "There is one law-giver that is able to save
and destroy; who art thou that judgest another?" Our wise and
merciful Shepherd has graciously taken care not to lay in our way
such a temptation to pride; he has cut up all such poison out of
our pasture; and therefore we should not desire to have it restored.
Blessed be his name, that he has not laid such a temptation in the
way of my pride! I know that in order to be fit for this business,
I must not only be vastly more knowing, but more humble than
I am.

Though I believe some of God's own children have of late been
very guilty in this matter, yet by what is said of it in the Scripture, it appears to me very likely that before these things which
God has lately begun have an end, God will awfully rebuke that
practice; may it in sovereign and infinite mercy be prevented, by
the deep and open humiliation of those that have openly practiced
it.

As this practice ought to be avoided, so should all such open,
visible marks of distinction and separation that imply it; as particularly, distinguishing such as we have judged to be in a converted state with the compellations of "brother" or "sister," 4 any
further than there is a visible ecclesiastical distinction. In those
places where it is the manner to receive such, and such only to the
communion of the visible church, as recommend themselves by
giving a satisfying account of their inward experiences, there Christians may openly distinguish such persons, in their speech and ordinary behavior, with a visible separation, without being inconsistent with themselves. And I don't now pretend to meddle with
that controversy, whether such an account of experience be requisite to church fellowship: but certainly, to admit persons to
communion with us as brethren in the visible church, and then
visibly to reject them, and to make an open distinction between

4. [The most charitable name for persons judged unconverted was "neighbor."
For harsher "compellations," see above, pp. 419–20.]

them and others by different names or appellations, is to be inconsistent with ourselves; 'tis to make a visible church within a visible church, and visibly to divide between sheep and goats, setting one on the right hand, and the other on the left.

This bitter root of censoriousness must be totally rooted out, as we would prepare the way of the Lord. It has nourished and upheld many other things contrary to the humility, meekness and love of the Gospel. The minds of many have received an unhappy turn, in some respects, with their religion: there is a certain point or sharpness, a disposition to a kind of warmth, that does not savor of that meek, lamb-like, sweet disposition that becomes Christians. Many have now been so long habituated to it, that they don't know how to get out of it; but we must get out of it; the point and sharpness must be blunted, and we must learn another way of manifesting our zeal for God.

There is a way of reflecting on others, and censuring them in open prayer, that some have; which though it has a fair shew of love, yet is indeed the boldest way of reproaching others imaginable, because there is implied in it an appeal to the most high God concerning the truth of their censures and reflections.

And here I would also observe by the way, that some have a way of joining a sort of imprecations with their petitions for others, though but conditional ones, that appear to me wholly needless and improper: they pray that others may either be converted or removed. I never heard nor read of any such thing practiced in the church of God till now, unless it be with respect to some of the most visibly and notoriously abandoned enemies of the church of God. This is a sort of cursing men in our prayers, adding a curse with our blessing; whereas the rule is, "Bless and curse not" [Rom. 12:14]. To pray that God would kill another is to curse him with the like curse wherewith Elisha cursed the children that came out of Bethel [II Kings 2:23-24]. And the case must be very great and extraordinary indeed to warrant it, unless we were prophets, and did not speak our own words but words indited by the immediate inspiration of the Spirit of God. 'Tis pleaded that if God has no design of converting others, 'tis best for them, as well as best for others, that they should be immediately taken away and sent to hell before they have contracted more guilt. To which I would say, that so it was best that those children that met Elisha, seeing God had no design of converting them, should die immediately as they did; but yet Elisha's imprecating that sudden death upon them was cursing them; and therefore would not have been lawful for one that did not speak in the name of the Lord as a prophet.

And then if we give way to such things as these, where shall we stop? A child that suspects he has an unconverted father and mother may pray openly that his father and mother may either be converted or taken away and sent to hell now quickly, before their guilt is greater. (For unconverted parents are as likely to poison the souls of their family in their manner of training them up, as unconverted ministers are to poison their people.) And so it might come to that, that it might be a common thing all over the country for children to pray after this manner concerning their parents, and brethren and sisters concerning one another, and husbands concerning their wives, and wives concerning husbands, and so for the persons to pray concerning all their unconverted friends and neighbors; and not only so, but we may also pray concerning all those saints that are not lively Christians, that they may either be enlivened or taken away; if that be true that is often said by some at this day, that these cold dead saints do more hurt than natural men, and lead more souls to hell, and that it would be well for mankind if they were all dead.

How needless are such petitions or imprecations as these! What benefit is there of them? Why is it not sufficient for us to pray that God would provide for his church and the good of souls, and take care of his own flock, and give it needful means and advantages for its spiritual prosperity? Does God need to be directed by us in what way he shall do it? What need we ask of God to do it by killing such and such persons, if he don't convert them—unless we delight in the thoughts of God's answering us in such terrible ways, and with such awful manifestations of his wrath to our fellow creatures?

And why don't ministers direct sinners to pray for themselves, that God would either convert them or kill them, and send them to hell now before their guilt is greater? In this way we should lead persons in the next place to self-murder, for many probably would soon begin to think that that which they may pray for, they may seek, and use the means of.

Some with whom I have discoursed about this way of praying have said that the Spirit of God, as it were, forces them to utter themselves thus, as it were forces out such words from their mouths, when otherwise they should not dare to utter them. But such a kind of impulse don't look like the influence of the Spirit of God. The Spirit of God sometimes strongly inclines men to utter words; but not by putting expressions into the mouth and urging to utter them; but by filling the heart with a sense of divine things, and holy affections; and those affections and that sense inclines the mouth to speak. That other way of men's being urged to use certain expressions by an unaccountable force, is very probably from the influence of the spirit of the Devil.

2. Another thing I would take notice of, in the management of which there has been much error and misconduct, is lay exhorting; about which there has been abundance of disputing, jangling, and contention.

In the midst of all the disputes that have been, I suppose that all are agreed as to these two things, viz. 1. that all exhorting one another of laymen is not unlawful or improper, but on the contrary, that some exhorting is a Christian duty: and 2. I suppose also, all will allow that there is something that is proper only for ministers; that there is some kind or way of exhorting and teaching or other, that belongs only to the office of teachers. All will allow that God has appointed such an office as that of teachers in the Christian church, and therefore doubtless will allow that something or other is proper and peculiar to that office, or some business of teaching that belongs to it, that don't belong as much to others as to them

If there be any way of teaching that is peculiar to that office, then for others to take that upon them is to invade the office of a minister; which doubtless is very sinful, and is often so represented in Scripture. But the great difficulty is to settle the bounds, and to tell exactly how far laymen may go, and when they exceed their limits; which is a matter of so much difficulty, that I don't wonder if many in their zeal have transgressed. The two ways of teaching and exhorting, the one of which ought ordinarily to be left to ministers, and the other of which may and ought to be practiced by the people, may be expressed by those two names of *preaching* and *exhorting* in a way of Christian conversation. But then a great deal of difficulty and controversy arises to determine what is preaching and what is Christian conversation. However, I will humbly offer my thoughts concerning this subject of lay exhorting, as follows.

(1) The common people in exhorting one another ought not to clothe themselves with the like authority with that which is proper for ministers. There is a certain authority that ministers have, and should exercise in teaching as well as governing the flock. Teaching is spoken of in Scripture as an act of authority, I Tim. 2:12. In order to a man's preaching, special authority must be committed to him, Rom. 10:15, "How shall they preach, except they be sent?" Ministers in this work of teaching and exhorting are clothed with authority, as Christ's messengers (Mal. 2:7) and as representing him, and so speaking in his name and in his stead, II Cor. 5:18–20. And it seems to be the most honorable thing that belongs to the officer of a minister of the Gospel, that to him is committed the word of reconciliation, and that he has power to preach the Gospel as Christ's messenger, and speaking in his name. The Apostle seems to speak of it as such, I Cor. 1:16–17. Ministers therefore in the exercise of this power, may clothe themselves with authority in speaking, or may teach others in an authoritative manner. Tit. 2:15, "These things speak and exhort, and rebuke with all authority: let no man despise thee." But the common people, in exhorting one another, ought not thus to exhort in an authoritative manner. There is a great deal of difference between teaching as a father amongst a company of children, and counseling in a brotherly way, as the children may kindly counsel and admonish one another. Those that are mere brethren ought not to assume authority in exhorting, though one may be better, and have more experience than another. Laymen ought not to exhort as though they were the ambassadors or messengers of Christ, as ministers do; nor should they exhort and warn and charge in his name, according to the ordinary import of such an expression when applied to teaching. Indeed, in one sense, a Christian ought to do everything he does in religion in the name of Christ; i.e. he ought to act in a dependence on him as his Head and Mediator, and do all for his glory: but the expression as it is usually understood, when applied to teaching or exhorting, is speaking in Christ's stead, and as having a message from him.

Persons may clothe themselves with authority in speaking, either by the authoritative words they make use of, or in the manner and authoritative air of their speaking: though some may think that this latter is a matter of indifferency, or at least of small importance, yet there is indeed a great deal in it. A person may go much out of his place, and be guilty of a great degree of assuming, in the manner of his speaking those words, which as they might be spoken, might be proper for him: the same words spoken in a different manner, may express what is very diverse. Doubtless there may be as much hurt in the manner of a person's speaking, as there may in his looks; but the wise man tells us that an high look is an abomination to the Lord, Prov. 21:4. Again, a man may clothe himself with authority in the circumstances under which he speaks; as for instance, if he sets himself up as a public teacher. Here I would have it observed that I don't suppose that a person is guilty of this merely because he speaks in the hearing of many: persons may speak, and speak only in a way of conversation, and yet speak in the hearing of a great number, as they often do in their common conversation about temporal things at feasts and entertainments, where women as well as others do converse freely together about worldly things in the hearing of a considerable number; and it may happen to be in the hearing of a great number, and yet without offense: and if their conversation on such occasions should turn on spiritual things, and they should speak as freely and openly, I don't see why it would not be as harmless. Nor do I think that if besides a great number's being present, persons speak with a very earnest and loud voice, this is for them to set up themselves as public teachers, if they do it from no contrivance or premeditated design, or as purposely directing themselves to a congregation or multitude, and not speaking to any that are composed to the solemnity of any public service; but speaking in the time of conversation, or a time when all do freely converse one with another, they express what they then feel, directing themselves to none but those that are near 'em and fall in their way, speaking in that earnest and pathetical manner, to which the subject they are speaking of and the affecting sense of their souls naturally leads them, and as it were constrains them: I say, that for persons to do thus, though many happen to hear them, yet it don't appear to me to be a setting themselves up as public teachers. Yea, if this be added to these other circumstances, that all this happens to be in a meetinghouse; I don't think that merely its being in such a place much alters the case, provided the solemnity of public service and divine ordinances be over, and the solemn assembly broke up, and some stay in the house for mutual religious conversation; provided also that they speak in no authoritative way, but in an humble manner, becoming their degree and station, though they speak very earnestly and pathetically.

Indeed, modesty might in ordinary cases, restrain some persons, as women, and those that are young, from so much as speaking when a great number are present; at least, when some of those present are much their superiors, unless they are spoken to: and yet the case may be so extraordinary as fully to warrant it. If something very extraordinary happens to persons, or if they are in extraordinary circumstances: as if a person be struck with lightning in the midst of a great company, or if he lies a dying, it appears to none any violation of modesty for him to speak freely before those that are much his superiors. I have seen some women and children in such circumstances, on religious accounts, that it has appeared to me no more a transgressing the laws of humility and modesty for them to speak freely, let who will be present, than if they were dying.

But then may a man be said to set up himself as a public teacher, when he in a set speech, of design, directs himself to a multitude, either in the meetinghouse or elsewhere, as looking that they should compose themselves to attend to what he has to say; and much more when this is a contrived and premeditated thing, without anything like a constraint, by any extraordinary sense or affection that he is then under; and more still, when meetings are appointed on purpose to hear lay persons exhort, and they take it as their business to be speakers, while they expect that others should come, and compose themselves, and attend as hearers; when private Christians take it upon them in private meetings to act as the masters or presidents of the assembly, and accordingly from time to time to teach and exhort the rest, this has the appearance of authoritative teaching.

When private Christians, that are no more than mere brethren, exhort and admonish one another, it ought to be in an humble manner, rather by way of entreaty, than with authority; and the more, according as the station of persons is lower. Thus it becomes women and those that are young, ordinarily to be at a greater distance from any appearance of authority in speaking than others: thus much at least is evident by that in I Tim. 2:9, 11–12.

That lay persons ought not to exhort one another as clothed with authority is a general rule, but it can't justly be supposed to extend to heads of families in their own families. Every Christian family is a little church, and the heads of it are its authoritative teachers and governors. Nor can it extend to schoolmasters among his scholars; and some other cases might perhaps be mentioned that ordinary discretion will distinguish, where a man's circumstances do properly clothe him with authority, and render it fit and suitable for him to counsel and admonish others in an authoritative manner.

(2) No man but only a minister that is duly appointed to that sacred calling ought to follow teaching and exhorting as a calling, or so as to neglect that which is his proper calling. An having the office of a teacher in the church of God implies two things: 1. a being invested with the authority of a teacher; and 2. a being called to the business of a teacher, to make it the business of his life. Therefore that man that is not a minister, that takes either of these upon him, invades the office of a minister. Concerning assuming the authority of a minister I have spoken already. But if a layman don't assume authority in his teaching, yet if he forsakes his proper calling, or doth so at least in a great measure, and spends his time in going about from house to house, to counsel and exhort, he goes beyond his line and violates Christian rules. Those that have the office of teachers or exhorters have it for their calling, and should make it their business, as a business proper to their office; and none should make it their business but such, Rom. 12:3–8, "For I say, through the grace given unto me, to every man that is among you, not to think of himself more highly than he ought to think; but to think soberly, according as God hath dealt to every man the proportion of faith. For as we have many members in one body, and all members have not the same office; so we being many, are one body in Christ. . . . He that teacheth, let him wait on teaching, or he that exhorteth, on exhortation." I Cor. 12:29, "Are all apostles? Are all prophets? Are all teachers?" I Cor. 7:20, "Let every man abide in the same calling wherein he was called." I Thess. 4:11, "And that ye study to be quiet, and to do your own business, and to work with your own hands, as we commanded you."

It will be a very dangerous thing for laymen, in either of these respects, to invade the office of a minister; if this be common among us we shall be in danger of having a stop put to the work of God, and the ark's turning aside from us, before it come to Mount Zion, and of God's making a breach upon us; as of old there was an unhappy stop put to the joy of the congregation of Israel, in bringing up the ark of God, because others carried it besides the Levites: and therefore David, when the error was found out, says, I Chron. 15:2, "None ought to carry the ark of God but the Levites only; for them hath the Lord chosen to carry the ark of God, and to minister unto him forever." And because one presumed to touch the ark that was not of the sons of Aaron, therefore the Lord made a breach upon them, and covered their day of rejoicing with a cloud in his anger.[5]

[(3)] Before I dismiss this head of lay exhorting, I would take notice of three things relating to it, upon which there ought to be a restraint.

A. Speaking in the time of the solemn worship of God, as public prayer, singing, or preaching, or administration of the sacrament of the Holy Supper; or any duty of social worship: this should not be allowed. I know it will be said that in some cases, when persons are exceedingly affected, they cannot help it; and I believe so too: but then I also believe, and know by experience, that there are several things that contribute to that inability besides merely and absolutely the sense of divine things they have upon their hearts. Custom and example, or the thing's being allowed, have such an influence that they actually help to make it impossible for persons under strong affections to avoid speaking. If it was disallowed, and persons at the time that they were thus disposed to break out had this apprehension that it would be a very unbecoming, shocking thing for 'em so to do, it would be a help to 'em as to their ability to avoid it. Their inability arises from their strong and vehement disposition; and so far as that disposition is from a good principle, it would be weakened by the coming in of this thought to their minds, viz. "What I am going to do will be for the dishonor of Christ and religion": and so that inward vehemence that pushed 'em forward to speak would fall, and they would be enabled to avoid it. This experience confirms.

B. There ought to be a moderate restraint on the loudness of

5. [I Chron. 13:5–14. Note that JE has telescoped two separated incidents.]

persons talking under high affections; for if there be not, it will grow natural and unavoidable for persons to be louder and louder, without any increase of their inward sense; till it becomes natural to 'em, at last, to scream and halloo to almost everyone they see in the streets, when they are much affected: but this is certainly a thing very improper, and what has no tendency to promote religion. The man Christ Jesus when he was upon earth, had doubtless as great a sense of the infinite greatness and importance of eternal things, and the worth of souls, as any have nowadays; but there is not the least appearance in his history of his taking any such course, or manner of exhorting others.

C. There should also be some restraint on the abundance of persons' talk under strong affections; for if persons give themselves an unbounded liberty to talk just so much as they feel an inclination to, they will increase and abound more and more in talk, beyond the proportion of their sense or affection; till at length it will become ineffectual on those that hear them, and by the commonness of their abundant talk, they will defeat their own end.

[(4)] One thing more I would take notice of before I conclude this part, is the mismanagement that has been in some places of the duty of singing praises to God. I believe it to have been one fruit of the extraordinary degrees of the sweet and joyful influences of the Spirit of God that have been lately given, that there has appeared such a disposition to abound in that duty, and frequently to fall into this divine exercise; not only in appointed solemn meetings, but when Christians occasionally meet together at each other's houses. But the mismanagement I have respect to, is the getting into a way of performing it without almost any appearance of that reverence and solemnity with which all visible, open acts of divine worship ought to be attended; it may be two or three in a room singing hymns of praise to God, others that are present talking at the same time, others about their work, with little more appearance of regard to what is doing than if some were only singing a common song for their amusement and diversion. There is danger, if such things are continued, of its coming to that by degrees, that a mere nothing be made of this duty, to the great violation of the third commandment.[6] Let Christians

6. [Exod. 20:7, "Thou shalt not take the name of the Lord thy God in vain."]

abound as much as they will in this holy, heavenly exercise, in God's house and in their own houses; but when it is performed, let it be performed as an holy act, wherein they have immediately and visibly to do with God. When any social open act of devotion, or solemn worship of God is performed, God should be reverenced as visibly present, by those that are present. As we would not have the ark of God depart from us, nor provoke God to make a breach upon us, we should take heed that we handle the ark with reverence.

With respect to companies singing in the streets, going to or coming from the place of public worship, I would humbly offer my thoughts in the following particulars.

A. The rule of Christ concerning putting new wine into old bottles does undoubtedly take place in things of this nature, supposing it to be a thing that in itself is good but not essential, and not particularly enjoined or forbidden. For things so very new and uncommon, and of so open and public a nature, to be suddenly introduced and set up and practiced in many parts of the country, without the matter's being so much as first proposed to any public consideration, or giving any opportunity for the people of God to weigh the matter, or to consider any reasons that might be offered to support it, is putting new wine into old bottles with a witness; as if it were with no other design than to burst them directly. Nothing else can be expected to be the consequence of this, than uproar and confusion, and great offense, and unhappy mischievous disputes, even among the children of God themselves: not that that which is good in itself, and is new, ought to be forborne till there is nobody that will dislike it; but it ought to be forborne till the visible church of God is so prepared for it, at least, that there is a probability that it will not do more hurt than good, or hinder the work of God more than promote it; as is most evident from Christ's rule and the apostles' practice. If it be brought in when the country is so unprepared that the shock and surprise on persons' minds, and the contention and prejudice against religion that it is like to be an occasion of, will do more to hinder religion than the practice of it is like to do to promote it, then the fruit is picked before 'tis ripe. And indeed, such an hasty endeavor to introduce such an innovation, supposing it to be good in itself, is the likeliest way to retard the effectual introduction of it; it will hinder its being extensively introduced, much more than it will promote it, and so will defeat its own end.

B. But as to the thing itself, if a considerable part of a congregation have occasion to go in company together to a place of public worship, and they should join together in singing praises to God, as they go, I confess that after long consideration and endeavoring to view the thing every way, with the utmost diligence and impartiality I am capable of, I cannot find any valid objection against it. As to the common objection from Matt. 6:5, "And when thou prayest, thou shalt not be as the hypocrites are; for they love to pray standing in the synagogues, and in the corners of the streets, that they may be seen of men": it is strong against a single person's singing in the streets or in the meetinghouse by himself, as offering to God personal worship; but as it is brought against a considerable company, their thus publicly worshipping God, it appears to me to have no weight at all; to be sure, it is of no more force against a company's thus praising God in the streets than against their praising him in the synagogue or meetinghouse, for the streets and the synagogues are both put together in these words of our Saviour, as parallel in the case that he had respect to. 'Tis evident that Christ speaks of personal, and not public worship. If to sing in the streets be ostentatious, then it must be because it is a public place, and it can't be done there without being very open; but it is no more public than the synagogue or meetinghouse is when full of people. Some worship is in its nature private, as that which is proper to particular persons, or families, or private societies, and has respect to their particular concerns: but that which I now speak of is performed under no other notion than a part of God's public worship, without any relation to any private, separate society, or any chosen or picked number, and in which every visible Christian has equal liberty to join, if it be convenient for him and he has a disposition, as in the worship that is performed in the meetinghouse. When persons are going to the house of public worship, to serve God there with the assembly of his people, they are upon no other design than that of putting public honor upon God; that is the business they go from home upon, and even in their walking the streets on this errand, they appear in a public act of respect to God; and therefore if they go in company with public praise, 'tis not a being public when they ought to be private. 'Tis one part of the beauty of public worship, that it be very public; the more public it is, the more open honor it puts upon God; and especially is it beautiful in that part of public worsip, viz. public praise; for the very notion of public praising of God is to declare abroad his glory, to publish his praise, to make it known, and proclaim it aloud, as is evident by innumerable expressions of Scripture. 'Tis fit that God's honor should not be concealed, but made known in the great congregation, and proclaimed before the sun, and upon the housetops, before kings and all nations, and that his praises should be heard to the utmost ends of the earth.

I suppose none will condemn singing God's praises merely because 'tis performed in the open air, and not in a close place: and if it may be performed by a company in the open air, doubtless they may do it moving as well as standing still. So the children of Israel praised God when they went to Mount Zion with the ark of God; and so the multitude praised Christ when they entered with him into Jerusalem a little before his passion; and so the children of Israel were wont, from year to year, to go up to Jerusalem when they went in companies from all parts of the land, three times in the year, when they often used to manifest the engagedness of their minds by traveling all night, and manifested their joy and gladness by singing praises with great decency and beauty, as they went towards God's holy mountain; as evident by Isa. 30:29, "Ye shall have a song, as in the night, when a holy solemnity is kept; and gladness of heart, as when one goeth with a pipe to come into the mountain of the Lord, to the Mighty One of Israel." And Ps. 42:4, "When I remember these things, I pour out my soul in me; for I had gone with the multitude, I went with them to the house of God, with the voice of joy and praise, with a multitude that kept holy day." Ps. 100:4, "Enter into his gates with thanksgiving, and into his courts with praise." When God's people are going to his house, the occasion is so joyful to a Christian in a lively frame (the language of whose heart is, "Come, let us go up to the house of the Lord," and who is glad when it is so said to him [Ps. 122:1]), that the duty of singing praises seems to be peculiarly beautiful on such an occasion. So that if the state of the country was ripe for it, and it should be so that there should be frequent occasions for a considerable part of a congregation to go together to the places of public worship, and there was in other respects a proportionable appearance of fervency of devotion, it appears to me that it would be ravishingly beautiful, if such things were practiced all over the land, and would have a great tendency to enliven, animate and rejoice the souls of God's saints, and greatly to propagate vital religion. I believe the time is coming when the world will be full of such things.

3. It seems to me to be requisite that there should be the consent of the governing part of the worshiping societies, to which persons have joined themselves and of which they own themselves a part, in order to the introducing of things in public worship, so new and uncommon, and not essential nor particularly commanded, into the places where those worshiping societies belong.[7] The peace and union of such societies seems to require it; seeing they have voluntarily united themselves to these worshiping societies, to that end that they might be one in the affairs of God's public worship, and obliged themselves in covenant to act as brethren and mutual assistants and members of one body, in those affairs, and all are hereby naturally and necessarily led to be concerned with one another in matters of religion and God's worship; and seeing that this is a part of the public worship, and worship that must be performed from time to time in the view of the whole, being performed at a time when they are meeting together for mutual assistance in worship, and therefore that which all must unavoidably be in some measure concerned in, so at least as to shew their approbation and consent, or open dislike and separation from them in it; I say, it being thus, charity and a regard to the union and peace of such societies seems to require a consent of the governing part in order to the introducing anything of this nature (unless they think those societies unworthy that they should be joined to them any longer, and so first renounce them as the worshiping societies of which they are members). Certainly if we are of the spirit of the Apostle Paul, and have his discretion, we shall not set up any such practice without it: he for the sake of peace conformed, in things wherein he was not particularly forbidden, to the Jews when among them; and so when among those that were without the law, conformed to them wherein he might.

7. [The ecclesiastical society in a colonial New England town was a corporation composed of all pewholders, and its officers were responsible for administering the affairs of the parish.]

To be sure, those go much beyond proper limits who, coming from abroad, do immediately of their own heads, in a strange place, set up such a new and uncommon practice among the people.

In introducing anything of this nature among a people, their minister especially ought to be consulted, and his voice taken, as long as he is owned for their minister. Ministers are pastors of worshiping societies, and their heads and guides in the affairs of public worship. They are called in Scripture, "those that rule over them"; and their people are commanded to obey them, because they watch for their souls, as those that must give account [Heb. 13:17]. If it belongs to these shepherds and rulers to direct and guide the flock in anything at all, it belongs to 'em so to do in the circumstantials of their public worship.

Thus I have taken particular notice of many of those things that have appeared to me to be amiss in the management of our religious concerns relating to the present revival of religion, and have taken liberty freely to express my thoughts upon them. Upon the whole, it appears manifest to me that things have as yet never been set a going in their right channel; if they had, and means had been blessed in proportion as they have been now, this work would have so prevailed as before this time to have carried all afore it, and have triumphed over New England as its conquest.

The Devil in driving things to these extremes, besides the present hindrance of the work of God, has, I believe, had in view a twofold mischief hereafter, in the issue of things; one with respect to those that are more cold in religion; to carry things to such an extreme that people in general, at length having their eyes opened by the great excess, and seeing that things must needs be wrong, he might take the advantage to tempt them entirely to reject the whole work as being all nothing but delusion and distraction. And another is with respect to those that have been very warm and zealous, of God's own children, that have been out of the way, to sink them down in unbelief and darkness. The time is coming, I doubt not, when the bigger part of them will be convinced of their errors; and then probably the Devil will take advantage to lead them into a dreadful wilderness, and to puzzle and confound them about their own experiences and the experiences of others; and to make them to doubt of many things that they ought not to doubt of, and even to tempt them with atheistical thoughts. I believe if all true Christians all over the land should now at once have their eyes opened fully to see all their errors, it would seem for the present to damp religion: the dark thoughts that it would at first be an occasion of, and the inward doubts, difficulties and conflicts that would rise in their souls, would deaden their lively affections and joys, and would cause an appearance of a present decay of religion. But yet it would do God's saints great good in their latter end; it would fit them for more spiritual and excellent experiences, more humble and heavenly love, and unmixed joys, and would greatly tend to a more powerful, extensive and durable prevalence of vital piety.

I don't know but we shall be in danger by and by, after our eyes are fully opened to see our errors, to go to contrary extremes. The Devil has driven the pendulum far beyond its proper point of rest; and when he has carried it to the utmost length that he can, and it begins by its own weight to swing back, he probably will set in, and drive it with the utmost fury the other way; and so give us no rest; and if possible prevent our settling in a proper medium. What a poor, blind, weak and miserable creature is man, at his best estate! We are like poor helpless sheep; the Devil is too subtle for us. What is our strength? What is our wisdom? How ready are we to go astray! How easily are we drawn aside into unnumerable snares, while we in the meantime are bold and confident, and doubt not but that we are right and safe! We are foolish sheep in the midst of subtle serpents and cruel wolves, and don't know it. Oh, how unfit are we to be left to ourselves! And how much do we stand in need of the wisdom, the power, the condescension, patience, forgiveness and gentleness of our good Shepherd!

PART V

SHEWING POSITIVELY WHAT OUGHT TO BE DONE
TO PROMOTE THIS WORK

IN considering of means and methods for promoting this glorious work of God, I have already observed, in some instances, wherein there has been needless objecting and complaining; and have also taken notice of many things amiss that ought to be amended. I now proceed in the third and last place [1] to shew positively what ought to be done, or what courses (according to my humble opinion) ought to be taken to promote this work. The obligations that all are under, with one consent to do their utmost, and the great danger of neglecting it, were observed before.[2] I hope that some, upon reading what was said under that head, will be ready to say, "What shall we do?" To such readers I would now offer my thoughts in answer to such an inquiry.

[*Stumbling Blocks Should Be Removed*]

And that which I think we ought to set ourselves about in the first place, is to remove stumbling blocks. When God is revealed as about to come gloriously to set up his kingdom in the world, this is proclaimed, "Prepare ye the way of the Lord, make straight in the desert an highway for our God," Isa. 40:3. And again, Isa. 57:14, "Cast ye up, cast ye up; prepare the way; take up the stumbling block out of the way of my people." And chap. 62:10, "Go through, go through the gates; prepare you the way of the people; cast up, cast up the highway; gather out the stones."

And in order to this, there must a great deal done at confessing of faults on both sides: for undoubtedly many and great are the faults that have been committed, in the jangling and confusions, and mixtures of light and darkness, that have been of late. There

1. [This sequence began at p. 385.]
2. [Above, pp. 370–83.]

is hardly any duty more contrary to our corrupt dispositions, and mortifying to the pride of man; but it must be done. Repentance of faults is, in a peculiar manner, a proper duty, when the kingdom of heaven is at hand, or when we especially expect or desire that it should come; as appears by John the Baptist's preaching. And if God does now loudly call upon us to repent, then he also calls upon us to make proper manifestations of our repentance. I am persuaded that those that have openly opposed this work, or have from time to time spoken lightly of it, cannot be excused in the sight of God, without openly confessing their fault therein; especially if they be ministers. If they have any way, either directly or indirectly, opposed the work, or have so behaved in their public performances or private conversation as has prejudiced the minds of their people against the work, if hereafter they shall be convinced of the goodness and divinity of what they have opposed, they ought by no means to palliate the matter and excuse themselves, and pretend that they always thought so, and that it was only such and such imprudences that they objected against, but they ought openly to declare their conviction, and condemn themselves for what they have done; for 'tis Christ that they have spoken against in speaking lightly of, and prejudicing others against this work; yea, worse than that, 'tis the Holy Ghost. And though they have done it ignorantly and in unbelief, yet when they find out who it is that they have opposed, undoubtedly God will hold them bound publicly to confess it.[3]

And on the other side, if those that have been zealous to promote the work have in any of the forementioned instances openly gone much out of the way, and done that which is contrary to Christian rules, whereby they have openly injured others, or greatly violated good order, and so done that which has wounded religion, they must publicly confess it and humble themselves, as they would gather out the stones, and prepare the way of God's people. They who have laid great stumbling blocks in others' way by their open transgression, are bound to remove them by their open repentance.

Some probably will be ready to object against this, that the opposers will take advantage by this to behave themselves insolently, and to insult both them and religion. And indeed, to the shame

3. [Cf. Matt. 12:31–32; I Tim. 1:13. On the unpardonable sin, see above, p. 55.]

of some, they have taken advantage by such things; as of the good spirit that Mr. Whitefield shewed in his retractations,[4] and some others. But if there are some embittered enemies of religion that stand ready to improve everything to its disadvantage, yet that ought not to hinder doing an enjoined Christian duty; though it be in the manifestation of humility and repentance after a fault openly committed. To stand it out, in a visible impenitence of a real fault, to avoid such an inconvenience, is to do evil to prevent evil. And besides, the danger of an evil consequence is much greater on the other side: to commit sin, and then stand in it, is what will give the enemy the greatest advantage. For Christians to act like Christians, in openly humbling themselves when they have openly offended, in the end brings the greatest honor to Christ and religion; and in this way are persons most likely to have God appear for them.

Again, at such a day as this, God does especially call his people to the exercise of extraordinary meekness and mutual forbearance: for at such a time Christ appears as it were coming in his kingdom, which calls for great moderation in our behavior towards all men; as is evident [in] Phil. 4:5, "Let your moderation be known unto all men: the Lord is at hand." The awe of the divine majesty that appears present or approaching should dispose us to it, and deter us from the contrary. For us to be judging one another, and behaving with fierceness and bitterness one towards another, when he who is the searcher of all hearts, to whom we must all give an account, appears so remarkably present, is exceeding unsuitable. Our business at such a time should be at home, searching ourselves and condemning ourselves, and taking heed to our own behavior. If there be glorious prosperity to the church of God approaching, those that are the most meek will have the largest share in it: for when Christ rides forth in his glory and his majesty, it is "because of truth, meekness and righteousness," Ps. 45:3–4. And

4. [Whitefield (above, pp. 48–49) was often guilty, especially during the youthful fervor of his first preaching tour in America, of rash and intemperate comments, which provoked several cries of outrage against him. To clarify his remarks and mollify his critics, he wrote such "retractations" as *A Letter from the Rev. Mr. Whitefield to Some Church Members of the Presbyterian Persuasion* (Philadelphia, 1740; reprinted in Boston the same year) and a letter of July 25, 1741, "To the Students, etc. under Convictions at the Colleges of Cambridge and New Haven," printed in *The Boston Gazette* for March 16, 1742 (also in his collected *Works*, *1*, 296–97).]

when God remarkably arises to execute judgment, it is "to save all the meek of the earth," Ps. 76:9. And 'tis the meek that "shall increase their joy in the Lord," Isa. 29:19. And when the time comes that God will give this lower world into the hands of his saints, it is the meek that "shall inherit the earth," Ps. 37:11 and Matt. 5:5. But "with the froward, God will shew himself unsavory" [II Sam. 22:27].

Those therefore that have been zealous for this work, and have greatly erred and been injurious with their zeal, ought not to be treated with bitterness. There is abundant reason to think that most of them are the dear children of God, for whom Christ died; and therefore that they will see their error. As to those things wherein we see them to be in an error, we have reason to say of 'em as the Apostle, Phil. 3:15, "If any are otherwise minded, God shall reveal this unto them." Their errors should not be made use of by us, so much to excite indignation towards them, but should influence all of us that hope that we are the children of God, to humble ourselves and become more entirely dependent on the Lord Jesus Christ, when we see those that are God's own people so ready to go astray. And those ministers that have been judged and injuriously dealt with, will do the part of Christ's disciples not to judge and revile again, but to receive such injuries with meekness and forbearance, and making a good improvement of them, more strictly examining their hearts and ways, and committing themselves to God. This will be the way to have God vindicate them in his providence, if they belong to him. We han't yet seen the end of things; nor do we know who will be most vindicated and honored of God in the issue. Eccles. 7:8, "Better is the end of a thing than the beginning thereof; and the patient in spirit is better than the proud in spirit."

Contrary to this mutual meekness is each party's stigmatizing one another with odious names; as is done in many parts of New England: which tends greatly to widen and perpetuate the breach. Such distinguishing names of reproach do as it were divide us into two armies, separated and drawn up in battle array, ready to fight one with another; which greatly hinders the work of God.[5]

And as such an extraordinary time as this does especially require of us the exercise of a great deal of forbearance, one towards another; so there is peculiarly requisite in God's people the exer-

5. [Cf. above, p. 65.]

cise of great patience, in waiting on God, under any special difficulties and disadvantages they may be under, as to the means of grace. The beginning of a revival of religion will naturally and necessarily be attended with a great many difficulties of this nature; many parts of the reviving church will, for a while, be under great disadvantages, by reason of what remains of the old disease of a general corruption of the visible church. We can't expect that after a long time of degeneracy and depravity in the state of things in the church, things should all come to rights at once; it must be a work of time: and for God's people to be overhasty and violent in such a case, being resolved to have everything rectified at once, or else forcibly to deliver themselves by breaches and separations, is the way to hinder things coming to rights as they otherwise would, and to keep 'em back, and the way to break all in pieces. Not but that the case may be such, the difficulty may be so intolerable, as to allow of no delay, and God's people can't continue in the state wherein they were without violations of absolute commands of God. But otherwise, though the difficulty may be very great, another course should be taken. God's people should have their recourse directly to the throne of grace, to represent their difficulties before the great Shepherd of the sheep, that has the care of all the affairs of his church; and when they have done, they should wait patiently upon him. If they do so, they may expect that in his time, he will appear for their deliverance: but if instead of that, they are impatient, and take the work into their own hands, they will bewray their want of faith, and will dishonor God, and can't have such reason to hope that Christ will appear for them, as they have desired, but have reason to fear that he will leave 'em to manage their affairs for themselves as well as they can: when otherwise, if they had waited on Christ patiently, continuing still instant in prayer, they might have had him appearing for them, much more effectually to deliver them. "He that believeth shall not make haste" [Isa. 28:16]; and 'tis for those that are found patiently waiting on the Lord, under difficulties, that he will especially appear, when he comes to do great things for his church, as is evident by Isa. 30:18 and chap. 40 at the latter end, and 49:23, and Ps. 37:9, and many other places.

I have somewhere, not long since, met with an exposition of those words of the spouse that we have several times repeated in the Book of Canticles, "I charge you, O daughters of Jerusalem, that ye stir not up, nor awake my love, till he please," which is the only satisfying exposition that ever I met with; which was to this purpose, viz. that when the church of God is under great difficulties and in distress, and Christ don't appear for her help but seems to neglect her as though he were asleep, God's people, or the daughters of Jerusalem, in such a case should not shew an hasty spirit; and not having patience to wait for Christ to awake for their help till his time comes, take indirect courses for their own deliverance and use violent means for their escape, before Christ appears to open the door for them; and so as it were, stir up and awake Christ before his time. When the church is in distress, and God seems not to appear for her in his providence, he is very often represented in Scripture as being asleep; as Christ was asleep in the ship, when the disciples were tossed by the storm, and the ship covered with waves [Matt. 8:23–27]: and God's appearing afterwards for his people's help is represented as his awaking out of sleep. Ps. 7:6, and 35:23, and 44:23, and 59:4, and 73:20. Christ has an appointed time for his thus awaking out of sleep: and his people ought to wait upon him; and not, in an impatient fit, stir him up before his time. 'Tis worthy to be observed how strict this charge is, given to the daughters of Jerusalem, which is repeated three times over in the Book of Canticles, chap. 2:7, and 3:5, and 8:4. In the 2d chapter and six first verses, is represented the supports Christ gives his church while she is in a suffering state, as the lily among thorns: in the 7th verse is represented her patience in waiting for Christ to appear for her deliverance, when she charges the daughters of Jerusalem not to stir up nor awake her love till he please, by the roes and the hinds of the field; which are creatures of a gentle, harmless nature, are not beasts of prey, do not devour one another, don't fight with their enemies, but fly from them; and are of a pleasant, loving nature, Prov. 5:19. In the next verse [Cant. 2:8], we see the church's success, in this way of waiting under sufferings with meekness and patience; Christ soon awakes, speedily appears, and swiftly comes. "The voice of my beloved! Behold, he cometh, leaping upon the mountains, skipping upon the hills!" [6]

6. [It does not seem possible to say precisely what "satisfying exposition" suggested to JE this view of Cant. 2:7, 3:5, and 8:4. He repeated the same interpretation, without attribution to any source, in his "Notes on the Scriptures," Book II, No. 395 (Yale MSS; printed in Dwight ed. of *Works*, *9*, 365–66). Among the commentaries following this line of thought one that he could have seen is John Robotham, *An Exposition on the Whole Book of Solomon's Song*

What has been mentioned hitherto has relation to the behavior we are obliged to, as we would prevent the hindrances of the work; but besides these, there are things that must be done more directly to advance it. And here it concerns everyone, in the first place, to look into his own heart and see to it that he be a partaker of the benefits of the work himself, and that it be promoted in his own soul. Now is a most glorious opportunity for the good of souls. 'Tis manifestly with respect to a time of great revival of religion in the world, that we have that gracious, earnest and moving invitation proclaimed, in the 55th [chapter] of Isaiah, "Ho, every one that thirsteth! etc.," as is evident by what precedes in the foregoing chapter, and what follows in the close of this. Here, in the 6th verse it is said, "Seek ye the Lord while he may be found; call upon him while he is near." And 'tis with special reference to such a time that Christ proclaims as he does, Rev. 21:6, "I will give unto him that is athirst, of the fountain of the water of life freely." And chap. 22:17, "And the Spirit and the bride say, Come; and let him that heareth say, Come; and let him that is athirst come; and whosoever will, let him take the water of life freely." And it seems to be with reference to such a time, which is typified by the Feast of Tabernacles, that Jesus at that feast stood and cried, as we have an account, John 7:37–38, "In the last day, that great day of the feast, Jesus stood and cried, saying, If any man thirst, let him come unto me and drink. He that believeth on me [. . .] out of his belly shall flow rivers of living water." And 'tis with special reference to God's freeness and readiness to bestow grace at such a time, that it is said in Isa. 60:11 of the spiritual Jerusalem, "Thy gates shall be open continually; they shall not be shut, day nor night."

[Orthodoxy Should Be Reaffirmed]

And though I judge not those that have opposed this work, and would not have others judge them, yet if any such shall happen

---

(London, 1651), which closely follows (nay, plagiarizes!) Henry Ainsworth, *Solomon's Song of Songs, in English Metre* (London, 1639). This particular way of allegorizing these verses, while a minority view, has been traced back as far as the Jewish Targum; see Richard Frederick Littledale, *A Commentary on the Song of Songs from Ancient and Medieval Sources* (London, 1869), pp. 83–84, though Littledale errs in including Philo of Carpasia (d. 374) in the lineage.]

to read this treatise, I would take the liberty to entreat them to leave off concerning themselves so much about others, and look into their own souls and see to it that they are the subjects of a true, saving work of the Spirit of God. If they have reason to think they never have been, or it be but a very doubtful hope that they have, then how can they have any heart to be busily and fiercely engaged about the mistakes and the supposed false hopes of others? And I would now beseech those that have hitherto been something inclining to Arminian principles, seriously to weigh the matter with respect to this work, and consider whether, if the Scriptures are the Word of God, the work that has been described in the first part of this treatise must not needs be, as to the substance of it, the work of God, and the flourishing of that religion that is taught by Christ and his apostles; and whether any good medium can be found, where a man can rest with any stability, between owning this work and being a Deist; and also to consider whether or no, if it be indeed so that this be the work of God, it don't entirely overthrow their scheme of religion; and therefore whether it don't infinitely concern 'em, as they would be partakers of eternal salvation, to relinquish their scheme. Now is a good time for Arminians to change their principles. I would now, as one of the friends of this work, humbly invite 'em to come and join with us, and be on our side; and if I had the authority of Moses, I would say to them as he did to Hobab, Num. 10:29, "We are journeying unto the place, of which the Lord said, I will give it you; come thou with us, and we will do thee good; for the Lord hath spoken good concerning Israel."

As the benefit and advantage of the good improvement of such a season is extraordinary great; so the danger of neglecting and misimproving it, is proportionably great. 'Tis abundantly evident by the Scripture, that as a time of great outpouring of the Spirit is a time of great favor to those that are partakers of the blessing; so it is always a time of remarkable vengeance to others. So in Isa. 61:2, the same that is called "the acceptable year of the Lord," is called also "the day of vengeance of our God." So it was amongst the Jews in the apostles' days: the Apostle in II Cor. 6:2 says of that time that it was "the accepted time," and "day of salvation"; and Christ says of the same time, Luke 21:22, "These are the days of vengeance." At the same time that the blessings of the kingdom of heaven were given to some, there was an ax laid at the root of the trees, that those that did not bear fruit might be "hewn down, and cast into the fire," Matt. 3:9–11. Then was glorified both the goodness and severity of God, in a remarkable manner, Rom. 11:22. The harvest and the vintage go together: at the same time that the earth is reaped, and God's elect are gathered into the garner of God, the angel that has power over fire thrusts in his sickle, and gathers the cluster of the vine of the earth, and casts it into the great winepress of the wrath of God, Rev. 14, at the latter end. So it is foretold that at the beginning of the glorious times of the Christian church, at the same time that the hand of the Lord is known towards his servants, so shall his indignation towards his enemies, Isa. 66:14. So when that glorious morning shall appear, wherein "the Sun of righteousness shall arise," to the elect, "with healing in his wings," the day "shall burn as an oven" to the wicked, Mal. 4:1–3. There is no time like such a time for the increase of guilt, and treasuring up wrath, and desperate hardening of the heart, if men stand it out; which is the most awful judgment, and fruit of divine wrath, that can be inflicted on any mortal. So that a time of great grace and pouring out of the Spirit and the fruits of divine mercy, is evermore also a time of great outpouring of something else, viz. divine vengeance on those that neglect and misimprove such a season.

[Older Persons Should Forsake Unbelief]

The state of the present revival of religion has an awful aspect upon those that are advanced in years. The work has been chiefly amongst those that are young; and comparatively but few others have been made partakers of it. And indeed, it has commonly been so, when God has begun any great work for the revival of his church; he has taken the young people, and has cast off the old and stiff-necked generation. There was a remarkable outpouring of the Spirit of God on the children of Israel in the wilderness, on the younger generation, their little ones that they said should be a prey, the generation that entered into Canaan with Joshua; which is evident by many things in Scripture [cf. Num. 14:1–38]. That generation seems to have been the most excellent generation that ever was in the church of Israel. There is no generation of which there is so much good and so little hurt spoken in Scripture, as might be shewn if it would not be too long. In that generation, that were under twenty years when they went out of Egypt, was that kindness of youth and love of espousals spoken of, Jer. 2:2–3. But the old generation were passed by, and remained obstinate and stiff-necked, were always murmuring, and would not be convinced by all God's wondrous works that they beheld. God by his awful judgments that he executed in the wilderness, and the affliction that the people suffered there, convinced and humbled the younger generation, and fitted them for great mercy, as is evident by Deut. 2:16; but he destroyed the old generation: "he swore in his wrath that they should not enter into his rest, and their carcasses fell in the wilderness" [Heb. 3:11, 17–18]. When it was a time of great mercy and pouring out of God's Spirit on their children, it was remarkably a day of vengeance unto them, as appears by the 90th Psalm.[7] Let the old generation in this land take warning from hence, and take heed that they don't refuse to be convinced by all God's wonders that he works before their eyes, and that they don't continue forever objecting, murmuring and caviling against the work of God, lest while God is bringing their children into a land flowing with milk and honey, he should swear in his wrath concerning them, that their carcasses shall fall in the wilderness.

So when God had a design of great mercy to the Jews, in bringing 'em out of the Babylonish Captivity and returning them to their own land, there was a blessed outpouring of the Spirit upon them in Babylon, to bring 'em to deep conviction and repentance, and to a spirit of prayer, to cry earnestly to God for mercy; which is often spoken of by the prophets: but it was not upon the old generation, that were carried captive. The Captivity continued just long enough for that perverse generation to waste away and die in their captivity; at least those of them that were adult persons when carried captive. The old generation and heads of families were exceeding obstinate, and would not hearken to the earnest repeated warnings of the prophet Jeremiah; but he had greater success among the young people; as appears by Jer. 6:10–11, "To whom shall I speak and give warning, that they may hear? Behold, their ear is uncircumcised, and they cannot hearken; behold, the word of the Lord is unto them a reproach: they have no delight in it. Therefore I am full of the fury of the Lord; I am weary with holding in; I will pour it out upon the children abroad,

7. [Psalm 90 is indeed attributed to Moses, and probably has reference to the subject of JE's discussion here; but Ps. 95:8–11 is much more to his point.]

and upon the assembly of the young men together; for even the husband with the wife (i.e. the heads of families, and parents of these children) shall be taken, the aged with him that is full of days." Blessed be God! There are some of the elder people that have been made partakers of this work: and those that are most awakened by these warnings of God's Word, and the awful frowns of his providence, will be most likely to be made partakers hereafter. It infinitely concerns them to take heed to themselves, that they may be partakers of it; for how dreadful will it be to go to hell, after having spent so many years in doing nothing but treasuring up wrath.

[Ministers Should Seek Grace, Zeal, and Courage]

But above all others whatsoever, does it concern us that are ministers to see to it that we are partakers of this work, or that we have experience of the saving operations of the same Spirit that is now poured out on the land. How sorrowful and melancholy is the case, when it is otherwise? For one to stand at the head of a congregation of God's people, as representing Christ and speaking in his stead, and to act the part of a shepherd and guide to a people in such a state of things, when many are under great awakenings and many are converted, and many of God's saints are filled with divine light, love and joy, and to undertake to instruct and lead 'em all under all these various circumstances, and to be put to it continually to play the hypocrite, and force the airs of a saint in preaching, and from time to time in private conversation and particular dealing with souls, to undertake to judge of their circumstances, to try to talk with those that come to him as if he knew what they said; to try to talk with persons of experience as if he knew how to converse with them, and had experience as well as they; to make others believe that he rejoices when others are converted, and to force a pleased and joyful countenance and manner of speech, when there is nothing in the heart, what sorrowful work is here! Oh, how miserably must such a person feel! What a wretched bondage and slavery is this! What pains, and how much art must such a minister use to conceal himself! And how weak are his hands!—besides the infinite provocation of the most high God, and displeasure of his Lord and Master, that he incurs by continuing a secret enemy to him in his heart, in such circumstances. I think there is a great deal of reason from the Scripture, to conclude that no sort of men in the world will be so low in hell, as ungodly ministers: everything that is spoken of in Scripture as that which aggravates guilt and heightens divine wrath, meets in them; however some particular persons, of other sorts, may be more guilty than some of these.

And what great disadvantages are unconverted ministers under to oppose any irregularities, or imprudences, or intemperate zeal, that they may see in those that are the children of God, when they are conscious to themselves that they have no zeal at all? If enthusiasm and wildness comes in like a flood, what poor weak instruments are such ministers to withstand it? With what courage can they open their mouths, when they look inward and consider how it is with them?

We that are ministers not only have need of some true experience of the saving influence of the Spirit of God upon our heart, but we need a double portion of the Spirit of God at such a time as this; we had need to be as full of light as a glass is, that is held out in the sun; and with respect to love and zeal, we had need at this day to be like the angels, that are a flame of fire [Ps. 104:4]. The state of the times extremely requires a fullness of the divine Spirit in ministers, and we ought to give ourselves no rest till we have obtained it. And in order to this, I should think ministers, above all persons, ought to be much in secret prayer and fasting, and also much in praying and fasting one with another. It seems to me it would be becoming the circumstances of the present day, if ministers in a neighborhood would often meet together and spend days in fasting and fervent prayer among themselves, earnestly seeking for those extraordinary supplies of divine grace from heaven, that we need at this day: and also if, on their occasional visits one to another, instead of spending away their time in sitting and smoking, and in diverting, or worldly, unprofitable conversation, telling news, and making their remarks on this and the other trifling subject, they would spend their time in praying together, and singing praises, and religious conference. How much do many of the common people shame many of us that are in the work of the ministry in these respects? Surely we do not behave ourselves so much like Christian ministers, and the disciples and ambassadors of Christ, as we ought to do. And while we condemn zealous persons for their doing so much at censuring ministers at this day, it ought not to be without deep reflections upon, and great condemnation of ourselves: for indeed, we do very much to provoke censoriousness, and lay a great temptation before others to the sin of judging: and if we can prove that those that are guilty of it do transgress the Scripture rule, yet our indignation should be chiefly against ourselves.

Ministers at this day, in a special manner, should act as fellow helpers in their great work. It should be seen that they are animated and engaged, and exert themselves with one heart and soul, and with united strength, to promote the present glorious revival of religion: and to that end should often meet together and act in concert. And if it were a common thing in the country for ministers to join in public exercises, and second one another in their preaching, I believe it would be of great service. I mean that ministers having consulted one another as to the subjects of their discourses before they go to the house of God, should there speak, two or three of them going, in short discourses, as seconding each other and earnestly enforcing each other's warnings and counsels. Only such an appearance of united zeal in ministers would have a great tendency to awaken attention, and much to impress and animate the hearers; as has been found by experience in some parts of the country.

Ministers should carefully avoid weakening one another's hands. And therefore everything should be avoided by which their interest with their people might be diminished, or their union with them broken. On the contrary, if ministers han't forfeited their acceptance in that character, in the visible church, by their doctrine or behavior, their brethren in the ministry ought studiously to endeavor to heighten the esteem and affection of their people towards them, that they may have no temptation to repent their admitting other ministers to come and preach in their pulpits.

Two things that are exceeding needful in ministers, as they would do any great matters to advance the kingdom of Christ, are zeal and resolution. The influence and power of these things to bring to pass great effects is greater than can well be imagined: a man of but an ordinary capacity will do more with them, than one of ten times the parts and learning without them: more may be done with them in a few days, or at least weeks, than can be done without them in many years. Those that are possessed of these qualities commonly carry the day in almost all affairs. Most of the great things that have been done in the world of mankind, the great revolutions that have been accomplished in the kingdoms and empires of the earth, have been chiefly owing to these things. The very sight or appearance of a thoroughly engaged spirit, together with a fearless courage and unyielding resolution, in any person that has undertaken the managing any affair amongst mankind, goes a great way towards accomplishing the effect aimed at. 'Tis evident that the appearance of these things in Alexander [the Great] did three times as much towards his conquering the world as all the blows that he struck. And how much were the great things that Oliver Cromwell did, owing to these things? And the great things that Mr. Whitefield has done everywhere, as he has run through the British dominions (so far as they are owing to means), are very much owing to the appearance of these things, which he is eminently possessed of. When the people see these things apparently in a person, and to a great degree, it awes them, and has a commanding influence upon their minds; it seems to them that they must yield; they naturally fall before them without standing to contest or dispute the matter; they are conquered as it were by surprise. But while we are cold and heartless, and only go on in a dull manner, in an old formal round, we shall never do any great matters. Our attempts, with the appearance of such coldness and irresolution, won't so much as make persons think of yielding: they will hardly be sufficient to put it into their minds; and if it be put into their minds, the appearance of such indifference and cowardice does as it were call for, and provoke opposition.

Our misery is want of zeal and courage; for not only through want of them does all fail that we seem to attempt, but it prevents our attempting anything very remarkable for the kingdom of Christ. Hence, oftentimes it has been that when anything very considerable that is new is proposed to be done for the advancement of religion, or the public good, many difficulties are found out that are in the way, and a great many objections are started, and it may be, it is put off from one to another; but nobody does anything. And after this manner good designs or proposals have oftentimes failed, and have sunk as soon as proposed. Whenas, if we had but Mr. Whitefield's zeal and courage, what could not we do, with such a blessing as we might expect?

Zeal and courage will do much in persons of but an ordinary capacity; but especially would they do great things if joined with great abilities. If some great men that have appeared in our nation had been as eminent in divinity as they were in philosophy, and had engaged in the Christian cause with as much zeal and fervor as some others have done, and with a proportionable blessing of heaven, they would have conquered all Christendom and "turned the world upside down" [Acts 17:6]. We have many ministers in the land that don't want for abilities; they are persons of bright parts and learning; they should consider how much is expected and will be required of them by their Lord and Master, and how much they might do for Christ, and what great honor and how glorious a reward they might receive, if they had in their hearts an heavenly warmth and divine heat proportionable to their light.

With respect to candidates for the ministry, I won't undertake particularly to determine what kind of examination or trial they should pass under, in order to their admission to that sacred work: but I think this is evident from the Scripture that another sort of trial, with regard to their virtue and piety, is requisite, than is required in order to persons being admitted into the visible church. The Apostle directs that hands be laid suddenly on no man; but that they should first be tried, before they are admitted to the work of the ministry [I Tim. 5:22]. But 'tis evident that persons were suddenly admitted by baptism into the visible church from time to time, on their profession of their faith in Christ, without such caution and strictness in their probation. And it seems to me, those would act very unadvisedly that should enter on that great and sacred work before they had comfortable satisfaction concerning themselves, that they had a saving work of God on their souls.

[Colleges Should Nurture Piety in Their Students]

And though it may be thought that I go out of my proper sphere to intermeddle in the affairs of the colleges, yet I will take the liberty of an Englishman (that speaks his mind freely concerning public affairs) and the liberty of a minister of Christ (who doubtless may speak his mind as freely about things that concern the kingdom of his Lord and Master) to give my opinion in some things with respect to those societies; the original and main design of which is to train up persons, and fit them for the work of the ministry. And I would say in general, that it appears to me that care should be taken, some way or other, that those societies should be so regulated, that they should in fact be nurseries of piety.

Otherwise, they are fundamentally ruined and undone as to their main design and most essential end. They ought to be so constituted that vice and idleness should have no living there: they are intolerable in societies whose main design is to train up youth in Christian knowledge and eminent piety, to fit them to be pastors of the flock of the blessed Jesus. I have heretofore had some acquaintance with the affairs of a college, and experience of what belonged to its tuition and government; [8] and I can't but think that it is practicable enough, so to constitute such societies that there should be no being there without being virtuous, serious and diligent. It seems to me to be a reproach to the land that ever it should be so with our colleges, that instead of being places of the greatest advantages for true piety, one can't send a child thither without great danger of his being infected as to his morals, as it has certainly sometimes been with these societies. 'Tis perfectly intolerable, and anything should be done rather than it should be so. If we pretend to have any colleges at all, under any notion of training up youth for the ministry, there should be some way found out that should certainly prevent its being thus. To have societies for bringing persons up to be ambassadors of Jesus Christ and to lead souls to heaven, and to have 'em places of so much infection, is the greatest nonsense and absurdity imaginable.

And as thorough and effectual care should be taken that vice and idleness ben't tolerated in these societies, so certainly the design of 'em requires that extraordinary means should be used in them for training up the students in vital religion and experimental and practical godliness, so that they should be holy societies; the very place should be as it were sacred: they should be, in the midst of the land, fountains of piety and holiness. There is a great deal of pains taken to teach the scholars human learning; there ought to be as much, and more care, thoroughly to educate 'em in religion, and lead 'em to true and eminent holiness. If the

8. [JE was at Yale as student 1716–20, graduate theologue 1720–22, and tutor 1724–26. His earlier observation of "monstrous impieties" on the part of students doubtless returned to memory here. Among the "acts of immorality lately committed," he had written to his father on March 21, 1721, were "stealing of hens, geese, turkies, pigs, meat, wood, etc.—unseasonable night-walking, breaking people's windows, playing at cards, cursing, swearing, and damning, and using all manner of ill language." The original letter is in the Andover Collection; it is printed in Ola E. Winslow, *Jonathan Edwards, 1703–1758* (New York, 1940), pp. 72–73.]

main design of these nurseries is to bring up persons to teach Christ, then it is of greatest importance that there should be care and pains taken to bring those that are there educated, to the knowledge of Christ. It has been common in our public prayers to call these societies "the schools of the prophets"; and if they are schools to train up young men to be prophets, certainly there ought to be extraordinary care there taken to train 'em up to be Christians.

And I can't see why it is not on all accounts fit and convenient for the governors and instructors of the colleges particularly, singly and frequently to converse with the students about the state of their souls; as is the practice of the Rev. Dr. Doddridge, one of the most noted of the present Dissenting ministers in England, who keeps an academy at Northampton, as he himself informs the Rev. Mr. Wadsworth of Hartford, in Connecticut, in a letter dated at Northampton, March 6, 1740/1, the original of which letter I have seen, and have by me an extract of it, sent to me by Mr. Wadsworth, which is as follows:

Through the divine goodness I have every year the pleasure to see some plants taken out of my nursery and set in neighboring congregations, where they generally settle with a unanimous consent, and that to a very remarkable degree, in some very large and once divided congregations. A circumstance in which I own and adore the hand of a wise and gracious God, and can't but look upon it as a token for good. I have at present a greater proportion of pious and ingenious youth under my care, than I ever before had; so that I hope the church may reasonably expect some considerable relief from hence, if God spare their lives a few years, and continue to them those gracious assistances which he has hitherto mercifully imparted. . . . I will not, Sir, trouble you at present with a large account of my method of academical education: only would observe, that I think it of vast importance to instruct them carefully in the Scriptures, and not only endeavor to establish them in the great truths of Christianity, but to labor to promote their practical influence on their hearts; for which purpose I frequently converse with each of them alone, and conclude the conversation with prayer. This does indeed take up a great deal of time, but I bless God, it's amply repaid in the pleasure I have, in seeing my labor is not in vain in the Lord.[9]

[*Wealth and Power Should Be Used for Religious Ends*]

There are some that are not ministers, nor are concerned immediately in those things that appertain to their office or in the education of persons for it, that are under great advantages to promote such a glorious work as this. Some laymen, though it be not their business publicly to exhort and teach, yet are in some respects under greater advantage to encourage and forward this work than ministers: as particularly great men, or men that are high in honor and influence. How much might such do to encourage religion, and open the way for it to have free course, and bear down opposition, if they were but inclined? There is commonly a certain unhappy shyness in great men with respect to religion, as though they were ashamed of it, or at least ashamed to do very much at it; whereby they dishonor and doubtless greatly provoke the King of kings, and very much wound religion among the common people. They are careful of their honor, and seem to be afraid of appearing openly forward and zealous in religion, as though it were what would debase their character and expose 'em to contempt. But in this day of bringing up the ark, they ought to be like David, that great king of Israel, who made himself vile before the ark; and as he was the highest in honor and dignity among God's people, so [he] thought it became him to appear foremost in the zeal and activity he manifested on that occasion; thereby animating and encouraging the whole congregation to praise the Lord, and rejoice before him with all their might: and though it diminished him in the eyes of scoffing Michal, yet it did not at all abate the honor and esteem of the congregation of Israel, but advanced it; as appears by II Sam. 6:22.

Rich men have a talent in their hands, in the disposal and improvement of which they might very much promote such a work

9. [Philip Doddridge (1702–51), English pietist and Congregationalist pastor, is known as the author of 370 hymns and ten volumes of collected writings on religious subjects. This letter, addressed to Daniel Wadsworth (1704–47), pastor of the First Church in Hartford 1732–47, includes greetings to "my worthy brother Mr. Edwards." Although the extract JE mentions was not found, the quoted passage follows the original letter, which is at the Connecticut Historical Society.]

as this, if they were so disposed. They are far beyond others under advantage to do good, and lay up for themselves treasures in heaven [Matt. 6:20]. What a thousand pities is it, that for want of a heart, they commonly have no share at all there, but heaven is peopled mostly with the poor of this world? One would think that our rich men, that call themselves Christians, might devise some notable things to do with their money, to advance the kingdom of their professed Redeemer, and the prosperity of the souls of men, at this time of such extraordinary advantage for it. It seems to me that in this age, most of us have but very narrow, penurious notions of Christianity, as it respects our use and disposal of our temporal goods. The primitive Christians had not such notions: they were trained up by the apostles in another way. God has greatly distinguished some of the inhabitants of New England from others, in the abundance that he has given 'em of the good things of this life. If they could now be persuaded to lay out some considerable part of that which God has given 'em for the honor of God, and lay it up in heaven instead of spending it for their own honor, or laying it up for their posterity, they would not repent of it afterwards.

How liberally did the heads of the tribes contribute of their wealth at the setting up the tabernacle, though it was in a barren wilderness? [Exod. 35:21–29] These are the days of the erecting the tabernacle of God amongst us. We have a particular account how the goldsmiths and the merchants helped to rebuild the wall of Jerusalem, Neh. 3:22. The days are coming, spoken of in Scripture,[1] and I believe not very far off, when the sons of Zion shall come from far, bringing their silver and their gold with them, unto the name of the Lord their God, and to the Holy One of Israel; and when the merchants of the earth shall trade for Christ more than for themselves, and their merchandise and hire shall be holiness to the Lord, and shall not be treasured or laid up for posterity, but shall be for them that dwell before the Lord, to eat sufficiently, and for durable clothing; and when the ships of Tarshish shall bring the wealth of the distant parts of the earth, to the place of God's sanctuary, and to make the place of his feet glorious; and the abundance of the sea shall be converted to the

1. [The turgid passage following is a mélange of phrases from Isa. 61:4, 9; 23:18; 61:13, 5, 16; Rev. 21:24; Matt. 21:8; Jas. 5:3, 2; Rev. 5:10; and I Sam. 2:30—in that order.]

use of God's church, and she shall suck the milk of the Gentiles, and suck the breasts of kings. The days are coming, when the great and rich men of the world shall bring their honor and glory into the church, and shall as it were strip themselves, to spread their garments under Christ's feet, as he enters triumphantly into Jerusalem; and when those that won't do so shall have no glory, and their silver and gold shall be cankered, and their garments moth-eaten; for the saints shall then inherit the earth, and they shall reign on earth, and those that honor God he will honor, and those that despise him shall be lightly esteemed.

If some of our rich men would give one-quarter of their estates to promote this work, they would act a little as if they were designed for the kingdom of heaven, and a little as rich men will act by and by, that shall be partakers of the spiritual wealth and glories of that kingdom. Great things might be done for the advancement of the kingdom of Christ at this day, by those that have ability, by establishing funds for the support and propagation of religion; by supporting some that are eminently qualified with gifts and grace, in preaching the Gospel in certain parts of the country that are more destitute of the means of grace; in searching out children of promising abilities, and their hearts full of love to Christ but of poor families (as doubtless there are such now in the land), and bringing them up for the ministry; and in distributing books that are remarkably fitted to promote vital religion and have a great tendency to advance this work; or if they would only bear the trouble, expense and loss of sending such books into various parts of the land to be sold, it might be an occasion that ten times so many of those books should be bought as otherwise would be; and in establishing and supporting schools in poor towns and villages, which might be done on such a foundation as not only to bring up children in common learning, but also might very much tend to their conviction and conversion, and being trained up in vital piety; and doubtless something might be done this way in old towns and more populous places, that might have a great tendency to the flourishing of religion in the rising generation.

[All Christians Should Honor God in Every Way]

But I would now proceed to mention some things that ought to be done, at such a day as this, that concern all in general.

[A] And here, the first thing I shall mention is fasting and prayer.

It seems to me that the circumstances of the present work do loudly call God's people to abound in this; whether they consider the experience God has lately given 'em of the worth of his presence, and of the blessed fruits of the effusions of his Spirit, to excite them to pray for the continuance and increase, and greater extent of such blessings, or whether they consider the great encouragement God has lately given 'em, to pray for the outpourings of his Spirit and the carrying on this work, by the great manifestations he has lately made of the freeness and riches of his grace; and how much there is, in what we have seen of the glorious works of God's power and grace, to put us in mind of the yet greater things of this nature that he has spoken of in his Word, and to excite our longings for those things and hopes of their approach; or whether we consider the great opposition that Satan makes against this work, and the many difficulties with which it is clogged, and the distressing circumstances that some parts of God's church in this land are under at this day on one account and another.

So [it] is God's will, through his wonderful grace, that the prayers of his saints should be one great and principal means of carrying on the designs of Christ's kingdom in the world. When God has something very great to accomplish for his church, 'tis his will that there should precede it the extraordinary prayers of his people; as is manifest by Ezek. 36:37, "I will yet for this be inquired of by the house of Israel, to do it for them"; together with the context. And 'tis revealed that when God is about to accomplish great things for his church, he will begin by remarkably pouring out "the spirit of grace and supplication," Zech. 12:10. If we are not to expect that the Devil should go out of a particular person that is under a bodily possession, without extraordinary prayer, or prayer and fasting [Matt. 17:21]; how much less should we expect to have him cast out of the land and the world without it?

I am sensible that considerable has been done in duties of this nature in some places; but I don't think so much as God, in the present dispensations of his providence, calls for. I should think the people of God in this land, at such a time as this is, would be in the way of their duty to do three times so much at fasting and prayer as they do; not only, nor principally, for the pouring out of the Spirit on those towns or places where they belong; but that God would appear for his church, and in mercy to miserable men, to carry on his work in the land and in the world of mankind, and to fulfill the things that he has spoken of in his Word, that his church has been so long wishing and hoping and waiting for. They that make mention of the Lord at this day ought not to keep silence, and should give God no rest, "till he establish, and till he make Jerusalem a praise in the earth," agreeable to Isa. 62:6–7. Before the first great outpouring of the Spirit of God on the Christian church, which began at Jerusalem, the church of God gave themselves to incessant prayer, Acts 1:13–14. There is a time spoken of, wherein God will remarkably and wonderfully appear for the deliverance of his church from all her enemies, and when he will "avenge his own elect": and Christ reveals that this will be in answer to their incessant prayers, or crying day and night, Luke 18:7. In Israel the Day of Atonement, which was their great day of fasting and prayer, preceded and made way for the glorious and joyful Feast of Tabernacles. When Christ is mystically born into the world, to rule over all nations, it is represented in the 12th chap. of Rev. as being in consequence of the church's crying and travailing in birth, and being pained to be delivered. One thing here intended, doubtless, is her crying and agonizing in prayer.

God seems now, at this very time, to be waiting for this from us. When God is about to bestow some great blessing on his church, it is often his manner, in the first place, so to order things in his providence as to shew his church their great need of it, and to bring 'em into distress for want of it, and so put 'em upon crying earnestly to him for it. And let us consider God's present dispensations towards his church in this land: a glorious work of his grace has been begun and carried on; and God has of late suffered innumerable difficulties to arise, that do in a great measure clog and hinder it, and bring many of God's dear children into great distress; and yet don't wholly forsake the work of his hand; there are remarkable tokens of his presence still to be seen, here and there; as though he was not forward to forsake us, and (if I may so say) as though he had a mind to carry on his work; but only was waiting for something that he expected in us, as requisite in order to it. And we have a great deal of reason to think that one thing at least is, that we should further acknowledge the greatness and necessity of such a mercy, and our dependence on God for it, in earnest and importunate prayers to him. And by the many errors that have been run into, and the wounds we have thereby given ourselves and the cause that we would promote, and the mischief and confusion we have thereby made, God has hitherto been remarkably shewing us our great and universal dependence on him, and exceeding need of his help and grace: which should engage our cries to him for it.

There is no way that Christians in a private capacity can do so much to promote the work of God, and advance the kingdom of Christ, as by prayer. By this even women, children and servants may have a public influence. Let persons be never so weak, and never so mean, and under never so poor advantages to do much for Christ and the souls of men otherwise; yet, if they have much of the spirit of grace and supplication, in this way they may have power with him that is infinite in power, and has the government of the whole world: and so a poor man in his cottage may have a blessed influence all over the world. God is, if I may so say, at the command of the prayer of faith; and in this respect is, as it were, under the power of his people; as princes, they have power with God, and prevail [cf. Gen. 32:28]. Though they may be private persons, their prayers are put up in the name of a Mediator, that is a public person, being the Head of the whole church and the Lord of the universe: and if they have a great sense of the importance of eternal things and concern for the precious souls of men, yet they need not regret it that they are not preachers; they may go in their earnestness and agonies of soul, and pour out their souls before One that is able to do all things; before him they may speak as freely as ministers; they have a great High Priest, through whom they may come boldly at all times [Heb. 4:14–16], and may vent themselves before a prayer-hearing Father, without any restraint.

If the people of God at this day, instead of spending time in fruitless disputing and talking about opposers, and judging of them and animadverting upon the unreasonableness of their talk and behavior, and its inconsistence with true experience, would be more silent in this way and open their mouths much more before God, and spend more time in fasting and prayer, they would be more in the way of a blessing. And if some Christians in the land, that have been complaining of their ministers and struggling in vain to deliver themselves from the difficulties they have complained of under their ministry, had said and acted less before men, and had applied themselves with all their might to cry to God for their ministers, had as it were risen and stormed heaven with their humble, fervent and incessant prayers for them, they would have been much more in the way of success.

God in his providence, appearing in the present state of things, does especially call on his people in New England to be very much in praying to him for the pouring out of the Spirit upon ministers in the land. For though it is not for us to determine, concerning particular ministers, how much they have of the Spirit of God; yet in the general, it is apparent that there is at this day need of very great degrees of the presence of God with the ministry in New England, much greater degrees of it than has hitherto been granted; they need it for themselves, and the church of God stands in extreme need of it.

In days of fasting and prayer, wherein the whole church or congregation is concerned, if the whole day, besides what is spent in our families, was not spent in the meetinghouse, but part of it in particular praying companies or societies, it would have a tendency to animate and engage devotion more than if the whole day were spent in public, where the people are no way active themselves in the worship, any otherwise than as they join with the minister. The inhabitants of many of our towns are now divided into particular praying societies; most of the people, young and old, have voluntarily associated themselves in distinct companies, for mutual assistance in social worship, in private houses: what I intend therefore is that days of prayer should be spent partly in these distinct praying companies. Such a method of keeping a fast as this, has several times been proved; viz. in the forenoon, after the duties of the family and closet, as early as might be, all the people of the congregation have gathered in their particular religious societies; companies of men by themselves, and companies of women by themselves; young men by themselves, and young women by themselves; and companies of children in all parts of the town by themselves, as many as were capable of social religious exercises; the boys by themselves, and girls by themselves. And about the middle of the day, at an appointed hour, all have met together in the house of God, to offer up public prayers, and to hear a sermon suitable to the occasion: and then, they have retired from the house of God again into their private societies, and spent the remaining part of the day in praying together there, excepting so much as was requisite for the duties of the family and closet in their own houses. And it has been found to be of great benefit to assist and engage the minds of the people in the duties of the day.

I have often thought it would be a thing very desirable, and very likely to be followed with a great blessing, if there could be some contrivance that there should be an agreement of all God's people in America, that are well affected to this work, to keep a day of fasting and prayer to God; wherein we should all unite on the same day in humbling ourselves before God for our past long continued lukewarmness and unprofitableness; not omitting humiliation for the errors that so many of God's people that have been zealously affected towards this work, through their infirmity and remaining blindness and corruption, have run into; and together with thanksgivings to God for so glorious and wonderful a display of his power and grace in the late outpourings of his Spirit, to address the Father of mercies, with prayers and supplications, and earnest cries, that he would guide and direct his own people, and that he would continue and still carry on this work, and more abundantly and extensively pour out his Spirit; and particularly that he would pour out his Spirit upon ministers; and that he would bow the heavens and come down [II Sam. 22:10; Ps. 18:9], and erect his glorious kingdom through the earth. Some perhaps may think that its being all on the same day is a circumstance of no great consequence; but I can't be of that mind: such a circumstance makes the union and agreement of God's people in his worship the more visible, and puts the greater honor upon God, and would have a great tendency to assist and enliven the devotions of Christians. It seems to me, it would mightily encourage and animate God's saints, in humbly and earnestly seeking to God for such blessings which concerns them all; and that it would be much for the rejoicing of all, to think that at the same time such multitudes of God's dear children, far and near, were sending up their cries to the same common Father for the same mercies. Christ speaks of agreement in asking, as what contributes to the prevalence [i.e. prevailing] of the prayers of his people. Matt. 18:19, "Again I say unto you, that if any two of you shall agree on earth as touching anything that they shall ask, it shall be done for them of my Father which is in heaven." If the agreement, or united purpose and appointment of but two of God's children, would contribute much to the prevalence of their prayers, how much more the agreement of so many thousands? Christ delights greatly in the union of his people, as appears by his prayer in the 17th of John:

and especially in the appearance of their union in worship lovely and attractive unto him.

I doubt not but such a thing as I have now mentioned is practicable without a great deal of trouble: some considerable number of ministers might meet together and draw up the proposal, wherein a certain day should be pitched upon, at a sufficient distance, endeavoring therein to avoid any other public day that might interfere with the design in any of the provinces, and the business of the day should be particularly mentioned; and these proposals should be published and sent abroad into all parts, with a desire that as many ministers as are disposed to fall in with 'em would propose the matter to their congregations, and having taken their consent, would subscribe their names, together with the places of which they are ministers, and send back the proposals thus subscribed to the printer (the hands of many ministers might be to one paper); and the printer having received the papers thus subscribed from all the provinces, might print the proposals again, with all the names; thus they might be sent abroad again with the names, that God's people might know who are united with 'em in the affair. One of the ministers of Boston might be desired to have the oversight of the printing and dispersing the proposals. In such a way, perhaps, might be fulfilled in some measure such a general mourning and supplication of God's people as is spoken of, Zech. 12, at the latter end, with which the church's glorious day is to be introduced. And such a day might be something like the Day of Atonement in Israel, before the joyful Feast of Tabernacles.

One thing more I would mention concerning fasting and prayer, wherein I think there has been a neglect in ministers; and that is, that although they recommend and much insist on the duty of secret prayer, in their preaching; so little is said about secret fasting. It is a duty recommended by our Saviour to his followers, just in like manner as secret prayer is; as may be seen by comparing the 5th and 6th vss. of the 6th chap. of Matt. with vss. 16–18. Though I don't suppose that secret fasting is to be practiced in a stated manner and steady course as secret prayer, yet it seems to me 'tis a duty that all professing Christians should practice, and frequently practice. There are many occasions of both a spiritual and temporal nature that do properly require it; and there are many particular mercies that we desire for ourselves or friends that it would be proper, in this manner, to seek of God.

[B] Another thing I would also mention, wherein it appears to me that there has been an omission with respect to the external worship of God. There has been of late a great increase of preaching the Word, and a great increase of social prayer, and a great increase of singing praises. These external duties of religion are attended much more frequently than they used to be; yet I can't understand that there is any increase of the administration of the Lord's Supper, or that God's people do any more frequently commemorate the dying love of their Redeemer in this sacred memorial of it, than they used to do: though I don't see why an increase of love to Christ should not dispose Christians as much to increase in this as in those other duties; or why it is not as proper that Christ's disciples should abound in this duty, in this joyful season, which is spiritually supper time, a feast day with God's saints, wherein Christ is so abundantly manifesting his dying love to souls, and is dealing forth so liberally of the precious fruits of his death. It seems plain by the Scripture, that the primitive Christians were wont to celebrate this memorial of the sufferings of their dear Redeemer every Lord's Day: and so I believe it will be again in the church of Christ, in days that are approaching. And whether we attend this holy and sweet ordinance so often now or no, yet I can't but think it would become us, at such a time as this, to attend it much oftener than is commonly done in the land.

[C] But another thing I would mention, which it is of much greater importance that we should attend to; and that is the duty that is incumbent upon God's people at this day, to take heed that while they abound in external duties of devotion, such as praying, hearing, singing, and attending religious meetings, there be a proportionable care to abound in moral duties, such as acts of righteousness, truth, meekness, forgiveness and love towards our neighbor; which are of much greater importance in the sight of God than all the externals of his worship: which our Saviour was particularly careful that men should be well aware of. Matt. 9:13, "But go ye and learn what that meaneth, I will have mercy and not sacrifice." And chap. 12:7, "But if ye had known what this meaneth, I will have mercy and not sacrifice, ye would not have condemned the guiltless."

The internal acts and principles of the worship of God, or the worship of the heart, in the love and fear of God, trust in God, and resignation to God, etc., are the most essential and important of all duties of religion whatsoever; for therein consists the essence of all religion. But of this inward religion, there are two sorts of external manifestations or expressions. The one sort are outward acts of worship, such as meeting in religious assemblies, attending sacraments and other outward institutions, and honoring God with gestures, such as bowing, or kneeling before him, or with words, in speaking honorably of him in prayer, praise, or religious conference. And the other sort are the expressions of our love to God by obeying his moral commands of self-denial, righteousness, meekness, and Christian love, in our behavior among men. And the latter are of vastly the greatest importance in the Christian life. God makes little account of the former in comparison of them. They are abundantly more insisted on by the prophets in the Old Testament, and Christ and his apostles in the New. When these two kinds of duties are spoken of together, the latter are evermore greatly preferred: as in Isa. 1:12–18, and Amos 5:21, etc., and Mic. 6:7–8, and Isa. 58:5–7, and Zech. 7, ten first verses, and Jer. 2, seven first verses, and Matt. 15:3, etc. Often, when the times were very corrupt in Israel, the people abounded in the former kind of duties, but were at such times always notoriously deficient in the latter; as the prophets complain, Isa. 58, four first verses; Jer. 6:13, compared with vs. 20. Hypocrites and self-righteous persons do much more commonly abound in the former kind of duties than the latter; as Christ remarks of the Pharisees, Matt. 23:14, 25, and 34. When the Scripture directs us to shew our faith by our works, it is principally the latter sort [that] are intended; as appears by Jas. 2, from [the] 8th vs. to the end, and I John 2d chap., vss. 3, 7–11. And we are to be judged at the last day, especially by these latter sort of works; as is evident by the account we have of the day of judgment, in the 25th [chapter] of Matt.

External acts of worship, in words and gestures and outward forms, are of little use but as signs of something else, or as they are a profession of inward worship: they are not so properly shewing our religion by our deeds; for they are only a shewing our religion by words, or an outward profession. But he that shows religion in the other sort of duties shews it in something more than a profession of words; he shews it in deeds. And though deeds may be hypocritical as well as words; yet in themselves they are of greater importance, for they are much more profitable to ourselves and our neighbor. We can't express our love to God by doing anything that is profitable to God; God would therefore have us do it in those things that are profitable to our neighbors, whom he has constituted his receivers: our goodness extends not to God, but to our fellow Christians. The latter sort of duties put greater honor upon God, because there is greater self-denial in them. The external acts of worship, consisting in bodily gestures, words and sounds, are the cheapest part of religion, and least contrary to our lusts. The difficulty of thorough external religion don't lie in them. Let wicked men enjoy their covetousness and their pride, their malice, envy and revenge, and their sensuality and voluptuousness, in their behavior amongst men, and they will be willing to compound the matter with God and submit to what forms of worship you please, and as many as you please; as is manifest in the Jews of old, in the days of the prophets, and the Pharisees in Christ's time, and the papists and Mahometans at this day.

At a time when there is an appearance of the approach of any glorious revival of God's church, God does especially call his professing people to the practice of moral duties. Isa. 56:1, "Thus saith the Lord; keep ye judgment, and do justice; for my salvation is near to come, and my righteousness to be revealed." So when John [the Baptist] preached that the kingdom of heaven was at hand, and cried to the people, "Prepare ye the way of the Lord, make his paths straight," as we have an account, Luke 3:4, the people asked him what they should do. He answers, "He that hath two coats, let him impart to him that hath none; and he that hath meat, let him do likewise." The publicans said, "What shall we do?" He answers, "Exact no more than that which is appointed you." And the soldiers asked him, "What shall we do?" He replies, "Do violence to no man, neither accuse any falsely; and be content with your wages" (vss. 10–14).

God's people at such a time as this ought especially to abound in deeds of charity, or almsgiving. We generally in these days seem to fall far below the true spirit and practice of Christianity with regard to this duty, and seem to have but little notion of it, so far as I can understand the New Testament. At a time when God is so liberal of spiritual things, we ought not to be strait-handed towards him, and sparing of our temporal things. So far as I can judge by the Scripture, there is no external duty whatsoever by which persons will be so much in the way, not only of receiving temporal benefits but also spiritual blessings, the influences of

God's Holy Spirit in the heart, in divine discoveries and spiritual consolations. I think it would be unreasonable to understand those promises made to this duty, in the 58th chap. of Isaiah, in a sense exclusive of spiritual discoveries and comforts. Isa. 58:7–11, "Is it not to deal thy bread to the hungry, and that thou bring the poor that are cast out to thy house? When thou seest the naked that thou cover him, and that thou hide not thyself from thine own flesh? Then shall thy light break forth as the morning, and thy health shall spring forth speedily, and thy righteousness shall go before thee, and the glory of the Lord shall be thy rearward; then shalt thou call, and the Lord shall answer; thou shalt cry, and he shall say, Here I am. If thou take away from the midst of thee the yoke, the putting forth of the finger, and speaking vanity; and if thou draw out thy soul to the hungry, and satisfy the afflicted soul; then shall thy light rise in obscurity, and thy darkness be as the noonday; and the Lord shall guide thee continually, and satisfy thy soul in drought, and make fat thy bones; and thou shalt be like a watered garden, and like a spring of water, whose waters fail not."

So that giving to the poor is the way to receive spiritual blessings is manifest [also] by Ps. 112:4–9, "Unto the upright there ariseth light in the darkness; he is gracious, and full of compassion, and righteous. A good man sheweth favor and lendeth; he will guide his affairs with discretion; surely he shall not be moved forever; the righteous shall be in everlasting remembrance; he shall not be afraid of evil tidings, his heart is fixed, trusting in the Lord; his heart is established, he shall not be afraid, until he see his desire upon his enemies: he hath dispersed, he hath given to the poor; [. . .] his horn shall be exalted with honor." That this is one likely means to obtain assurance is evident by I John 3:18–19, "My little children, let us not love in word, neither in tongue, but in deed, and in truth; and hereby we know that we are of the truth, and shall assure our hearts before him."

We have a remarkable instance in Abraham, of God's rewarding deeds of charity with sweet discoveries of himself, when he had been remarkably charitable to his brother Lot, and the people that he had redeemed out of captivity with him, by exposing his life to rescue them, and had retaken not only the persons but all the goods, the spoil that had been taken by Chedorlaomer and the kings that were with him; and the king of Sodom offered him that if he would give him the persons, he might take the goods to himself: Abraham refused to take anything, even so much as a thread or shoelatchet, but returned all. He might have greatly enriched himself, if he had taken the spoils to himself, for it was the spoils of five wealthy kings and their kingdoms, yet he coveted it not; the king and people of Sodom were now become objects of charity, having been stripped of all by their enemies; therefore Abraham generously bestowed all upon them, as we have an account in Gen. 14, and four last verses. And he was soon rewarded for it, by a blessed discovery that God made of himself to him; as we have an account in the next words, "After these things, the word of the Lord came unto Abram in a vision, saying, Fear not, Abram, I am thy shield, and thy exceeding great reward." [Gen. 15:1] "I am thy shield, to defend thee in battle, as I have now done; and though thou hast charitably refused to take any reward, for exposing thy life to rescue this people, yet fear not; thou shalt not lose, thou shalt have a reward; I am thy exceeding great reward." [2]

When Christ was upon earth he was poor, and an object of charity; and during the time of his public ministry he was supported by the charity of some of his followers, and particularly certain women, of whom we read, Luke 8:2–3. And these women were rewarded by being peculiarly favored with gracious manifestations which Christ made of himself to them. He discovered himself first to them after his resurrection, before the twelve disciples: they first saw a vision of glorious angels, who spake comfortably to them; and then Christ appeared to 'em and spake peace to 'em, saying, "All hail, be not afraid"; and they were admitted to come and hold him by the feet, and worship him, Matt. 28:9. And though we can't now be charitable in this way to Christ in person, who in his exalted state is infinitely above the need of our charity; yet we may be charitable to Christ now, as well as they then; for though Christ is not here, yet he has left others in his room, to be his receivers; and they are the poor. Christ is yet poor in his members; and he that gives to them, lends to the Lord [Prov. 19:17]: and Christ tells us that he shall look on what is done to them, as done to him [Matt. 25:40].

Rebekah, in her marriage with Isaac, was undoubtedly a remarkable type of the church in her espousals to the Lord Jesus. But she found her husband in doing deeds of charity, agreeable

2. [JE's paraphrastic interpretation of Gen. 15:1.]

to the prayer of Abraham's servant, who prayed that this might be the thing that might distinguish and mark out the virgin that was to be Isaac's wife [Gen. 24]. So Cornelius was brought to the knowledge of Christ in this way. He was "a devout man, and one that feared God with all his house, which gave much alms to the people, and prayed to God alway." And an angel appeared to him and said to him, "Thy prayers and thine alms are come up for a memorial before God; and now send men to Joppa, and call for one Simon, whose surname is Peter, etc.," Acts 10, at the beginning. And we have an account in the following parts of the chapter, how God, by Peter's preaching, revealed Christ to Cornelius and his family, and of the Holy Ghost's descending upon them, and filling their hearts with joy, and their mouths with praises.

Some may possibly object that for persons to do deeds of charity, in hope of obtaining spiritual blessings and comforts in this way, would seem to shew a self-righteous spirit, as though they would offer something to God to purchase these favors. But if this be a good objection, it may be made against every duty whatsoever. All external duties of the First Table will be excluded by it, as well as those of the Second.[3] First-Table duties have as direct a tendency to raise self-righteous persons' expectations of receiving something from God, on account of them, as Second-Table duties; and on some accounts more, for those duties are more immediately offered to God, and therefore persons are more ready to expect something from God for them. But no duty is to be neglected for fear of making a righteousness of it. And I have always observed that those professors that are most partial in their duty, exact and abundant in external duties of the First Table, and slack as to those of the Second, are the most self-righteous.

If God's people in this land were once brought to abound in such deeds of love, as much as in praying, hearing, singing, and religious meetings and conference, it would be a most blessed omen. There is nothing would have a greater tendency to bring the God of love down from heaven to the earth: so amiable would be the sight, in the eyes of our loving and exalted Redeemer, that it would soon as it were fetch him down from his throne in heaven, to set up his tabernacle with men on the earth, and dwell with them. I don't remember ever to have read of any remarkable outpouring of the Spirit that continued any long time, but what

3. [I.e., of the Decalogue; see above, p. 395 n.]

was attended with an abounding in this duty. So we know it was with that great effusion of the Spirit that began at Jerusalem in the apostles' days: and so in the late remarkable revival of religion in Saxony, which began by the labors of the famous Professor Francke, and has now been carried on for above thirty years, and has spread its happy influences into many parts of the world; it was begun, and has been carried on, by a wonderful practice of this duty.[4] And the remarkable blessing that God has given Mr. Whitefield, and the great success with which he has crowned him, may well be thought to be very much owing to his laying out himself so abundantly in charitable designs.[5] And it is foretold that God's people shall abound in this duty in the time of the great outpouring of the Spirit that shall be in the latter days. Isa. 32:5 and 8, "The vile person shall no more be called liberal, nor the churl said to be bountiful. . . . But the liberal deviseth liberal things, and by liberal things shall he stand."

[D] To promote a reformation with respect to all sorts of duties among a professing people, one proper means, and that which is recommended by frequent Scripture examples, is their solemn, public renewing their covenant with God.[6] And doubtless it would greatly tend to promote this work in the land, if the congregations of God's people could generally be brought to this. If a draft of a covenant should be made by their ministers, wherein there should be an express mention of those particular duties that the people of the respective congregations have been observed to be most prone to neglect, and those particular sins that they have heretofore especially fallen into, or that it may be apprehended they are especially in danger of, whereby they may prevent or resist the motions of God's Spirit, and the matter should be fully proposed and explained to the people, and they have sufficient op-

4. [August Hermann Francke (1663–1727) may be credited with institutionalizing the Pietistic movement in German Lutheranism begun by Philipp Jakob Spener (1635–1707). Appointed to a professorship at the University of Halle (in Saxony) in 1691, Francke by the time of his death had made the school a center of Pietism. His influence was multiplied many times over through educational foundations, philanthropic institutions, and evangelistic missions throughout the world.]

5. [In America, chiefly the Georgia orphanage, for which Whitefield received an offering nearly everywhere he preached.]

6. [JE had led his own congregation to do this in March 1742; see above, pp. 85–86, and below, pp. 550–54.]

portunity given them for consideration, and then they should be led, all that are capable of understanding, particularly to subscribe the covenant, and also should all appear together on a day of prayer and fasting, publicly to own it before God in his house, as their vow to the Lord; hereby congregations of Christians would do that which would be beautiful, and would put honor upon God, and be very profitable to themselves.

Such a thing as this was attended with a very wonderful blessing in Scotland, and followed with a great increase of the blessed tokens of the presence of God, and remarkable outpourings of his Spirit; as the author of *The Fulfilling of the Scripture* informs, p. 186, 5th edition.[7]

A people must be taken when they are in a good mood, when considerable religious impressions are prevailing among 'em; otherwise they will hardly be induced to this; but innumerable will be their objections and cavils against it.

[E] One thing more I would mention, which if God should still carry on this work, would tend much to promote it, and that is that an history should be published once a month, or once a fortnight, of the progress of it, by one of the ministers of Boston, who are near the press and are most conveniently situated to receive accounts from all parts.[8] It has been found by experience that the tidings of remarkable effects of the power and grace of God in any place, tend greatly to awaken and engage the minds of persons in other places. 'Tis great pity therefore, but that some means should be used for the most speedy, most extensive and certain giving information of such things, and that the country ben't left only to the slow, partial and doubtful information and false representations of common report.

Thus I have (I hope, by the help of God) finished what I proposed. I have taken the more pains in it because it appears to me that now God is giving us the most happy season to attempt an universal reformation, that ever was given in New England.

7. [For the identification of this work, see above, p. 307 n. The passage cited here refers to the National Covenant of February 1638 against Archbishop William Laud's abortive attempt to impose the Anglican liturgy on Scotland. It is interesting that JE should read this event as a spiritual revival and not a nationalistic uprising; even his source remarks that "an enlarged heart did appear for the public cause."]

8. [See above, p. 59.]

And 'tis a thousand pities that we should fail of that which would be so glorious, for want of being sensible of our opportunity, or being aware of those things that tend to hinder it, or our taking improper courses to obtain it, or not being sensible in what way God expects we should seek it. If it should please God to bless any means for the convincing the country of his hand in this work, and bringing them fully and freely to acknowledge his glorious power and grace in it, and engage with one heart and soul, and by due methods, to endeavor to promote it, it would be a dispensation of divine providence that would have a most glorious aspect, happily signifying the approach of great and glorious things to the church of God, and justly causing us to hope that Christ would speedily come to set up his kingdom of light, holiness, peace and joy on earth, as is foretold in his Word. "Amen: even so, come, Lord Jesus!" [Rev. 22:20].

SOME LETTERS RELATING TO
THE REVIVAL

TO DEACON LYMAN OF GOSHEN, CONNECTICUT

Original in Andover Collection of Edwards MSS.

Northampton, Aug. 31, 1741

Dear Friend,

In my prodigious fullness of business, and great infirmity of body, I have time to write but very briefly concerning those things you mention. Concerning the great stir that is in the land, and those extraordinary circumstances and events that it is attended with, such as persons crying out, and being set into great agonies, with a sense of sin and wrath, and having their strength taken away, and their minds extraordinarily transported with light, love and comfort, I have been abundantly amongst such things, and have had great opportunity to observe them, here and elsewhere, in their beginning, progress, issue and consequences; and however there may be some mixtures of natural affection, and sometimes of temptation, and some imprudences and irregularities, as there always was, and always will be in this imperfect state; yet as to the work in general, and the main of what is to be observed in these extraordinary things, they have all the clear and incontestable evidences of a true divine work. If this ben't the work of God, I have all my religion to learn over again, and know not what use to make of the Bible.

As to any absolute promises made to natural men, the matter is exceeding plain. God makes no promises of any future eternal good to fallen man in any other covenant but the covenant of grace; but how can they have any interest in the promises of the covenant of grace, that have no interest in the Mediator of that covenant, and never have performed the condition of that covenant, which is faith in the Mediator? The Scripture is ignorant of any other way of coming to a title to any promises of God, but only laying hold of the promises by faith, which surely men that have no faith don't do.

As to the ministers that go about the country to preach, I believe most of the clamor that is made against them must needs be from some other principle than a regard to the interest of religion; because I observe now there is vastly a greater outcry against ministers riding about to preach the Gospel, than used to be heretofore when ministers rode about on the business of a physician, though that be so much more alien from their proper work and though they were gone from their own people five times as much. But I observe that nowadays no irregularities are so much cried out against as exceeding in religion. As to ministers that ride about the country, I can't say how the case is circumstanced with all of 'em, but I believe they are exceedingly misrepresented. Mr. Pomeroy [1] and Mr. Wheelock [2] have been cried out as much as most, and by particular opportunity I have had to know how it has been with them, they scarcely ever are absent from their people on the Sabbath, and are very careful not to leave them destitute; and are not wont to go abroad but only where they are invited, and not to go into other ministers' pulpits without their consent, and rarely without having [it] desired of them; and at the same time are more abundant in labors among their own people than ever.

I rejoice to hear of the flourishing of the work of God in your parts: I hope God will cause it to prevail against all opposition. Let us look to God to plead his own cause, and to get to himself the victory. Seek to him to direct you and give you wisdom, and humility, and zeal. I desire your prayers for me. I am your sincere and entire friend,

Jonathan Edwards.

P.S. The Rev. Mr. Williams [3] of Hatfield died this morning.

1. [Benjamin Pomeroy, pastor at Hebron, Conn.; see above, p. 108 n. 4.]
2. [Eleazar Wheelock, pastor at Lebanon Crank (now Columbia), Conn.; see above, p. 120 n. 4.]
3. [William Williams, JE's uncle; see above, p. 8 n. 6.]

TO THE REV. JAMES ROBE OF KILSYTH, SCOTLAND

Printed in The Christian Monthly History, *ed. by James Robe, vol. 5, no. 5 (Edinburgh, Aug. 1745), pp. 126–31. (See above, p. 84.)*

Northampton, May 12, 1743

Rev. and Dear Sir,

Last week I was surprised with the unexpected favor of your letter, with one from Mr. MacLaurin.[1] It may well make me blush at the consideration of my vileness, to receive such undeserved testimonies of respect from servants of the Lord, at so great a distance, and that have been so highly favored and honored of God as you have been. Pleasant and joyful are the accounts which we have lately had from Scotland, concerning the kingdom of our God there, for which we and the world are specially indebted to you, who have honored your dear Lord, and refreshed and served his church, by the accounts you have published in your narrative and journals of the work of God in Kilsyth, and other parts in the West of Scotland.[2] Future generations will own themselves indebted to you for those accounts. I congratulate you, dear Sir, on the ad-

1. [John MacLaurin (1693–1754) was a prominent Scottish Presbyterian minister, pastor in the Ramshorn parish of northwest Glasgow 1723–54.]

2. [James Robe, *A Faithful Narrative of the Extraordinary Work of the Spirit of God at Kilsyth, and Other Congregations in the Neighborhood near Glasgow* (Glasgow, 1742). Robe continued the story of the Scottish revivals by adding sporadic installments serially to his account, and it became known popularly as "The Kilsyth Narrative." Some were published occasionally in his *Christian Monthly History* (Edinburgh, 1743–46), and the final one (Part 8) was printed in 1751 as a separate pamphlet which also incorporated a letter of attestation from William McCulloch of nearby Cambuslang (see below, p. 539). All the pieces were collected later and published as *A Narrative of the Extraordinary Work of the Spirit of God at Cambuslang, Kilsyth, etc., Begun 1742. Written by James Robe and Others. With Attestations by Ministers, Preachers, etc.* (Glasgow, 1790). JE probably read "The Kilsyth Narrative" in Thomas Prince's *Christian History*, which began publication in March 1743 with reprints of Robe's early installments (*1*, 3–56, 87–93, 300–36, 341–52; *2*, 173–215).]

vantages God has put you under to favor the church of God with a narrative of his glorious works, by having made you the instrument of so much of them, and giving you such glorious success in your own congregation. The accounts which we have received from you are, on some accounts, more pleasant and agreeable than what we have had to send to you: the work of God with you has been less mixed with error and extravagance; you have taken a more wise and prudent care to prevent things of that nature, or to suppress them as soon as they have appeared; and ministers that have been the principal promoters of the work, have seemed to be more happily united in their sentiments, and so under greater advantage to assist one another, and to act as co-workers and fellow helpers.

You have heard great things from New England of late, which, I doubt not, have refreshed and rejoiced your hearts; and indeed, great and wonderful have the things been in which God has passed before us. But now we have not such joyful news to send you; the clouds have lately thickened, and our hemisphere is now much darkened with them. There is a great decay of the work of God amongst us, especially as to the awakening and converting influence of the Spirit of God; and the prejudices there are, in a great part of the country, are riveted and inveterate. The people are divided into two parties, those that favor the work and those that are against it, and the distinction has long been growing more and more visible, and the distance greater, till there is at length raised a wall between them up to heaven; so that one party is very much out of the reach of all influence of the other.[3] This is very much owing to imprudent management in the friends of the work, and a corrupt mixture which Satan has found means to introduce, and our manifold sinful errors by which we have grieved and quenched the Spirit of God.

It can scarcely be conceived of what consequence it is, to the continuance and propagation of a revival of religion, that the utmost care be used to prevent error and disorder among those that appear to be the subjects of such a work; as also, that all imaginable care be taken by ministers in conducting souls under the work; and particularly that there be the greatest caution used in comforting and establishing persons, as being safe and past danger of hell. Many among us have been ready to think that all high rap-

3. [Cf. above, p. 65.]

tures are divine; but experience plainly shews that it is not the degree of rapture and ecstasy (though it should be to the third heavens), but the nature and kind that must determine us in their favor. It would have been better for us, if all ministers here had taken care diligently to distinguish such joys and raised affections, as were attended with deep humiliation, brokenness of heart, poverty of spirit, mourning for sin, solemnity of spirit, a trembling reverence towards God, tenderness of spirit, self-jealousy and fear, and great engagedness of heart after holiness of life, and a readiness to esteem others better than themselves; and that sort of humility that is not a noisy showy humility, but rather this which disposes to walk softly and speak trembling; and if we had encouraged no discoveries or joys but such as manifestly wrought this way, it would have been well for us.

And I am persuaded we shall generally be sensible, before long, that we run too fast when we endeavor by our positive determinations to banish all fears of damnation from the minds of men, though they may be true saints, if they are not such as are eminently humble and mortified, and (what the Apostle calls) "rooted and grounded in love" [Eph. 3:17]. It seems to be running before the Spirit of God. God by his Spirit does not give assurance any other way, than by advancing these things in the soul: he does not wholly cast out fear, the legal principle, but by advancing and filling the soul full of love, the evangelical principle. When love is low in the true saint, they need the fear of hell to deter them from sin, and engage them to exactness in their walk, and stir them up to seek heaven; but when love is high, and the soul full of it, we don't need fear. And therefore a wise God has so ordered it that love and fear should rise and fall like the scales of a balance: when one rises, the other falls, as there is need, or as light and darkness take place of each other in a room, as light decays, darkness comes in, and as light increases and fills the room, darkness is cast out; so love, or the spirit of adoption, casts out fear, the spirit of bondage. And experience convinces me, that even in the brightest and most promising appearances of new converts, it would have been better for us to have encouraged them only as it were conditionally, after the example of the Apostle, Heb. 3:6, "Whose house are we, if we hold fast the confidence and the rejoicing of the hope firm unto the end"; and vs. 14, "For we are made partakers of Christ, if we hold the beginning of our confidence steadfast unto the end." And after the example of Christ, Rev. 2:10, "Be thou faithful unto death, and I will give thee a crown of life." So Luke 21:34–36, and in many other places.

'Tis probable that one reason why God has suffered us to err, is to teach us wisdom, by experience of the ill consequence of our errors. What you relate of the opposition of the Seceding ministers is very surprising; especially of the two Erskines, whose writings, especially Mr. Ralph Erskine's *Gospel Sonnets,* have been in great repute among God's people here: [4] but this is a day of wonders of various kinds. I have reason to admire divine condescension in making any use of anything I have written for the defense of the work of God in Scotland.

As to what you propose concerning my writing a narrative, etc., I am not conveniently situated for it, living in an extreme part of the land, and an hundred miles from the press, as well as on many other accounts unfit for it. But Mr. Prince of Boston, who is every way fit, and under good advantages for it, has already undertaken it, and, I suppose, will prosecute the undertaking, so far as it shall be thought for God's glory.[5]

I hope, dear Sir, you'll remember me in your prayers. Never was I so sensible in any measure how vain a creature man is; what a leaf driven of the wind, what dry stubble, what poor dust, a bubble, a shadow, a nothing, and more vain than nothing; and what a vain and vile helpless creature I am, and how much I need God's help in everything, as of late. Dear Sir, don't forget New England; and don't forget your affectionate and obliged brother and servant, and unworthy fellow laborer,

Jonathan Edwards.

4. [Ebenezer Erskine (1680–1754) and others withdrew from the Church of Scotland in 1733 to form the Secession Church. His brother Ralph (1658–1752), who also seceded, was of a poetic turn, although his enormously popular *Gospel Sonnets* (Edinburgh, 1720; 25th ed., 1798), contained no sonnets but the outlines of a theological system in verse.]

5. [JE refers to *The Christian History,* which began publication in March 1743; see above, p. 59.]

TO THE REV. WILLIAM McCULLOCH OF CAMBUSLANG, SCOTLAND

Original in Andover Collection; printed (with minor changes) in Dwight,
Life of President Edwards, *pp. 196–98. (See above, pp. 84–85.)*

Northampton, May 12, 1743

Rev. and Dear Sir,

Mr. MacLaurin [1] of Glasgow, in a letter he has lately sent me,
informs me of your proposing to write a letter to me, and being
prevented by the failing of the expected opportunity: I thank you,
Rev. Sir, that you had such a thing in your heart. We were informed the last year, by the printed and well attested narrative of
the glorious work of God in your parish, which we have since understood has spread into many other towns and parishes in that
part of Scotland; especially are we informed of this by Mr. Robe's
Narrative,[2] and I perceive by some papers of the *Weekly History,*[3]
sent me by Mr. MacLaurin of Glasgow, that the work has continued to make glorious progress at Cambuslang, even till it has
prevailed to a wonderful degree indeed. God has highly favored
and honored you, dear Sir, which may justly render your name
precious to all that love our Lord Jesus Christ.

We live in a day wherein God is doing marvellous things; in
that respect we are distinguished from former generations. God
has wrought great things in New England, which, though exceeding glorious, have all along been attended with some threatening

1. [See above, p. 535 n. 1.]
2. [See above, p. 535 n. 2.]
3. [*The Glasgow Weekly History Relating to the Late Progress of the Gospel
at Home and Abroad; Being a Collection of Letters, Partly Reprinted from*
The London Weekly History *and Partly Printed First Here at Glasgow. For
the Year 1742* (Glasgow, 1743). Published during 1742 only, this periodical
"seems to have been chiefly under Mr. McCulloch's management" (D. MacFar-
lan, *The Revivals of the Eighteenth Century, Particularly at Cambuslang* {Edin-
burgh, ca. 1845}, p. 112). A copy is at the Massachusetts Historical Society, and
is described in *PMHS*, 53 (1920), 192–217.]

clouds; which from the beginning caused me to apprehend some great stop or check to be put to the work, before it should be begun and carried on in its genuine purity and beauty, to subdue all before it, and to prevail with an irresistible and continual progress and triumph; and it is come to pass according to my apprehensions. But yet I cannot think otherwise, than that what has now been doing, is the forerunner of something vastly greater, more pure, and more extensive. I can't think that God has come down from heaven, and done such great things before our eyes, and gone so much beside and beyond his usual way of working, and wrought so wonderfully, and that he has gone away with a design to leave things thus. "Who hath heard such a thing? Who hath seen such things?" And will God, when he has wrought so unusually, and made the earth "to bring forth in one day, [. . .] bring to the birth and not cause to bring forth?" And shall he "cause to bring forth and shut the womb?" (Isa. 66:8–9) I live upon the brink of the grave, in great infirmity of body, and nothing is more uncertain than whether I shall live to see it: but I believe God will revive his work again before long, and that it will not wholly cease till it has subdued the whole earth.

But God is now going and returning to his place, till we acknowledge our offense, and I hope to humble his church in New England, and purify it, and so fit it for yet greater comfort, that he designs in due time to bestow upon it. God may deal with his church, as he deals with a particular saint; commonly after his first comfort, the clouds return, and there [is] a season of remarkable darkness, and hidings of God's face, and buffetings of Satan; but all to fit [him] for greater mercy; and as it was with Christ himself, who presently after the heavens were opened over his head, and the Spirit was poured out upon him, and God wonderfully testified his love to him, was driven into the wilderness to be tempted of the Devil forty days [Matt. 3:16—4:1 and parallels]. I hope God will show us our errors, and teach us wisdom by his present withdrawings: now in the day of adversity we have time and cause to consider, and begin now to have opportunity to see the consequences of our conduct. I wish that God's ministers and people everywhere would take warning by our errors, and the calamities that are the issue of them. I have mentioned several things in my letters to Mr. MacLaurin and Mr. Robe; [4] another I might have

4. [Above, pp. 536–38.]

mentioned, that most evidently proves of ill consequence, i.e. we have run from one extreme to another, with respect to talking of experiences; that whereas formerly there was too great a reservedness in this matter, of late many have gone to an unbounded openness, frequency and constancy in talking of their experiences, declaring almost everything that passes between God and their own souls, everywhere and before everybody. Among other ill consequences of such a practice this is one, that religion runs all into that channel; and religion is placed very much in it, so that the strength of it seems to be spent in it; that other duties that are of vastly greater importance, have been looked upon [as] light in comparison of this, so that other parts of religion have [been] really much injured thereby; as when we see a tree excessively full of leaves, we find so much less fruit; and when a cloud arises with an excessive degree of wind, we have the less rain. How much, dear Sir, does God's church at such a day need the constant gracious care and guidance of our good Shepherd, and especially we that are ministers?

I should be glad, dear Sir, of a remembrance in your prayers, and also of your help, by information and instructions, by what you find in your experience in Scotland. I believe it to be the duty of one part of the church of God thus to help another.

I am, dear Sir, your affectionate brother and servant in Jesus Christ.

Jonathan Edwards

TO THE CONVOCATION OF EVANGELICAL PASTORS

A published testimony "From Seven Rev. Pastors in the County of Hampshire," printed in The Christian History *for August 6, 1743 (vol. I, no. 23). After the antirevival faction published its* Testimony *of May 25, 1743, evangelicals hastily summoned a convocation to issue a counter-testimony, and invited prorevival pastors who could not attend to submit letters of attestation and support. (See above, p. 79.) JE did not attend, presumably for reasons stated in this letter, but joined six fellow ministers of his area in sending the brief testimony printed below.*

County of Hampshire, June 30, 1743

Rev. and Honored Sirs,

Whereas an advertisement hath lately been published, wherein it is signified, that it is the desire of a number of ministers that there should be a meeting of all such ministers in this province as are persuaded that there has of late been a happy revival of religion in the land, at Boston, the day after [Harvard's] Commencement, to give a joint testimony to the late glorious work of God's grace, and to consult what should be done to promote this work, and to suppress those things that bring a reproach upon it and hinder it; and in the same advertisement it is desired that if any such ministers are not able to be present at this interview, they would not fail to send their testimony and thoughts in writing: we whose names are subscribed to this, living at a great distance, and our circumstances not well allowing us to go so great a journey at the time proposed, would hereby signify; that according to what understanding we have of the nature of Christianity, and the observation we have had opportunity to make, we judge that there has been within the last two years and an half, a blessed outpouring of the Spirit of God in this county, in awakening and converting sinners, and in enlightening, quickening and building up saints in faith, holiness and comfort; which has been attended in great numbers with an abiding alteration and reformation of disposition and behavior. And particularly we would hereby declare to the glory of God's grace, that we judge that there has been a happy revival of religion in the congregations that have been committed to our pastoral care, and that there are many in them that, by abiding manifestations of a serious, religious and humble spirit, and a conscientious care and watchfulness in their behavior towards God and man, give all grounds of charity towards them, as having been sincere in the profession they have made. And however there has been, especially in some places, a mixture of enthusiasm and false religion, and some have run into great errors in their conduct, and some have fallen away, and there is a declension in others that is to be lamented; yet we think the effect has been such, and still continues to be such, as leaves no room reasonably to doubt of God's having been wonderfully in the midst of us, and such as has laid us under great obligations forever to admire and extol the riches of his grace in doing such great things for us.

Thus, Rev. Sirs, begging of him that he would be with you in your meeting, and guide you in your thoughts and conclusions with respect to these things, and direct you to that which may be for his glory and the prosperity of Zion, and desiring your prayers to God for us, and the flocks committed to our care, we remain, honored and dear Sirs, your brethren and fellow servants in the Gospel ministry.

> Stephen Williams, pastor of a church in Springfield
> Peter Reynolds, pastor of the church in Enfield
> Jonathan Edwards, pastor of the church in Northampton
> Samuel Allis, pastor of the church in Somers
> John Woodbridge, pastor of the Second Church in Hadley
> David Parsons, Jr., pastor of the Third Church in Hadley
> Edward Billing, pastor of the church in Cold Spring [1]

1. [The Revs. Timothy Woodbridge of Hatfield and Chester Williams of Hadley First Church sent a separate letter, dated June 29, 1743, concurring with the sentiments of their Hampshire colleagues. See *The Christian History, 1,* 180.]

TO THE REV. THOMAS PRINCE OF BOSTON

Evidently intended for publication, this letter was entitled "The State of Religion at Northampton in the County of Hampshire, About a Hundred Miles Westward of Boston," and published in The Christian History, I *(Jan. 14, 21, and 28, 1743/44), 367–81. It is also in Dwight,* Life of President Edwards, *pp. 160–70. (See above, pp. 85–86.)*

Northampton, Dec. 12, 1743

[Rev. and Dear Sir,]

Ever since the great work of God that was wrought here about nine years ago, there has been a great abiding alteration in this town in many respects. There has been vastly more religion kept up in the town, among all sorts of persons, in religious exercises and in common conversation, than used to be before: there has remained a more general seriousness and decency in attending the public worship; there has been a very great alteration among the youth of the town, with respect to reveling, frolicking, profane and unclean conversation, and lewd songs; instances of fornication have been very rare; there has also been a great alteration amongst both old and young with respect to tavern-haunting. I suppose the town has been in no measure so free of vice in these respects, for any long time together, for this sixty years, as it has been this nine years past. There has also been an evident alteration with respect to a charitable spirit to the poor (though I think with regard to this, we in this town, as the land in general, come far short of Gospel rules). And though after that great work nine years ago there has been a very lamentable decay of religious affections, and the engagedness of people's spirit in religion, yet many societies for prayer and social religion were all along kept up, and there were some few instances of awakening and deep concern about the things of another world, even in the most dead time.

In the year 1740 in the spring, before Mr. Whitefield came to this town,[1] there was a visible alteration: there was more serious-

1. [Whitefield visited Northampton October 17–20, 1740; see above, pp. 48–49.]

ness and religious conversation, especially among young people. Those things that were of ill tendency among them were more foreborne; and it was a more frequent thing for persons to visit their minister upon soul accounts, and in some particular persons there appeared a great alteration about that time. And thus it continued till Mr. Whitefield came to town, which was about the middle of October following: he preached here four sermons in the meetinghouse (besides a private lecture at my house), one on Friday, another on Saturday, and two upon the Sabbath. The congregation was extraordinarily melted by every sermon; almost the whole assembly being in tears for a great part of sermon time. Mr. Whitefield's sermons were suitable to the circumstances of the town; containing just reproofs of our backslidings, and in a most moving and affecting manner, making use of our great profession and great mercies as arguments with us to return to God, from whom we had departed. Immediately after this the minds of the people in general appeared more engaged in religion, shewing a greater forwardness to make religion the subject of their conversation, and to meet frequently together for religious purposes, and to embrace all opportunities to hear the Word preached. The revival at first appeared chiefly among professors, and those that had entertained the hope that they were in a state of grace, to whom Mr. Whitefield chiefly addressed himself, but in a very short time there appeared an awakening and deep concern among some young persons that looked upon themselves as in a Christless state; and there were some hopeful appearances of conversion; and some professors were greatly revived. In about a month or six weeks there was a great alteration in the town, both as to the revivals of professors, and awakenings of others. By the middle of December a very considerable work of God appeared among those that were very young, and the revival of religion continued to increase; so that in the spring, an engagedness of spirit about things of religion was become very general amongst young people and children, and religious subjects almost wholly took up their conversation when they were together.

In the month of May 1741, a sermon was preached to a company at a private house. Near the conclusion of the exercise one or two persons that were professors were so greatly affected with a sense of the greatness and glory of divine things, and the infinite importance of the things of eternity, that they were not able to conceal it; the affection of their minds overcoming their strength, and having a very visible effect on their bodies. When the exercise was over, the young people that were present removed into the other room for religious conference; and particularly that they might have opportunity to inquire of those that were thus affected what apprehensions they had; and what things they were that thus deeply impressed their minds: and there soon appeared a very great effect of their conversation; the affection was quickly propagated through the room: many of the young people and children that were professors appeared to be overcome with a sense of the greatness and glory of divine things, and with admiration, love, joy and praise, and compassion to others that looked upon themselves as in a state of nature; and many others at the same time were overcome with distress about their sinful and miserable state and condition; so that the whole room was full of nothing but outcries, faintings and such like. Others soon heard of it, in several parts of the town, and came to them; and what they saw and heard there was greatly affecting to them; so that many of them were overpowered in like manner: and it continued thus for some hours; the time being spent in prayer, singing, counseling and conferring. There seemed to be a consequent happy effect of that meeting to several particular persons, and in the state of religion in the town in general.

After this were meetings from time to time attended with like appearances. But a little after it, at the conclusion of the public exercise on the Sabbath, I appointed the children that were under sixteen years of age to go from the meetinghouse to a neighbor house; that I there might further enforce what they had heard in public, and might give in some counsels proper for their age. The children were there very generally and greatly affected with the warnings and counsels that were given them, and many exceedingly overcome; and the room was filled with cries: and when they were dismissed, they, almost all of them, went home crying aloud through the streets, to all parts of the town. The like appearances attended several such meetings of children that were appointed. But their affections appeared by what followed to be of a very different nature: in many they appeared to be indeed but childish affections; and in a day or two would leave 'em as they were before: others were deeply impressed; their convictions took fast hold of them, and abode by them: and there were some that from one meeting to another seemed extraordinarily affected for some time, to but little purpose, their affections presently vanishing from time to time, but yet afterwards were seized with abiding convictions, and their affections became durable.

About the middle of the summer, I called together the young people that were communicants, from sixteen to twenty-six years of age to my house; which proved to be a most happy meeting: many seemed to be very greatly and most agreeably affected with those views which excited humility, self-condemnation, self-abhorrence, love and joy: many fainted under these affections. We had several meetings that summer of young people attended with like appearances. It was about that time that there first began to be cryings out in the meetinghouse; which several times occasioned many of the congregation to stay in the house after the public exercise was over, to confer with those who seemed to be overcome with religious convictions and affections; which was found to tend much to the propagation of their impressions, with lasting effect upon many; conference being at these times commonly joined with prayer and singing. In the summer and fall the children in various parts of the town had religious meetings by themselves for prayer, sometimes joined with fasting; wherein many of them seemed to be greatly and properly affected, and I hope some of them [were] savingly wrought upon.

The months of August and September [1741] were the most remarkable of any this year, for appearances of conviction and conversion of sinners, and great revivings, quickenings, and comforts of professors, and for extraordinary external effects of these things. It was a very frequent thing to see an house full of outcries, faintings, convulsions and such like, both with distress, and also with admiration and joy. It was not the manner here to hold meetings all night, as in some places, nor was it common to continue 'em till very late in the night: but it was pretty often so that there were some that were so affected, and their bodies so overcome, that they could not go home, but were obliged to stay all night at the house where they were. There was no difference that I know of here, with regard to these extraordinary effects, in meetings in the night and in the daytime: the meetings in which these effects appeared in the evening, being commonly begun, and their extraordinary effects, in the day, and continued in the evening; and some meetings have been very remarkable for such extraordinary effects that were both begun and finished in the daytime.

There was an appearance of a glorious progress of the work of God upon the hearts of sinners in conviction and conversion this summer and fall; and great numbers, I think we have reason to hope, were brought savingly home to Christ. But this was remarkable: the work of God in his influences of this nature seemed to be almost wholly upon a new generation; those that were not come to years of discretion in that wonderful season nine years ago, children, or those that were then children: others that had enjoyed that former glorious opportunity without any appearance of saving benefit, seemed now to be almost wholly passed over and let alone. But now we had the most wonderful work among children that ever was in Northampton. The former great outpouring of the Spirit was remarkable for influences upon the minds of children, beyond all that had ever been before; but this far exceeded that. Indeed, as to influences on the minds of professors, this work was by no means confined to a new generation: many of all ages partook of it; but yet, in this respect it was more general on those that were of the younger sort. Many that had formerly been wrought upon, that in the times of our declension had fallen into decays, and had in a great measure left God, and gone after the world, now passed under a very remarkable new work of the Spirit of God, as if they had been the subjects of a second conversion. They were first led into the wilderness, and had a work of conviction, having much greater convictions of the sin of both nature and practice than ever before (though with some new circumstances, and something new in the kind of conviction); in some with great distress, beyond what they had felt before their first conversion. Under these convictions they were excited to strive for salvation, and the kingdom of heaven suffered violence from some of them in a far more remarkable manner than before: and after great convictions and humblings, and agonizings with God, they had Christ discovered to them anew as an all-sufficient Saviour; and in the glories of his grace, and in a far more clear manner than before, and with greater humility, self-emptiness and brokenness of heart, and a purer and higher joy, and greater desires after holiness of life, but with greater self-diffidence, and distrust of their treacherous hearts.

One circumstance wherein this work differed from that which had been in the town five or six years before, was that conversions were frequently wrought more sensibly and visibly; the impressions stronger, and more manifest by external effects of them; and the progress of the Spirit of God in conviction, from step to step, more apparent; and the transition from one state to another more sensible and plain; so that it might, in many instances, be as it were seen by bystanders. The preceding season had been very remarkable on this account beyond what had been before; but this [was] more remarkable than that. And in this season these apparent or visible conversions (if I may so call them) were more frequently in the presence of others, at religious meetings, where the appearances of what was wrought on the heart fell under public observation.[2]

After September 1741, there seemed to be some abatement of the extraordinary appearances that had been; but yet they did not wholly cease, but there was something of them from time to time all winter.

About the beginning of February 1741/2, Mr. Buell came to this town, I being then absent from home, and continued so till about a fortnight after.[3] Mr. Buell preached from day to day, almost every day, in the meetinghouse (I having left to him the free liberty of my pulpit, hearing of his designed visit before I went from home) and spent almost the whole time in religious exercises with the people, either in public or private, the people continually thronging him. When he first came, there came with him a number of the zealous people from Suffield, who continued here for some time. There were very extraordinary effects of Mr. Buell's labors; the people were exceedingly moved, crying out in great numbers in the meetinghouse, and great part of the congregation commonly staying in the house of God for hours after the public service, many of them in uncommon circumstances. Many also were exceedingly moved in private meetings, where Mr. Buell

2. [JE had compared the Northampton awakenings of 1735 and 1741 in *The Distinguishing Marks*; see above, p. 268.]

3. [Samuel Buell (1716–98) was graduated from Yale in 1741 and licensed to preach by the New Haven Ministers' Association shortly thereafter. During the Great Awakening he itinerated widely before settling as pastor of the Presbyterian church at East Hampton, L. I., in 1746. JE preached the installation sermon. For Buell's visit to Northampton in 1742, see above, p. 69.]

was: and almost the whole town seemed to be in a great and continual commotion, day and night; and there was indeed a very great revival of religion. But it was principally among professors; the appearances of a work of conversion were in no measure equal to what had been the summer before. When I came home I found the town in very extraordinary circumstances, such in some respects as I never saw it in before. Mr. Buell continued here a fortnight or three weeks after I returned: there being still great appearances attending his labors; many in their religious affections being raised far beyond what they ever had been before: and there were some instances of persons lying in a sort of trance, remaining for perhaps a whole twenty-four hours motionless, and with their senses locked up; but in the meantime under strong imaginations, as though they went to heaven, and had there a vision of glorious and delightful objects. But when the people were raised to this height, Satan took the advantage, and his interposition in many instances soon became very apparent: and a great deal of caution and pains were found necessary to keep the people, many of them, from running wild.

In the month of March I led the people into a solemn public renewal of their covenant with God.[4] To that end I made a draft of a covenant, and first proposed it to some of the principal men in the church; then proposed it to the people in their several religious societies, in various parts of the town; and then proposed it to the whole congregation in public; and then deposited a copy of it in the hands of each of our four deacons, that all that desired it might resort to them, and have opportunity to view and consider it. Then the people in general that were above fourteen years of age first subscribed the covenant with their hands, and then on a day of fasting and prayer, all together presented themselves before the Lord in his house, and stood up, and solemnly manifested their consent to it, as their vow to God. The covenant was as follows:

> *A Copy of a Covenant Entered into and Subscribed by the People of God at Northampton, and Owned Before God in His House As Their Vow to the Lord, and Made a Solemn Act of Public Worship, by the Congregation in General That Were Above Fourteen Years of Age, on a Day of Fasting and*

4. [See above, pp. 85–86.]

Prayer for the Continuance and Increase of the Gracious Presence of God in That Place, March 16, 1741/2

Acknowledging God's great goodness to us, a sinful, unworthy people, in the blessed manifestations and fruits of his gracious presence in this town, both formerly and lately, and particularly in the very late spiritual revival; and adoring the glorious majesty, power, and grace of God, manifested in the present wonderful outpouring of his Spirit in many parts of this land, and in this place; and lamenting our past backslidings and ungrateful departings from God; and humbly begging of God that he would not mark our iniquities, but for Christ's sake come over the mountains of our sins, and visit us with his salvation, and continue the tokens of his presence with us, and yet more gloriously pour out his blessed Spirit upon us, and make us all partakers of the divine blessings he is at this day bestowing here and in many parts of this land; we do this day present ourselves before the Lord, to renounce our evil ways, and put away our abominations from before God's eyes, and with one accord to renew our engagements to seek and serve God: and particularly do now solemnly promise and vow to the Lord as follows:

In all our conversation, concerns, and dealings with our neighbor, we will have a strict regard to rules of honesty, justice, and uprightness; that we don't overreach or defraud our neighbor in any matter, and either willfully or through want of care, injure him in any of his honest possessions or rights; and in all our communication, will have a tender respect, not only to our own interest, but also to the interest of our neighbor; and will carefully endeavor in everything to do to others as we should expect, or think reasonable, that they should do to us, if we were in their case and they in ours.

And particularly we will endeavor to render to everyone his due; and will take heed to ourselves, that we don't wrong our neighbor, and give them a just cause of offense, by willfully or negligently forbearing to pay our honest debts.

And wherein any of us, upon strict examination of our past behavior, may be conscious to ourselves that we have by any means wronged any of our neighbors in their outward estate; we will not rest till we have made that restitution, or given that satisfaction, which the rules of moral equity require: or if we are, on a strict and impartial search, conscious to ourselves that we have in any other respect considerably injured our neighbor; we will truly endeavor to do that which we, in our consciences, suppose Christian rules require, in order to a reparation of the injury and removing the offense given thereby.

And furthermore we promise that we will not allow ourselves in backbiting; and that we will take great heed to ourselves to avoid all violations of those Christian rules, Tit. 3:2, "Speak evil of no man"; Jas. 4:11, "Speak not evil one of another, brethren"; and II Cor. 12:20, "Lest there be [. . .] strifes, backbitings, whisperings": and that we will not only not slander our neighbor, but also will not, to feed a spirit of bitterness, ill will, or secret grudge against our neighbor, insist on his real faults needlessly, and when not called to it; or from such a spirit speak of his failings and blemishes with ridicule, or an air of contempt.

And we promise that we will be very careful to avoid doing anything to our neighbor from a spirit of revenge. And that we will take great care that we do not, for private interest, or our own honor, or to maintain ourselves against those of a contrary party, or to get our wills, or to promote any design in opposition to others, do those things which we, on the most impartial consideration we are capable of, can think in our consciences will tend to wound religion and the interest of Christ's kingdom.

And particularly that so far as any of us, by divine providence, have any special influence upon others, to lead them in the management of public affairs; we will not make our own worldly gain, or honor, or interest in the affections of others, or getting the better of any of a contrary party, that are in any respect our competitors, or the bringing or keeping them down, our governing aim, to the prejudice of the interest of religion and the honor of Christ.

And in the management of any public affair wherein there is a difference of opinions, concerning any outward possessions, privileges, rights or properties: we will not wittingly violate justice for private interest; and with the greatest strictness and watchfulness, will avoid all unchristian bitterness, vehemence, and heat of spirit; yea, though we should think ourselves injured by a contrary party: and in the time of the management of such affairs, will especially watch over ourselves, our spirits, and our tongues, to avoid all unchristian inveighings, reproachings, bitter reflectings, judging and ridiculing others, either in public meetings, or in private conversation, either to men's faces, or behind their backs; but will greatly endeavor, so far as we are concerned, that all should be managed with Christian humility, gentleness, quietness and love.

And furthermore, we promise that we will not tolerate the exercise of enmity and ill will, or revenge in our hearts, against any of our neighbors; and we will often be strictly searching and examining our hearts with respect to that matter.

And if any of us find that we have an old secret grudge against any of our neighbors, we will not gratify it, but cross it, and endeavor to our utmost to root it out, crying to God for his help; and that we will make it our true and faithful endeavor, in our places, that a party spirit may not be kept up amongst us, but that it may utterly cease; that for the future we may all be one, united in undisturbed peace and unfeigned love.

And those of us that are in youth do promise never to allow ourselves in any youthful diversions and pastimes, in meetings or companies of young people, [anything] that we in our consciences, upon sober consideration, judge not well to consist with, or would sinfully tend to hinder the devoutest, and most engaged spirit in religion; or indispose the mind for that devout and profitable attendance on the duties of the closet, which is most agreeable to God's will, or that we in our most impartial judgment, can think tends to rob God of that honor which he expects, by our orderly, serious attendance on family worship.

And furthermore we promise that we will strictly avoid all freedoms and familiarities in company, so tending either to stir up or gratify a lust of lasciviousness, that we cannot in our consciences think will be approved by the infinitely pure and holy eye of God; or that we can think on serious and impartial consideration, we should be afraid to practice, if we expected in a few hours to appear before that holy God, to give an account of ourselves to him, as fearing they would be condemned by him as unlawful and impure.

We also promise, with great watchfulness, to perform relative duties, required by Christian rules, in the families we belong to; as we stand related respectively, towards parents and children, husbands and wives, brothers and sisters, masters or mistresses and servants.

And we now appear before God, depending on divine grace and assistance, solemnly to devote our whole lives to be laboriously spent in the business of religion: ever making it our greatest business, without backsliding from such a way of living; not hearkening to the solicitations of our sloth and other corrupt inclinations, or the temptations of the world, that tend to draw us off from it; and particularly, that we will not abuse an hope, or opinion that any of us may have of our being interested in Christ, to indulge ourselves in sloth, or the more easily to yield to the solicitations of any sinful inclinations; but will run with perseverance the race that is set before us [Heb. 12:1], and work out our own salvation with fear and trembling [Phil. 2:12].

And because we are sensible that the keeping [of] these solemn vows may hereafter, in many cases, be very contrary to our corrupt inclinations and carnal interests; we do now therefore appear before God, to make a surrender of all to him, and to make a sacrifice of every carnal inclination and interest to the great business of religion, and the interest of our souls.

And being sensible of our own weakness, and the deceitfulness of our own hearts, and our proneness to forget our most solemn vows and lose our resolutions; we promise to be often strictly examining ourselves by these promises, especially before the sacrament of the Lord's Supper; and beg of God that he would, for Christ's sake keep us from wickedly dissembling in these our solemn vows; and that he who searches our hearts [Rom. 8:27] and ponders the path of our feet [Prov. 4:26] would from time to time help us in trying ourselves by this covenant, and help us to keep covenant with him, and not leave us to our own foolish wicked and treacherous hearts.

In the beginning of the summer 1742, there seeeemed to be some abatement of the liveliness of people's affections in religion: but yet many were often in a great height of them. And in the fall and winter following there were at times extraordinary appearances. But in the general people's engagedness in religion and the liveliness of their affections have been on the decline: and some of the young people especially have shamefully lost their liveliness and vigor in religion, and much of the seriousness and solemnity of their spirits. But there are many that walk as becometh saints [Eph. 5:2–3]; and to this day, there are a considerable number in the town that seem to be near to God, and maintain much of the life of religion, and enjoy many of the sensible tokens and fruits of his gracious presence.

With respect to the late season of revival of religion amongst us, for three or four years past; it has been observable that in the former part of it, in the years 1740 and 1741, the work seemed to be much more pure, having less of a corrupt mixture, than in the former great outpouring of the Spirit in 1735 and 1736. Persons seemed to be sensible of their former errors, and had learnt more of their own hearts, and experience had taught them more of the tendency and consequences of things: they were now better guarded, and their affections were not only greater, but attended with greater solemnity, and greater humility and self-distrust, and greater engagedness after holy living and perseverance; and there were fewer errors in conduct. But in the latter part of it, in the year 1742, it was otherwise: the work continued more pure till we were infected from abroad: our people hearing, and some of them seeing the work in other places, where there was a greater visible commotion than here, and the outward appearances were more extraordinary; were ready to think that the work in those places far excelled what was amongst us; and their eyes were dazzled with the high profession and great shew that some made who came hither from other places.

That those people went so far beyond them in raptures and violent emotions of the affections, and a vehement zeal, and what they called boldness for Christ; our people were ready to think was owing to their far greater attainments in grace, and intimacy with heaven: they looked little in their own eyes in comparison of them, and were ready to submit themselves to 'em, and yield themselves up to their conduct, taking it for granted that everything was right that they said and did. These things had a strange influence on the people, and gave many of them a deep and unhappy tincture, that it was a hard and long labor to deliver 'em from, and which some of them are not fully delivered from to this day.

The effects and consequences of things amongst us plainly shews the following things, viz. that the degree of grace is by no means to be judged of by the degree of joy, or the degree of zeal; and that indeed we can't at all determine by these things, who are gracious and who are not; and that it is not the degree of religious affections, but the nature of them that is chiefly to be looked at. Some that have had very great raptures of joy, and have been extraordinarily filled (as the vulgar phrase is) and have had their bodies overcome, and that very often, have manifested far less of the temper of Christians, in their conduct since, than some others that have been still, and have made no great outward show. But then again there are many others, that have had extraordinary joys and emotions of mind, with frequent great effects on their bodies, that behave themselves steadfastly as humble, amiable, eminent Christians.

'Tis evident that there may be great religious affections, that may in shew and appearance imitate gracious affections, and have the same effects on their bodies, but are far from having the same effect in the temper of their minds, and course of their lives. And likewise there is nothing more manifest by what appears amongst us, than that the goodness of [a] person's state is not chiefly to be judged of by any exactness of steps, and method of experiences, in what is supposed to be the first conversion; but that we must judge more by the spirit that breathes, the effect wrought on the temper of the soul, in the time of the work, and remaining afterwards.[5] Though there have been very few instances among professors amongst us, of what is ordinarily called scandalous sin, known to me; yet the temper that some of them shew, and the behavior they have been of, together with some things in the kind and circumstances of their experiences, make me much afraid lest there be a considerable number that have woefully deceived themselves. Though on the other hand, there is a great number whose temper and conversation is such as justly confirms the charity of others towards them; and not a few in whose disposition and walk, there are amiable appearances of eminent grace. And notwithstanding all the corrupt mixtures that have been in the late work here;

5. [On JE's view of the stages in conversion, see above, pp. 25–29.]

there are not only many blessed fruits of it in particular persons, that yet remain, but some good effects of it upon the town in general. A party spirit has more ceased: I suppose there has been less appearance these three or four years past, of that division of the town into two parties, that has long been our bane, than has been these thirty years; and the people have apparently had much more caution, and a greater guard on their spirit and their tongues, to avoid contention and unchristian heats, in town meetings and on other occasions. And 'tis a thing greatly to be rejoiced in, that the people very lately have come to an agreement and final issue, with respect to their grand controversy relating to their common lands; which has been above any other particular thing, a source of mutual prejudices, jealousies, and debates, for fifteen or sixteen years past. The people are also generally of late in some respects considerably altered and meliorated in their notions of religion: particularly they seem to be much more sensible of the danger of resting in old experiences, or what they were subjects of at their supposed first conversion; and to be more fully convinced of the necessity of forgetting the things that are behind, and pressing forward [Phil. 3:13–14], and maintaining earnest labor, watchfulness and prayerfulness as long as they live.

[Jonathan Edwards]

TO WILLIAM McCULLOCH

The main purpose of this letter was to expound JE's postmillennial views regarding an historical millennium and the events which he thought were to precede it. (See above, pp. 71–72.) It is somewhat lengthy, and only the paragraphs describing the revival and its decline are reproduced here. The original letter is in the Andover MSS, and is printed—with the customary editorial liberties—in Dwight, Life of President Edwards, *pp. 211–19. A critical text of the entire piece will appear in the "Letters" volume of the Yale edition of* The Works of Jonathan Edwards.

Northampton, March 5, 1743/4

Rev. and Dear Sir,

I return you thanks for your most obliging, entertaining and instructive letter, dated Aug. 13, 1743,[1] which I received about the latter end of October: my answering which has been unhappily delayed, by reason of my distance from Boston, and not being able to find any opportunity to send thither till the ship was gone that brought your letter; which I much regretted. My delaying to answer has been far from arising from any indifference with respect to this correspondence, by which I am sensible I am highly honored and privileged.

'Tis probable that you have been informed by other correspondents before now what the present state of things in New England is. It is indeed on many accounts very melancholy: there is a vast alteration within this two years; for about so long, I think it is, since the Spirit of God began to withdraw, and this great work has been on the decline. Great numbers in the land about two years ago were raised to an exceeding great height, in joy and elevations of mind, and through want of watchfulness and sensibleness of the danger and temptation that there is in such circumstances, many were greatly exposed, and the Devil taking the ad-

1. [McCulloch's letter is printed in Dwight, *Life of President Edwards,* pp. 198–200. See above, pp. 84–85.]

vantage, multitudes were soon, and to themselves insensibly, led far away from God and their duty. God was provoked that he was not sanctified in this height of advancement, as he ought to have been; he saw our spiritual pride and self-confidence, and the polluted flames that arose of intemperate, unhallowed zeal; and he soon in a great measure withdrew from us; and the consequence has been that "the enemy has come in like a flood" [Isa. 59:19], in various respects, until the deluge has overwhelmed the whole land. There had from the beginning been a great mixture, especially in some places, of false experiences, and false religion with true; but from about this time, the mixture became much greater; many were led away with sad delusions; and this opened the door for "the enemy to come in like a flood" in another respect; it gave great advantage to the enemies and opposers of this work, furnished them with weapons, and gave 'em new courage, and has laid the friends of the work under such disadvantage, that nothing that they could do would avail anything to withstand their violence. And now it is come to that, that the work is put to a stop everywhere, and it is the day of the enemies' triumph, but I believe also a day of God's people's humiliation, which will be better to 'em in the end than their elevations and raptures. The time has been amongst us when "the sower went forth to sow" [Matt. 13:3], and we have seen the spring, wherein the seed sprang up in different sorts of ground, appearing then fair and flourishing; but this spring is past, and we now see the summer, wherein the sun is up with a burning heat, that tries the sorts of ground; and now appears the difference: the seed in stony ground, where there was only a thin layer of earth on a rock, withers away, the moisture being dried out; and the hidden seeds and roots of thorns in unsubdued ground, now springs up and chokes the seed of the Word. Many high professors are fallen, some into gross immoralities, some into the opinions of sectaries, some into a rooted spiritual pride, enthusiasm, and an incorrigible wildness of behavior, some into a cold, carnal frame of mind, showing a great indifference to things of religion. But there are many, and I hope those the greater part of those that were professed converts, [who] appear hitherto like the good ground. And nothwithstanding the thick and dark clouds that so soon follow that blessed sunshine that we have had, yet I cannot but steadfastly maintain an hope and persuasion that God will revive his work, and that what has been so great and very extraordinary is a forerunner of a yet more glorious and extensive work.

It has been slanderously reported and printed concerning me, that I have often said that the millennium was already begun, and that it began at Northampton; a doctor of divinity in New England has ventured to publish this report to the world, from a single person, who is concealed and kept behind the curtain;[2] but the report is very diverse from what I have ever said. Indeed, I have often said, as I say now, that I looked upon the late wonderful revivals of religion as forerunners of those glorious times so often prophesied of in the Scripture, and that this was the first dawning of that light, and beginning of that work which, in the progress and issue of it, would at last bring on the church's latter-day glory: but there are many that know that I have from time to time added, that there would probably be many sore conflicts and terrible convulsions, and many changes, revivings and intermissions, and returns of dark clouds, and threatening appearances, before this work shall have subdued the world, and Christ's kingdom shall be everywhere established and settled in peace, which will be the lengthening of the millennium, or day of the church's peace, rejoicing and triumph on earth, so often spoken of. . . .

You inquire of me, Rev. Sir, whether I reject all those for counterfeits that speak of visions and trances. I am far from doing of it: I am, and always have been, in that matter, of the same opinion that Mr. Robe expresses in some of those pamphlets Mr. Mac-Laurin sent me,[3] that persons are neither to be rejected, nor approved on such a foundation. I have expressed the same thing in my discourse on *The Marks of a Work of the True Spirit*,[4] and han't changed my mind.

. . . Dear Brother, asking your earnest prayers for me and for New England, I am your affectionate brother and engaged friend and servant,

Jonathan Edwards.

2. [Charles Chauncy, *Seasonable Thoughts*, p. 372. See above, p. 71 n.]
3. [See above, p. 535.]
4. [*Distinguishing Marks*; above, pp. 235–38, 278–82.]

TO THE REV. THOMAS GILLESPIE OF
CARNOCK, SCOTLAND[1]

*The original is in the Andover MSS, and is printed (with some revisions)
in Dwight,* Life of President Edwards, *pp. 462–68. The main subject of
the letter is JE's dismissal from Northampton (above, pp. 87–88), but much
of it describes conditions in the town which bore importantly on the
revivals. Approximately half the letter is reproduced below; the complete
piece will appear in the "letters" volume of the Yale edition of* The
Works of Jonathan Edwards.

Stockbridge, July 1, 1751

Rev. and Very Dear Sir,

I am very greatly obliged to you for your most kind, affectionate,
comfortable and profitable letter of Feb. 2, 1751. I thank you,
Sir, for your sympathy with me under my troubles, so amply
testified, and the many suitable and proper considerations you
suggest to me for my comfort and improvement. May God enable
me to make a right improvement of them.

'Tis not to be wondered at, dear Sir, that you are shocked and
surprised at what has happened between me and the people of
Northampton. 'Tis very surprising to all impartial and considerate persons that live near, and have the greatest advantage to know
the circumstances of the affair, and the things that preceded this
event and made way for it: but no wonder if it be much more so
to strangers at a distance. I doubt not, but that God intends his
own glory, and the safety and prosperity of Zion, and the advancement of the interest of religion, in the final issue of this event: and
that shall be very good.[2] But [it] is best that the true state of the

1. [Gillespie (1708–74) studied at the University of Edinburgh and at Philip
Doddridge's Northampton Academy (see above, p. 512). Pastor at Carnock from
1741 to 1752, when he was deposed for refusing to help settle a minister
resisted by the people, Gillespie founded the Relief Church of Scotland in
1761.]

2. [The last five words of this sentence are uncertain, their legibility being
obscured in a fold of the paper. Not even Dwight could make them out, and
the present restoration should be regarded as tentative.]

case should be known, and that it should be viewed as it is, in order
to receiving that instruction, which divine providence holds forth
in it, and in order to proper reflections and a right improvement.

As there is a difference among particular persons as to their
natural temper, so there is some difference of this kind to be observed in different countries, and also in different cities and towns.
The people of Northampton are not the most happy in their
natural tempers. They have, ever since I can remember, been
famed for a high-spirited people, and close, and of a difficult, turbulent temper. However, though in some respects they have been a
stiff-necked people, yet God has been pleased in times past to bestow many special and distinguishing favors upon them. The town
has stood now near an 100 years. Their first minister, Mr. Eleazar
Mather [3] (brother to Dr. Increase Mather [4] of Boston, and Mr.
Samuel Mather [5] of Dublin, in Ireland), was a very eminent man
of God. After him came Mr. Stoddard,[6] my grandfather; a very
great man, of strong powers of mind, of great grace, and great authority, of a masterly countenance, speech and behavior. He had
great success in his ministry; there being many seasons in his day
of general awakening among his people. He continued in the ministry at Northampton about 60 years. But God was pleased, in
some respects, especially to manifest his power in the weakness of
his successor, there having been a more remarkable awakening
since his death than ever had been till then in that town; although
since that, also a greater declension, and more awful departures
from God, in some respects, than ever before: and so the last minister has had more to humble him than either of his predecessors.
May the effect be answerable to God's just expectations!

The people having from the beginning been well instructed, have
had a name, for a long time, for a very knowing people; and many
have appeared among them [as] persons of good abilities; and
many that have been born in the town have been promoted to
places of public improvement: they have been a people distinguished on this account. These things have manifestly been abused

3. [See above, p. 114 n. 4.]

4. [1639–1723; father of the famous Cotton Mather (1663–1728).]

5. [1626–71; on his importance to religious thought in America, see Mason I.
Lowance, Jr., "Introduction" to Samuel Mather, *The Figures or Types of the
Old Testament* (New York: Johnson Reprint Corp., 1969).]

6. [See above, pp. 15–17.]

to nourish the pride of their natural temper, which had made 'em more difficult and unmanageable. There were some mighty contests and controversies among them in Mr. Stoddard's day; which were managed with great heat and violence; some great quarrels in the church, wherein Mr. Stoddard, great as his authority was, knew not what to do with them. In one ecclesiastical controversy in Mr. Stoddard's days, wherein the church was divided into two parties, the heat of spirit was raised to such a height, that it came to hard blows; a member of one party met the head of the opposite party, and assaulted him and beat him unmercifully. In later times the people have had more to feed their pride; they have grown a much greater and more wealthy people than formerly, and are become more extensively famous in the world, as a people that have excelled in gifts and grace, and had God extraordinarily among them: which has insensibly engendered and nourished spiritual pride, that grand inlet of the Devil into the hearts of men, and avenue of all manner of mischief among a professing people. Spiritual pride is a most monstrous thing. If it ben't discerned and vigorously opposed in its beginning, it very often soon raises persons above their teachers, and supposed spiritual fathers, and sets 'em out of the reach of all rule and instruction; as I have seen in innumerable instances. And there is this inconvenience attends the publishing of narratives of a work of God among a people: such is the corruption that is in the hearts of men, and even of good men, that there is great danger of their making it an occasion of spiritual pride.[7] There is great reason to think that Northampton people have provoked God greatly against them by trusting in their privileges and attainments; and the consequences may well be a warning to all God's people far and near, that hear of them.

Another thing which probably has contributed in some measure to the unhappiness of the people's manners, was that Mr. Stoddard, though an eminently holy man, was naturally of a dogmatical temper; and the people being brought up under him, and with a high veneration for him, naturally were led to imitate him: especially their officers and leading men seemed to think it an excellency to be like him in this respect.

It has been a very great wound to the church of Northampton

7. [JE refers to his *Faithful Narrative*. He himself had taken unconcealed pride in the notoriety it brought to him and his church; see above, pp. 88, 210.]

that there has for forty or fifty years been a sort of settled division of the people into two parties, somewhat like the Court and Country party in England (if I may compare small things with great). There have been some of the chief men in the town, of chief authority and wealth, that have been great proprietors of their lands; who have had one party with them. And the other party, which commonly has been the greatest, have been of those who have been jealous of them, apt to envy 'em, and afraid of their having too much power and influence in town and church. This has been a foundation of innumerable contentions among the people from time to time, which have been exceeding grievous to me; and by which doubtless God has been dreadfully provoked, and his Spirit grieved and quenched, and much confusion, and many evil works have been introduced.

Another thing that evidently has contributed to our calamities is, that the people had got so established in certain wrong notions and ways in religion, which I found them in and never could beat them out of. Particularly it was too much their method to lay almost all the stress of their hopes on the particular steps and method of their first work, i.e. the first work of the Spirit of God on their hearts in their convictions and conversion, and to look but little at the abiding sense and temper of their hearts, and the course of their exercises, and fruits of grace, for evidences of their good estate. Nor had they learned, and many of them never could be made to learn, to distinguish between impressions on the imagination, and truly spiritual experiences. And when I came among them, I found it to be too much a custom among them without discretion, or distinction of occasions, places, or companies, to declare and publish their own experiences; and oftentimes to do it in a light manner, without any air of solemnity. This custom has not a little contributed to spiritual pride, and many other evils. When I first settled among the people, being young and of but little experience,[8] I was not thoroughly aware of the ill consequences of such a custom; and so allowed it, or at least did not testify against it as I ought to have done.

And here I desire it may be observed that I would be far from so laying all the blame of the sorrowful things that have come to pass, to the people, as to suppose that I have no cause of self-re-

8. [He was 23 years old and had a scant eight months of pastoral experience, gained at a small Presbyterian church in New York, N.Y.]

flection and humiliation before God on this occasion. I am sensible that it becomes me to look on what has lately happened, as an awful frown of heaven on me, as well as on the people. God knows the wickedness of my heart and the great and sinful deficiencies and offenses which I have been guilty of in the course of my ministry at Northampton. I desire that God would discover them to me more and more, and that now he would effectually humble me and mortify my pride and self-confidence, and empty me entirely of myself, and make me to know how that I deserve to be cast away as an abominable branch, and as a vessel wherein is no pleasure; and if it may consist with his holy will, sanctify me, and make me a vessel more meet for my Master's use [II Tim. 2:21], and yet improve me as an instrument of his glory and the good of the souls of mankind.

One thing that has contributed to bring things to such a pass at Northampton, was my youth and want of more judgment and experience, in the time of that extraordinary awakening about sixteen years ago. Instead of a child, there was want [i.e. need] of [a] giant in judgment and discretion among a people in such an extraordinary state of things. In some respects, doubtless my confidence in myself was a great wrong to me; but in other respects, my diffidence of myself injured me. It was such that I durst not act my own judgment, and had no strength to oppose received notions and established customs, and to testify boldly against some glaring false appearances and counterfeits of religion, till it was too late. And by this means as well as others, many things got footing, which have been a dreadful source of spiritual pride, and other things that are exceeding contrary to true Christianity. If I had had more experience and ripeness of judgment and courage, I should have guided my people in a better manner, and should have guarded them better from Satan's devices, and prevented the spiritual calamity of many souls, and perhaps the eternal ruin of some of them; and should have done what would have tended to lengthen out the tranquility of the town.

However, doubtless at that time there was a very glorious work of God wrought in Northampton, and there were numerous instances of saving conversion; though undoubtedly many were deceived, and deceived others; and the number of true converts was not so great as was then imagined. Many may be ready from things that are lately come to pass to determine that all Northampton religion is come to nothing, and that all the famed awakenings and revivals of religion in that place prove to be nothing, but strange tides of a melancholy and whimsical humor. But they would draw no such conclusion if they exactly knew the true state of the case, and would judge of it with full calmness and impartiality of mind. . . .

I am, Sir, your most affectionate friend and brother,

Jonathan Edwards.

THE PREFACE TO TRUE RELIGION
BY JOSEPH BELLAMY

True RELIGION *delineated;*

OR,

EXPERIMENTAL RELIGION,

As diftinguifhed from FORMALITY on the one Hand, and ENTHUSIASM on the other, fet in a Scriptural and Rational Light.

In Two DISCOURSES.

In which fome of the principal Errors both of the ARMINIANS and ANTINOMIANS are confuted, the Foundation and Superftructure of their different Schemes demolifhed, and the Truth as it is in JESUS, explained and proved.

The whole adapted to the weakeft Capacities, and defigned for the Eftablifhment, Comfort and Quickening of the People of GOD, in thefe Evil Times.

By *Jofeph Bellamy,* A. M.
Minifter of the Gofpel at *Bethlem* in *Connecticut.*

With a Preface by the Rev. Mr. EDWARDS.

Ifai. xxx. 21. *And thine Ears fhall hear a Word behind thee, faying, This is the Way, walk ye in it, when ye turn to the right Hand, and when ye turn to the left.*
Matth. vii. 13, 14. *Enter ye in at the ftrait Gate ; for wide is the Gate, and broad is the Way that leadeth to Deftruction, and many there be which go in thereat : Becaufe ftrait is the Gate, and narrow is the Way which leadeth unto Life, and few there be that find it.*

BOSTON:
Printed and Sold by S. KNEELAND, in Queen-Street. 1750

TEXT OF THE PREFACE TO *TRUE RELIGION*

Joseph Bellamy (1719–90) was JE's pupil, friend, and colleague. In 1750 he published his first major work, True Religion Delineated, *a book of 421 pages. Drawing the same battle lines as those which had characterized the controversies of the 1740s (see above, pp. 64–65), he positioned experiential piety on middle ground between the opposite extremes of "Formality," which he equated with Arminianism, and "Enthusiasm," which he equated with Antinomianism. Just as he finished writing, JE was cashiered out of the Northampton pulpit, in effect becoming a casualty of the conflict Bellamy was describing. At his friend's urging, JE wrote a commendatory preface for the new book shortly after preaching his farewell sermon (see above, pp. 88–89). The text below is that of the first edition, issued from the Boston press of Kneeland and Green.*

THE Being of God is reckoned the first, greatest and most fundamental of all things that are the objects of knowledge or belief. And next to that must be reckoned the nature of that religion which God requires of us, and must be found in us, in order to our enjoying the benefits of God's favor: or rather this may be esteemed of like importance with the other; for it in like manner concerns us to know how we may honor and please God, and be accepted of him, as it concerns us to know that he has a being. This is a point of infinite consequence to every single person; each one having to do with God as his supreme judge, who will fix his eternal state, according as he finds him to be with or without true religion. And this is also a point that vastly concerns the public interests of the church of God.

It is very apparent, that the want of thorough distinction in this matter, through the defect either of sufficient discerning or care, has been the chief thing that has obscured, obstructed and brought to a stand all remarkable revivals of religion, which have been since the beginning of the Reformation; the very chief reason why the most hopeful and promising beginnings have never come to any more than beginnings; being nipped in the bud, and soon followed with a great increase of stupidity, corrupt principles, a profane and atheistical spirit, and the triumph of the open enemies of religion. And from hence, and from what has been so evident from time to time in these latter ages of the church, and from the small acquaintance I have with the history of preceding times; I can't but think, that if the events which have appeared from age to age should be carefully examined and considered, it would appear that it has been thus in all ages of the Christian church from the beginning.

They therefore who bring any addition of light to this great subject, *the nature of true religion and its distinction from all counterfeits,* should be accepted as doing the greatest possible service to the church of God. And attempts to this end ought not to be despised and discouraged, under a notion that it is but vanity and arrogance in such as are lately sprung up in an obscure part of the world, to pretend to add anything on this subject to the information we have long since received from their fathers, who have lived in former times in New England and more noted countries. We cannot suppose that the church of God is already possessed of all that light, in things of this nature, that ever God intends to give it; nor that all Satan's lurking-places have already been found out. And must we let that grand adversary alone in his devices, to ensnare and ruin the souls of men, and confound the interest of religion amongst us; without attempting to know anything further of his wiles than others have told us; though we see every day the most fatal effects of his hitherto unobserved snares; for fear we shall be guilty of vanity or want of modesty, in attempting to discern anything that was not fully observed by our betters in former times? And that, whatever peculiar opportunities God gives us, by special dispensations of his providence, to see some things that were overlooked by them?

The remarkable things that have come to pass in late times, respecting the state of religion, I think, will give every wise observer great reason to determine that the counterfeits of the grace of God's Spirit are many more than have been generally taken notice of heretofore; and that therefore we stand in great need of having the certain and distinguishing nature and marks of genuine religion more clearly and distinctly set forth than has been usual; so that the difference between that and everything that is spurious may be more plainly and surely discerned, and safely determined.

As inquiries of this nature are very important and necessary in themselves, so they are what the present state of religion in New England and other parts of the British dominions do in a peculiar manner render necessary at this season; and also do give peculiar opportunity for discoveries beyond what has been for a long time. Satan transforming himself into an angel of light [II Cor. 11:14] has shewn himself in many of his artifices more plainly than ordinary; and given us opportunity to see more clearly and exactly the difference between his operations and the saving operations and fruits of the Spirit of Christ: and we should be much to blame if we did not improve such an advantage.

The author of the ensuing treatise has not been negligent of these opportunities. He has not been an unwary or undiscerning observer of events that have occurred these ten years past. From the intimate acquaintance with him, which I have been favored with for many years, I have abundant reason to be satisfied that what has governed him in this publication is no vanity of mind, no affectation to appear in the world as an author,[1] nor any desire of applause; but a hearty concern for the glory of God, and the kingdom and interest of his Lord and Master Jesus Christ; and that as to the main things he here insists on, as belonging to the distinguishing nature and essence of true religion, he declares them, not only as being satisfied of them from a careful consideration of important facts (which he has had great opportunity to observe) and very clear experience in his own soul; but the most diligent search of the Holy Scriptures, and strict examination of the nature of things; and that his determinations concerning the nature of genuine religion, here exhibited to the world, have not been settled and published by him without long consideration, and maturely weighing all objections which could be thought of, taking all opportunities to hear what could be said by all sorts of

---

1. [Bellamy had already appeared in print, having published a sermon entitled *Early Piety Recommended* (Boston, 1748) two years previously. (The only copy known is at the Presbyterian Historical Society.) But this was only a small pamphlet of 56 pages, whereas *True Religion* was a much more ambitious work aimed at a wide audience. It is not surprising, therefore, that JE should reveal his sensitivity regarding neophyte authors—a diffidence dating from his youth, when he advised himself to maintain "a superabundance of modesty" because "mankind are by nature proud and exceeding envious and evermore jealous of such upstarts, and it exceedingly irritates and affronts them to see them appear in print" (shorthand notes on the cover of "Notes on Natural Science," Yale MSS; translated by William P. Upham in *PMHS*, 2d ser., *15* {1901–02}, 515).]

persons against the principles here laid down, from time to time conversing freely and friendly with gentlemen in the Arminian scheme, having also had much acquaintance and frequent long conversation with many of the people called Separatists,[2] their preachers and others.

And I cannot but express my sincere wishes, that what is here written by this reverend and pious author may be taken notice of, read without prejudice, and thoroughly considered: and I verily believe, from my own perusal, it will be found a discourse wherein the proper essence and distinguishing nature of saving religion is deduced from the first principles of the oracles of God, in a manner tending to a great increase of light in this infinitely important subject; discovering truth, and at the same time shewing the grounds of it; or shewing what things are true, and also why they are true; manifesting the mutual dependence of the various parts of the true scheme of religion, and also the foundation of the whole; things being reduced to their first principles in such a manner, that the connection and reason of things, as well as their agreement with the Word of God, may be easily seen; and the true source of the dangerous errors concerning the terms of God's favor and qualifications for heaven, which are prevailing at this day, is plainly discovered; shewing their falsehood at the very foundation, and their inconsistence with the very first principles of the religion of the Bible.

Such a discourse as this is very seasonable at this day. And although the author (as he declares) has aimed especially at the benefit of persons of vulgar capacity; and so has not labored for such ornaments of style and language as might best suit the gust[3] of men of polite literature; yet the matter or substance that is to be found in this discourse is what, I trust, will be very entertaining and profitable to every serious and impartial reader, whether learned or unlearned.

Jonathan Edwards

Northampton
August 4, 1750

2. [Evangelicals who withdrew from the standing churches to form "Strict Congregational" or "Separate Baptist" churches ostensibly composed only of converted persons.]

3. [In the nineteenth-century American reprints (above, p. 93) this word is changed to "taste."]

Few references to biblical characters and events appear in the General Index, and where they do the entries are selective; such matters may be located more conveniently through the Index of Scriptures. *Since JE refers to the Deity an overwhelming number of times, the Index entries for "God," "Jesus Christ," "Holy Spirit," and their synonyms are likewise limited to pages where he offers extended discussions of specific aspects.*

Dedham, England, 311
Deerfield, Mass., 22, 102, 103, 119, 153, 208, 312 n.
Deism, 58, 78, 262, 503
Delusions. *See* Enthusiasm
Devil: mimics or infiltrates the work of God, 108, 226, 243–44, 246, 259–60, 277, 385, 563; not the author of all spectral phenomena, 237; opposes Christ and his work, 250, 271, 540, 571; thwarted by revivals, 250–53, 258; opposes Bible, 253–54; prince of darkness, 255; provokes extremism, 269, 410–13, 494–95; work of Christ attributed to, 55, 271, 275; the Great Awakening not his work, 330, 344; possessed pre-Christian America, 354; father of the unconverted, 390; his kingdom to be overthrown, 398; ensnares the proud, 414–16, 558–59; tradition regarding origin of, 416–17; finds opportunities among enthusiasts, 432–33, 439; takes advantage of defects in Christians, 462–63, 467–71, 477, 550; takes advantage of external customs, 471–73; inspires hateful affections, 483; exorcised by prayer and fasting, 516; mentioned, 162, 301, 345, 458, 461, 570
Devotion, Ebenezer, 22; attests FN-3, 41, 143
Diary of Joshua Hempstead, 52 n.
"Diary of Michael Wigglesworth" (ed. Morgan), 26 n.
Diary of Stephen Williams. *See* Williams, Stephen
Discipline of the Methodist Episcopal Church, 83 n.
Discourses on Various Important Subjects (JE), 19–21, 168
Dispensations of history, 215–17
Dissenters, English, 513
"Dissertation on the State of Religion," 17 n.
Distinguishing Marks (JE): place in the Great Awakening, 52–56; published in Boston, 57, 213; creates a new vocabulary, 57–58; published in Great Britain, 60; answered by Rand, 64; arguments expanded in ST, 66–78, 289; early distribution, 90; later editions, 91; text, 226–88
Doctrine of the Instituted Churches (Stoddard), 15 n., 16 n.
Doddridge, Philip (1702–51), 512, 513 n., 561 n.
Doolittle, Benjamin, 22
Durham, Conn., 23, 110, 120, 154
Dutch Reformed Church, 156–57

Dutch Calvinistic Pietism (Tanis), 1–2 n., 157 n.
Duty and Interest of a People (Williams), 33 n., 111, 130 n.
Dwight, Sereno E., 8 n., 33 n., 45–46, 57 n., 70 n., 84 n., 88 n., 89 n., 134 n., 501 n., 539, 544, 558, 561

Early Piety Recommended (Bellamy), 571 n.
Earthquakes, 21, 31, 131, 133, 139
East Jersey Presbytery, 156 n.
East Lyme, Conn., 50, 51 n.
East Windsor, Conn.: early awakenings, 4; revival of 1735, 23, 102, 120, 154
Easthampton, L.I., 57, 549 n.
Ed (Heb., altar), 317
Edict of Nantes, 63 n.
Edinburgh, University of, 561
Education: to be respected, 56, 224, 282–83; for ministers, 456–67; for children, 515. *See also* Colleges
Edward Taylor's Treatise (ed. Grabo), 16 n.
Edwards, Esther Stoddard (JE's mother), 103 n.
Edwards, Jerusha (JE's daughter), 57 n., 73 n.
Edwards, Jonathan (1703–58): relation to revival tradition, 1, 2; "Personal Narrative," 4, 30–31; compares his revivals with Stoddard's, 5, 174, 181, 190, 268, 562; opposes Arminianism, 7–8, 17–20, 100–01, 116, 148; letter to Pepperell, 8; family feud with Williamses, 8, 37; on the Halfway Covenant, 14; on visible sainthood, 15, 43, 76–77, 286–87; on justification by faith, 20–21; on the morphology of conversion, 25–32, 43–44, 263–70; Boston lecture, 25; on evidences of conversion, 28, 121, 556; writes FN, 32–37, 130, 143; illness in self and family, 34, 155, 210; handwriting, 35, 45; corrects first edition of FN, 38–45; on suicides, 46–47; attempts to revive the revival, 47–48; defends revival at Yale commencement, 52–56; tries to counteract Davenport's fanaticism, 61; on the French Prophets, 63, 313, 330, 341, 468; stands between opposing parties, 64–65, 88, 569; expands arguments of DM in ST, 65–78, 289; describes wife's religious experiences, 68–70, 331–41; millennial speculations, 71–72, 84–85, 280–82; theory of preaching, 72–73, 246–48, 385–94; religious experiences of his children, 73; admits and rebukes errors among revivalists, 74–77,

INDEX OF SCRIPTURES